CAMBRIDGE GREEK AND LATIN CLASSICS

MENANDER

SAMIA

(THE WOMAN FROM SAMOS)

EDITED BY

ALAN H. SOMMERSTEIN

Professor of Greek
University of Nottingham

CAMBRIDGE
UNIVERSITY PRESS

CAMBRIDGE
UNIVERSITY PRESS

University Printing House, Cambridge CB2 8BS, United Kingdom

Published in the United States of America by Cambridge University Press, New York

Cambridge University Press is part of the University of Cambridge.

It furthers the University's mission by disseminating knowledge in the pursuit of
education, learning and research at the highest international levels of excellence.

www.cambridge.org
Information on this title: www.cambridge.org/9780521735421

© Cambridge University Press 2013

First published 2013

Printed and bound in the United Kingdom by Clays, St Ives plc

A catalogue record for this publication is available from the British Library

Library of Congress Cataloguing in Publication data
Menander, of Athens.
[Samia. English]
Samia (the Woman from Samos) / Menander ; edited by Alan H. Sommerstein,
Professor of Greek, University of Nottingham.
pages cm
Includes bibliographical references and indexes.
ISBN 978-0-521-51428-6 (hard back)
1. Athens (Greece) – Drama. 2. Illegitimate children – Drama. 3. Fathers and
sons – Drama. 4. Mistresses – Drama. I. Sommerstein, Alan H. II. Title.
PA4246.E4 2013
882'.01 – dc23 2013016269

ISBN 978-0-521-51428-6 Hardback
ISBN 978-0-521-73542-1 Paperback

D.M.
virorum comicorum
Geoffrey Arnott
Colin Austin
Kenneth Dover
Eric Handley
Douglas MacDowell

CONTENTS

PREFACE

This edition represents the first appearance of Menander in the *Cambridge Greek and Latin Classics*. Next to *Dyskolos*, *Samia* is the play of Menander that in its present state comes nearest to completeness: we have virtually the whole of the last three Acts, and in the first two, although almost half the text is completely lost and much of the remainder is badly damaged, it is almost always possible to infer with considerable confidence what was done, and often also the substance of what was said, in the missing portions. I hope that this edition will serve to encourage the study (especially at undergraduate level) of Greek New Comedy, the ancestor of an entire western tradition of light drama.

My thanks are due above all to Pat Easterling and Richard Hunter, first for inviting me to undertake this edition and then for all the help they have given me in the course of its preparation. They have read the whole edition in draft and made many valuable suggestions. I have not felt able to adopt all of them, but responsibility for any errors or infelicities is entirely mine. I have received much assistance from other scholars who had often been working on Menander far longer than I, among whom particular mention is due to Horst-Dieter Blume, to Christophe Cusset and especially to Richard Green, who kindly made available to me his images of the fragmentary Brindisi mosaic (see Introduction §11) and shared with me his ideas about it: my disagreement with these ideas does not diminish my respect or my gratitude.

The completion of this edition was greatly accelerated by an award of research leave by the School of Humanities of the University of Nottingham, where I have had the privilege of working for nearly forty years, and of an additional semester by the Arts and Humanities Research Council under a scheme which has now unfortunately been terminated.

ABBREVIATIONS

Ancient authors and texts, and collections of papyri, are generally abbreviated as in LSJ or its *Revised Supplement*, although longer abbreviations are used in some cases; other deviations, where not self-evident, are listed below. Fragments of tragedy are cited from *TrGF*, those of comedy from *PCG*; for fragments of other authors the name of the editor, or the abbreviated title of the collection, is given. References to the plays of Menander contained in Sandbach 1990 are to that edition wherever possible; where Arnott 1979 + 1996a + 2000 has a different line-numbering, both references are given, distinguished as S and A respectively.

The comedies of Plaut(us) and Ter(ence) are abbreviated as follows:

Ad.	*Adelphoe*	*Eun.*	*Eunuchus*
Amph.	*Amphitruo*	*Hec.*	*Hecyra*
Andr.	*Andria*	*HT*	*Heauton Timorumenos*
Asin.	*Asinaria*	*Men.*	*Menaechmi*
Aul.	*Aulularia*	*Merc.*	*Mercator*
Bacch.	*Bacchides*	*Phorm.*	*Phormio*
Capt.	*Captivi*	*Poen.*	*Poenulus*
Cas.	*Casina*	*Pseud.*	*Pseudolus*
Cist.	*Cistellaria*	*Trin.*	*Trinummus*
Curc.	*Curculio*		

Sigla used in the critical apparatus to denote papyri are given in the discussion of each papyrus in section 13 of the Introduction. In addition the following abbreviations appear as superscripts to these sigla:

ac	*ante correctionem* (before correction)
pc	*post correctionem* (after correction)
s	*supra lineam* (above the line)

Other abbreviations are listed below. Modern works not listed are referred to by author and date, and particulars given in the Bibliography; but the editions of Arnott 2000, Austin 1969–70, Dedoussi 2006, Gomme & Sandbach 1973,[1] Jacques 1971 and Lamagna 1998 are normally referred to by the editor's name alone.

Note on line references: references in the form '47–8' are to the two (or more) lines so numbered; references in the form '57/8' are to the lacuna

---

[1] In references to passages in the Gomme-Sandbach commentary that must have been written, or fundamentally rewritten, after the appearance of the Bodmer papyrus, Sandbach's name is used alone.

between these lines, or to actions that take place between the end of one spoken line and the beginning of the next.

Ant.	Antiphon
Apoll.	Apollodorus[2]
Fab. Inc.	Menander, *Fabula Incerta* (Sandbach) = *Fabula Incerta 1* (Arnott)
FGrH	F. Jacoby et al., *Die Fragmente der griechischen Historiker* (Berlin/Leiden, 1923–)
h. Dem.	*Homeric Hymn to Demeter*
IC	M. Guarducci, *Inscriptiones Creticae* (Rome, 1935–50)
IG	*Inscriptiones Graecae*
Karch.	Menander, *Karchedonios*
Koster	W. J. W. Koster et al., *Scholia in Aristophanem* (Groningen, 1960–2007)
LGPN	M. J. Osborne and S. G. Byrne, *A lexicon of Greek personal names. Vol. 2: Attica* (Oxford, 1994)
LIMC	*Lexicon iconographicum mythologiae classicae* (Zurich, 1981–99)
LSJ	H. G. Liddell and R. Scott, *A Greek-English lexicon*, 9th edn rev. by H. Stuart Jones (Oxford, 1926–40) with *Revised Supplement* by P. G. W. Glare (Oxford, 1996)
Lyc. *Leocr.*	Lycurgus [not Lycophron], *Against Leocrates*
OCD[4]	S. Hornblower, A. J. W. Spawforth and E. Eidinow, eds. *The Oxford classical dictionary*, 4th edn (Oxford, 2012)
OED	*Oxford English dictionary* (online edition: www.oed.com)
PAA	J. S. Traill, *Persons of ancient Athens* (Toronto, 1994–)
PBingen	H. Melaerts, ed. *Papyri in honorem Johannis Bingen octogenarii (P. Bingen)* (Leuven, 2000)
PCG	R. Kassel and C. F. L. Austin, *Poetae comici Graeci* (Berlin, 1983–2001)
RE	*Paulys Real-Encyclopädie der classischen Altertumswissenschaft: Neue Bearbeitung* (Stuttgart, 1894–1980)

---

[2] If the name is in square brackets, the reference is to the mythographer.

Rhodes and Osborne	P. J. Rhodes and R. G. Osborne, *Greek historical inscriptions, 404–323 B.C.* (Oxford, 2003)
schol.	scholium or scholia
SH	H. Lloyd-Jones and P. J. Parsons, *Supplementum Hellenisticum* (Berlin, 1983)
Sik.	Menander, *Sikyonioi*
SVF	H. F. A. von Arnim, *Stoicorum veterum fragmenta* (Leipzig, 1903–24)
test.	testimonium
TrGF	*Tragicorum Graecorum fragmenta* (Göttingen, 1971–2004)

INTRODUCTION

1 MENANDER'S LIFE AND CAREER

Menander, son of Diopeithes (of the Athenian deme of Cephisia) and his wife Hegestrate,[1] was born in the Athenian year 342/1 BC;[2] he was thus about three years old when Macedonian hegemony over Greece was firmly established with Philip II's defeat of the Athenians and Thebans at Chaeronea, and came of age, at eighteen, in the year (324/3) near the end of which Alexander the Great died in Babylon. In accordance with the practice of the time ([Arist.] *Ath.Pol.* 42), he spent the following two years (323/2 and 322/1) living the semi-segregated life of an 'ephebe' (cf. 10n.) in the company of his age-mates, one of whom was destined for a fame equalling his own – the future philosopher Epicurus;[3] these years witnessed the crushing of an Athenian-led anti-Macedonian revolt in the so-called Lamian War, followed by the disfranchisement of the poorer citizens (many of whom were deported to Thrace) by command of the Macedonian regent Antipater, who also ordered several leading demo-cratic politicians, including Demosthenes and Hypereides, to be executed without trial, and placed a Macedonian garrison at the Peiraeus.[4] From then on, despite repeated regime changes including several restorations of democracy, Athens always remained dependent on one or another of the Macedonian dynasts who fought each other for shares of Alexander's empire.[5]

Menander, it seems, had chosen the profession of a comic poet at an early age; one source claims that he attached himself to an established dramatist, Alexis of Thurii, to learn the craft.[6] At any rate he was still an

[1] Apollodorus *FGrH* 244 F 43; *IG* XIV 1184; Paus. 1.2.2; *Suda* μ 89. His father was probably born in 385/4, since a Diopeithes of Cephisia is named in a list of public arbitrators for the year 325/4 (*IG* II² 1926.17–19) during which his sixtieth birthday must therefore have fallen ([Arist.] *Ath.Pol.* 53.4).

[2] *IG* XIV 1184; confirmed by D.L. 10.14 (= Apollodorus *FGrH* 244 F 42), which gives this as the birth-date of Menander's exact contemporary (see below) Epicurus.

[3] Strabo 14.1.18. Epicurus had then only recently come to Athens, his parents having been Athenian settlers (cleruchs) on Samos (ibid. and D.L. 10.1).

[4] Plut. *Phoc.* 27.7–29.1, *Dem.* 28–29; D.S. 18.18.4–5. Demosthenes avoided exe-cution by suicide. Political rights were limited to those possessing property worth at least 2000 drachmae.

[5] For the political history of these decades see Habicht 1997, Bayliss 2011 and Waterfield 2011, also Lape 2004: 40–67 and (for the period down to 307) O'Sullivan 2009.

[6] *Prolegomena de Comoedia* III 57–58 Koster. The *Suda* (α 1138) even asserts, impossibly, that Alexis was Menander's paternal uncle. See Arnott 1996b: 11–13.

ephebe when, in 321, he produced *Orge (Anger)*,[7] the first of his 108 plays.[8]
We do not know for certain when he won his first victory; it may not have
been until 316, when he was successful at the Lenaea with *Dyskolos*.[9] The
following year he won at the City Dionysia for the first time;[10] in total, however, he was to gain in his career only eight victories[11] – though this may
still have been more than any of his numerous rivals achieved in the same
period.[12] It should be remembered that little more than half of Menander's plays can have been produced at the two main Athenian festivals
during his thirty years of activity, even supposing that he applied and was
selected to compete on every possible occasion; the remainder must have
been staged at some of the many other dramatic festivals which by the late
fourth century were being held in Attica and elsewhere.[13]

Once, but apparently only once, Menander found himself in danger
for political reasons. When Demetrius of Phalerum, who had been effectively the sole ruler of Athens for ten years under the aegis of Antipater's
son Cassander, was overthrown in 307 by the intervention of two other
Macedonian dynasts (Antigonus Monophthalmus and his son Demetrius
Poliorcetes) and democracy was restored, there was a wave of vengeful leg-
islation and litigation against the ex-tyrant's friends or supposed friends.
Demetrius had been a pupil of Theophrastus and a follower of the Peri-
patetic school of philosophy, and a law was passed, on the proposal of one

---

[7] *Prolegomena de Comoedia* III 58–59 Koster – which appears to say he was the first
ephebe ever to do so (quite plausible, since the full-blown ephebic system was only
thirteen years old: D. M. Lewis 1973: 254; Sommerstein 2010: 48–49). The one
manuscript gives the date as that of the archonship of Diocles; there was no archon
of this name in the relevant period, and the name is usually emended to Philocles
(322/1) – the only plausible alternative, Anticles (325/4), is incompatible with our
transmitted birth dates both for Menander and for Epicurus. Different versions of
the chronicle of Eusebius give the date 322/1 and 321/0 for this production; they
state (probably wrongly) that it was victorious. See Schröder 1996.
[8] So *Prolegomena de Comoedia* III 60 Koster; Apollodorus *FGrH* 244 F 43 gives the
number as 105. We know the titles of about 98 plays.
[9] Hypothesis to *Dyskolos*. The papyrus names the archon as Didymogenes; this is
usually emended to Demogenes, the archon of 317/16.
[10] *Marm.Par. (FGrH* 239 B 14).
[11] A. Gellius 17.4.4, citing Apollodorus. At least four of these successes were at
the City Dionysia (cf. *IG* ii² 2325.160).
[12] Philemon, widely regarded in antiquity as second only to Menander in the
genre (Quintilian 10.1.72), gained only three Lenaean victories in a career of some
sixty-five years (*IG* II² 2325.161). In the Lenaean victor-list, Menander and Philemon are eighth and ninth in a sequence of fifteen wholly or partly preserved names
(lines 153–167); at least eight of these fifteen dramatists gained only one win each,
and probably none had more than three (unless Menander had four – against his
name only the first unit-stroke survives). See Konstantakos 2008.
[13] On the spread of theatre in the fourth century, see Csapo 2010: 83–103; on
the Hellenistic period, Le Guen 1995 and many of the contributors to P. J. Wilson
2007.

Sophocles of Sunium, that no one was to be allowed to maintain a philosophical school unless authorized to do so by the Council and Assembly,
whereupon Theophrastus and his followers left Athens.[14] Menander was
not a philosopher (though according to one source he too had studied
with Theophrastus),[15] but he had been, or was believed to have been, a
friend of Demetrius,[16] and he is said to have 'come close to being put on
trial' for that reason[17] but was 'begged off' by Telesphorus, a kinsman of
Antigonus and his son.[18]

Menander appears never to have married, and there is no record of
his having any children. In later centuries he was believed to have lived
with a *hetaira* named Glykera, and Alciphron (2nd/3rd century AD), the
writer of fictional letters from classical and early Hellenistic Athens, created a letter of Menander to Glykera and a reply;[19] but when we find that
Menander is also said to have had another mistress named Thaïs (Martial
Epigr. 14.187–8), suspicion is aroused, since *Glykera* and *Thaïs* were the
titles of two of Menander's plays.[20] Alciphron's letters are built around an
invitation that Menander is supposed to have received from King Ptolemy
(I of Egypt), which he intends to decline;[21] that he received, and refused,
such invitations from Ptolemy and also from an unidentified king of Mace-
donia is also stated by the elder Pliny (*HN* 7.111).

We do not have enough datable material to be able to follow the development of Menander's technique and style, except in a few respects such
as the virtual disappearance of personal satire in his middle and later works
(see §8). Plutarch, however, who clearly did know the sequence of many
of the plays,[22] says (*Mor.* 853f) that while Menander right from the start of

---

[14] D.L. 5.38; cf. Athen. 610e-f, Pollux 9.42, Alexis fr. 99, and see Arnott 1996b:
259–265, 858–9 (who makes the law sound more innocuous than it was). The law
was annulled a year later, and Sophocles heavily fined (despite being defended by
Demochares, nephew of Demosthenes).

[15] D.L. 5.36, citing Pamphile.

[16] It is striking that Menander's only two datable victories came in the first two
years of Demetrius' rule.

[17] No doubt in the actual indictment, had things got so far, some allegation of
an actual legal offence would have been concocted.

[18] D.L. 5.79.   [19] Alciphr. 4.18–19.

[20] Accordingly Alciphron makes Glykera speak of 'the play you've put me into'
(4.19.20).

[21] Menander writes from the Peiraeus, and says he is in indifferent health
(4.18.4); apparently we are meant to infer that these are the last letters that passed
between him and Glykera.

[22] Very likely from synopses (Hypotheses) either prefixed to play-texts or com-
piled into books on their own; in a surviving fragment of such a book (*POxy*
1235.103–12) we are told, not only that *Imbrioi* was to have been produced at the
Dionysia of 301 (but the festival, or at least the comic contest, was not held owing
to a political upheaval), but also that it was 71st (or 73rd or 76th or 79th) in the

his career was adept at matching each character's language to his or her age and personality,

> when he died he was at his peak as a poet and producer, at the time of life when, according to Aristotle, authors show the greatest improvement as regards style. If one compares the earliest plays of Menander with those of his middle and his last periods, one will realize from that how much further he would have advanced had he lived.

Menander died in his fifty-second year (291/0);[23] according to a tradition known to Ovid (*Ibis* 591), which may go back to Menander's near-contemporary Callimachus (fr. 396 Pfeiffer), he was drowned while swimming at the Peiraeus.[24] He was buried beside the Athens-Peiraeus road, where his tomb was seen by Pausanias more than four centuries later (Paus. 1.2.2). Soon afterwards he was honoured with a seated statue in the theatre (Paus. 1.21.1; see Papastamati-von Moock 2007, Zanker 1995: 78–83);[25] its inscribed base survives (*IG* II^2 3777), naming its makers as Cephisodotus and Timarchus, sculptors of the early third century and sons of the great Praxiteles (Pliny *HN* 34.51, 36.24). Many surviving sculptures and other images appear to be direct or indirect copies of this statue.[26]

2 NEW COMEDY

The periodization of Athenian comedy into 'Old', 'Middle' and 'New' phases, though it goes well back into antiquity,[27] is necessarily artificial,

---

sequence of Menander's plays – roughly where we should expect it to be, coming about two-thirds of the way through his career.

[23] All our sources (Apollodorus *FGrH* 244 F 43; *IG* xiv 1184; *Prolegomena de Comoedia* III 60 Koster) agree on Menander's age at death. Those that give a date for it (*IG* XIV 1184, and two versions of Eusebius' chronicle) place it in 292/1 (*IG* XIV 1184 names the Athenian archon, Philippus, and adds that it was the thirty-second year of Ptolemy I); this, however, would be only the fifty-first year of Menander's life, and it is likely that the attempt to equate dates in calendars that began their year at different seasons has led to a slippage of one year (see Schröder 1996: 35–42).

[24] The identification of the comic poet who, in Ovid's words, *liquidis periit, dum nabat, in undis*, as Menander, and the statement that Callimachus wrote an epigram on his death, both depend on a scholium in a single MS of dubious authority (see Pfeiffer 1949: 324–5); but *dum nabat* 'while swimming' does not fit the stories of the death by drowning of Eupolis (Cicero, *Ad Atticum* 6.1.18; *Suda* ε 3657) or of Terence (Suetonius, *Life of Terence* 4–5), and there is nothing surprising in a middle-aged Athenian going swimming for pleasure, for exercise, or to maintain an important survival skill (see Hall 1993).

[25] Zanker argues that many features of the statue, as reconstructed from later copies, suggest that it was designed to associate Menander with an elitist, anti-democratic ideology.

[26] On these see Blume 1998: 12–15.

[27] Possibly as far as Aristophanes of Byzantium in the second century BC (Nesselrath 1990: 180–7, Olson 2007: 22–6).

particularly since it was conventional to assign any given poet exclusively to one of the three periods. What can be said is that when Menander's career began, the dominant form of comedy was already in essentials the type with which he is exclusively associated. Aristotle, who died in 322, discusses in the ninth chapter of his *Poetics* the distinction between poetry (by which he means epic or dramatic poetry) and history: history tells what happened to particular persons on particular occasions ('what Alcibiades did or what was done to him'), poetry tells 'the sort of thing that tends to happen' (οἷα ἂν γένοιτο) or 'what kinds of things will inevitably or probably be said or done by what kind of person'.[28] And Aristotle continues:

> This has now become clear (ἤδη ... δῆλον γέγονεν) in the case of comedy; for they put together their plot using probable events and then apply random names [to the characters], and do not write about individuals in the manner of the iambic poets. In the case of tragedy, on the other hand, the poets stick to real names.[29]

The characterization of contemporary comedy in this passage fits Menander's practice very well, if we assume – as we must in the case of tragedy also – that in speaking of 'probable' events Aristotle is not thinking of the situations which, as it were, generate the plot, and which often, both in comedy and in tragedy, involve highly implausible coincidences,[30] but the decisions and actions of the characters in response to these situations ('what ... will inevitably or probably be said or done') and their consequences. And it clearly distinguishes this type of comedy from two other types. One is the type associated with Aristophanes and his contemporaries who often 'wr[o]te about individuals in the manner of the iambic poets' in plays focusing directly and openly on topical events, issues and personalities. Comedy of that kind was not entirely obsolete in Aristotle's time,[31]

---

[28] Arist. *Poet.* 1451a36-b11.

[29] Arist. *Poet.* 1451b11–16. By 'real names' (τῶν γενομένων ὀνομάτων) Aristotle means the names of persons whom we would now call mythical.

[30] Such as that two travellers who meet and quarrel fatally on a lonely road should be a father and the son whom he had ordered should be left to die at the age of two days; or that (as in both the *Aspis* and *Misoumenos* of Menander) after soldier A had borrowed an item of equipment from soldier B, the former should be killed and the latter taken prisoner, with the result that B is mistakenly reported dead.

[31] Timocles, who stands next but one before Menander in the Lenaea victor-list, wrote several plays whose titles recall fifth-century comedies or their themes – *Demosatyroi* (i.e. womanizing politicians, cf. fr. 5?), *Dionysiazusae, Dionysus, Heroes, Orestautokleides, Philodikastes* (i.e. a lover of jury service, cf. Ar. *Wasps*) – and his forty-two surviving fragments contain no less than forty-nine references to thirty-seven different contemporary individuals, including Demosthenes (frr. 4, 12, 41), Hypereides (frr. 4, 17) and about a dozen other men active in public affairs. At an even later date, probably in 302/1, Philippides, himself active in politics and diplomacy (*IG* II² 657), attacked Stratocles, the leading figure in Athenian politics

and even in *Samia* there are three passages satirizing contemporary individuals,[32] but as a broad generalization Aristotle's statement holds true.[33] The other declining variety of comedy was the burlesque treatment of mythical or tragic stories, which had been so popular in the mid-fourth century that it formed the majority of the output of a dramatist like Eubulus;[34] there are still a few such plays in the output of Menander's older contemporaries Diphilus and Philemon,[35] but Menander himself wrote none.

Of the comedy of his day we possess a sample that is substantial in absolute terms though small in comparison with the total output of the dramatists of the time,[36] comprising papyrus fragments, ancient quotations, and more than a score of comedies by the Roman dramatists Plautus and Terence adapted from plays by Menander, his contemporaries and their successors.[37] This evidence suggests that the genre was dominated (though

at the time, and his patron Demetrius Poliorcetes (Philippides frr. 25, 26) – though he may have prudently left Attica shortly afterwards (O'Sullivan 2009: 64–78; Sommerstein forthcoming (*a*) 290–1), and in general, after 322, the only political figures mentioned disparagingly in comedy were safe targets – that is, men who were either not in Athens (and not in control of Athens) or else completely out of favour with the current regime (606–8n.)

[32] Diomnestus (504–5), Chaerephon (603–4) and Androcles (606–8).

[33] So prominent and controversial a politician as Demosthenes is mentioned only twice in comic fragments not attributed to Timocles (Antiphanes fr. 167, *com. adesp.* 149); in the 339 fragments of Alexis, whose career had begun over thirty years before Menander's, only four political figures are mentioned – one (nine times) for his love of expensive food, one (three times) for his extreme thinness, one (twice) for his legislative harassment of fishmongers, and one (just possibly) for his political activity (Aristogeiton, Alexis fr. 211; cf. Dem. 25 and 26 and Deinarchus 2).

[34] Hunter 1983: 22 n.3 lists 28 mythological titles out of a total of 57, to which should possibly be added *Echo*.

[35] Diphilus' sixty-two known titles include *The Danaids, Heracles, Theseus, The Lemnian Women, The Daughters of Pelias* and *Pyrrha* (wife of the Flood hero Deucalion); to these should be added *Sappho*, since the great woman poet, dead more than two centuries, had become a quasi-mythical figure. Philemon's sixty-one known titles include *The Myrmidons* and possibly *Apollo* and *Palamedes*.

[36] We know that both at the City Dionysia of 312 (*IG* II[2] 2323a.36–9) and at the Lenaea of 285 (*IG* II[2] 2319.56–9) the number of competing comedies was five. If this was the regular number throughout the period, then over Menander's thirty-year career a total of 300 plays will have been accepted for performance at these major Athenian festivals alone, and perhaps as many more (cf. p. 2 above) were performed elsewhere and their scripts preserved.

[37] For twelve of the twenty-one plays of Plautus, and for all six of those of Terence, a Greek source is identified (in the script or by an ancient commentator) or can be inferred with reasonable confidence. Of the Plautine plays, *Bacchides, Cistellaria* and *Stichus* are based on plays of Menander; *Casina, Rudens* and *Vidularia* on Diphilus; *Mercator* and *Trinummus* on Philemon; *Poenulus* and perhaps *Aulularia* (see Arnott 1996b: 859–64) on Alexis, *Asinaria* on the otherwise unknown Demophilus, and *Miles Gloriosus* on a play named *Alazon* by an unidentified poet

not monopolized)[38] by plots in which the driving force was heterosexual love, usually (though not invariably)[39] viewed from the male perspective, and the goal of the action was either the achievement of a desired union (sometimes a marriage, sometimes a relationship with a *hetaira*) against opposition from one or more quarters or (as happens in *Epitrepontes, Misoumenos* and *Perikeiromene*) the re-establishment of an existing union after it had been disrupted. *Samia* includes both (the disrupted and re-established union being that of Demeas and Chrysis),[40] but is unusual inasmuch as during the greater part of the play there is no opposition whatsoever to the projected marriage between Moschion and Plangon: all the difficulties that arise are caused by the *mistaken belief* of Moschion and his confederates that one or both of the young people's fathers will be opposed to the match, together with their correct belief that at least one of the fathers will fall into uncontrollable rage if he comes to know why it is essential that the marriage take place, with the result that 'the young man unwittingly becomes his own obstructor' (Goldberg 1980: 21).

The formal structure of New Comedy is very simple. Every play, it seems, consisted of five acts, separated by choral interludes. The chorus was still

(the title is not otherwise attested). Terence adapted four of his plays from Menander and the other two, *Phormio* and *Hecyra*, from Apollodorus of Carystus, a dramatist of the following generation. One play of Plautus, *Amphitruo*, has a myth-based plot, and its Greek source may be of somewhat earlier date.

[38] In two plays of Plautus, *Captivi* and *Menaechmi*, the action instead centres on an attempt to reunite separated kinsfolk; in *Menaechmi* the love interest is subordinate, in *Captivi* there is none at all. The (re)union of family members who had been long separated, or who had been unaware of each other's identity, is an important feature in many other plays also, including *Samia* (see §3).

[39] In Plautus' *Cistellaria* (59–95), which is known to have been adapted from Menander's *Synaristosai*, the young woman Selenium declares herself to be hopelessly in love with Alcesimarchus, who is living with her and has sworn to marry her even though she is believed to be of foreign birth; the marriage eventually becomes possible when Selenium is discovered to be a citizen (of Sicyon, where the action is set, not of Athens). If, as is likely, *PHeid* 175 (= *com. adesp.* 1074 K-A) comes from *Synaristosai* (see Arnott 2000: 325–37), it would appear that Plautus is here keeping quite close to his original, though we cannot be quite sure that Selenium's Greek counterpart (whose name, as we know from a Mytilene mosaic, was either Plangon or Pythias) was represented as having such passionate feelings or expressing them so strongly.

[40] In featuring *two* united or reunited couples, *Samia* appears to be typical of Menander's practice. With the possible exception of *Misoumenos* (but cf. *Mis.* 270–4 S = 671–5 A where Kleinias speaks of 'a girl of mine' about whom he is 'in agony' and for whom, if she does not come to his party, he will be searching all over the city), all Menander's seven best preserved plays seem to end with the union/reunion of two couples: in *Dyskolos*, we have Sostratos and Knemon's daughter, and Gorgias and Sostratos' sister; in *Epitrepontes*, Charisios and Pamphile, Chairestratos and Habrotonon (see n. 72 below); in *Perikeiromene*, Polemon and Glykera, Moschion and the daughter of Philinos (1025–6). See Blanchard 2007: 131–4.

an essential part of the performance (737n.) but had virtually no role
in the drama; it was conventional for a character to remark, at the end
of the first act, on the approach of (usually) a band of drunken youths
(119a/b n.), and then to make an exit so as to avoid getting in their way,
but in the surviving Menandrian texts the chorus is never, after that point,
mentioned at all, except that at each act-break there is a notation χοροῦ
('<performance> of the chorus'). We cannot even tell by direct evidence
whether the chorus only danced or whether they also sang (probably the
latter, if only because bands of drunken youths are more usually noisy than
silent), nor what they did during the acts,[41] nor whether they departed
after their last interlude or remained to the end of the play (probably the
latter, since they would then be able to sing appropriately in accompaniment to the festive final exit of the principals).

Within the acts, almost all the verse was spoken, except for an occasional
solo song,[42] though the piper who accompanied the choral interludes may
also have played during, and given a stricter rhythm to, at least some of
the passages written in iambic or trochaic tetrameters.[43] The action was
in principle continuous within each act, though sometimes the scene may
be briefly empty of actors between an exit and the next entrance.[44] No
more than three speaking characters are ever on stage at any one time,[45]
and it is likely, though not certain, that the plays were written so as to be
performable by a troupe of three actors (see §10).

The imaginary location of the action was normally a street or other public space outside two (sometimes possibly three) private houses;[46] each of
these houses might belong to a head of family (like Demeas and Nikeratos
in *Samia*), to a bachelor (like young Chairestratos in *Epitrepontes*, elderly
Smikrines in *Aspis*, or the soldiers in *Misoumenos* and *Perikeiromene*), or to
a *hetaira* (as in *Dis Exapaton* and *Synaristosai*). Other persons or families
of significance to the action might be imagined as living at a little distance (like Kallippides in *Dyskolos*, Smikrines in *Epitrepontes*, or the farmer

---

[41] Possibly they retired to an inconspicuous position at the edge of the *orchestra*;
there is some reason to believe that choruses sometimes did this even in Aristophanes' time (see Sommerstein 1990: 202).

[42] E.g. *Theoph.* 6–27 S = 36–57 A; *Leukadia* 11–16 A.

[43] See opening note to Act IV.

[44] In *Samia* this happens only in the first act, once for certain at 95/96 (exit
Moschion, then enter Demeas and Nikeratos with servants) and probably also in
the lacuna between 57 and 58 (exit Moschion, then enter Chrysis; see 57/58n.).
In *Dyskolos* it occurs in all five acts, seven times in all (49/50, 392/3, 455/6, 521/2,
638/9, 665/6, 873/4).

[45] Whereas in Aristophanes there are several scenes involving four speaking
characters (MacDowell 1994).

[46] The third door, in the centre, could also represent the entrance to another
kind of interior space (e.g. a cave-shrine in *Dyskolos*, a temple in *Leukadia*).

Kleainetos in *Georgos*) or may arrive during the play as visitors from further afield (like Demeas in *Misoumenos*). The action of the drama is essentially the *inter*action of these family members and individuals.

The characters are usually assignable to a limited number of stock types, who appear to have been fairly readily recognizable, even before they spoke or were spoken to, by their masks and costumes (see §10). The main categories were: young citizen men (unmarried or newly-married); older citizen men[47] (of an age to have marriageable children); marriageable maidens (or recently married wives), and young women of obscurer status who are eventually discovered to be marriageable; *hetairai*; professional soldiers; parasites (men who tried to live, so far as possible, at other people's expense);[48] brothel-keepers, male or female (*pornoboskoi*); cooks; slaves or ex-slaves of both sexes and all ages. This is a very limited and skewed sample of society – but it is all that is needed to make a typical New Comedy plot work; and in Menander's hands it was capable of almost infinite variety, because, in the words of Louis MacNeice,[49] he knew 'all the tricks of the virtuosos who invert the usual': he delighted in creating characters who failed to behave in the manner expected of a person of their type[50] and putting them to work in generating new plot structures.

New Comedy resembled tragedy, and differed markedly from what we know of Old Comedy, in that it was usually in broad terms predictable how a play would end. The young man in love would gain the bride he desired; the couple on the point of splitting up would come back together; the soldier reported dead would come back alive and well. Frequently, too, the audience, early in the play, would be let into secrets that remained unknown to the characters, or most of them, by means of a prologue spoken by an omniscient divinity – sometimes at the outset of the play (as in *Dyskolos*), more often, it seems, after an opening scene or scenes had aroused their curiosity. With the conclusion therefore largely known in advance, most of the plot interest would lie in uncertainty about how it would be reached and in the detours that might arise along the way.[51]

---

[47] There are virtually no citizen males of intermediate age in New Comedy, just as there are virtually no children who have passed babyhood but not reached adolescence.

[48] Such as the real-life figure of Chaerephon (603n.).

[49] Cited by Turner 1979: 108.

[50] Consider even the minor figure of the Cook in *Samia*, who seems at first a thoroughly conventional example of his self-important, narrowly professional type, but who ends (383–90) by persistently attempting, despite repeated rebuffs, to intervene to prevent an injustice.

[51] In *Aspis*, for instance, we are told in the delayed prologue (97–148), by the goddess Chance, that the supposedly dead Kleostratos will come back alive, and that Smikrines' scheme to marry the young man's sister (now, after her brother's presumed death, a substantial heiress) will fail. Kleostratos actually returns towards

In *Samia* some very important facts are unknown to one part of the cast (Demeas and Nikeratos, returning from abroad), but they are known to the other part (their households back in Athens), and there is no need for a divine prologue; instead Moschion is made to explain the initial situation to us himself – and in doing so, to reveal much to us about his personality and his weaknesses.

3 THE PLOT OF *SAMIA*

Although only about half of the first two acts has survived, the essentials of the action can be reconstructed with very little uncertainty, not least because in the early part of the play the action appears to have been rather slow-moving.

Demeas,[52] a wealthy, unmarried[53] Athenian, adopted Moschion[54] as his son when Moschion was a young child[55] (cf. 7–9) and brought him up in affluence (13–16). After Moschion had grown up, Demeas, by then fairly

---

the end of Act IV (491–509). Up to that point the action has been built almost entirely around a scheme, conceived by Kleostratos' loyal slave Daos, to fake the death of Smikrines' very wealthy brother Chairestratos so that Smikrines will transfer his marital ambitions to Chairestratos' daughter (heiress to a far larger fortune). Kleostratos returns just as this scheme is proving successful – Smikrines learns of Chairestratos' 'death' (471–3) and apparently agrees to renounce his right to marry Kleostratos' sister in favour of Chaireas, whom she knows well and who loves her (484ff, see Arnott 1979: 83–5, Ireland 2010: 104–5) – and thereby makes it unnecessary; but it is Daos' scheme that has been the core of the play, producing some fine comic scenes (especially, in the surviving portions, those involving the bogus doctor), exposing Smikrines' blind avarice and making a thorough fool of him.

[52] One of the names regularly employed for old men in New Comedy; it is found in *Dis Exapaton, Misoumenos, Imbrioi* (fr. 190), in Alexis' *Pyraunos* (fr. 205), in several papyrus fragments of unidentified comedies (*com. adesp.* 1008, 1014, 1093), and in Terence's *Adelphoe.*

[53] It is not clear from the surviving text whether he is a bachelor or a childless widower.

[54] Moschion ('Bullock') is the most frequent name in Menander for a young man in love (cf. Choricius of Gaza 32.2.73 Foerster-Richtsteig = Men. test. 141 *PCG*); it appears in at least six other plays of his and in several unattributed papyrus fragments (*com. adesp.* 1063, 1096, 1098, 1129, 1130), but seems to have been avoided by Roman dramatists. It was a fairly common name in the Athens of his time, being borne by a tragic dramatist (*TrGF* I, no. 97) and by a parasite who is mentioned several times in comic and quasi-comic texts (Alexis fr. 238, Axionicus fr. 4.14, Machon fr. 6.46 Gow) and who may have been the title character of a comedy by Callicrates.

[55] In ancient Athens the primary purpose of adoption was not to provide a home for an orphaned or unwanted child, but to provide a direct heir for a family that lacked one; accordingly an adopted child had to be of legitimate citizen birth, and a man who already had a son could not adopt another. For Athenian laws and customs regarding adoption see Harrison 1968: 82–96; MacDowell 1978: 99–101; Rubinstein 1993.

advanced in years,[56] fell in love with a *hetaira* from Samos named Chrysis,[57] and Moschion encouraged him to take her into his house (19–28).

Moschion himself fell in love[58] with Plangon,[59] the daughter and only child of Nikeratos,[60] Demeas' much poorer neighbour. Apparently, however, he at first took no steps to seek her hand in marriage, possibly because he was afraid his father would object to his choosing a bride who would bring little or nothing by way of dowry. Then Demeas and Nikeratos went away together on a long business trip[61] to the Black Sea region – which ruled out any possibility of marriage until such time as they returned. Plangon's mother and Chrysis struck up a friendship (35–8), which led to their holding an all-night women's party together at Demeas' and Moschion's house for the festival of the Adonia (38–46) – during which Moschion raped Plangon (see §5) with the result that she became pregnant (47–50). He immediately went to see Plangon's mother and made a sworn promise to marry her when her father returned (53n.).

But Demeas and Nikeratos did not return for many months – so long, indeed, that the baby (a boy)[62] was born while they were still away. Its parents, together with Plangon's mother, Chrysis, and Moschion's slave Parmenon,[63] decided to conceal the birth until Moschion and Plangon were

---

[56] The Cook calls him a γέρων (361), but this may only mean that he is old enough to have an adult son. Oedipus speaks of the man he killed on the road as a πρέσβυς (Soph. *OT* 805, 807) when, according to Iocaste, Laius' hair was 'just becoming sprinkled with grey' (ibid. 742).

[57] Chrysis ('Goldie') was a common name for *hetairai* both in real life (*Kolax* F 4; Timocles fr. 27.4; title of a play by Antiphanes; Plut. *Dem.* 24.1) and in comedy (see note on *PBerol* 8450 = *com. adesp.* 1131 at end of commentary).

[58] He probably made this clear in the lacuna between 29 and 30 (see 29/30n.).

[59] Plangon ('Dolly') was a name commonly given to Athenian girls (see e.g. Dem. 39.9) and could also be borne by *hetairai* (Anaxilas fr. 22.8; title of play by Eubulus; Timocles fr. 27.2). As a fictive name in comedy, however, it seems always to be applied to young women who are, or eventually prove to be, of citizen birth and marriageable (*Dysk.* 430, see Sandbach 1973: 203; *Heros* 24, 37; and the Mytilene mosaic of *Synaristosai*, where Plangon probably corresponds to Selenium in Plautus' *Cistellaria* who proves to be of Sicyonian citizen birth and can marry her lover Alcesimarchus).

[60] This common Athenian name, most famously borne by the father of the fifth-century statesman and general Nicias, is not found elsewhere in Menander (unless *com. adesp.* 1017 – in which Nikeratos appears to be a *young* man – is his); it appears in a cook's speech (Strato fr. 1.13), alongside the names Moschion and Philinos (*Perik.* 1026), in a list of diners.

[61] We are never, in the surviving text, actually told their purpose of the journey, but it certainly was for business and not for pleasure: both men found the climate, the food and the people distasteful (96–111, 417).

[62] We learn the baby's gender only at 132, but Menander's audience would probably have guessed it long before; in a Menandrian comedy, a baby recently born, or born during the course of the play, is invariably male.

[63] Parmenon ('Steadfast', literally 'Remaining by one's side' – ironically inappropriate to this particular character) had been a regular name for comic slaves at least since the early fourth century (Ar. *Eccl.* 868). Menander used it in *Theophoroumene*

safely married; their reason for doing this is lost in the lacuna between 57 and 58, but given the temperament of Nikeratos as we see it later (492–584), it is highly likely that they were terrified of what he might do if he discovered that his daughter had had a child out of wedlock (see 54n.). As it happened, Chrysis, about the same time or a little earlier, had herself given birth, but her baby had died (55–6n.). It thus became possible for the baby to be taken into her house and for her to suckle it[64] and pretend it was her own. As we shall discover later, everyone in the house knows who the baby's real parents are.

This is the situation when the action of the play begins. Parmenon, who has been sent to the harbour, returns (61) with the news that Demeas' and Nikeratos' ship has arrived, and Moschion knows that for him the crisis is imminent. He resolves, despite considerable apprehension, to ask Demeas immediately for permission to marry Plangon; in the meantime the pretence will be maintained that Chrysis is the baby's mother. Moschion goes off to practise the speech he will have to make to his father, and thus misses Demeas' and Nikeratos' homecoming. From the two men's conversation we learn that they have already agreed (on Demeas' initiative, 117–18) to marry their children to each other, and it may almost seem as though the play is over before it has properly begun. (Act I ends here.)

Demeas is angered to discover that Chrysis has apparently had a child and kept it instead of exposing it (132n.), and threatens to throw them both out of his house (133–4) but is persuaded by Moschion to relent. He then asks Moschion whether he is willing to marry Plangon, and is surprised and delighted by his enthusiastic agreement. Demeas next half persuades, half bullies Nikeratos into agreeing to hold the wedding this very day (167–88); Moschion, evidently not wanting to face Nikeratos before he has to, has gone off to the Agora. Parmenon is sent off to make the necessary purchases for the wedding feast and to hire a cook (189–95), and shortly afterwards Nikeratos also goes shopping. Once again all problems seem to have been solved. (Act II ends here.)

In the midst of the wedding preparations, Demeas overhears an old freedwoman talking half to the baby and half to herself, in terms that make it clear that Moschion is the baby's father; immediately afterwards he sees Chrysis suckling the child, seemingly confirming that she is its mother. Moschion, it seems, must have cuckolded Demeas in his absence. The returning Parmenon is forced to confess that the baby is Moschion's,

---

(Mytilene mosaic), *Plokion* (fr. 300), *Hypobolimaios* (fr. 373), and doubtless other plays (frr. 798, 901).

[64] Though Plangon would be able to visit the house from time to time and give the baby some feeds, thus maintaining her milk flow and her bond with the child (57/58n.)

but when threatened with a savage flogging (321–3) he runs away, leaving Demeas in possession of only half the truth. Demeas, being certain that Moschion is of virtuous character, argues himself into believing that the supposed affair must be all Chrysis' fault, and – though still very much in love with her (350, 356) – he resolves to expel her from his house, and immediately does so; for the sake of Moschion's reputation, however, he pretends that he is punishing her only for keeping the baby (374–5). Nikeratos returns home shortly afterwards, hears what has happened to Chrysis, and sympathetically takes her into his house. (Here Act III ends.)

Nikeratos, on his wife's insistence (421), decides to intercede with Demeas on behalf of Chrysis; but when Moschion returns from town, Nikeratos asks him to make the first approach. Demeas sees Moschion's intervention as proof that in the supposed affair with Chrysis, Moschion had not after all been an innocent victim, and that the two are still in league; and there follows a long argument at cross-purposes, in which almost everything Moschion says makes Demeas more and more certain of his guilt, until he loses control of himself and begins to shout, thus revealing the quarrel and its cause to Nikeratos. Nikeratos now denounces Moschion in ferocious terms and declares that he would not now dream of letting him marry Plangon (502–5); and he hardly needs Demeas' urging (517–18) to rush into his house with the intention of expelling Chrysis. Moschion hastily takes the opportunity to confess the truth to his father: the baby is his, but its mother is Plangon. Almost before Demeas can take this in, Nikeratos reappears, thunderstruck at having seen Plangon suckling the baby. Demeas, now sure that Moschion has told the truth, apologizes for his suspicions; Moschion, terrified of what Nikeratos may now do, takes to his heels. Demeas is left to cope as best he can with a near-insane Nikeratos who threatens at one moment to burn the baby alive (553–5), at another to kill Chrysis who is protecting it and encouraging Plangon and her mother to put up a united front (556–62), at another, after Demeas has helped Chrysis escape back into his own house, to kill his wife (580–1). At more than one moment Demeas has to resist or restrain his neighbour by physical force (574–6, 581–2nn.), but eventually Nikeratos is mollified by a combination of soothing assurances that Moschion will marry Plangon forthwith (586, 599, 610) and an absurd attempt to 'prove' that the baby's father was really a god. Final preparations for the wedding can now be completed, and Demeas can thank the gods that his suspicions have proved unfounded (614–15). (Here Act IV ends.)

Moschion returns, indignant that his father should have suspected him, and decides to give Demeas a fright by pretending he is about to go abroad as a mercenary soldier. Demeas, however, does not plead and beseech as Moschion had hoped (664–7) but gives him a lecture on his duty as a son

(694–712). Nikeratos then comes out in search of the bridegroom and, finding him apparently about to decamp, threatens to imprison him as a seducer, at which Moschion draws his sword; but Demeas calms everyone down, the bride is brought out, and the pair are formally betrothed (726–8), after which all depart in the torchlit procession with which a comedy customarily ended, the final words being, as usual, an appeal to the audience for applause and to the goddess Nike for victory in the festival competition.

4 THE CHARACTERS AND THEIR RELATIONSHIPS

(a) Adoptive father and adopted son

As soon as the Bodmer papyrus made it possible to view and understand *Samia* more or less as a whole, it was quickly perceived (Treu 1969; Mette 1969; Jacques 1971: xxviii–xli; Lloyd-Jones 1972) that the relationship between Moschion and Demeas was a crucial feature, perhaps *the* crucial feature, of the play, even though it is rather rare for them to be on stage together.[65] A major determinant of Moschion's actions, evident from the prologue on, is his awareness of how much he owes to his adoptive father, and his sense of shame at having acted in a way that would lower him in his father's estimation. An even stronger determinant of Demeas' actions is his desire to believe the best of his son if at all possible, to avoid quarrelling with him, and to avoid doing anything that might injure his reputation. In Act II this leads Demeas to condone Chrysis' apparent offence against him (in rearing 'her' baby instead of exposing it, 132n.), contrary to his original intentions, when Moschion urges him to, and then to put pressure on a reluctant Nikeratos to have Moschion and Plangon married that very day; in Act III it leads him to expel Chrysis from his house on the mere presumption that Moschion, being a person of good character, could not have committed a serious sexual wrong, and also to avoid telling her the real reason for her expulsion; in Act IV, and again in Act V, it leads him to apologize (537–8, 702–3) for an 'injustice' that was at least as much Moschion's fault as his own.

Clearly these features of the father-son relationship are to be understood as connected in some way with Menander's unusual decision to make this relationship an adoptive rather than a biological one. One can see at

---

[65] They appear together in the first half of Act II (120–62), during a long stretch of Act IV (440–539), and in the concluding scene of the play (690–737). All three of these passages, as it happens, are preserved in the Bodmer papyrus alone.

bound to choose the son.[68] Moschion, for his part, must know that
he could hardly wound Demeas more deeply than by pretending he is
about to go abroad as a soldier, putting in grave jeopardy the life that
meant so much to his father: no wonder he expects that Demeas will
beg and beseech him not to go.

(3) In addition to the above considerations, Moschion is also keenly aware
that his adoptive father is a very rich man and has given him an
extremely affluent upbringing (7–18). We do not know whether anything was said about his birth family in the lost opening of the prologue, but even if nothing was stated explicitly, Moschion's emphasis
on the fact that he owes his social status entirely to Demeas (17 δι'
ἐκεῖνον ἦν ἄνθρωπος) clearly implies that his natural father was much
less well off. Owing so much to Demeas, Moschion knows that it is
his duty to repay him by leading his life in a way that will redound
to Demeas' credit (17–18), and he is deeply ashamed to have failed
in this (47–8, 67); to a large extent, this is what makes him reluctant
to admit this failure to his father, and hesitant to seek his consent to
a marriage that can bring the family no social or economic benefit.
We may find ourselves wondering whether he would ever, despite the
oath he swore to Plangon's mother (53), have plucked up courage to
do so, had not the same marriage been already agreed upon by the
two fathers and presented to Moschion, as it were, on a plate.

For Moschion, like several of Menander's young men (Zagagi 1979;
Lamagna 1998: 58–9), is a rather weak character. He is terrified of Nikeratos and twice runs away from him (161–2, 539). He has to be urged and
shamed by his slave into fulfilling his sworn promise to do his duty by Plangon (63–76); in this connection he becomes the only free man in all of
known Greek drama to call himself a coward (65n.). When waiting to put
into action his plan to frighten Demeas by pretending to go abroad, he gets
cold feet, too late (682–6), on thinking of the possibility that Demeas may
not react as planned and may thereby force him into a humiliating climb-
down. His generosity to those less fortunate than himself (15–16, 30–4n.)
is an attractive trait, but he is being generous with Demeas' money, not his
own; his swift confession of his rape of Plangon, and his oath to marry her
as soon as possible, seem an impressive acceptance of responsibility, but
we had probably been told that he was already set on marrying her if he
could, and his confession appears to be presented as partly motivated by
awareness that he was in any case the obvious suspect (50–1n.).

[68] Even when Demeas has come to believe that Moschion has grievously wronged
him and is continuing to conspire with Chrysis against him (cf. 456–8, 469–70,
474–5, 481 ἐνθυμεῖσθε), though he rages verbally against Moschion, he seeks to take
punitive action only against Chrysis (517–18).

However, Moschion does have some qualities that are beginning (to use language that is thematic in the play) to make a man of him (64n.), qualities that we can see germinating under the stimulus of fatherhood. It is when his son is under threat that he is seen displaying moral and even physical courage (Sommerstein 2012). When Demeas is about to throw Chrysis and the baby out of his house (130–4), Moschion, hitherto so afraid to face him, says immediately 'Don't!' (134) and challenges his father's assumption that a bastard child is *ipso facto* inferior; we have only the first few lines of his argument and enigmatic fragments of the rest (137–43m), but we know that his persuasion was successful. When Chrysis has actually been expelled, again with the baby, Moschion urges his father to allow her to return, and persists in doing so in the face of strong indications that Demeas' anger is being increasingly aroused. And when it is Nikeratos' turn to want to expel her (once more, with the baby), Moschion attempts, though ineffectively, to prevent him from doing so by physically blocking him from entering his own house (519–20nn.). He has his limits: he flees from Nikeratos when the latter discovers that Plangon is the baby's mother, and it is left to Demeas and the three women to protect the child from its maternal grandfather.

It may at first seem that Moschion's feelings towards Plangon are only those of passionate desire (ἔρως) – which, in view of her citizen status, could find fulfilment on a long-term basis only through marriage. But in this respect, too, he can be seen to mature. In mentioning the reasons that are impelling him to stay in Athens and marry Plangon (624–5), he places first not desire (πόθος) but his oath; and when the formal betrothal finally takes place, Moschion's response to it – his last significant utterance in the play – is the fullest and most moving such response in surviving New Comedy: ἔχω, λαμβάνω, στέργω (728–9). Moschion may have begun the play as a spoilt post-adolescent; he ends it as a man capable of playing the role he now holds, that of head of a nuclear family.

Demeas is a man of conventional ethical principles who, like Moschion, has a strong sense of shame, being particularly anxious that it shall not be *known* that he or his son has done anything improper.[69] It is symptomatic that when Nikeratos is raging at Moschion (495–505), comparing him to the worst sexual criminals of myth, telling Demeas he should have put out his son's eyes as Amyntor did those of Phoenix, and saying he would rather marry his daughter to a blackmailer (?) like Diomnestus (504n.) than to Moschion, the only thing Demeas says to his son (500) is 'It's *your* doing that all this has come out into the open'; and that in the centre of his later

---

[69] In this he strikingly resembles Phaedra in Euripides' *Hippolytus* (see §6); cf. *Hipp.* 321, 393–7, 403–4, 420, 428–30, 687–8, 717–21.

moral lecture (703–9) he places a contrast between his own behaviour during the crisis – keeping the truth under wraps for Moschion's sake, and not making it public 'for our enemies to gloat over' – with the way Moschion is now publicizing their quarrel and 'making people into witnesses against me of my own folly'. Much earlier, out of shame (23) and likewise fearing that Moschion's reputation would be compromised (27), he had been reluctant to avow his passion for Chrysis and even more reluctant to take her into his house, until Moschion himself had persuaded him to do so (28n.). He had not been able to conceal the passion itself from Moschion (23–4), and this points us to another leading characteristic of Demeas: he is very liable to be overpowered by strong emotions. One of these is his passion for Chrysis, with which he has a hard struggle when he expels her (350, 356); another, as we have seen, is his love of Moschion. The third, and sometimes the most powerful, is anger. In the surviving text this is first mentioned in the context of Chrysis' pretence that she is the mother of the baby: Moschion says (80) that Demeas will be angry with her (for not having exposed it), but Chrysis is sure he is so much in love with her that he will be unable to remain angry for long. This proves to be a misjudgement: Demeas does relent from his initial intention to throw Chrysis out, but it is his love of Moschion, not of Chrysis, that mollifies him.

In Act III we see to the full how devastating Demeas' anger can be – and also that he is aware of its power and strives hard to control it. When he first comes on stage he is outwardly 'very calm' (cf. 263), though his words show that he is in fact distraught (206–18), and there follows a long, factual narrative (219–66) and a reflective, logical argument (266–79) – until his rage breaks through in the two words ἐξέστηχ' ὅλως (279). But then he immediately resumes control again as he sees Parmenon and the Cook approaching. His interrogation of Parmenon is well managed, particularly the smoothly expressed menace of 306–7 ('For many reasons, I have no wish to flog you'), until Parmenon, believing that he knows all, confesses that an attempt was being made to deceive him (320 λανθάνειν). At this he at once calls for a strap, threatens to beat Parmenon black and blue (323n.) and thereby prevents himself from getting any more information as Parmenon flees. But again, after some paratragic exclamations (325–6; for a detailed discussion of this passage, see Fountoulakis 2011), he calms himself down, and reasons himself into a conviction that Moschion cannot have intentionally wronged him. All his anger is therefore channelled against Chrysis (348–98), taking perhaps an extra edge from the need for him to master his erotic passion, and he takes, or professes to take, a vindictive delight in her present and likely future sufferings; he is so much in the grip of this emotion that the Cook (361, 363), Chrysis herself (415), and Nikeratos when he learns what has happened (416–20), all think he has gone at least temporarily insane.

But there is still Moschion to be thought of, still a wedding to be held; and when we next see him (440–51) Demeas is doing his best to 'swallow' his anger (447) so that no one becomes aware of his and Moschion's shame: he finds a safety-valve, as it were, by briefly letting fly at the servants (440–4). His control is sorely tried by Moschion's innocent intervention on behalf of Chrysis, but he just about maintains it by alternating between indignant asides (454, 456, 457–8) and desperate appeals to Moschion to leave him alone (454–5, 460, 465–6, 470–1); it is already wearing thin, though, by 461–2, after which Moschion and Nikeratos both feel it necessary to warn him that it is not always good to yield to anger, and by 469–70 he is coming close to revealing the 'truth' that he has been so anxious to conceal. His last throw is to reveal to Moschion alone what he thinks he knows (476–9), but Moschion's baffled replies seem to him like the final proof that his son has lost all moral sense, and he denounces him at the top of his voice (481–4), no longer caring whether Nikeratos can hear (cf. 489). After this Nikeratos largely takes over the role of angry old man – in a more comic mode – and Demeas says little.

After Moschion's confession, soon followed by his rapid departure, we see a different side to Demeas as he finds himself fighting (sometimes almost literally so) to save the lives of his partner and his grandson. From now on two of his three powerful emotions fade out of the picture. He no longer yields to anger (not even in face of Moschion's provocations, though Moschion fears he may, 682–4), and as for his passion for Chrysis, if only 568–737 had survived of the play we might almost have thought Chrysis was merely Demeas' housekeeper.[70] His love for Moschion, on the other hand, is as strong as ever (he even loves him for being angry, 695–6). But what comes to the fore in this last part of the play is Demeas' ability to reason and to persuade, which he employs to good effect upon Nikeratos at the end of Act IV (see §4(c)) as in Act III he had employed it, to less good effect, upon himself. And it is this rational side of Demeas that is most prominent at the end, as he explains his view of the father-son relationship to Moschion (694–712) and in a few words (720–1, 723) makes sure that Moschion's play-acting and Nikeratos' indignation do not hamper the completion of the wedding – though not without having a little fun at the expense of them both as he pretends to Nikeratos that Moschion really is meaning to abandon Plangon and go abroad (715–16). Demeas too, then, has learned from this experience. He was enraged with Chrysis

---

[70] It is, however, highly significant that a little earlier (561) Demeas had referred to her as his wife (τῆς γυναικός). She can never actually be that, of course, but in contrast with his earlier sarcastic description of her as a γαμετὴ ἑταίρα (130), he is now apparently going to give her the respect due to the lady of the house – as the women, free and slave, in both households, have been doing for a long time (35–8, 258n.)

and then enraged with Moschion, when neither of them had in fact seriously wronged him at all: he himself now says he was wrong, foolish, even
mad (703, 708). Moschion, as his son, ought not to have rebuked him as
he did at 462–3; nevertheless, the rebuke was a deserved one, and Demeas
now understands why.

(b) Chrysis

Chrysis gives her name, or rather her nationality, to the play, but we should
not attach vast importance to this fact. *Samia* is one of no less than eighteen Menandrian plays (one-sixth of the dramatist's entire output) that
are named after a person or persons who are actually or supposedly of
non-Athenian origin, most often a woman,[71] either a *hetaira* (or ex-*hetaira*)
or else, as in Menander's and Terence's *Andria*, a young woman at first
believed to be a foreigner but eventually discovered to be Athenian and
marriageable. *Andria* provides a good example to show how little significance need be attached to the status of 'title character': in Terence's play,
and very likely in Menander's too, the 'girl from Andros' (called Glyc-
erium by Terence) never appears on stage, though she is heard once from
offstage, crying out in labour (Ter. *Andr.* 473, cf. Men. fr. 38). Titles of
this type (unlike some other Menandrian titles such as *Dyskolos, Aspis* and
Perikeiromene) may be no more than identifying labels. However, Chrysis
certainly is in fact an important character in *Samia*; in particular, she is
the most striking figure of what was probably its most famous scene, the
one portrayed on the Mytilene mosaic (§11), though she fades out almost
completely well before the play ends.

   It is not clear in the surviving text – indeed Menander may never have
made it clear – whether it was she who originated the plan whereby she was
to pretend to be the mother of Moschion's and Plangon's baby (57/58n.);
but it is certainly she who has the main responsibility, and takes the main
risk, in carrying the plan out. The risk is a grave one, too; as a *pallake* (§5)
she can be dismissed by her partner without notice or reason given, and
she will then revert to her previous life as a self-employed *hetaira* dependent on her personal charms (as long as they last) and her willingness to
make them available to anyone who can pay (cf. 390–7), unless she has
the good fortune to captivate another rich man's heart. So far as we can
tell, her motive for running this risk is simply fondness for the baby and
reluctance to see it suffer (84–6n.); she has nothing to gain by it, except
the gratitude of Moschion and Plangon. For doing them this service she

---

[71] In ten of these titles the ethnic is feminine (always singular); in eight it is
masculine (three of these are singular, three plural, and in two cases our sources
are in disagreement).

is nearly thrown into the street as soon as Demeas comes home, and actually suffers this fate not long afterwards; she finds refuge with Nikeratos, but later has to flee for her life from *him*. Throughout the play she is presented as the main guardian of the baby. She has it with her every time she appears on stage (except at the very end, if she does appear then: 730n.), though when indoors it may be cared for by others, including its real mother (241–50, 535–43), or by nobody (225–6). When its life is in danger from the fury of Nikeratos, she snatches it from the frightened Plangon (559) and declares she will never give it up; and it is in her arms that, shortly afterwards, Plangon's son makes the last of his journeys in the play, returning to the house in which he began it, now known to be his true home.

Chrysis' resourcefulness is a trait that she shares with other Menandrian *pallakai* such as Glykera in *Perikeiromene* and Habrotonon in *Epitrepontes*[72] (Traill 2008, Sommerstein forthcoming (*d*)); so is her ability to form a network of support among persons of more assured social status. Nikeratos' wife and daughter treat her as a friend (35–8); so do other women of the neighbourhood (40–1); so does Nikeratos himself, until he learns of her supposed affair with Moschion. The slaves in Demeas' house look up to her as their mistress (258n.), and she acts as their manager and supervisor (301–4n., 730). It is only vis-à-vis Demeas himself that she is powerless – or rather, has only as much power as Eros can confer on her, which in this play proves to be very little.

For, considering that Chrysis is a professional *hetaira*, her actual role in the play is a remarkably unsexualized one. Demeas and Nikeratos at certain times find it easy, because of her background, to *think* of her as a promiscuous seductress or a cheap whore (348 χαμαιτύπη); but at no time does she *act* as one. Far from her winning Demeas back by erotic machinations, he simply takes it for granted, once he knows she is innocent, that she can return to her old position in his home – and when he tells her to take refuge there (569ff), she is at first baffled and hesitant, despite Nikeratos' threats and pursuit, because she does not understand, and is not told, why he has changed his attitude. When she re-enters his house, she almost steps out of the play; she is briefly mentioned in the verbal crossfire between Demeas and Nikeratos (577–8) and is then completely forgotten until 730 when she is matter-of-factly told to organize a women's procession as part of the wedding celebrations; it is not even made clear whether she herself comes back on stage as part of it (though she

---

[72] During most of *Epitrepontes* Habrotonon is actually a *hetaira*, and a slave; but it is likely that during the play Charisios (believing her to be the mother of his child) purchased her freedom, and that she finally became the *pallake* of his friend Chairestratos (Arnott 2004: 274–5; Furley 2009: 134, 208–9, 241–2).

probably does). Overall, her role in the play is less like that of a *hetaira* than like that of a wife (cf. 561) – but a wife who lacks the vital safeguard of an assured refuge from ill-treatment or neglect in the home of her natal family, and of a dowry which they can reclaim if her marriage breaks up for any reason.[73] She does nothing improper or unworthy at any point in the play, not even in what many might think justified retaliation for the atrocious way she was treated by Demeas and then by Nikeratos. And she risks, and nearly endures, expulsion and ruin in order to help a child who is not even hers – and in all her tribulations it never occurs to her to try and save her skin by revealing that it is not hers (Keuls 1973: 16–17). She is the most admirable character in *Samia*.

(c) Demeas and Nikeratos

The two fathers are generally seen either together or in parallel scenes, and they make a contrasting pair. Demeas is mostly presented in a serious light: we may pity him for his mistakes (though probably not as much as we pity the victims of those mistakes), we do not laugh at him. Nikeratos does make us laugh, usually without any such intention on his part; his actions and words are consistently inappropriate or incongruous. And, while both men are liable to bursts of anger, Nikeratos' rages, whether verbal or physical, are regularly far more extreme; in Act IV he repeatedly goes to the very brink of murder.

Whereas Demeas is a rich man, Nikeratos is poor. In the script as we have it, this only becomes apparent at 593,[74] when Demeas asks him whether any part of his roof is leaky and he replies 'Most of it'. In performance it will have been evident as soon as the pair first appear, from the contrast in their clothing, the scantiness of Nikeratos' luggage, and probably from his having at most one slave to carry it (96–119a n.). It is not explained in the surviving text why Demeas chose Nikeratos as his companion on a long business voyage, but there would be opportunities for such an explanation, by Demeas himself or by Moschion, in several of the lacunae in Acts I and II. The quality most needed in a business partner is honesty, and whatever else may be said about Nikeratos, he is almost

---

[73] It is true that Demeas when expelling Chrysis says to her (381–2) that 'you've got everything that's your own' and that he is also giving her 'maids and jewellery'; but this statement, if taken seriously, differs so sharply in tone and attitude from everything else Demeas says that it should probably be understood as sarcastic (381–2n.). Chrysis came to Demeas with virtually nothing (377–9), and she is leaving with the baby, one old woman servant (301–4, 372–3nn.), and the clothing and jewellery that she is actually wearing.

[74] The description of Athens in 101 as having καθαρὰ πενήτων ἀγαθά, even if uttered by Nikeratos, would not necessarily prove that he was a poor man (see 98–101n.).

incapable of deception: he even feels it necessary to give Demeas prior warning of his intention to murder Chrysis (560–3)! Another quality that might recommend him to Demeas is his tendency to defer to the richer man's views: once Demeas is able to draw Nikeratos into conversation, the outcome is almost inevitably what Demeas wishes it to be. It was Demeas who had first proposed to arrange a marriage between his son and Nikeratos' daughter (117–18), and Nikeratos had readily agreed (cf. 115–17); nothing is said about the financial arrangements, on which in any real-life marriage negotiations an agreement would have had to be reached, but the audience will have realized that Demeas cannot have expected Nikeratos to be able to give a large dowry.[75] In Act II Demeas undertakes to arrange the wedding for this very day, and succeeds, after some resistance, in pressuring Nikeratos into agreeing to this (186–7), though Nikeratos had previously insisted that it was 'impossible' (176); it seems likely that Demeas boldly asserts the blatant falsehood that the two men had already agreed on an immediate marriage (170–1n.), and that Nikeratos, once he perceives Demeas' determination, allows him to get away with the lie. 'That's very sensible of you' (νοῦν ἔχεις), says Demeas (187) on securing Nikeratos' compliance. Demeas uses the same words again, twice (605, 611), when Nikeratos agrees to proceed with the wedding despite having discovered the truth about the baby; he is well aware that Moschion is its father (585–6, 599, 612; cf. 717), but assents to Demeas' absurd pretence that the child is really the son of a god, because he does not wish to 'fight with [him] to no purpose' (604–5). Earlier in the scene, Nikeratos had twice (at 547 and 563) broken away from attempts by Demeas to engage him in dialogue, and rushed into his house intent on violence; at 582, when he is about to do this for a third time, Demeas succeeds in holding him back long enough for him to cool down a little, and from then on the wealthier man begins to regain his mastery. At the end of the play (723) it is Demeas who puts a stop to the bickering between Nikeratos and Moschion, which still looks as though it may lead to another physical confrontation (721–2n.), by ordering Nikeratos to bring out his daughter for the formal betrothal.

Nikeratos' distinctive personality does not emerge very clearly in his earlier appearances[76] – though we may have been told something in the

---

[75] In the end Moschion receives no dowry at all, but that may be in effect his punishment for the rape (726–8n.).

[76] Regardless of how we divide his first dialogue with Demeas (98–101n.): the two are in agreement that they are thankful to be back in Athens and away from the Black Sea region, and in their remarks about the lack of sunshine there it is Nikeratos who is flatly prosaic (the sun was obscured by fog, 109) and Demeas who is humorously picturesque (the sun didn't shine more than he had to because there was nothing of consequence for him to see, 110–11).

prologue about his fiery temper (29–30, 54nn.); at the end of Act III, and
at the beginning of Act IV, his treatment of Chrysis is humane and sympathetic, and his diagnosis of Demeas' mental condition differs little from
that offered by other characters, while his one intervention in the first forty
lines of the dialogue between Moschion and Demeas (463) merely echoes
a statement of conventional wisdom by Moschion (though one that Nikeratos himself will soon be forgetting!). Everything changes at 492, when
he has come to understand that Demeas is accusing Moschion of having
had an affair with Chrysis, and that Moschion is apparently admitting this
and yet brazenly asserting that he has done Demeas no serious wrong and
that Chrysis has done him no wrong at all (481–90). At this point Nikeratos bursts out in a frenzied denunciation of the young man whom he was
just about to make his son-in-law, and from here to the end of Act IV his
seemingly uncontrollable rage is the central feature of the drama.

   He begins by wildly exaggerating Moschion's offence, claiming[77] that
it dwarfs all the most heinous sexual crimes of myth or tragedy, including
those of Tereus, Oedipus and Thyestes (495–7nn.), telling Demeas that
he ought to put out his son's eyes (498–500) or sell both him and Chrysis
(illegally) into slavery (508–10), and absurdly describing what the pair
are alleged to have done as 'murder' (514–15). This time Demeas has
no need to bend Nikeratos to his will, for what he wants Nikeratos to do
(expel Chrysis) is exactly what Nikeratos was intending to do in any case
(516–18), and he goes inside determined to do it.

   But if we thought that the tone and content of Nikeratos' words were
rather extreme, they are nothing to what we are shortly going to see, when
a fresh discovery strikes him a blow under which he can do nothing but
lash out blindly and indiscriminately. It is one thing to learn that one's
intended son-in-law is a bad lot; one can always find another. It is another
thing to learn that one's unmarried daughter has borne a child: it can
mean irretrievable ruin for her and for the family's reputation. Nikeratos
had urged Demeas to take violent action: now he takes, or tries to take,
even more violent action himself, three times declaring his intention of
committing murder (553–4, 560–3, 580–1) – the last prospective victim,
his wife, being apparently chosen mainly as a substitute for Chrysis and
the baby who are no longer accessible, as if the only thing that can satisfy
him will be to have killed *somebody*. There is something ridiculous about
this, as there is when he takes pains to give notice to Demeas that he is
about to murder Chrysis (563); at the same time, lives really are in danger,
and nobody knows how to control Nikeratos until Demeas applies physical force, prevents Nikeratos from taking any action, and so compels him

----

[77] With much use of paratragic language (492, 493, 495–7, 498–500, 507–8,
516, 517nn.).

to engage in talk – which, as on earlier occasions, leads inevitably to his surrender.

It is striking that during Nikeratos' violent phase, he completely forgets about Moschion; Moschion is present when Nikeratos first comes out (532) after seeing his daughter suckling the baby, but that sight has so devastated him that he no longer remembers that he knows who the baby's father is, and Moschion can escape (539) unnoticed or at any rate unchallenged. Only when Nikeratos is in course of being brought back to reason (585–6) does he manage to put his two pieces of knowledge together,[78] and even then he needs to be assured repeatedly by Demeas that Moschion will certainly marry Plangon (586, 599, 610) and thereby put all to rights in the only way it can be done – which does not stop him from muttering darkly about what he would have done to Moschion if he had caught him at the time of the rape (612).[79] When he does come face to face with Moschion (712–28), any threatening edge is taken off the confrontation by the presence of Demeas, and it is hard (and was probably hard for the original audience) to judge whether Nikeratos still hopes to hurt Moschion somehow or whether he only wishes to frighten and embarrass him. His announcement 'before witnesses' (726) of a zero dowry, which is almost the last thing he says in the play, might seem to leave him with the upper hand – but there is no sign that Moschion was ever interested in a dowry, or in anything else except winning Plangon as his wife. And the *very* last thing he says in the play (727–8) again points up his relatively limited intelligence: first of all he explicitly mentions the prospect of his death, on an occasion when nothing of ill omen should be said,[80] then in an attempt to correct this he adds 'which god forbid – may I live for ever', a prayer that he should know can never be granted.

The word that best sums Nikeratos up is the word Demeas uses of him at 550, αὐθέκαστος. In context it means 'harsh' (550n.); but it can also mean – and does mean, elsewhere in comedy – 'one who tells it like it is'. He is naive, easily manipulated, and subject to fits of completely irrational rage; but he is also the only significant character in the play who never tells or acts a lie, and he does desire what is best for his daughter, however poor

---

[78] Demeas, by contrast, when he first overheard talk indicating that Moschion was the baby's father (248, 253–4) and then saw Chrysis suckling it (265–6), saw at once what the obvious conclusion was, though because of his love of Moschion he was reluctant actually to draw it.

[79] We may well suspect that, given the opportunity, he would have killed the young man (612n.) without reflecting that he was thereby depriving Plangon of the only husband who would probably ever be willing to take her.

[80] As he himself had been aware when he complained that an evil omen had occurred in the midst of the wedding preparations, with the arrival of the expelled Chrysis causing distress and tears among the womenfolk, including presumably the bride Plangon (423–6).

may be his judgement of how to secure it. It may not be an accident that she is the one person in his house whom in 532–585 he does not explicitly threaten to kill.

(d) Nikeratos' wife and daughter

Nikeratos' daughter, Plangon, can hardly be said to be a character in the play. Like many marriageable girls in New Comedy, she exists almost entirely as an object whose fate is determined by others. She is a rape victim, but the effect of the crime on her (and on her attitude to its perpetrator) is never given any attention (see further §5); she is a bride, but her role in the ceremony is simply to be handed over; she comes on stage for the first time at that moment (725), a dozen lines from the end of the play, and does not speak a word. From time to time (37–41, 67–8, 410, 426, 558–9) she is referred to in the company of, and doing the same things as, her mother; when they are named separately, the mother is usually named first, and we may assume that her daughter simply followed her lead. Only once do we hear of Plangon doing anything individually. This is at a crucial moment of the plot (535–43), when her father sees her suckling the baby; and on realizing he now knows her secret, she immediately faints. She will presumably have been giving the baby at least one feed a day on a regular basis (57/58n.), but there is no sign that anything has been said about this.

Nikeratos' wife (never named) comes across far more vividly as quite a strong character, stronger in some ways than her husband, though she never appears on stage. We probably met her first in a lost section of Moschion's prologue (29/30n.), since by the time our text resumes we are clearly expected to know all about the family living next door. We next learn about the friendship between her and Chrysis, culminating in their joint celebration of the Adonia (35–41). When Moschion learned that Plangon was pregnant, he went to see her mother, promised to marry her as soon as Nikeratos returned, and swore an oath to do so (51–3); he may have volunteered the oath, but it is at least as likely that we are meant to infer that Plangon's mother prudently demanded it. When Moschion is hesitant about approaching his father, saying he feels ashamed to face him, Parmenon asks him whether he is not ashamed to face 'the girl you've wronged, and her mother' (67–8) – and this has its effect on Moschion, who trembles (69). It is evidently not a good idea to incur this woman's hostility. She must, too, have agreed to the arrangement under which Chrysis cared for the baby, knowing that one of its objectives was to keep Nikeratos in the dark until the baby's parents were safely married.

Demeas, it seems, knows of her strong-willed nature. When he and Nikeratos have agreed to hold the wedding this day, Nikeratos says (196–8) that he will go inside, tell his wife to get things ready in the house, and then follow Parmenon (to the Agora); in his absence, Demeas reflects that 'talking his wife round will give him some trouble' (200–1), and when Nikeratos comes out again he may be grumbling about his wife's loud complaints and saying she is interfering in matters that are not her concern (203–5n.). She evidently feels that if *she*, rather than her husband, had been able to talk to Demeas, the wedding (much as she desires it) would not have been arranged at such absurdly short notice.

At the end of Act III, Nikeratos takes Chrysis into his house, saying 'Come this way, with me, to my wife' (418). At the beginning of Act IV (421), his wife has evidently been urging him, to his exasperation, to tackle Demeas about his treatment of Chrysis, which suggests that left to himself, he might well not have done so (and as it is, he is glad to let Moschion take the lead).

When the baby is in danger (553ff), its mother and grandmother stand firm in its defence under the leadership of Chrysis (556–60) and refuse to answer any of Nikeratos' questions about it. Nikeratos for the time being focuses his anger on the ringleader, Chrysis, but when she has found sanctuary in Demeas' house, with Nikeratos unable to get near her or the baby, he decides that the only thing left for him to do is to kill his wife (580–1) – who must, he realizes, have been a party to the concealment from him of the pregnancy and birth. It is just as well for him that she never gets to know of this. Our last indirect glimpse of her (713) is of a piece with what has gone before: Nikeratos comes out of his house, talking back to someone within, and saying 'don't pester me'.

Thus Nikeratos, who is so easily dominated by Demeas, seems also to be somewhat in awe of his wife; she can usually get her way on issues that matter to her, except when she can be presented with a *fait accompli*, as at the end of Act II – and even then she may complain very vocally. Ancient audiences may have interpreted this more to the discredit of Nikeratos than to the credit of his wife – but they will have noted her devotion to the welfare of her daughter, and of the baby whose grandfather wanted to put him to the flames.

(e) The slaves and the Cook

In contrast with some other Menandrian slaves (the loyal and ingenious Daos in *Aspis*, for example, or the talkative and nervous Onesimos in *Epitrepontes*), Parmenon is not so much a dramatic character as a figure who can perform, at need, any of the dramatic and comic functions typically associated with slaves. In Act I he is a valuable adviser, reminding Moschion of his duty (63–76; cf. 86/87n.) and probably raising the issue of what to do about the baby now that Demeas and Nikeratos have come home

(77–9n.). In Act II he appears only briefly to be sent out shopping. In Act III, under interrogation by Demeas, he first swears his innocence with suspiciously emphatic repetition (310–11) and then hedges his reply in a way that makes it obvious that he is not telling the truth (315: when asked who is the father of Chrysis' baby, he replies 'you are, *she says*'), finally betraying his young master[81] by a confession (320) – a confession both of paternity and of deception – and confirming his guilt (and Moschion's), if confirmation were needed, by running away. He does not return till Act V, when he is given an entrance-monologue (641–57), arguing unconvincingly that he had done no wrong at any time in the matter of the baby and ought never to have run away; this monologue is entirely unnecessary to the action and indeed impedes it (Moschion very much wants to make use of him, 639–40, but stands doing nothing for the next seventeen lines), but it is highly amusing and serves as a farcical pendant to Moschion's monologue which preceded it. He is then sent to fetch a sword and cloak, disobeys his orders for Moschion's own good, gets his lip cut open for his pains (679), obeys his orders at the second time of asking, and finally (691–4) plays along with Moschion's pretence of going abroad, whether because he thinks this is what Moschion wants him to do or whether he has divined that Moschion *doesn't* actually want to go abroad and is trying to embarrass him (690–4n.). It is not meaningful to attempt to combine these vignettes into a consistent character.

Two other slaves, and one ex-slave, have significant roles in the play, though not as speaking characters in the ordinary sense: Moschion's old nurse, now a free woman but still living in her former owner's house (235–61), whose loose tongue (λαλιά, cf. 241, 255, 261) revealed to Demeas that Moschion was the baby's father; the quick-witted young girl (251–9) who tried to silence her and then did what she could to cover up the blunder; and another old woman slave[82] who is sent away with Chrysis (373) and thus appears in the memorable expulsion scene. The first two are very effectively characterized in a short space of time by the direct quotation of their words (six speeches, mostly short, by the ex-nurse and four by the girl).

---

[81] He is, admittedly, in a very difficult position. He has the confidence of Moschion, is in a conspiracy with him and others, and owes them loyalty; but it is clear that Demeas is his actual owner, with unlimited power of physical punishment.

[82] She cannot be the same person as the nurse, since she is referred to as a slave in 382; she may be the drink-addicted old woman of 302–3, whom Demeas takes an opportunity to be rid of (301–4n.). After the expulsion scene there is no indication that she ever appears again; the audience are presumably expected to have forgotten her by the time their attention is called back, at 516, to Chrysis' position in Nikeratos' house.

A character who seems at first purely conventional, but who is then exploited in an unusual way, is the Cook,[83] apparently represented as an African (283–390n.). In his first short scene he seems like any other comic cook, boring other characters with his professional talk (286–92) and the butt of endless puns on the verb κόπτειν (285, 292). But when he comes outside again at 357, initially in search of Parmenon, he soon finds himself a spectator of Demeas' expulsion of Chrysis – and eventually (383–90) more than a spectator, as he twice makes an attempt to intervene, only to be cut off each time (the last time with a threat of violence) before he can get out more than two words. His motive is not clear (283–390, 383nn.), but in view of 383 (τὸ πρᾶγμ' ὀργή τίς ἐστι) it is at least possible that we are to understand him as acting out of sympathy for one whom he sees as the victim of a temporary fit of anger (Nikeratos too thinks that Demeas will come back to his senses and change his mind, 416–20).

(f) The baby

When a baby[84] is born shortly before, or (as in *Georgos*, or in Terence's *Andria* and *Adelphoe*) actually during, the action of a New Comedy play, it may become a very important silent character[85] as it progresses towards the recovery of its true identity and/or its true home: witness the itinerary of Pamphile's baby in *Epitrepontes*, from its mother to Sophrone,[86] to the woods, to Daos, to Syriskos and his wife, to Habrotonon, and back to Pamphile (and, for the first time, also to its father Charisios). Eventually the baby will always prove to be legitimate (or capable of being made so forthwith) and a citizen of Athens by birth; it is, moreover, invariably male, and therefore also the heir of the family (οἶκος) in whose house (οἰκία) it finally finds its proper place.

In *Samia*, as we have seen, the baby (the child of Moschion and Plangon) goes where Chrysis goes;[87] it never appears except in her arms, and she never appears without it – except perhaps at the very end of the play, when at last it no longer needs her protection. It was born, of course, in Nikeratos' house where its mother lived; Moschion, its father, soon took it

[83] He is accompanied by one or more assistants (cf. 282 τούτους οὓς ἄγει, 295 παράγετ').
[84] On the role of the baby in *Samia*, see especially Heap 2003.
[85] Silent while on stage, that is; it can be allowed to cry while indoors, as at 226, 239 and *Epitr.* 853–4.
[86] There is no direct evidence that it was Sophrone who took the baby to the woods, but she would be the obvious choice for the task: she is the servant who is most in Pamphile's confidence, as is evident from Smikrines' choice of her to accompany him (which she does very reluctantly) on his final attempt to persuade Pamphile to leave her husband (*Epitr.* 1062–77).
[87] The following analysis of the baby's movements is based on that by Cusset 2000: 222.

into his own house (54), which was in fact its true home, but it was passed off for the time being as the bastard son of Demeas and Chrysis. This unexpectedly brought it into peril (132–4) until Moschion persuaded Demeas to accept it. Then, unknown to its father, it became in Demeas' mind (but only in Demeas' mind, since he told nobody else) the bastard son of *Moschion* and Chrysis, and as a result it was expelled, together with Chrysis, from the house to which it belonged, and was taken instead into the house of its maternal grandfather, Nikeratos. He thought, at that point, that its parents were Demeas and Chrysis; everyone else in his house knew its real parentage. Then Nikeratos learned that the baby's father was Moschion – and immediately his attitude towards it became the same as that of Demeas, only more so. At that point (516–20), for a minute or two, it seems likely that the baby will lose *both* its homes, the citizenship to which it is entitled by birth, and even its life. Then Moschion confesses the truth to Demeas. Demeas has always known that he was either the father or the grandfather of the baby, but now for the first time he knows it can be made legitimate and becomes its unconditional ally, at the very moment when Nikeratos becomes the most dangerous enemy it has had – and, paradoxically, does so by virtue of the discovery that *he* is its grandfather. Chrysis protects the baby at her own peril, and to her surprise a refuge opens up for her back in Demeas' house. Thus the baby finally returns to its true home. Nikeratos demands its surrender (578–9). 'Nonsense,' says Demeas, 'it's mine.' — 'No, it's not yours.' – 'Yes, it is.' In fact it belongs to *both* of them – though it will take another thirty or forty lines for Demeas to make Nikeratos understand this. The baby's travels and travails, however, are now at an end. But at this moment neither his father nor his mother is at home with him. Indeed, as the play ends, there is only one person, other than slaves, in the house of Demeas – and that is the infant who will one day be its master.

5 LOVE, MARRIAGE – AND RAPE

Heterosexual[88] desire focused on a specific person – what Greeks called ἔρως[89] – may or may not be a human universal, but certainly its favoured

---

[88] Homoerotic passions, relationships and activities appear to have been completely absent from Menander (except for a passing joke or two, e.g. *Dysk.* 891–2); cf. Plut. *Mor.* 712c. They remained very much part of Athenian life, and figured in the comedies of some of Menander's contemporaries (Diphilus wrote a *Paiderastai*, Antiphanes a *Paiderastes* and a *Ganymedes*; cf. also Baton fr. 7, Damoxenus fr. 3).

[89] Reasonably translatable as 'love' in the sense in which it appears in phrases like 'in love with', 'love story' and 'love song'. In view, however, of the ambiguities of the English word and the strong suggestion it carries of reciprocity, I shall often in this section render ἔρως as 'desire'.

forms of expression and paths to fulfilment, whether in real life or in artistic imagination, vary enormously between cultures, and within the same culture they can change profoundly in comparatively short periods. In Western popular fiction today – whether in novel, drama or film – the typical pattern is for desire to be felt by one party and sooner or later reciprocated by the other, after which a sexual relationship is established which may or may not lead to cohabitation and eventually marriage. As recently as the 1950s this pattern was almost unknown, and would have led many readers/spectators to take a disparaging view of the morality of the characters concerned (especially the woman) and possibly of the author's morality too: fictional courtship was expected to be chaste, and the sexual relationship was (tacitly) taken to be part of the marital bond that was typically established right at the end of the story.[90] With a contrast like this in mind, we may be better prepared for the assumptions about ἔρως that we find in New Comedy.

These assumptions depend crucially on the status and upbringing of the woman concerned. In New Comedy there are basically two possible modes of life for a free woman; which one of them she adopts is determined almost entirely by the manner in which she is brought up, and this in turn is largely determined by whether she was known or believed to be of citizen birth. One was the life of a *hetaira*,[91] who in principle was prepared to sleep with anyone for a suitable payment, but who would usually prefer, if possible, to become, as Chrysis does, the live-in partner (παλλακή, 508n.) of an unmarried man on a more or less permanent basis – though, as Chrysis discovers, such a position did not in itself confer any security on her, and it was the man's exclusive right to decide whether any children she might bear could be reared or whether they had to be exposed (132n.). A man may, and often does, fall in love with a *hetaira*, as Demeas did with Chrysis (19–22, 81–2, 350); the *hetaira* herself is usually thought of as more hard-headed, since she always has to consider how best to make her living, precarious as that necessarily is. However, a young woman brought up among *hetairai* may feel strong desire for a particular man, as Plangon/Selenium does in *Synaristosai/Cistellaria* (Plaut. *Cist.* 59–95).

The other mode of life was that of the citizen maiden, whose destiny was marriage, and who at her marriage was expected to be a virgin. To her, ἔρως

---

[90] As a Frank Sinatra song of 1955 put it: 'Love and marriage, love and marriage / Go together like a horse and carriage; / This I tell ya, brother, / You can't have one without the other!'

[91] Literally 'female companion' (compare the modern euphemistic use of 'escort'). There are good discussions of the classical and Hellenistic *hetaira* by Davidson 1997, McClure 2003, and the contributors to Faraone and McClure 2006.

was supposed to be irrelevant; indeed she had no right even to choose her husband, for she could be validly and bindingly betrothed without her consent or even her knowledge, her disposition being in the hands of her κύριος (her father if alive, otherwise a brother or else a guardian who might or might not be a relative). Thus in *Georgos*, young Gorgias, who has been working on Kleainetos' farm and done him good service, has accepted an offer by Kleainetos to marry his sister (*Georg.* 43–84) – neither of them knowing that Gorgias' sister was in an advanced stage of pregnancy, having been raped (see below) by another young man who has apparently, like Moschion in *Samia*, promised her mother (the father being evidently dead) that he will marry her (*Georg.* 1–3, 15–19, 29–30); and Gorgias and Kleainetos, we hear (*Georg.* 76–7), are even now on their way to Gorgias' home so that Kleainetos can take Gorgias' sister back to his farm. All this has been done without a word being said either to the prospective bride or to her mother; the latter is informed for the first time on the very day of the planned wedding, and not by Gorgias or Kleainetos but by another man's slave – and there is no suggestion that Gorgias has done anything seriously wrong. The question of the young woman's own preferences is hardly ever raised.[92]

A young man too might find that a marriage had been made for him by his family without his consent or knowledge; this indeed is the situation of the second young man in *Georgos*, who comes back from abroad to find that preparations are in full swing for his marriage next day to his half-sister[93] (*Georg.* 7–12). A man was in a slightly better position than a woman to say no to an imposed marriage, since he could always leave home temporarily (as the young man in *Georgos* does) or permanently (as Moschion pretends to be doing in the last act of *Samia*);[94] but he would still be disobeying his

---

[92] The nearest approach is perhaps in *Aspis* (253–83), where Chairestratos tries to persuade his brother Smikrines not to exercise his legal right to marry their niece, the sister of the supposedly dead Kleostratos, arguing that he is too old for her (*Aspis* 258–9) and that Chaireas, who had been about to marry her when the report arrived of Kleostratos' death, had known her from childhood (262–3); but even here no attempt is made actually to consult the girl, and while we are invited to share her fiancé's distress (*Aspis* 284–98) and that of Chairestratos (299–315) we learn nothing of her own state of mind.

[93] The daughter of his father by a second marriage. At Athens a man could marry his half-sister provided the two were born of different mothers.

[94] A woman who tried to do likewise would find herself with no means of leading a respectable life. A passage of Aristophanes (*Knights* 1300–15, especially 1311–12) suggests that she would have the right to flee to sanctuary, but that might in practice be the equivalent of going on hunger strike in the hope that her parents would relent in order to save her life (cf. Christensen 1984 on the taking of sanctuary by slaves).

parents in a matter of considerable consequence and thereby breaking an important social rule.[95]

If all marriages had been made in this way, most of Menander's comedies could never have been written. They normally centre on a young man who succeeds in obtaining, against opposition either from older or richer people or from circumstances, the marriage that he himself desires. There are two principal devices by which such a plot can operate (they may sometimes be combined).

One possibility is that a man may fall in love with a young woman whose true parentage is unknown; he may even take her to live with him, as Polemon does in *Perikeiromene*, Thrasonides in *Misoumenos*, and Alcesimarchus in Plautus' *Cistellaria* (based on Menander's *Synaristosai*) – though plays of this subtype tend to be set in cities other than Athens. When the woman's true identity is discovered (a process which normally includes the identification of a father or brother who can lawfully give her in marriage), she can be married to her lover; for a bride in Menander need not be a virgin, so long as she has known *no man other than him who marries her*.[96]

The other scenario is based, as in *Samia*, on rape.[97] Together with the acceptance of slavery (and the master's right to inflict any form of physical ill-treatment for any reason or none, cf. 306–7, 321–4, 679) as part of the natural order of things, the attitude taken to rape – and the very fact of its being treated as a routine plot device in a *comic* drama – is to every modern mind the hardest feature to tolerate in Menander's dramatic world.

Rape in Menander's Athens was in fact as serious a crime in law as it is today.[98] Gorgias in *Dyskolos*, probably the most level-headed person in

[95] Cf. Men. fr. 492 'Obey your mother and marry your kinswoman.' The thirty-year-old speaker of Lysias 19 claims it as a virtue that he has never taken part in litigation or politics *and has never contradicted his father*.

[96] In order to ensure that this is the case, some rather implausible assumptions sometimes have to be made: the girl is regularly said to have been brought up 'well and chastely' (*bene et pudice*) or 'like a daughter', even though in some cases she has grown up in a *hetaira* household. Cf. *Perik.* 130–1; Plaut. *Cist.* 171–3; Ter. *Andr.* 274, *HT* 226.

[97] Since it has sometimes been suggested that Moschion's impregnation of Plangon is represented as a seduction rather than a rape (Lape 2004: 144–5, Dedoussi 2006: 113; more cautiously Arnott 2001: 84), it should be pointed out that there is no clear case in New Comedy of the consensual seduction of a woman known to be of citizen status: such a woman would have shown herself to be of bad character, unfit to be the wife or mother of a citizen, and unfit to participate in civic religion (cf. [Dem.] 59.85–6). Parmenon, moreover, speaks of Plangon (67–68; cf. also 646–7) as 'the girl you wronged', treating her as purely a victim and not a consenting participant.

[98] Omitowoju 2002, in arguing that a woman's consent was irrelevant to Greek definitions of sexual crimes, ignores much of the evidence (see Sommerstein 2006).

that play, thinks that to be executed only once is not a sufficient punishment for it (*Dysk.* 291–3). Rape was the paradigm case of the crime of *hybris*,[99] and *hybris* was punishable by death if the prosecutor demanded it and the jury agreed.[100] And yet this is certainly not how actual rape and its actual perpetrators are treated in Menander's plays.[101] Moschion is allowed to say to his father 'It's not such a terrible thing – thousands have done it, surely!' (485–7); Demeas is extremely indignant, but only because he thinks Moschion is referring to the seduction (not rape) of Chrysis. When Nikeratos thinks Moschion has committed the offence just mentioned, he is appalled beyond measure at the idea of having him for a son-in-law (501–4); when Nikeratos understands the truth, Demeas knows that the best way to mollify him is to assure him constantly that Moschion will certainly marry his daughter. And it is not that the victim's perspective is being ignored; rather, it is being assumed that the victim's perspective will be the same. In *Epitrepontes*, Pamphile has been raped by a (then) unknown man at the Tauropolia festival, has subsequently been married to Charisios, and has given birth to a son five months later (while Charisios was away from home). The baby was exposed. When Charisios heard of this, he moved out of his house to stay with his friend Chairestratos; Pamphile is told by her father (inaccurately but sincerely) that Charisios has taken up with the music-girl Habrotonon, and probably that she has borne him a son. She refuses, however, to end her marriage. Then Habrotonon, carrying 'her' baby, accidentally comes face to face with Pamphile, and recognizes her as the girl who had been raped at the previous year's Tauropolia which she (Habrotonon) had attended; Pamphile in turn recognizes the baby, from its clothes, as her own child. The dialogue continues:

---

[99] That the drafter of the law of *hybris* had sexual violence at the front of his mind is evident from the sequence in which he lists the possible victims of the crime, παῖδα ἢ γυναῖκα ἢ ἄνδρα (Dem. 21.47; Aeschines 1.15 puts ἄνδρα before γυναῖκα, the conventional order in almost all other contexts). The text of the law is probably a later insertion in Dem. 21 (Canevaro 2013), but that does not in itself prove that it is not authentic (cf. Sommerstein forthcoming (*b*), on Andoc. 1.96–8), and it is most unlikely that a forger would have written γυναῖκα ἢ ἄνδρα when the context in Demosthenes is not concerned with sexual violence at all, and when the victim of the principal act of alleged *hybris* under discussion was a man (Demosthenes himself).

[100] 'Whoever the court convicts, it shall immediately assess about him what penalty it thinks he deserves to suffer or pay' (Dem. 21.47, cf. Aeschines 1.15); as always in the Athenian courts when a penalty was not fixed by law, this assessment was done by the 'pendulum' method, each side making a proposal and the jury being required to choose between them, and this did sometimes result in a death sentence (Dem. 21.49).

[101] On the treatment of rape in Menander see especially Rosivach 1998: 13–50.

PAMPHILE: But who's the father?

HABROTONON: Charisios.

PAMPHILE: Darling, are you absolutely sure of that?

HABROTONON: I know it for certain. But aren't you the newly-married lady who lives in there?

PAMPHILE: That's right.

HABROTONON: Happy lady, some god has taken pity on you both!

(Epitr. 870–4)

Pamphile and Habrotonon now know that the man who raped Pamphile is the man who is now married to her – and both of them clearly see this as the best thing that could possibly have happened! This, indeed, is the regular view of virtually all characters, of both genders, in New Comedy; the attitude of Gorgias in *Dyskolos* is to be explained by his (mistaken) assumption that Sostratos is a rich playboy bent on mere sexual predation. Rape, it is assumed, is completely atoned for by an offer of marriage; and such an offer is never refused. A rapist is only treated as a villain if he refuses (or is thought to have refused) to do the right thing by the woman, and by the child if there is one (e.g. *Georg.* 25–30; cf. E. M. Harris 2006: 320–7).

One can understand why this should be so, in a society where great importance is attached to the virginity of a bride. A rape might lead to a pregnancy, or it might not. If it did not, the best thing to do was to conceal it: a prosecution would only advertise the fact that the victim was no longer a virgin, and make it harder to find her a husband. If the rape did lead to a pregnancy, it would probably be possible to coerce the perpetrator into marrying the victim (if he needed coercing) by the mere *threat* of prosecution – and even less likely that anyone else could be induced to marry her; moreover, the child would then become legitimate[102] and would not need to be exposed. With the high rate of infant and child mortality, one would not have wished to expose a healthy first-born, especially a son, if it could respectably be avoided. Thus to treat marriage as wiping out the guilt of rape served the interests of *everyone* concerned, including the

---

[102] Throughout New Comedy it is taken for granted that a child conceived, or even born, out of wedlock becomes legitimate when its parents lawfully marry each other, at least if, as is always the case, neither was married to a third party at any material time. At one point in *Epitrepontes*, indeed (566–70), the slave Onesimos speculates that if his master Charisios finds that he has a son by a citizen woman who is not his wife, he will divorce Pamphile and marry the other woman – which he would hardly be able to do if the child was not thereby made legitimate, even though at the time of its birth Charisios had been married to Pamphile. But this is a scenario that never materializes, and we may well not be expected to work out all its implications (cf. Brown 1983: 416–20).

victim – provided that the perpetrator's behaviour, before and after the
crime, gave evidence that he was not naturally vicious but had been provoked into a wrongful act by some combination of desire, drink and youth-
ful exuberance (*amor, vinum, adulescentia*: Ter. *Ad.* 470). In Moschion's case
such evidence is amply available – his general good character (18, 273–4,
343–7), probably his earlier generosity to Nikeratos' family (30–4n.), his
immediate offer of marriage (50–3), his taking the baby into his house
(54), and probably professions of devotion to Plangon that were transpar-
ently sincere (cf. 623–32) – and it was clearly enough to convince Plangon's mother that marriage to him was her daughter's best prospect. As
usual, nothing is said about Plangon's own feelings, but the parallel of
Epitrepontes (see above) suggests that they would have been assumed to be
much the same.

6 TRAGIC THEMES AND REMINISCENCES: HIPPOLYTUS AND OTHERS[103]

That Menander's drama, and New Comedy generally, owes much to fifth-
century tragedy, especially Euripides, was already recognized in antiquity (cf. Satyrus *POxy* 1176 fr. 39 col. 7); indeed, according to Quintilian (10.1.69), it was recognized openly by Menander himself, who 'both
greatly admired [Euripides], *as he often testifies*,[104] and followed his lead,
though in a different genre'. In modern times it has often been observed
that many of Menander's plays have strong intertextual links with particular tragedies,[105] and in the case of *Samia* a close relationship has long been
observed with Euripides' *Hippolytus*,[106] with Demeas, Moschion and Chrysis corresponding to Theseus, Hippolytus and Phaedra respectively. In
both plays a quick-tempered father, returning from abroad, wrongly comes
to believe that in his absence his son (a bastard son in one case, an adopted
son in the other) has slept with his (the father's) wife or concubine. In
both plays the son is proud of his virtuous character. In both, owing partly
to deception, partly to the father's 'over-confidence in his own reasoning'

[103] This section is adapted from Sommerstein forthcoming (*c*).
[104] In what survives of Menander there is only one reference to Euripides
by name, at *Aspis* 427, where he is indeed praised, but only on a par with the
fourth-century tragedian Chaeremon. Presumably some of his characters elsewhere
expressed themselves in terms like those found in two passages of his contemporary Philemon ('If the dead really have sensation...I'd hang myself so as to meet
Euripides', Philemon fr. 118; 'Euripides, the one true master of language', fr. 153).
[105] See generally Katsouris 1975a, 1975b, Hurst 1990, Gutzwiller 2000, Cusset
2003, Furley 2009: 2–8, and on individual plays (other than *Samia*) Anderson 1982,
Belardinelli 1984, Porter 2000, Cannatà Fera 2003, Karamanou 2005.
[106] See e.g. Katsouris 1975a: 131–5; Jaekel 1982; S. R. West 1991: 16–22; Lamagna 1998: 64–7; Cusset 2003: 163–8; Troupi 2006: 48–77; Omitowoju 2010.

(S. R. West 1991: 18), the situation develops in such a way that the son finds it impossible to convince his father that his suspicions are groundless. Many detailed parallels can also be perceived,[107] most notably between the father-son confrontations in *Samia* 452–538 and *Hippolytus* 902–1101. Since *Samia* is a comedy, the truth naturally comes out in time to prevent any truly evil consequences, and several other features of the Euripidean play undergo inversion. The Hippolytus and Phaedra figures – Moschion and Chrysis – are at no time hostile to one another; in fact they are allies in a scheme to deceive Demeas, and Moschion intensifies Demeas' suspicions of himself by speaking in *defence* of Chrysis (453–75). Hippolytus is falsely accused of rape; Moschion is really guilty of it, but is never suspected (in regard to Plangon, that is) until he confesses. Hippolytus is in a sense a surplus son – he is not his father's heir, and can indeed be perceived as a potential threat to his half-brothers, Phaedra's children (*Hipp.* 304–10, cf. 1010–20);[108] Moschion, as we have seen (§4(a)), is the only legitimate son Demeas has or is ever likely to have. And whereas Theseus is convinced that Hippolytus' professions of virtue are bogus (*Hipp.* 916–57), Demeas for long takes it for granted that Moschion is truly virtuous – more virtuous, indeed, than he really is – and takes drastic action against Chrysis on the strength of that belief. It is striking, too, that whereas Demeas and Nikeratos are very free in referring to mythological figures and stories which they see as paralleling the events they are passing through – Helen (337), Tereus, Oedipus, Thyestes and Amyntor (495–500), Acrisius and Danaë (589–98) – they never make any direct reference to Phaedra or Hippolytus. Other features of character or action are transferred from one of the chief figures to another: thus the expulsion of Chrysis from Demeas' house corresponds to the banishment of Hippolytus, who, however, unlike Chrysis, does think fleetingly of revealing the truth that has been concealed from Theseus/Demeas, even though in his case this would involve breaking an oath (*Hipp.* 1060–3).[109]

There were also, however, other fifth-century tragedies that dramatized the same story or a story of similar pattern; and at least two of them appear also to have been intertexts for *Samia*.[110]

---

[107] See for example 14–15, 47, 50, 209, 325–56, 356, 362, 452–520, 492, 507–8, 537, 601–2, 612–13, 719nn.

[108] His position in Theseus' family corresponds to that which would have been occupied in Demeas' family by a son born to Chrysis.

[109] See Troupi 2006: 55.

[110] Of a third, Sophocles' *Phaedra* (see Talboy and Sommerstein 2006, Casanova 2007a), not enough is known for us to be able to identify any relationship, unless (Cusset 2003: 167 n. 20) Demeas' visit to a land where the sun hardly shone, whence he has now thankfully returned to Athens (101–11), might recall Theseus' visit to the underworld, whence he returns during the action of *Phaedra* (Soph. frr. 686–7).

Not long after the first substantial parts of *Samia* were recovered thanks
to the Cairo papyrus, Sehrt (1912: 29–31) drew attention to parallels
between its plot and that of Euripides' *Phoenix* (498–500n.), and much
later Jacques (1971: xxiv) pointed out that *Sam.* 343–7[111] were very close
in sense to a surviving fragment of that play (Eur. fr. 812), where a speaker
defending Phoenix (accused of raping his father's concubine) argues
from his own rich experience that when witnesses contradict each other,
the best criterion for judging the truth is the character and manner of
life of the individuals concerned. In Euripides' play, too, much was made
of the fact that Amyntor was an old man, and of the great age difference
between him and his wife (Eur. frr. 804, 805, 807); Demeas too is an old
man who has taken a much younger partner.[112] There may well have been
other echoes of *Phoenix* in *Samia* which we cannot now detect, not least
because we know little of the structure of its plot.

Considerably more can now be said about the relationship between
Samia and another Euripidean play, *Hippolytos Kalyptomenos* (henceforth
HippK), his earlier[113] treatment of the Phaedra–Hippolytus story, thanks
to the availability of two papyri[114] presenting slightly different versions of a
Hypothesis to the play, whose evidence can be combined with that of about
nineteen quoted fragments and of other statements about Euripides' version of the story that are not compatible with the surviving play.[115] At the
start of *HippK* Theseus was away in Thessaly, probably visiting his friend
Peirithous. Phaedra, in love with Hippolytus, made a direct approach
to him, proposing not only an adulterous affair but also that he should
attempt to seize political power. Being rebuffed, and doubtless fearing he
would denounce her, she then, on Theseus' return, accused Hippolytus of
rape and of plotting to overthrow him. Hippolytus was given a chance to
defend himself, but as in the surviving play he was unable to do so effectively because Phaedra had bound him by an oath of secrecy. Theseus ban-
ished Hippolytus from his dominions and prayed to Poseidon to destroy
him. After Hippolytus had driven away in his chariot, Theseus began to

[111] 515–19 in Jacques' numbering.
[112] See Jouan and van Looy 2002: 327, Cusset 2003: 165 n. 7. Theseus, on the
other hand, is never to our knowledge spoken of as an old man in any of the Hippolytus–Phaedra plays, and in the generally accepted account his mother long out-
lived him (*Little Iliad* fr. 17 West, *Sack of Troy* Arg. §4 West).
[113] That *HippK* was produced before the surviving *Hippolytus*, as is stated in the
'Aristophanic' Hypothesis to the latter, is argued (against Gibert 1997, Hutchinson
2004: 24–5, Zwierlein 2004: 57 n.2) by Talboy and Sommerstein 2006: 266–72.
[114] *PMich* inv. 6222A and *POxy* 4640 (*HippK* test. ii *TrGF*; Collard and Cropp
2008: 474–7).
[115] For a detailed justification of the following partial reconstruction of *HippK*,
see Talboy and Sommerstein 2006: 255–66 (updates in Sommerstein and Talboy
2012: 265–6).

have second thoughts, perhaps prompted by a slave who advised him not to believe a woman 'even when she tells the truth' (Eur. fr. 440), and he decided to test Phaedra (who did not know of Hippolytus' departure). He dressed the slave in Hippolytus' clothes and had him approach Phaedra, with his face covered, and ask for some true proof of her love for him; this induced Phaedra to utter words that revealed the truth about her passion. But the discovery came too late to save Hippolytus, whose death through the action of Poseidon's bull was now reported; Phaedra committed suicide, Hippolytus' body was brought back for burial, and a god or goddess ordained the establishment of a cult in his honour.

At least four features of *Samia* appear to be specifically and strongly reminiscent of *HippK* rather than of the surviving *Hippolytus* or any other tragedy.[116]

(1) In *HippK*, Theseus learns the truth from the unguarded words of Phaedra, spoken indoors ('at the hearth', according to the Hypothesis) when she is unaware that potentially unfriendly ears are listening; probably he was himself eavesdropping from concealment on the conversation between her and the disguised slave. In *Samia* (228–61) Demeas learns the truth – or rather a misleading portion of the truth – by overhearing, indoors and unseen, the unguarded words of a woman (Moschion's old nurse).

(2) Demeas is led by his judgement of Moschion's character to conclude that Chrysis must be the villain in the supposed affair between her and Moschion. Of the two Euripidean plays, it is only in *HippK* that Phaedra is a villain, and only in *HippK* that Theseus ever believes her to be one.

(3) In the surviving *Hippolytus*, Theseus learns the truth about Phaedra only from Artemis, almost at the end of the play (*Hipp.* 1298–1312). In *HippK* he apparently began to suspect it much sooner (though still, as it turned out, too late), thanks to a shrewd slave. In *Samia* there are two humble characters who are candidates for the role of this slave, but neither of them is allowed to take it successfully, in both cases because of Demeas' fierce temper. The first is Parmenon, who knows the truth but, when questioned, at first (313–15) sticks to the false story that Chrysis is the baby's mother; when Demeas tells him that he knows Moschion to be the father, Parmenon may or may not be on the point of revealing the full truth (320) when Demeas interrupts him and calls for a strap to flog him, whereat Parmenon runs away. The other is the Cook (§4e), whose attempts to make Demeas think twice before expelling Chrysis and the baby are brusquely cut short by Demeas. The

---

[116] For possible further echoes of *HippK* see 137–143a, 514, 632nn.

Theseus of *HippK*, we know, despite his anger against Hippolytus, *was* prepared to listen to the slave and to think it possible that he himself might be mistaken.

(4) *Samia* 343–7 is reminiscent not only of Eur. fr. 812 from *Phoenix* but also of Eur. fr. 1067, of which it seems to contain some verbal echoes (underlined below):

> τὸν σὸν δὲ παῖδα σωφρονοῦντ' ἐπίσταμαι
> χρηστοῖς θ' ὁμιλοῦντ' εὐσεβεῖν τ' ἠσκηκότα·
> πῶς οὖν ἂν ἐκ τοιοῦδε λήματος[117] κακὸς
> γένοιτ' ἄν; οὐδεὶς τοῦτό μ' ἂν πίθοι ποτέ.

I know that your son behaves modestly, associates with good men, and practises piety. How, then, out of such a character as that, could he become wicked? No one will ever persuade me that he could.

In Stobaeus (4.29.47) this extract is not ascribed to a specific play. It is, however, one of a group of ten successive Euripidean passages, eight of which *are* cited from specific plays, all of them except the first being in alphabetical order of play-titles; and its position in this listing implies that it comes from a play whose title begins with theta or iota. Only one such play[118] contained, as significant figures in the drama, a father and an adult son – namely *HippK*, to which this fragment was in fact attributed two centuries ago (Monk 1813: 154); it would work very well as part of the same scene (maybe the same speech) as Eur. fr. 440, the slave trying to persuade Theseus that Hippolytus is innocent and that he should not believe Phaedra's allegation. Here Demeas is trying to persuade *himself*, and succeeds – in reaching a wrong conclusion.

Various other possible reminiscences of plays of Euripides (and in one case Sophocles) are discussed in the Commentary.[119]

7 RICH AND POOR

An important element of the situation out of which the action of *Samia* arises is the disparity in economic circumstances between the two households involved, between the wealth of Demeas and the poverty of

---

[117] Düntzer: σώματος codd., which makes both syntax and sense problematic, and is probably due to a copyist's eye or mind wandering to σωφρονοῦντ' two lines above.

[118] Other than the surviving *Hippolytus* and *Ion*, which obviously do not come into consideration.

[119] See notes on 47 (*Aeolus*), 137–143a (*Antigone* or *Antiope*, also Sophocles' *Aleadai*), 325–6 (*Oedipus* and *Orestes*), 552–4 (*Melanippe the Wise*), 572–3 and 580 (both *Telephus*), 591 (*Danaë*), and 732–3 (*Trojan Women*). All plays referred to are by Euripides unless otherwise stated.

Nikeratos: this will manifest itself in the clothing of the characters, in the contrast between the retinue and luggage of the two old men when they arrive home (96–119a n.), in the fact that Nikeratos has to do his own shopping (196–8) whereas Demeas sends one of his many slaves, in the poor quality of his sacrificial animal (399–404) and, at the end (727–8), in Nikeratos' inability to give any dowry with his daughter.[120] This disparity also helps explain some key features of the action, such as Moschion's hesitancy in seeking his father's permission to marry Plangon (see §3) and Nikeratos' willingness, when not mastered by anger, to accept (sometimes after token resistance) almost any assertion or proposal made by Demeas (see §4(c)).

Yet to Demeas the wealth gap seems irrelevant, except when he exploits it to get Nikeratos to fall in with his wishes (and even when he does this, the agreed action is always also in Nikeratos' interests, or at least not contrary to them). In particular, he has chosen Nikeratos as his companion on a long business voyage, and he has taken the initiative in proposing a marriage alliance which in economic terms is far better than anything Nikeratos could reasonably have expected for his daughter, and far inferior to what a rich man would normally seek for his son.[121] He may have explained his motives in a lost soliloquy (119a/b, 166/167nn.). In any case they are paralleled elsewhere in Menander. In *Dyskolos*, after Gorgias has betrothed his sister to Sostratos (*Dysk.* 761–2) on the latter's somewhat airy assurance that his father will not oppose the match (761) despite the wide socioeconomic gap between them, Sostratos presents his father Kallippides with the *fait accompli* and Kallippides readily agrees, perceiving how deeply his son is in love (786–90). Kallippides at first refuses Sostratos' suggestion that his (Sostratos') sister should at the same time be given in marriage to Gorgias ('I don't want to have a destitute daughter-in-law *and* a destitute son-in-law – one's quite enough for us!', *Dysk.* 795–6) but is rather easily persuaded out of this by Sostratos, who argues that wealth is impermanent and

---

[120] While the absence of a dowry is doubtless in part due to the fact that, for more than one reason, Moschion needs no inducement to marry Plangon (see §5 and 726–8n.), it may also indicate that Nikeratos simply cannot afford a dowry – or at any rate that he cannot afford a dowry big enough to be respectable by the standards of New Comedy (726–8n.). Sostratos in *Dyskolos* declares that he is willing to marry Gorgias' sister without a dowry (*Dysk.* 306–8), but Gorgias nevertheless offers one (844–6) when he is in a position to do so. This was not only a matter of self-respect but also of prudence, since it served as a deterrent against ill-treatment or arbitrary divorce: if a marriage was dissolved for any reason (with the possible exception of adultery) and the wife returned to her natal family, the dowry had to be returned also (Schaps 1979: 74–84).

[121] He also, it seems, when Nikeratos is hesitant about holding the wedding immediately, offers to bear the whole expense of it (176–7n.) or at least the lion's share.

I say, father, that for such time as you are master of it, you ought to
use it generously, to give help to all, to make as many other people
well-off as your resources allow. That is something that never dies,
and if you eventually come to grief, it will result in your getting the
same thing back in your turn. Far better to have a friend in plain
sight than concealed riches that you bury and hoard. (*Dysk.* 805–12)

And in the end, the main resistance to Sostratos' proposal comes from
Gorgias himself, who is reluctant to 'luxuriate on other people's toil'
(829–31); but he too is persuaded – and by Kallippides, who gives him
a dowry of three talents and refuses his offer of a dowry for his own sister
(842–7).

The lecture Sostratos gives his father may be rather priggish and unfil-
ial, but it seems to represent an ethic that is pervasive in Menander. When
Moschion says that his father 'made a man of him' (17), being a 'man' for
him included not only hunting, riding, and putting on fine shows (13–15)
but also being 'able to give reasonable assistance to friends who were in
need of it' (15–16), and he seems to have given such assistance to Plangon
and her mother while Nikeratos was abroad (30–4n.). Smikrines in *Aspis*
is condemned by the prologue-goddess (*Asp.* 114–21) and everyone else
in the play for putting self-enrichment above all human and family considerations, and his namesake in *Epitrepontes* forfeits much audience sympathy, and in the end is subjected to ridicule by a slave (*Epitr.* 1078–1130),
because in his daughter's marital crisis he seems to be thinking more about
his dowry than about her welfare.[122]

As Konstan 1995: 104 puts it, 'harmony between rich and poor is…a
premise of New Comedy': he points out that while there are many New
Comic plots in which an otherwise impossible marriage becomes possible
when a girl previously thought to be a foreigner is discovered to be a citizen (§5), there are none in which objections to a marriage are overcome
when the prospective bride or groom, already known to be of citizen status,
is discovered to belong to a wealthy instead of a poor family. The fundamental distinction is always that between citizens and non-citizens, and it
is wrong to despise the poor citizen.[123]

[122] *Epitr.* 127–40, 153–4 (?), 601 (Charisios' possible gambling losses), 687–8,
749–51, 1078–9. A similar ethical position is apparent in the so-called Didot rhesis
(*com. adesp.* 1000) – probably not by Menander – in which a young wife whose
husband has fallen into poverty argues against her father's attempt to take her
away from him and give her to another man: 'If the man who's going to marry me
now…if *he* in turn loses his property, will you give me to a third husband? And if
the same happens again, to a fourth? How long will you go on testing out fortune
on *my* life?' (*com. adesp.* 1000.27–33).
[123] It is typical of the Smikrines of *Epitrepontes* (see above) that he should con-
demn the two men who ask him to arbitrate their dispute, because they presume to

This orientation has been seen (as by Lape 2004, especially 19–39) as a quasi-political stance, democratic and egalitarian, and opposed to undemocratic regimes such as that of Demetrius of Phalerum. If such, however, was Menander's ideology, it does not seem to have been understood by Demetrius, intellectual though he was: Menander was notably successful in the first years of Demetrius' rule, winning first prizes both in 316 (with *Dyskolos*) and in 315, and when Demetrius fell, Menander was in some peril as a supposed friend of his (§1).[124] Demetrius himself, indeed, claimed to be a democrat, saying that far from destroying Athenian democracy he had put it back on its feet;[125] and his extensive sumptuary laws seem to have been designed, at least in part, to curb 'conspicuous waste' by the rich.[126] There is no reason why he should not have looked with favour on voluntary transfers of wealth whereby the better-off directed some of their resources away from their own consumption towards making possible a more secure livelihood for some of those less prosperous, thus increasing social cohesion and reducing social discontent; and the financial arrangements accompanying marriages provided a useful mechanism for such transfers. The egalitarian Phaleas of Chalcedon had suggested that inequalities of wealth could be gradually removed by a legal requirement that dowries should be given only when the bride's family was richer than the groom's;[127] such a compulsory scheme would probably in practice be unworkable,[128] but encouragement of voluntary arrangements on the same principle was another matter. And it is striking that both in *Dyskolos* and in *Samia* the dowry arrangements are as Phaleas would have them:

engage in litigation when their dress shows them to be poor (*Epitr.* 228–30). The disputants, Daos and Syriskos, are in fact slaves, but Smikrines does not know that.

[124] This last point was noted by reviewers of Lape's book such as Major 2004 and Golden 2005: 454.

[125] οὐ μόνον οὐ κατέλυσε τὴν δημοκρατίαν ἀλλὰ καὶ ἐπηνώρθωσε (Strabo 9.1.20, referring to Demetrius' own writings about the political system over which he presided). In Strabo's very next sentence, however, Demetrius' fall is ascribed to 'jealousy and hatred of the ὀλίγοι'. Demetrius is perhaps the first dictator who is known to have openly described his regime as a democracy, a practice not yet obsolete.

[126] For example by limiting the number of guests at a wedding (Athen. 245a–c, citing Men. fr. 208 and Timocles fr. 34), the size of funeral monuments (Cicero, *De Legibus* 2.66), and the expenditure of *choregoi* (13n.). See most fully O'Sullivan 2009: 45–103, 168–85.

[127] Arist. *Pol.* 1266a39–b5. Phaleas' language (or Aristotle's) could also be read in the more radical sense of requiring there to be a transfer from the richer to the poorer of the two families involved, regardless of which was the bride's family and which the groom's.

[128] At first every family would seek a marriage alliance with a richer one, in order to receive (or not to have to give) a dowry; but the rich would soon find that they could best avoid compulsory transfers by marrying only each other, and the end result would be undiminished inequality and greater class exclusiveness.

of the three marriages that are made, only one involves any dowry payment
(the marriage of Gorgias to Sostratos' sister), and that is the only one of
the three in which the bridegroom's family is the poorer of the two.

This ethic is 'egalitarian' (Lape 2004: 30) only in a very limited sense.
All citizens are equal qua citizens: Moschion as an ephebe was, as he puts
it, 'no different from anyone else, just what they call "one of the *hoi polloi*"'
(10–11). But the difference in lifestyle between him and his father on the
one hand, and Nikeratos on the other, is enormous, and has clearly not
been much diminished, nor is it likely to be, by the generosity that he and
Demeas have displayed and no doubt will continue to display. Only in the
next generation will things have changed. When Nikeratos dies[129] there
will no longer, in this little world, be any poor people. Nobody can have
seriously thought the recipe here applied could be generalized to cover a
whole community; there would simply not be enough rich men available
whose resources could continue to support them in affluence while also
lifting another family out of poverty. But it remains true, in the eyes of
Menander (it would seem) and of his audience, that generosity is good
and praiseworthy – that it is better to be a Demeas than a Smikrines.

8 THE DATE OF *SAMIA*

No explicit information survives about the date when *Samia* was produced,
and we are forced to rely on internal evidence. This has led different analysts to somewhat different conclusions,[130] often based on rather equivocal
evidence, but nearly always[131] placing the play somewhere in the first half
of Menander's career.

The most cogent evidence for an early date is the presence of satirical
references to three contemporary Athenians, Diomnestus, Chaerephon
and Androcles (504, 603, 606–8nn.). There are no such references in any
of the other plays of Menander preserved on papyri (not even in the virtually complete, and relatively early, *Dyskolos*), and only ten in the 'book'
fragments. Of these ten, four (frr. 264–6, 268) come from *Orge*, Menander's first play; two (frr. 224, 225) from *Methe*, which must date from 318 or
earlier;[132] one from *Androgynos* (fr. 55), also likely to be early, since it refers
(fr. 51) to the Lamian war of 322; and two from *Kekryphalos* (frr. 215, 216),

---

[129] His wife, if she survives him, will doubtless be taken into her son-in-law's
house.
[130] See Jacques 1971: xlviii–lxv (earlier than *Dyskolos* [316], but perhaps not
much earlier); (Gomme and) Sandbach 1973: 542–3 (uncertain, but probably
between 315 and 309); Lamagna 1998: 37–45 (close to *Dyskolos*, perhaps earlier);
Arnott 2000: 7–13 (*c*.314); Dedoussi 1970: 160, 2006: 26*–31* (310 or perhaps
later).
[131] An exception was W. Ludwig in Turner 1970: 174.
[132] Since fr. 224.14 refers to Callimedon, who in that year fled from Athens and
was sentenced to death *in absentia* (Plut. *Phoc.* 35.5).

which probably dates from the first year or two of Demetrius of Phalerum's rule.[133] Thus, apart from *Samia*, we have only one possible reference to a contemporary Athenian in a play that may be later than *c.*315 – fr. 385, from *Hypobolimaios*, which mentions one Amphietides, whose name had become proverbial for imbecility (and who may therefore not have been a contemporary at all).[134] This is very strong evidence that *Samia* was produced no later than *c.*314 – that is, in the first seven years or so of Menander's career – and, in the absence of any objective evidence requiring a later date,[135] this evidence should be accepted.

It is more difficult to place *Samia* within this period. We cannot place it before *Dyskolos* on the ground of the absence in *Dyskolos* of satirical references to individuals, since *Kekryphalos*, which does have such references, is likely to be later than *Dyskolos*.[136] And there are a couple of passages in *Samia* which, it has been argued (Arnott 2000: 10–12),[137] would have a particularly topical ring in the year 315/14, though in neither case is the evidence decisive.

(1) Moschion envisages going to Caria to fight as a mercenary (628), and there is no specific surviving reference to fighting in Caria between Menander's début and 315 when Ptolemy I (then an ally of Cassander, the ultimate master of Demetrian Athens) sent a large mercenary force there under an Athenian commander named Myrmidon (D.S. 19.62.4–5). However, our sources are likely to record, in this period, mainly campaigns fought by the Macedonian dynasts (or their surrogates) against each other, and much mercenary activity in this

---

[133] Men. fr. 208, which refers to Demetrius' law limiting the numbers of guests at weddings as 'new', must be very close in time to Timocles fr. 34 – which, among the many references by Timocles to contemporary persons and events, is the only one that is datable later than 322.

[134] Compare the case of Melitides (or Meletides), another proverbial imbecile, who is mentioned in *Aspis* (269) and whom we might have taken for a contemporary had he not also been mentioned in Aristophanes' *Frogs* (991).

[135] I discount arguments based on the supposed maturity or immaturity of Menander's technique, since these are hopelessly subjective (compare Lamagna 1998: 41–45 with Dedoussi 2006: 30*-31*). It is true that Plutarch (see §1) says that Menander's middle and late plays were greatly superior to his early ones, but we do not know what criteria he was using: Dedoussi herself (2006: 26*) is of the opinion that in *Dyskolos* Menander's dramatic and theatrical techniques are 'already well developed'.

[136] Demetrius of Phalerum became governor of Athens towards the end of the Athenian year 318/17 (D.S. 18.74.3; see O'Sullivan 2009: 39–41), so that *Dyskolos*, produced at Lenaea 316, will have been the very first play that Menander composed for performance at Athens under his rule.

[137] Arnott mentions one or two other points which carry less weight; the most important of these – the reference (13) to Moschion having been a *choregos*, which he takes to allude to Demetrius' abolition of the *choregia* in 317/6 or 316/5 – has been thrown into grave doubt by subsequent scholarship (13n.).

unstable region will have taken the form of expeditions against the native peoples (often for the purpose of plundering rather than with any political or strategic aim), like the Lycian campaign in which Kleostratos is reported killed in *Aspis* (23–82).

(2) Demeas' exclamation μονομαχήσω τήμερον (570) may allude to the competition in μονομαχία that formed part of the games held by Cassander at Aegae in 316/15 (570n.); but armed single combat as an exercise or an entertainment, at funeral games and on other occasions, was far from new to the Greek world (ibid.).

While, therefore, it may be taken as virtually certain that *Samia* was produced no later than 314, we cannot fix its date more precisely than this, though *Samia*'s thematic similarity to *Dyskolos* (a rich man agreeing to, or himself arranging, the marriage of his son to a poorer man's daughter, with whom no dowry is to be given – cf. *Dysk.* 784–847) might suggest that the two plays were fairly close in date to each other.

9 LANGUAGE AND METRE

The language of Menander's comedy is essentially the Attic Greek of his day. This has changed in some respects from what we think of as the classical norm; for example, γίνομαι and γινώσκω have largely supplanted γιγν-, and οὐθείς (with μηθείς, οὐθαμῶς, etc.) has established itself as a competitor with οὐδ-, μηδ- (a competition which the newer forms are destined eventually to lose). There have been many changes in vocabulary and lexical usage (far fewer in inflection or syntax), often found already in the speeches of Demosthenes and his contemporaries; these are discussed where they occur in the Commentary.[138]

Menander's language seems in most respects, by comparison with that of Old Comedy, much closer to the language of conversational prose. The exuberant compounds and neologisms of Aristophanes are gone; almost, though not quite, gone are poetic alternative inflectional forms such as –οισι, -αισι and –μεσθα,[139] and asyndeton is very frequent. The loose relationship between sentence-structure and verse-structure (see below) also adds to the colloquial feel of the diction. However, the language of

---

[138] In Acts I and II see for example (on lexical matters) 5–6, 14, 17, 51, 54, 55, 96, 104–5, 129nn.; (on accidence) 98n. (ἰχθῦς nom.), 141n. (-αις, -αι aor. opt.); (on syntax) 12, 413nn. (the 'connecting relative'). For a comprehensive study of the language of Menander see Cartlidge forthcoming.

[139] These endings occur altogether four times in the plays of Menander known from papyri; there is only one instance in *Samia* (516, in a distinctly paratragic context) and none in *Dyskolos*. In Aristophanes they appear between them 79 times in *Birds* alone, and 17 times even in his latest play, *Wealth*. See Willi 2002: 115–16.

New Comedy has its own conventions and mannerisms: a notable one is the tendency to postpone connective particles, especially γάρ, to remarkably late positions in the sentence.[140]

The principal metre of Menandrian comedy, as of all other Greek drama, is the iambic trimeter, and its scansional structure is the same as in Old Comedy, namely:

$$\overset{1}{\times\ \overline{\smile}\ \smile\ \overline{\smile}}\quad\overset{2}{\times\ \overline{\smile}\ \smile\ \overline{\smile}}\quad\overset{3}{\times\ \overline{\smile}\ \smile\ -}$$

Where two short syllables take the place of a long ('resolution'), they must normally both be part of the same word. Any half-*metron* can be replaced by the sequence ⏑⏑ –, in which all three syllables must normally be part of the same word (this is known as 'anapaestic substitution').[141]

Caesura (a word-break within the second *metron*) is optional, though usual: of the last 100 lines of Act III (321–420) about 79 have a caesura after the first and/or before the last element of this *metron* (the so-called penthemimeral and hephthemimeral caesuras, one of which is almost invariably present in a tragic iambic verse), sixteen have a caesura at the midpoint of the *metron*, and five have none at all.[142] There may be a sentence-break, or a change of speaker, at any point or points in the line,[143] although such breaks do not usually occur after the very first element or before the very last.[144] There is a strong tendency to run units of syntax and sense over from one line to the next: to use a rough measure, of the 100 lines referred to above, forty-four have no punctuation at the end in this edition, compared with twenty-four of the first 100 trimeters in Aristophanes' *Wealth*.[145]

Throughout Act IV and in the latter part of Act V (670–737), a total of 263 lines, the metre used is the trochaic tetrameter catalectic (see opening note to Act IV). In comedy the rhythm of this metre is significantly stricter than that of the iambic trimeter. Leaving aside the very rare substitution of – ⏑⏑ for a half-*metron* (the equivalent in this metre of 'anapaestic

[140] See 43–4, 92nn. and Dover 1985: 337–40 (= 1987: 59–63).

[141] For these rules, and the principal types of exceptions thereto, see M. L. West 1982: 89–90. An interesting exception in *Samia* is πικρὰ πάντ' (100) – or should we read it as πίκρ' ἅπαντ', with elision softening the word-break?

[142] Different analysts may arrive at slightly different figures, according to their decisions about which words to treat as prepositive or postpositive (i.e., for purposes of versification, part of the following or preceding word respectively).

[143] Thus one speech by Demeas (138–9 σὺ μὲν | παίζεις) consists of the last two syllables of one line and the first two of the next.

[144] Yet note 256 (ending with the one-word sentence ποῦ;), 385–6 (νὴ | καὶ τοῖς θεοῖς θύσει).

[145] Text used: Sommerstein 2001.

substitution' in the iambic trimeter),[146] the schema of the trochaic tetrameter is:

$$
\begin{array}{cccc}
1 & 2 & 3 & 4 \\
\overline{}\,\smile\,\overline{}\,\times & \overline{}\,\smile\,\overline{}\,\times\,| & \overline{}\,\smile\,\overline{}\,\times & \overline{}\,\smile\,-
\end{array}
$$

There is almost always a word-break between the second and third *metra.*[147]

10 PERFORMANCE

Assuming that it was produced at the Lenaea or City Dionysia, *Samia* will have been performed in the Theatre of Dionysus as reconstructed in stone during the administration of Lycurgus (*c.*336–324).[148] The basic elements of the theatre environment – the 'dancing-place' (*orchestra*) in which the chorus performed, but which could also be used by the actors; side-passages (*eisodoi*, later *parodoi*)[149] for entrances from, and exits towards, places at a distance; and a building at the back (still called 'booth', *skene*, despite being now a permanent and imposing edifice with a columniated front and projecting wings) representing up to three houses or other interior spaces that played a role in the action – were much the same as they had been for a century before him.[150] In *Samia*, as in many other Menandrian comedies, only two of the three *skene* doors are in use – doubtless the two lateral doors, one representing the entrance to the house of Demeas, the other to that of Nikeratos.[151]

---

[146] This occurs in *Samia* only at 731, to accommodate the semi-formulaic expression δᾶιδα καὶ στεφάνους (731n.).

[147] The only clear exception – in all of Menander that survives – is 484 (see 484n.).

[148] To be precise, the reconstruction was *completed* under Lycurgus; it had been begun before he took office (Paus. 1.29.16), perhaps as early as *c.*360 (Goette 1999). On the dating of Lycurgus' administration, see D. M. Lewis 1997: 221–9.

[149] The later term appears first, in connection with a theatre, in an inscription from Eretria of about the time of Menander's death (*IG* XII[9] 207.55), but since this passage speaks of 'the' *parodos* as if there were only one, it probably refers to the approach to the theatre used by spectators. In this edition the side-passages are called *eisodoi*. On the question whether the two *eisodoi* conventionally denoted specific destinations, or whether their significance had to be established afresh for each play, see note at start of Commentary.

[150] Fourth-century vase paintings from southern Italy show the actors performing on a platform elevated above the *orchestra* at first by four steps, later by six to eight (Green 2010: 86–7); in late classical and Hellenistic stone theatres in the Greek west, correspondingly, the doors in the *skene* were at second-storey level, and most of a play's action must have taken place at this level. In Greece proper, contrariwise, the *skene* doors seem always to have been at ground-floor level. See Moretti 2001: 156–83; Gogos 2008: 75–82, especially 76 n. 344.

[151] In *Dyskolos*, on the other hand, all three doors are used, the central door representing the entrance to the sanctuary of Pan and the Nymphs, with the houses of Knemon and of Gorgias on each side of it.

All Menander's plays, so far as we know, can be performed, if necessary, by three actors,[152] provided that it was considered acceptable for the same role to be played by different actors in different scenes – and we know that this sometimes *was* acceptable in the Athenian theatre, for it is necessary in at least one *tragic* drama – Sophocles' *Oedipus at Colonus*, produced posthumously in 401 BC. And there are passages which look as though they were written specifically to give time for an actor to change mask and costume before appearing in another role. Moschion's monologue before his final exit in Act I (only eight lines survive, 88–95, but it is likely to have been considerably longer) enables the actors who have exited (into the *skene*) as Chrysis and Parmenon to change and re-enter (via an *eisodos*) as Demeas and Nikeratos; and in Act V, Parmenon's not very well motivated departure at 694 will enable the actor to change and reappear as Nikeratos at 713. In several papyri, notably *PSI* 1176 (*com. adesp.* 1063), the parts of the three actors are indicated in the margin by the letters A B Γ, and in at least one, *PBerol* 21119 (*com. adesp.* 1118), we also find the letter Δ,[153] suggesting that this text has been marked up for performance by *four* actors. This seemingly contradictory evidence is readily explicable on the assumption that, while for many performances only three actors would be available (and we know that this was the regular strength of a touring troupe, whether for tragedy or for comedy)[154], there would sometimes be four (as we know was the case in the comic competitions at the major Athenian festivals in Aristophanes' time: MacDowell 1994). If this was so, dramatists would normally write their plays so that they *could* be performed by three actors, but would use a fourth when the opportunity arose. There are various possible three-actor schemes for *Samia*, for example:

(1) Parmenon (Act I), then Demeas throughout.
(2) Moschion throughout, also Parmenon (Acts II and III), Chrysis (Acts III and IV).
(3) Chrysis (Act I), then Nikeratos throughout, also Cook (Act III) and Parmenon (Act V).

Even with four actors, it would still be necessary to split the part of Parmenon, since he is on stage in the company of all the four major characters at different times – with Chrysis in Act I, with Moschion in Acts I and V, with Demeas in Acts II, III and V, and with Nikeratos in Act II – but, as we have seen (§4(e)), Parmenon cannot be said to have been given a

<hr>

[152] Though at *Sik.* 270–3 this requires us to assume a fairly prolonged dumb-show (see Arnott 2000: 260 n. 26) or a rather lengthy interval during which the stage was empty.
[153] There is also an isolated Δ in the margin at line 15 of *PVindob* 29811 (*com. adesp.* 1081), but it is not clear what this signifies; see Lowe 1962: 35.
[154] Pickard-Cambridge 1968: 155–6; Gomme and Sandbach 1973: 16.

consistent personality. It is therefore quite likely that Menander envisaged the following four-actor arrangement for *Samia*:

(1) Demeas.
(2) Moschion and Cook.
(3) Chrysis, also Parmenon (from Act II onwards).
(4) Parmenon (Act I), then Nikeratos.

We have a good deal of evidence about the masks and costumes worn by New Comic performers (see especially Webster, Green and Seeberg 1995, Green 2010), in particular from vase-paintings (which, however, give out at about the time of Menander), from some monumental reliefs, from many terracotta masks and figurines, from later paintings, mosaics etc., based on near-contemporary originals (see §11), and from an extensive catalogue of masks, and a brief digest of costumes, in the *Onomasticon* of the lexicographer Julius Pollux (second century AD) (Pollux 4.118–20, 143–54). Both masks and costumes certainly gave clear signals about the broad stock type to which each character belonged, but – in spite of the impression given by Pollux's catalogue – the masks do not appear to have formed a fixed repertoire (Poe 1996). The costumes were much closer in form to those of ordinary life than had been the case in Old Comedy. Free men and all women, including *hetairai*, wore their clothes long; slaves and cooks were more skimpily dressed (and might have bellies fattened by padding, as the Cook seems to have in the Mytilene mosaic of *Samia*), but the phallus, which had been ubiquitous in earlier comedy, was no longer to be seen.

11 *SAMIA* IN ART

One of the series of mosaics, probably of the fourth century AD, discovered in the early 1960s in the so-called House of the Menander at Mytilene on Lesbos (Charitonides et al. 1970: 38–41 and pl. 4.1) declares itself to be a representation of Act III of *Samia* (Σαμίας μέ(ρος) Γ) and labels the characters, from left to right, as Μάγειρος, Δημέας and Χρυσίς. The scene illustrated is that of the expulsion of Chrysis from Demeas' house (369–83). Demeas (white-haired, white-bearded, and wearing a long, belted, sleeved robe), is advancing towards Chrysis, with his right arm outstretched and his stick raised threateningly in the other hand; his mouth is open. Chrysis, who is holding the baby, is very richly dressed: both her long inner garment, and her shorter outer one, are multi-coloured, her hair is elaborately styled, and she appears to be wearing a tiara and a necklace. She looks slightly towards Demeas as he speaks to her. The Cook, who is a black man (283–390n.) and has something of a pot belly, wears a brown outer garment cut very short and, it would appear, trousers; he is watching and listening intently, and perhaps thinking of intervening (his left foot is turned towards Demeas and Chrysis), but has not yet done so. If one particular moment is represented, it may be 382–3,[155] when Demeas for the third time orders Chrysis to go away (ἐκ τῆς οἰκίας ἄπιθι) and the Cook is on the point of resolving to go up to him (προσιτέον) and protest.

This group of mosaics almost certainly reflects, not contemporary productions of Menander (if any), but an iconographic tradition that goes back almost to the dramatist's own time (Csapo 1999; idem 2010: 140–67), probably to a set of paintings of scenes from his plays commissioned in Athens not long after his death (Green 2010: 93–102). A considerable number of works in this tradition, in various media, are known from the centuries between, notably several wall-paintings and mosaics from Pompeii and its vicinity, as well as relief sculptures, gems, terracotta figurines of individual characters, etc. Until recently, though, no earlier representation of the *Samia* scene was known.

Now, however, a damaged mosaic, probably of the early second century AD, has been found under the Palazzo Nervegna in Brindisi, and Green (forthcoming) has identified it as an earlier version of our *Samia* scene.[156] Only the two left-hand figures (who would be the Cook and Demeas) survive, and only their lower halves. There are some differences which may make one doubt whether the two scenes are in fact one and the same. In particular, the feet of the cook (or slave) are close together in the Brindisi mosaic, so that he does not seem about to make a move; and the back leg of the old man is at a significantly greater angle from the vertical. Comparing a fragmentary sarcophagus lid in the Louvre (Ma 3192; Webster, Green and Seeberg 1995 no. 6RS2), Green argues that in the Brindisi mosaic, and in the original painting, Demeas was *supplicating* Chrysis, begging her forgiveness, and that by the time of the Mytilene mosaic the tradition had become garbled. There is, however, no such scene in *Samia*, and no point in the second half of the play (let alone in Act III, to which the Mytilene mosaic specifically refers) at which one could plausibly suppose that one had been lost. Moreover, in the Louvre fragment the old man's stick is held down at his side, whereas in the Brindisi mosaic it is not visible at all – presumably, as in the Mytilene mosaic, it was held high, hardly the act of a suppliant. I conclude that the Louvre fragment is irrelevant, and that if the Brindisi mosaic does represent *Samia*, it is not necessarily, despite

[155] Ferrari 2004: 128–9 suggests 383–4; but the Cook's pose is not an active one – his left arm is down by his side, his right arm concealed under his garment – and Demeas has not yet noticed him.

[156] I am most grateful to Richard Green for making the draft of his article available to me and enabling me to view images of the Brindisi mosaic and other works discussed in the article, though my interpretation of the evidence differs widely from his.

its greater age, more faithful to its ultimate original than its Mytilene counterpart.

12 THE RECOVERY OF MENANDER

Menander's comedies[157] continued to be widely read throughout antiquity (though interest increasingly concentrated on a relatively small number of plays)[158], and a few surviving papyri, including one of *Samia* (A2), date from as late as the turn of the sixth/seventh century AD. But then the Arab conquest cut Egypt and Syria off from the Byzantine Greek world, and in the Byzantine empire itself the eighth century in particular was a time of neglect for all learning that did not have either a practical or a religious application: the only pagan Greek poetry that continued to be read was that which was studied in the schools. Menander had by then ceased to be a school author, except for the so-called *Sententiae* or *Monosticha*, single-line maxims of very mixed origin which as a corpus had come to be associated with his name and which have survived in numerous medieval manuscripts (Jaekel 1964, Pernigotti 2008). That his actual plays were no longer used as school texts may have been due to several factors: their Attic dialect was not considered to be as pure as that of Aristophanes (Blanchard 1997); their sexual morality may have seemed dubious, especially from a Christian point of view (Easterling 1995: 156–8); and unlike Homer, Pindar, the tragedians and Aristophanes, they had hardly ever been thought difficult enough to be worth equipping with a commentary (N. G. Wilson 1983: 20).[159] At any rate the plays ceased to be copied and soon ceased to be read; the very few early medieval 'Menander manuscripts' that exist are palimpsests, i.e. the original writing (of the late antique period) has been partly scraped off and the surface reused for the writing of a different text.[160]

To the scholars of the Renaissance and for over three centuries after, therefore, Menander remained 'a shadow with a great name'. It was known

[157] Blume 1998: 16–45 gives an excellent account of the disappearance and rediscovery of Menander. On his reception in antiquity, see Nervegna 2013.

[158] On this process see Blume 1998: 24–33.

[159] For all the other authors mentioned, systematic commentaries survive, mostly in the form of marginal annotations (scholia) in late-antique or medieval manuscripts, but with some fragments of separate commentary volumes from earlier centuries. For Menander we have nothing of the kind, only a few isolated notes in one or two of the papyri (e.g. in B on *Samia* 325 and 656).

[160] Thus pages from a Menander manuscript of the fourth century (bearing parts of *Dyskolos* and *Titthe*), along with others from many books in various languages, were reused in the eighth century and then reused again in 886 for a Syriac theological text (D'Aiuto 2003: 266–83). The page bearing the Sinai fragment of *Epitrepontes* (see below) was likewise reused (in the eighth century) for a Syriac text.

that he had been greatly admired in antiquity: Plutarch[161] had said that he was vastly superior to Aristophanes, Julius Caesar[162] that his 'comic punch' (*vis comica*) made him twice as good as his Roman imitator Terence, Quintilian[163] that he was exceptionally skilled in matching language to character and a near-ideal model for the budding orator, and the great Alexandrian scholar Aristophanes of Byzantium,[164] apostrophizing Menander and 'life', had wondered which of the two had been imitating the other. It was believed (wrongly), on the basis of the *Sententiae*, that he had been a master of the pithy one-liner. But of his actual plays very little was known. There were several hundred ancient quotations, but they were not likely to be representative: they were quoted, not because they were typical of Menander, but because in expression or content they illustrated some matter in which the quoting author was interested. There were the Latin adaptations of some plays by Terence (whose commentator Donatus provided some useful information on the changes he had made) and, more dubiously, those by his less urbane, more rumbustious predecessor Plautus (see §2). And that was about all.

Then in 1844 the biblical scholar Konstantin Tischendorf, investigating manuscripts at St Catharine's monastery on Mount Sinai, found two leaves of a fourth-century manuscript of Menander (now known to contain parts of *Epitrepontes* and *Phasma*) glued into the cover of another book (so that Tischendorf could only read, and transcribe, one of the two sides of each leaf). They were eventually separated by another scholar, Archbishop Porfiry Uspensky, and taken to St Petersburg, where they lay neglected for decades. The texts were published in part in 1876 from Tischendorf's transcript (Cobet 1876), and in full, from the original manuscript, fifteen years later (Jernstedt 1891);[165] but they made little impact.

Over the following decade and a half, a period full of major papyrus discoveries in Egypt, several more fragments of Menandrian plays were published, but the first such fragment – eighty-seven mostly well preserved lines of *Georgos* (Nicole 1898) – remained the most extensive. The breakthrough came in 1907 with the publication by Gustave Lefebvre of the fifth-century Cairo codex (C), found at Aphroditopolis in the Thebaid,

---

[161] *Comparison of Aristophanes and Menander = Mor.* 853a–854d.
[162] Quoted by Donatus, *Life of Terence* 7 (Men. test. 64 K-A).
[163] 10.1.69–72.
[164] *Comm. in Call.* fr. 5 Nauck-T7 Slater (Men. test. 83 K-A).
[165] The fragments were long thought to have disappeared (Gomme and Sandbach 1973: 289 still say 'They *were* at Petrograd, now Leningrad'), but they were in fact all the time in the Saltykov-Shchedrin State Public Library (now the National Library of Russia) in what is now again St Petersburg (Turner 1969: 310; Arnott 1998c: 35–7).

which contained substantial parts of five plays of Menander,[166] including *Samia*, and also of the *Demes* of the Old Comic poet Eupolis. An explosion of editions and studies followed, including within three years the first Teubner text (Körte 1910),[167] soon rendered out of date by further papyrus publications, which have continued to the present day. By far the most important advance, however, was the discovery in 1958, in the private collection of Martin Bodmer at Geneva, of a manuscript containing *Dyskolos* virtually complete, together with most of *Samia* and a large portion of *Aspis*[168] – though publication of the latter two plays was long delayed, at Bodmer's wish, in the vain hope that more of the manuscript might be found (Kasser and Austin 1969: 5). Today there are over a score of identifiable Menandrian plays from which we have papyrus fragments of significant extent (and probably an even larger number of others from which we have such fragments but which we have not been able to identify) and seven of which we possess more than one-third of the total number of lines,[169] and Menander has fully taken his place as one of the five major Athenian dramatists.[170]

13 TEXT AND TITLE

The text of *Samia* depends mainly on the two sources mentioned in the previous section.

Samia was the first of the three plays contained in the Bodmer codex (B), known for this play as *PBodm* 25, a papyrus book of the late third or early fourth century AD (published with photographs by Kasser and Austin 1969).[171] The codex is damaged at beginning and end, and it can

---

[166] One of these has still not been identified, and is traditionally labelled *Fabula Incerta* (in Arnott 2000 it is *Fabula Incerta 1*).

[167] This edition was revised and expanded from time to time, most recently as Körte and Thierfelder 1957.

[168] Eighty-three lines of this play had been known since 1913 from another papyrus (*PSI* 126), but had not been identified; the play had been referred to as the *Comoedia Florentina*. The Bodmer codex contained four passages (20–1, 30–1, 72–3, 326–7) which had been cited from *Aspis* by ancient authors.

[169] *Aspis, Dyskolos, Epitrepontes, Misoumenos, Perikeiromene, Samia, Sikyonioi*.

[170] Though still much less intensively studied – or at least much less written about – than his longer-known colleagues. For the five years 2005–2009, *L'Année Philologique* (http://www.annee-philologique.com) records 467 publications on Aeschylus, 439 on Sophocles, 781 on Euripides, 457 on Aristophanes and 99 on Menander.

[171] A torn-off fragment of one leaf of this codex, containing parts of lines 399–410 and 446–57, has survived separately and is now at Barcelona (*PBarcelona* 45); this fragment is included in the transcript and photographs of Kasser and Austin 1969, and in the apparatus of this and other editions it is treated as part of B.

be estimated (Arnott 1999) that up to line 253 (from which point onwards every line of B's text of the play survives at least in part) something like 160 lines are missing from B and not supplied by C (not counting the space, equivalent to about five or six lines, that would have been occupied by the breaks at the end of Acts I and II, including the word χοροῦ); in other words, the complete text of the play was just under 900 lines in length – not much shorter than *Dyskolos* (969) once allowance is made for *Samia's* higher proportion of tetrameters.

The Cairo codex (C; *PCair* J43227; republished photographically by Koenen et al. 1978) was written, again on papyrus, in the fifth century and taken apart in the sixth, its leaves being used by its then owner, Flavius Dioscorus, to cover important documents kept in an amphora. Those which survive contain portions of *Epitrepontes, Heros, Perikeiromene, Samia,* the *Fabula Incerta,* and Eupolis' *Demes;* when the codex was intact, it almost certainly contained one or more other plays as well. From *Samia* C preserves most of Act III (216–416) and a section straddling Acts IV and V (547–686); in many passages the text is badly abraded and very hard to read.

B and C appear to have a common source considerably more recent than Menander's time. In the 320-odd lines for which they are both available, they agree in significant error thirteen times,[172] and in two of these passages the true reading has been preserved in another surviving source.[173] When there is a real choice to be made between them, they are about equally likely to be right,[174] though B is disfigured by a greater number of crude blunders (many of them afterwards corrected, either by the scribe himself or by a supervisor). Both normally mark change of speaker in the same way, by a horizontal line (*paragraphos*) under the beginning of the verse in, or after, which a change occurs (regardless of whether the line contains one speaker-change or more than one) and the symbol : (*dicolon*) at the actual point of change.[175] B also normally gives the names

---

[172] 267, 304, 341 (loss of τις), 342, 385, 394, 407, 548, 554, 573, 590, 653, 675. Probably 375 should be added if, as the present state of B suggests may be the case, the different corruptions in B and C are attempts to regularize the metre after the speaker-abbreviation μαγειρ. had been incorporated in the text.

[173] At 385 in the considerably older O16 (see below); at 573 in B's supralinear variant.

[174] In the apparatus of this edition (which generally does not record passages where one codex is alone in manifest error, see below), thirty-four passages appear in which B and C are in substantive disagreement, B is right in fifteen of these, C in eighteen (including B's omission of 606–11), and in the very corrupt line 674 each preserves a part of the truth.

[175] The *dicolon* may also be used to mark a change of *addressee,* including the beginning or end of an aside or soliloquy.

of speakers, usually in abbreviated form, when they first speak in a scene, and occasionally elsewhere; C, in *Samia*, does so only once, at 616.[176]

Three other papyri preserve small parts of the play:

> *POxy* 2943 (O17), of the second century, contains the ends of nine lines (119b-125), and the beginnings of twenty-two more (134–143m), from the early part of Act II, and throws some uncertain light on the process whereby Moschion persuades his father not to expel Chrysis (143b-m nn.).
>
> *PBingen* 23 (= *PAntinoop.* inv. 4) (A2), of the sixth or seventh century – one of the latest of all Menandrian papyri – contains the beginnings or ends of ten lines (312–15, 345–50) from the middle of Act III.
>
> *POxy* 2831 (O16), of the first or second century, contains the ends of lines 385–90; in this short stretch it twice differs from BC, once in truth (385), once in error (386).

On *PBerol* 8450 (= *com. adesp.* 1131), which has sometimes been attributed to *Samia*, see note at end of Commentary.

The title of the play is given as Σαμία in the *subscriptio* at the end of B's text and in the legend of the Mytilene mosaic; thanks to the designation of Chrysis as 'the Samian woman' in two passages found in C (265, 354) the play had already in 1907 been identified by Lefebvre as the one previously known from a single ancient citation (F 1; see end of Commentary) – though that citation is of a line that has not survived in any papyrus and may not in fact be from *Samia* at all.[177] An alternative title can be inferred from two other citations, both by Stobaeus (1.6.9 and 4.29.10), which were revealed by the Bodmer codex to come from *Samia* (163–4 and 140–2 respectively). Stobaeus' manuscripts give the play's title variously as Κνηδία, Κηδεία and Ἀκήδεια, and it had been usual to regard these as corruptions of Κνιδία (*The Woman from Cnidus*);[178] the new evidence showed that this was impossible, and it was quickly seen[179] that Κηδεία (*The Marriage Alliance*) would be an appropriate alternative title for *Samia*. To be sure, most New Comedies end with the making of a marriage alliance between two families, but it is usually one which, during most of the play, had been opposed by the older generation in at least one of these families (as for

---

[176] This is the opening of Act V, the only act-beginning that survives in C. C has considerably more speaker-names in some other plays.

[177] There are also several words or phrases cited by grammarians and others simply from Menander, or without an author's name, which can be ascribed with varying degrees of confidence to *Samia*; the clearest case is ἐξήραξε κἀνεχαίτισεν (209), cited from Menander by Favorinus, *On Exile* 25.3 Barigazzi. Other possible citations are discussed by Dedoussi 2006: 37*–38* (nos. 4–11).

[178] Alexis wrote a play of this name (Alexis fr. 110).

[179] Kasser and Austin 1969: 25 n. 2.

example in *Georgos* or *Synaristosai/Cistellaria*). The distinctive feature of this play is that the deceptive intrigue set on foot by Moschion, Plangon (with her mother) and Chrysis, to conceal the birth of a child to Moschion and Plangon until the two fathers have come home and been persuaded to agree to their marriage, proves to be unnecessary because the fathers have already, while abroad, themselves agreed to arrange a marriage between their children – but by the time those at home learn of this, it is too late to call off the deception. The whole action of the play stems from this collision between two schemes planned independently to bring about the same result. The subtitle Κηδεία denotes one of these two schemes; the main title Σαμία denotes the principal agent in the other scheme.[180]

The critical apparatus of this edition notes only those passages where the user needs to be warned that the text adopted is conjectural or otherwise uncertain: thus there will not normally be an apparatus note where one of the two main witnesses (B and C) is manifestly in error while the other preserves the true reading. In the many lines that are only partially preserved, conjectural supplements are indicated in the conventional manner by square brackets in the text; those which were proposed soon after the relevant papyrus evidence became available, and have not been seriously disputed since, are generally not noted in the apparatus (for full attributions of these, see the apparatus of Arnott 2000). Angled brackets in the text enclose conjectural restorations of material lost from the transmitted text through scribal error; where a restoration is judged to be certain, it is not bracketed (cf. Barrett 1964: vii). Information about *paragraphoi* and *dicola* (see above) is not given in the apparatus except for special reasons.

---

[180] Gaiser 1976 argued for Ἀκήδεια 'uncaringness, neglect of a duty of care' as the subtitle, but he had to suppose, without any direct evidence, that Moschion had been entrusted by Nikeratos with the responsibility of caring for his wife and daughter, and that his rape of Plangon was primarily to be viewed as a breach of this trust – as if any ancient Greek father, let alone one of Nikeratos' character, would entrust the care of his daughter to an unrelated young man, without first ensuring that he married her.

ΜΕΝΑΝΔΡΟΥ ΣΑΜΙΑ

ΤΑ ΤΟΥ ΔΡΑΜΑΤΟΣ ΠΡΟΣΩΠΑ

ΜΟΣΧΙΩΝ
ΧΡΥΣΙΣ
ΠΑΡΜΕΝΩΝ
ΔΗΜΕΑΣ
ΝΙΚΗΡΑΤΟΣ
ΜΑΓΕΙΡΟΣ

ΜΕΝΑΝΔΡΟΥ ΣΑΜΙΑ

ΜΕΡΟΣ Α'

(desunt versus ca. vii)

ΜΟΣΧΙΩΝ

]...ε̣. [.]υ̣περ[
]ο̣νετι λυπῆσαί με δε̣ῖ
ὀδ]υ̣νηρόν ἐστιν· ἡμάρτηκα γάρ,
ὥστ᾿ αὐτ]ὸ̣ τοῦτό <γ᾿> ἐσόμενον λογίζομαι.
]δὲ τοῦτ᾿ ἂν εὐλόγως ὑμῖν ποεῖν   5
]τὸν ἐκείνου διεξελθὼν τρόπον.
ὡς μὲ]ν ἐτρύφησα τῶι τότ᾿ εὐθέως χρόνωι
ὢν παι]δίον, μεμνημένος σαφῶς ἐῶ·
εὐεργέ]τ̣ει γὰρ ταῦτά μ᾿ οὐ φρονούντά πω.
ὡς δ᾿ ἐν]εγράφην οὐδὲν διαφέρων οὐδενός,   10
τὸ λεγό]μενον δὴ τοῦτο " τῶν πολλῶν τις ὤν" –
ὃς γέγον]α μέντοι νὴ Δί᾿ ἀθλιώτερος ·
αὐτοὶ] γάρ ἐσμεν — τῶι χορηγεῖν διέφερον
καὶ τῆι] φιλοτιμίαι· κύνας παρέτρεφέ μοι,
ἵππο]υς· ἐφυλάρχησα λαμπρῶς· τῶν φίλων   15
τοῖς] δεομένοις τὰ μέτρι᾿ ἐπαρκεῖν ἐδυνάμην.
δι᾿ ἐκεῖνον ἦν ἄνθρωπος. ἀστείαν δ᾿ ὅμως
τούτων χάριν τιν᾿ ἀπεδίδουν· ἦν κόσμιος.
μετὰ τοῦτο συνέβη – καὶ γὰρ ἅμα τὰ πράγματα
ἡμῶν δίειμι πάντ᾿· ἄγω γάρ πως σχολήν –   20
Σαμίας ἑταίρας εἰς ἐπιθυμίαν τινὰ
ἐλθεῖν ἐκεῖνον, πρᾶγμ᾿ ἴσως ἀνθρώπινον.
ἔκρυπτε τοῦτ᾿, ἠισχύνετ᾿· ἠισθόμην <δ᾿> ἐγὼ
ἄκοντος αὐτοῦ διελογιζόμην θ᾿ ὅτι
ἂν μὴ γένηται τῆς ἑταίρας ἐγκρατής,   25

2–3 [γέγ]ονε· τί...δεῖ | [αὐτόν;] Austin   4 [ὥστ᾿] Sommerstein, [αὐτ]ὸ̣ Barigazzi
τοῦτό <γ᾿> Sandbach: τουτο B   5 [δῆλον] Barigazzi, [σαφὲς] Austin   6 [ἔχοιμι]
Lamagna   7 [ὡς μὲ]ν Oguse: [οἷς μὲ]ν Austin   8 [ὢν] Jacques, Oguse: [παι]δίον
Photiadis   ]δίων B^{ac}   10 [ὡς δ᾿ ἐν]εγράφην Kamerbeek, Luppe: [εἶτ᾿ ἐν]εγράφην
multi   11 δὴ Austin: δὲ B   12 [ὃς] Arnott, [γέγον]α Austin   13 suppl.
Oguse   14 suppl. Kasser et Austin   παρέτρεφέ Jacques: γαρέτρεφέ B   21 ἐπιθυμίαν Photiadis: εθυμιαν B   τινα B: τινὸς Jacques   22 ἴσως Austin: ισωσδε B
23 τοῦτ᾿ Austin: τουτομ᾿ B   <δ᾿> add. Rossi

ὑ[π]' ἀντεραστῶν μειρακίων ἐνοχλήσεται,
τοῦτο <δὲ> ποῆσαι δι' ἐμ' ἴσως αἰσχύνεται.
...]ω λαβεῖν ταύτην τὸ μεγ.. [.] .. π. [
...] . οσε. [.] . [

(desunt versus ca. xxiii)

].[....].[..].[30
] . φέροντ' ἰδὼν
]αυτὸς προσετίθην πανταχοῦ
] . ησθε, πρὸς τὸν γείτονα
]α συνθλάσας τὸ σημεῖον σφόδρα
φ]ιλανθρώπως δὲ πρὸς τὴν τοῦ πατρὸς   35
Σαμί]αν διέκειθ' ἡ τῆς κόρης μήτηρ, τά τε
πλεῖ]στ' ἦν παρ' αὐταῖς ἤδε, καὶ πάλιν ποτὲ
αὗτ]αι παρ' ἡμῖν. ἐξ ἀγροῦ δὴ καταδραμὼν
.....] .. γ' εἰς Ἀδώνι' αὐτὰς κατέλαβον
συν]ηγ[μ]ένας ἐνθάδε πρὸς ἡμᾶς μετά τινων   40
ἄλλω]ν γυναικῶν. τῆς δ' ἑορτῆς παιδιὰν
πολλὴ]ν ἐχούσης, οἷον εἰκός, συμπαρὼν
ἐγι]νόμην, οἴμοι, θεατής· ἀγρυπνίαν
ὁ θ]όρυβος αὐτῶν ἐνεπόει γὰρ μοί τινα·
ἐπὶ] τὸ τέγος κήπους γὰρ ἀνέφερόν τινας,   45
ὠρχο]ῦντ', ἐπαννύχιζον ἐσκεδασμέναι.
ὀκν]ῶ λέγειν τὰ λοίπ'· ἴσως δ' αἰσχύνομαι
οἷς] οὐδὲν ὄφελος· ἀλλ' ὅμως αἰσχύνομαι.
ἐκύ]ησεν ἡ παῖς· τοῦτο γὰρ φράσας λέγω
καὶ] τὴν πρὸ τούτου πρᾶξιν. οὐκ ἠρνησάμην   50
τὴν] αἰτίαν σχών, ἀλλὰ πρότερος ἐνέτυχον
τῆι] μητρὶ τῆς κόρης, ὑπεσχόμην γαμεῖν
...]υνεπανέλθηι ποθ' ὁ πατήρ, ὤμοσα.

27 <δὲ> add. Arnott, Sandbach   28 [εἶσ]ω vel [ἐγ]ὼ Sandbach: [λέγ]ω Jacques:
[οὖτ]ω West   31 [συ]μφέροντ' Nardelli: [προ]σφέροντ' e.g. Dedoussi   32 vel
ουτος   —τίθην Austin: —τιθειν B   33 [ἵνα πάντα πυνθά]νησθε Kamerbeek: aliq-
uid (πάντα?) a scriba omissum esse coniecit Lamagna   34 [καὶ ταῦτ]α Sbordone: [ἤνεικ]α Kamerbeek   35 init. [κακῶς] Gaiser   36 suppl. Austin   38
[αὗτ]αι Jacques: [αὕτ]η legit Dedoussi   39 interpretatio vestigiorum incerta: [ὡς
ἔτυ]χ[ε] Sandbach: [ὑπὸ νύ]κτα Dedoussi   Ἀδώνι' Photiadis: ἀδώνει' B   43 οἴμοι
Arnott, Jacques (cf. οιχουσης Bᵃᶜ in 42): οιμε B   45 ἀνέφερόν Austin: ἐνέφερον B
48 [οἷς] Lowe: [ὅτ'] Post: [ἵν'] Ferrari   ἀλλ' Bˢ: ἐστ' (sic) B   52 ὑπεσχόμην Photiadis: ὑποσχόμην B   53 [καὶ ν]ῦν, ἐπὰν ἔλθηι Handley: [ἂν σ]υνεπανέλθη (et mox
<ἐπ>ὤμοσα praeeunte Kassel) Sandbach

ΣΑΜΙΑ　　　　　　　　63

τὸ π]αιδίον γενόμενον εἴληφ’, οὐ πάλαι·
ἀπὸ] ταὐτομάτου δὲ συμβέβηκε καὶ μάλα　　　　　55
εὔκαιρο]ν· ἡ Χρυσίς – καλοῦμεν τοῦτο γὰρ
] . [.] . . . νον εὖ πάλαι

(desunt versus ca. xxvi–xxvii)

ΧΡΥΣΙΣ
　　　　　　　] .. [. . .] . [
σπουδῆι πρὸς ἡμᾶς . [. . .]δ[
ἐγὼ δ’ ἀναμείνασ’ ὅ τι λέγουσ’ ἀ[κούσομαι.　　　60

Μο. ἑόρακας αὐτὸς τὸν πατέρα σύ, Παρμέν[ων;
ΠΑΡΜΕΝΩΝ
　　　οὔκουν ἀκούεις; φημί.
Μο.　　　　　　　καὶ τὸν γείτονα;
Πα. πάρεισιν.
Μο.　　　　εὖ γ’ ἐπόησαν.
Πα.　　　　　　ἀλλ’ ὅπως ἔσει
ἀνδρεῖος εὐθύς τ’ ἐμβαλεῖς περὶ τοῦ γάμου
λόγον.
Μο.　　　τίνα τρόπον; δειλὸς ἤδη γίνομαι,　　　65
ὡς πλησίον τὸ πρᾶγμα γέγονε.
Πα.　　　　　　πῶς λέγεις;
Μο. αἰσχύνομαι τὸν πατέρα.
Πα.　　　　　τὴν δὲ παρθένον
ἣν ἠδίκηκας τήν τε ταύτης μητέρα;
ὅπως — τρέμεις, ἀνδρόγυνε.
Χρ.　　　　　τί βοᾶις, δύσμορε;
Πα. καὶ Χρυσὶς ἦν ἐνταῦθ’. ἐρωτᾶις δή με σὺ　　70
τί βοῶ; γελοῖον. βούλομ’ εἶναι τοὺς γάμους
ἤδη, πεπαῦσθαι τουτονὶ πρὸς ταῖς θύραις
κλάοντα ταύταις μηδ’ ἐκεῖν’ ἀμνημονεῖν
ὧν ὤμοσεν, θύειν, στεφανοῦσθαι, σησαμῆν
κόπτειν παρελθὼν αὐτός. οὐχ ἱκανὰς ἔχειν　　75

56 [εὔκαιρο]ν Sandbach: [ἔτικτε]ν ἡ Χρ. Austin　57 init. [αὐτήν] Sandbach
]όμενον legit Lamagna　ευ Bˢ: οὐ B　59 ἐ[νθά]δ’ Jacques: ν[ῦν] δ[οκῶ] Barigazzi
60 suppl. Barigazzi, Sandbach (qui tamen ἀ[κροάσομαι] maluit)　64 ἐμβαλεῖς
multi: αμβαλεῖς B　69 ὅπως B: ὣ πῶς Del Corno: οὔ; πῶς Gronewald: οὔ; πῶς;
Lamagna: πῶς οὐ Arnott　72 πεπαῦσθαι multi: πεπαυσθαιτε B

προφάσεις δοκῶ σοι;
Μο.   πάντα ποιήσω· τί δεῖ
λέγειν;
Χρ.   ἐγὼ μὲν οἴομαι.
Πα.   τὸ δὲ παιδίον
οὕτως ἐῶμεν ὡς ἔχει ταύτην τρέφειν
αὐτήν τε φάσκειν τετοκέναι;
Χρ.   τί δὴ γὰρ οὔ;
Μο.   ὁ πατὴρ χαλεπανεῖ.
Χρ.   <τί δέ;> πεπαύσεται πάλιν.   80
ἐρᾶι γάρ, ὦ βέλτιστε, κἀκεῖνος κακῶς,
οὐχ ἧττον ἢ σύ· τοῦτο δ᾽ εἰς διαλλαγὰς
ἄγει τάχιστα καὶ τὸν ὀργιλώτατον.
πρότερον δ᾽ ἔγωγε πάντ᾽ ἂν ὑπομεῖναι δοκῶ
ἢ τοῦτο τίτθην ἐν συνοικίαι τινὶ   85
ε........ [   ] . �‚[
                (desunt versus ca. xxi–xxii)
Μο.   ] . [
βο]ύλομαι
λά]βοις
γ]ὰρ ἀθλιώτερον   90
]πάντων· οὐκ ἀπάγξομαι ταχύ;
ῥ]ήτωρ μόνος γὰρ φιλόφρονος
]ότερός εἰμ᾽ ἔν γε τοῖς νυνὶ λόγοις.
ἀ]πελθὼν εἰς ἐρημίαν τινὰ
γυμν]άζομ᾽· οὐ γὰρ μέτριος ἀγών ἐστί μοι.   95

ΔΗΜΕΑΣ
ἆ]ρ᾽ οὖν μεταβολῆς αἰσθάνεσθ᾽ ἤδη τόπου,
ὅσον διαφέρει ταῦτα τῶν ἐκεῖ κακῶν;
Πόντος· παχεῖς γέροντες, ἰχθῦς ἄφθονοι,
ἀηδία τις πραγμάτων. Βυζάντιον·

77 οἴομαι Austin: οιμαι B   παιδίον Austin: παιδιονεχειν (cf. 75, 78) B   79
φάσκειν Photiadis: φάσκει B   80 χαλεπανεῖ Austin: χαλεπαϊνεῖ B   <τί δέ;> add.
West: <σοι> (Moschioni continuatum) Sandbach   85 τίτθην Lloyd-Jones: τιθην
B   86 ἔχουσ[αν ἐκτρέφειν] e.g. Lamagna   89, 90 suppl. Austin   92 init.
[δέω κριτοῦ] Barigazzi: [δεῖται κριτοῦ] mallem, si suppeditaret spatium   93 [καὶ
φαυλ]ότερός Barigazzi: [ἔτ᾽ ἀπειρ]ότερός Austin (ἀπειρ. iam Luschnat)   94 init. [τί
δ᾽ οὐκ] Kassel, Oguse   96 [ἆ]ρ᾽ οὖν Arnott: [τί] οὖν; Sisti: [οὔ]κουν Austin   98
ἰχθῦς Arnott: ἰχθύες B

ἀψίνθιον, πικρὰ πάντ'. Ἄπολλον. ταῦτα δὲ   100
καθαρὰ πενήτων ἀγάθ'. Ἀθῆναι φίλταται,
πῶς ἂν [γ]ένοιθ' ὑμῖν ὅσων ἔστ' ἄξιαι,
ἵν' ὦμεν ἡμεῖς πάντα μακαριώτατοι
οἱ τὴν πόλιν φιλοῦντες. εἴσω παράγετε
ὑμεῖς. ἀπόπληχθ', ἕστηκας ἐμβλέπων ἐμοί;   105

ΝΙΚΗΡΑΤΟΣ
      ἐκ[ε]ῖν' ἐθαύμαζον μάλιστα, Δημέα,
      τῶν περὶ ἐκεῖνον τὸν τόπον· τὸν ἥλιον
      οὐκ ἦν ἰδεῖν ἐνίοτε παμπόλλου χρόνου·
      ἀὴρ παχύς τις, ὡς ἔοικ', ἐπεσκότει.
Δη.   οὔκ, ἀλλὰ σεμνὸν οὐδὲν ἐθεᾶτ' αὐτόθι,   110
      ὥστ' αὐτὰ τἀναγκαῖ' ἐπέλαμπε τοῖς ἐκεῖ.
Νι.   νὴ τὸν Διόνυσον, εὖ λέγεις.
Δη.   καὶ ταῦτα μὲν
      ἑτέροις μέλειν ἐῶμεν· ὑπὲρ ὧν δ' ἐλέγομεν
      τί δοκεῖ ποεῖν σοι;
Νι.   τὰ περὶ τὸν γάμον λέγεις
      τῶι μειρακίωι σου;
Δη.   πάνυ γε.
Νι.   ταῦτ' ἀεὶ λέγω.   115
      ἀγαθῆι τύχηι πράττωμεν, ἡμέραν τινὰ
      θέμενοι.
Δη.   δέδοκται ταῦτ';
Νι.   ἐμοὶ γοῦν.
Δη.   ἀλλὰ μὴν
      κἀμοὶ προτέρωι σου.
Νι.   παρακάλει μ' ὅταν ἐξίηις.
Δη. (?)   ]ιγαστυ[119a

        (desunt versus ca. x-xi inter quos periit notatio ΧΟΡΟΥ)

                      ΜΕΡΟΣ Β'

Δη. (?)   ].   119b
                               ] . α.   119c
                               ]ται   119d

100 fort. πίκρ' ἄπαντ' (vide Introd. §9)   117 γοῦν Austin: γουμ B   119a [ε]ῖς
ἄστυ Dedoussi   119b–125 fines versuum praebet O17   119d [ἔρχε]ται vel
[προσέρχε]ται Arnott

Δη. vel Μο. (?)]..ῠ̣τ̣ο̣ει καὶ δι.[

Μο. οὐδὲ] ἔν 120
ἐ]γὼ μελετήσας ὧν τό[τ᾿ ἐνόουν ἔρ]χομαι.
ὡς ἐγενόμην γὰρ ἐκπ[οδὼν αὐτὸς μ]όνος,
ἔθυον, ἐπὶ τὸ δεῖπνον [ἐκάλουν τοὺς φίλ]ους,
ἐπὶ λούτρ᾿ ἔπεμπον τὰς γ[υναῖκα]ς, περιπατῶν
τὴν σησαμῆν διένεμον· ἦ[ιδον ἐνί]οτε 125
ὑμέναιον, ἐτερέτιζον· ἦν ἀβέλτ[ε]ρο[ς.
ὡς δ᾿ οὖν ἐνεπλήσθην –. ἀλλ᾿, Ἄπολλον, οὑτοσὶ
ὁ π]ατήρ. ἀκήκο᾿ ἆρα. χαῖρέ μοι, πάτερ.
Δη. ν]ὴ καὶ σύ γ᾿, ὦ παῖ.
Μο. τί σκυθρωπάζεις;
Δη. τί γάρ;
γ]αμετὴν ἑταίραν, ὡς ἔοικ᾿, ἐλάνθανον 130
ἔχ]ων.
Μο. γαμετήν; πῶς; ἀγνοῶ <γὰρ> τὸν λόγον.
Δη. λάθ]ριό[ς τι]ς ὑός, ὡς ἔοικε, γέγονέ μοι·
ἡ δ᾿] ἐς [κόρ]ακας ἄπεισιν ἐκ τῆς οἰκίας
ἤ]δη λαβ[ο]ῦ̣σ̣α.
Μο. μηδαμῶς.
Δη. πῶς μηδαμῶς;
ἀλλ᾿ ἦ μ[ε θ]ρέψειν ἔνδον ὑὸν προσδοκᾷς 135
νόθον; [λόγο]ν γ᾿ οὐ τοῦ τρόπου τοὐμοῦ λέγεις.
Μο. τίς δ᾿ ἐ̣σ̣τ̣ὶ̣ν̣ ἡμῶν γνήσιος, πρὸς τῶν θεῶν,
ἢ τίς νόθο̣ς̣, γενόμενος ἄνθρωπος;
Δη. σὺ μὲν
παίζεις.
Μο. μὰ τὸν Διόνυσον, <ἀλλ᾿> ἐσπούδακα.
οὐθὲν γένος γένους γὰρ οἶμαι διαφέρειν, 140
ἀλλ᾿ εἰ δικαίως ἐξετάσαι τις, γνήσιος

120 denuo incipit B [οὐδὲ] Gallo 122 ἐκπ[οδὼν] Sisti [αὐτὸς] Dedoussi [μ]όνος Austin (qui etiam ἐκτὸ[ς ἄστεως]) 125 διένεμον Austin: διενιμον B ἦ[ιδον] Austin [ἐνί]οτε Sandbach 126 ἐτερέτιζον Photiadis: ετερεθιζον B 128 χαῖρέ μοι Austin: χαιρεαμοι B 131 <γὰρ> add. Photiadis: <σὸν> (post τὸν) Arnott 132 ὑός, ὡς Austin: υωσ B 133 [ἡ δ᾿] Webster: [ὄν] Turner: [ὄν γ᾿] Austin 134–143m initia versuum praebet O17 135 ἀλλ᾿ ἦ Austin: aut αλλη aut αλλω O17: ἄλλωι Turner 136 [λόγο]ν Turner: [μανία]ν Austin: [κενό]ν Dedoussi: [μιαρό]ν Arnott γ᾿ ου B: κοὐ Kasser [λέγω]ν τοῦτ᾿ οὐ Handley 139 ἀλλ᾿ add. Arnott, Sandbach 140–2 citat Stobaeus 4.29.10 ex Menandri Κηδία (sic: Κηδεία Austin) 140]σγενουσ B: γένους γένος Stobaeus 141 εξετασαιτισ·γνησιοσ B: ἐξετάσεις καὶ γνησίως Stobaeus post 143a deficit B post 143b, 143e, 143g, 143i paragraphi in O17

	ὁ χρηστός ἐστιν, ὁ δὲ πονηρὸς καὶ νόθος	142
	καὶ δοῦλος. [ ].[..]ς	143a
	λεγωνεαν[	143b
Δη.	ἀλλ' ἀργύριον[	143c
	ἔστ' αὐτὸ μεῖγ[αι	143d
	εἶναι πολ ... [	143e
Μο.	σὺ ταῦτα συγχ[	143f
	τοῦτον λαβ.. [	143g
Δη.	ἄδηλον εἶπ[ας	143h
	πᾶσαν ἀπο[	143i
Μο.	(?) πολὺ μ[ἄλλον	143j
	τοιοῦτον[	143k
	κατα[	143l
	. [	143m

(desunt versus ca. xvi)

	] .. [	144
Δη.	] ἐσπούδακας;	145
Μο.	]ν γαμεῖν ἐρῶ	
	]ν μὴ τοὺς γάμους	
	[ ].	
Δη.	[ ].ως, παῖ.	
Μο.	βούλομαι	
	] δοκεῖν.	
Δη.	καλῶς ποεῖς.	
Μο.	]..	
Δη.	ἂν διδῶσ' οὗτοι, γαμεῖς;	150
Μο.	πῶς ἄν, π]υθόμενος μηδὲ ἓν τοῦ πράγματος,	
	ἐσπο]υδακότα μ' αἴσθοιο συλλάβοις τέ μοι;	
Δη.	ἐσπουδακότα; μηδὲν πυθόμενος; καταν[οῶ	
	τὸ πρᾶγμα, Μοσχίων, ὃ λέγεις. ἤδη τρέχω	
	πρὸς τουτονὶ καὶ τοὺς γάμους αὐτῶι φράσω	155

143b i.e. λέγων ἐὰν vel λέγων ἐᾶν vel λέγω νέαν   143d vel ἔσται τὸ   suppl. nescio-
quis   143e πολίτ[ης] Turner (possis etiam πολίτην)   143f vel συλλ[fort.
συγχ[ωρεῖς;]   143h, 143j suppl. Turner   144 denuo incipit B   146 fort.
[νῦ]ν (Austin) vel [τήμερο]ν   147 fort. [ἆ]ν μή   149 [εἶναι δίκαιος κοὺ] δοκεῖν
Austin: fort. e.g. [γενναῖος εἶναι καὶ] δοκεῖν   150 incertum utrum vestigium dicoli
ante αν legatur: (Δη.) ἐπὰν Dedoussi   διδῶσ' Lowe: δίδωσ' B   152 τέ μοι Photiades: γεμοι B

ποεῖν· τὰ παρ᾿ ἡμῶν γὰρ <παρ>έσται.

Μο.   ταῦ[τά γ᾿ εὖ

λέγεις. περιρρανάμενος ἤδη παρα[γαγὼν
σπείσας τε καὶ λιβανωτὸν ἐπιθεὶς [τὴν κόρην
μέτειμι.

Δη.   μήπω δὴ βάδιζ᾿, ἄχ[ρι ἂν μάθω
εἰ ταῦτα συγχωρήσεθ᾿ ἡμῖ[ν οὑτοσί.   160

Μο.   οὐκ ἀντερεῖ σοι. παρενοχλε[ῖν δ᾿ ὑμῖν
ἐμὲ συμπαρόντ᾿ ἐστ᾿ ἀπρε[πές

Δη.   ταὐτόματόν ἐστιν ὡς ἔοικέ που θεὸς
σώιζει τε πολλὰ τῶν ἀοράτων πραγμάτων.
ἐγὼ γὰρ οὐκ εἰδὼς ἔχοͅ[τα τουτονὶ   165
ἐρωτικῶς τᾳ[τ

              (desunt versus ca. xxvii)

        ]εͅ[..] ἐκεῖνον βούͅ[λομαι
        δεῦ]ρ᾿ εἰς τὸ πρόσθεν, δ[ε]ῦρό μοι,
Νικήρατ᾿, ἔξελθ᾿.]

Νι.   ἐπὶ τί;
Δη.   χαῖρε πολλὰ σύ.
Νι.   ]ν.
Δη.   μνημονεύεις, εἰπέ μοι,   170
           ]ν ἐθέμεθ᾿ ἡμέραν;
Νι.   ἐγώ;
Δη.   τ]αυτ[α]γί· τὴν τήμερον
οἶ]σͅθ᾿ ἀκριβῶς.
Νι.   ποῦ; πότε;
Δη.   γ]ίͅνεσθαι ταχύ
        ]εͅρον.

156–9 sic inter personas divisit Arnott: B paragraphos habet sub vv. 156 et 158, dicola scripta sed postmodo deleta post ποεῖν (156) et λέγεις (157)   156 γὰρ <παρ>έσται Austin: γαρεσται B   ταῦ[τά γ᾿ εὖ] Jacques: ταῦ[θ᾿ ἃ σύ] Sandbach, oratione Demeae usque ad ἐπιθεὶς (158) continuata   157 suppl. Oguse (παρ᾿ ᾳ[B) 158 σπείσας Photiades: επεισασ B   160 suppl. Austin   161 suppl. Austin: dein [πάτερ] idem, [ἴσως] Oguse   162 suppl. Photiades: dein [ἀλλ᾿ ἀπέρχομαι] West, [ἀλλ᾿ εἴμ᾿ ἐκποδών] Barigazzi   163–4 citat Stobaeus 1.6.9, Menandri Κηδείαν laudans: initia versuum usque ad εοικ[et αορατ[praebet B   166 suppl. Kasser et Austin   168 init. [ἔξω καλεῖν] Arnott   [δεῦ]ρ᾿ Austin   δ[ε]ῦρό μοι Handley: δ[.]ͅυρομαι B, littera vel litteris (ο?) super α scripta   169 suppl. Barigazzi   170 [καὶ σύ γε. τί (δ᾿ Barigazzi) ἐστι]ν; Barigazzi, Arnott   171 [εἰς τοὺς γάμους ἦ]ν Blume: [ὡς οὐχὶ πρότερο]ν (et mox ἐγώ.) Sandbach, similia alii   172 [τ]αυτ[α]γί Dedoussi   173 [οἶ]σθ᾿ (vel [ἴ]σθ᾿) Austin

Νι.   τρόπωι τίνι;   175
Δη. [   ]
Νι.   ἀλλ' ἔστ' ἀδύνατον.
Δη.   ἐ]μοί, σοὶ δ' οὐδὲ ἕν.
                       ]γειν.
Νι.   ὦ Ἡράκλεις.
(?)   ]ϛ· οὕτω σοι φράσαι
                       ] . ν· ἀλλὰ <–> τοδὶ λέγειν   180
                       ]ν.
Νι.   πρὶν εἰπεῖν τοῖς φίλοις
                       ]δοκεῖν·
Δη.   Νικήρατε,
                       ἐμ]οὶ χαρίσηι.
Νι.   πῶς γνώσομαι;
Δη.   ] . τυχόντος μοι φίλον
        [   ]
Νι.   τοῦτ' ἐσπούδακας;   185
Δη. [   ]
Νι.   ἀ]λλὰ συγχωροῦντά σοι
                       ἐ]στιν φιλονικεῖν.
Δη.   νοῦν [ἔχ]εις.
                       ]ν συνοίσει σοι.
Νι.   λέγεις
                       ]ϛ.
Δη.   Παρμένων, παῖ, Παρμέν[ων,
              στε]φάνους, ἱερεῖον, σήσαμα,   190
                       ] πάντα τὰξ ἀγορᾶς ἁπλῶς
        πριάμενος ἧ]κε.
Πα.   πάντ'· ἐμοὶ <≈>, Δημέα,
                       ]αλίπηι
Δη.   καὶ ταχέως· ἤδη λέγω.

175 [τήμ]ερον Jacques: [αἱρετώτ]ερον Dedoussi   176 e.g. [οὐκοῦν μελήσει ταῦτ' ἐ]μοί ([οὐκοῦν μέλει τοιαῦτ' ἐ]μοί iam Barigazzi)   179–80 incertum quis quando loquatur   180 <δεῖ> add. Austin, <καὶ> Sisti   183] χαρισ:ηι (litteris οι super χα scriptis) B: [ἐμ]οὶ Austin: [χάριν εἴσομ', ἂν ἐμ]οὶ Kamerbeek   184 possis e.g. [ἔξω σε μᾶλλον το]ῦ τυχόντος μοι φίλον   187 φιλονικεῖν Austin: φιλονεικειν B   190 init. fort. [σφυρίδα λαβὼν] (ita Blume in 191)   ἱερεῖον Austin: ἱέρειονα B   191 [δᾳδας, λιβανωτόν,] e.g. Dedoussi   192 init. suppl. Austin   <μὲν> Austin: <δὴ> Arnott: fort. <γοῦν>: <δ' ἵνα> Dedoussi, Niceratum scilicet hic loqui censens   193 [ἄν τις παρ]αλίπηι – Austin: [μηδὲν παρ]αλίπηι; Dedoussi   ἤδη Austin: ηδε B

ἄγε καὶ μ]άγειρον.
Πα.　　　καὶ μάγειρον· πριάμενος
[　;]
Δη.　　　π]ριάμενος.
Πα.　　　ἀργύριον λαβὼν τρέχω.　　　　　　　　195
Δη.　σὺ δ᾽ οὐδ]έπω, Νικήρατ᾽;
Νι.　　　　　εἰσιὼν φράσας
πρὸς τ]ὴν γυναῖκα τἄνδον εὐτρεπῆ ποεῖν
διώξομ᾽ εὐθὺς τοῦτον.
Πα.　　　　　　　　οὐκ οἶδ᾽ οὐδὲ ἕν,
πλήν προστέτακται ταῦτα συντείνω τ᾽ ἐκε[ῖ
ἤδη.
Δη.　　τὸ πεῖσαι τὴν γυναῖκα πράγματα　　　200
αὐτῶι παρέξει· δεῖ δὲ μὴ δοῦναι λόγον
μηδὲ χ[ρ]όνον ἡ[μ]ᾶς. παῖ, διατρίβεις. οὐ δραμεῖ;
Νι.(?)　　　　　　　　　].[..]γος ἡ γυνὴ
] ἱκετεύω· τί οὖν;
]..[..]ς᾽ ἡλίκον　　　205
(desunt versus ca. x inter quos periit notatio ΧΟΡΟΥ)

ΜΕΡΟΣ Γ´

Δη.　　　　　　] . δρόμου καλο[ῦ
χει]μὼν ἀπ[ροσδ]όκητος ἐξαίφνης [μέγας
ἐλθών· ἐκεῖνος τοὺς ἐν εὐδίαι ποτὲ
θέοντας ἐξήραξε κἀνεχαίτισεν.
τοιοῦτο γὰρ καὶ τοὐμόν ἐστι νῦν· ἐγώ,　　　210
ὁ τοὺς γάμους ποῶν, ὁ θύων το[ῖ]ς θεο[ῖς,
ὧι πάντα κατά νοῦν ἀρτίως ἐγίν[ετο,
οὐδ᾽ εἰ βλέπω, μὰ τὴν Ἀθηνᾶν, οἶδ[α νῦν
καλῶς ἔτ᾽· οὔκ, [ἀ]λλ᾽ ἐπὶ τὸ πρόσθεν π[
ὀδύν]ην τιν᾽ ἀνυπέρβλητον ἐξ[αίφνης λαβών.　　215

194 ita suppl. Austin ([λαβὲ καὶ μ]άγειρον Dedoussi)　195 [ταυτί] Dedoussi: [ἃ δεῖ] Arnott　202 δραμεῖ Kassel: δαραμει B　203 [περ]ί[ερ]γος Barigazzi　205 haec prima dispexit Dedoussi: in initio proximi versus [λαλεῖ] vel [βοᾶι] stetisse putavit Arnott　206 [ἐ]κ Arnott　207 ἐξαίφνης Austin: εξέφνης B　[μέγας] Sisti 209 ἐξήραξε καὶ ἀνεχαίτισεν citat Favorinus de exilio 25.3 Barigazzi　-χαίτ- Favorinus: -χέτ- Bᵖᶜ: -χειτ- Bᵃᶜ.　213 οἶδ[α] Austin, [νῦν] LloydJones　214 καλῶς ἔτ᾽ Austin: καλωετ B　ἐπὶ τὸ Austin: ἐπιό B: εἰς τὸ Sandbach　π[ρόαγομαι] Austin: π[εριπατῶ] Dedoussi　215 [ὀδύν]ην Kasser et Austin: [πληγ]ὴν Jacques　-βλητον Austin: -βοлητον B　[λαβών] Lloyd-Jones

ἢ ᾽στ[ὶ] πιθανόν; σκέψασθε πότερο[ν εὖ φρονῶ
ἢ μαίνομ᾽, οὐδέν τ᾽ εἰς ἀκρίβειαν [
λαβὼν ἐπάγομαι μέγ᾽ ἀτύχημα [διὰ κενῆς.
ὡς γὰρ τάχιστ᾽ εἰσῆλθον, ὑπερεσπουδακὼς
τὰ τοῦ γάμου πράττειν, φράσας τὸ πρᾶγμ᾽ ἁπλῶς   220
τοῖς ἔνδον ἐκέλευσ᾽ εὐτρεπίζειν πάνθ᾽ ἃ δεῖ,
καθαρὰ ποεῖν, πέττειν, ἐνάρχεσθαι κανοῦν.
ἐγίνετ᾽ ἀμέλει πάνθ᾽ ἑτοίμως, τὸ δὲ τάχος
τῶν πραττομένων ταραχήν τιν᾽ αὐτοῖς ἐνεπόει,
ὅπερ εἰκός. ἐπὶ κλίνης μὲν ἔρριπτ᾽ ἐκποδὼν   225
τὸ παιδίον κεκραγός, αἱ δ᾽ ἐβόων ἅμα
" ἄλευρ᾽, ὕδωρ, ἔλαιον ἀπόδος, ἄνθρακας."
καὐτὸς διδοὺς τούτων τι καὶ συλλαμβάνων
εἰ[ς τ]ὸ ταμιεῖον ἔτυχον εἰσελθών, ὅθεν
πλείω προαιρῶν καὶ σκοπούμενος σ[230
οὐκ εὐθὺς ἐξῆλθον. καθ᾽ ὃν δ᾽ ἦν χρόνον ἐγὼ
ἐνταῦθα, κατέβαιν᾽ ἀφ᾽ ὑπερώιου τις γυνὴ
ἄνωθεν εἰς τοὔμπροσθε τοῦ ταμιειδίου
οἴκημα· τυγχάνει γὰρ ἱστεών τις ὤν,
ὥσθ᾽ ἥ τ᾽ ἀνάβασίς ἐστι διὰ τούτου τό τε   235
ταμιεῖον ἡμῖν. τοῦ δὲ Μοσχίωνος ἦν
τίτθη τις αὕτη, πρεσβυτέρα, γεγονυῖ᾽ ἐμὴ
θεράπαιν᾽, ἐλευθέρα δὲ νῦν. ἰδοῦσα δὲ
τὸ παιδίον κεκραγὸς ἠμελημένον
ἐμέ τ᾽ οὐδὲν εἰδυῖ᾽ ἔνδον ὄντ᾽, ἐν ἀσφαλεῖ   240
εἶναι νομίσασα τοῦ λαλεῖν, προσέρχεται
καὶ ταῦτα δὴ τὰ κοινὰ " φίλτατον τέκνον"
εἰποῦσα καὶ " μέγ᾽ ἀγαθόν· ἡ μάμμη δὲ ποῦ;"
ἐφίλησε, περιήνεγκεν. ὡς δ᾽ ἐπαύσατο
κλᾶον, πρὸς αὑτήν φησ[ι]ν " ὦ τάλαιν᾽ ἐγώ,   245
πρώην τοιοῦτον ὄντα Μοσχίων᾽ ἐγὼ
αὐτὸν ἐτιθηνούμην ἀγαπῶσα· νῦν δ᾽ [ἐπεὶ
παιδίον ἐκείνου γέγον[ε]ν, ἤδη καὶ τόδ[ε

216 incipit C   initium sic Sandbach: ηστ[C,]πιθανὸν B   finem suppl. Austin
217 τ᾽ Austin: γ᾽ B: periit C   [τότε] Austin   218 suppl. Austin   225 ἐκποδὼν
Lefebvre: ευθυσεκποδῶ C: periit B   230 καισκοπ- C: καισυνκοπ- (σ super νκ scriptum) B: συσκοπ- Dedoussi   σ[υχνὰ] Hense, Wilamowitz: σ[χολῆι Sudhaus   233
ταμιειδίου Croenert: ταμειῖου C: τα[B   246–53 periit B   248 ἤδη legit Sudhaus

(desunt versus ii vel iii)

]ạ καὶ
γεγο]νέναι."   250

.....].[....]... καὶ θεραπαινιδίωι τινὶ
ἔξωθεν εἰστρέχοντι " λούσατ', ὦ τάλαν,
τὸ παιδίον" φησίν· " τί τοῦτ'; ἐν τοῖς γάμοις
τοῖς τοῦ πατρὸς τὸν μικρὸν οὐ θεραπεύετε;"
εὐθὺς δ᾽ ἐκείνη " δύσμορ', ἡλίκον λαλεῖς"   255
φήσ᾽· " ἔνδον ἐστὶν αὐτός." " οὐ δήπου γε· ποῦ;"
" ἐν τῶι ταμιείωι." καὶ παρεξήλλαξέ τι·
" αὐτὴ καλεῖ, τίτθη, σε", καὶ " βάδιζε καὶ
σπεῦδ'· οὐκ ἀκήκο᾽ οὐδέν· εὐτυχέστατα."
εἰποῦσ᾽ ἐκείνη δ᾽ " ὦ τάλαινα τῆς ἐμῆς   260
λαλιᾶς" ἀπῆιξεν ἐκποδών, οὐκ οἶδ᾽ ὅποι.
κἀγὼ προήιειν τοῦτον ὅνπερ ἐνθάδε
τρόπον ἀρτίως ἐξῆλθον, ἡσυχῆι πάνυ,
ὡς οὔτ᾽ ἀκούσας οὐδὲν οὔτ᾽ ἠισθημένος·
αὐτὴν δ᾽ ἔχουσαν αὐτὸ τὴν Σαμίαν ὁρῶ   265
ἔξω διδοῦσαν τιτθίον παριὼν ἅμα·
ὥσθ᾽ ὅτι μὲν αὐτῆς ἐστι τοῦτο γνώριμον
εἶναι, πατρὸς δ᾽ ὅτου ποτ᾽ ἐστίν, εἴτ᾽ ἐμὸν
εἴτ᾽ − οὐ λέγω δ᾽, ἄνδρες, πρὸς ὑμᾶς τοῦτ᾽ ἐγώ −
οὐχ ὑπονοῶ, τὸ πρᾶγμα δ᾽ εἰς μέσον φέρω   270
ἅ τ᾽ ἀκήκο᾽ αὐτός, οὐκ ἀγανακτῶν οὐδέπω.
σύνοιδα γὰρ τῶι μειρακίωι, νὴ τοὺς θεούς,
καί κοσμίωι τὸν πρότερον ὄντι χρόνον ἀεὶ
καὶ περὶ ἔμ᾽ ὡς ἔνεστιν εὐσεβεστάτωι.
πάλιν δ᾽, ἐπειδὰν τὴν λέγουσαν καταμάθω   275
τίτθην ἐκείνου πρῶτον οὖσαν, εἶτ᾽ ἐμοῦ
λάθραι λέγουσαν, εἶτ᾽ ἀποβλέψω πάλιν
εἰς τὴν ἀγαπῶσαν αὐτὸ καὶ βεβιασμένην
ἐμοῦ τρέφειν ἄκοντος, ἐξέστηχ᾽ ὅλως.
ἀλλ᾽ εἰς καλὸν γὰρ τουτονὶ προσιόνθ᾽ ὁρῶ   280
τὸν Παρμένοντ᾽ ἐκ τῆς ἀγορᾶς· ἐατέον

251 init. [τοιαῦ]τ᾽ [ἐλάλ]ησε Sudhaus   261 ἀπῆιξεν Austin: απηιξ Β: απηλθεν C
262 προήιειν Β: προηλθον C   266 sic C: ἔξω καθ᾽ αυτην (καὶ add. Photiades)
διδοῦσαν τι᾽θίον Β   267 αὐτῆς ἐστι τοῦτο multi: εστι τουτο αυτησ fere ΒC   270
ουχ᾽ Β: ουθ᾽ C   280 τουτονὶ προσιόνθ᾽ Β: τουτον π[.]ρọνθ᾽ C sec. Sandbach: τουτονὶ
παρόνθ᾽ van Leeuwen: τοῦτον εἰσιόνθ᾽ Körte

αὐτὸν παραγαγεῖν ἐστι τούτους οὓς ἄγει.

Πα. μάγειρ', ἐγώ, μὰ τοὺς θεούς, οὐκ οἶδα σὺ
ἐφ' ὅ τι μαχαίρας περιφέρεις· ἱκανὸς γὰρ εἶ
λαλῶν κατακόψαι πάντα πράγματ'.
ΜΑΓΕΙΡΟΣ
                   ἄθλιε   285
   ἰδιῶτ'.
Πα.   ἐγώ;
Μα.   δοκεῖς γέ μοι, νὴ τοὺς θεούς.
εἰ πυνθάνομαι πόσας τραπέζας μέλλετε
ποεῖν, πόσαι γυναῖκές εἰσι, πηνίκα
ἔσται τὸ δεῖπνον, εἰ δεήσει προσλαβεῖν
τραπεζοποιόν, εἰ κέραμός ἐστ' ἔνδοθεν   290
ὑμῖν ἱκανός, εἰ τοὐπτάνιον κατάστεγον,
εἰ τἄλλ' ὑπάρχει πάντα –
Πα.   κατακόπτεις γέ με,
εἰ λανθάνει σε, φίλτατ', εἰς περικόμματα,
οὐχ ὡς ἔτυχεν.
Μα.   οἴμωζε.
Πα.   καὶ σύ, τοῦτό γε
παντὸς ἕνεκ'. ἀλλὰ παράγετ' εἴσω.
Δη.   Παρμένων.   295
Πα. ἐμέ τις κέκληκε;
Δη.   ναιχί.
Πα.   χαῖρε, δέσποτα.
Δη. τὴν σφυρίδα καταθεὶς ἧκε δεῦρ'.
Πα.   ἀγαθῆι τύχηι.
Δη. τοῦτον γὰρ οὐδέν, ὡς ἐγῶιμαι, λανθάνοι
τοιοῦτον ἂν πραττόμενον ἔργον· ἔστι γὰρ
περίεργος, εἴ τις ἄλλος. ἀλλὰ τὴν θύραν   300
προϊὼν πέπληχε.
Πα.   δίδοτε, Χρυσί, πάνθ' ὅσ' ἂν
ὁ μάγειρος αἰτῆι· τὴν δὲ γραῦν φυλάττετε
ἀπὸ τῶν κεραμίων, πρὸς θεῶν. τί δεῖ ποεῖν,
δέσποτα;
Δη.   τί δεῖ ποεῖν <σε>; δεῦρ' ἀπὸ τῆς θύρας·

---

294 ετυχεν C: ετυχες B   302 δε C: τε B   304 ποεῖν <σε>: Ellis, Wilamowitz:
ποεῖν; <ἴθι> Leo, Mazon: ποειν BC (σε in C in fine versus dispicere se credidit
Sudhaus)

        ἔτι μικρόν.
Πα.   ἤν.
Δη.   ἄκουε δή μου, Παρμέν[ων.   305
ἐγώ σε μαστιγοῦν, μὰ τοὺς δώδεκα θεού[ς,
οὐ βούλομαι διὰ πολλά.
Πα.   μαστιγοῦν; τί δὲ
πεπόηκα;
Δη.   συγκρύπτεις τι πρός μ᾽, ἤι[σ]θημ᾽.
Πα.   ἐγώ;
μὰ τὸν Διόνυσον, μὰ τὸν Ἀπόλλω τουτονί,
μὰ τὸν Δία τὸν σωτῆρα, μὰ τὸν Ἀσκληπιόν –   310
Δη.   παῦ᾽ μηδὲν ὄμνυ᾽· οὐ γὰρ εἰκάζων λέγω.
Πα.   ἢ μήποτ᾽ ἄρ᾽ –
Δη.   οὗτος, βλέπε δεῦρ᾽.
Πα.   ἰδού, βλέπω.
Δη.   τὸ παιδίον τίνος ἐστίν;
Πα.   ἤν.
Δη.   τὸ παιδίον
τίνος ἔ[στ᾽, ἐρ]ωτῶ.
Πα.   Χρυσίδος.
Δη.   πατρὸς δὲ τοῦ;
Πα.   σόν, φ[ησίν].
Δη.   ἀπόλωλας· φενακίζεις μ᾽.
Πα.   ἐγώ;   315
Δη.   εἰδότα γ᾽ ἀκριβῶς πάντα καὶ πεπυσμένον
ὅτι Μοσχίωνός ἐστιν, ὅτι σύνοισθα σύ,
ὅτι δι᾽ ἐκεῖνον αὐτὸ νῦν αὕτη τρέφει.
Πα.   τίς φησι;
Δη.   πάντες. ἀλλ᾽ ἀπόκριναι τοῦτό μοι·
ταῦτ᾽ ἐστίν;
Πα.   ἔστι, δέσποτ᾽, ἀλλὰ λανθάνειν –   320
Δη.   τί " λανθάνειν" ; ἱμάντα παίδων τις δότω
ἐπὶ τουτονί μοι τὸν ἀσεβῆ.
Πα.   μή, πρὸς θεῶν.
Δη.   στίξω σε, νὴ τὸν Ἥλιον.
Πα.   στίξεις ἐμέ;

305 μου B: νυν C   308 aut προσμ᾽ aut πραγμ᾽ C: πραγμ᾽ B   εγω in initio v.
309 habet C, habebat olim B ut videtur   312–15 fines versuum praebet A2
315 φ[ησίν] Sandbach: φ[ασίν] Sudhaus

Δη. ἤδη γ'.
Πα.   ἀπόλωλα.
Δη.   ποῖ σύ, ποῖ, μαστιγία;
     λάβ' αὐτόν. " ὦ πόλισμα Κεκροπίας χθονός,   325
     ὦ ταναὸς αἰθήρ, ὦ —" τί, Δημέα, βοᾶις;
     τί βοᾶις, ἀνόητε; κάτεχε σαυτόν, καρτέρει·
     οὐδὲν γὰρ ἀδικεῖ Μοσχίων σε. παράβολος
     ὁ λόγος ἴσως ἔστ', ἄνδρες, ἀλλ' ἀληθινός.
     εἰ μὲν γὰρ ἢ βουλόμενος ἢ κεκνισμένος   330
     ἔρωτι τοῦτ' ἔπραξεν ἢ μισῶν ἐμέ,
     ἦν ἂν ἐπὶ τῆς αὐτῆς διανοίας, ἔτι θρασὺς
     ἐμοί τε παρατεταγμένος· νυνὶ δέ μοι
     ἀπολελόγηται τὸν φανέντ' αὐτῶι γάμον
     ἄσμενος ἀκούσας. οὐκ ἐρῶν γάρ, ὡς ἐγὼ   335
     τότ' ὠιόμην, ἔσπευδεν, ἀλλὰ τὴν ἐμὴν
     Ἑλένην φυγεῖν βουλόμενος ἔνδοθέν ποτε.
     αὕτη γάρ ἐστιν αἰτία τοῦ γεγονότος·
     παρέλαβεν αὐτόν που μεθύοντα δηλαδή,
     οὐκ ὄντ' ἐν ἑαυτοῦ· πολλὰ δ' ἐξεργάζεται   340
     ἀνόητ' ἄκρατος καὶ νεότης, ἂν <τις> λάβηι
     τὸν συνεπιβουλεύσοντα τούτοις πλησίον.
     οὐδενὶ τρόπωι γὰρ πιθανὸν εἶναί μοι δοκεῖ
     τὸν εἰς ἅπαντας κόσμιον καὶ σώφρονα
     τοὺς ἀλλοτρίους εἰς ἐμὲ τοιοῦτον γεγονέναι,   345
     οὐδ' εἰ δεκάκις ποιητός ἐστι, μὴ γόνωι
     ἐμὸς ὑός· οὐ γὰρ τοῦτο, τὸν τρόπον δ' ὁρῶ.
     χαμαιτύπη δ' ἄνθρωπος, ὄλεθρος. ἀλλὰ τί;
     οὐ γὰρ περιέσται. Δημέα, νῦν ἄνδρα χρὴ
     εἶναί σ'· ἐπιλαθοῦ τοῦ πόθου, πέπαυσ' ἐρῶν,   350
     καὶ τἀτύχημα μὲν τὸ γεγονὸς κρύφθ' ὅσον
     ἔνεστι διὰ τὸν ὑόν, ἐκ τῆς δ' οἰκίας
     ἐπὶ κεφαλὴν ἐς κόρακας ὦσον τὴν καλὴν
     Σαμίαν. ἔχεις δὲ πρόφασιν, ὅτι τὸ παιδίον
     ἀνείλετ'· ἐμφανίσηις γὰρ ἄλλο μηδὲ ἕν,   355
     δακὼν δ' ἀνάσχου, καρτέρησον εὐγενῶς.

332 ἦν ἂν multi: ην[.]ν C: γενεν B   341 ἂν <τις> Luppe: εαν B: οταν C   342
-σοντα Jacques: -σαντα BC   345–50 initia versuum praebet A2   347 ὑός A2:
υιος BC   353 επι B: επι την C   356 ευγενως C: δ' ευγενως B

Μα. ἀλλ᾽ ἄρα πρόσθε τῶν θυρῶν ἐστ᾽ ἐνθάδε;
παῖ, Παρμένων. ἄνθρωπος ἀποδέδρακέ με,
ἀλλ᾽ οὐδὲ μικρὸν συλλαβών.
Δη.   ἐκ τοῦ μέσου
ἄναγε σεαυτόν.
Μα.   Ἡράκλεις, τί τοῦτο; παῖ.   360
μαινόμενος εἰσδεδράμηκεν εἴσω τις γέρων·
ἢ τί τὸ κακόν ποτ᾽ ἐστί; τί δέ μοι τοῦτο; παῖ.
νὴ τὸν Ποσειδῶ, μαίνεθ᾽, ὡς ἐμοὶ δοκεῖ·
κέκραγε γοῦν παμμέγεθες. ἀστεῖον πάνυ,
εἰ τὰς λοπάδας ἐν τῶι μέσωι μου κειμένας   365
ὄστρακα ποήσαι. πάνθ᾽ ὅμοια. τὴν θύραν
πέπληχεν. ἐξώλης ἀπόλοιο, Παρμένων,
κομίσας με δεῦρο. μικρὸν ὑπαποστήσομαι.

Δη. οὔκουν ἀκούεις; ἄπιθι.
Χρ.   ποῖ γῆς, ὦ τάλαν;
Δη. ἐς κόρακας ἤδη.
Χρ.   δύσμορος.
Δη.   ναί, δύσμορος.   370
ἐλεεινὸν ἀμέλει τὸ δάκρυον. παύσω σ᾽ ἐγώ,
ὡς οἴομαι –
Χρ.   τί ποοῦσαν;
Δη.   οὐδέν. ἀλλ᾽ ἔχεις
τὸ παιδίον, τὴν γραῦν· ἀποφθείρου ποτέ.
Χρ. ὅτι τοῦτ᾽ ἀνειλόμην;
Δη.   διὰ τοῦτο καὶ –
Χρ.   τί " καί" ;
Δη. διὰ τοῦτο.
Μα.   τοιοῦτ᾽ ἦν τι τὸ κακόν· μανθάνω.   375
Δη. τρυφᾶν γὰρ οὐκ ἠπίστασ᾽.
Χρ.   οὐκ ἠπιστάμην;
τί δ᾽ ἔσθ᾽ ὃ λέγεις;
Δη.   καίτοι πρὸς ἔμ᾽ ἦλθες ἐνθάδε
ἐν σινδονίτηι, Χρυσί – μανθάνεις; – πάνυ
λιτῶι.

357 προσθε B: προσθεν C   366 ομοια C: ετοιμ[B   371 ἐλεεινὸν BC: ἐλεινὸν van
Herwerden   373 ποτε B: ταχυ C   375 τοιοῦτ᾽ ἦν τι multi: τουτ᾽ ην τι B: τοιουτ᾽
ην C   376 ηπιστασ᾽…ηπισταμην C: επιστασο…επισταμην B

Χρ.   τί οὖν;
Δη.   τότ᾽ ἦν ἐγώ σοι πάνθ᾽, ὅτε
φαύλως ἔπραττες.
Χρ.   νῦν δὲ τίς;
Δη.   μή μοι λάλει.   380
ἔχεις τὰ σαυτῆς πάντα· προστίθημί σοι
ἐγώ θεραπαίνας, χρυσί᾽. ἐκ τῆς οἰκίας
ἄπιθι.
Μα.   τὸ πρᾶγμ᾽ ὀργή τίς ἐστι· προσιτέον.
βέλτισθ᾽, ὅρα –
Δη.   τί μοι διαλέγει;
Μα.   μὴ δάκηις.
Δη.   ἑτέρα γὰρ ἀγαπήσει τὰ παρ᾽ ἐμοί, Χρυσί· νὴ   385
καὶ τοῖς θεοῖς θύσει.
Μα.   τί ἐστιν;
Δη.   ἀλλὰ σὺ
ὑὸν πεπόησαι· πάντ᾽ ἔχεις.
Μα.   οὔπω δάκνει.
ὅμως –
Δη.   κατάξω τὴν κεφαλήν, ἄνθρωπέ, σου,
ἄν μοι διαλέγηι.
Μα.   νὴ δικαίως γ᾽. ἀλλ᾽ ἰδού,
εἰσέρχομ᾽ ἤδη.
Δη.   τὸ μέγα πρᾶγμ᾽· ἐν τῆι πόλει   390
ὄψει σεαυτὴν νῦν ἀκριβῶς ἥτις εἶ.
αἱ κατὰ σέ, Χρυσί, πραττόμεναι δραχμὰς δέκα
μόνας †ἑταῖραι† τρέχουσιν ἐπὶ τὰ δεῖπνα καὶ
πίνουσ᾽ ἄκρατον ἄχρι ἂν ἀποθάνωσιν, ἢ
πεινῶσιν ἂν μὴ τοῦθ᾽ ἑτοίμως καὶ ταχὺ   395
ποῶσιν. εἴσει δ᾽ οὐδενὸς τοῦτ᾽, οἶδ᾽ ὅτι,
ἧττον σύ, καὶ γνώσει τίς οὖσ᾽ ἡμάρτανες.
ἔσταθι.
Χρ.   τάλαιν᾽ ἔγωγε τῆς ἐμῆς τύχης.

Νι.   τουτὶ τὸ πρόβατον τοῖς θεοῖς μὲν τὰ νόμιμα

---

380 λάλει C: διαλέγου (ex 389) B   382 χρυσι᾽ B: χρυσι C: Χρυσί Robert
385–90 fines versuum praebet O16   385 νη O 16: νυν BC   386 τι C: τις B
συ BC: τι O16   387 πεπόησαι B: πεπόηκας C   389 νη δικαιως γ᾽ B: και δικαιως C
392 αἱ C: οὐ B   393 εταιραι B^{ac}C: ετεραι B^{pc}: ἀεὶ Leo   394 ἄχρι ἂν Headlam:
αχρισαν BC

ἅπαντα ποιήσει θυθὲν καὶ ταῖς θεαῖς.   400
αἷμα γὰρ ἔχει, χολὴν ἱκανήν, ὀστᾶ καλά,
σπλῆνα μέγαν, ὧν χρεία 'στὶ τοῖς Ὀλυμπίοις.
πέμψω δὲ γεύσασθαι κατακόψας τοῖς φίλοις
τὸ κώιδιον· λοιπὸν γάρ ἐστι τοῦτό μοι.
ἀλλ', Ἡράκλεις, τί τοῦτο; πρόσθε τῶν θυρῶν   405
ἕστηκε Χρυσὶς ἥδε κλάουσ'· οὐ μὲν οὖν
ἄλλη. τί ποτε τὸ γεγονός;
Χρ.   ἐκβέβληκέ με
ὁ φίλος ὁ χρηστός σου· τί γὰρ ἄλλ';
Νι.   ὦ Ἡράκλεις.
τίς; Δημέας;
Χρ.   ναί.
Νι.   διὰ τί;
Χρ.   διὰ τὸ παιδίον.
Νι. ἤκουσα καὐτὸς τῶν γυναικῶν ὅτι τρέφεις   410
ἀνελομένη παιδάριον. ἐμβροντησία.
ἀλλ' ἔστ' ἐκεῖνος ἡδύς. οὐκ ὠργίζετο
εὐθύς; διαλιπὼν δ', ἀρτίως;
Χρ.   ὃς καὶ φράσας
εἰς τοὺς γάμους μοι τἄνδον εὐτρεπῆ ποεῖν
μεταξύ μ' ὥσπερ ἐμμανὴς ἐπεισπεσὼν   415
ἔξωθεν ἐκκέκλεικε.
Νι.   Δημέας χολᾶι.
ὁ Πόντος οὐχ ὑγιεινόν ἐστι χωρίον.
πρὸς τὴν γυναῖκα δεῦρ' ἀκολούθει τὴν ἐμήν.
θάρρει· τί βούλει; παύσεθ' οὗτος ἀπομανείς,
ὅταν λογισμὸν ὧν ποεῖ νυνὶ λάβηι.   420

ΧΟΡΟΥ

ΜΕΡΟΣ Δ΄

Νι. παρατενεῖς, γύναι. βαδίζω νῦν ἐκείνωι προσβαλῶν.
οὐδ' ἂν ἐπὶ πολλῶι γενέσθαι τὸ γεγονός, μὰ τοὺς θεούς,
πρᾶγμ' ἐδεξάμην. μεταξὺ τῶν γάμων ποουμένων
συμβέβηκ' οἰωνὸς ἡμῖν ἄτοπος. ἐκβεβλημένη

400 θυθεν BC: τυθὲν van Leeuwen   407 ποτε τὸ multi: ποτ' εστι το BC   post
416 deficit C   419 θάρρει Austin: θαρσει B

εἰσελήλυθεν πρὸς ἡμᾶς παιδάριον ἔχουσά τις· 425
δάκρυα γίνεθ', αἱ γυναῖκες τεθορύβηνται. Δημέας
σκατοφαγεῖ· νὴ τὸν Ποσειδῶ καὶ θεούς, οἰμώξεται
σκαιὸς ὤν.

Μο.   οὐ μὴ δύηι ποθ' ἥλιος; τί δεῖ λέγειν;
ἐπιλέλησθ' ἡ νὺξ ἑαυτῆς. ὦ μακρᾶς δειλῆς. τρίτον
λούσομ' ἐλθών· τί γὰρ ἔχοιμ' ἂν ἄλλο ποιεῖν;

Νι.   Μοσχίων, 430
χαῖρε πολλά.

Μο.   νῦν ποοῦμεν τοὺς γάμους; ὁ Παρμένων
εἶπεν ἐν ἀγορᾶι περιτυχὼν ἄρτι μοι. τί κωλύει
μετιέναι τὴν παῖδά μ' ἤδη;

Νι.   τἀνθάδ' ἀγνοῶν πάρει;

Μο.   ποῖα;

Νι.   ποῖ'; ἀηδία τις συμβέβηκεν ἔκτοπος.

Μο.   Ἡράκλεις· τίς; οὐ γὰρ εἰδὼς ἔρχομαι.

Νι.   τὴν Χρυσίδα 435
ἐξελήλακ' ἔνδοθέν σου, φίλταθ', ὁ πατὴρ ἀρτίως.

Μο.   οἷον εἴρηκας.

Νι.   τὸ γεγονός.

Μο.   διὰ τί;

Νι.   διὰ τὸ παιδίον.

Μο.   εἶτα ποῦ 'στι νῦν;

Νι.   παρ' ἡμῖν ἔνδον.

Μο.   ὦ δεινὸν λέγων
πρᾶγμα καὶ θαυμαστόν.

Νι.   εἴ σοι δεινὸν εἶναι φαίνεται –

Δη.   ἂν λάβω ξύλον, ποήσω τὰ δάκρυ' ὑμῶν ταῦτ' ἐγὼ 440
ἐκκεκόφθαι. τίς ὁ φλύαρος; οὐ διακονήσετε
τῶι μαγείρωι; πάνυ γάρ ἐστιν ἄξιον, νὴ τὸν Δία,
ἐπιδακρῦσαι· μέγα γὰρ ὑμῖν ὤιχετ' ἐκ τῆς οἰκίας
ἀγαθόν· αὐτὰ τἄργα δηλοῖ. χαῖρ', Ἄπολλον φίλτατε,
ἐπ' ἀγαθῆι τύχηι τε πᾶσι τοὺς γάμους οὓς μέλλομεν 445
<νῦν> ποεῖν ἡμῖν γενέσθαι δὸς σύ. – μέλλω γὰρ ποεῖν
τοὺς γάμους, ἄνδρες, καταπιὼν τὴν χολήν. – τήρ[ει δέ με,
δέσποτ', αὐτὸς ἵνα γένωμαι μὴ 'πίδηλος μηδ[ενί,

---

426 τεθορύβηνται Austin: τεθορύβηται B   434 ποῖ ' Austin: ποιαφηις B   445 οὓς
Austin: om. B   446 νῦν Austin: om. B   447 τήρ[ει] Austin, dein [δέ με] Sommerstein, [δὲ σύ] vel [μόνον] idem Austin

ἀλλὰ τὸν ὑμ[έν]αιον ᾄδειν εἰσανάγκασόν με σύ.
ἅ]ξ[ομ᾽ ο]ὺκ ἄριστ᾽ ἐγὼ <γὰρ> ὡς ἔχω νῦν. ἀλλὰ τί;   450
.......]νελθοι.

Νι.   σὺ πρότερος, Μοσχίων, πρόσελθέ μου.
Μο. νὴ Δί᾽. ὦ π]άτερ, τί ποιεῖς ταῦτα;
Δη.   ποῖα, Μοσχίων;
Μο. ποῖ᾽, ἐρωτ]ᾷς; διὰ τί Χρυσὶς οἴχετ᾽ ἀπιοῦσ᾽; εἰπέ μοι.
Δη. ......] πρεσβεύεταί τις πρός με· δεινόν. – οὐχὶ σό[ν,
μὰ τὸν Ἀ]πόλλω, τοὖργον ἐστίν, ἀλλὰ παντελ[ῶς ἐμόν·   455
τίς ὁ φλύ]αρος; – δεινὸν ἤδη· συναδικεῖ μ᾽ οὗτος –
Μο.   [τί φῄς;
Δη. – περιφα]νῶς. τί γὰρ προσέρχεθ᾽ ὑπὲρ ἐκείνης; ἀσ[μένωι
χρῆν γὰρ αὐτῶι τοῦτο δήπου γε[γονέναι.
Μο.   τί τ]οὺς φίλους
προσδοκᾷς ἐρεῖν πυθομένους;
Δη.   . [.....]κω Μοσχίων
τοὺς φίλους – ἔα μ᾽.
Μο.   ἀγεννὲς ἂν ποι[οίη]ν ἐπιτρέπων.   460
Δη. ἀλλὰ κωλύσεις μ᾽;
Μο.   ἔγωγε.
Δη.   τοῦθ᾽ – ὁρᾶ[θ᾽; – ὑ]περβολή·
τοῦτο τῶν δεινῶν ἐκείνων δεινό[τερο]ν.
Μο.   [ο]ὺ πάντα γὰρ
ἐπιτρέπειν ὀργῆι προσήκει.
Νι.   Δημέα, κ[αλ]ῶς λέγει.
Μο. ἀποτρέχειν αὐτῆι φράσον δεῦρ᾽ εἰσιών, Νικήρατε.
Δη. Μοσχίων, ἔα μ᾽, ἔα με, Μοσχίων· τρίτον λέγω   465
τουτογί· πάντ᾽ οἶδα.
Μο.   ποῖα πάντα;
Δη.   μή μοι διαλέγου.
Μο. ἀλλ᾽ ἀνάγκη, πάτερ.

450 [ἅ]ξ[ομ᾽ ο]ὺκ Barigazzi: [ἄρ]ξ[ομ᾽ ο]ὺκ Arnott   <γὰρ> Roca-Puig: om. B:
<μὲν> Austin   451 [οὺκ ἂν ἐπα]νέλθοι (sc. Chrysis) Jacques: [πάντα νῦ]ν ἔλθοι
Sandbach: [εἴθε μόνο]ν ἔλθοι (sc. Moschion) Dedoussi   452 [νὴ Δί᾽. ὦ π]άτερ
Barigazzi ([π]άτερ iam Kasser et Austin): [εἴέν. ὦ π]άτερ Sandbach   454 [δηλαδὴ]
Fernández Galiano: [Ἡράκλεις] e.g. Austin   με Jacques: εμὲ   456 dicolon post
ουτος praebet B   457 [περιφα]νῶς Lloyd-Jones: [καταφα]νῶς Jacques   ἀσ[μένωι]
Sandbach: ἀν[ακρινῶν] Dedoussi   458 χρῆν Austin: εχρην B   αυτῶ B: αὐτὸν
Dedoussi   γε[γονέ<ναι>]]Jacques: γ᾽ ε[ἰδέναι] Dedoussi   459 π[ροσδο]κῶ <γὼ>
Sandbach: π[ροσδο]κῶ <μοι> Austin   461 sic suppl. Oguse: ὁρᾶ<ι>[ς, ὑ]π-
Kasser et Austin   466 τουτογί Austin: τουτογε B

Δη.   ἀνάγκη; τῶν ἐμῶν οὐ κύριος
ἔσομ' ἐγώ;
Μο.   ταύτην ἐμοὶ δὸς τὴν χάριν.
Δη.   ποίαν χάριν;
οἷον ἀξιοῖς μ' ἀπελθεῖν αὐτὸν ἐκ τῆς οἰκίας
καταλιπόνθ' ὑμᾶς δύ' ὄντας. τοὺς γάμους ἔα ποεῖν,   470
τοὺς γάμους ἔα με ποιεῖν, ἂν ἔχῃς νοῦν.
Μο.   ἀλλ' ἐῶ·
βούλομαι δὲ συμπαρεῖναι Χρυσίδ' <ἡμῖν>.
Δη.   Χρυσίδα;
Μο. ἕνεκα σοῦ σπεύδω μάλιστα τοῦτο.
Δη.   ταῦτ' οὐ γνώριμα,
οὐ σαφῆ; μαρτύρομαί σε, Λοξία· συνόμνυται
τοῖς ἐμοῖς ἐχθροῖς τις. οἴμοι· καὶ διαρραγήσομαι.   475
Μο. τί δὲ λέγεις;
Δη.   βούλει φράσω σοι;
Μο.   πάνυ γε.
Δη.   δεῦρο δή.
Μο.   λέγε.
Δη. ἀλλ' ἐγώ. τὸ παιδίον σόν ἐστιν. οἶδ'· ἀκήκοα
τοῦ συνειδότος τὰ κρυπτά, Παρμένοντος. μηκέτι
πρὸς ἐμὲ παῖζ'.
Μο.   ἔπειτά σ' ἀδικεῖ Χρυσίς, εἰ τοῦτ' ἔστ' ἐμόν;
Δη. ἀλλὰ τίς; σύ;
Μο.   τί γὰρ ἐκείνη γέγονεν αἰτία;
Δη.   τί φῄς;   480
οὐδὲν ἐνθυμεῖσθε;
Μο.   τί βοᾷς;
Δη.   ὅ τι βοῶ, κάθαρμα σύ;
τοῦτ' ἐρωτᾷς; εἰς σεαυτὸν ἀναδέχει τὴν αἰτίαν,
εἰπέ μοι, καὶ τοῦτο τολμᾷς ἐμβλέπων ἐμοὶ λέγειν;
παντελῶς οὕτως ἀπεγνωκώς με τυγχάνεις;
Μο.   ἐγώ;
διὰ τί;
Δη.   " διὰ τί" φῄς; ἐρωτᾶν δ' ἀξιοῖς;

472 Χρυσίδ' <ἡμῖν> Austin: χρυσιδ' (sic) B   476 δή Austin: ηδη B   478 μηκέτι
Austin: ωστεμηκετι B: ὥστε μὴ idem Austin   481 οὐδὲν (Demeae orationem con-
tinuantes) Handley, Sandbach: ουδεν:ουδεν B: (Μο.) οὐδέν. dein (Δη.) ἐνθυμεῖσθε
Austin   482–3 εἰπέ μοι huc transp. multi: ante ειˬσεαυτὸν (sic) exhibet B

Μο.   τὸ πρᾶγμα γάρ   485
ἔστιν οὐ πάνδεινον, ἀλλὰ μυρίοι δήπου, πάτερ,
τοῦτο πεποήκασιν.
Δη.   ὦ Ζεῦ, τοῦ θράσους. ἐναντίον
δή σ᾽ ἐρωτῶ τῶν παρόντων· ἐκ τίνος τὸ παιδίον
ἐστί σοι; Νικηράτωι τοῦτ᾽ εἶπον, εἰ μή σοι δοκεῖ
δεινὸν <εἶναι>.
Μο.   νὴ Δί᾽ ἀλλὰ δεινὸν οὕτω γίνεται   490
τοῦτο πρὸς τοῦτον λέγειν με· χαλεπανεῖ γὰρ πυθόμενος.
Νι. ὦ κάκιστ᾽ ἀνδρῶν ἁπάντων· ὑπονοεῖν γὰρ ἄρχομαι
τὴν τύχην καὶ τἀσέβημα τὸ γεγονὸς μόλις ποτέ.
Μο. τέλος ἔχω τοίνυν ἐγώ.
Δη.   νῦν αἰσθάνει, Νικήρατε;
Νι. οὐ γάρ; ὦ πάνδεινον ἔργον· ὦ τὰ Τηρέως λέχη   495
Οἰδίπου τε καὶ Θυέστου καὶ τὰ τῶν ἄλλων, ὅσα
γεγονόθ᾽ ἡμῖν ἐστ᾽ ἀκοῦσαι, μικρὰ ποιήσας —
Μο.   ἐγώ;
Νι. τοῦτ᾽ ἐτόλμησας σὺ πρᾶξαι, τοῦτ᾽ [ἔ]τλης; Ἀμύντορος
νῦν ἐχρῆν ὀργὴν λαβεῖν σε, Δ[η]μέα, καὶ τουτονὶ
ἐκτυφλῶσαι.
Δη.   διὰ σὲ τούτωι γέγονε πάν[τ]α καταφανῆ.   500
Νι. τίνος ἀπόσχοι᾽ ἂν σύ; ποῖον οὐκ ἂν [   ].[
εἶτ᾽ ἐγώ σοι δῶ γυναῖκα τὴν ἐμαυτ[οῦ θυγατέρα;
πρότερον — εἰς κόλπον δέ, φασί· τὴν αδ[—
ἐπὶ Διομνήστωι γενοίμην νυμφίωι [
ὁμολογουμένην ἀτυχίαν.
Δη.   ταῦ[τ   505
ἠδικημένος κατεῖχον.
Νι.   ἀνδράποδ[ον εἶ, Δημέα.
εἰ γὰρ ἐμὸν ἦισ[χυνε λέ]κτρον, οὐκ ἂν εἰς ἄλλον ποτέ
ὕβρισ᾽, οὐδ᾽ ἡ συγ[κλ]ιθεῖσα· παλλακὴν δ᾽ ἂν αὔριον
πρῶτος ἀνθρώπ[ω]ν ἐπώλουν, συναποκηρύττων ἅμα
υἱόν, ὥστε μηθὲ[ν εἶ]ναι μήτε κουρεῖον κενόν,   510

490 <εἶναι> Austin: om. B   491 χαλεπανεῖ... πυθόμενος Austin: χαλεπαινει...
πευθομενοσ B   492 ἁπάντων Austin: παντων B   497 γεγονόθ᾽ Kassel: γεγο-
νασ᾽ B: γεγον᾽, ὅσ᾽ Handley   501 [αἰσχύνοις λ]έχ[ος] Arnott: [ἐργάσαι᾽ ἔ]τι Austin
503 Ἀδ[ράστειαν] Lloyd-Jones, dein [σέβω] Austin   504 [γὼ πενθερός] Austin:
fort. e.g. [γωγ᾽ ἀντὶ σοῦ]   505 ἀτυχίαν Austin: την ατυχια B   ταῦ[τ᾽ ἀκούσας τὴν
χολὴν] Arnott (ταῦ[τα] iam Austin): ταῦ[τα τῶν γάμων χάριν] Weissenberger   506
ἀνδράποδ[ον εἶ, Δημέα] Sandbach: ἀνδράποδ[ον ἄρ᾽ ἦσθα σύ] Austin

      μὴ στοάν, κ[αθη]μένους δὲ πάντας ἐξ ἑωθινοῦ
      περὶ ἐμοῦ λαλ[ε]ῖν, λέγοντας ὡς ἀνὴρ Νικήρατος
      γέγον᾽, ἐπεξελθὼν δικαίως τῶι φόνωι.
Δη.   ποίωι φόνωι;
      φόνον ἐγὼ κρίνω τὰ τοιαῦθ᾽ ὅστις ἐπαναστὰς π[ο]εῖ.
Μο. αὖός εἰμι καὶ πέπηγα τῶι κακῶι, νὴ τοὺς θεούς.   515
Νι.   ἀλλ᾽ ἐγὼ πρὸς τοῖσιν ἄλλοις τὴν τὰ δείν᾽ εἰργασμένην
      εἰσεδεξάμην μελάθροις τοῖς ἐμοῖς.
Δη.   Νικήρατε,
      ἔκβαλ᾽, ἱκετεύω· συναδικοῦ γνησίως, ὡς ἂν φίλος.
Νι.   ὃς διαρραγήσομ᾽ ἐπιδών. ἐμβλέπεις μοι, βάρβαρε,
      Θρᾶιξ ἀληθῶς; οὐ παρήσεις;
Μο.   πάτερ, ἄκουσον, πρὸς θεῶν.   520
Δη.   οὐκ ἀκούσομ᾽ οὐθέν.
Μο.   οὐδ᾽ εἰ μηδὲν ὧν σὺ προσδοκᾶις
      γέγονεν; ἄρτι γὰρ τὸ πρᾶγμα κατανοῶ.
Δη.   πῶς μηδὲ ἕν;
Μο. οὐχὶ Χρυσίς ἐστι μήτηρ οὗ τρέφει νῦν παιδίου,
      ἀλλ᾽ ἐμοὶ χαρίζεται τοῦθ᾽ ὁμολογοῦσ᾽ αὐτῆς.
Δη.   τί φήις;
Μο. τὰς ἀληθείας.
Δη.   διὰ τί δὲ τοῦτό σοι χαρίζεται;   525
Μο. οὐχ ἑκὼν λέγω μέν, ἀλλὰ μείζον᾽ αἰτίαν φυγὼν
      λαμβάνω μικράν, ἐὰν σὺ τὸ γεγονὸς πύθηι σαφῶς.
Δη.   ἀλλ᾽ ἀποκτενεῖς πρὶν εἰπεῖν;
Μο.   ἔστι τῆς Νικηράτου
      θυγατρός ἐξ ἐμοῦ· λαθεῖν δὲ τοῦτ᾽ ἐβουλόμην ἐγώ.
Δη.   πῶς λέγεις;
Μο.   ὥσπερ πέπρακται.
Δη.   μή με βουκολεῖς ὅρα.   530
Μο. οὗ λαβεῖν ἔλεγχον ἔστι; καὶ τί κερδανῶ πλέον;
Δη.   οὐθέν. ἀλλὰ τὴν θύραν τις –
Νι.   ὦ τάλας ἐγώ, τάλας·
      οἷον εἰσιδὼν θέαμα διὰ θυρῶν ἐπείγομαι
      ἐμμανὴς ἀπροσδοκήτωι καρδίαν πληγεὶς ἄχει.
Δη.   τί ποτ᾽ ἐρεῖ;

514 ὅστις Handley: οσατισ B   516 εἰργασμένην Kasser et Austin: εργασμενη[ν] B^{pc}: εργασαμην B^{ac} 519 διαρραγήσομ᾽ ἐπιδών Lloyd-Jones: διαραγήσομ᾽ ἴδων B   521 οὐδ᾽ εἰ μηδὲν Arnott: νηδι᾽οὐδεν B

Νι.   τὴν θυγατέρ᾽ <ἄρτι> τὴν ἐμὴν τῶι παιδίωι   535
τιτθίον διδοῦσαν ἔνδον κατέλαβον.

Δη.   τοῦτ᾽ ἦν ἄρα.

Μο. πάτερ, ἀκούεις;

Δη.   οὐδὲν ἀδικεῖς, Μοσχίων, μ᾽, ἐγὼ δὲ σέ,
ὑπονοῶν τοιαῦτα.

Νι.   πρὸς σέ, Δημέα, πορεύομαι.

Μο. ἐκποδὼν ἄπειμι.

Δη.   θάρρει.

Μο.   τουτονὶ τέθνηχ᾽ ὁρῶν.

Δη. τί τὸ πάθος δ᾽ ἐστίν;

Νι.   διδοῦσαν τιτθίον τῶι παιδίωι   540
ἀρτίως ἔνδον κατέλαβον τὴν ἐμαυτοῦ θυγατέρα.

Δη. τυχὸν ἔπαιζεν.

Νι.   οὐκ ἔπαιζεν. ὡς γὰρ εἰσιόντα μ[ε
εἶδεν, ἐξαίφνης κατέπεσεν.

Δη.   τυχὸν ἴσως ἔδοξε [

Νι. παρατενεῖς " τυχὸν" λέγων μοι πάντα.

Δη.   τούτων αἴτιό[ς
εἰμ᾽ ἐγώ.

Νι.   τί φῄς;

Δη.   ἄπιστον πρᾶγμά μοι δοκεῖς λέγε[ιν.   545

Νι. ἀλλὰ μὴ[ν] εἶδον.

Δη.   κορυζᾷς.

Νι.   οὗτος οὐκ ἔστιν λόγος.
ἀλλὰ πάλιν ἐλθών –

Δη.   τὸ δεῖνα· μικρόν, ὦ τᾶν – οἴχετ[αι.
πάντα πράγματ᾽ ἀνατέτραπται· τέλος ἔχει. νὴ τὸν Δία,
οὑτοσὶ τὸ πρᾶγμ᾽ ἀκούσας χαλεπανεῖ, κεκράξεται·
τραχὺς ἄνθρωπος, σκατοφάγος, αὐθέκαστος τῶι τρόπωι.   550
ἐμὲ γὰρ ὑπονοεῖν τοιαῦτα τὸν μιαρὸν ἐχρῆν, ἐμέ;
νὴ τὸν Ἥφαιστον, δικαίως ἀποθάνοιμ᾽ ἄν. Ἡράκλεις,
ἡλίκον κέκραγε. τοῦτ᾽ ἦν· πῦρ βοᾶι· τὸ παιδίον
φησὶν ἐμπρήσειν ἀπειλῶν. υἱδοῦν ὀπτώμενον
ὄψομαι. πάλιν πέπληχε τὴν θύραν. στρόβιλος ἢ   555

535 <ἄρτι> add. Austin: om. B (θυγατερατην)   537 μ᾽ add. Sandbach: om.
B   543 ἔδοξε [σοι] Kasser et Austin: ἔδοξε [γάρ –] Sandbach   547 denuo adest
C   548 πάντα van Herwerden, Wilamowitz: παντατα C:] τατα B   554 υἱδοῦν
Richards: υιωδουν BC

σκηπτὸς ἄνθρωπός τίς ἐστι.

Νι.   Δημέα, συνίσταται
ἐπ' ἐμὲ καὶ πάνδεινα ποιεῖ πράγμαθ' ἡ Χρυσίς.

Δη.   τί φής;

Νι. τὴν γυναῖκά μου πέπεικε μηθὲν ὁμολογεῖν ὅλως
μηδὲ τὴν κόρην, ἔχει δὲ πρὸς βίαν τὸ παιδίον
οὐ προήσεσθαί τέ φησιν· ὥστε μὴ θαύμαζ', ἐὰν   560
αὐτόχειρ αὐτῆς γένωμαι.

Δη.   τῆς γυναικὸς αὐτόχειρ;

Νι. πάντα γὰρ σύνοιδεν αὕτη.

Δη.   μηδαμῶς, Νικήρατε.

Νι. σοὶ δ' ἐβουλόμην προειπεῖν.

Δη.   οὑτοσὶ μελαγχολᾷ.
εἰσπεπήδηκεν. τί τούτοις τοῖς κακοῖς τις χρήσεται;
οὐδεπώποτ' εἰς τοιαύτην ἐμπεσών, μὰ τοὺς θεούς,   565
οἶδα ταραχήν. ἔστι μέντοι τὸ γεγονὸς φράσαι σαφῶς
πολὺ κράτιστον. ἀλλ', Ἄπολλον, ἡ θύρα πάλιν ψοφεῖ.

Χρ. ὦ τάλαιν' ἐγώ, τί δράσω; ποῖ φύγω; τὸ παιδίον
λήψεταί μου.

Δη.   Χρυσί, δεῦρο.

Χρ.   τίς καλεῖ μ';

Δη.   εἴσω τρέχε.

Νι. ποῖ σύ, ποῖ φεύγεις;

Δη.   Ἄπολλον· μονομαχήσω τήμερον,   570
ὡς ἔοικ', ἐγώ. τί βούλει; τίνα διώκεις;

Νι.   Δημέα,
ἐκποδὼν ἄπελθ'· ἔα με γενόμενον τοῦ παιδίου
ἐγκρατῆ τὸ πρᾶγμ' ἀκοῦσαι τῶν γυναικῶν.

Δη.   μηθαμῶς.

Νι. ἀλλὰ τυπτήσεις μ';

Δη.   ἔγωγε. θᾶττον εἰσφθάρηθι σύ.

Νι. ἀλλὰ μὴν κἀγώ σε.

Δη.   φεῦγε, Χρυσί· κρείττων ἐστί μου.   575

Νι. πρότερος ἅπτει μου σὺ νυνί· ταῦτ' ἐγὼ μαρτύρομαι.

Δη. σὺ δ' ἐπ' ἐλευθέραν γυναῖκα λαμβάνεις βακτηρίαν
καὶ διώκεις.

Νι.   συκοφαντεῖς.

573 μηθαμως Bˢ: μαίνομαι B et ut vid. C   575 καγωσε B: καγ[ω]ς[ε] vel καγ[ω]γ[ε]
C

Δη.   καὶ σὺ γάρ.
Νι.   τὸ παιδίον
ἐξένεγκέ μοι.
Δη.   γελοῖον· τοὐμόν;
Νι.   ἀλλ᾽ οὐκ ἔστι σόν.
Δη.   ἐμόν.
Νι.   ἰὼ 'νθρωποι.
Δη.   κέκραχθι.
Νι.   τὴν γυναῖκ᾽ ἀποκτενῶ   580
εἰσιών· τί γὰρ ποήσω;
Δη.   τοῦτο μοχθηρὸν πάλιν·
οὐκ ἐάσω. ποῖ σύ; μένε δή.
Νι.   μὴ πρόσαγε τὴν χεῖρά μοι.
Δη.   κάτεχε δὴ σεαυτόν.
Νι.   ἀδικεῖς, Δημέα, με, δῆλος εἶ,
καὶ τὸ πρᾶγμα πᾶν σύνοισθα.
Δη.   τοιγαροῦν ἐμοῦ πυθοῦ,
τῆι γυναικὶ μὴ 'νοχλήσας μηδέν.
Νι.   ἆρ᾽ ὁ σός με παῖς   585
ἐντεθρίωκεν;
Δη.   φλυαρεῖς· λήψεται μὲν τὴν κόρην,
ἔστι δ᾽ οὐ τοιοῦτον. ἀλλὰ περιπάτησον ἐνθαδὶ
μικρὰ μετ᾽ ἐμοῦ.
Νι.   περιπατήσω;
Δη.   καὶ σεαυτόν γ᾽ ἀνάλαβε.
οὐκ ἀκήκοας λεγόντων, εἰπέ μοι, Νικήρατε,
τῶν τραγωιδῶν, ὡς γενόμενος χρυσὸς ὁ Ζεὺς ἐρρύη   590
διὰ τέγους καθειργμένην τε παῖδ᾽ ἐμοίχευσέν ποτε;
Νι.   εἶτα δὴ τί τοῦτ';
Δη.   ἴσως δεῖ πάντα προσδοκᾶν. σκόπει,
τοῦ τέγους εἴ σοι μέρος τι ῥεῖ.
Νι.   τὸ πλεῖστον. ἀλλὰ τί
τοῦτο πρὸς ἐκεῖν᾽ ἐστί;
Δη.   τοτὲ μὲν γίνεθ᾽ ὁ Ζεὺς χρυσίον,
τότε δ᾽ ὕδωρ. ὁρᾶις; ἐκείνου τοὔργον ἐστίν. ὡς ταχὺ   595
εὕρομεν.
Νι.   καὶ βουκολεῖς με;
Δη.   μὰ τὸν Ἀπόλλω 'γὼ μὲν οὔ.

590 χρυσὸς ὁ Ζεὺς multi: οζευσχρύσοσ B: οζ[.]υ[.]χρ[. . .]σ C   591 τε B: δε C

        ἀλλὰ χείρων οὐδὲ μικρὸν Ἀκρισίου δήπουθεν εἶ·
        εἰ δ᾽ ἐκείνην ἠξίωσε, τήν γε σήν –
Νι.   οἴμοι τάλας·
        Μοσχίων ἐσκεύακέν με.
Δη.   λήψεται μέν, μὴ φοβοῦ
        τοῦτο· θεῖον δ᾽ ἔστ᾽, ἀκριβῶς ἴσθι, τὸ γεγενημένον.   600
        μυρίους εἰπεῖν ἔχω σοι περιπατοῦντας ἐν μέσωι
        ὄντας ἐκ θεῶν· σὺ δ᾽ οἴει δεινὸν εἶναι τὸ γεγονός;
        Χαιρεφῶν πρώτιστος οὗτος, ὃν τρέφουσ᾽ ἀσύμβολον,
        οὐ θεός σοι φαίνετ᾽ εἶναι;
Νι.   φαίνεται· τί γὰρ πάθω;
        οὐ μαχοῦμαι διὰ κενῆς σοι.
Δη.   νοῦν ἔχεις, Νικήρατε.   605
        Ἀνδροκλῆς ἔτη τοσαῦτα ζῆι, τρέχει, πηδᾶι, πολὺ
        πράττεται, μέλας περιπατεῖ· λευκὸς οὐκ ἂν ἀποθάνοι,
        οὐδ᾽ ἂν εἰ σφάττοι τις αὐτόν. οὗτός ἐστιν οὐ θεός;
        ἀλλὰ ταῦτ᾽ εὔχου γενέσθαι [σ]υμφέροντα, θυμία,
        σπένδε· τὴν] κόρην μέ[τε]ισ[ιν] οὑμὸς ὑὸς αὐτίκα.   610
Νι.   ἐξ ἀνάγκης ἐστὶ τοῦ[τ]ο.
Δη.   πολλ[αχ]ῆι μὲν νοῦν ἔχει[ς –
Νι.   εἰ δ᾽ ἐλήφθη τότε –
Δη.   πέπαυσο· μὴ παροξύνου· πόει
        τἄνδον εὐτρεπῆ.
Νι.   ποήσω.
Δη.   τὰ παρ᾽ ἐμοὶ δ᾽ ἐγώ.
Νι.   πόει.
Δη.   κομψὸς εἶ. χάριν δὲ πολλὴν πᾶσι τοῖς θεοῖς ἔχω,
        οὐθὲν εὑρηκὼς ἀληθὲς ὧν τότ᾽ ὤιμην γεγονέναι.   615

                        ΧΟΡΟΥ

                    ΜΕΡΟΣ Ε΄

Μο.   ἐγὼ τότε μὲν ἧς εἶχον αἰτίας μάτην
        ἐλεύθερος γενόμενος ἠγάπησα καὶ
        τοῦθ᾽ ἱκανὸν εὐτύχημ᾽ ἐμαυτῶι γεγονέναι

598 ειδ᾽ BᵃᶜC: ωσ Bᵖᶜ   γε C: τε B   606–11 om. B   606 πηδα Cᵖᶜ: παιδα Cᵃᶜ
608 ἐστιν οὐ C: οὐκ ἔστιν Sandbach   610 [σπένδε] suppl. Sudhaus   κόρην edd.,
qui olim]νκορην se in C legere credebant: τεκορην C sec. Riad   611 τοῦ[τ]ο leg.
et suppl. Riad: ταῦ[τ]α leg. et suppl. Jensen   πολλ[αχ]ῆι μὲν leg. et suppl. Riad (ut
prius Jensen incertioribus vestigiis fretus)

ὑπέλαβον· ὡς δὲ μᾶλλον ἔννους γίνομαι
καὶ λαμβάνω λογισμόν, ἐξέστηκα νῦν   620
τελέως ἐμαυτοῦ καὶ παρώξυμμαι σφόδρα
ἐφ᾽ οἷς μ᾽ ὁ πατὴρ ὑπέλαβεν ἡμαρτηκέναι.
εἰ μὲν καλῶς οὖν εἶχε τὰ περὶ τὴν κόρην
καὶ μὴ τοσαῦτ᾽ ἦν ἐμποδών, ὅρκος, πόθος,
χρόνος, συνήθει᾽, οἷς ἐδουλούμην ἐγώ,   625
οὐκ ἂν παρόντα γ᾽ αὖθις ἡτιάσατο
αὐτόν με τοιοῦτ᾽ οὐδέν, ἀλλ᾽ ἀποφθαρεὶς
ἐκ τῆς πόλεως ἂν ἐκποδὼν εἰς Βάκτρα ποι
ἢ Καρίαν διέτριβον αἰχμάζων ἐκεῖ·
νῦν δ᾽ οὐ ποήσω διὰ σέ, Πλαγγὼν φιλτάτη,   630
ἀνδρεῖον οὐθέν· οὐ γὰρ ἔξεστ᾽, οὐδ᾽ ἐᾶι
ὁ τῆς ἐμῆς νῦν κύριος γνώμης Ἔρως.
οὐ μὴν ταπεινῶς οὐδ᾽ ἀγεννῶς παντελῶς
παριδεῖν με δεῖ τοῦτ᾽, ἀλλὰ τῶι λόγωι μόνον,
εἰ μηθὲν ἄλλ᾽, αὐτὸν φοβῆσαι βούλομαι,   635
φάσκων ἀπαίρειν. μᾶλλον εἰς τὰ λοιπὰ γὰρ
φυλάξεθ᾽ οὗτος μηθὲν εἴς μ᾽ ἀγνωμονεῖν,
ὅταν φέροντα μὴ παρέργως τοῦτ᾽ ἴδηι.
ἀλλ᾽ οὑτοσὶ γὰρ εἰς δέοντά μοι πάνυ
καιρὸν πάρεστιν, ὃν μάλιστ᾽ ἐβουλόμην.   640

Πα. νὴ τὸν Δία τὸν μέγιστον, ἀνόητόν τε καὶ
εὐκαταφρόνητον ἔργον εἴμ᾽ εἰργασμένος·
οὐθὲν ἀδικῶν ἔδεισα καὶ τὸν δεσπότην
ἔφυγον. τί δ᾽ ἦν τούτου πεποηκὼς ἄξιον;
καθ᾽ ἓν γὰρ οὑτωσὶ σαφῶς σκεψώμεθα.   645
ὁ τρόφιμος ἐξήμαρτεν εἰς ἐλευθέραν
κόρην· ἀδικεῖ δήπουθεν οὐδὲν Παρμένων.
ἐκύησεν αὕτη· Παρμένων οὐκ αἴτιος.
τὸ παιδάριον εἰσῆλθεν εἰς τὴν οἰκίαν
τὴν ἡμετέραν· ἤνεγκ᾽ ἐκεῖνος, οὐκ ἐγώ.   650
τῶν ἔνδον ὡμολόγησε τοῦτό τις τεκεῖν·
τί Παρμένων ἐνταῦθα πεπόηκεν κακόν;
οὐθέν. τί οὖν οὕτως ἔφυγες, ἀβέλτερε

καὶ δειλότατε; γελοῖον· ἠπείλησέ με
στίξειν· μεμάθηκας; διαφέρε[ι δ᾿ ἀ]λλ᾿ οὐδὲ γρῦ   655
ἀδίκως [πα]θεῖν τοῦτ᾿ ἢ δικαίως, ἔστι δὲ
πάντα τρόπον οὐκ ἀστεῖον.

Μο.   οὗτος.
Πα.   χαῖρε σύ.
Μο. ἀφεὶς ἃ φλυαρεῖς ταῦτα θᾶττον εἴσιθι.
ε ἴσω.
Πα. τί ποήσων;
Μο.   χλαμύδα καὶ σπάθην τινὰ
ἔνεγκέ μοι.
Πα.   σπάθην ἐγώ σοι;
Μο.   καὶ ταχύ.   660
Πα. ἐπὶ τί;
Μο.   βάδιζε καὶ σιωπῆι τοῦθ᾿ ὅ σοι
εἴρηκα ποίει.
Πα.   τί δὲ τὸ πρᾶγμ᾿;
Μο.   εἰ λήψομαι
ἱμάντα –
Πα.   μηδαμῶς· βαδίζω γάρ.
Μο.   τί οὖν
μέλλεις; πρόσεισι νῦν ὁ πατήρ· δεήσεται
οὗτος καταμένειν δηλαδή. δεήσεται   665
ἄλλως μέχρι τινός· δεῖ γάρ. εἶθ᾿, ὅταν δοκῆι,
πεισθήσομ᾿ αὐτῶι. πιθανὸν εἶναι δεῖ μόνον
ὃ μὰ τὸν Διόνυσον οὐ δύναμαι ποεῖν ἐγώ.
τοῦτ᾿ ἔστιν· ἐψόφηκε προϊὼν τὴν θύραν.
Πα. ὑστερίζειν μοι δοκεῖς σὺ παντελῶς τῶν ἐνθάδε   670
πραγμάτων, εἰδώς τ᾿ ἀκριβῶς οὐθὲν οὐδ᾿ ἀκηκοὼς
διὰ κενῆς σαυτὸν ταράττεις εἰς ἀθυμίαν τ᾿ ἄγεις.
Μο. οὐ φέρεις;
Πα.   ποοῦσι γάρ σοι τοὺς γάμους· κεράννυται,
θυμιᾶτ᾿, ἐνῆρκτ᾿, ἀνῆπται θύμαθ᾿ Ἡφαίστου φλογί.
Μο. οὗτος, οὐ φέρεις;

653 οὕτως ἔφυγες complures: εφυγεσουτωσ C: εφευγεσουτοσ B   654] με B: μοι C:
(-ησ᾿) ἐμὲ Sandbach   665 καταμενειν B: καταμενεινμου C   δεήσεθ᾿ οὗτος καταμένειν
μου δηλαδή Sudhaus   666 ἄλλως complures: αλλ᾿ως BC   668 ὁ C: ου B   671
τ᾿B: δ᾿C   οὐδ᾿C: ουτ᾿B   672 εισαθυ- C: εισθαυ-B^{ac}: εισταθυ-B^{pc}, unde εἴς τ᾿ἀθυμίαν
ἄγεις Jacques

90 ΜΕΝΑΝΔΡΟΥ

Πα.   σὲ γάρ, <σὲ> περιμένουσ᾿ οὗτοι πάλαι.   675
μετιέναι τὴν παῖδα μέλλεις; εὐτυχεῖς· οὐδὲν κακόν
ἐστί σοι· θάρρει· τί βούλει;
Μο.   νουθετήσεις μ᾿, εἰπέ μοι,
ἱερόσυλε;
Πα.   παῖ, τί ποιεῖς, Μοσχίων;
Μο.   οὐκ εἰσδραμὼν
θᾶττον ἐξοίσεις ἅ φημι;
Πα.   διακέκομμαι τὸ στόμα.
Μο. ἔτι λαλεῖς, οὗτος;
Πα.   βαδίζω. νὴ Δί᾿ ἐξεύρηκά γε   680
τόδε κακόν.
Μο.   μέλλεις;
Πα.   ἄγουσι τοὺς γάμους ὄντως.
Μο.   πάλιν;
ἕτερον ἐξάγγελλέ μοί τι. νῦν πρόσεισιν· ἂν δέ μου
μὴ δέητ᾿, ἄνδρες, καταμένειν, ἀλλ᾿ ἀπορ γισθεὶς ἐᾶι
ἀπιέναι – τουτὶ γὰρ ἄρτι παρέλιπον – τί δεῖ ποεῖν;
ἀλλ᾿ ἴσως οὐκ ἂν ποήσαι τοῦτ᾿. ἐὰν δέ; πάντα γὰρ   685
γίνεται. γελοῖος ἔσομαι, νὴ Δί᾿, ἀνακάμπτων πάλιν.
Πα. ἤν· χλαμὺς πάρεστιν αὕτη καὶ σπάθη· ταυτὶ λαβέ.
Μο. δεῦρο δός. τῶν ἔνδον οὐθείς σ᾿ εἶδεν;
Πα.   οὐθείς.
Μο.   οὐδὲ εἷς
παντελῶς;
Πα.   οὔ φημι.
Μο.   τί λέγεις; ἀλλά σ᾿ ὁ Ζεὺς ἀπολέσαι.
Πα. πρόαγ᾿ ὅποι μέλλεις. φλυαρεῖς.
Δη.   εἶτα ποῦ ᾿στιν, εἰπέ μοι;   690
παῖ, τί τοῦτο;
Πα.   πρόαγε θᾶττον.
Δη.   ἡ στολὴ τί β[ούλετα]ι;
τί τὸ πάθος; μέλλεις ἀπαίρειν, εἰπέ μ[οι   ;

674 θυμιατ᾿ B: θυμιαματ᾿ C   ἐνῆρκτ᾿, ἀνῆπται Kassel (ἐνήρκται iam Austin):
ανηπτ᾿ανηρται (-ρκαι Bᵃᶜ) B: [.....]ατ᾿αναπτεται C (sed εγηρκτ᾿αναπτεται legit Riad)
θυμματ᾿ (sic) C: σπλαγχναθ B   φλογι BᵖᶜC: πυρι Bᵃᶜ   675 <σὲ> add. Sudhaus:
om. BC   683 αλλ᾿αποργισθεισ C: αλλαπαροργισθεισ B   post 686 deficit C   691
πρόαγε Austin: προαγεῖθι B   β[ούλετα]ι Kasser et Austin   692 μ[οι] Kasser et
Austin, dein [σύ, Μοσχίων] Austin (possis etiam e.g. [πρὸ τῶν γάμων])

Πα. ὡς ὁρᾶις, ἤδη βαδίζει κἄστὶν ἐν ὁδῶ[ι. νῦν δὲ δεῖ
     κἀμὲ τοὺς ἔνδον προσειπεῖν· ἔρχο[μ' εἴσω.
Δη.   [Μοσχίων,
     ὅτι μὲν ὀργίζει, φιλῶ σε, κοὐχ[695
     εἰ λελύπησαι γὰρ ἀδίκως αἰτίαν. [
     ἀλλ' ἐκεῖν' ὅμως θεώρει· τίνι πικρῷ[
     εἰμὶ γὰρ πατήρ. ἐ[γώ ποτ' ἀν]αλαβών σε παιδίον
     ἐξέθρεψ'· εἴ σοι χ[ρόνος τι]ς γέγονεν ἡδὺς τοῦ βίου,
     τοῦτόν εἰμ' ὁ δοὺς [ἔγωγε], δι' ὃν ἀνασχέσθαι σε δεῖ   700
     καὶ τὰ λυπήσαντα [παρ' ἐ]μοῦ καὶ φέρειν τι τῶν ἐμῶν
     ὡς ἂν ὑόν. οὐ δικαί[ως] ἠιτιασάμην τί σε·
     ἠγνόησ', ἥμαρτον, ἐμάνην. ἀλλ' ἐκεῖνορ[
     εἴς τε τοὺς ἄλλους ἁμαρτὼν σοῦ πρόνοιαν ἡλίκη[ν
     ἔσχον, ἐν ἐμαυτῶι τ' ἐτήρουν τοῦθ' ὃ δή ποτ' ἠγνόουν·   705
     οὐχὶ τοῖς ἐχθροῖς ἔθηκα φανερὸν ἐπιχαίρειν· σὺ δὲ
     τὴν ἐμὴν ἁμαρτίαν νῦν ἐκφέρεις, καὶ μάρτυρας
     ἐπ' ἐμὲ τῆς ἐμῆς ἀνοίας λαμβάνεις. οὐκ ἀξιῶ,
     Μοσχίων. μὴ μνημονεύσηις ἡμέραν μου τοῦ βίου
     μίαν ἐν ἧι διεσφάλην τι, τῶν δὲ πρόσθεν ἐπιλάθηι.   710
     πόλλ' ἔχων λέγειν ἐάσω· καὶ γὰρ οὐ καλῶς ἔχει
     πατρὶ μόλις πιθέσθ', ἀκριβῶς ἴσθι, τὸ δ' ἑτοίμως καλόν.

Νι. μὴ 'νόχλει μοι· πάντα γέγονε – λουτρά, προτέλει', οἱ γάμοι –
     ὥστ' ἐκεῖνος, ἄν ποτ' ἔλθηι, τὴν κόρην ἄπεισ' ἔχων.
     παῖ, τί τοῦτ';
Δη.   οὐκ οἶδ' ἔγωγε, μὰ Δία.
Νι.   πῶς οὐκ οἶσθα σύ;   715
     χλαμύς· ἀπαίρειν οὑτοσί που διανοεῖται.
Δη.   φησὶ γοῦν.
Νι. φησὶν οὗτος; τίς δ' ἐάσει, μοιχὸν ὄντ' εἰλημμένον,
     ὁμολογοῦντ'; ἤδη σε δήσω, μειράκιον, οὐκ εἰς μακράν.
Μο. δῆσον, ἱκετεύω.

693 suppl. West (νῦν δὲ χρὴ iam complures)   694 suppl. Kasser et Austin
(ἔρχομ' ἤδη. – Μοσχίων), Barigazzi (εἴσω)   695 κοὐχ[ὶ μέμφομαί τί σοι] Austin
696 ἔ[γωγ' ἔχω] Austin: ϲ[χών, εὔλογον] Sandbach   697 πικρὸ[ς σύ γ' εἶ; πατρί]
Dedoussi: πικρῷ[ς οὕτως ἔχεις;] Kamerbeek: πικρῷ[ς χρῆσθαι δοκεῖς;] Lamagna
698 ita suppl. Lowe (ἐ[γὼ γὰρ ἀν]αλαβὼν iam Webster)   699 σοι multi (σο[ΒᵖC]):
ϲη vel συ Βᵃᶜ   χ[ρόνος τι]ς Barigazzi   700 ita suppl. complures: [ἐγώ σοι] Handley   σεδει Β sine elisionis nota: σ' ἔδει Austin   703 ἐκεῖν' ὀρ[θῶς σκόπει] Austin
704 τε Β: γε Sandbach   705 ἐν add. multi: om. Β   712 πιθεσθ' Β: πείθεσθ'
Arnott, Mette

Νι.   φλυαρεῖς πρός μ' ἔχων. οὐ καταβαλεῖς
τὴν σπάθην θᾶττον;
Δη.   κατάβαλε, Μοσχίων, πρὸς τῶν θεῶν· 720
μὴ παροξύνηις.
Μο.   ἀφείσθω· καταλελιπαρήκατε
δεόμενοί μου.
Νι.   σοῦ δεόμενοι; δεῦρο δή.
Μο.   δήσεις μ' ἴσως;
Δη. μηδαμῶς. ἔξω κόμιζε δεῦρο τὴν νύμφην.
Νι.   δοκεῖ;
Μο. πάνυ μὲν οὖν. – εἰ τοῦτ' ἐποίεις εὐθύς, οὐκ ἂν πράγματα
εἶχες, ὦ πάτερ, φιλοσοφῶν ἄρτι.
Νι.   πρόαγε δὴ σύ μοι. 725
μαρτύρων ἐναντίον σοι τήνδ' ἐγὼ δίδωμ' ἔχειν
γνησίων παίδων ἐπ' ἀρότωι, προῖκα τἀμὰ πάνθ' ὅταν
ἀποθάνω γ', ὃ μὴ γένοιτ', ἀλλ' <εἰσ>αεὶ ζώιην.
Μο.   ἔχω,
λαμβάνω, στέργω.
Δη.   τὸ λοιπόν ἐστι λουτρὰ μετιέναι.
Χρυσί, πέμπε τὰς γυναῖκας, λουτροφορον, αὐλητρίδα. 730
δεῦρο δ' ἡμῖν ἐκδότω τις δᾶιδα καὶ στεφάνους, ἵνα
συμπροπέμπωμεν.
Μο.   πάρεστιν ὅδε φέρων.
Δη.   πύκαζε σὺ
κρᾶτα καὶ κόσμει σεαυτόν.
Μο.   ἀλλ' ἐγώ.
Δη.   παῖδες καλοί,
μειράκια, γέροντες, ἄνδρες, πάντες εὐρώστως ἅμα
πέμψ[α]τ' εὐνοίας προφήτην Βακχίωι φίλον κρότον. 735
ἡ δὲ κα]λλίστων ἀγώνων πάρεδρος ἄφθιτος θεὰ
εὐμε]νὴς ἕποιτο Νίκη τοῖς ἐμοῖς ἀεὶ χοροῖς.

720 κατάβαλε multi: καταβε B 721 παροξύνηις Lloyd-Jones, Sandbach: παροξ-
υνοσ B 722 δεῦρο δή multi: δευροηδη B 724 πάνυ μὲν οὖν Moschioni tribuit
Sommerstein, Demeae nominatim B ἐποίεις multi: εποισεισ B 725 εἶχες multi:
εχεισ B σύ μοι Austin: συδευρομοι B (δεῦρο ex 722, 723) 727 παίδων multi: των-
παιδων B τἀμὰ πάνθ' Handley: ταμανθ' B 728 γ' ὃ μὴ multi: τομη B <εἰσ>αεὶ
West, Sandbach: αει B: <εἴθ'> ἀεὶ Austin

Fragmentum alibi citatum

F 1

φέρε τὴν λιβανωτόν· σὺ δ᾽ ἐπίθες τὸ πῦρ, Τρυφή.

Τρυφή Scaliger: τρυφῆι cod.

haec Μένανδρος ἐν τῆι Σαμίαι φησί teste Phrynicho (*Ecl.* 157
Fischer), qui poetam laudat quia tus λιβανωτόν, non λίβανον
vocavit: sed cum in fabula nostra mentio fiat λιβανωτοῦ
v. 158, suspicandum est grammaticum hanc eclogam e
fonte hausisse qui *duos* versus comicos e diversis fabulis
citasset, neglegenterque omisisse et Samiae versum et
alterius fabulae nomen

COMMENTARY

The action takes place in front of two houses, those of Demeas and Nikeratos. In the Lycurgan theatre (see Introduction §10) it will probably no
longer have been possible, as it might have been in Aristophanes' time,
to use painted panels hung on the *skene* front to give an impression of
the affluence of one house and the dilapidation (593) of the other (see
Moretti 1997: 17–25); instead, Demeas' wealth is quickly made evident by
Moschion's description of his luxurious upbringing (7–17), and he will
probably also have mentioned the poverty of Nikeratos' family in the lost
portion of the prologue (29/30n.) In addition to the houses, there are
three other off-stage locations that are of importance to the play:

(1) The harbour, towards which Moschion goes at the end of the prologue
to look for Parmenon (57/58n.), returning with him at 61, and from
which Demeas and Nikeratos arrive at 96. This is also the direction
in which Moschion would have to exit in Act V if he were to fulfil his
threat to go abroad as a mercenary soldier; in 691–4 he moves as if
about to make such an exit, but does not actually do so.

(2) The 'lonely place' (94), perhaps outside the city walls (122n.), where
Moschion goes at 95 with the intention (not fulfilled) of rehearsing
what he will say to his father, returning at 120 or shortly before.

(3) The city centre. Both Parmenon on behalf of Demeas, and Nikeratos
on behalf of himself, go to the Agora (191, 198, 281) to buy what
they need for the wedding (Parmenon also to hire a cook); Moschion
also departs in that direction at 162, for we learn later (431–2) that
he had met Parmenon in the Agora. On the exits of Parmenon at 324 and
Moschion at 539, see below.

It will be seen that in Act I directions (1) and (2) are opposed to each
other, while in Act V directions (2) and (3) are opposed (since Moschion
and Parmenon must arrive from opposite directions, and neither of them
is coming from the harbour). It follows that of the theatre's two wing-
entrances (εἴσοδοι or πάροδοι), one (called Eisodos A in this commentary)
will be used for directions (1) and (3) – the harbour (in Act I, and towards
the end of Act V) and the city centre (in the rest of the play) – and the
other (Eisodos B) for direction (2) – the countryside. These directionali-
ties would have to be established afresh for each play: there was no fixed
convention. In *Aspis*, for example, all arrivals and departures seem to be
to or from the Agora or harbour, and one would not want them to be
all on the same side; even more cogently, in *Kitharistes* (35–52) a character, probably Phanias, enters from the harbour (it is clear from 42–7 that
he has arrived by sea), orders his luggage to be taken into a house (51–2),

and then departs towards the Agora (cf. 49–50). Ancient sources (e.g. Pollux 4.126–7; Vitruvius 5.6.8; *Prolegomena de Comoedia* Xa. 1–3, XIc.71–3, 87–90 Koster) assert that there was a fixed convention, but only Pollux mentions all three of the key directions (harbour, city centre, countryside), and his account is either confused or corrupt, placing all three directions on the same side of the performing area (the other side is used, he says, for arrivals from 'elsewhere', a non-existent category).

Barigazzi 1970: 260–1 argues that we can infer from 428–31 that Demeas' house is the one nearer to Eisodos A: otherwise Nikeratos, moving from his own house towards Demeas' house, would have had his back to Moschion approaching along Eisodos A, and would not have taken the initiative in greeting him at 430–1. If so, Moschion will flee along Eisodos A when Nikeratos, coming from the direction of his own house, advances towards him and Demeas at 538–9; and therefore Parmenon, who must return from the other side at 641, will have fled from the angry Demeas at 324 along Eisodos B. It may also be possible to infer from 716 (see 715n.) that Eisodos A is to the spectators' left.

ACT I

The first act brings all the main characters on stage – indeed, all the characters except the Cook (who speaks only some twenty lines and contributes nothing to the plot). In general it seems to have been Menander's practice to bring at least one important character into the play late, sometimes as late as the fourth act (Kleostratos in *Aspis*; Pamphile *and* Charisios – both of whom have been just offstage, in separate houses, the whole time – in *Epitrepontes*). His failure to do so in this play *might* be an indication that it was written early in his career, but it could also be an artistic choice: all the complications of the plot arise not from new developments impinging from outside, but from successive misunderstandings of the situation as it already existed when Demeas and Nikeratos returned from abroad. By the end of Act I the audience are fully informed of this situation. So are Moschion, Chrysis and Parmenon, except for one important fact of which they are ignorant, namely that the two fathers have agreed to arrange a marriage between their children – a fact which they will learn in the next act. Demeas and Nikeratos, contrariwise, know this fact and nothing else – and the other members of their households are determined that they shall remain, for the time being, in this state of ignorance, as they might have done had not one elderly ex-slave woman been loose of tongue (236–54).

Act I also gives us a good initial idea of most of the personalities involved. We observe Moschion's self-centredness and timidity; Chrysis' devotion to the well-being of the baby; Demeas' dominant position in his relationship with Nikeratos (96–119a, 98–101nn.), and the latter's apparent willingness to accept it (though we shall find later that this has its limits). The presentation of the two old men in their first scene helps to assure us of the basic decency of both of them, so that when they act unjustly or even cruelly later on, we are unlikely to regard either as a villain. We learn, too, something of the relationship between Moschion and his adoptive father, mainly as seen from the son's point of view but to some extent also from the father's: Moschion vividly aware of how much he owes to Demeas (5–18), Demeas reluctant to pursue a liaison for fear that it might compromise Moschion's reputation (19–27), each with a strongly developed sense of shame about anything that might lower him in the eyes of the other (23, 27, 67). These characteristics will do much to determine the course of the play's action. And yet at the end of Act I it will appear that the action has nowhere to go – that when Moschion returns to plead with his father for permission to marry Plangon, he will find himself forestalled as Demeas asks *him* to do that very thing, with the play still nearly four acts from its conclusion. Menander's audiences normally know from the start, in broad terms, the kind of ending for which a play is headed; often they are told this explicitly in a divine prologue (1–57n.). Usually they are left wondering 'how on earth are we going to get to that conclusion, starting from here?' In *Samia*, by contrast, the question is 'how on earth, starting from here, are we going to *avoid* getting to that conclusion far too soon?'

1–57 Prologue. The most common pattern for the opening of a Menandrian play appears to consist of an opening scene that excites the audience's interest but gives them only partial information, followed by a 'delayed prologue' in which a divine personage reveals the full situation, giving the audience crucial information which is not known to the characters on stage. This form of opening is preserved in full in *Aspis* and in part in *Perikeiromene*, is attested by the list of *dramatis personae* in *Heros*, and is highly probable also in *Epitrepontes* and *Misoumenos*; its origin can be traced to a combination of two patterns found in fifth-century drama – the expository divine prologues of some tragedies (such as Euripides' *Alcestis*, *Hippolytus* and *Ion*), which however always come at the very beginning of the play, and the practice in several plays of Aristophanes (*Knights*, *Wasps*, *Peace*, *Birds*) of beginning with a lively but mystifying scene and then having one of the characters involved in that scene explain to the audience what is going on. In *Dyskolos* and in *Samia* the regular arrangement would be inappropriate, since there is no important information of which all the characters are unaware. In *Dyskolos* it is still necessary to have a divine prologue, since it is important that the audience should understand from the start what manner of man Knemon is – Sostratos does not yet know this, and Knemon is not the sort of person to explain it at length himself; in addition Pan can make it clear (*Dysk.* 34–44) that *he* is working to bring about the happy outcome which Knemon's daughter deserves for her virtuous character and her reverence for himself and the Nymphs. In *Samia*, however, all the information the audience need is already in the possession of Moschion – except for one fact, namely that his father and Plangon's father have already decided to arrange a marriage between their children; and Menander wishes to keep this up his sleeve. To have Moschion deliver the prologue himself has the advantage that he is made to reveal a great deal to the audience about his personality, his virtues and his weaknesses (details in notes below).

The prologue introduces us to four of the five main characters in the play – Moschion himself, Demeas, Nikeratos, Chrysis – and also to Plangon and her mother, who have no role in the onstage action but of whom much will be heard in the course of the play, especially in Act IV. There was probably also brief mention of the other significant character, Parmenon, in the lost conclusion of the speech (see 57/58n.) and perhaps also at the beginning (see 20n.) As is usual in Menandrian prologues, most of the characters are only described, not named: in each of the three prologues that are fully (or almost fully) preserved, only one name is mentioned, and the person named is either the title character (Chrysis here [56], Knemon in *Dyskolos* [6]) or a character with a strong link to the play's title (Kleostratos, owner of the eponymous shield, in *Aspis* [110]). It is likely that Menander's audiences did not identify characters primarily by their names – though in view of the play's imperfect state of preservation, it would be unwise to make any inference from the fact that, for example, Nikeratos' name is not mentioned until 182; probably (cf. B's list of *dramatis personae* for *Dyskolos*) they would think of the character named Moschion as 'the lover', of Nikeratos as 'the girl's father', and so forth.

The play begins with Moschion coming out of his (or rather Demeas') house. Throughout its duration he will never re-enter that house; all his exits will be via the wing-entrances (Eisodos A at some point in the lacuna between 57 and 58, and also at 162; Eisodos B at 95 and 539).

1 Probably about seven lines are lost before this (for the calculations on which this is based, see Arnott 1999). In these a good deal must have been said about Demeas, who is referred to in 6 by the pronoun ἐκείνου: right from the start we are put on notice that the father-son relationship will be central to the play. The phrase τότ᾽ εὐθέως 'immediately after that' in 7 furthermore suggests strongly that in the opening lines mention was made of the fact that Demeas had adopted Moschion; in the surviving text, at least, we do not hear of this again until 346, and it too is a matter very important to our understanding of the situation (see Introduction §4(a)). Possibly Moschion may have explained briefly why Demeas had decided to adopt a son – whether he was a bachelor who thought himself past the age for a first marriage, or a widower who was childless or whose only child had died. Before this he may have said something to indicate why he had come out of his house (e.g. to see whether Parmenon had returned from the harbour; cf. Dworacki 1989: 201); he could then mention the expected arrival of his father, and his fear of coming face to face with him (but without as yet explaining the cause of this fear, beyond the one word ἡμάρτηκα (3)).

2–6 In the first preserved phrases, Moschion is reflecting that something is, or will be, 'painful' to himself and/or to another (undoubtedly Demeas), because he (Moschion) has done something wrong, and deciding that the best way to explain why this is the case will be to describe Demeas' character. The thing that will be painful is almost certainly the thing that he can never in this play bring himself to do until it is nearly too late, namely to confess the truth about Plangon and her baby to Demeas. Even in monologue it takes him till line 49 – really about the eightieth line of his speech – to state, indirectly, what is the wrong that he has done.

2 If the first complete word preserved is τί, it is very tempting to restore the previous word as [γέγ]ονε (Austin), in which case Moschion will no doubt have been thinking about the prospect of explaining '[what] has happened' either to the audience (cf. 5 ὑμῖν) or to Demeas. An alternative possibility is that the words should be divided as]ον ἔτι, but no plausible restoration/interpretation along these lines has been offered.   με is probably the subject of λυπῆσαι; the object, either expressed ([αὐτὸν] Austin at the start of the next line) or understood, is Demeas, and Moschion is expressing his reluctance to cause distress to a father who has done so much for him (7–18). Gallo 1983 thought that με was object of the infinitive, and offered the restoration τί λυπῆσαί με δεῖ [τοῦτ'· ἀλλ' ὁδ]υνηρόν ἐστιν ('why should this distress me? But it *is* painful...') This certainly fits well with Moschion's general self-centredness throughout the play; but for him to ask such a question would imply, implausibly, that he thinks many people would find it surprising that he should be distressed by the thought of asking his father for permission to marry a poor man's daughter who has already given birth to his child. On this reading, too, line 4 (see below) would be little but a repetition of ὀδυνηρόν ἐστιν (3). Austin 2010: 13 proposed [αὐτόν] at the start of 3, giving the sense 'why should I distress myself?' (for αὐτόν as a first-person reflexive cf. fr. 632); but then ὀδυνηρόν ἐστιν would be redundant.

3 ὀδ]υνηρόν ἐστιν: sc. to me.   ἡμάρτηκα: Parmenon will use the stronger term ἠδίκηκας, to his young master's face (68); but at least Moschion accepts that he has done what he ought not. In *Epitrepontes*, when it is discovered that an as yet unidentified citizen girl has probably been made pregnant by an act of rape, Habrotonon speaks of the perpetrator as τὸν ἀδικοῦντα (499, 508); but when the actual perpetrator, Charisios, finds his crime brought home to him by Habrotonon's false claim to be the mother of his baby, and is then put to shame by his wife's refusal to leave him in the face of her father's bullying, he speaks not of ἀδικία or even ἁμαρτία but of an ἀτύχημα (921, cf. 891, 898, 914–15, 918). For these three grades of 'harm' (βλάβη) see Arist. *EN* 1135b16–25 (ἀτύχημα, when the harmful effect was not to be expected; ἁμάρτημα, when it was predictable but not intended; ἀδίκημα, when it was intended or – worse – premeditated); cf. also [Arist.] *Rhet. ad Alex.* 4.8–9.

4 What does Moschion 'reckon' (LSJ λογίζομαι II.2) will happen? If με (2) is subject of λυπῆσαι (as argued above), τοῦτο will refer back to the most recent expression he has used that clearly speaks of an anticipated future event, viz. λυπῆσαι (sc. Δημέαν).   **[ὥστ' αὐτ]ό:** this restoration makes explicit the logical connection between Moschion's three statements: because he has done something wrong (3b), telling the truth about it will distress Demeas (4), which in turn will be painful for Moschion (3a). Alternative possibilities include [ἀλλ' αὐτ]ὸ (Barigazzi) and [σαφὲς αὐτ]ὸ (Sisti); other proposals, such as Jacques' [οἴσω δ' ἐγ]ὼ τοῦτ' εἰς μέσον, require us to read the first partly preserved letter in the line as ω, which is unlikely given the curvature of its surviving portion.   **τοῦτό <γ'>:** Sandbach's insertion of γ' is all but essential, since it is otherwise hard to find any convincing restoration of the beginning of the line. Note that B writes τουτο without elision, and that Γ could easily have been lost before E.   **ἐσόμενον:** λογίζομαι also governs a participle at Hdt. 3.65.5 Σμέρδιν τὸν Κύρου μηκέτι ὑμῖν ἐόντα λογίζεσθε. The preference for the participial construction (which normally guarantees the truth of the statement being made) over that with the infinitive may be designed to convey the speaker's strong conviction that his 'calculation' is correct; see Fraenkel on Aesch. *Ag.* 269.

5–6 clearly constitute a sentence, whose main verb must have been lost at the beginning of either the first or the second line. If we associate ἄν (5) with this main verb, the verb must be a first-person optative (ἔχοιμι Lamagna, θέλοιμι Sbordone) and must have stood at the beginning of line 6, giving the sense 'I will be able (*or* I would like) to make this —— to you by explaining his character' – in which case the missing word is likely to have meant something like 'clear, evident' (e.g. [δῆλον] Barigazzi, [σαφὲς] Austin 2010: 13). If instead we take ἄν with ποεῖν, the main verb could be [οἶμαι] (Austin, Lloyd-Jones) at the start of line 5, but then no plausible supplement is available in 6: [ἅπαντα] (Lloyd-Jones) would require us to change τοῦτ' to ταῦτ'.

5 εὐλόγως: most likely 'probably'; this sense of εὔλογος was already established in the fourth century (Arist. *Metaph.* 1060a18). If so, [ἔχοιμι] in the sense 'be able' will be the best restoration at the start of 6. **ὑμῖν:** addressed to the audience. Prologue speeches by *gods* are always so addressed, and our evidence, so far as it goes, suggests that this was taken as a matter of course, second-person plural pronouns and verbs being used (e.g. *Dysk.* 1, *Aspis* 113) without any introductory vocative expression (ἄνδρες or the like). We do not have any other prologue speeches by *characters* for comparison (*com. adesp.* 1001, which has ἄνδρες in line 3, though clearly the beginning of a speech, is not necessarily from a prologue), but in other parts of Menandrian plays characters who, as it were, turn away from the action to address the audience normally use ἄνδρες to signal that they are doing so (cf. 269, 329, 447, 683). We therefore cannot tell whether or not Moschion used ἄνδρες at the lost beginning of his speech. The second person plural appears again at 33 (where see note), and as late as 47–8 Moschion's embarrassment makes it evident that his speech is still thought of as addressed to the audience, not as a soliloquy (cf. also perhaps 13 if we adopt Oguse's supplement).

6 τρόπον: a favourite word of Menander's to denote a person's character (e.g. 136, 347, 550; *Dysk.* 13, 254, 742, 770; *Epitr.* 1093, 1106), though it is found in this sense as early as the *Theognidea* (964). As Luppe 1972 observed, Moschion does not in fact, in the text we have, describe Demeas' character directly, but this does not (as he argued) justify positing a lacuna between 9 and 10: Moschion describes his father's character by giving an account of his actions.

7 [ὡς μὲ]ν ἐτρύφησα 'in what luxury I lived'. The verb τρυφᾶν normally has a slightly pejorative tone, suggesting *excessive* luxury (e.g. *Dysk.* 357, 755; *Georg.* F 2.4); but this does not apply where a speaker is using the word to describe good treatment from which he has benefited, just as in English 'You're really spoiling me!' is a grateful compliment, not a reproach (cf. Eur. *Bacch.* 969). Nevertheless we may come to wonder whether Demeas may indeed have been over-indulgent to his adopted son, unintentionally encouraging him to believe that the comforts and pleasures of life were his automatic entitlement. For the alternative restoration [οἷς] the best parallel would be *Dysk.* 830, where B reads τρυφαίνειν ἀλλοτρίοις πόνοις, but τρυφαίνειν is nowhere else attested and Maas's τρυφᾶν ἐν (cf. Euphron fr. 11.2) is now widely adopted.   **τῶι τότ' εὐθέως χρόνωι** 'in the time immediately after that' (i.e. after his adoption). In conjunction with μεμνημένος σαφῶς below, this shows that we are to imagine Moschion as having been adopted when he was old enough to retain a permanent memory of his experiences. It may well have been the general practice to adopt boys only after they had survived the infant stage with its high mortality rate. We

hear later (246–7) that Moschion's nurse, who is still in Demeas' household, had been with him from babyhood; we can if we wish assume that
Demeas had purchased her from Moschion's natural father so that the
child might not be parted from her, but it may be that Menander simply
did not trouble about consistency in this peripheral matter.

8 μεμνημένος σαφῶς: concessive, 'although I remember it clearly'.

9 This is not terribly convincing as a reason for passing lightly over the
subject, and one may suspect that Menander's main concern was not to
lengthen further a speech that was already very long indeed. Including
the lost portions it must have extended to 90–100 lines – not far short
of the longest known speech in Menander, the report of the debate in
the Eleusinian deme assembly in *Sikyonioi* (176–271), which appears to
have contained originally 102–104 lines.   **οὐ φρονοῦντα:** i.e. not having
a matured intelligence; cf. Aeschines 1.39 (saying he will concentrate on
Timarchus' misdeeds when ἤδη φρονῶν καὶ μειράκιον ὤν and disregard those
he committed παῖς ὤν), Soph. *Aj.* 554–5.

10–16 Moschion passes from the benefactions his adoptive father had
conferred on him in boyhood to those he has received as a young adult. He
is fully conscious of their extent and of the obligation he accordingly owes
to Demeas (17–18), but in this passage he is curiously inexplicit in credit-
ing the benefactions to their giver: in the listing in 13–16 the first person
singular is prominent (διέφερον, ἐφυλάρχησα, ἐδυνάμην) and Demeas figures
only once and then as the unexpressed subject of a verb (παρέτρεφε 14).
All the actions that would help to give Moschion a reputation for public-
spirited munificence he speaks of as his own, though he knows well that
it was Demeas' money that was being spent on them. Even in an excur-
sus whose objective is to praise Demeas, Moschion cannot help giving evidence of his self-centredness.

10–14 'When I was registered <as a citizen> no different from any other,
"one of the many" as the saying goes – though as we're alone, <I can
say that> I've <now> become more wretched <than any of them> – I
excelled as a *choregos* and in other honourable services.'
    For a broad understanding of what Moschion is trying to say here, and
for the restoration of the text, the crucial question is how ἀθλιώτερος (12)
fits into its context.
    In the first place, ἀθλιώτερος is a strong word. It cannot merely mean
'less happy', as for example ἀμαθέστερος can mean 'less clever' (Ar. *Frogs*
1445) without implying that the person referred to is positively stupid;
rather, if one says that A is ἀθλιώτερος than B, one is implying that even B

is miserable enough to be called ἄθλιος and asserting that A is more miserable still. Cf. *Mis.* A4 S = 4 A, Men. fr. 400, and (though here the comparative form is not used) *Perik.* 532–6 – all, it may be noted, referring to persons unhappy *in love*. This at once tells us that the comparison is being made, not with Moschion's own boyhood (for by his account he certainly was not unhappy then), but with his contemporaries, the οἱ πολλοί of 11. Presumably he regards them (or most of them) as ἄθλιοι because they lack his material advantages.

Secondly, is Moschion saying that he *is* 'more wretched' than οἱ πολλοί, or that he *is not?* The fact that in backing his statement with an oath he says νὴ Δί' rather than μὰ Δί' creates a very strong presumption in favour of the former alternative; nowhere in Menander, so far as we know, is the oath-particle νὴ used with a negative statement.

Now there is only one respect in which Moschion could with any plausibility at all claim to be more wretched than most people, namely the complications and embarrassments that have resulted from his rape of Plangon: once again, as in the passages cited above, ἄθλιος is being applied to the unhappy lover (so rightly Dedoussi). The remark is prompted by his statement that on coming of age he was treated as 'one of the many': here he says that in one way, which matters very much to him, he was *not* one of the many. He does not, however, follow this up by proceeding at once to speak of his love-troubles, but reverts to the affluence and social prominence of his ephebic and post-ephebic years (see below). In other words, line 12 and the first half of line 13 form a parenthesis, and the following words, τῶι χορηγεῖν διέφερον κτλ., do not continue their thought but rather that of 10–11.

This makes it desirable to restore the beginning of this passage in such a way as to make 10–13a (minus the parenthesis) into a single continuous sentence, i.e. as [ὡς δ' ἐν]εγράφην (Kamerbeek, Luppe); at 12, when the expected main clause fails to arrive, the hearer will know that the sentence has been interrupted and will expect a resumption. If we adopted a supplement (such as the popular [εἶτ' ἐν]εγράφην) which made 10–11 into an independent sentence, the hearer would not at once realize that 12–13a was a parenthesis and would be confused by the sudden reversion to the previous topic.

10 [ἐν]εγράφην 'I was registered', sc. in the citizen list of my deme, on reaching the age of eighteen ([Arist.] *Ath.Pol.* 42.1; Dem. 18.261). Since 334, the following two years would be spent living the semi-segregated life of an ephebe ([Arist.] *Ath.Pol.* 42.2–5; Lyc. *Leocr.* 76; see Parker 1996: 253–5); at some point in the early Hellenistic era the period of service was reduced to one year, but this seems to have happened after the latest likely date for the production of *Samia* (see Introduction §8; the

earliest date proposed for the change in the ephebic law is 307, Habicht
1992).   οὐδὲν διαφέρων οὐδενός: the point is that whereas in his home
life Moschion was privileged and pampered, in his capacity as a citizen
he was no different from any other citizen; in particular, for the next two
years he would wear the same uniform as the other ephebes, eat the same
food (purchased, on behalf of all the ephebes of his tribe, by their adult
σωφρονιστής), and take part alongside them in weapon training, garrison
duties, frontier patrols, etc. But the point would probably not have been
worth making except as preparation for Moschion's statement (12–13a)
of the one respect in which he now *differs* from his contemporaries – to his
disadvantage.

11 τὸ λεγό|μενον δὴ τοῦτο: almost formulaic for introducing a proverb or
idiom, cf. frr. 296.8, 450, *com. adesp.* 78, Pl. *Gorg.* 514e.   τῶν πολλῶν τις
'just an ordinary person': for this phrase (or its synonym εἷς τῶν πολλῶν)
cf. *Dysk.* 484–5, Dem. 21.96, Isoc. 2.50.

12 [ὅς γέγον]α 'but I have <now> become'. If 12–13a is a parenthesis (see
10–14n.), a verb is required here, and γέγονα is vastly preferable to πέφυκα
(Photiadis), which is not found in any Menander papyrus or any book
fragment now accepted as genuine. A monosyllable is then required to
begin the line, and [ὅς] (Arnott) works best: for the 'connecting relative'
(to use a term familiar from Latin syntax) cf. 413, 519, *Aspis* 176, and especially *Dysk.* 163 where, as here, the connection comes with a contrastive
or concessive tinge. As in Latin, sentences introduced by such a relative
are not felt as subordinated relative clauses, otherwise μέντοι could hardly
have been used (Denniston 1954: 403–4, 406). Of other restorations, [ὧι]
(Sandbach) gives unsuitable sense (Moschion's misery is not the result of
his being τῶν πολλῶν τις), and [νῦν] (Austin) is too long for the space.
μέντοι could here be either affirmative ('definitely'; cf. *Dysk.* 151, *Epitr.*
510) or adversative ('on the other hand', cf. probably 566); the latter is
perhaps preferable, as making explicit the contrast between Moschion's
present and his previous state.   ἀθλιώτερος: understand either τῶν πολλῶν (from 11) or πάντων τῶν ἄλλων (since οὐδὲν διαφέρων οὐδενός, 10, is
equivalent to ὅμοιος ὢν πᾶσι τοῖς ἄλλοις).

13 [αὐτοὶ] γάρ ἐσμεν 'we [i.e. you – the audience – and I] are all by ourselves'; cf. Ar. *Ach.* 504, *Thesm.* 472, Herodas 6.70, Plaut. *Cas.* 197 *nos
sumus*); this does not, of course, explain Moschion's misery, but it does
explain the fact that he feels able to mention it. Other restorations interpret the first person plural differently, but all have disadvantages. With
παχεῖς 'rich' (Arnott 1998a: 37–8; lit. 'fat', cf. Ar. *Wasps* 287, *Peace* 639)
'we' would mean 'my father and I', and the point would be that Demeas'
wealth makes it unlikely that he will consent to his son's marrying a poor

man's daughter; but παχύς is not otherwise found in this sense in Menander, and in any case this adjective, like English 'fat cat', is not normally applied by rich people to *themselves* (Austin 2010: 13). Even less attractive are proposals that identify 'we' as the whole human race ([θνητοί] Lloyd-Jones, [οὐδὲν] Dedoussi), since Moschion has just been *contrasting* himself with other people (12n.). **τῶι χορηγεῖν:** the expensive and prestigious activity of financing choruses for dramatic, dithyrambic or other competitions at state or deme festivals (on which see P. J. Wilson 2000); cf. Dem. 18.257 where χορηγεῖν is paired with another 'liturgy', the trierarchy, and linked (as here) with the broader concept of φιλοτιμία. It has usually been supposed that the *choregia* was abolished, at least for state festivals, early in the administration of Demetrius of Phalerum, perhaps in 316 (see P. J. Wilson 2000: 307–8); but Wilson and Csapo 2012 (see also O'Sullivan 2009: 168–85) have shown that our evidence is compatible with, and even favours, the view that *choregoi* continued to function – though under the supervision of an administrator (*epimeletes*) of the festival – at least until 311 and quite possibly until shortly after Demetrius' fall in 307 (in 307/6 their role had been taken over by an *agonothetes*: *IG* II² 3073). Our passage therefore cannot be used to assign this play to a very early date (see Introduction §8). It was forbidden for anyone under forty to be the *choregos* of a boys' chorus (Aeschines 1.11, [Arist.] *Ath.Pol.* 56.3), but we hear nothing of any age limit for *choregoi* of adult choruses: in 411/10 the speaker of Lysias 21 had undertaken two *choregiai* within a few months of his coming of age (Lys. 21.1). Once the new-model *ephebeia* was established, ephebes were exempt from all liturgies ([Arist.] *Ath.Pol.* 42.5); we are not explicitly told that they were *disqualified* from undertaking them, but the explanation given for the ban on their engaging in most lawsuits – 'that they may have no excuse for leaving [their guard postings]' – would be equally cogent in justifying such a disqualification. Moschion may thus be passing lightly over his ephebic service and speaking of his activities after it ended (i.e. from the age of twenty onwards) – which, it is to be understood, were all paid for by his adoptive father (cf. 17). **διέφερον** 'I excelled' (i.e. my activities as *choregos* and in other forms of φιλοτιμία were exceptionally numerous and/or lavish) echoes and reverses οὐδὲν διαφέρων οὐδενός: at eighteen and nineteen Moschion may have been just another ephebe, but thereafter he soon made plain both his privileged status and his desire to make a name for himself in the community.

14 φιλοτιμίαι: in the later fourth century this means activity likely to earn public honour and motivated by the desire for it (see Dover 1974: 230–3, Whitehead 1983, MacDowell 1990: 378–9), in particular material benefactions to the community or to individuals in need (cf. Dem. 18.257).

14–15 κύνας . . . | [ἵππο]υς: these would be used in the élite pursuits of hunting and riding, so much praised by Xenophon (in *Cynegeticus, Hipparchicus* and *Peri Hippikēs*). The Euripidean Hippolytus was likewise devoted to hound and horse equally (Eur. *Hipp.* 17–18, 52, 109–12, 1093, 1127–36, 1397). Youths of the 'better' class (οἱ χρηστοί) trading on their physical charms would ask their older male admirers for horses or hunting dogs as presents (Ar. *Wealth* 153–9). In *Dyskolos* the wealthy young Sostratos sees, and falls in love with, Knemon's daughter when he comes to Phyle on a hunting trip (*Dysk.* 42, 71, 522–3). Hunting and riding, it should be added, were to an ancient Greek entirely separate activities: hounds were followed on foot, not on horseback.   **παρέτρεφε** 'he [Demeas] maintained in addition' (sc. to those he kept for his own use); cf. [Arist.] *Ath.Pol.* 62.2, Plut. *Mor.* 830e. B's γὰρ ἔτρεφε would imply that keeping horses and hounds was a species of φιλοτιμία: but by this time 'a reputation [for φιλοτιμία] could not be won by conspicuous private luxury' (Dover 1974: 231, citing Dem. 21.159).

15 ἐφυλάρχησα: a φύλαρχος was the commander of a tribal contingent of cavalry ([Arist.] *Ath.Pol.* 61.5, Xen. *Hipparch.* 1.8). In the fifth century, like other office-holders, they had to be at least thirty years old ([Arist.] *Ath.Pol.* 30.2 – admittedly from an alleged draft constitution that never came into operation). Most of the rank and file, however, will have been younger men (Bugh 1988: 62–5, 172; Spence 1993: 198–202), and it is not too surprising to find that with Athens under Macedonian domination, active warfare unlikely, and the cavalry having more of a ceremonial than a military role, the tribal command might be given to a rich young man who, at formal parades, could 'not only make it his concern that he himself should look splendid (λαμπρός, cf. λαμπρῶς here), but rather that all those who follow him should be a sight worth looking at' (Xen. *Peri Hippikēs* 11.10, cf. *Hipparch.* 1.22).

15–16 τῶν φίλων | . . . ἐδυνάμην: helping friends (and others) in need was another recognized component of φιλοτιμία (see Dover 1974: 177–8), and the verb ἐπαρκεῖν was often used in this connection; cf. Ar. *Wealth* 829–30, Soph. *El.* 322, Dem. 18.268, 36.58–9, Arist. *EN* 1163a33–4. Contrast Theophrastus' 'illiberal' man (ἀνελεύθερος), who displays 'a lack of φιλοτιμία where this involves expense' (*Char.* 22.1) and who 'when a friend is seeking a contribution to an interest-free loan (ἔρανος) and has talked to him about it, will turn into a side street when he sees the friend approaching and go the long way home' (*Char.* 22.9).

16 τὰ μέτρι' 'to a reasonable extent', i.e. not so lavishly as to cross the boundary between liberality (ἐλευθεριότης) and prodigality (ἀσωτία), cf. Arist. *EN* 1119b22–1121b12.

17 δι' ἐκεῖνον ἦν ἄνθρωπος: for Menander, to be fully human is, among other things, to recognize the claims of society and of other individuals, and do one's best to aid them; Knemon in *Dyskolos*, that ἀπάνθρωπος... ἄνθρωπος σφόδρα (*Dysk.* 6), falls badly short of this standard, as does Smikrines in *Aspis* (260). Moschion, however, is here speaking not of his *willingness* to display generosity but, as the preceding lines show, of his *ability* to do so, and it is surprising and revealing that he should imply that had he been poor he would not have been fully human. Whereas here being 'human' is for Moschion a mark of excellence, only five lines later (22) it will be an excuse for weakness, when he says it was ἴσως ἀνθρώπινον that Demeas fell in love with Chrysis (cf. also 138). Later in the play the male characters will be exercised, not by the question of what it means to be an ἄνθρωπος, but by that of what it means to be an ἀνήρ (64n.)   **ἀστείαν** 'proper' (cf. *Kith.* F 6, Men. fr. 340); this adjective, literally 'of the town' (as opposed to the countryside) whence 'sophisticated', 'clever', 'witty' etc., has a tendency to get watered down semantically into a vague term of approval (cf. 364 (ironic), 657).   **ὅμως:** since everyone was supposed to respond with gratitude and respect when treated well – and especially so a son to his father – it is at first sight surprising to find this adverb here (and Jacques conjectured ὅλως). But 'perhaps seemly behaviour is unexpected in a rich, indulged young man' (Sandbach).

18 ἦν κόσμιος 'I was well-behaved'; the κόσμιος is one who 'does not do anything unseemly' (Philemon fr. 4.4). Moschion's κοσμιότης has made a very strong impression on Demeas (273, 344). But he himself speaks of it here in the imperfect, not the present, tense: he knows that he has recently behaved in a manner very far from κόσμιον.

19–20 καὶ γάρ... σχολήν: the story of how Chrysis became Demeas' live-in παλλακή is not strictly relevant to explaining Moschion's embarrassment at the prospect of facing his father – but from Menander's point of view, it is necessary for the audience to know it. The digression will also serve to increase their suspense as they wait (im)patiently to learn what the cause of his embarrassment actually is.

20 ἄγω γάρ πως σχολήν: he is waiting for the return of Parmenon from the harbour, where he had sent him to learn whether Demeas and Nikeratos had arrived from abroad. (He may, indeed, have originally come out of his house to see whether Parmenon was on his way; if so, this would have been mentioned in the lost first line or two of the play, 1n.).

21ff 'An ironical reversal of the conventional situation, where it is the fathers who need to be persuaded to accept their sons' amours' (Arnott 1975: 11, comparing Ar. *Wasps* 1341–87).

21 Σαμίας: 'Menander likes to insert the title of his play somewhere in the opening lines' (Arnott 1993:29, comparing *Aspis* 16, *Dysk.* 6 – one might add *Mis.* A43-4 S = 43-4 A). Samos was famous for its *hetairai* (Diphilus fr. 49; Plaut. *Bacch.* 200; Ter. *Eun.* 107; Athen. 220f, 593a, 594c); one of them, Lampito, had Demetrius of Phalerum as one of her lovers (Athen. 13.593e-f). *Samia* had already been the title of a comedy by Anaxandrides, and a Samian *hetaira* was probably a character in Menander's *Dis Exapaton* (cf. Plaut. *Bacch.* 200, 574). It is thus possible that the word Σαμία in itself carried connotations of mercenary or promiscuous sexuality. In Act III Chrysis will twice be referred to (not addressed) as ἡ Σαμία by Demeas when he believes she has been unfaithful to him with Moschion (265, 354).

21-2 εἰς ἐπιθυμίαν...ἐλθεῖν: cf. Pl. *Critias* 113d τῆς κόρης... εἰς ἐπιθυμίαν Ποσειδῶν ἐλθὼν συμμείγνυται.

21 τινά: cf. 43-4 ἀγρυπνίαν...τινά, *Aspis* 390 πιθανότητα...τινα, *Dysk.* 38 ἐπιμέλειαν...τινα. Jacques' τινός is attractive (the corruption would be very easy) but not clearly superior to the transmitted reading.

22 πρᾶγμ' ἴσως ἀνθρώπινον: cf. 17n.

23 ἔκρυπτε τοῦτ': imperfect rather than aorist, indicating an (unsuccessful) *attempt* to conceal his passion (both from Moschion and from the world in general): Goodwin 1912: 12. Concealment would of course be impossible if he took Chrysis into his home. Later we shall see Demeas attempting resolutely to conceal from the world, and in particular from Nikeratos and his family, the shaming 'fact' of Chrysis' supposed affair with Moschion, and later explaining to Moschion (704-6) that he did so largely for the latter's own sake (cf. 27 δι' ἔμ'). **ἠισχύνετ':** probably on account of his age; cf. Lys. 3.4, Pherecrates fr. 77, and see W. V. Harris 1997: 364-5 on 'the derision which was aimed at those who formed sexual liaisons with persons much younger than themselves'. Compare Theophrastus' ὀψιμαθής (an old man acting less than half his age) who 'falls in love with a *hetaira*, attacks her door with battering-rams, gets beaten up by a rival and takes him to court' (Thphr. *Char.* 27.9).   **<δ'>:** B's asyndeton presents no great stylistic difficulty, but the insertion of δ' helps account for the non-sensical δε – presumably a misplaced correction – which appears in B in the previous line (after ἴσως).

24 διελογιζόμην 'I reckoned, I reasoned'. Elsewhere in Menander (*Aspis* 2, *Epitr.* 253, 564) this verb takes an internal accusative, but it governs an indirect statement in Dem. 23.26, 25.25 (both with ὅτι) and 44.35 (infinitive construction). The indirect statement covers the whole of 25-7, as the tenses of the verbs in 26 and 27 show.

25 ἂν μὴ γένηται τῆς ἑταίρας ἐγκρατής: i.e. unless he took her into his home, where rivals would no longer have any means of access to her. At any rate that was what Demeas ultimately did, doubtless at Moschion's urging. Dedoussi 1970: 161 thought that the meaning was rather 'unless he made an agreement with her giving him the exclusive right to her services' (such as Simon allegedly made with the adolescent Plataean boy Theodotus, Lys. 3.22–6; cf. also Plaut. *Asin.* 746–809); but how could he enforce this agreement, except by one of the two methods envisaged in Lys. loc.cit. – bringing legal proceedings, which would involve widespread and unwelcome publicity (cf. 23n.), or violence, in which at his age he would stand little chance against the ἀντερασταὶ μειράκια?

26 ἐνοχλήσεται: middle with passive meaning, 'he would be harassed'.

27 δι' ἔμ': because it would harm Moschion's reputation if he was living in the same house as a *hetaira*, or because Chrysis would be the equivalent of a stepmother to him (cf. Plaut. *Epid.* 165–73, where Periphanes says he would feel it shameful to remarry because 'I respect my son', *revereor filium*)?

28 About the only things we can say with confidence about this line are that it begins a new sentence (since there is nothing in what precedes for λαβεῖν to depend on) and that λαβεῖν ταύτην has Demeas as its subject and means 'to take Chrysis into his home' (cf. *Mis.* 306 παρθένον σ' εἴληφ' ἐγώ). Jacques' [λέγ]ω 'I told him to ...' is attractive, but there may not be enough space to accommodate the three letters.

29/30 In this lacuna, Moschion must have (i) completed the story of how Chrysis came into his father's house (though without mentioning her name, which at 56 is clearly being given for the first time); (ii) described the family of Nikeratos which lived next door, perhaps with mention of Nikeratos' fiery character (see 54n.); (iii) explained how he had fallen in love with Plangon (for he undoubtedly *is* genuinely in love with her – note what he says in soliloquy at 622–32 – and it is important that the marriage has not been forced on him by Plangon's pregnancy but is one that he passionately desires); perhaps (iv) added that he had been reluctant to ask his father for permission to marry her because of Nikeratos' poverty; and then (v) told how Demeas and Nikeratos had gone away together on a long business trip to the Black Sea region (which ruled out any possibility of a marriage until they had returned). By the time the text resumes, the audience are clearly in possession of these facts, with the possible exception of (iv): 'the neighbour' (33) and 'the girl' and her mother (36) are spoken of in a way that shows we are already familiar with them, Nikeratos' and Demeas' absence is also presupposed (53), and in the narrative of what happened at the Adonia (38–50) there is no suggestion that Moschion's passion for Plangon had only just been kindled.

30–4 The best clue to this puzzling passage comes in the last line: συν-θλάσας τὸ σημεῖον 'smashing the seal' suggests that Moschion broke open a storeroom, cupboard or chest in his house, which Demeas had sealed before his departure (cf. *Aspis* 197, 358; Aesch. *Ag.* 609–10; Dem. 42.2; Pl. *Laws* 954a); the mention of 'the neighbour' in the previous line, and of 'the girl's mother' in the next sentence, makes it likely that he did so in order to give money or goods to Plangon and her mother, who may well have been in some hardship in Nikeratos' absence, or to make purchases on their behalf; this interpretation finds some support in προσ-ετίθην (32) which can mean 'I spent money' (Pl. *Euthph.* 3d9, Arist. *EN* 1130a25). Such taking of his father's property behind his father's back was not exactly the action of a κόσμιος son (18), particularly since it is likely to have been motivated in part by stronger emotions than mere pity with respect to Plangon; but Moschion, who was anyway used to being generous with his father's money (15–16), could reasonably feel that Demeas would not have wanted Nikeratos' family to be left destitute because the head of the household had gone abroad in his company (and probably at his suggestion). If so, he was essentially right, as we will discover when we learn that Demeas is prepared, and indeed eager (117–18), to have his son marry Plangon with, at best, a far smaller dowry than could easily have been gained elsewhere. Even then, though, we may continue to wonder how Demeas will react when he discovers the broken seal; but so far as we can tell, he never does discover it during the action of the play, and by the end, with Plangon now Demeas' daughter-in-law and the mother of his grandson, the matter has ceased to be of any significance.

31 With συμφέροντ' (Nardelli 1972: 462 n.12; cf. Gaiser 1976: 107–8) the meaning will probably be that Moschion 'saw that [a particular course of action] was for the benefit [of Nikeratos' wife and daughter]', the participle being neuter plural; with προσφέροντ' the participle will more probably be masculine singular and refer to someone (maybe a creditor) 'applying' some form of pressure to extract from Plangon and her mother money which they did not have.

32 πανταχοῦ: probably 'on every occasion', 'at every opportunity' (cf. *Heros* F 3, Men. fr. 317).

33].ησθε can only be a second-person plural ending, and the verb must have formed part or all of a parenthetical remark addressed to the audience (cf. 5n.) Kamerbeek's [ἵνα πάντα πυνθά]νησθε gives excellent sense (cf. 19–20) and also conveys a slight reluctance on Moschion's part to reveal facts that might be seen as discreditable to him. There is not enough space to accommodate these letters, but the same would apply to virtually any other restoration (since the metre requires at least five syllables), and probably the text was defective before the papyrus was damaged: πάντα could well have fallen out before πυνθα-. **πρὸς τὸν γείτονα** may go with προσετίθην (32) – though προστίθημι normally takes a dative of the bene-ficiary – or with a first-person verb (e.g. [ἤνεικ]α [Kamerbeek]) at the start of 34. In the latter case πρός will mean in effect 'to the house of' (cf. 40 πρὸς ἡμᾶς), since Nikeratos himself was away from home.

34 σφόδρα may have intensified another adverb or equivalent, now lost at the start of 35; but it may also have modified συνθλάσας directly, cf. Alexis fr. 272.3 (of a cup) ὦτα συντεθλασμένον σφόδρα.

35 [φ]ιλανθρώπως: an appropriate word: Plangon's mother treated Chrysis not as a *hetaira* but as a fellow human being, regularly making her welcome in her home.

36 ἡ τῆς κόρης μήτηρ: this – at least in the surviving text – is our first introduction to a person who, for a non-speaking (and probably non-appearing) character, will be quite a significant figure in the play (see Introduction §4(d)).

36–8 Chrysis' visits to Nikeratos' house were more frequent than the reciprocal visits of Plangon and her mother (contrast τά ... πλεῖστα with ποτέ 'sometimes'); it was one thing for Chrysis to visit an all-female house-hold, and another for her neighbours, women of citizen status, to enter the home of an unrelated (and unmarried) young man, unless they could be sure he would be out of the house for the duration of their visit (see below).

37 ἥδε: ὅδε is often used both in tragedy and in comedy to refer (doubtless with the aid of a gesture) to persons who are imagined as being within the *skene* (Dale 1964: 166; Taplin 1977: 150–1); in Menander this usage occurs at *Aspis* 123 and probably also at *Dysk.* 185.

38 αὐτ]αι or αὐτ]η? The traces are slight and ambiguous, and either read-ing would be intelligible in terms of the situation and the social conven-tions. On the one hand, one could reasonably argue, as Dedoussi does, that Plangon's mother would be even more reluctant to risk bringing her daughter into contact with a young male citizen than she would be to make the visit herself. On the other hand, Moschion would be out of the house for much of the time – as he is in this play, where in fact he never enters it at all – and when he went off to his father's country property (39n.) he would be away all day, so that from time to time there would be opportuni-ties for the two women to visit Chrysis without any risk of embarrassment. Nothing can be inferred from παρ' ἡμῖν, which merely means 'at our house' and does not imply that Chrysis and Moschion were both in the house at the time of the visit(s).

38–50 The rape (Introduction §5) of an unmarried girl of citizen status at a nocturnal festival was a cliché of New Comedy; we find it in *Epitrepontes* (the Tauropolia; again a παννυχίς, *Epitr.* 452, 474) and *Phasma* (94–99 S = 194–9 A; yet another παννυχίς, at the Brauronia). In Euripides' *Ion* (545–55) Xuthus recalls an occasion when he succumbed to 'the pleasures of Bacchus' while celebrating with a θίασος of maidens at Delphi. At such celebrations a young woman might plausibly be caught off guard, alone or nearly so (46n.), in a place to which men had access. In this play the festival in question was the Adonia, properly a women's commemoration of the death of Adonis, the mortal youth who was loved by Aphrodite – though by Menander's time its mournful origins seem to have been largely forgotten, and it had become particularly popular with *hetairai* (cf. Diphilus frr. 42.39–41; 49). The cult was already well established in late seventh-century Lesbos (Sappho frr. 140, 168 Lobel-Page), but two centuries later it had not received official recognition at Athens (for an Assembly meeting could be held during the festival: Ar. *Lys.* 389–97; Plut. *Nic.* 13.11, *Alc.* 8.5), and there is no good evidence that it ever did. The distinctive rite of the festival was the planting of 'Adonis-gardens' in pots which were taken up to the house-roof (45n.). Almost all our evidence (see especially the Plutarch passages just cited and Pl. *Phdr.* 276b, where note ἑορτῆς χάριν) indicates that the Adonia was held in high summer (see Weill 1966), as in the Semitic lands whence it had come to Greece (and where the Babylonian month usually corresponding to June/July bore Adonis' Semitic name of Dumuzi or Tammuz); Ar. *Lys.* 389–97 does not prove otherwise (see Sommerstein 1990: 173), nor (*pace* Dillon 2002: 168) does Thphr. *HP* 6.7.3 or *CP* 1.12.2 imply that Adonis-gardens were sown in spring. Thus the return home of Demeas and Nikeratos, and the action of our play, which must come some ten months after this fateful Adonia, will be taking place in the spring, soon after the opening of the sailing season (which began at the time of the City Dionysia – though only a bore would bother to say so: Thphr. *Char.* 3.3). See further Weill 1970; Detienne 1972; Winkler 1990: 189–93; Dillon 2002: 162–9; 2003; Parker 2005: 283–8.

38 ἐξ ἀγροῦ: Demeas, then, owns a house and land in the countryside as well as his town house, like (for example) Kallippides in *Dyskolos* or Euphiletus, the speaker of Lysias 1 (Lys. 1.11, 20), and in his absence Moschion will have to go there from time to time to look after the farm.   **δή** 'well then', 'mark[ing] a new stage in a narrative' (Denniston 1954: 238). **καταδραμών:** why was Moschion in a hurry? Since, according to his story, he only became a spectator of the women's celebration because their noise was keeping him awake (43–4), we are probably to understand that the celebration began in the evening (and was intended to continue all night, 46); and since, when Moschion arrived home, he found the women already assembled there (40), the simplest explanation for his haste is that he was anxious to get home before it was too dark (e.g. to avoid robbers; cf. Ar. *Birds* 493–8; 1490–3, Antiphon 2.2.5). Possibly this was made a little clearer by the lost opening word or two of 39 (see below); but it is at least as likely that the audience were assumed to know that women's Adonia parties normally began around nightfall.

39 The traces of what preceded γ' are highly ambiguous. Turner proposed [περυ]σινά, but (i) when the name of a festival is *qualified*, a definite article is required, and (ii) the departure of Demeas and Nikeratos for the Black Sea must have occurred no more than a year ago (since Chrysis must have given birth not long before Plangon did, 56n.), so the time-indication 'last year', if it was given at all, will have been attached to their departure, not to the Adonia. So far as sense is concerned, Sandbach's [ὡς ἔτυ]χ[ε] and Dedoussi's [ὑπὸ νύ]κτα would both be satisfactory; in both cases γ' would lay a mild stress on, and draw attention to, the point Moschion is making – with Dedoussi's restoration, that he arrived home unusually late; with Sandbach's, that it was only by chance that he found himself in the house with a large group of women (evidently he did not know they were going to be holding an Adonia party, otherwise he might have decided to go to a friend's house for the night).   **εἰς Ἀδώνι'** is to be taken with συνηγμένας.

40 πρὸς ἡμᾶς 'at our house' (33n.).

41 ἑορτῆς: this word is never aspirated in Attic inscriptions (Threatte 1980–96: I 500–1).   **παιδιάν:** cf. *Epitr.* 478 in another festival rape narrative.

43 οἴμοι: once again (cf. 23n.) a correction in an ancestor (quite likely the immediate exemplar) of B appears to have been inserted a line too early, so that in 42 the scribe of B initially wrote οιχουσης instead of εχουσης. For οἴμοι in late Middle and New Comedy cf. Timocles frr. 11.5 (parenthetical, as here) and 10; Philemon fr. 6. Moschion bitterly regrets his decision to become a 'spectator' of the Adonia revelry, which (as he leaves us to infer for ourselves) led to his viewing Plangon in circumstances which aroused desires that he found himself unable to control, and so was the cause of all his present troubles and anxieties. The rival conjectures are unsatisfactory: οἶμαι, θεατής (Photiadis) makes Moschion, absurdly, unsure whether he was a spectator of the celebrations or not; Sandbach's ingenious suggestion οἴμ', ἐνθεαστής ('possessed') might be an attempt on Moschion's part to extenuate his guilt, but this would come too early in his narrative and would not be explained (γάρ 44) by his statement that he could not sleep.

43-4 ἀγρυπνίαν|... τινα: had he hoped to go to bed early, tired by the long walk home from the countryside (cf. Lys. 1.13)?

44 γάρ is often placed late, even (as here) after non-cohering words, in Middle and New Comedy (Denniston 1954: 97; Dover 1985: 338-41 = 1987: 61-4, who calls this 'a quite distinctive artificial feature of comedy'); cf. *Aspis* 138-9, *Dysk.* 692-3, *Perinth.* 13-14, frr. 17, 64.5-6.

45 κήπους: these 'gardens of Adonis' were pots, or fragments of pots, sown with fast-growing seeds (fennel and lettuce, according to Hesychius α 1231); the women carried them up to the roof and there sang laments for Adonis (cf. Ar. *Lys.* 392-6); cf. Parker 2005: 285 fig. 15 (Karlsruhe, Badische Landesmuseum B39 = *LIMC* Adonis 47), where, significantly, the 'garden' is being handed to a rather scantily clad woman by a winged Eros. After the festival the 'gardens' withered quickly and were thrown away into springs, so that 'more barren than an Adonis-garden' became a proverb (Zenobius 1.49).

46 [ὠρχο]ῦντ': dancing was part of the ritual (Ar. *Lys.* 392), but we are doubtless also meant to imagine that the women engaged in informal group-dances as part of their παιδιά: dancing features in rape narratives in *Epitr.* 1120 and *Phasma* 95 = 195.   **ἐπαννύχιζον:** all-night revels by women alone appear to have been a common and accepted phenomenon both at religious festivals and in connection with other kinds of celebration such as a betrothal feast (*Dysk.* 857) or a wedding (Poseidippus fr. 28.19-23).   **ἐσκεδασμέναι:** so that at one moment Plangon was alone; this element too is found in another comic rape narrative (*Epitr.* 486-7, 1120).

47 ἴσως: there is no 'perhaps' about Moschion's feeling ashamed, as his preceding and following sentences show; what he is uncertain about is whether feeling ashamed is οὐδὲν ὄφελος.   **αἰσχύνομαι:** Moschion, who had encouraged Demeas to overcome his shame over his passion for Chrysis (23-7) and who, as we shall soon hear, took the initiative in making what was considered appropriate atonement for his crime (50-3), cannot bring himself to confess that crime in so many words even to the uninvolved theatre audience, let alone to his father (cf. 65-9). On the importance of the theme of αἰδώς in this play, and its echoes of Euripides (especially *Hippolytus*), see Introduction §6 and Jäkel 1982.

48 [οἷς]: for αἰσχύνομαι with a causal dative cf. Ar. *Clouds* 992, Dem. 4.42. There is little to choose between [οἷς] and [ἵν'] (Ferrari 1998) 'where, in circumstances in which'.   **οὐδὲν ὄφελος** (sc. αἰσχύνεσθαι) 'no benefit' (*Theoph.* F 1.15; fr. 690), not 'no need' (Arnott), which would seem insensitive and out of character.   **ἀλλ'** (B above the line) or ἐσθ' (ἐστ' B in text)? B's failure to aspirate ἐστ' before ὅμως suggests that its exemplar had ἐστ' ἀλλ' in its text. Neither word is indispensable, but ἐστ' is the more open to suspicion of being interpolated: elsewhere (see above) Menander does not use ἐστι with ὄφελος.

49 τοῦτο…φράσας 'by saying that'; if the present participle φράζων had been used, the meaning would have been something like 'in the process of saying that'.

50 πρᾶξιν: πράττω and its derivatives are often used euphemistically to refer to sexual activity, e.g. *Dysk.* 292, Eur. *Hipp.* 1004, Aeschines 1.132, 158, Theocr. 2.143.

50–1 οὐκ ἠρνησάμην | [τὴν] αἰτίαν σχών: most likely 'I didn't wait to be accused and then deny the charge' (so in effect Lamagna; for αἰτίαν ἔχειν 'be accused' cf. Aesch. *Eum.* 99, Pl. *Apol.* 38c), though a grammatically possible alternative is 'Having incurred the responsibility, I didn't deny it' (so Sandbach; for this sense of αἰτίαν ἔχειν cf. *Ant.* 1312, Aesch. *Eum.* 579). The choice between these interpretations depends upon whether it would be reasonable for Moschion to expect that suspicion would focus on him. It probably would. In a typical case of nocturnal rape in New Comedy, such as that of Pamphile in *Epitrepontes*, neither the victim nor anyone else present would have been able to identify the attacker. Here, however, the rape took place at or very close to Moschion's home, and he would have been the only free male known to have been on the scene. His swift confession may thus be perceived less as a noble acceptance of the consequences of his action than as a move to pre-empt (cf. πρότερος) an accusation that was bound to come; what is more, we know (29/30n.) that the marriage which he now pledges himself to make was one for which he was in any case longing. Aeschinus in Terence's *Adelphoe* (471–3) made a similar confession and a similar sworn promise to the mother of the girl he had raped, but did nothing about fulfilling it because, although (unlike Demeas) his father was at home, Aeschinus (like Moschion) was afraid and ashamed to speak to him about the matter (*Ad.* 690).

51 πρότερος 'I took the initiative and…'　　**ἐνέτυχον:** the meaning of ἐντυγχάνω developed from 'meet by chance' to simply 'meet' (Pl. *Apol.* 41b, *Phd.* 61c) and then 'talk to' (*Dysk.* 751, *Perik.* 302).

52 [τῆι] μητρὶ τῆς κόρης: see 36n.　　**ὑπεσχόμην γαμεῖν:** throughout New Comedy it is assumed that the rape of an unmarried woman is completely atoned for by an offer to marry her (Omitowoju 2002: 184, 205; E. M. Harris 2006: 299–305, 320–31); see Introduction §5.

53 A line with multiple textual problems. Two things are fairly certain. (1) ὁ πατήρ is Plangon's father (who alone has the legal right to give her in

marriage), not Moschion's adoptive father (who would not be a party to
the marriage contract at all). (2) Moschion will have promised to marry
Plangon *when* her father returned, not *if* he returned – firstly because
he was not, and would not wish to appear to be, a reluctant bridegroom
looking for a get-out clause; secondly because it would distress his future
mother-in-law if he raised by implication the possibility that her husband
might never return; and thirdly because if he said 'if' it would raise in
spectators' minds the distracting and irrelevant issue of Plangon's possibly becoming an *epikleros* (like Kleostratos' sister in *Aspis*) on her father's
presumed death, obliged to marry the nearest relative who claimed her.
Hence the clause about Nikeratos' return must be introduced not by ἄν
but by ἐπάν. Of proposals so far made along these lines the best is [καὶ
ν]ῦν, ἐπὰν ἔλθῃ ποθ' ὁ πατήρ (Handley), which would require us to assume,
probably rightly (20n.), that we already know that Moschion is expecting
Demeas and Nikeratos to arrive home very soon: Moschion first says he
promised to marry Plangon 'right now' and then clarifies his meaning by
adding 'when her father eventually (ποτε) comes' (Arnott 1998a: 38–9).
Restorations involving [σ]υνεπανέλθῃ (Sandbach), giving the approximate
sense 'when her father comes home with <mine>', are considerably less
satisfactory, since Demeas has not been mentioned for over twenty lines.
ὤμοσα: Parmenon will remind Moschion of this oath at 74, and he himself,
at 624, will name it as the first of many reasons why he cannot abandon
Plangon and go abroad as a mercenary. It is one of only two occasions in
Menander (both events in the dramatic past) when a person reinforces
with a solemn oath a promise made to another person (the oath in Men.
fr. 239 is not a promise but a threat); the other is *Perik.* 791, where again
the promise was made to a woman.

54 [τὸ π]αιδίον: we are not for the present told the baby's gender; but in
New Comedy children born in circumstances like these are always male.
This will be confirmed at 132 (if not earlier in one of the lost passages).
εἴληφ': understand εἰς τὴν οἰκίαν (28n.): cf. 649–50 τὸ παιδάριον εἰσῆλθεν
εἰς τὴν οἰκίαν | τὴν ἡμετέραν· ἤνεγκ' ἐκεῖνος (sc. Moschion). The full phrase
appears in Men. fr. 315.3 and Strato fr. 1.1–2. It is not, in the surviving
text, explained why Moschion took this action and thereby created problems about how to feed the baby. Treu 1969: 237 (see also S. R. West
1991: 13–14) observed that, given the character of Nikeratos as we see
it later, there would have been good grounds to fear dangerous violence
if he came home – as he might at any time, now it was spring (38–50n.) –
and discovered what had happened; if this was the reason for the decision
to move the baby, it will probably have been made clearer in lost sections
of the prologue, with Moschion saying something about Nikeratos' character in the last lacuna (29/30n.) and something about the family's fears
in the next one.

55–6 What was the fortuitous event that occurred at this point? There can be little doubt that the early editors were right in supposing that Chrysis had also given birth (perhaps a month or two before Plangon, since her child must have been conceived before Demeas' departure) and that her baby had died, thus enabling her both to suckle Plangon's baby (78, 265–6) and to pass it off temporarily as her own (79). Dedoussi 1970 objected that if Chrysis had been able to breast-feed the baby, Plangon would not later have had to take the risk of being seen by her father doing so (535–43); that is indeed an illogicality, but unlikely to be noticed amid all the hurly-burly of the latter part of Act IV. What is more, if Chrysis had *not* been able to breast-feed, the whole deception could not have worked: as S. R. West 1991: 11–12 pertinently asks, how otherwise could the baby have been fed at night, when Plangon could not visit it? And if the fortuitous event was not the birth and/or the death of Chrysis' baby, what was it? It cannot have been simply the presence of Chrysis in Moschion's house (as Dedoussi supposes), since she had been there for at least a year. For the motif of a mother whose baby dies and who then rears someone else's child as her own, cf. *Epitr.* 265–9, Hdt. 1.112–13 (Cyrus).

55 ταὐτομάτου: ταὐτόματον in Menander is almost a synonym of τύχη (163, *Epitr.* 1108, *Perik.* 151, Men. fr. 376 (cf. fr. 372.2–6)), and the equivalence is made explicit in Philemon fr. 125. On the importance of τύχη in this play see Jäkel 1982: 24–6, who points particularly to 228–36: Demeas overheard the careless talk of Moschion's old nurse because he 'happened' to have gone into the store-room in search of something needed for the wedding preparations (229), and because the steps to the upper floor, from which the old woman descended, led into a room which 'happened' to be immediately adjacent to the store-room (234–6).

56 [εὔκαιρο]ν 'opportune', cf. *Dysk.* 668 where an equally self-centred Sostratos speaks thus of the near-drowning of Knemon. That no one (so far as we know) expresses sympathy for Chrysis over the loss of her baby is not too surprising – it would have had to be exposed anyway; but we are probably meant to notice that Moschion sees the event only as something that can be turned to his advantage.   **Χρυσίς:** see 1–57n.

57/8 In this lacuna (probably of some 26–7 lines) Moschion must have explained the scheme whereby Chrysis was to suckle the baby and pretend it was hers – though Plangon will probably have continued to visit the house fairly regularly (with her mother, naturally, as before) and on those occasions given the baby a feed herself. We may or may not have been told whose idea the scheme was. It can hardly have been Moschion's, as he would not have had 'the ingenuity . . . or the courage' to conceive or implement it (Lloyd-Jones 1972: 128); and Parmenon is at any rate able to convince himself that the whole business had nothing to do with him

(644–54). S. R. West 1991 is probably right to hold that the idea was Chrysis' own (see also Krieter-Spiro 1997: 99–100). It is she who will shortly insist that the ruse must be carried on (84–5), and the same passage gives her a clear motive (pity for the baby) for embarking on this risky scheme; the strength of character which this implies will be displayed again in Act IV (556–61) when, at peril of her own life, she takes the lead in protecting the child from Nikeratos' rage.

When the text resumes, Chrysis is on stage, and sees Moschion and Parmenon approaching. Parmenon has come, evidently from the harbour, with news of the arrival of Demeas and Nikeratos, and has met Moschion on the way, for they enter in mid-conversation. Thus Moschion must have decided to go to the harbour and see for himself whether his father had returned – having no doubt become impatient with Parmenon's long absence. It is not clear whether Chrysis' entry immediately followed Moschion's exit, or whether she entered while he was still on stage and exchanged a few words with him. Lamagna, favouring the latter view, argues that a sequence of two monologues might risk losing the audience's attention; but there are other instances of a prologue speech being followed by another (shortish) monologue (*Aspis* 97–163, *Perik.* 121–80), and Chrysis would hardly need to eavesdrop on Moschion's conversation with Parmenon (as she does in 60–9) if she had herself been talking with Moschion only a few minutes before.

It is not certain whether Chrysis has the baby with her in this scene, as she almost always does subsequently (see Introduction §4(*b*)). Probably she should, since she is posing as its mother; οὕτως (78) and τοῦτο (85) give a measure of support to this view. The 'baby' will have been a doll (Arnott 2001: 82), since real babies cannot be relied upon to remain silent. The baby may have provided a motive for Chrysis to come out of doors; cf. *Epitr.* 853–4 where a baby has been crying persistently and Habrotonon brings it outside in the hope of soothing it.

We cannot tell what Chrysis said while she was alone on stage, but she could well have spoken about her affection for the baby (cf. 84–5) and her concern for Plangon; this would have made a sharp contrast with the self-centred speech of Moschion. Another possibility is raised by the proposal of Gaiser 1976: 100–1 n.2 to find a place in this lacuna for F 1; he supposes that Chrysis came out with a female servant (named in the fragment as Tryphe) to make an offering and prayer for Demeas' safe return (see note on F 1 at end of commentary).

59 πρός ἡμᾶς: 33n.

60 ἀ[κούσομαι] (for which cf. *Mis.* 283 S = 684 A) is preferable to ἀ[κροάσομαι], since the simple verb ἀκροάομαι is not attested in Menander, only the compound ἐπακροάομαι (*Epitr.* 938) and the derivative ἀκροατής (*Kith.* F 6).

Chrysis withdraws to a spot where Moschion and Parmenon are not likely to notice her. She has no very obvious reason for eavesdropping on their conversation rather than asking immediately after their news, but from the dramatist's point of view this device makes possible the revealing exchange between Parmenon and his young master in 63–9.

61 Moschion and Parmenon enter from the direction of the harbour (Eisodos A), ostensibly in mid-conversation, like Demeas and Nikeratos (96), Parmenon and the Cook (283), Demeas and Chrysis (369), and various pairs of characters in other Menandrian plays, e.g. Smikrines and Chairestratos, *Aspis* 250; Myrrhine and Philinna, *Georgos* 22; Chaireas and Sostratos, *Dysk.* 50; Daos and Syriskos, *Epitr.* Act II fr. nov. (Furley 2009: 38). Almost always, as here, the initial exchanges are so framed as to make it very rapidly clear to the audience what is being talked about (see Frost 1988: 10–11). Here, evidently, we are to suppose that on his way to the harbour Moschion has encountered Parmenon hurrying back to the house with news of the arrival of Demeas and Nikeratos. In his first questions (or the first that we hear) Moschion is trying to make sure that Parmenon's news is not a mere second-hand report – even though Parmenon has apparently already told him (62 οὔκουν ἀκούεις;) that he has seen with his own eyes that Demeas has arrived.

62 οὔκουν in a 'surprised or indignant question' (Denniston 1954: 432); cf. 369 (where again the speaker is evidently repeating something he has already said), Ar. *Clouds* 1377 (angry that his father should resent being beaten up for disparaging Euripides), *Wealth* 257 (the chorus angry at being told to hurry when they are already coming as fast as they can). φημί 'yes' (*Epitr.* 361, *Fab. Inc.* 31; Ar. *Frogs* 1205, *Wealth* 395; frequent in Plato, who uses it 20 times in *Gorgias* alone).

63 πάρεισιν 'they're here' (from εἰμί), not 'he's coming' (from εἶμι), as is shown by Moschion's reply (in the third person plural). Parmenon suspects from Moschion's repeated questions that he is not quite prepared to accept that Demeas and Nikeratos really have arrived – and, as his own next words show, he has guessed the reason why. So instead of answering Moschion's question about Nikeratos, he condenses his whole message, already delivered, into a single word and reiterates it, in the hope that it will at last get through to Moschion.   εὖ γ' ἐπόησαν: expressing pleasure at the news, cf. *Dysk.* 629 (referring to Knemon's fall into the well), Eur. *Med.* 472, *IA* 642. The pleasure, as we soon find, is more conventional than heartfelt: the return of the two travellers means that Moschion's long-delayed marriage is at last imminent – but only if he can pluck up courage to confess the truth to his father, a prospect that in fact terrifies him. ὅπως ἔσει 'make sure you are' (Goodwin 1912: 94–5); one of only two preserved instances in Menander (the other is *Epitr.* 1110–11) of a construction very common in Aristophanes (e.g. *Ach.* 253, 741, 746). This particular phrase functions in comedy virtually as a periphrastic imperative of εἰμί. The true imperative of this verb, ἴσθι, occurs fairly freely in Aeschylus (*Seven* 238, *Ag.* 512, *Cho.* 147, *Eum.* 91), but soon afterwards it was squeezed out by its more frequent (and morphologically more transparent) homonym, the imperative of οἶδα; in Sophocles and Euripides ἴσθι 'be' is confined to the single phrase εὔφημος ἴσθι (Soph. fr. 478; Eur. *Hipp.* 724, *Or.* 1327) and in comedy, though not (as Sandbach supposed) entirely absent, it appears only at Eupolis fr. 341 (two separate passages) and Ar. *Knights* 860.

64 ἀνδρεῖος: Moschion has said that his father made him an ἄνθρωπος (17); but does he deserve to be considered an ἀνήρ? Within five lines Parmenon will be taunting him as ἀνδρόγυνε (69). The question of what it means to 'be a (real) man' will be a recurring one in the play; all the principal male characters, at one time or another, will behave as though 'being a man' meant acting drastically on impulse without consideration – Demeas at 349–53 (expelling Chrysis from his home), Nikeratos at 508–13 (selling her as a slave and disowning Moschion as a son), Moschion himself at 630–1 (going abroad as a mercenary, to punish Demeas for wrongly suspecting him). The slave Parmenon arguably has a better understanding of 'manliness' than any of them – though he still runs away to avoid a flogging (324), for which he, like Moschion at 65, will later brand himself a coward (654). The tone he adopts towards his master in this scene suggests that he is considerably the older man of the two; it has been suggested (Krieter-Spiro 1997: 15) that we are meant to suppose that he had been Moschion's παιδαγωγός (cf. *Aspis* 14).

65 τίνα τρόπον; is probably to be taken as a despairing rhetorical question (in effect meaning 'I can't, no way'). We may momentarily suppose that Moschion is asking Parmenon for advice, as if he were a *servus callidus* like Daos in *Aspis* (compare Sostratos' misplaced confidence in Getas at *Dysk.* 181–5); in fact, so far as we know, Parmenon neither takes nor suggests any useful initiative throughout the play.   δειλός 'cowardly' is the regular antonym of ἀνδρεῖος, and not an epithet that people often apply to themselves (δειλία was, after all, a legal crime punishable by loss of citizen rights: Andoc. 1.74, Lys. 14.5–9, Aeschines 3.175–6; see Carey 1989: 143–4). There appears, indeed, to be no other case, in comedy or tragedy, of a free male calling himself δειλός, unless Eur. fr. 854 (τὸ μὲν σφαγῆναι δεινόν ... τὸ μὴ θανεῖν δὲ δειλόν) is spoken by Phrixus (the only known male to have been designated as a human sacrifice in a non-extant Euripidean drama); in comedy no other character of any gender or status applies this

epithet to himself except Parmenon later in this play (654). As a well educated young man, Moschion must know how disgraceful δειλία was considered to be; if he is prepared to admit to it, he must be very afraid indeed.

66 ὡς πλησίον τὸ πρᾶγμα γέγονε = ὅτι οὕτω πλησίον τὸ πρᾶγμα γέγονε
'because the thing has come so close at hand'; cf. Pl. *Crito* 43b ηὐδαιμόνισα
(σε) τοῦ τρόπου... ἐν τῆι νῦν παρεστώσηι συμφόραι, ὡς ῥαιδίως αὐτὴν καὶ
πράιως φέρεις ('that you take it so easily and gently'), *Phd.* 58e.

67 αἰσχύνομαι τὸν πατέρα 'I am ashamed to face my father': see 47n.

67–8 τὴν δὲ παρθένον | ... τήν τε ταύτης μητέρα; With this punctuation (see
69n. for other possibilities) we must understand αἰσχύνει: 'and what about
the girl you've wronged, and her mother – are you ashamed to face *them*?'
By confessing to his father, Moschion will be violating Demeas' reasonable
and confident expectation that he would behave κοσμίως and eventually
make a socioeconomically appropriate marriage; by failing to do so, he
would be violating a sworn promise to Plangon and her mother (as Parmenon makes explicit at 73–4) and failing in his duty to his child (contrast
Chrysis' devotion to a child not hers, 84–5). Parmenon is right to imply
that between these alternatives only one choice is morally possible.

68 ἠδίκηκας: 3n.

69 ὅπως: if sound, this must be the beginning of a sentence or clause
which Parmenon never completes, breaking off (an *aposiopesis*) on perceiving that Moschion is trembling; had he continued, ὅπως would have
been followed by a future indicative (e.g. μὴ προδώσεις) in a strongly imperative sense (63n.). It is perhaps best to make this interrupted sentence
grammatically independent by punctuating at the end of 68; the alternative (Sandbach, Casanova 2007b: 11–12) is to treat 'the girl and her
mother' as the object of the verb that would have followed ὅπως – a structure which might well be hard for a listener to understand, given that the
verb itself is never heard. Several emendations have been proposed (see
apparatus), but none is free from difficulty. Against the proposal of Del
Corno (1975: 756), note that ὤ is not found in Menander (or indeed any-
where in drama) introducing a question; against that of Arnott (1998a:
40), that a Moschion who remained unmoved at the thought of betraying Plangon and her mother would have been not so much ἀνδρόγυνος as
ἀναιδής or ἀναίσθητος; against those of Gronewald 1997 and of Lamagna,
that sentence-final οὖ is never elsewhere in Menander enjambed on its
own at the start of a line.   **τρέμεις:** here, as Chrysis' reaction shows, Parmenon suddenly raises his voice, in anger or contempt. Two characters in
Menander speak of *themselves* as 'trembling' – Thrasonides (*Mis.* 266 S =

667 A) at the prospect of meeting for the first time the father of the girl whom he loves and who hates him, Glykera (*Perik.* 805) when her newly rediscovered father is about to explain why he exposed her in infancy. **ἀνδρόγυνε:** Moschion has failed the test of being ἀνδρεῖος (64). The epithet ἀνδρόγυνος likewise implies 'coward' (and is likewise contrasted with ἀνδρεῖος) on its only other known occurrence in the text of Menander, *Aspis* 242 (cf. 244), where the Thracian τραπεζοποιός absurdly applies it to Daos, who has brought his (supposedly dead) master's booty home from Lycia instead of absconding with it. Similarly in the late fifth century Ἀνδρόγυνοι was an alternative title for Eupolis' Ἀστράτευτοι (Storey 2003: 74–81), in which reference was made to the alleged cowardice of Peisander (Eupolis fr. 35); and in the comic myth on the origin of sexual orientations told by 'Aristophanes' in Pl. *Symp.* 189c-193d, the ἀνδρόγυνοι (189e, 191d), ancestors of heterosexuals, are contrasted with the pure males whose homosexual descendants are ἀνδρειότατοι ... φύσει (192a). Nothing is known of the title character of Menander's Ἀνδρόγυνος ἢ Κρής (we do not even know whether the two titles referred to the same person).   **τί βοᾶις, δύσμορε;** is to be taken as a rebuke, not (despite Parmenon's response) as a request for information, since Chrysis can infer from the conversation, at least as easily as the audience can, what has aroused Parmenon's indignation. As a form of address in Menander, δύσμορε is used exclusively by women (255, *Epitr.* 468; see Bain 1984: 36), and seems always to convey reproof (though at 370 Chrysis calls herself δύσμορος in self-pity); in Old Comedy and in fifth-century tragedy (especially Sophocles) the adjective had been used by men and women alike, always to convey pity and/or grief (e.g. Aesch. *Seven* 837; Soph. *Aj.* 923, *OC* 557, 1109; Eur. *Med.* 1218, *Tro.* 793; Ar. *Birds* 7; at Soph. *OC* 804 Creon is *pretending* to pity Oedipus, cf. 740, 744–7).

70–1 Parmenon turns and notices Chrysis, who now comes forward to join him and Moschion.

70 ἦν: imperfect referring to a state of affairs which has existed for some time, though the speaker has only now become aware of it (Goodwin 1912: 12–13). In earlier Greek this use of the imperfect was usually associated with the particle ἄρα (Denniston 1954: 36–7), but cf. Ar. *Birds* 1048 (ἔτι γὰρ ἐνταῦθ' ἦσθα σύ;), 1051, Eur. *Ion* 184–7. The usage seen here, when one character notices the onstage presence of another, seems to have been semi-formulaic in New Comedy; there are no other Greek examples, but cf. Ter. *Phorm.* 857–8 *oh tu quoque aderas, Phormio?*, *Ad.* 901 *ehem, pater mi, tu hic eras?* See Bain 1977: 160–1.

70–1 ἐρωτᾶις | ... τί βοῶ; The sentence is best taken as a question, with the slightly indignant tone often conveyed by δή with pronouns, 'particularly in the case of σύ (especially in questions)' (Denniston 1954: 207–8), cf. Eur. *Hipp.* 948–9, *Andr.* 324–5. For the idiom of echoing a direct question with an indirect question (or equivalent) governed by ἐρωτᾶις; cf. 481–2 (the same question!), Crobylus fr. 5, Ar. *Ach.* 288, *Lys.* 493, Xen. *Cyr.* 1.6.10, Pl. *Phdr.* 258e.

71 γελοῖον 'that's ridiculous' constitutes a complete sentence, as here, at 579, 654, *Georg.* F 4, and (πάνυ γ.) *Fab. Inc.* 53.

72–3 πεπαῦσθαι 'to be finished with'. The subject is τουτονί = Moschion.

73–4 πρὸς ταῖς θύραις | κλάοντα evokes the notion of the παρακλαυσίθυρον (on which see Copley 1956, especially 1–27). That *term* is not attested in Greek until much later (Plut. *Mor.* 753a), but the idea of the weeping or singing lover haunting his beloved's door day and night was already a cliché (Ar. *Eccl.* 959–63, Eur. *Cycl.* 502, Pl. *Symp.* 183a, 203d and perhaps already Alcaeus fr. 374 Lobel-Page). In the present case, however, Moschion is being kept outside Plangon's door only by his own fear and embarrassment vis-à-vis his father. At the beginning of *Misoumenos* we are presented with the paradox of a rejected lover (Thrasonides) pacing about in distress outside *his own* door.

73–4 ἐκεῖν' ἀμνημονεῖν | ὧν ὤμοσεν: cf. 53. Like other verbs of remembering and forgetting, ἀμνημονεῖν can take either a genitive (e.g. Eur. *IT* 361, Thuc. 3.40.7, Isoc. 12.253, Aeschines 1.72) or an accusative (Thuc. 5.18.1, Dem. 6.12, [Dem.] 7.19, Aeschines 3.221). Here the verb governs an accusative, but the relative pronoun introducing the following clause is 'attracted' into the genitive as if ἐκείνων had preceded.

74–5 Moschion's oath was simply to marry Plangon as soon as her father returned; Parmenon mentions three specific ritual or customary actions forming part of the wedding preparations or celebrations. That at least two of these are connected with food does not necessarily show that Parmenon's primary interest in the wedding is as an occasion for feasting (as Sandbach and Lamagna suppose); Moschion himself, when daydreaming about the wedding a little later (122–6), refers to a sacrifice, a dinner and sesame-cake. The three actions are mentioned in no particular order: one would put a garland on one's head before performing a sacrifice (Eur. *El.* 778, Aeschines 3.77; see Burkert 1985: 56) and when the wedding eventually takes place garlands are distributed to all present at the outset (731).

74 θύειν probably refers to the sacrifice from which would come the meat for the wedding feast; note the close connection at 123 between ἔθυον and the inviting of friends to dinner. Arnott 1998a: 40–1 takes the reference to be to the προτέλεια, but that sacrifice was a matter purely for the bride's family (713, Eur. *IA* 733; see Oakley and Sinos 1993: 11–12, Parker 2005: 440–1).

74–5 σησαμῆν | κόπτειν: the σησαμῆ, a spherical cake made of honey, oil and crushed sesame seeds (Athenaeus 14.646f), was regularly eaten at weddings, doubtless (schol. Ar. *Peace* 869) because the many seeds served as a symbol of fecundity; see Oakley and Sinos 1993: 23. According to Photius s.v. σήσαμον it had at one time been customary to take or send it round to friends (as was done with portions of sacrificial meat, 403–4n., and as is sometimes done today with portions of wedding cake), whereas in his own time (or that of his source) it was served (only) at the wedding feast itself; but Photius' source may well have misunderstood a passage like 124–5 περιπατῶν τὴν σησαμῆν διένεμον, which may refer simply to taking the cakes round to the diners at the feast.

75 κόπτειν doubtless refers to the process of crushing the seeds into a paste which was then, with the addition of honey and oil, shaped (ξυμπλάτ-τεται, Ar. *Peace* 869) into cakes. It is neither attested nor likely that the bridegroom was expected to take part personally in the preparation of this delicacy; but Parmenon wants everything to happen as quickly as possible (ἤδη 72) and wants Moschion to be as eager as he is to hurry things on. In reality it would be wholly improper for the wedding preparations to be started before Nikeratos had agreed to his daughter's marriage.   **παρελθὼν αὐτός** 'going inside himself': nominative, despite τουτονί, because everything that follows ὤμοσεν is being treated as though it were governed by that verb. When used in this sense παρελθεῖν is usually accompanied by εἴσω or something equivalent (e.g. *Aspis* 95, *Perik.* 349; Ar. *Clouds* 853), but cf. Eur. *HF* 599. In itself the wording of this phrase leaves it unclear whether Moschion is being urged to enter his own house or that of Nikeratos (though in performance this could be clarified by gesture); but the contrast with πρὸς ταῖς θύραις | κλάοντα ταύταις strongly suggests that Nikeratos' house is meant. B actually punctuates after παρελθών, and Sandbach accordingly takes αὐτός to be the first word of the following sentence, in which case it would refer to Parmenon; but that would imply an irrelevant contrast between Parmenon and some other person who would have even more justification for shouting at Moschion. Kamerbeek 1972: 381–2 construed παρελθὼν αὐτός with ὤμοσεν, taking it to refer to Moschion's visit to Plangon's mother (51–3) when he swore to marry her; but then αὐτός would again have little point – one could not swear an oath by proxy, and it would be foolish to send a slave to make an offer of marriage (cf. *Dysk.* 70–7) – and in any case it is doubtful whether a listener (as opposed to a reader) would be able to understand the sentence in this way.

75–6 ἱκανάς...| προφάσεις: sc. τοῦ βοᾶν.

76–7 τί δεῖ | λέγειν; 'Why need I say?', i.e. 'that goes without saying', cf. Eur. *Andr.* 920. This and other parallels (e.g. Aesch. *Ag.* 598, *Eum.* 826; Plat. *Symp.* 217c) show that in this idiom the subject of λέγειν is με (hence not 'why must you preach?' [Arnott]).

77 ἐγὼ μὲν οἴομαι: Chrysis perceives how deeply Moschion is in love with Plangon (cf. 81–2) and is confident he will do whatever is necessary to ensure that he marries her. μέν is *solitarium* (Denniston 1954: 380–2), implying 'whatever others may think'.

77–9 'And the baby – are we to let her [Chrysis] look after it, just as she's doing now, and pretend she's its mother?' This question has here been given to Parmenon rather than Moschion. Its attitude to the ruse is non-committal but with a slight bias in its favour, underplaying the new and risky feature – the deception of the two fathers (see below on οὕτως ἐῶμεν ὡς ἔχει) – which has Moschion worried enough (80) to require consider-able reassurance, and some impassioned eloquence (84–85), from Chry-sis. The fact that the speaker refers to Chrysis in the third person (78 ταύτην) points the same way: Moschion would be more likely to address Chrysis directly, when she has just commented favourably on a remark of his.

In this edition it is assumed that the plan whereby Chrysis pretends to be the mother of the baby is only a temporary device, and that the audience will take it for granted – if indeed it was not made explicit in one of the lost passages, perhaps by Chrysis after 86 (Barigazzi 1970: 158) – that once Moschion and Plangon are married the true parentage of the baby will be revealed, in the confident expectation that the situation will then be accepted by its two grandfathers. The actual outcome shows that that expectation would have been justified. When Moschion confesses the truth (528–9), *before* being married, and confesses also to having con-cealed the facts from Demeas, Demeas tells Moschion that he has done no wrong (537); Nikeratos, as a father dishonoured by the violation of his daughter's virginity, is rather harder to persuade (585–613), but soon acquiesces. The view taken here has been that of most critics, but Sand-bach 1986 argued that the conspirators' plan is to pass the baby off *perma-nently* as the child of Demeas and Chrysis, pointing out *inter alia* that when in Act II Moschion finds his longed-for marriage presented to him on a plate, he does not take the opportunity to tell his father the truth about the baby. Sandbach is refuted by Dedoussi 1988, who argues (1) that Mos-chion's oath (53) to marry Plangon ('for the procreation of legitimate children', 727) can hardly be regarded as compatible in the letter, and certainly is incompatible in spirit, with an intention to begin that marriage by leaving their first child to be brought up as another man's bastard; (2) that there is no case in New Comedy of the acceptance of 'a child borne by a foreign *hetaira* to an Athenian citizen'; and (3) that Moschion's silence on the subject of the baby in Act II is necessary for the plot (one might add, more cogently, that it is thoroughly motivated by his character and the shame he feels about the whole matter (47–8, 67)). Throughout New Comedy it is taken for granted that a child born to an Athenian father and mother who are not at the time married (either to each other or to a third party) becomes legitimate if its parents subsequently marry (Ogden 1996: 125). To pass off such a child permanently as the child of a foreign *hetaira* would be to cheat him both of legitimacy and of citizenship, and a Moschion who was prepared to do this could not hope to win the respect of the audience and would not have deserved that of Demeas. We will learn, moreover (236–61), that everyone in Demeas' house is aware that Moschion is the baby's father; it would be worse than foolhardy to expect them all to be capable of keeping this secret in perpetuity. That the intention all along was eventually to declare the baby to be Moschion's and Plangon's child is further evidenced by the fact that Plangon was giving it some of its feeds (535–6); if she was in the end to be recognized as its mother, this would help maintain both her milk supply and the mother-child bond; if she was not, it was both unnecessary and cruel.

Both Sandbach and Dedoussi bind together this issue of whether Chrysis was to pose as the baby's mother temporarily or permanently with the issue of whether Chrysis had had and lost a baby of her own (55–6n.); in fact either answer to the first question is consistent with either answer to the second, and the view taken here agrees with Sandbach in holding that Chrysis had indeed given birth, and with Dedoussi in holding that she was caring for Plangon's baby, and pretending it was hers, only for the time being.

78 οὕτως ἐῶμεν ὡς ἔχει ought logically to govern only τρέφειν – but syntactically it governs αὐτὴν... φάσκειν τετοκέναι also, conveying the suggestion that for Chrysis to pretend the baby is hers is merely a continuation of the status quo. This is not the case. As we shall learn in Act III (242–54) – if we were not told it already in the lacuna at 57/58 – everyone in both households knows who the baby's real parents are, so Chrysis has not so far 'pretended to be its mother' at all, except perhaps (but we hear nothing of this) to outsiders. Now she will have to deceive her partner and protector – and 'admit', moreover, that she has disobeyed him (79n.) – while Moschion and Plangon, at least by silence, will have to be party to the deception of their fathers, normally a serious delinquency.   τρέφειν 'look after'. In relation to children, τρέφειν means in effect 'perform the function of a parent in child-rearing'. In most contexts this is equivalent to 'rear, bring up' (e.g. *Epitr.* 251, 469, 1117; *Perik.* 794, 800, 812), but here Chrysis is *in loco parentis* only on a temporary basis. Since the child is very young, τρέφειν will include breast-feeding, but the expression that specifically denotes breast-feeding in this play is διδόναι τιτθίον (266, 536).

79 τί δὴ γὰρ οὔ; 'Why ever not?', 'Of course!' Chrysis does not hesitate for a moment; it seems to her too obvious for words that the right thing to do is to continue acting as though the baby were her own. Moschion's response will indicate (if we have not been told this already) that this will annoy Demeas; probably the audience will be able to guess that he had given instructions that any child Chrysis might bear him should be exposed, not reared (130–6, 374, 410–11).

80 The line as transmitted is metrically incomplete, either one long or two short syllables having been lost between χαλεπανεῖ and πεπαύσεται. West's <τί δέ;> 'so what?' 'but what does that matter?' is the best supplement (cf. *Aspis* 376). It has the advantage over <σοι> (Sandbach) that it places the speaker-break at the penthemimeral caesura; elsewhere in the iambic trimeters of this play there are over twenty lines with a speaker-break at this point and only three (117, 374, 386) which have such a break at the end of the third foot.   χαλεπανεῖ is used absolutely, as at 491, 549, *Fab. Inc.* 48; at *Dysk.* 171, on the other hand, it governs a dative.   **πεπαύσεται** sc. χαλεπαίνων. But later Demeas will admonish himself πέπαυσ᾽ ἐρῶν (349).

81–3 Chrysis speaks confidently of the workings of ἔρως, on which she is of course an expert. In Act II it will at first appear that she is wrong, but before long Demeas' anger will subside, easily soothed by the persuasion of Moschion (137ff). When he discovers that Moschion is the baby's father, indignation does defeat ἔρως, though only after a hard struggle (49–350) and only in alliance with his love for his adopted son.

81 ὦ βέλτιστε: in Menander this is almost always used in addressing a superior. Slaves use it in speaking to strangers (*Aspis* 431, *Dysk.* 476, *Epitr.* 224, 308, 370; *Mis.* 229 S = 630 A) and occasionally to their masters (*Dysk.* 144), a poor young man in addressing a rich one (*Dysk.* 319, 338, 342), a younger brother to an elder (*Aspis* 251); it is a comic absurdity when the cook Sikon recommends that if one wants to borrow some utensil from a stranger's house, and a slave answers the door, one should flatter him by calling him βέλτιστε (*Dysk.* 496–7). Here, however, Chrysis seems to be using it in a manner more common in Plato and Xenophon, 'with slightly patronizing connotations' (Dickey 1996: 133; see generally ibid. 107–45) as one conscious of her superior knowledge. With one exception (Eubulus fr. 105) this is the only place in surviving comedy where βέλτιστε is used by a woman.   **κακῶς** 'desperately'. In *Dysk.* 53–4 Sostratos, whose passion is being treated by his friend Chaireas as matter for amusement, tells him κακῶς ἔχω 'I'm in a bad way'; the same phrase is used in a similar context by Dionysus in Ar. *Frogs* 58 in reference to his passion for Euripides (of which both he and Heracles are speaking in erotic terms). The underlying idea – that being in love is a sickness – also appears in *Mis.* 361 S = 762 A and *Perik.* 488–9 (cf. Ter. *Andr.* 309, *Heaut.* 100); it is a cliché in Euripides (e.g. Eur. *Hipp.* 38–40, 392–4; Ar. *Thesm.* 1116–18, in a parody of Euripides' *Andromeda*).

82–3 τοῦτο δ'...|...τὸν ὀργιλώτατον: cf. fr. 790 ὀργὴ φιλούντων ὀλίγον ἰσχύει χρόνον, Ter. *Andr.* 555 *amantium irae amoris integratiost.* We cannot tell whether the audience had already before 80 (perhaps in the missing section between 29 and 30) learned from Moschion about Demeas' irascible temperament. If they had not, they may for the time being take Chrysis' words merely as an implicit a fortiori argument ('since love can soothe even the angriest temper, it will certainly soothe the more moderate temper of a Demeas').

84–6 'I think I would sooner undergo absolutely anything than for this child [to be looked after by] a wet-nurse in some tenement block.' Chrysis expresses very strongly her affection for Moschion's and Plangon's baby and her determination to ensure that it shall be properly cared for. The surviving text offers no direct explanation of why she should show such devotion to the well-being of a child not hers, but Menander seems to assume that women in general have a natural fondness for young children; cf. 242–8, 253–4, 558–69, *Epitr.* 466–70, 856.

84 πρότερον...πάντ' ἂν ὑπομεῖναι δοκῶ: cf. *Epitr.* 401–2 ἀποσφαγείην πρότερον ἂν δήπουθεν ἢ | τούτωι τι καθυφείμην ('I'm sure I'd sooner have my throat cut than give in at all to this fellow').

85–6 Chrysis is thinking here of what would happen to the baby in the short term – until its parents were safely married – if she did not continue to care for it herself: it would have to be entrusted for the time being to some poor woman hired as a wet-nurse (cf. Dem. 57.35 and 42–5 on this 'lowly and slavelike' occupation), who might well neglect it. There was a stereotype of the τίτθη as negligent, greedy and bibulous (Men. fr. 412; Ar. *Knights* 716–18; Cratinus fr. 5; Pl. *Rep.* 343a), though this will have applied primarily to *hired* wet-nurses like the mother of Demosthenes' client; wet-nurses who were family slaves were often highly regarded and eventually set free (236–8, [Dem.] 47.55), and τίτθη (often τίτθη χρηστή) is by far the most common occupational designation in Athenian tomb-inscriptions commemorating women of no known citizenship or ethnicity (e.g. *IG* II² 10843, 11647, 12387, 12559). Our passage has generally (except by Dedoussi) been thought to relate to the *long-term* future of the baby, assumed to be 'already too old to be exposed' (Sandbach), if Demeas refuses to have it in his house; but the baby can hardly be more than a month old (38–50n.), and there is no reason to doubt that Demeas on his return could have ordered Chrysis to expose it forthwith (after all, but for Moschion's intercession in 134ff, he would have taken even more drastic action than that).

85 τοῦτο sc. τὸ παιδίον.   **συνοικίαι:** a residential building divided into several separate housing units (Aeschines 1.124), generally inhabited by poor people, including women living on their own (like the owner of the stolen cockerel in Ar. *Frogs* 1331–63, who appeals to her ξύνοικοι to witness to the theft, 1342), or by visiting foreigners ([Xen.] *Ath.Pol.* 1.17, Aeschines 1.43), or by prostitutes (Isaeus 6.19). Such buildings had a bad reputation (see Fisher 2001: 260–2); like their later equivalents, the *insulae* of Rome (Juvenal 3.197–202), they could be fire-traps and were doubtless often insanitary, a hazard to the health of all and particularly of infants.

86 An infinitive (τρέφειν or a synonym), to which τίτθην will have been subject and τοῦτο object, must have stood in this line (Pieters 1971: 97). The letter-traces, while very scanty, suggest that the infinitive was not the first word, pointing rather to something like ἔχουσ[αν] (Lamagna). In that case the next word must have begun with a vowel, but no solution readily suggests itself: Lamagna's [ἐκτρέφειν] would mean 'rear to maturity', which is not the scenario that is being imagined (85–6n.) and which, in any case, a τίτθη, as such, could not do.

86/7 When the text resumes, Moschion is alone. Chrysis and Parmenon will have gone back into the house, either together or separately: Chrysis is presumably in the house at 133, and Parmenon is certainly there at 189. Possibly Chrysis went inside first, and Parmenon then gave his master a second reminder (cf. 63–77) that he must now find the courage to face his father – who will be arriving any moment – and ask permission to marry Plangon. We have the last few lines of what may have been a fairly long monologue by Moschion in which he apparently considered, to little effect, how he could go about this task; as Dedoussi notes, this will have given time for the actors who had played Chrysis and Parmenon not only to change masks and costumes for the roles of Demeas and Nikeratos, but also to get from the *skene* to the distant wing from which they will enter.

88–9 It is not possible to establish, even approximately, what Moschion is saying here. The surviving (parts of) words are consistent with an imagined conversation between him and Demeas (cf. *Epitr.* 929–32) in which he says to his father 'I want [to marry our neighbour's daughter]' and Demeas curtly replies [οὐκ ἂν λά]βοις 'you can't marry her'; but they are consistent with many other possibilities also.

90 ἀθλιώτερον: ἄθλιος is a cliché word for distressed lovers in Menander (12n.). Moschion may well be saying something like 'Whom in the world could one imagine being more wretched than me?' (e.g. – partly following Barigazzi 1970: 159 – [ἐμοῦ τίν' ἂν λέγοις γ]ὰρ ἀθλιώτερον | [ἀνδρῶν ἁ]πάντων;).

91 οὐκ ἀπάγξομαι ταχύ; This is a prediction (idiomatic English 'won't I ...?'), not a deliberative question ('shan't I ...?'), since the latter would require a subjunctive (ἀπάγξωμαι), and hence the verb is more likely to mean 'choke' (with grief) than 'hang myself' (so too *Perik.* 505).

92 In view of what precedes and follows, this line is likely to have been a sentence on its own; if so, its lost beginning must have included a verb that governs a genitive and also a noun for φιλόφρονος to qualify, the two words together containing no more than nine or ten letters. Barigazzi's [δέω κριτοῦ] is the proposal that comes nearest meeting these criteria; it presupposes the existence of a proverb (not otherwise attested) 'A lone pleader needs a friendly judge', and makes Moschion say that he is in the position of that 'lone pleader' – and imply that he expects his 'judge', Demeas, to be far from friendly. Its weakness is that personal active forms of δέω 'lack, need' are rare in Attic (and unattested in Menander) except in the idiom πολλοῦ δέω 'I am very far from ...' and variants thereof. The middle form of the same verb is more common, but [δεῖται κριτοῦ] probably will not fit into the space available.   **ῥήτωρ:** not here 'habitual public speaker' or 'person with oratorical skills' (as in *Epitr.* 236), but simply 'person arguing a case'; cf. *com. adesp.* 947 ἀγροίκου μὴ καταφρόνει ῥήτορος.   **γάρ** placed late: 43-4n.

93 The word ending in]ότερος, whatever it is, cannot be a 'true' comparative, since there is no room in the line to specify what Moschion is comparing himself to; it must therefore bear the sense 'rather —' or 'too —'. About seven or eight letters are lost at the beginning of the line; no plausible adjective has a stem as long as this, so an extra word is needed. The best solution offered so far is Barigazzi's [καὶ φαυλ]ότερός, giving the sense 'and I'm not good enough (literally, too bad) in the sort of speaking that I'll have to do now'. It was routine in Greek to use the comparative of an adjective or adverb to indicate, not necessarily a high degree of the quality it denoted, but a low degree of the opposite quality, e.g. ἀμαθέστερον 'less cleverly' (Ar. *Frogs* 1445), χεῖρον 'less good' (e.g. Pl. *Men.* 98c). Another possibility is [ἔτ' ἀπειρ]ότερός (Austin after Luschnat) 'I'm still not very experienced in ...', though that would raise by implication the irrelevant prospect of Moschion's *one day becoming* a practised and eloquent speaker.

94-5 [ἀ]πελθὼν εἰς ἐρημίαν τινὰ | [γυμν]άζομ': so in Terence's *Andria* (406-8) Simo is seen arriving 'from some lonely place, where he's been thinking and hopes he's worked out a speech that will tear [his son Pamphilus] to pieces'; for εὑρετικὸν εἶναί φασι τὴν ἐρημίαν | οἱ τὰς ὀφρῦς αἴροντες ('the highbrows [i.e. philosophers] say that solitude helps you find solutions') (Men. fr. 37). In *Perikeiromene*, similarly, another Moschion goes to an out-of-the-way part of his house to think what to do next and practise what he will say in the event of his receiving a message from Glykera (*Perik.* 537-41, 550 ἐμελέτων λόγον); our Moschion cannot be allowed to do that, since if he did, his first meeting with his father would take place indoors, out of sight of the audience (Barigazzi 1970: 159).

95 [γυμν]άζομ': this restoration is supported by μελετήσας in 121. If the supplement [τί δ' οὐκ] in 94 is correct, the present tense here is idiomatic; the present is always used in comedy after τί (δ') οὐ where the speaker is urging a course of action on another and/or on himself (*Epitr.* F 3.1; Ar. *Ach.* 358, *Birds* 149, 828, *Thesm.* 1193, 1221). Possibly the original, literal meaning of the idiom was 'Why am I (are you) not (sc. now) doing X?', implying 'I (you) ought to do X at once'.   **οὐ γὰρ μέτριος ἀγών ἐστί μοι:** Pat Easterling compares Soph. *Aj.* 1163 ἔσται μεγάλης ἔριδός τις ἀγών where the chorus correctly anticipate an angry and perilous confrontation between Teucer and Agamemnon (cf. also Eur. *Hel.* 1090). If our passage does recall this, the echo will prove to be ironic: before Moschion has returned, we will have learned that he will, at most, be pushing at an open door.

Moschion departs by Eisodos B – that is, in the direction opposite to that from which he knows his father will be arriving. His apprehensions will undoubtedly have led most spectators to expect that Demeas will be far from well disposed to his request to marry Plangon (Ireland 1983: 45-6); they are about to be taken by surprise.

96-119a It is common in Menander for the plot to take a new turn towards the end of an act (Handley 1970: 11-12, Zagagi 1994: 76-9). In our play this also occurs at the end of Act III (405-20: Chrysis takes refuge with Nikeratos); in *Dyskolos* we find it in all the first four acts (Daos sees Sostratos talking to Knemon's daughter, 212-20; the first members of the sacrificial party arrive at the shrine, 393-426; Knemon's mattock falls down the well and he decides to go down and retrieve it himself, 574-601; Kallippides arrives, 773-83). Here the arrival of Demeas and Nikeratos was foreseen, though we probably expected that Moschion would stay to meet them. What no one will have expected is that after some amusing, and patriotically uplifting, but dramatically irrelevant dialogue, we would learn that the two fathers had already agreed to make the very marriage between their children which Moschion is anxiously preparing to request, and for whose sake Chrysis is engaging in a scheme of deception at some risk to herself. It had seemed as though the play would be about 'the traditional struggle to obtain the father's consent to the wedding of his son' (Zagagi 1994: 118); now this expectation has been swept away, and the action seems about to end almost before it has begun, leaving the audience wondering what new complications Menander will devise to keep it going.

Demeas and Nikeratos enter by Eisodos A; their costumes will signal their contrasting economic status. Several mute performers accompany them, as the plurals αἰσθάνεσθ' (96) and παράγετε ὑμεῖς (104–5); most, possibly all, of these will be slaves of Demeas, carrying his extensive luggage. Blume 1974: 35–6 suggests that Nikeratos had one slave, and that Demeas' angry words in 105 are addressed to him; but Demeas would not speak, in Nikeratos' presence, as though he were entitled to give orders to Nikeratos' slave (and if he did, the fiery-tempered Nikeratos would probably complain). It is not impossible that Nikeratos is represented as being so poor that he has no male slave at all (cf. Ar. Eccl. 593) and has to carry his own (very limited) luggage; certainly there is no indication in the rest of the play that there are any male slaves in his house – where Demeas speaks of his slaves collectively in the masculine gender (221), Nikeratos speaks only of 'the women' (410, 426, 573), and even that might refer only to his wife and daughter, though it is perhaps more likely that we are to suppose he has also one female slave, like Knemon in Dyskolos (there are no known slaveless households in Menander: Krieter-Spiro 1997: 72). In any case the audience will immediately recognize that the man who is better dressed and has a large retinue must be Moschion's adoptive father.

The arrival of a large travelling party with much luggage may be compared to the arrival, at the start of Aspis, of Daos with his master's captives and booty, or to that of Phanias at Kitharistes 35ff; in Dyskolos Menander doubles the effect by having the household of Sostratos' mother, with the requisites for their sacrifice and meal, arrive in two instalments – first Sikon and Getas with the sheep and most of the luggage (393–426) and then the rest of the party (430–41). Such scenes have their ancestry partly in Old Comedy (where it is normally the chorus that makes a spectacular mass entrance) and partly in tragedy (cf. Aesch. Eum. 1003–31 – temple-staff of Athena Polias, with sacrificial animals; Soph. Trach. 225–90 – Lichas with captive women; Eur. Hel. 1165 – Theoclymenus with huntsmen, hounds and nets). It is not clear whether the slaves enter ahead of Demeas and Nikeratos or after them (there is a similar uncertainty in Aspis, see Goldberg 1980: 27, Frost 1988: 21, Beroutsos 2005: 21 n. 25), though 104–5 will play more easily if the slaves at that moment are nearer to Demeas' door than Demeas is himself.

96 μεταβολῆς … τόπου: this and related expressions appear frequently in Aristotle (e.g. Cat. 15a14) in the sense 'locomotion', but by Menander's time it seems to have become an everyday phrase denoting any substantial change of location; in Men. fr. 835.9 it refers to migration, here to the experience of returning to Athens after spending many months abroad.

97 ταῦτα: the word was doubtless accompanied by a vague gesture to indicate that what was meant were the sights, sounds and smells of Athens; so again 100.   **τῶν ἐκεῖ κακῶν:** specified in the following lines.

98–101 are here taken as a continuation of Demeas' speech, which is thus unbroken from 96 to 105; B has no indication of change of speaker within these ten lines. From Sandbach 1970: 121 onwards, however, many have preferred to give 98–101 (as far as ἀγάθ') to Nikeratos. In support of this view have been cited inter alia: the staccato style of the passage (cf. e.g. 410–13, 425–7); the praise of Athens as having καθαρὰ πενήτων ἀγαθά, which is prima facie more appropriate to a poor speaker and might even be thought tactless in Demeas' mouth; and the fact that subsequently (106–9, 417) it is only Nikeratos who makes hostile remarks about the Pontic environment (Fountoulakis 2008: 471–2). On the other hand, Demeas' words in 96–7 cry out for some specification of what τὰ ἐκεῖ κακά were, and the person who apostrophizes Ἀθῆναι φίλταται (101) ought to be the same person who had warmly praised Athens a moment before. Arnott 1998a: 42–3 pointed out that Demeas too can speak in a staccato style (e.g. 324–7, 380–3, 547–50) and that πενήτων ἀγαθά may have been proverbial (cf. Synes. Epist. 148.130 Hercher, where it seems to mean something like 'simple good living'); we may add that Demeas is himself a 'fat old man' (98) – he will certainly have been made to look much better nourished than Nikeratos (cf. Ar. Wealth 557–62) – so that for Nikeratos to refer to such people disparagingly would be to risk insulting his companion. On balance it is best to retain B's assignment of the lines. Demeas will thus establish himself immediately as the dominant member of the pair; his superiority is confirmed when he is the first to (re)introduce the topic of the planned marriage (113) and when we learn that he had been the one to propose it originally (117–18).

98 παχεῖς γέροντες: the stereotype that inhabitants of the Black Sea region were obese must have been long current, for the Hippocratic treatise *Airs, Waters, Places* (15, 19), referring to the Phasians (on the east coast of the Black Sea) and the Scythians (on the north coast and in its hinterland), ascribes it to the region's misty atmosphere (cf. 106–9, where note the phrase ἀὴρ παχύς); see Collard 1989.   **ἰχθῦς ἄφθονοι:** the Black Sea was famous for the abundance and variety of its fish, for which Byzantium was the most important market; see e.g. Diph. fr. 17.14; Sopater fr. 11; Archestratus frr. 22, 34, 35, 37, 38, 40; Euthydemus *SH* 455; Strabo 7.6.2. High-quality fish is normally regarded in comedy as a prized delicacy, but

Demeas is presumably complaining (with obvious comic exaggeration) that in the Black Sea region one cannot get anything *else* to eat. The nominative plural ἰχθῦς (Eubulus fr. 108.3, Antiphanes fr. 233.3, Alexis fr. 263.9; cf. ἰχθῦ [dual] Antiphanes fr. 192.15) became established in Attic in place of the older ἰχθύες (Telecleides fr. 1.6, Archippus fr. 30) in the first third of the fourth century, when likewise μῦς (Antiphanes fr. 191.1) was replacing μύες (Anaxandrides fr. 42.61).

99 ἀηδία τις πραγμάτων: lit. 'a distastefulness of business'; it is not clear whether Demeas has found his business activities in the Black Sea distasteful because he was dealing with men of dubious honesty, or because he found them physically repulsive (cf. 98), or whether he has merely had his fill of business (cf. Ter. *Eun.* 403–4 *satietas hominum aut negoti... odium*) and longs for home and leisure.

100 ἀψίνθιον: a bitter-tasting aromatic herb (wormwood, *Artemisia absinthium*) which Byzantines, according to the (as usual, exaggerated) statement of a cook in Diphilus fr. 17.11–15, expected to be used to flavour every dish they ate; it was also widely used in medicinal preparations (Thphr. *CP* 3.1.3, 6.4.6; Pliny *HN* 27.46–52). When Βυζάντιον and ἀψίνθιον were mentioned together, the similarity in sound doubtless made their association seem particularly appropriate (Pieters 1971: 97).   **πικρὰ πάντ':** wormwood has a tendency to spread its bitterness to other plants in its vicinity, a fact of which the ancients were aware (Philostratus, *Life of Apollonius* 1.21). But Demeas is doubtless also to be understood as meaning that the literal bitterness of Byzantium's favourite herb is matched by the metaphorical bitterness of life there in general; similarly Ovid writes from Tomi *tristia deformes pariunt absinthia campi,* | *terraque de fructu quam sit amara docet* (*Ex Ponto* 3.8.15–16).   **Ἄπολλον:** Demeas utters this invocation twice again (567, 570), where it is clearly an appeal to Apollo ἀποτρόπαιος (cf. Ar. *Wasps* 161, *Birds* 61, *Wealth* 359, 854; also *Peace* 238, *Wealth* 438) to avert imminent danger (Nikeratos is going berserk and threatening murder). Elsewhere in Menander we find Apollo invoked to disavow an imputation (*Aspis* 85 – that Smikrines' interest in the booty is motivated by greed; *Dysk.* 293 – that Sostratos has dishonourable intentions towards Knemon's daughter; *Perik.* 1018 – that Polemon has not learned from his experiences) or to avert an evil omen (*Dysk.* 415, provoked by the report of a dream in which Sostratos' mother had seen Pan putting fetters on her son). Here perhaps Demeas is vividly recalling his 'bitter' experiences abroad, and hoping that Apollo will remove even the memory of them. Blume 1974: 36 n. 62 thinks he is merely greeting (the pillar of) Apollo Agyieus in front of his house (444n.); but that would require χαῖρε or the like.   **ταῦτα:** life at Athens (97n.).

101 καθαρὰ πενήτων ἀγάθ': 98–101n.: the good, simple food of Athens (which all of the theatre audience could afford) is contrasted with the cloying, unhealthy luxuries and unpleasant seasonings of the Black Sea region (which most of them could not).

101–4 It is common, both in tragedy and in comedy, for travellers returning from abroad to greet their native land (in comedy, this is normally Attica) with effusive joy; cf. *Aspis* 491, Men. frr. 1, 247, Plaut. *Bacch.* 170–3, Aesch. *Ag.* 503–21, Soph. fr. 202, Eur. fr. 558. But here the greeting immediately turns into a wish that Athens may have 'all that [she] deserve[s]' and so make her patriotic citizens happy – clearly implying that at present Athens is not in that blessed position. This is not useful evidence for dating the play, since at virtually any time in Menander's career it would be true that Athens did not have the power or prosperity that most Athenians would consider she deserved.

102 πῶς ἄν 'if only…!', cf. e.g. Ar. *Ach.* 991, Eur. *Hipp.* 345. **γένοιθ' ὑμῖν ὅσων ἔστ' ἄξιαι** 'you could get all that you deserve' (literally, 'there could come to be for you as much as you are worthy of'). The plural concord of Ἀθῆναι is regular (cf. Ar. *Knights* 1329–30 ὦ ταὶ λιπαραὶ…Ἀθῆναι, δείξατε…; *AP* 7.256.3–4 χαίρετ', Ἀθῆναι, γείτονες Εὐβοίης), though it could have been overridden had the predicate been a singular noun (cf. Plato com. fr. 217 πατρὶς <δ'> Ἀθῆναι μοῦστιν <αἱ> χρυσάμπυκες). Isocrates twice says (7.66, 15.234) that thanks to Pericles' building programme 'visitors to the city, even today, think she is worthy to rule not only over the Greeks but over the whole of mankind'.

103 ἵν' ὦμεν: when a sentence expressing a wish, with an optative verb, governs a final clause, the verb of the final clause may be either optative (e.g. Eur. *Hipp.* 732–4) or, as here, subjunctive (e.g. Eur. *Ion* 671–2); see Goodwin 1912: 60–1. **πάντα** 'in all respects', 'in every way'.

104–5 εἴσω παράγετε | ὑμεῖς: addressed to his slaves; the phrase is a set idiom (295, *Epitr.* 405). Their exit into Demeas' house clears the stage for his ensuing private conversation with Nikeratos. Some compounds of ἄγω had long been used intransitively in the sense 'go', 'move' (e.g. Ar. *Wasps* 290 ὕπαγε, *Birds* 383 ἄναγ'), and in Menander παράγω joins this group.

105 One slave is slower than the rest to obey Demeas' order, and is angrily told (perhaps with a threatening gesture) to get on with it. The bullying of a sluggish slave was a comic cliché; cf. *Dysk.* 441, Ar. *Birds* 1317–36, *Lys.* 426–7. This is our first direct evidence that Demeas *can* be roused to anger when he perceives himself to have cause for it: Moschion's apprehensions, we may feel, are not entirely misplaced. **ἀπόπληχθ'** (= ἀπόπληκτε): sarcastically pretending that the slave must be paralysed.

ἕστηκας ἐμβλέπων ἐμοί; Herodas 5.40 is almost identical; elsewhere (*Dysk.* 441, Ar. *Lys.* 426) attention may be drawn to the slave's foolishly open mouth (κέχηνας) rather than to his foolishly staring eyes.

106–9 Nikeratos, now alone with Demeas, speaks for the first time (98–101n.). Their first exchange, besides further flattering the audience's sense of Athenian superiority (this time at the expense of the Pontic climate), may suggest that he is willing to accept his own social and intellectual inferiority to Demeas, as he repeatedly does hereafter (see Introduction §4(c)). There is probably also an ironic point to the passage (see Stoessl 1969: 198, 1973: 23; Collard 1989: 102): Demeas and Nikeratos think they have returned from a land of mist and fog to a land of clear air and bright sunshine – but during most of the rest of the play we shall be watching them go badly astray in a fog of ignorance and misapprehension.

109 ἀὴρ παχύς τις: in the northern and western parts of the Black Sea fog is frequent (75–80 days a year) and can sometimes stay unbroken for a week or more (Danoff 1962: 949). Conditions tend to be worst near the coasts, where ancient travellers would normally sail.   ὡς ἔοικ᾽: this surprising expression of diffidence is probably merely designed by the poet to serve as a 'feed' for Demeas' jesting response.

110–11 The basic idea behind Demeas' joke (the Sun doesn't care to visit the Black Sea region much, because there's nothing worth seeing there) is as old as the *Odyssey* (12.377–83), where the Sun demands that the companions of Odysseus be punished for slaughtering his sacred cattle, 'in whom I used to delight every time I entered the starry sky or turned back from heaven to earth', and threatens that otherwise he will 'sink down to the realm of Hades and shine among the dead'; it reappears in Ar. *Clouds* 584–6 where the Sun is said to have threatened not to shine on the Athenians if Cleon was elected as a general (there was indeed an eclipse a few weeks after that election).

110 σεμνὸν οὐδέν: from 'nothing worthy of respect' this comes to mean 'nothing worthy of special note' (Ar. *Knights* 777, Ar. fr. 729, Arist. *EN* 1146a15).   αὐτόθι 'there', i.e. in the Black Sea region; this adverb can sometimes refer to the place where the speaker is (e.g. Ar. *Knights* 119), but in Attic it much more often refers to some other place (e.g. Ar. *Frogs* 274, Antiphanes frr. 126, 164, Philemon fr. 49, Pl. *Prot.* 314b).

111 αὐτὰ τἀναγκαῖ᾽ 'just to the extent that was unavoidable', i.e. 'as little as possible'; cf. Diphilus fr. 4.

112–18 The division of speakers shown here is that favoured by most editors: B marks no speaker change before καὶ ταῦτα μὲν (112), before ταῦτ᾽ ἀεὶ λέγω (115), or before ἐμοὶ γοῦν (117). We have a secure starting point in 114b–15a, which must be spoken by Nikeratos since he refers to the prospective bridegroom, Moschion, as 'your lad'. He is asking about the meaning of the question in 113b–14a, and it must therefore be Demeas who asks that question. The answer to it comes in 115b–17a, which will thus be spoken by Nikeratos after Demeas has confirmed (πάνυ γε) that he was indeed asking about the planned marriage. So far as the sense is concerned, we could then either continue δέδοκται ταῦτ᾽ ἐμοὶ γοῦν (as a statement) to Nikeratos or make the first two words a question by Demeas and the last two Nikeratos' reply; the latter is livelier (and avoids our having to disregard one of the speaker-changes that B *does* mark). The resulting dialogue gives Demeas the initiative at every stage (98–101, 106–9nn.): he had been the first to decide the marriage should be made, he raises the issue for discussion now, and he asks for a firm decision from Nikeratos.

113 ἐῶμεν: subjunctive, 'let us leave'.   **ὑπὲρ ὧν … ἐλέγομεν:** by the regular rules of relative attraction (Smyth 1956: 567) this is equivalent to ὑπὲρ ('about', LSJ ὑπέρ A III) ἐκείνων ἃ ἐλέγομεν. It is not clear whether the previous conversation referred to is to be imagined as taking place within the last hour or so, or at an earlier time, e.g. during the sea voyage.

114 τὰ περὶ τὸν γάμον: the accusative is regular in Menander after τὰ περί 'the things having to do with…', 'the matter of…' (623, *Aspis* 251, *Epitr.* 567).

115 τῶι μειρακίωι σου: the dative is unusual, but can be paralleled by *Aspis* 130–1 μακροτέραν ὁρῶν ἐκείνωι τὴν ἀποδημίαν. Menander was straining to avoid the sequence τοῦ μειρακίου σου: out of several hundred instances of enclitic μου and σου in comedy, only one (at Ar. *Frogs* 1200) is preceded by a word ending in –ου (and even there, there is a variant reading σοι). **ταῦτ᾽ ἀεὶ λέγω** tells us that Nikeratos had also strongly supported the plan when it was discussed previously.

116 ἀγαθῆι τύχηι: a common formula (297, *Aspis* 381, *Dysk.* 422, *Epitr.* 223; Ar. *Birds* 435, 675, *Eccl.* 131), used in state decrees from the fifth century on (e.g. *IG* I³ 40.40, 93.3) and frequently in Menander's time (e.g. *IG* II² 338.10, 380.12, 448.64, 467.24), and tantamount to a prayer that the outcome of an action or decision may be favourable. At *Dysk.* 816, as here, it is used (with the verb πράττειν) by a father consenting to the marriage of his daughter.

116–17 ἡμέραν τινὰ | θέμενοι: then as now, 'fixing the day' – and issuing invitations (cf. 123, 181) – would make the commitment into a firm one, and make a breach of it into a major embarrassment. Nikeratos, for whom the proposed match is very advantageous, is anxious to finalize it.

117 δέδοκται ταῦτα; 'Is that your final decision?' The perfect δέδοκται
(and its participle δεδογμένον) have an air of irrevocability about them; cf.
Men. fr. 64.4, Ar. *Wasps* 485, Soph. *Ant.* 576, Eur. *Med.* 1236, *Bacch.* 1350.
ἀλλὰ μήν 'indicating a favourable reaction to the previous speaker's words'
(Denniston 1954: 343); cf. Ar. *Birds* 385, Pl. *Phd.* 58d.

118 κἀμοὶ προτέρωι σου: it was, then, Demeas who first thought of the
idea of a marriage between Moschion and Plangon. In the surviving text
we never learn what his reason was. Menander had an opportunity to let
him tell us when he was alone on stage after Nikeratos' exit (119a/b n.),
but it is not clear whether he used this opportunity; we might, however,
have learned more if Demeas' long monologue in Act II had survived
(166/167n.). We may at any rate note, firstly that Demeas thought well
enough of Nikeratos' character to make him his companion on a long
business trip, and secondly that Menander regularly encourages his audience to take a favourable view of marriage alliances between rich and poor
families (see Introduction §7).   **παρακάλει μ' ὅταν ἐξίηις:** clearly Nikeratos at this point exits into his own house, and expects that Demeas will
likewise be going into his. Both have to greet their families (Moschion
and Chrysis on the one hand – neither of the fathers is aware that Moschion is not at home – Plangon and her mother on the other) and let
them know of the proposed marriage; Nikeratos' expectation will be that
by the time Demeas comes out having done this, he himself will also be
ready to confirm the arrangement and agree a date. This is more or less
what happens in 168–87, though Nikeratos will be taken aback when he
learns what date Demeas wants. Rather similarly in *Dysk.* 781–3, when Sostratos wants to speak to his father Kallippides about his intended marriage
to Knemon's daughter (and also – but neither Gorgias nor the audience
know this – about his plan to marry his own sister to Gorgias), he asks
Gorgias to 'wait inside', saying he will call for him soon, which he does at
820 after Kallippides has agreed to the two marriages.

119a As there is no *dicolon* (:) to mark a change of speaker at the end
of 118 in B, it is possible that Nikeratos' exit-speech continued into 119;
but it is also possible that the *dicolon* has been omitted by error, as several others have been in the previous few lines (112–18n.). If (which is
doubtful) the reading and restoration [ε]ἰς ἄστυ (Dedoussi) is correct, the
speaker at that point is likely to be Demeas, since Nikeratos is not expecting the wedding to be fixed for this very day and will have no special reason for going shopping in town; but Demeas too is not likely to be thinking now about doing so (or rather about sending Parmenon to do so),
since he has important matters to see to in his house first (see previous
note).

119a/b Demeas is alone on stage, and the apparent length of the lacuna (only some ten lines, excluding those needed to mark the act-break) makes it unlikely that anyone joined him before the end of Act I. He will have had a short soliloquy, perhaps briefly explaining why he has chosen to make a marriage alliance with Nikeratos' family, perhaps reflecting on the difficulties he (wrongly) expects to have in persuading Moschion to go along with his plan (compare his words in 200–2 about the difficulties he expects Nikeratos to have in persuading his wife); then, as happens at the end of every Menandrian first act whose conclusion survives (*Aspis* 245–8, *Dysk.* 230–2, *Epitr.* 169–71, *Perik.* 261–2; cf. *com. adesp.* 1153.8–9), he will have seen approaching a band of drunken young men (the cho-rus) and prudently withdrawn into his house. The chorus will then have danced, and probably sung; the words of their songs (if any), in this as in other plays, were not included in the script, which merely had the note χοροῦ '<performance> of the chorus' at each act-break (in *Samia* this note appears at the two act-breaks where the text has survived, 420/421 and 615/616).

ACT II

We had expected that the next event to take place would be a meeting between Moschion and Demeas. Instead, in Moschion's absence, Demeas' first encounter on his return home has been with Chrysis and the baby that she is pretending is her own. As predicted (80), Demeas is angry; but before his passion for Chrysis can soften his anger (80–3) it is softened instead by Moschion, who proves surprisingly eloquent and persuasive, considering that he finds himself unexpectedly in the position of plead-ing against the banishment from his home of his own child, without being able to admit that it *is* his own child. A long lacuna (for little can be made of the twelve line-beginnings, 143b–m, that survive only in O17) leaves it formally uncertain what eventually causes Demeas to relent, but Demeas' later behaviour makes it highly likely that his affection for his adopted son moved him to yield to the latter's wishes. With this difficulty out of the way, the situation is back where it was at the end of Act I, and when B resumes it is evident that Demeas has told Moschion of his intention to marry him to Plangon and that Moschion has agreed with enthusiasm and pleasure. The main features of the rest of Act II were a long monologue by Demeas, now mostly lost (166/167n.); a poorly preserved scene in which he overbears, rather than persuades, Nikeratos into agreeing to hold the wedding this very day (167–89); and the beginning of preparations for the event as Parmenon and Nikeratos go off on their shopping expeditions. Once again, and even more strongly than at the end of Act I, it appears that there is nothing left in the situation that can impede the marriage or sustain the momentum of a comic plot. There are indications (200–1, 203) that Nikeratos' wife is making difficulties, but we know (as Nikeratos and Demeas do not) that she is strongly committed to the marriage and that any objections she may have can only be to the haste with which she is being required to prepare for it.

Some things in this act, however, may in retrospect be seen as ironically foreshadowing later developments. Moschion, in the unnoticed presence of Demeas, utters words (123–6) that would make it clear to any listener that he is hoping to be married very soon – but there are no untoward consequences, because Demeas has not heard him; the outcome will be very different when the old freedwoman utters other careless words in the unnoticed presence of Demeas (236–54). Soon afterwards Demeas angrily declares his intention to expel Chrysis and the baby he believes (wrongly) to be his son, but then yields to Moschion's dissuasion, probably out of paternal affection; this prefigures the scene in Act III when Demeas actually does expel Chrysis and the baby – whom he now believes (rightly) to be his grandson – an action largely *caused* by the paternal affection which makes him unable to believe that Moschion could be a guilty party in the supposed liaison between him and Chrysis (328–47). His statement in that speech (343–7) that what matters is a son's character, not whether he is one's biological or adopted child, echoes Moschion's argument (137–43a) that what matters is not whether someone is legitimately born or not, but whether he is a good or a bad person. Moschion's sudden departure at 162, apparently from shame and/or fear at the prospect of meeting Nikeratos (161–2n.), will be mirrored by his even more sudden departure at 539 in much more justified fear of a Nikeratos who is almost insane with shock and rage. Demeas' monologue begins (163–4) with the reflection that ταὐτόματον ('chance', 55n.) is in a way a divine power that causes 'many things we do not see' to come out right: in the next act a chance event – Demeas' overhearing of the freedwoman – will trigger a chain reaction that threatens to make things come out utterly *wrong* and to wreck the marriage that Demeas himself so much desires, and the situation will be saved not by chance but by human will – first Demeas' determination to go through with the wedding for his son's sake (444–50), then Moschion's realization that he has no choice but to tell the truth (520–31), and finally Demeas' ability to hold Nikeratos at bay, then to humour him, until he is ready to see reason. There may well have been more such ironically apposite remarks in the lost portion of Demeas' monologue.

119b–d Act II probably began with the re-entrance of Demeas (for at 127–8 Moschion says 'here's father' rather than 'father's coming out' or the like, implying that Demeas is already on stage); he can only have spoken some three or four lines – perhaps enough to show that he is angry, maybe that he is angry with Chrysis in particular, but not enough to make clear the reason why – when he sees Moschion approaching. A few letters from the ends of three lines (119b-d) survive in O17 before the point at which B resumes; O17 also usefully supplements the defective B at the ends of lines 120–5. The three surviving letters of line 119d,]ται, look like a verbal ending, and since Moschion is speaking before the end of the next line, Arnott 1998b: 7–8 may well have been right to suppose that the verb was ἔρχεται or προσέρχεται, indicating that Demeas has caught sight of the approach of Moschion (cf. *Georg.* 31, *Dysk.* 405, 607, *Sik.* 123–4). One would normally expect him, after such a long absence, to greet his son immediately; instead he does and says nothing until Moschion notices him. Possibly Menander made him explain why (e.g. because he felt it better that the reunion should not take place when he was in an angry mood, or because he was uncertain how to broach the subject of a marriage which he expected might well be uncongenial to Moschion); but it is at least as likely that he expected his audience would simply accept it as a convention that the entering character could be allowed a short monologue before being engaged in conversation by the character already present (cf. 60/61n., 428–30, 641–57).

120 It is not clear whether the early part of this line was spoken by Demeas or Moschion, and no plausible restoration has been suggested.

120–6 It now proves that solitude has not after all been conducive to constructive thinking for Moschion (94–5n.); he has merely been indulging in daydreams about the wedding, instead of focusing on the task of making sure that there is one. As Blume 1974: 58–9 notes, most of the things he imagines himself as doing were not normally done by a bridegroom at all but by other members of his or the bride's family. All of them are described in the imperfect tense, suggesting either that Moschion has been carrying out these activities, in his imagination, over and over again, or that he was vividly picturing himself *in the midst of the process* of carrying them out.

122 ἐκπ[οδὼν αὐτὸς μ]όνος: ἐκποδὼν appears to have been in regular use to refer to a person going off to think something out in solitude (*Perik.* 540, *Georg.* 20). For αὐτὸς μόνος cf. *Dysk.* 331, *Epitr.* 244. Austin's ἐκτὸ[ς ἄστεως] is less likely, though (*contra* Dedoussi) ἐκτὸς does appear to occur once in Menander (*Epitr.* 612): the solitary thinker is not elsewhere described as going outside the city.

123 ἔθυον: i.e. I imagined myself sacrificing. In fact the sacrifices will be conducted by the heads of the two families: Demeas will describe himself (211) as ὁ θύων τοῖς θεοῖς, and Nikeratos, despite his poverty, will buy a sheep to sacrifice (399–404). And as things turn out, Nikeratos' sacrifice will have been completed (713), and Demeas' will at least be well under way (674), before Moschion has even begun to take any part in the proceedings.

124 ἐπὶ λούτρ': not to bathe themselves, but to fetch water for the ritual baths taken by both bride and groom (Oakley and Sinos 1993: 15–16). The water was brought from the Enneakrounos fountain-house near the Acropolis (Thuc. 2.15.5; see Travlos 1971: 204). When the wedding is actually about to take place (729–30) it will be Demeas who sends 'the women' for the bathing water (or rather instructs Chrysis to do so).   **τὰς γ[υναῖκας]:** i.e. the women slaves. Carrying water from the spring or well to the home was seen as a quintessentially feminine task (see S. Lewis 2002: 71–5) – as it usually is to this day in places having no piped supply – and, being heavy work, it would be done by slaves if they were available (*Iliad* 6.457–8, *Odyssey* 3.427–9; Eur. *Tro.* 205–6; Ar. *Lys.* 330), though the chorus of old women of citizen status in Aristophanes' *Lysistrata* (319–49) do it in an emergency, and the Euripidean Electra (Eur. *El.* 54–66) does it as an act of protest.

124–5 περιπατῶν | τὴν σησαμῆν διένεμον: 74–5n.

125–6 ἦ[ιδον ἐνί]οτε | ὑμέναιον: the ὑμέναιος was a song sung to (not by) the bridal couple as they travelled to their new home, understood at least from the time of Pindar (fr. 139.6 Snell-Maehler) as an invocation of a wedding-god Hymen or Hymenaeus. Two literary versions of such songs, with a refrain Ὑμὴν Ὑμέναι' ὤ *vel sim.*, are sung at the end of Aristophanes' *Peace* (1329–56) and *Birds* (1731–54). If the text as given here is correctly punctuated and restored, it will mean that while fantasizing about his coming wedding, Moschion from time to time – actually, not in imagination (otherwise ἐνίοτε would have no point) – sang (or hummed, see next note) the song that would be sung to him when the wedding eventually took place. Text and punctuation are disputed. B has a raised dot after ὑμέναιον (and no punctuation at the end of 125), and this arrangement is followed here. It makes the restoration ἦ[ιδον] almost inevitable; the next word must be an adverb, and [ἐνί]οτε works best (τότε has figured in some proposals, but then an extra syllable is required, and δή [Turner] would place undue emphasis on the *time* at which Moschion sang). The alternative would be to take ὑμέναιον as the object of ἐτερέτιζον; this, however, does not produce satisfactory results. If we keep the above wording, punctuating either before or after ἐνίοτε, it would imply that Moschion sang something other than the ὑμέναιος (for one cannot understand ὑμέναιον with ἦιδον, when the word has not yet been used), and the sentence would then have no relevance to a wedding. Lamagna preferred to remove all punctuation, producing a single sentence, e.g. ἡ[γεμὼν τ]ότε ὑμέναιον ἐτερέτιζον 'I hummed a wedding-song at that time as leader of a chorus': a plausible solution on these lines may exist, but this is not it – a lone daydreamer might hum the tune of a ὑμέναιος instead of singing it, but the leader of a chorus would not.

126 ἐτερέτιζον: understand ὑμέναιον. The verb means 'hum': cf. Thphr. *Char.* 19.10 on the (impious, inconsiderate) kind of man who, when a piper is playing, 'alone of the other [listeners] will clap his hands [to the beat] and συντερετίζειν'; also Phrynichus com. fr. 14 (vocalizing a pipe melody); Euphro fr. 1.34 πρὸς τὸ δίχορδον (two-stringed instrument) ἐτερέτιζες. For singing and humming as alternatives cf. Aesch. *Ag.* 16 ὅταν δ' ἀείδειν ἢ μινύρεσθαι δοκῶ.   ἦν ἀβέλτ[ε]ρο[ς]: Moschion now realizes that he has wasted his opportunity, and will have to approach his father (whom, not yet having seen him, he doubtless assumes to be inside the house) without any rehearsal.

127 δ' οὖν 'well, anyway', dismissing the topic and returning to the main subject (Denniston 1954: 462–4). We never learn precisely what Moschion was going to say, for on catching sight of his father he abruptly stops (and drops his tone so as not to be overheard), but it could have been something like 'I suddenly realized that father would be home by now and that I'd better get back quickly.'   Ἄπολλον: 100n. Here the invocation expresses shock, alarm, and Moschion's hope and prayer that no evil will result from his unguarded words.

128 ἀκήκο' ἄρα: either a statement ('Then he's heard!') or a question ('Has he heard, then?') In either case Moschion is thinking about the words he himself has just been speaking, and their implications: if Demeas has heard and understood them, then Moschion has inadvertently revealed his desires and intentions too soon. Sandbach thought that Moschion was assuming Demeas had heard that Chrysis had (supposedly) had a baby; but it was always certain, and expected (80), that Demeas would learn this as soon as he came home – and would learn about it, not by hearing the talk of others, but by seeing the baby in his house. In either case, also, ἄρα is probably not the interrogative particle but the inferential particle, equivalent to the more common ἄρα (Denniston 1954: 44–6) and found at *Aspis* 356, *Epitr.* 1092, *Perik.* 504 (question and answer), and in yes/no questions at Strato fr. 1.21 and Philemon fr. 108.1. Both statement and question would make good sense, but perhaps it will add more to the tension of the moment if Moschion jumps straight to an alarming conclusion (only later discovered, by him and by us, to be erroneous) than if he merely expresses uncertainty. In point of fact Demeas has not heard, or has not heeded, what Moschion said, probably because he is wrapped up in thoughts about Chrysis and the baby (he cannot even raise a smile to greet his son, 129); it is clear from 145–6 that he is surprised by Moschion's eagerness to marry.   χαῖρέ μοι is found only here in comedy, and even in tragedy it is confined to lyric (Eur. *Hipp.* 63, 70, *IA* 1509), to poignant adieux (Eur. *Tro.* 45, Poseidon to Troy; 458, Cassandra to Hecuba; *Ba.* 1379, Agaue to Cadmus – all parting for ever) and to poignant reunions (Eur. *Ion* 561, Ion to a 'father' he has never met before). Is Moschion trying hard – maybe too hard – to strike an appropriate note in greeting his father after about a year's absence? The pronoun μοι is a so-called ethic dative, expressing the speaker's personal interest in the message being conveyed (Schwyzer 1950: 149, Smyth 1956: 342–3). B's surprising corruption χαιρεα may indicate that its scribe was copying the three plays contained in the codex (*Samia, Dyskolos* and *Aspis*) for a second time within a fairly short period: both *Dyskolos* and *Aspis* contain a character named Chaireas, and the vocative form of the name appears in both scripts (*Dysk.* 54, *Aspis* 300, 374).

129 [ν]ὴ καὶ σύ γ' 'The same to you': a regular, colourless response to the greeting χαῖρε (also *Georg.* 41), several times imitated by Lucian (e.g. *Timon* 46, *Dearum Iud.* 7); see Macleod 1970.   τί σκυθρωπάζεις; It is often necessary for the audience to be informed verbally about characters' facial expressions (cf. *Dis Ex.* 103–4, *Sik.* 124; Ar. *Lys.* 7–8, 707; Eur. *Med.* 271, *Hipp.* 1152, *Phoen.* 1333), since a character's face as seen by the spectator was an unchanging mask, with the lips usually parted in an artificial attitude that was neither a frown nor a smile (see Webster, Green and Seeberg 1995: 6–51, esp. 9–16 on the masks of old men).   τί γάρ; 'You ask me why?': cf. *Aspis* 171, *Georg.* 85, *Dysk.* 553, 636, *Epitr.* 261. Aristophanes would have written ὅ τι; (e.g. *Ach.* 106, *Knights* 742).

130 γ]αμετὴν ἑταίραν is a sarcastic oxymoron. Demeas means that Chrysis, who was a *hetaira* until he took her into his house (21, 25) and is now his παλλακή (508), is behaving as if she were his wife. He explains himself more specifically (though still not very clearly) next time he speaks (132n.).

131 ἀγνοῶ <γάρ> τὸν λόγον: a syllable is missing in B, and this restoration, the first to be proposed, is best (cf. Eur. *Phoen.* 707). The alternative, ἀγνοῶ τὸν <σὸν> λόγον (Arnott), puts undue emphasis (as Dedoussi notes) on the second-person possessive when there is no implied contrast between Demeas and anyone else.

132 Demeas is not, of course, angry merely because Chrysis has (he believes) borne a child; he is angry, as Chrysis says later (374), because she is rearing it. This explains why he speaks of the child as [λάθ]ριό[ς τι]ς υἱός: Chrysis cannot reasonably be said to have *given birth* to the baby behind Demeas' back (for all he knows, she might not even have known she was pregnant at the time of his departure, and if she had, he would hardly have required her to induce an abortion), but if she knew that he desired that any child she might bear should be exposed, and yet kept the baby, she could certainly be said to have *given him a son* by deception. It is nowhere made explicit in the surviving text that Demeas had given such orders, and there is no particular reason to suppose that this was stated in a lost passage; probably the audience were relied on to take it for granted. Exposure of unwanted, especially illegitimate, children appears to have been a common practice (Eyben 1980/1: 12–19, 48–9; Patterson 1985; Garland 1990: 84–93; Ogden 1996: 102–3, 106–10). At Athens it seems to have been viewed with a certain squeamishness, for it is hardly ever referred to except in drama (e.g. *Epitr. passim*; Ar. *Clouds* 530–2; Eur. *Ion* 16–27, 898–966), and Isocrates (12.121–3) goes so far as to claim that it had never occurred at Athens even in mythical times; but Plato (*Tht.* 160e–161a) can take it for granted that a baby 'not worthy of rearing' would be 'put away'. According to Aristotle (*Pol.* 1335b21–2) 'the ordinance of custom' did not countenance the exposure of infants 'on account of the number of children' (i.e. as a means of family limitation), but Aristotle says nothing about exposure performed for other reasons, and indeed himself recommends that there should be a law 'that no maimed child be reared' (ibid. 19–21). Demeas' view of the situation, we now see, is that by keeping 'her' child Chrysis has treated him as if he were a legitimate son, who would normally always be reared.   ὡς ἔοικε: again sarcastic, as in 130; but he speaks more truly than he knows – it is indeed only *in appearance* that a son has been born to Demeas!

133 [ἡ δ'] is slightly preferable to [ὅν] (Turner), which is probably too short for the available space: [ὅν γ'] (Austin) might be an even better fit, but Menander scarcely ever uses γε after forms of ὅς (only *Mis.* 249 S = 650 A, reinforcing an affirmative answer to a question). It is easy enough to supply the unexpressed object of λαβοῦσα (the baby) from the context.   ἐς [κόρ]ακας ἄπεισιν: later, when Demeas actually does expel Chrysis, he similarly says to her ἄπιθι...ἐς κόρακας ἤδη (369–70); the phrase ἐς κόρακας 'to blazes, to hell' (literally, 'to the ravens', i.e. to the fate of a corpse left unburied to be devoured by birds) also appears at 353 when he declares his intention of expelling her. No other character in Menander uses the phrase more than once; it occurs five times in all outside this play (*Dysk.* 112, 432; *Epitr.* 160, *Heros* 70, *Perik.* 396). Demeas' anger towards Chrysis is evidently being presented as extremely strong even now, when her supposed offence is much less grave than that of which he will later believe her guilty.

134 [ἤ]δη 'right now'.

135-6 To rear one's bastard child in one's home was abnormal (Ogden 1996: 100–10), though neither in law nor in social practice was it impossible, as witness the case of the son of Pericles and Aspasia (who was made legitimate by an Assembly decree only after Pericles' two older, legitimate sons had died in the plague of 430, Plut. *Per.* 37.2–5). Demeas' reaction here is actually a little illogical, since he does not know whether Moschion is objecting to the expulsion of the baby, the mother or both; but the audience know that it is for the child – his child – that Moschion is concerned, and his argument (or the few lines of it that we are able to follow) is relevant only to the position of the child.

135 ἀλλ' ἦ 'giv[es] lively expression to a feeling of surprise or incredulity' (Denniston 1954: 27); English expressions with a comparable effect, variously nuanced, include 'What,...?', 'You don't mean to say...?' and 'You don't seriously mean...?' Cf. *Epitr.* 1064–6: 'Taking away my daughter too hastily, am I, you villainous old woman? What, am I to wait (ἀλλ' ἦ περιμένω) until that fine husband of hers has eaten up the whole of my dowry?' and Aesch. *Cho.* 220, Eur. *Hipp.* 932, Ar. *Ach.* 1111–12. The reading of the papyrus (here O17; B lacks the beginning of the line) is uncertain, but in any case ἄλλωι does not give satisfactory sense (Kassel 1973: 8–9); theoretically the masculine could refer generically to Chrysis as 'another person' (cf. 342, Eur. *Alc.* 634), but a hearer will almost inevitably take it as indicating that Demeas already suspects that the baby's father is someone other than himself – which at this stage he certainly does not.   ἔνδον 'in my house', cf. 438, 651, [Dem.] 59.118 ἀλλ' οὐ γυναῖκα εἶναι αὐτοῦ [sc. φήσει], ἀλλὰ παλλακὴν ἔχειν ἔνδον;

136 [λόγο]ν γ' οὐ τοῦ τρόπου τοὐμοῦ λέγεις 'you are saying something not in accordance with my character', i.e. 'that's not the way I do things'. For λόγον X λέγειν, where X is an adjective or a phrase equivalent to one, cf. Men. fr. 704 χρηστὸν ὅταν εἴπηι λόγον, Aesch. *Supp.* 246 εἴρηκας...ἀψευδῆ λόγον, Soph. *Trach.* 63 εἴρηκεν δ' ἐλεύθερον λόγον 'she [a slave] has spoken like a free person'; for τοῦ τρόπου τοὐμοῦ cf. *Aspis* 368, Ar. *Wasps* 1002, *Thesm.* 93. The particle γε emphasizes the whole object phrase, not just the word it follows; cf. Ar. *Birds* 378 παρ' ἀνδρῶν γ' ἔμαθον ἐχθρῶν κοὐ φίλων (Denniston 1954: 149). Most alternative restorations (e.g. those of Austin, Dedoussi and Arnott) make the second word of the line a noun or adjective in asyndetic coordination with οὐ τοῦ τρόπου τοὐμοῦ (but this phrase and its variants are elsewhere always linked to a preceding coordinate expression with καί or τε) or else emend the surviving text (κοὐ Kasser). Handley's proposal (*ap.* Turner 1972: 3–4) [λέγω]ν τοῦτ' οὐ τρόπου τοὐμοῦ λέγεις, involving a gentler emendation (ΤΟΥ for ΓΟΥ) and a different division of words, gives a sense almost identical to that of Turner's restoration adopted here, and may be right.

137–43a Moschion, unexpectedly having to improvise an argument, apparently takes one from tragedy. In Sophocles' *Aleadai* (fr. 87), Telephus, the son of Heracles and Auge, taunted with his bastardy and asked how he can be reckoned equal to a legitimate son, replies ἅπαν τὸ χρηστὸν γνησίαν ἔχει φύσιν: in Euripides' *Antigone* (or should it be *Antiope*? – the two titles are often confused by scribes), someone says (Eur. fr. 168) ὀνόματι μεμπτὸν τὸ νόθον, ἡ φύσις δ' ἴση. There may well have been several other passages of similar import in other lost tragedies; perhaps Euripides' *Hippolytos Kalyptomenos* (see Introduction §6) contained one of them, especially if Phaedra in that play encouraged her bastard stepson Hippolytus to usurp the Athenian throne (see Talboy and Sommerstein 2006: 259, discussing Eur. fr. 434). Time-honoured as such sentiments now were, and whatever philosophical validity they may have been thought to possess, they neither had had nor were likely to have any effect on law, social convention, or popular attitudes to legitimacy and bastardy at Athens (cf. Ogden 1996: 204). Indeed another Euripidean character, in *Andromeda* (fr. 141), while asserting that bastards are 'in no way inferior' to those of legitimate birth, says that because bastards 'are handicapped by convention' (νόμωι νοσοῦσιν) it is inadvisable to bring them into the world.

138 γενόμενος ἄνθρωπος: so, in a similar though not identical argument, Philemon fr. 22 (spoken by a slave) 'though a man be a slave, he is none the less a man, ἂν ἄνθρωπος ἦι'.   **μέν** *solitarium* (76–7n.) used with a personal pronoun 'impl[ies] a contrast with other people' (Dunbar 1995: 138, on Ar. *Birds* 12; see Denniston 1954: 381–2), in this case with Chrysis. Demeas knows, he thinks, why Chrysis has kept the baby – maternal feeling, and a desire to elevate her own status (130); but what serious reason could Moschion have for wanting to share his adoptive home with a bastard half-brother, a type of situation which 'above all [others] sowed discord in Greek families' (Ogden 1996: 189)?

139 ἐσπούδακα 'I'm serious': the perfect tense of this verb is very commonly used from the late fifth century onwards to describe the subject's present state of mind (e.g. 152–3, 185, *Dysk.* 148; Ar. *Thesm.* 572, *Frogs* 813; Xen. *Symp.* 2.17, *Lac.* 14.4; Pl. *Symp.* 217a, *Phdr.* 234d, 236b).

140 οὐθέν: in Attic inscriptions of Menander's time οὐθ- is invariably used in all masculine and neuter (but never in feminine) forms of this pronoun (Threatte 1980–96: I 472). He himself, if we may trust the papyri, mostly wrote οὐδ-, which appears at least eighteen times (against ten for οὐθ-) in *Samia* (in *Dyskolos* οὐθ- is found only once). There was certainly some tendency for οὐθ- to be replaced by οὐδ- (standard both in the Koine and in classical Attic literature) in the course of transmission: four times in *Samia* (615, 643, 653, 671) B reads οὐθ- where the later C has οὐδ-. However, papyri of the Hellenistic age show no consistency; indeed one of the oldest, *PKöln* 203 (= *com. adesp.* 1147 = Men. *Fab. Inc.* no. 8 Arnott) of the third century BC, has only οὐδ- (6, 38). It seems likely, therefore, that Menander wavered between the orthography that had been regular in the literary tradition and one that better reflected the pronunciation of his own day. He sometimes got into a habit of using one or the other spelling exclusively or almost exclusively: 140 is the only surviving instance of οὐθ- in the first three acts of *Samia*, whereas in the fourth and fifth acts it is more frequent than οὐδ- (9:5). **γένος γένους:** γένος here means 'birth, ancestry, descent' (not 'offspring'), as in *Aspis* 15, 124, 201, *Dysk.* 65, *Epitr.* 337, *Perik.* 129, *Sik.* 248, 347; Men. frr. 835, 877. For the polyptoton (repetition of the same lexical item in different inflected forms) cf. *Dysk.* 46, 721; the device is much less frequent in Menander than in Euripides (on whose use of it see Denniston 1939: 91), and indicates a degree of rhetorical elevation (or here, perhaps, pretentiousness). **διαφέρειν:** not just 'differ' (since the ancestry of some people obviously *does* differ from that of others) but 'make a difference', 'differ so as to matter'; cf. *Epitr.* 410 οὐδὲ ἕν μοι διαφέρει 'it makes no difference to me', 'I don't mind in the least', and (ironically) *Dysk.* 516.

141–2 A 'mixed conditional' with the verb of the protasis in the optative and that of the apodosis in the present indicative. Spelled out, the logic of the sentence is that good people *are* the truly legitimate, and bad people are the real bastards and slaves, and that *if* people were to examine the matter fairly (as most do not), they would find this to be the case. Similarly in English, the protasis 'If the truth were known' is normally followed (or preceded) by an apodosis stating the allegedly unrecognized truth in the present or past indicative (e.g. 'Faith, if the truth were known, I was begot | After some gluttonous dinner' [Thomas Middleton and/or Cyril Tourneur, *The Revenger's Tragedy* I.ii.179 ed. Foakes 1996]).

141 ἐξετάσαι: Menander, unlike the fifth-century dramatists, uses -αις, -αι (e.g. 366, 685, 689; *Dysk.* 203, 251, 252, 269, 335, 511, 605) more frequently than -ειας, -ειε (*Dysk.* 368, 620–1 etc.; no instances in *Samia*). Menander *might* have written the future indicative ἐξετάσει (-σεις Stobaeus), but B's reading, giving a seemingly anomalous but easily intelligible 'mixed conditional' (see above), should be preferred as *lectio difficilior.*

142–3a καὶ … | καί 'both … and'.

143a δοῦλος: the claim that a wicked man is a *slave* is also known from tragedy (Eur. fr. 57), and it lurks at the back of Aristotle's mind in his discussion of 'natural slavery' (*Pol.* 1254a13–1255b15), coming to the surface at 1255a39–40 ('When they say this, they are defining the slave and the free man purely in terms of virtue and vice'). It is irrelevant to Moschion's argument, since Chrysis is certainly free and therefore her child will be free also.

143b–m Of these twelve lines we have only (from O17) the beginnings (maximum eleven letters), with four horizontal lines (*paragraphoi*) which show that there was at least one change of speaker during, or at the end of, 143b, 143e, 143g and 143i. Probably there was only one speaker change at each of these points, at least the first three; at any rate ἄδηλον εἶπ[ας] (143h) sounds like Demeas declaring himself baffled by some obscure remark of Moschion's. Very little can be gleaned from the rest of the passage, except that in his first speech (143c) Demeas made prominent mention of money (ἀργύριον). Was he reminding Moschion that the maintenance of the child would involve expenditure and thus diminish Moschion's inheritance (so Dedoussi)? Possibly, but Demeas is nowhere else shown as being obsessed (like the Smikrines of *Aspis* or of *Epitrepontes*) with the monetary aspects of a family situation – and he has recently taken the initiative (117–18) in arranging for his son a marriage that will bring him little or nothing by way of dowry. Or is he suggesting that Chrysis might be sent away with a lump sum or allowance to assist her in bringing up the child independently? This would not satisfy Moschion, but it might pave the way for further concessions, as Demeas' anger cooled, leading eventually to his agreeing that Chrysis and the baby could remain in his home. At any rate he must have so agreed, presumably during the sixteen or so lines that are completely lost before B again becomes available: when he does eventually expel Chrysis, it is for her supposed infidelity, and his complaint that she had failed to expose the baby, which had caused him to threaten expulsion in Act II, has become a mere 'pretext' (354) to protect Moschion's reputation and ensure that his marriage can go ahead.

In the text of this edition, a new speaker (alternately Moschion and Demeas) has been indicated at the start of the line following each of the four *paragraphoi*. In the first three cases we can be fairly confident that the indication is correct, since (i) the preserved opening words of the three lines concerned (143c, 143f, 143h) would each time make a good beginning for a new speech and (ii) the content of the third opening (143h) suggests that the speaker is Demeas (see above). At 143i–j, however, we cannot tell whether there was one speaker change or two, nor whether the surviving first word of 143j was or was not the first word of a speech, so the speaker-indication here is flagged as tentative.

143c ἀργύριον: 143b–m n.

143d ἔστ' αὐτὸ μεῖγ[αι]: if this reading and restoration are correct, Demeas is talking about the possibility of the baby remaining in his home – if only, perhaps, to say that this was out of the question (if e.g. 143c ended with οὐδαμῶς).

143e Turner's reading and restoration, if correct or approximately so (which is very uncertain), would indicate that Demeas was raising the (horrendous) possibility that Chrysis' child might eventually lay claim to citizen status. This may prima facie seem absurd, but we know of a prosecution in the late 340s (that of Neaera and Stephanus, [Dem.] 59) where the case rested almost entirely on the allegation that the defendants had fraudulently insinuated the children of a foreign ex-*hetaira* into the citizen body.

143f If the restoration tentatively proposed in the apparatus ('You're agreeing to that?') is correct, it might support the suggestion made above (143b–m n.) that Demeas had offered to contribute to the child's maintenance provided it was taken away from his home.

143h ἄδηλον εἶπ[ας: 143b–m n.

144–6 When the text resumes, the topic of conversation has changed: the subject is now Moschion's marriage. In 145 one character is asking the other whether he is serious; in 146 someone (obviously Moschion) is speaking about marriage and saying he passionately desires it. Has Moschion after all taken the plunge and asked for permission to marry Plangon, or has Demeas, to his amazement, saved him the trouble by asking *him* if he is willing to marry her? The latter is much the more probable scenario. Having just succeeded, with some difficulty, in persuading Demeas not to expel Chrysis and the baby, the timid Moschion is even less likely to risk angering him again by asking him to accept an almost penniless daughter-in-law (cf. *Dysk.* 794–6). Evidently in the latter part of the lacuna, after agreeing that Chrysis and the baby could remain in his home, Demeas had changed the subject and raised the issue of a marriage for Moschion. If he did so initially in general terms, Moschion's response will have been cautious, but when he mentioned Plangon (or rather 'our neighbour's daughter' or the like; one did not refer to a respectable woman by her name in the presence of men not members of her family, see Sommerstein 1980) Moschion will have agreed to the match with alacrity and enthusiasm. This would take Demeas by surprise, in view of the poverty of Nikeratos' family, and it is probably he who asks 'are you serious?' in 145. In the next few lines Demeas must have suggested, or agreed to a suggestion by Moschion, that the wedding should take place that very day (this is presupposed by 156–9).

146 γαμεῖν ἐρῶ 'I passionately long to marry' (perhaps he added 'now' or 'today', see apparatus); for ἐρᾶν + infinitive cf. Ar. *Ach.* 147, *Wealth* 1009. Austin and Arnott punctuate between these words and take ἐρῶ to mean

'I'm in love'; but, as Dedoussi points out, Demeas' words at 335–6 imply that Moschion did not himself say this – rather, Demeas *inferred*, from other things he said, that he was in love with Plangon. Dedoussi herself takes ἐρῶ to be the future of λέγω, but does not explain in what connection Moschion could be saying 'I will say...'

147 The end of this line cannot be the end of Moschion's speech (nor does B have a *dicolon* to mark a change of speaker). If we restore [ἂ]ν, Moschion may be saying something like 'I'll burst with impatience if we don't have the wedding straight away' (e.g. [ἂ]ν μὴ τοὺς γάμους [ποῶμεν αὐτίκ]).

148–9 Demeas is apparently still finding it difficult to understand why Moschion is so eager for the marriage, but now a statement by Moschion of what he desires or intends (**βούλομαι...**) wins his father's warm approval. Proposed restorations of the first half of 149 have mostly been variations on Austin's [εἶναι δίκαιος κοὐ] δοκεῖν 'to be honest and not <merely> seem so', an expression found in Philemon (fr. 97.8) and based on Aesch. *Seven* 592 οὐ γὰρ δοκεῖν ἄριστος ἀλλ᾽ εἶναι θέλει (of Amphiaraus), a passage which had been quoted and discussed by Plato (*Rep.* 361b, 362a–b) with particular reference to the virtue of δικαιοσύνη. A declaration in Austin's terms would certainly appeal to Demeas, but it would be a very risky thing for Moschion to say: for what reason – other than the true reason, which he dare not reveal – should anyone think that *justice* demands that he marry Plangon? More appropriate sense might be given by West's [εἶναί τε χρηστὸς καὶ] δοκεῖν, but this may be too long for the available space. One might suggest [γενναῖος εἶναι καὶ] δοκεῖν: γενναῖος is a synonym of χρηστός in *Theoph.* F 1.14–15, and in *Dysk.* 805–8 Sostratos urges his father to use his wealth γενναίως by spreading it as widely as possible and in particular by agreeing to make the far from affluent Gorgias his son-in-law. By marrying Plangon, Moschion will be *both* displaying liberality to those poorer than himself (as on previous occasions: 15–16, 30–4nn.) *and* making it obvious to all that he is doing so, thus enhancing both his own reputation and that of the father who brought him up to behave thus. 'Goodness divorced from a reputation for goodness was of limited interest' (Dover 1974: 226).

150 ἂν διδῶσ᾽: B has a low dot before αν which may or may not be the remnant of a *dicolon* marking change of speaker; we cannot therefore tell from it precisely where Demeas' speech began, and Dedoussi's ἐπὰν is compatible with the visible traces. It may also seem more compatible with the situation than ἄν, since the audience know that Nikeratos has in fact already agreed to the marriage; but in the lacunose state of the text we cannot tell whether or not Demeas has mentioned this to Moschion, and he would have a motive for not doing so, since he 'may want to avoid giving the impression that everything has been arranged behind his son's back' (Sandbach), particularly since he apparently still cannot quite believe (see below on γαμεῖς;) that Moschion really is willing and eager to make the marriage.   οὗτοι probably denotes vaguely 'the people in there' (cf. *Mis.* 431 S = 961 A διδόασί σοι γυναῖκα); shortly afterwards (154–6, 160–1) both Demeas and Moschion are assuming that the decision will in fact be made by Nikeratos alone, and this makes it less likely that Demeas is here referring specifically to Nikeratos and his wife (on the latter's personality as indicated in the play, see Introduction §4(d)).   γαμεῖς; This must be a question ('you'll marry her?'). If the sentence were read as a statement, it would sound as though Demeas was laying down the law to his son, and that would not fit the context, in which Moschion has repeatedly expressed his eagerness for the marriage and Demeas has praised his attitude. To take it as a question also suits the interpretation of 151–2 which can be shown to be best on independent grounds (see below). It seems that Demeas, who is in effect being requested to ask Nikeratos to hold the wedding at very short notice, is anxious to be absolutely sure that the request is being made seriously; his reluctance to accept this stands in marked contrast to his almost instant decision to expel Chrysis from his house (130–4).

151–2 'I wish you'd stop asking me questions about this business, realize that I'm serious about it, and cooperate with me.' Moschion is getting impatient with his father's persistent failure to grasp how strongly he desires an immediate marriage to Plangon, and perhaps afraid that under further questioning he might inadvertently blurt out something that could give Demeas an inkling of the truth about the baby.

151 [πῶς ἄν]: this restoration has been almost universally accepted, but its consequences for the interpretation of the sentence have not always been understood. The construction πῶς ἄν + optative is 'the equivalent of a wish' (Sandbach) or of an earnest request; see 101–4n. If the meaning were 'how could you know I was serious?' (Arnott), the verb would be imperfect or aorist indicative. There is, to be sure, an alternative interpretation that is grammatically possible, taking πῶς as a true interrogative, πυθόμενος as a conditional participle, and the potential optative as a weak future: 'how are you going to realize that I'm serious, and cooperate with me, unless you find out something about the matter?' (so in effect Stoessl 1969: 200 and many after him). But what, in context, could this mean? Stoessl himself thought that Moschion was here on the point of confessing the truth to Demeas; but there is absolutely no reason for him to do so, when the marriage is not yet an accomplished fact and Demeas has just demonstrated the unreliability of his temper. Kassel (*ap.* Austin ad loc.) thought Moschion was impatiently demanding that Demeas sound out Nikeratos – which would be odd, when with ἂν διδῶσ'οὗτοι Demeas has just clearly implied his intention of doing so. Note that however we interpret πυθόμενος… τοῦ πράγματος, Stoessl's construal, like that adopted here, presupposes that Demeas does not yet 'realize that [Moschion] is serious', and is therefore inconsistent with his having stated just previously that Moschion can marry Plangon if her parents agree (150n.).   [π]υθόμενος μηδὲ ἓν τοῦ πράγματος: literally, 'not inquiring at all about the matter' (LSJ πυνθάνομαι I 3): μηδέ rather than οὐδέ because this is part of what Moschion is requesting. Logically he should have said 'not inquiring *further*', since Demeas has already asked him two or three questions about it at least (145, 148–9n., 150), but this kind of illogic was and is frequent in conversation; cf. 311 μηδὲν ὄμνυ᾿ interrupting a string of four oaths.

152 |ἐσπο]υδακότα: Demeas has already asked Moschion whether he is in earnest (145), and has received an affirmative answer, of which, so it seems to Moschion, he has taken no notice.

153–4 Demeas at last, as he supposes, understands the situation: Moschion is desperately in love with Plangon (cf. 165–6). This is, of course, true (and very convenient for Demeas' plans), but it is far from the whole truth.

153 ἐσπουδακότα; μηδὲν πυθόμενος; Demeas repeats the words of Moschion's that have convinced him that his son is indeed in earnest.

153–4 καταγ[οῶ] | τὸ πρᾶγμα: the audience know better, as for the second time in a single scene Demeas is successfully deceived. Later (335–6) he will realize that he was in error – but, thanks to the first deception, he will identify the error wrongly, and so will discard a true belief (that Moschion is in love with Plangon) while retaining a false one (that Chrysis is the mother of the baby, whose father he by then knows to be Moschion). For other examples of Demeas' excessive confidence in his own intellect cf. 267–8, 316–18, 466, 477 (Katsouris 1975b: 108). Later still (522) we shall hear the words τὸ πρᾶγμα κατανοῶ again, from Moschion, when he at last becomes aware of this misapprehension of his father's – for which, of course, he had been partly responsible – and confesses the full truth.

154–6 τρέχω indicates the urgency with which Demeas is now ready to help fulfil his son's wishes. Normally, 'running' to serve another is something that slaves do (195, 202, 678, *Mis.* 237 S = 638 A, *Perik.* 1009; Ar. *Birds* 76–9, *Wealth* 222, 229, 1103; cf. Ter. *HT* 31, 37, *Eun.* 36), though in Old Comedy a character who feels himself to be holding the whip-hand may give such orders to an equal or superior (in Ar. *Wealth* 1133 a slave does so to a god!). Nowhere else, however, in the comic corpus, does a parent 'run' to serve his or her adult son. Demeas' behaviour here is perhaps best compared with that of the delighted husband in Ar. *Thesm.* 510, who 'runs' out of the room at his wife's urgent demand, believing her about to give birth at last after a ten-day labour, thus enabling her to produce from concealment a baby boy who had been bought for her in the slave market. Demeas too is delighted that Moschion's desires so happily coincide with his own.

155 τουτονί: with a gesture towards Nikeratos' house; cf. 549, *Aspis* 139, *Mis.* 301 S = 702 A.

155–6 τοὺς γάμους... | ποεῖν: 'today' is left to be understood; this would be easy if Moschion had already indicated that he wished for the wedding to be held immediately (147n.), and Moschion's response (156–8) shows that he does indeed understand Demeas' intention.

155 αὐτῶι φράσω 'I'll ask him': φράζω, like English 'tell', does not necessarily imply that the addressee is obliged to obey; in Aristophanes it often denotes a request (*Peace* 98) or recommendation (*Clouds* 1009, *Birds* 711, *Lys.* 1009, 1012, *Wealth* 46) which may or may not be complied with.

156–9 On the division of parts adopted here, Moschion says that he will immediately begin preparations for the wedding, about which he had earlier been fantasizing (123–6; cf. also the urgings of Parmenon, 74–5), and then go to fetch his bride home, thereby completing the marriage; he is, of course, jumping the gun, and has to be warned to wait.

B's indications of speaker-change are confused, and the scribe evidently changed his mind at least once. There are *paragraphoi* (horizontal strokes) under lines 156 and 158, which ought to indicate a change of speaker in, or at the end of, each of these lines. The scribe also originally marked the precise position of speaker-changes with *dicola* after ποεῖν (156) and λέγεις (157) – indications not wholly consistent with those given by the *paragraphoi* – but subsequently deleted them. We cannot tell whether he left the *paragraphoi* in place intentionally or only by oversight, or whether he had had it in mind to insert new *dicola* in different places but neglected to do so. Perhaps the relevant markings in his exemplar were badly faded at this point. At any rate, what he has done with them gives us no help in dividing the passage between speakers.

It is certain, however, that [τὴν κόρην] μέτειμι (158–9) is spoken by Moschion, and the words immediately following by Demeas; and all but certain that τὰ παρ' ἡμῶν γὰρ <παρ>έσται (156), spoken in the first person plural in the name of the household, are the words of Demeas speaking as its head.

Lamagna, following Austin and Blume 1974: 66, continues the whole of 156–8 as far as ἐπιθείς to Demeas; but whether one envisages Demeas as stating what he himself intends to do (which is Lamagna's own view) or as giving instructions to Moschion, he cannot embark, or allow Moschion to embark, on the preliminary rituals of a wedding when he has as yet no idea (159–60) whether Nikeratos will be willing to hold it today. This consideration forces us to give περιρρανάμενος...μέτειμι all to Moschion, and leaves uncertain only the assignment of ταυ[◡ –] λέγεις (on which see below).

156 τὰ παρ' ἡμῶν: a general expression covering (1) willingness and readiness to hold the wedding forthwith, (2) performance of all the ritual acts incumbent on the bridegroom and his family (such as those mentioned in 157–8), and (3) the appurtenances and accessories which it was customary or (in view of Demeas' greater wealth) convenient for the bridegroom's family to provide, including those which Parmenon is sent to market to purchase (189–202) and those which the household staff are soon busy preparing (219–25). **παρέσται:** παρ- has been lost in B, leaving the line unmetrical; it could easily have dropped out after γάρ.

156–7 ταῦ[τά γ' εὖ] | λέγεις: if this restoration (Jacques), or something like it, is correct, Moschion is expressing his pleasure that his father has fallen in with his wishes. The most plausible alternative would be to restore e.g. ταῦ[θ' ἅ σὺ] λέγεις, continued to Demeas, which would probably require us to suppose that 'Moschion [had] asked, in the gap before 145, for some of the concomitants of a wedding' (Sandbach). He may have done, but there is no other evidence that he did.

157 περιρρανάμενος 'after giving myself a ritual sprinkling', a purification rite preliminary to a sacrifice or to entering a sanctuary (Parker 1983: 19–20). Sandbach suggests that Moschion, in his hurry, is skimping on the normal requirement for the bridegroom to bathe all over (124n.); but schol. Eur. *Phoen.* 347 ('In former times it was the custom for bridegrooms to bathe in their local rivers and [= or?] to take water from rivers and springs and sprinkle themselves with it') indicates that it may have been a legitimate alternative form of the ritual (Christian baptism provides an obvious parallel). When in Aristophanes' *Lysistrata* the female semichorus throw water from their pitchers at the male semichorus – water brought, we are probably to understand, from the Enneakrounos (Sommerstein 1990: 170) – they say they are giving them 'a nuptial bath' (*Lys.* 378). **παρα[γαγών]** 'going inside' (104n.; *Dysk.* 556, 780, 859; *Perik.* 525). B has an apostrophe after παρ-, indicating an (internal) elision and thus ruling out the restoration παρα[γενοῦ] (West, Sandbach). As we have seen, Moschion will never in fact go into his own house throughout the play.

158 σπείσας τε καὶ λιβανωτὸν ἐπιθείς: libations, and the placing (and burning) of incense on altars, were accompaniments to many ritual acts, from prayers (e.g. *Dysk.* 660–1; Ar. *Wasps* 860–91, *Peace* 433–8, *Frogs* 871–94) upwards, and in particular to sacrifices (e.g. *Kolax* F 1); at 674 Parmenon reports that incense is being burned in connection with a sacrifice in Demeas' house. Earlier (123) Moschion was imagining himself performing, or taking part in, a sacrificial ritual; here, however, he may be envisaging something less time-consuming (cf. above on περιρρανάμενος), perhaps merely a quick prayer before going over to his bride's house.

158–9 [τὴν κόρην] μέτειμι 'I'll go to fetch the girl', sc. and bring her home; this is the act that will definitively make the pair husband and wife (Oakley and Sinos 1993: 28). When Moschion returns in Act IV, this is still the first thing on his mind (433–4). Yet when all obstacles to the marriage are at last removed, we find he is brooding on other things (616–40); Parmenon has to urge him – in vain – to go and fetch his bride immediately (676), and by 714 Nikeratos is saying that all is ready for him to do so 'if he ever comes'. In the end, with Moschion still keeping up a pretence of reluctant compliance, it will be Demeas who asks for the bride to be brought out of her father's house (723).

Here Moschion presumably makes to go into his (i.e. Demeas') house, but Demeas stops him.

160 εἰ ταῦτα συγχωρήσεθ': i.e. whether he will agree to hold the wedding today.

161 οὐκ ἀντερεῖ σοι: a bad prediction in any case – Nikeratos' initial reaction to Demeas' proposal is that it is 'impossible' (176), and only at 186–7 does he agree to it – and an absurdly optimistic one if, as is on balance likely (150n.), Moschion is unaware that Demeas and Nikeratos have already agreed on the marriage in principle and now have only to fix the date. A similarly confident prediction is made in similar terms (οὐδὲν ὁ πατὴρ ἀντερεῖ [μοι]) by Sostratos in *Dysk.* (761) about his own father's reaction to the news of his betrothal to Knemon's daughter, but that prediction is a correct one (785–90) – or would have been, had not Sostratos proposed in addition that his own sister should be married to Gorgias. Moschion's rapid departure, and the evidence we already have of his timidity (65–76, 80, 94–5, 128), suggest strongly that we are to understand that he is not really as confident as his words imply, but is eager to encourage his father to put his proposal to Nikeratos without delay.

161–2 παρενοχλε[ῖν] ... | ... ἀπρε[πές] 'It's improper for me to get in your way by being present together with you.' Probably this would have seemed to the audience a rather lame excuse, particularly since Demeas has made no request for Moschion to absent himself: in *Aspis* 250ff Chaireas does not speak while his stepfather and guardian, Chairestratos, is urging Smikrines to allow their niece, the sister of the supposedly dead Kleostratos, to marry Chaireas, but Smikrines, while adamantly insisting on his right to marry the heiress himself, makes no objection to Chaireas' presence at the inter-view. Evidently Moschion does not want to come face to face with Nikeratos (from whom he has much to conceal) unless it is absolutely unavoidable. He could, admittedly, have avoided Nikeratos just as well by going into his own house – but Menander needs to get him completely off the scene if his plot for the drama is to work.

Moschion departs by Eisodos A (see note at start of play). It is not cer-tain whether an exit in this direction will in itself signal that his destination is the city centre (ibid.), but at present it is in any case only important *that* he is going, not *where* he is going.

163 ταὐτόματον: 55n. **θεός:** to call an entity or concept a god is to say that it has 'power to affect [humans]' (Dover 1974: 142–3, citing this pas-sage and also Men. fr. 838); Euripides had been particularly fond of this trope (e.g. *Hel.* 560*, *Phoen.* 506, 531–2, *Or.* 398–9), but he did not origi-nate it (cf. Hes. *Works* 763–4; Aesch. *Cho.* 59–60*; Soph. frr. 605, 922; Hdt. 8.111.2–3) and, as the two asterisked passages show, it was perfectly possi-ble to personify and deify an abstract concept even if it was expressed as an infinitival phrase or, as here, a nominalized neuter adjective; see Stafford 2000: 9–13. Τύχη, a synonym of ταὐτόματον (55n.), is of course frequently so treated (Burkert 1985: 185–6), and she is the prologue-speaker in *Aspis* (97–148); already before Menander's time there was a cult of Ἀγαθὴ Τύχη in Athens (Parker 1996: 227–37, especially 231–2).

164 '…and causes many things that one does not see to turn out safely', thus entitling it to the divine epithet σωτήρ: cf. Aesch. *Ag.* 664 Τύχη…σωτήρ; Pind. *Olymp.* 12.2.

165–6 Evidently Demeas is here saying that thanks to ταὐτόματον he has been able to give Moschion the marriage on which, unknown to him, Mos-chion had already set his heart. Note that underlying his words is the assumption that, other things being equal, it is good that a young man should marry the girl (of citizen status) with whom he is in love; cf. *Dysk.* 788–90 where Kallippides says that this helps to ensure that the marriage will be durable. In our passage a similar principle appears to be presup-posed rather than asserted, which strongly suggests that it would not be as 'striking to a fourth-century audience' as Sandbach (on *Dysk.* 788) sup-posed (see Brown 1993).

166/7 When B resumes at 167, Demeas is still alone on stage, and nothing in the remainder of the play requires or even suggests that any other char-acter appeared during the lost passage. Accordingly it has been generally accepted that the monologue by Demeas which began at 163 continued right through the lacuna, being thus in all some 33–34 lines in length. Demeas may have explained, if he had not done so already (119a/b n.),

why he had proposed to Nikeratos a marriage alliance between their families (cf. Holzberg 1974: 33 n. 102), and/or explained why he thought Moschion was deserving of the good fortune which he, Nikeratos and ταὐτόματον between them had conferred on him (for both these suggestions
see Barigazzi 1970: 164–5). The latter topic in particular would provide
good opportunities for dramatic irony. At 167 Demeas' reflections have
evidently come to an end and he is about to make his approach to Nikeratos. If he has decided to deceive Nikeratos by speaking as though they
had already agreed to hold the wedding immediately (170–1n.), he will
probably, immediately before 167, have given some indication, in general
terms, of what he was intending to do and why he expected his ploy to be
successful.

168–9 With the restorations adopted here (in text or apparatus), Demeas
calls to Nikeratos to come out of his house (cf. *Dysk.* 637–8; Ar. *Ach.* 404–6,
749, 823), perhaps also knocking at his door; the repetition of δεῦρο will
indicate his urgency (cf. 154–6n.; Ar. *Knights* 148, *Clouds* 866, 1485).
Austin, reading the last six letters of 168 as]χρομαι, thought that the second half of that line was spoken by Nikeratos, coming out of his own accord
(perhaps annoyed by Demeas' apparent delay) and saying εἰς τὸ πρόσθεν δ'
[ἔ]ρχομαι: in the ensuing dialogue, however, Demeas is clearly taking the
initiative (note especially 170–1), and one would therefore expect him to
be the one who causes the conversation to take place. Nikeratos' ἐπὶ τί;
(169) also suggests that Demeas has called him out.

169 [Νικήρατ']: as the passages cited in the previous note show, when calling a person out of his house, it was usual to address him by name (otherwise a slave might answer the call). This may have been the first mention
of Nikeratos' name in the play: he is not named in the earlier dialogue
between the two fathers (96–119) and probably was not named in the prologue (1–57n.). Nikeratos comes out of his house.   ἐπὶ τί; 'for what purpose?' (cf. 661).   χαῖρε πολλὰ σύ: it is surprising to find Demeas using
this extra-hearty version of the regular greeting χαῖρε when he and Nikeratos have only recently parted after travelling together for many months
(contrast 431, *Mis.* 213; also *com. adesp.* 1017.7, 77, where Phaidimos has
evidently just arrived from abroad); presumably, being about to make a
proposal which may anger Nikeratos, he wishes to appear exceptionally
friendly.

170–1 Nikeratos' bewildered response ποῦ; πότε; (173) strongly suggests
that Demeas has here said, not 'You remember that we didn't fix a day?'
but, with a *suggestio falsi*, 'You remember what day we fixed?', and then
gone on to say that the date agreed was today (172 τὴν τήμερον) and, reinforcing his bluff, that Nikeratos knows this well (173 [οἶ]σθ' ἀκριβῶς). If

Demeas were avowedly making for the first time a proposal to hold the wedding today, Nikeratos might well object, but it would make no sense for him to ask 'where? when?' If, on the other hand, Demeas is claiming that he and Nikeratos have already agreed on today as the date, Nikeratos, who of course has no recollection of making any such agreement, will very naturally ask where and when it was made.

Why, though, should Demeas lie? Presumably we are to understand that he fears that if the proposal is presented as a new one, Nikeratos will reject it, whereas if Nikeratos can be persuaded that he has already given his word, he will be reluctant to break it. But if Nikeratos realizes that Demeas is trying to trick him, will he not be even more hostile to the proposal, maybe even to the extent of calling off the marriage altogether? Demeas' ploy is only explicable if he is confident of successfully fooling Nikeratos, 'not rating his friend's intellectual ability very highly' (Blume 1974: 71); and in order for the audience to understand this, he would probably have had to explain in advance to them why he expected his plan to succeed (166/7n.). Later on (586–611), when Nikeratos has realized the truth about Moschion, Plangon, and the baby, Demeas will placate him with the absurd pretence that the baby's real father may be a god; there (604–5), as here (186–7), Nikeratos eventually surrenders, and both times Demeas compliments him for acting intelligently (νοῦν ἔχεις).

Thus Demeas joins the play's large company of deceivers, which already includes Moschion, Plangon and her mother, Chrysis, Parmenon, and all of Demeas' domestic staff (and Nikeratos' too, if he has any, 96–119a n.) – everyone in both households, in fact, except Nikeratos himself. Demeas will later deceive Chrysis (354–6, 374–5) and the world in general (446–9) in order to conceal what he believes to be a grave offence against him by Moschion.

170 εἰπέ μοι is in this play a mannerism of Demeas, who uses it five times in all (also 483, 589, 690, 692) out of a total of seven occurrences (Sandbach 1970: 122–3).

171 ἐγώ; 'Do I <remember that>?' In response either to a statement or to a 'yes/no' question, ἐγώ; expresses bafflement (484) and is often tantamount to a denial (286, 308, 315, 497). If Demeas' question were to be restored as 'You remember that we didn't fix a day?' (see previous note), we would have to take ἐγώ as declarative rather than interrogative and as equivalent to an affirmative answer (cf. 733, *Epitr.* 858).

172 [τ]αὐτ[α]γί: this restoration is very uncertain: the first partly surviving letter may be λ rather than α, the ι is a correction above the line, and the horizontal stroke of γ (if that is what it is) is continuous with that of the following τ. If the letters are correctly read, Demeas may have said

something like '[Yes,] that [was agreed on].'   τὴν τήμερον *sc.* ἡμέραν: cf.
com. adesp. 1014.20. In fourth-century prose (e.g. Xen. *Anab.* 4.6.9; Dem.
4.40, 9.28; Lyc. *Leocr.* 2; Dein. 1.22) ἡμέραν is never omitted, but here there
is not sufficient space in 173 for it to be restored, and it can easily be
understood from 171.

173–86 It is rarely possible in this passage to make even a plausible guess
at the wording of the lost first half of each line, but the gist of the
exchanges is clear, as Nikeratos gradually yields in the face of Demeas'
evidently immovable determination that the wedding shall be held today.

174–5 [γ]ίνεσθαι ταχύ: apparently Demeas makes no further attempt to
keep up his pretence that the date has already been agreed, and says
instead that (for unspecified reasons) it is best, or is his wish, that the
marriage take place 'speedily'.   ]ερον might be the remnant of τήμερον
(which, however, would be somewhat repetitive after τὴν τήμερον 172 and
ταχύ 174) or of a comparative such as αἱρετώτερον 'preferable' (for which
cf. *Mis.* A13 S = 13 A). In the former case, Nikeratos with τρόπωι τίνι; will
be asking how the wedding can be arranged so quickly; in the latter, he
will be asking in what way it is preferable for it to be held today.

176–7 Demeas chooses to assume that by ἀλλ' ἔστ' ἀδύνατον Nikeratos
means that he will not be able to afford all the requisites for the wedding, and assures him that he need not concern himself with that as he,
Demeas, will see to everything. With the restoration proposed cf. Ar. *Peace*
149, 1041, 1311 ἐμοὶ μελήσει ταῦτά γ'.

178 ὦ Ἡράκλεις: this interjection is very common in Menander (five times
more in this play alone: 360, 405, 408, 435, 552), usually indicating surprise, amazement or annoyance. Such feelings are here more appropriate
to Nikeratos, irritated with Demeas' persistence and probably unable to
understand his impatience, than they would be to Demeas. Nikeratos is
also the speaker at 405 and 408; no one else in the play uses the expression more than once.

179–81 Little can be made of the two lines and a half down to the middle
of 181, and it is not clear who speaks what. In 180 a long monosyllable must
have dropped out of the text, which as we have it is unmetrical. The words
that follow, τοδὶ λέγειν, ought to point forwards to a following sentence
or clause, and there will only be space for such a sentence or clause if
there is a syntactic break at the end of 180, i.e. if the second half of 180
is syntactically complete; hence <δεῖ> is the most likely supplement, and
the speaker at this point is probably Demeas.

181–2 Nikeratos raises a further practical objection. He may have asked: '[Am I to hold the wedding] before inviting my friends [cf. 123], [so as] to seem [mean]?'

182–3 On Kamerbeek's reading and restoration, Demeas gives up attempting to argue Nikeratos into agreeing to an immediate wedding and instead asks him to agree as a favour, assuring him that he will be grateful (with an implicit promise of reciprocal favours later on): for χάριν εἴσομαι in such contexts cf. Ar. *Wasps* 1420. If χάριν did appear earlier in the line, it may help explain B's error in placing a *dicolon*, marking change of speaker, in the middle of the word χαρίσ-ηι instead of at the end. B also, it seems, at first omitted ἐμοί, inserting it afterwards above the line (the last two letters have survived).

183 πῶς γνώσομαι; 'How shall I decide?' Nikeratos wavers: it is difficult to refuse a request for a favour, when one has already received many favours from the person making the request.

184 Demeas reinforces his plea by an explicit appeal to friendship: 'help friends, harm enemies' was a basic principle of popular Greek ethics (e.g. Soph. *Ant.* 641–4, Ar. *Birds* 419–20, Pl. *Rep.* 332a–b; see Dover 1974: 180–4, M. W. Blundell 1989: 26–59).   τυχόντος: Demeas may be using the quasi-adjective ὁ τυχών 'random, ordinary, average' and assuring Nikeratos that he regards him (or will regard him, if he acts as Demeas wishes in the matter of the marriage) as 'no ordinary friend' but an exceptionally close one: he perhaps said something like [ἔξω σε μᾶλλον το]ῦ τυχόντος μοι φίλον 'I will treat you as more of a friend than the average <friend>'. In view of the great difference in wealth between the two men, this offer shows how strong is Demeas' desire to gratify his son's wishes: Aristotle (*EN* 1158b33–5) even holds that 'if a great gap arises [between two friends] in … prosperity or anything else … they cease to be friends or even to think it appropriate that they should be'. If our interpretation of 170–3 is correct, it is highly ironic that Demeas should make such an offer to Nikeratos so soon after shamelessly lying to him. He will appeal to Nikeratos as a φίλος again at 518, when he asks him to expel Chrysis from his house; not long afterwards, though (570–6, 582–3), the two men will be applying physical force to each other, before Demeas once again cajoles Nikeratos into complying with his wishes.

185–7 For the reason stated in the previous note, Nikeratos cannot quite believe that Demeas really means what he has just said, and so echoes the question that Demeas had asked Moschion not long before (145, cf. 138–9). Demeas presumably confirms that he is indeed 'serious', and Nikeratos surrenders and is complimented by Demeas for doing so. Supplementation in 186–7 is particularly difficult; but Lamagna's [ἐμὲ νῦν ἄλογόν ἐ]στιν may at any rate be close to the sense, making Nikeratos say 'since I am in agreement with you [*sc.* that our two children should marry], it's absurd for me to be disputatious now [*sc.* on the issue of *when* this marriage should take place]', though its wording is unlikely to be right (ἄλογος occurs only once in Menander, at *Aspis* 415 in what is evidently a tragic quotation).

187 φιλονικεῖν 'be (sc. unduly) determined to win', i.e. 'be contentious, prolong a dispute unreasonably'. Not φιλονεικεῖν (B), which would mean much the same if it existed: the adjective from which this verb is derived invariably appears, in texts of the classical and Hellenistic periods, as φιλόν(ε)ικος of the second declension (e.g. Men. fr. 636), not φιλον(ε)ίκης of the third, showing that it is derived from νίκη rather than νεῖκος, and similarly the abstract noun is always φιλον(ε)ικία (e.g. *Aspis* 318), not φιλον(ε)ίκεια.   **νοῦν ἔχεις:** Demeas will say this again to Nikeratos, twice in quick succession, at the climax of his successful attempt to humour him out of his fury against Moschion (605, 611); earlier (470–1) he warns Moschion that, ἂν ἔχῃς νοῦν, he should abandon his plea for Chrysis to be allowed to return to their home. In all four passages Demeas is concerned that nothing should prevent the wedding from being held as quickly as possible, and they are the only occurrences of the phrase νοῦν ἔχειν in the play.

188 συνοίσει σοι 'it will be to your advantage'; in what way, we cannot tell, though Nikeratos, in his mostly lost reply, may have made a (humorous?) guess, e.g. that a wedding without invited guests (181) will be comparatively cheap (Dedoussi, comparing Men. fr. 340).

Demeas goes to the door of his house and calls loudly for Parmenon, who is to go to the Agora, buy the supplies needed for the wedding, and hire a cook.

189 παῖ: a regular form of address to a male slave, of any age (again 202, 358; see Dickey 1996: 70–7, 232–5); Daos, who is so addressed in *Aspis* 305, is apparently middle-aged at least (*Aspis* 11–12). *Puer* was similarly used in Latin from early times (giving rise to compound names like *Marcipor* 'Marcus' boy', Pliny *HN* 33.26).

190–1 When Parmenon returns at 283, he is carrying a basket (σφυρίδα 297) containing his purchases; hence the proposal of Blume 1974: 73 to restore [σφυρίδα λαβὼν σύ] at the start of 191. The participial phrase would perhaps, however, be better placed in 190 at the beginning of the sentence; then the otiose σύ could be dispensed with, and the summing-up phrase πάντα τἆξ ἀγορᾶς ἁπλῶς could directly follow the detailed shopping list.

190 [στε]φάνους, ἱερεῖον, σήσαμα: cf. 74–5 (the speaker is Parmenon!) θύειν, στεφανοῦσθαι, σησαμῆν κόπτειν; sesame-cakes were also mentioned at 125. As Blume 1974: 72 saw, already from these words Parmenon will have understood that a wedding is in prospect (cf. also 431–2), and it may be added that the presence of Nikeratos would strongly suggest that the bride is to be Plangon; but for one thing this will have seemed almost too good to be true, and for another, even if it is true, Parmenon cannot tell whether the marriage has come about as a result of Moschion's persuasion or of Demeas' or Nikeratos' discovery of the truth about the baby. Accordingly he acts a little stupid with Demeas (192–5) and ensures that no careless words shall reach his ears (198–200n.) – though in his absence another member of the household will spill some of the beans. At the beginning of 191 some further items, probably two, will have been added to the list; for Dedoussi's suggestions (torches and incense) cf. 731 and 158 respectively.

191 πάντα τὰξ ἀγορᾶς ἁπλῶς: he means 'absolutely everything that's needed for a wedding' (ἁπλῶς as in Diphilus fr. 87.5, Philemon fr. 114.2, Ar. *Ach.* 873, *Wasps* 538), but has forgotten that he has not actually said anything about a wedding, so that strictly speaking he is instructing Parmenon to buy (at least) some quantity of every commodity sold in the Agora!

192–3 That Parmenon addresses his master as Δημέα rather than δέσποτα (296, 304, 320) need not arouse suspicion; cf. *Dysk.* 247, *Sik.* 135, 142, and see Dickey 1996: 235. If something like Austin's restoration is correct, Parmenon begins to say what he will do if complete discretion about what to buy is left to him (LSJ παραλείπω II, 'leave to another' and thence 'allow') but is cut off in mid-sentence by Demeas. Dedoussi gives this speech to Nikeratos, asking whether Demeas really intends to leave nothing in the market for *him* to buy; but Nikeratos never in this scene takes the conversational initiative with Demeas, and if he were to complain here, Demeas, anxious throughout to secure his cooperation, would not have ignored him.

193 καὶ ταχέως 'and (sc. go) quickly'; cf. Ar. *Frogs* 166 'Pick up the luggage.' – πρὶν καὶ καταθέσθαι· – καὶ ταχέως μέντοι πάνυ.   ἤδη λέγω 'I mean right now'; cf. 133–4nn., 370–1.

194 [ἄγε καὶ μ]άγειρον: there is nothing to choose between ἄγε 'bring' and λαβέ 'get, hire' (for the latter cf. Alexis fr. 216, Euphron fr. 1.15). The audience are thus explicitly notified that that favourite character, the comic cook, will be making an appearance before very long.   καὶ μάγειρον; We must punctuate after these words, making them an echo question of a type characteristic of Parmenon (cf. 306–7, 323, 659–660: Macua Martínez 1997: 155–6). Parmenon is professing not to understand his orders entirely – but he cannot reveal what he is actually uncertain about (is Moschion being married, and to whom?) and so, rather absurdly, he asks for confirmation that he is to hire a cook *as well as* make the purchases mentioned, when he would have known perfectly well that if an animal is to be sacrificed and eaten, a cook is needed to kill, butcher and prepare it (283–390n.). If we did not punctuate, Parmenon would be pretending, with at least equal absurdity, that he was being asked to *buy* a cook: it is imaginable that he might do so – but not that Demeas would confirm that such was indeed his wish ([π]ριάμενος 195). It would not, in fact, have been impossible to buy a cook, since some cooks were slaves (Poseidippus fr. 25; see Krieter-Spiro 1997: 27–9); but that would be far too large a transaction to be entrusted to a slave (who might run away with the cash, on which he could live for several months). A century earlier, when prices generally were lower, a donkey driver could fetch 155 drachmae, a τραπεζο-ποιός (certainly less valuable than a cook: *Dysk.* 647, Antiphanes fr. 150) 215, and a goldsmith 360 (*IG* I³ 422.71–78).

195 ἀργύριον λαβὼν τρέχω: Parmenon perceives (doubtless from Demeas' tone and perhaps gesture) that he cannot safely prevaricate any longer, and using the 'prophetic' present tense (Goodwin 1912: 11) he assures Demeas that he will 'run' (154–6n.) to the Agora as soon as he has the money for the purchases. He then goes into the house to get the money (and a shopping-basket), returning at 198. Demeas then turns to Nikeratos.

196 [σὺ δ' οὐδ]έπω: in the third person, expressions of this type normally mean 'he hasn't *come* yet' (*Dysk.* 867, Ar. *Thesm.* 846), but that would not make sense in the second person (except in a letter), and here the context, and especially Parmenon's words just before, make it clear that Demeas means 'aren't you *going* yet?' He can, it seems, safely assume that Nikeratos will be willing, despite his poverty, to make at least some contribution to the wedding; but his words may well be taken to betray some impatience, indicating a continuing anxiety to ensure that, in accordance with Moschion's wishes, everything will be completed today. Nikeratos' reply makes it clear that there will be no unnecessary delay on his part.

197 [πρὸς τ]ὴν γυναῖκα: Demeas, in contrast, gives similar instructions τοῖς ἔνδον (221), i.e. to his large household of male and female slaves. Nikeratos probably has no male slaves, and may not even have a female one (96–119a n.): most of the work of preparing for the wedding will fall upon his wife, and he must also do his own shopping.

198 διώξομ' 'I will follow quickly after' (not 'I will pursue'), as in *Dysk.* 378, Xen. *Hell.* 1.1.13; in Pl. *Phd.* 61b8-d5 διώκειν and ἕπεσθαι are treated as interchangeable.

Nikeratos goes into his house; almost immediately Parmenon (with shopping-basket and purse) comes out of Demeas' house, talking back to those within (for similar entrances cf. 301, 421, 440–4, 713–14; *Aspis* 164–6, *Dysk.* 427–9, 874–8, *Epitr.* 430–1; see Frost 1988: 7–8). Note the rapid succession of exits and entrances as this act approaches its end: Parmenon comes out of the house (189), goes back in (195), Nikeratos goes in (198), Parmenon comes out again (198) and departs towards the Agora (202), after which, in the lost final verses, Nikeratos must come out and likewise leave for the Agora, and Demeas must go back inside his house – altogether eight movements by three characters within, at most, twenty-odd lines.

198–200 Parmenon has evidently asked (Chrysis?) for money for his purchases, and has been asked in reply why they are being made; he professes complete ignorance, not wishing to say anything that might give Demeas an inkling that he knows, or has guessed, more than Demeas has told him.

199 συντείνω 'I'm hurrying' (in fact he will be rather slow to depart, 200–2n.). This sense of συντείνω, first attested here, appears to have remained a colloquialism for several centuries: it is not used by Polybius or Diodorus, but appears in Dionysius of Halicarnassus (*Ant.Rom.* 3.40.5, 11.37.3) and is common in Plutarch (e.g. *Nic.* 30.2, *Philop.* 18.6, *Brut.* 6.4).

200–1 τὸ πεῖσαι... | ... παρέξει: Demeas is both wrong and right. On the one hand, he little knows that Nikeratos' wife is eager for the marriage to take place and had in fact virtually arranged for it in her husband's absence. On the other hand, Nikeratos' words in 203–5 – if they are indeed his – suggest that she has been grumbling about being ordered to make rushed preparations for it at a moment's notice.

201–2 μὴ δοῦναι λόγον | μηδὲ χ[ρ]όνον 'not allow [sc. to Nikeratos' wife] any say in the matter [cf. Xen. *Hell.* 5.2.20 ἐδίδοσαν Λακεδαιμόνιοι τοῖς συμμάχοις λόγον καὶ ἐκέλευον συμβουλεύειν], or any time'.

202 ἡ[μ]ᾶς may be equivalent to ἐμέ (as in *Dysk.* 70, *Epitr.* 694), or it may be a genuine plural, including Nikeratos. The latter is more likely, since only Nikeratos has the right to insist that his wife obey him.   **παῖ, δια-τρίβεις:** Parmenon has probably been dallying to listen to Demeas' reflections, intrigued by his apparent determination to hasten things as much as possible and perhaps hoping he may drop some words that will give further information about the planned wedding.   **οὐ δραμεῖ;** See 154–6, 195nn. At this further sign of Demeas' impatience, which is probably accompanied by a threatening gesture, Parmenon realizes that he cannot safely stay any longer and departs, with reasonable rapidity, in the direction of the city centre (by Eisodos A). It is possible that Demeas then immediately goes into his house without speaking again; but one would expect him to express some satisfaction at having achieved his purpose (not least to contrast with the state of distress in which he will reappear at the start of the next act), so it is more likely that he remains on stage and has a brief monologue after Nikeratos' departure.

203–5 The reference to ἡ γυνή makes it highly likely that the speaker here is Nikeratos, commenting on his wife's reaction to the news he brought her and the instructions he gave. The reading and supplement [περ]ἱ[ερ]γος, though very uncertain, would be appropriate: Menander uses this adjective and its derivatives several times (300; *Epitr.* F 2; *Epitr.* 262, 575) in reference to persons (normally slaves; once a cook) who interfere in, or seek information about, matters which 'ought' to be no concern of theirs. Barigazzi 1970: 167–8 and Arnott may well be right to suppose that with ἱκετεύω Nikeratos is directly quoting his wife's words to him: the word is normally in Menander used in situations of urgency or distress (e.g. 518, *Dysk.* 86, 123, *Epitr.* 430, *Perik.* 510), most often by slaves or anguished lovers, and would suit a wife begging her husband for more time to complete a task. Arnott may also be right in suggesting that if ἡλίκον is correctly read in 205, the reference is to the loudness of the wife's voice as she complains.

After a few more words of soliloquy, and perhaps a brief exchange with Demeas, Nikeratos departs through Eisodos A as Parmenon had done. Demeas may then express his satisfaction at having persuaded Nikeratos to hold the wedding immediately, and his pleasure at having been able to do this favour for his adopted son: for the second time in rapid succession (cf. 163–6), things have gone just the way he wished. He then goes into his house (perhaps saying that he is doing so in order to instruct the household to make preparations for the wedding, cf. 219–22), and the second choral interlude follows.

Already at the beginning of Act II every member of both households had been committed to the marriage taking place, though Demeas and Nikeratos had reached their decision separately from those at home and unknown to them. Now, far from any obstacles having arisen, those which Moschion (and probably, to a lesser extent, Demeas) had apprehended have proved illusory, and all those whose opinion formally counts (i.e. the three free adult males) have agreed that the wedding is to be held forthwith. With three acts to go, the audience can be virtually certain that some kind of obstacle will nevertheless appear, but few if any of them can have guessed its nature.

ACT III

With everything seemingly settled, a storm bursts out of a cloudless sky
(206–9) as Demeas, in the play's second major monologue, tells of his
accidental discovery, through the careless talk of an old freedwoman, that
the baby being cared for (and, he now sees, suckled: 265–6) by Chrysis
is not, as he had supposed, his own child but Moschion's. He is at first
reluctant to believe this (267–79), in spite of what most would consider
to be decisive evidence, because of Moschion's previous excellent character (272–4); but Parmenon, returning from the market, is partly bul-
lied, partly bluffed, into admitting Moschion's paternity (320), and then
is not allowed to give any further explanation, as an angry Demeas fright-
ens him into fleeing. This completes the 'pseudo-recognition' sequence,
as Jäkel 1982: 25–6 calls it, comparing it to the episode in Euripides' *Ion*
(517–635) in which Xuthus is deceived (by Apollo) into 'recognizing' Ion
as his son.

Demeas now finds a way to reconcile his deep-seated belief in Moschion's good character with the facts as he now thinks he knows them:
since Moschion cannot possibly be to blame for what has happened (328),
it must have been Chrysis who seduced him. He even manages to see Moschion's eagerness to marry Plangon as evidence for this, taking it as having
been motivated by a desire to escape the clutches of Chrysis (333–7). He
does not refer to any feature of Chrysis' character or past behaviour in
justification of this conclusion, either in his soliloquy (325–56) or later
when speaking to Chrysis herself – except that at 348 he calls her a cheap
whore (χαμαιτύπη), implying that as an ex-*hetaira* she must necessarily be
incapable of remaining faithful to one partner. He does, on the other
hand, again lay emphasis on *Moschion's* character (343–7). These reflections lead him to the fateful decision to expel Chrysis from his home,
even though he still loves her (350, 356), but to do so without telling
her the real reason for his action (351–5). The scene in which he carries out this decision (359–98) appears to have been the most memorable
part of the play, and found its way into the iconographic tradition represented for us, some seven centuries later, by the Mytilene mosaic (see
Introduction §11).

But that mosaic itself, by the presence in it of the Cook, reminds us
that side by side with this plot-line (whose tragic potentialities are empha-
sized by reminiscences of at least three Euripidean plays; see Introduction §6), the wedding preparations are going on as though nothing untoward were happening. Demeas himself, indeed, is determined that they
should, for the sake of the supposedly innocent and virtuous Moschion;
and other characters, knowing nothing of what is in his mind beyond
what he may willingly or inadvertently reveal, proceed as if nothing were

amiss. Demeas' opening monologue portrays for us (219–30) the bustle in his house (which led to the baby being laid aside, 225–6, and thus indirectly to the old woman's unguarded remarks). Presently the return of Parmenon, with his shopping and the hired Cook, provides an opportunity for a hackneyed joke – which can nevertheless, it seems, still raise a laugh *twice* (282–4, 292–4nn.) – and for an equally typical display of professional superiority by a practitioner of this far from exalted occupation (285–92); yet the Cook will later be given a more than merely comic function, when he attempts ineffectively to intervene on Chrysis' behalf (384–9) – even if we have reasonable grounds for suspecting that his main motive for doing so is fear of losing a day's wages (cf. 367–8), fear which proves to be unfounded (his final exit is into Demeas' house, 390). Towards the end of the act we are given another *topos* of comic festivity as Nikeratos arrives with a skinny sheep for his sacrifice (399–404n.); he is also able to save Chrysis (and, unbeknown to him, his own grandson) from what might have been a catastrophic fate (foretold by Demeas in 390–6, though without reference to the baby) by giving them shelter in his own home. Like the Cook (361) and Chrysis (415) he thinks Demeas is mad (416, 419) – and perhaps they are not so wrong; Demeas himself, speaking of his response to the evidence pointing to Moschion as the baby's father, had said ἐξέστηχ' ὅλως (279).

A noteworthy feature of this act is the absence from it of Moschion. He departed at 162, not because he had business elsewhere (like Parmenon and Nikeratos, who went off to do shopping) but merely to avoid being present at the impending conversation between Demeas and Nikeratos about his marriage. He would have no reason to believe that that conversation would be very prolonged, and many would have expected him to be the first character to return in Act III, especially in view of his earlier eagerness to be married as soon as possible. If he had arrived back, say, at the end of Demeas' opening monologue, the action might have taken a very different turn. Instead it is Parmenon and the Cook who appear, followed some time later by Nikeratos. During this latter part of Act III, Menander seems to be doing what he can to prevent us from wondering why Moschion has not returned, by dividing the action into short stretches (the longest, the scene of Chrysis' expulsion, amounts to forty-two lines) each of which gives us much to think about, or much to laugh at, or both.

The text of the last three acts is in a much better state of preservation than that of the first two. Through most of them, including almost the whole of Act III (216–416), we have C as well as B available, and at the same time B itself becomes better preserved with much less damage to its pages (in which state it will continue throughout *Dyskolos* and into the third act of *Aspis*). There are only two passages in Demeas' opening monologue (at its beginning, and between 248 and 251) where the text has suffered serious loss, and none at all in the rest of the act.

Demeas comes out of his house, slowly and calmly (cf. 262–3), though it will quickly become evident that he is in a state of violent agitation which he is with difficulty endeavouring to control.

206–82 This monologue will have required a virtuoso performance, being comparable in this respect to the report of the Eleusinian assembly meeting in *Sikyonioi* (176–271). On the one hand Demeas is struggling to control his own emotions, anxious as he is to let nobody be aware of his suspicions (cf. 263–4); for the most part he succeeds, but at the very end he bursts out with ἐξέστηχ' ὅλως (279), only to have to restrain himself again on seeing Parmenon approaching with the Cook. On the other hand, he is reporting lively and sometimes agitated conversation among other persons (all women), often presenting their words in direct speech (between 242 and 261 he quotes at least ten separate utterances), almost in a miniature drama within the play in which he, a dramatic character himself, acts the parts of two other characters – one of whom (the young slave) is herself at one point playing a part (at 258 when she calls out αὐτὴ καλεῖ, τίτθη, σε in the middle of a series of half-whispered warnings and instructions to the old nurse), so that here we have an actor playing an actor playing an actress. In the end, after all that Demeas has heard and seen, he still professes not to be sure what the truth is (216–18, 267–79), though he has no rational ground for doubt except his unquestioning faith in Moschion's good character. The audience, for their part, are kept in suspense until 248 before they know what it is that has so devastated Demeas.

206–8 The next sentence but one ('for my present situation is similar to that', 210) suggests that this damaged sentence must originally have run something like this (supplements, which are for illustration only, in italics): '*I now understand what it must be like when, after* fair sailing weather, a *great* storm, coming on suddenly and unexpectedly, *strikes a ship*.' Storm imagery is of course very common in poetry of all kinds; this particular variant (a storm arising suddenly out of fine weather) is surprisingly rare before Menander (cf. however Soph. *Aj.* 1148 ('from a small cloud'), *Ant.* 415–21 (a dust-storm) and Xen. *Hell.* 2.4.14) – though according to schol. Aesch. *Cho.* 1067 there was a special word for a storm of this kind (γονίας, used in the passage commented on). Our passage was later imitated (and part of 209 quoted) by Favorinus (*On Exile* 25.3 Barigazzi). In New

Comedy, we find elaborate storm images of different kinds in Philemon fr. 28 and *com. adesp.* 1063.4–16.

206 δρόμου καλοῦ: just as θεῖν (209, Ar. *Eccl.* 109 οὔτε θέομεν οὔτ᾽ ἐλαύνομεν) and δραμεῖν (Soph. *Aj.* 1083) can mean 'travel under sail', so δρόμος can mean 'sailing' (cf. Theopompus *FGrH* 115 F 74 ναῦν οὐριοδρομοῦσαν 'a ship sailing under fair winds' and, in metaphor, Soph. *Aj.* 889 οὐρίωι… δρόμωι).

207 [χει]μών… [μέγας]: a frequent collocation (Arnott 1998b: 11), e.g. Eur. fr. 781.58; Hdt. 7.188.2 (a storm springing up ἐξ αἰθρίης τε καὶ νηνεμίης); Pl. *Prot.* 344d. A popular alternative suggestion has been λάβρος (Austin), but that adjective does not normally pair with χειμών and is moreover unattested in comedy of any period.

208 ἐλθών is followed in B by what appears to be a punctuation mark. For the use of this verb to denote the 'coming on' of a storm cf. *Iliad* 9.5–6 Βορέης καὶ Ζέφυρος… ἐλθόντ᾽ ἐξαπίνης. **ἐκεῖνος:** sc. ὁ χειμών.

209 This is the only three-word iambic trimeter in *Samia*; they appear sporadically in other Menandrian plays without necessarily implying tragic reminiscence (e.g. *Dysk.* 668, 965). Here, however, at the end of a passage which (so far as it survives) has strictly observed the metrical rules of tragedy, such reminiscence is inherently likely, and our line may well be designed to echo Eur. *Hipp.* 1232 ἐς τοῦθ᾽ ἕως ἔσφηλε κἀνεχαίτισεν (describing the wrecking of Hippolytus' chariot by a monstrous bull sent by Poseidon). Leurini 1994: 94–5 points out that the whole narrative of Hippolytus' disastrous drive (*Hipp.* 1173–1254) is full of references to the sea, and Hippolytus himself is compared to a sailor (1221, 1224) and his reins to a ship's helm (1227). **κἀνεχαίτισεν:** the earliest recorded meaning of ἀναχαιτίζω is 'rear up', of a horse (Soph. fr. 179; [Eur.] *Rhes.* 786); it then acquired the transitive sense 'throw (one's rider)', whence more broadly 'cause to capsize, upset, wreck' both literally (Eur. *Hipp.* loc. cit.; Philostr. *Imag.* 2.17 θάλαττα… ἀναχαιτίζουσα) and metaphorically (Anaxandrides fr. 3; Dem. 2.9).

211 Demeas is not yet 'holding the wedding' or 'sacrificing to the gods' (the sacrificial victim, which Parmenon was ordered to buy (190), has still to arrive), but the present tense is justified because he has begun preparations for both (219–22).

212 κατὰ νοῦν (+ dative) = 'agreeably to the desires of'; cf. Soph. *OC* 1768; Pl. *Phd.* 97d, *Symp.* 193c, *Rep.* 358b, and (with the dative omitted, the beneficiary being easily identifiable from the context) Men. fr. 845.7; Ar. *Knights* 549, *Peace* 762, 940.

213–14 'I don't even know now, by Athena, whether I'm still seeing straight!' So far as grammar goes, καλῶς could be taken either with βλέπω or with οἶδα. The former choice requires the two related words to be separated by several unrelated ones, but this hyperbaton is not as violent as it may seem (the oath μὰ τὴν Ἀθηνᾶν being parenthetical) and is far from the most extreme in Menander (compare e.g. *Dysk.* 236–8 τοῦτο τοῦ λοιποῦ χρόνου | εἰπεῖν θ᾽ ὅπως μηδείς ποτ᾽ αὐτὸν ὄψεται | ποιοῦντα 'and tell him that no one should ever see him doing that in future'). The decision should therefore be made on the basis of sense. If καλῶς is taken with οἶδα the meaning will be 'I don't properly know any more whether I can see' (so Lamagna) or '... whether I'm alive' (Dedoussi). The fact that such a statement would be wildly exaggerated is less important than the fact that it would not fit well with what Demeas says shortly afterwards (216–18), when he asks for help in determining, not whether he is capable of receiving sense-impressions, but whether his mind has gone awry and grossly misinterpreted those which he has received. Both recent editors point out that Demeas' distress has been primarily caused by evidence that came to his ears, not to his eyes – the words of the old freedwoman; what he saw afterwards – Chrysis suckling the baby – merely confirmed, or seemed to confirm, that she was the child's mother, as he already believed her to be. However, we should remember that until he saw this, he had no clear evidence that she *was* its mother. There was at least one young female slave in his house (the θεραπαινίδιον of 251–9) and probably several (cf. 226–7): Demeas, always eager to believe the best of Moschion, would be free to suppose that he had had a fling with one of these – improper, no doubt (since they belonged to Demeas, not to him), but nowhere near as heinous as if Chrysis were the woman concerned. If he is not 'seeing straight' – if his belief that he had seen Chrysis suckling the baby was either an error or a hallucination caused by some kind of mental disorder (ἢ μαίνομ᾽ 217) – then things are not after all as bad as they seem.

213 μὰ τὴν Ἀθηνᾶν: oaths by Athena, very rare in Old Comedy (only Ar. *Peace* 218), become fairly frequent from the mid fourth century (Nicostratus fr. 29) onwards, and there are at least seven other instances in Menander (*Aspis* 319; *Kolax* F 2.5; *Perik.* 303; *Sik.* 116; frr. 96, 296.13–14, 420.1), in two of which the name of Athena is coupled with that of Olympian Zeus. All the speakers are male; the oath does not appear to have any particular function, except that it adds a degree of emphasis to the statement made, as do all oaths more substantial than νὴ/μὰ (τὸν) Δία. The oath by Athena has largely replaced that by Poseidon, which was very frequent in Old Comedy but in Middle and New Comedy appears only three times, twice in this play (363, 427) and once in *Heros* (87); the two oaths are of the same metrical shape, but from a versifier's point of view, νὴ/μὰ τὸν Ποσειδῶ had the disadvantage that it had to be followed by a word beginning with a consonant.

214 οὐκ 'no, I don't', tantamount to an emphatic reiteration of the preceding negative sentence, as in Ar. *Ach.* 421, *Clouds* 1470, *Frogs* 1308, Dem. 21.112.   **ἐπὶ τὸ πρόσθεν:** εἰς is more usual in this phrase, but ἐπὶ appears in *Dysk.* 522, Arist. *PA* 695a26, 712b17. Prima facie one would expect the verb (lost, but for one uncertainly read letter, at the end of the line) to be a verb of motion, but it is difficult to find a convincing one: προάγομαι is not found elsewhere, as προάγω is (690, 691, 725, *Dysk.* 363, 866, *Kith.* 50), in the intransitive sense 'come (forward)', and the present tense is also doubtfully appropriate since Demeas came out of the house at least ten lines ago. Thus Dedoussi's π[εριπατῶ] 'I'm pacing about' (cf. *Georg.* 85; *Mis.* A7, A21 S = 7, 21 A; Ar. *Lys.* 709) is tempting; but it would require us to take ἐπὶ τὸ πρόσθεν as locative ('in front' sc. of the house) rather than directional ('to the front'), and for this Dedoussi offers no parallel.

215 'Having suddenly been struck by a distress that could not have been greater' (lit. 'unsurpassable').   **[ὀδύν]ην:** this noun and its derivatives are fairly common in Menander in the metaphorical sense of grief or distress (3, *Dysk.* 88, 606, *Epitr.* 754 and F 10); the alternative restoration [πληγ]ὴν, on the other hand, is used in comedy only in reference to actual physical blows.   **ἀνυπέρβλητον:** this adjective is applied to grief/distress in Arist. *Rhet.* 1370b31 οἱ δ᾽ ὀργιζόμενοι λυποῦνται ἀνυπερβλήτως μὴ τιμωρούμενοι. It was a favourite with Isocrates, who was using it as early as *c.*380 (Isoc. 4.71), and appears occasionally in other fourth-century prose writers; in poetry it is found before Menander only in Antiphanes fr. 166.5.   **[λαβών]** should probably be preferred to ἔχων (Austin), since after ἐξ[αίφνης] – if that is the correct restoration – we should expect an aorist participle (referring to an event) rather than a present participle (referring to a state of affairs): ὀδύνην … λαβών is not exactly paralleled, but note *Dysk.* 606 (an Attic farmer cultivating rocky fields) ὀδύνας ἐπισπᾶτ᾽ οὐδὲν ἀγαθὸν λαμβάνων.

216 ἦ 'στ[ὶ] πιθανόν; 'Is it credible?' It is not clear whether Demeas is to be understood as talking to himself or, as in the next sentence (see below), to the audience; either way, they will have no idea what the proposition is whose credibility he doubts.   **ἦ** is the likeliest reading of the vertical stroke which is all that is left of the first letter of C's first surviving line. As an interrogative particle it is much less frequent in fourth-century than in fifth-century drama, but it appears in *Dysk.* 53 and *Epitr.* 1065, each time adding a touch of incredulity or indignation to the question.   **σκέψασθε:** addressed to the audience (cf. 5–6n.), though the vocative ἄνδρες is used only at 269. The audience, once Demeas tells them what he has heard and seen, will know that he is not mad – but also that he *is* badly mistaken and that he *is* distressing himself for no good reason.

217 ἢ μαίνομ': here Demeas is wondering whether his belief in the truth of what he has heard and/or seen is the *result* of insanity; at the end of this speech, having reasoned his way to the conclusion that it is likely to be true, he says that this has *caused* him to go out of his mind (279). **τ' (γ´ B),** linking οὐδὲν . . . [διὰ κενῆς] with μαίνομαι to form together the second wing of the alternative indirect question governed by σκέψασθε, is necessary; otherwise Demeas would be stating *as a fact* that his distress was unwarranted.

217–18 εἰς ἀκρίβειαν . . . | λαβών 'having understood correctly'. The phrase εἰς ἀκρίβειαν is found earlier only in philosophical texts (Pl. *Euthyd.* 288a, *Laws* 809c, 967b, [Pl.] *Epin.* 983c; Arist. *Pol.* 1331a1–2 εὑρημένων τῶν περὶ τὰ βέλη καὶ τὰς μηχανὰς εἰς ἀκρίβειαν πρὸς τὰς πολιορκίας 'now that inventions have been perfected in the field of missiles and engines for siege warfare').

218 ἐπάγομαι 'I am bringing on myself', cf. Thuc. 6.10.1, Dem. 54.1 παραινούντων μὴ μείζω πράγματ' ἢ δυνήσομαι φέρειν ἐπάγεσθαι: the middle of this verb occurs, before Menander, only in prose. **[διὰ κενῆς]** 'pointlessly', 'to no purpose', a phrase that will be applied later to the behaviour of Nikeratos (605) and Moschion (672).

219–66 The narrative of what Demeas did, saw and heard inside the house (during the time covered by the choral interlude between Acts II and III). As in many tragic narratives (e.g. Soph. *El.* 681–756, Eur. *Bacch.* 1043–1147) the climax is long delayed; it eventually comes almost casually (248) in the middle of the old nurse's inconsequential babble. For possible echoes of Euripides' *Hippolytos Kalyptomenos*, see Introduction §6.

220–1 ἁπλῶς is probably to be taken with πάνθ' ('absolutely everything'), cf. 191. Most editors have taken it with φράσας in the sense 'simply, without going into detail' (as Jacques puts it, 'en deux mots'), and Lamagna explains that this is important for the plot because the household do not know the full facts and so have no alternative but to maintain the 'fiction' that Chrysis is the baby's mother; but the deception scheme in any case requires that the fiction be maintained until the marriage is an accomplished fact. We are to understand that Demeas said to the household 'We're celebrating Moschion's wedding today; hurry up and get everything ready.' Menander has not enabled us to infer from Demeas' words whether or not he identified the bride, and presumably therefore he does not consider it important that we should know this.

221 τοῖς ἔνδον would be mostly slaves, but included at least two free people (Chrysis and the old nurse, 236–8) who, however, were still Demeas' dependants and expected to obey his orders; a minority of the slaves were male (and so the whole group is spoken of in the masculine gender here and at 224), but most were women (so that the voices heard calling loudly for this or that item to be fetched were, or seemed to be, all female, 226–7).

222 καθαρά ποεῖν 'clean up', 'make the place spick and span'. Lamagna sees a reference to purification rites, but this is unlikely: even Josephus, who as a Jewish priest knew a great deal about purification rites and has much to say about them, on the only occasion when he uses the phrase καθαρά ποιεῖν (*AJ* 3.9.1) is referring simply to the cleansing of a carcass (or possibly to skinning, cf. Leviticus 1.6).   **πέττειν:** baking bread and cakes; cf. Ar. *Peace* 869 (in a list of wedding preparations) ὁ πλακοῦς πέπεπ-ται.   **ἐνάρχεσθαι κανοῦν** 'dedicate a sacrificial basket' by placing in it barley grains (to be thrown on the altar fire and on the head of the victim), a garland (to adorn the victim), and the sacrificial knife; the basket would be carried round the altar and its contents taken out as they were needed for the ritual, the knife last. See Ar. *Peace* 948; Eur. *El.* 800–14, *IA* 1470–2, 1563–9; *Odyssey* 3.441–52; Denniston 1939: 147–8, Burkert 1983: 3–5, 1985: 55–7. The use of the verb ἐνάρχεσθαι 'make a beginning' (Eur. *El.* 1142, *IA* 955, 1472; Aeschines 3.120) indicates that the preparation of the basket was the first of the acts that constituted the sacrifice, and probably that once it had been done, the sacrifice itself had without fail to be proceeded with; if so, Demeas by giving this order has committed himself irrevocably to going ahead with the wedding.

223 ἐγίνετ': the imperfect tenses and present participles, from here to 228 inclusive, describe the *state* of affairs (general bustle, in which Demeas himself was involved) up to and including the beginning of the series of *events* to be narrated, the moment when Demeas went into the store-room (229).   **ἀμέλει** 'certainly', 'to be sure' (371, *Aspis* 388); the transition from the original sense 'don't worry' (imperative of ἀμελέω) is well illustrated by Ar. *Eccl.* 799–800 ἢν δὲ μὴ κομίσωσι, τί; – ἀμέλει κομιοῦσιν, where the reply to 'And what if they don't bring in [their property]?' can equally well be understood as 'Don't worry, they will' or as 'They certainly will'. Here the adverb has almost become a particle (González Merino 1983: 171–2) equivalent to a stronger version of μέν.   **ἑτοίμως** 'willingly', 'without hesitation' (395, 712, *Aspis* 152, *Dysk.* 518).

223–4 τὸ δὲ τάχος | ...ἐνεπόει 'but the speed with which things were being done was creating some confusion among them'.

225–6 The baby must have been left in the 'weaving-room' (233–6), where the old nurse will see it and comfort it. Chrysis at that moment will have been too busy to look after it: if Demeas himself had to lend a hand with the preparations (228–30), a fortiori Chrysis, his inferior both in status and in gender, would be fully occupied. She did pick up the baby not long afterwards; to be precise, she must have done so in the short interval between the disappearance of the old nurse (261) and Demeas' emergence into the courtyard (265–6).

227 Here, as more extensively in 242–61, Demeas will imitate the voices of those whose words he quotes – in this case the voices of several women calling more or less at once (226 ἅμα) for ingredients needed for the making of bread or cakes (222) and fuel to heat the oven(s).   ἔλαιον ἀπόδος is best rendered 'give me my oil', i.e. the oil I need for cooking. Though usually translatable as 'give back' or 'pay', ἀποδίδωμι strictly speaking means 'give to another what (s)he justifiably demands'. In *Heros* (28–31) Laches' slave Daos tells how the freedman Tibeios, unable to support himself in old age, borrowed a mina from Laches, then another mina, and then died; on which his interlocutor, Getas, comments 'Perhaps because your master οὐκ ἀπεδίδου the third mina', probably with the arch implication (Gomme and Sandbach 1973: 390) that Tibeios regarded it as Laches' duty to lend him whatever money he asked for. In the present scene, the household are under orders to prepare the wedding feast quickly, and therefore any of the slaves may justifiably demand that any fellow-slave do whatever is necessary to ensure that these orders are fulfilled.

228 διδούς...καὶ συλλαμβάνων: probably a hendiadys, 'in the course of helping out by giving them some of these things'; it is unlikely that Demeas is to be envisaged as doing anything other than fetch supplies, since that task alone would occupy him fully (particularly since he was apparently not very familiar with the layout of the store-room, 230).

229 ταμιεῖον 'store-room', used especially, in ordinary households, for the storage of non-perishable food (Ar. fr. 897; Xen. *Peri Hippikēs* 4.1; Thphr. *Char.* 4.9).   ἔτυχον: 55n.

230 πλείω 'several <different> things', cf. Men. fr. 219.7, Poseidippus com. fr. 30, Philippides fr. 6.   προαιρῶν: this had long been the regular word for taking food out of a store-room (Ar. *Thesm.* 418–420, Pherecrates fr. 74.1, Thphr. *Char.* 4.9).   καὶ σκοπούμενος σ[: Demeas evidently had to hunt around the store-room for the things he required, not knowing exactly where to find each item: organizing the stores was women's business (Xen. *Oec.* 8–9), and Demeas, moreover, has been away from home for many months. B's reading implies the existence of a variant συσκοπού-μενος: but the middle of συσκοπέω is not otherwise attested before the late antique period, and the prefix συ- probably results from the wandering of a copyist's eye or mind to συλλαμβάνων (228), or perhaps to σ[υχνά] 'a lot' if that is to be restored at the end of the present line (it is the best restoration; the popular alternative σ[χολῆι] would mean 'unhurriedly', which would be quite inappropriate for the ὑπερεσπουδακώς Demeas).

232 κατέβαιν' ἀφ' ὑπερώιου: the house, then, had an upper storey (not necessarily, or even probably, as extensive as the lower); we are not told what it was used for, but perhaps there were living quarters there for the old freedwoman and for some or all of the household slaves, particularly the women. Women's quarters were often on an upper storey, if the house had one; see e.g. *Odyssey* 1.328–31 (and many other passages about Penelope), Lys. 1.9, [Dem.] 47.57. On Greek house plans see Cahill 2002 (analysing the extensive evidence from Olynthus).   **τις γυνή:** we have to wait more than three lines, through an elaborate explanation of the layout of the relevant rooms, before we learn who this woman is (236–8).

233–4 εἰς τοὔμπροσθεν τοῦ ταμιειδίου | οἴκημα 'into the room in front of the store-room', i.e. the room through which one had to pass to reach the store-room (235–6). The diminutive form ταμιειδίου (an easy correction of C's unmetrical reading, though attested otherwise only in grammarians and lexicographers, e.g. *Suda* τ 64) should probably not be given any special significance – though a store-room, whatever its actual size, will have *felt* small because it would be hard to move about in, being rather dark (for coolness) and full of storage vessels.

234 τυγχάνει: 55n.   **ἱστεών** 'a weaving-room' (literally, 'loom-place'), in which the women of the household made clothes. The Attic form was ἱστών (Phryn. *Ecl.* 137), which is cited by Pollux (7.28) from a letter ascribed to Olympias (mother of Alexander the Great) and, in oblique cases, by two lexicographers (Hsch. ι 1011, *Suda* ι 703). It is noteworthy that the *koine* form (originally Ionic), condemned by Phrynichus loc. cit., was already in common use in Menander's Athens. If the women slaves slept on the upper floor (232n.), it would be convenient and efficient for them to be able to descend directly into the weaving-room. Cahill 2002: 169–79 shows, from the find-spots of loom-weights, that weaving, which 'requires a sheltered but well-lit space', was usually carried on 'in enclosed or semienclosed spaces adjoining the courtyard or other source of light'.

235 ὥσθ' 'so located that...'   **ἡ...ἀνάβασις** 'the staircase' (Hdt. 1.181.4; LXX 1 Kings 6.8). Many classical and Hellenistic houses, at Olynthus and elsewhere, appear to have had true staircases to their upper floors, the stone bases for which have survived; see Nevett 1999: 56, 75, 92, 105, 116, 121, 130, 144, and Cahill 2002: 94, 103, 109, 118, 125, 131. They probably did not have banisters or handrails, and the actual ascent and descent might still be hazardous, especially at night: Euphiletus exchanged the men's and women's quarters in his house so that his wife 'wouldn't have to run the risk of going downstairs every time the baby needed a wash' (Lys. 1.9).

235–6 ἐστι...|...ἡμῖν 'we have'.

236–8 The old ex-nurse was as familiar a character in New Comedy as she had been in fifth-century tragedy; sometimes, as here, she has been manumitted (85–6n.), sometimes (like Sophrone in *Epitrepontes*) she is still a slave.

237 πρεσβυτέρα probably means only that she was past the usual age of menopause, reckoned to be between 40 and 50 (Arist. *HA* 585b2–5); she might thus have been in her twenties or early thirties when Moschion was a small child.

237–8 γεγονυῖ' ἐμὴ | θεράπαιν' could mean either 'who had *been* my slave' (cf. *Heros* 22) or 'who had *become* my slave'; from this passage alone, therefore, nothing can be deduced about whether this woman had already been Moschion's nurse before his adoption (rather than, say, having been bought at the time of the adoption for the specific purpose of caring for the child) or, consequently, about Moschion's age when adopted; but see 7, 246nn.

238 ἐλευθέρα: but still living in Demeas' house and dependent on him: it was considered a duty to house and maintain one's former nurse if she had no other means of support ([Dem.] 47.56) and, Moschion not yet having a household of his own, this duty devolved on his father. This woman appears not to be expected to perform domestic tasks: she reproaches the women slaves for not washing the baby (252–4), but it does not occur to her to wash him herself. Similarly the freedwoman ex-nurse of the speaker of [Dem.] 47 is treated with considerable respect by the family, taking her meals with them while the women slaves remain in their quarters ([Dem.] 47.55–6).

239 τὸ παιδίον κεκραγὸς ἠμελημένον: probably to be taken as equivalent to ὅτι τὸ παιδίον κεκραγὸς ἠμέλητο ('that the baby had been ignored while/although it was crying') rather than to ὅτι τὸ παιδίον ἐκεκράγει ἠμελημένον ('that the baby was crying because it had been ignored'): the baby had, we gather, been crying since before Demeas went into the store-room (225–6), and nobody had done anything about it.

240 οὐδὲν εἰδυῖ': because she had been upstairs; the other members of the household were almost all in and around the kitchen, and knew that Demeas was going back and forth to the store-room. ἔνδον here and in 256 probably means 'in the building' (as opposed to the courtyard), rather than merely 'on the premises' (as in *Aspis* 213, 218, 227). If Demeas had been out in the courtyard, even though the weaving-room adjoined it (252 ἔξωθεν εἰστρέχοντι), he would have been unlikely to hear what the old nurse was saying indoors, unless she was shouting (of which there is no sign).

240–1 ἐν ἀσφαλεῖ | …τοῦ λαλεῖν 'in a safe situation for chattering', 'in a safe place to speak freely'; the genitive 'defines the field of reference of ἐν ἀσφαλεῖ (Gomme and Sandbach 1973, comparing Xen. *Hell.* 6.2.9 κεῖσθαι τὴν Κέρκυραν … ἐν καλῶι …τοῦ τὴν Λακωνικὴν χώραν βλάπτειν 'Corcyra was well placed for the purpose of inflicting damage on Spartan territory').

242 ταῦτα δὴ τὰ κοινά 'those things that everyone says', cf. *Epitr.* 526. There may be a tinge of disparagement in δή (as if to say 'this is the way women always cackle over babies'); δή often strikes a note of this kind when it follows οὗτος (Denniston 1954: 208–9), cf. Thuc. 6.92.5 τοῦτον δὴ τὸν ὑφ' ἁπάντων προβαλλόμενον λόγον; Pl. *Rep.* 338b (Thrasymachus) αὕτη δή…ἡ Σωκράτους σοφία.   **φίλτατον τέκνον:** τέκνον in Menander is used almost exclusively by women (*Mis.* 214 S = 615 A is the only provable exception) in addressing younger people of whom they are fond; see Bain 1984: 38–9. Dickey 1996: 65–9 points out that usage in post-classical prose is different, but none of her evidence (1996: 267) comes from within 250 years of Menander's time.

243 μέγ' ἀγαθόν 'you great treasure'; cf. Lucian *Dial. Deorum* 11.1 (the infant Hermes) καλόν τέ ἐστι καὶ προσμειδιᾷ πᾶσι καὶ δηλοῖ ἤδη μέγα τι ἀγαθὸν γενόμενον. The phrase was also used in speaking to and about adults: Ar. *Thesm.* 737 (of women) ὦ μέγα καπήλοις ἀγαθὸν ἡμῖν δ' αὖ κακόν, Xen. *Cyr.* 5.3.20 ὦ μέγα ἀγαθὸν σὺ τοῖς φίλοις Κῦρε. Demeas himself will use it in bitter sarcasm at 443–4 (μέγα γὰρ ὑμῖν ὤιχετ' ἐκ τῆς οἰκίας ἀγαθόν): he is referring there to Chrysis – but the baby also left his house at the same time, and, as his soon-to-be-legitimate grandson, it truly is a μέγα ἀγαθόν for his *oikos*.   **ἡ μάμμη δέ ποῦ;** 'but where's your mummy?' For μάμμη and related words in Greek baby-talk see Golden 1995: 20–1; it was a mark of ἀηδία for an adult to address his mother thus (Thphr. *Char.* 20.7). By 'your mummy' the old nurse, unaware of the need to guard her tongue, means Plangon, but Demeas will take her to mean Chrysis.

244 ἐφίλησε, περιήνεγκεν 'she kissed him and (sc. picked him up and) carried him about'.

244–5 ἐπαύσατο | κλᾶον: the baby, then, was crying primarily for attention – though this does not preclude the possibility of his also being in need of a wash (252–3) and/or a feed (266). Note that the subject changes from the old nurse (ἐφίλησε, περιήνεγκεν) to the baby and back (φησιν) without any formal indication; the hearer is each time left to infer the new subject from the sense (it was the baby that had been crying; it is adults who soliloquize) and from the gender of words referring to the subject (κλᾶον neuter; αὐτήν feminine).

245 ὦ τάλαιν' ἐγώ: everywhere else in Menander a woman who speaks of herself as τάλαινα is referring to some actual or apprehended misfortune affecting her (in *Epitr.* 529 a misfortune she is *pretending* to have suffered), and it is therefore likely that the same is true in this passage. Her first sentence is very much focused on herself, and the second, now incomplete, probably was as well (248n.). Did she, in the lost lines that followed, lament that, having cared for Moschion twenty-odd years ago and now for Moschion's son, she had never had the opportunity to care for a child of her own?

246 πρώην 'not long ago'. In the other two Menandrian attestations of this adverb (*Georg.* 47, *Epitr.* 633) the interval referred to is one measured in days, not in months or years, let alone, as here, in decades. Such exaggeration is more commonly associated with the phrase χθές (τε) καὶ πρώην (e.g. Dem. 18.130, referring – if it refers to any actual event at all – to Aeschines' entry into political life at least eighteen years before the date of the speech). In modern English, however, one might well say 'It seems like only the other day that...'   **τοιοῦτον ὄντα** implies that this woman had been Moschion's nurse from his earliest infancy, i.e. even before Demeas adopted him (7n.).

247 ἐτιθηνούμην 'I nursed': this may include suckling (e.g. *Epitr.* 464 – Syriskos' wife had lost her own baby, 268, shortly before taking charge of the baby who proves to be Pamphile's), but need not (e.g. *h.Dem.* 142, spoken by Demeter disguised as a woman past childbearing age, cf. 101–2).

248 παιδίον ἐκείνου γέγον[ε]ν: now at last we learn what it is that has so distressed Demeas – or so we suppose. The long and lively dialogue with the young maid (251–61) will rivet the audience as they await possible further revelations, but there prove to be none – until Demeas goes out into the courtyard.   **ἤδη καὶ τόδ[ε]:** καὶ indicates that all or part of the statement that has just been made about Moschion also applies to his child (τόδε *sc.* τὸ παιδίον); the statement was that the speaker had nursed and cherished Moschion, so the broken sentence must have gone on to say that she is performing (some of) the functions of a loving nurse for his son as well.

The next two or three lines are completely lost in C (B has lost the whole of 246–53); the preserved remnants of the following two lines (249–50) are too scanty for anything to be inferred from them. We cannot even be sure that the old nurse's speech extends to the end of 250, unless Sudhaus's restoration in 251 (see apparatus) is correct. For a suggestion as to what the lost lines may have contained, see 245n.

251 θεραπαινιδίωι: this diminutive occurs otherwise in comedy (and indeed in Attic literature) only in *Dysk.* 460, where it refers disparagingly

to allegedly lazy (but actually non-existent) slaves of Knemon. Here it
may indicate that the maid is junior both in age and in household rank.
We never see her, and she only speaks twenty words (no sentence longer
than four), but we are made vividly aware that she is quick-moving (252
εἰστρέχοντι), quick-thinking, and something of an actress.

252 ἔξωθεν: from the courtyard (Arnott 1998b: 12).   **λοῦσατ':** she
assumes that the baby has soiled himself. The plural imperative indicates
that the maid is being told, not necessarily to wash the baby herself, but
to see to it that one or more of the household staff do so; cf. 301–2 δίδοτε,
Χρυσί, πάνθ' ὅσ' ἂν | ὁ μάγειρος αἰτῆι.   **ὦ τάλαν:** in Attic comedy, of all
periods, this vocative is used only by women (or men imitating women's
speech); sometimes it functions as an interjection expressing 'self-pity or
sympathy', but in several passages (e.g. *Epitr.* 546; *Mis.* A56 S = 56 A, 132
S = 532 A) it serves as a true address form and can convey, as here, 'a hint
of rebuke' (Bain 1984: 33; see also McClure 1995: 45–8, Sommerstein
1995/2009: 22–3).

255–9 Demeas, imitating the speech of the maid as he had heard it, will
speak her words in an urgent 'stage whisper' except for αὐτὴ καλεῖ, τίτθη,
σε which is said loudly (as is signalled by the implicit stage-direction καὶ
παρεξήλλαξέ τι).

255 δύσμορ': 69n.   **ἡλίκον λαλεῖς** 'how loudly you're talking!' (cf. 553),
equivalent to ὡς μέγα φωνεῖς (cf. Aesch. *Eum.* 936, Soph. *Phil.* 574).

256 ἔνδον ἐστὶν αὐτός: to judge by the silence of commentators, Menander
estimated correctly that his audience would not ask themselves how the
maid could know this – a question to which there is no good answer; they
will be too engrossed in the way the situation is developing – the maid's
desperate attempt to keep the secret safe, the old nurse's horrified realization that she has very probably spilled the beans, and the effect that
all this is having on Demeas, especially as the exchanges between the two
women make it increasingly certain that his household has been deliberately concealing important information from him. The pronoun αὐτός was
used by slaves to refer to their master, both in talking among themselves
and in addressing visitors (e.g. Pl. *Prot.* 314d); in Ar. *Clouds* 219 a student
of Socrates' *phrontisterion* similarly refers to Socrates as αὐτός.   **οὐ δήπου**
γε 'surely not!' 'he can't be!' Cf. Dem. 20.167, where Demosthenes uses
the identical expression to emphasize the incredibility of the idea that the
Athenians, who punish counterfeiters of coinage with death, should give
ear to those 'who are trying to make the whole city counterfeit and untrust-
worthy', and Xen. *Mem.* 4.6.11.

257 παρεξήλλαξέ τι 'she changed <her voice> somewhat'.

258 "αὐτή καλεῖ, τίτθη, σε": this is spoken loudly, with the object of ascertaining whether Demeas can hear what is said in the weaving-room (cf. 259) and also of encouraging the old nurse to leave the room before she can commit further indiscretions. The maid succeeds in her second aim, but it was almost inevitable that she would fail in the first: if Demeas has in fact heard compromising remarks, his obvious course of action is to remain silently where he is until the weaving-room is empty and he can leave unnoticed.   αὐτή shows that the slaves regard Chrysis as the lady of the house (256n.); one may reasonably suppose that she, rather than Moschion, has been in effective charge of most of the household activities during Demeas' long absence (Blume 1974: 91 n. 24). This perception of her is reinforced by the easy relations that have existed for some time between her and the women of Nikeratos' family (35–46). That Parmenon uses her name in addressing her (301) and in referring to her in her presence (70), rather than calling her δέσποινα (*Heros* F 2) or κεκτημένη, need not be taken as counter-evidence, seeing that he can address his owner as Δημέα (192). But her status, respected as it is, remains precarious; as we have already seen (132–4), Demeas has the right to dismiss her from his home at a moment's notice and without any obligation to provide for her in any way thereafter (cf. 390–7).

258–9 βάδιζε καὶ | σπεῦδ' 'off with you (661, *Epitr.* 376), hurry!' The maid has reverted to her previous low tone of voice.

259 οὐκ ἀκήκο' οὐδέν is *doubly* mistaken, as Lamagna notes: not only has Demeas heard everything (indeed the maid's well-meaning intervention has actually made things worse by providing evidence of a conspiracy to conceal), but he has also been placed on the way to making, from what he has heard, not a true inference (as the women will have feared) but a false inference that will anger him far more than the truth could ever have done.   εὐτυχέστατα 'that's very lucky'.

260–1 The old nurse is now fully aware of her blunder; the words that now escape her suggest that she is not at all confident that Demeas has 'heard nothing' – but at the same time, if spoken aloud (as they probably are), they actually make things worse by telegraphing the fact that she has revealed something that was supposed to have been kept secret.

260 ὦ τάλαινα: she has considerably more cause now to call herself τάλαινα than at 245; but as a result of her indiscretion, Chrysis will soon have far more serious cause yet to do so (398, 568).

260–1 τῆς ἐμῆς | λαλιᾶς: for the genitive of cause after an exclamatory vocative cf. 398, *Dysk.* 189, Ar. *Birds* 1423 ὦ μακάριε τῆς τέχνης.

261 ἀπῆιξεν: obeying, too late, the maid's instruction βάδιζε καὶ σπεῦδ᾽. Barigazzi 1970: 170 argues that ἀπῆιξεν is not appropriate to an old woman, but Dedoussi rightly compares Soph. *Trach.* 190 (where the speaker is an old man, cf. 184). In neither passage need we suppose that the old person ran (indeed in *Trach.* 179 the approaching messenger was seen στείχονθ᾽), only that they moved as fast as their legs could carry them.

262 προήιειν 'I was on my way out in front <of the house>': the imperfect indicates that this movement was *in progress* (i.e. that Demeas was coming through the courtyard towards the front door) when he saw Chrysis suckling the baby, and is thus preferable to C's aorist προῆλθον (doubtless a copyist's anticipation of ἐξῆλθον in 263). He was presumably intending to do what he has actually since then done – go out of the house where he could reflect alone on what he had heard and its possible implications, before letting anyone else know or taking any action.

262–3 τοῦτον ὅνπερ... | ...ἡσυχῆι πάνυ: more detail is given here than the audience need, since they saw the manner in which Demeas came out of the house at the beginning of this act; but the passage serves as an implicit stage-direction, indicating to the actor how he is to make that entrance.

264 ὡς = ὥσπερ: ὡς οὔτ᾽ ἀκούσας thus means literally 'like one who had neither heard...', i.e. 'as if I had neither heard...' (but 'the participle is not felt to be conditional in Greek, as is shown by the negative οὐ᾽ (Goodwin 1912: 343). Cf. *Iliad* 23.429–30, where during the chariot-race Menelaus warns Antilochus not to try to overtake at a narrow point of the track but Antilochus only presses his horses on even harder ὡς οὐκ ἀΐοντι ἐοικώς (the text there indicating twice over that he is only pretending not to have heard).

265 αὐτήν (cf. 267 αὐτῆς) echoes 258, but to Demeas Chrysis is now not 'the lady of the house' but a dependent *hetaira* who has certainly been guilty of disobedience and perhaps of sexual infidelity too.   **ἔχουσαν** 'holding'.   **αὐτό,** i.e. τὸ παιδίον: the baby has not been mentioned since 254, but it is still at the front of Demeas' mind. All the same, one would expect it to be more clearly identified; this is the first of numerous, and increasingly frequent, indications in the latter part of Demeas' speech that emotional agitation is causing him to express himself obscurely or clumsily (266, 271, 275, 276–7, 278, 282nn.).   **τὴν Σαμίαν:** after the first mention of Chrysis' name (56) everyone except Demeas – even an infuriated Nikeratos on the point of threatening to murder her (557, cf. 560–1) – uses the name both in addressing her and in referring to her in the third person. Demeas too *addresses* her repeatedly by name in the expulsion scene (378, 382, 385, 392) just as he does after he knows the truth (569, 575, 730); but in her absence he never *refers* to her as 'Chrysis' (except in an echo-response to Moschion, 472) but as 'the Samian' (here and 354) or 'my Helen' (336–7). Probably his use of the ethnic designation here should be felt as betraying some degree of alienation: he is already thinking of Chrysis not as 'my partner' but as 'that foreign woman'.   ὁρῶ: the historic present tense marks a key moment in the narrative: cf. *Aspis* 49 (the sudden enemy attack), 108 (the death of the man who had taken Kleostratos' shield). See Sicking and Stork 1996, especially 165: 'The primary function of the [historic present] is to lift out from their context those narrative assertions that are essential for what the speaker has stated to be his immediate concern.' The use of ὁρῶ(μεν) in this function is almost formulaic in first-person narratives in tragedy (e.g. Aesch. *Pers.* 205, *Ag.* 659, *Eum.* 40; Soph. *El.* 894, 900, *Trach.* 912, 915, 930; Eur. *Supp.* 653, *Or.* 871, 879, *Bacch.* 680, 1063); in Menander it appears at *Sik.* 189, a passage partly modelled on Eur. *Or.* 871–83.

266 is one of the rare passages (674 is perhaps the only comparable one, apart from B's omission of 606–11) where B's text and C's differ widely and both have found defenders (see Casanova 2007c). C's reading has here been preferred. The discrepancy probably resulted from the omission or loss of part of the line in one branch of the tradition, followed by the insertion of a stopgap phrase to fill the line out; and it would be much easier to hit upon καθ' αὑτήν as a stopgap than upon παριὼν ἅμα. Apart from this consideration, either reading would have been acceptable, except that B's text leaves the line a syllable short and requires the insertion of <καὶ>.   ἔξω i.e. in the courtyard.   διδοῦσαν τιτθίον reappears at 536 and 540, where it is Plangon who is breastfeeding the baby and Nikeratos who is traumatized by the sight of it. The sequence ἔχουσαν ... διδοῦσαν lacks something in elegance, but is not necessarily to be suspected on that ground, especially in this part of Demeas' speech (265n.); it is the equivalent, in the accusative-and-participle construction, of what would be ἔχουσα ... δίδωσι in direct speech.   παριὼν ἅμα 'just as I was passing by' (for ἅμα with present participle in this sense cf. Pl. *Phd.* 76c εἰ μὴ ἄρα ἅμα γιγνόμενοι λαμβάνομεν ... ταύτας τὰς ἐπιστήμας) serves to explain how Demeas came to see what Chrysis was doing. We are probably to imagine that she was standing near the wall of the building at one side of the courtyard, with her back to the door from which Demeas emerged, and that he got a glimpse of the baby at her breast as he passed her on his way towards the street door.

267–8 ὥσθ' ... |εἶναι: the construction is ὥστε γνώριμον εἶναι ὅτι τοῦτό [*sc.* τὸ παιδίον] ἐστι [*sc.* υἱὸς] αὐτῆς. Ironically, what Demeas thinks he 'knows' the audience know to be false, and what he suspects but cannot bring himself to believe (268–79) they know to be true. If a woman was lactating, one could at once infer that she must have given birth (Arist. *Rhet.*

1357a14–16), as automatically as one could infer that a person who was feverish must be suffering from a disease; but of course it did not follow that she must have given birth *to the baby she was suckling!*

267 αὐτῆς: 265n.   **γνώριμον:** from 'known' (*Epitr.* 865, cf. Arist. *Poet.* 1451b20–6) this has come to mean, in Demeas' mouth, 'certain' (as again at 473, where likewise the proposition of which Demeas is 'certain' is entirely false).

268–70 'As to who the baby's father might be, whether it's mine or whether it's – no, gentlemen, I'm not saying it in front of you! – <as to that,> I'm making no conjectures...' This edition follows Barigazzi 1970: 170–1 in taking οὐ λέγω κτλ. as a parenthesis, and οὐχ ὑπονοῶ as governing the indirect question πατρὸς...ὅτου ποτ' ἐστίν. Editors have preferred to assume an anacoluthon (a complete break in the syntax) and treat οὐχ ὑπονοῶ as parallel to οὐ λέγω: thus Jacques translates 'cela, messieurs, je ne vous le dis pas, je ne forme pas de soupçon'. The syntactic irregularity would be acceptable coming from Demeas in his present state (265n.), but it is not necessary to assume it, since ὑπονοῶ can mean 'conjecture, guess, infer' (492, *Karch.* F 2, Alexis fr. 269.6), and this gives good sense. Moreover, Demeas certainly *does* have suspicions that Moschion may be the baby's father, otherwise why is he so agitated? What he is not going to do is form an *opinion*, even as a guess, about who the father is, until he has further evidence.

269 εἶτ' – οὐ λέγω δ'...: aposiopesis (69n., 326, 372, 374); he cannot bring himself to say εἶτε Μοσχίωνος. Casanova 2007b argues that this figure is particularly characteristic of *Samia* and especially of Demeas, always concerned to conceal what may discredit his adopted son, and claims that no other play of Menander contains more than one genuine instance of the phenomenon (he recognizes only *Epitr.* 1120 and *Perik.* 269).   **ἄνδρες:** addressed to the audience (5–6n.). Menander can perhaps here be said to embrace, rather than evade, the paradox of the soliloquy – that it is spoken in front of a large gathering by a character who in the dramatic fiction is supposed to be alone. The solution of the paradox is that the theatre audience are physically present but are completely outside the dramatic action, on which they can exercise no influence: in one sense they are there, but in another sense they are not there. Hence it is possible for Demeas first to present, in front of this audience, a report of his overhearing utterances which he quotes verbatim and which name Moschion as the baby's father, then to refuse to mention explicitly before them even the possibility of his being so, and then, a moment later, to say he is 'bringing the matter before the public' (270) and rehearse in their presence the evidence telling both against and for Moschion's guilt.

270 τὸ πρᾶγμα: if this stood on its own it might denote all the facts of the case, but with ἅ τ᾽ ἀκήκο᾽ αὐτός following it must refer to the one fact that Demeas did not 'hear' but *saw* – the fact that Chrysis was suckling the baby. **εἰς μέσον φέρω** 'bring before the public', cf. Eur. *Supp.* 438–9 (adapted from the herald's call for speakers to come forward and address the *ekklesia*) τίς θέλει πόλει | χρηστόν τι βούλευμ᾽ ἐς μέσον φέρειν ἔχων;, *Hel.* 1542 δόλιον οἶκτον ἐς μέσον φέρων 'putting on a deceptive public display of pity', Dem. 18.139, Ar. *Eccl.* 602 τοῦτ᾽ εἰς τὸ μέσον καταθήσει 'he will deposit it [his money] in the public store'.

271 οὐδέπω: this is the third consecutive line ending in –ω, following immediately upon two lines ending in –μον. Demeas is particularly liable to rhyme the ends of his lines (Feneron 1974: 94–5; cf. e.g. 153–5, 328–30), but this passage, with successive rhymes covering altogether five lines, is in Menander second only to *Dysk.* 729–33, where five successive lines of Knemon's end in –ω. The jingle may be designed to seem careless (265n.).

272 σύνοιδα: once again Demeas speaks of what he 'knows' to be true, but this time he does not speak beyond his actual knowledge, referring only to Moschion's behaviour during τὸν πρότερον…χρόνον, i.e. before he (Demeas) went abroad. Nevertheless he clearly treats this as strong presumptive evidence, assuming, as according to Aristotle (*EN* 1144b4–6) 'everyone' did, that basic character traits are innate ('if we are just or self-controlled or courageous, we have these qualities right from birth'). **τῶι μειρακίωι:** Davidson 2006: 46–9 argues that the transition from μειράκιον to ἀνήρ was thought of as taking place at the age of twenty, i.e. that μειράκιον was more or less synonymous with ἔφηβος; but this is refuted by Men. fr. 494 παῖς γέγον᾽, ἔφηβος, μειράκιον, ἀνήρ, γέρων and by the very fact that Menander's young men in love, who are regularly called μειράκια, are always in a position to marry at short notice and are never in surviving plays described as ephebes, or associated with ephebic activities or clothing. From Moschion's brief autobiographical remarks (see especially 13–15nn.) one would gather that he was a few years past the end of his *ephebeia*, maybe about twenty-three.

273 ὄντι: as τὸν πρότερον…χρόνον shows, this is an 'imperfect' participle (cf. Goodwin 1912: 47–8) and thus makes the same statement that Moschion himself made in the prologue (18 ἦν κόσμιος).

274 Moschion had not only shown himself κόσμιος in general but particularly respectful towards Demeas, which makes it all the more incredible that he should commit such a heinous offence against him as is suggested by the evidence of what Demeas has heard and seen.   **ὡς ἔνεστιν εὐσεβεστάτωι** 'showing the greatest possible respect'; cf. 352 κρύφθ᾽ ὅσον ἔνεστι, Xen. *Mem.* 3.8.4 'a good shield (good for protection) is ὡς ἔνι (= ἔνεστι) ἀνομοιοτάτη to a good javelin (good for throwing far and fast)'.

275–9 Demeas now itemizes the circumstantial evidence pointing to the credibility of the old nurse's words.

275 πάλιν 'on the other hand' (*Dysk.* 285, Men. fr. 607.4, Pl. *Rep.* 507b). The word appears again in a different sense later in this sentence (277), another indication that Demeas is not in full control of his language (265n.). **καταμάθω** 'I consider' (LSJ καταμανθάνω 4), cf. Xen. *Cyr.* 7.5.80 'if anyone wonders what good it does to achieve our desires, if we are still going to have to endure hunger and thirst, toil and care, ἐκεῖνο δεῖ καταμαθεῖν ὅτι τοσούτωι τἀγαθὰ μᾶλλον εὐφραίνει ὅσωι ἂν μᾶλλον προπονήσας τις ἐπ' αὐτὰ ἴηι'.

276 τίτθην ἐκείνου πρῶτον οὖσαν: and therefore not likely to concoct, or believe, falsehoods to his discredit.

276–7 εἶτ'...εἶτ': normally, in enumerations, successive occurrences of εἶτα (or ἔπειτα) are syntactically parallel; these are not – the first opens the second half of the indirect statement governed by καταμάθω, the other opens the second of two clauses introduced by ἐπειδάν. Once again Demeas' use of language betrays his growing agitation.   **ἐμοῦ | λάθραι λέγουσαν:** this may not seem strictly logical, since the nurse's words would have gained, not lost, credibility if she had spoken them knowing Demeas to be present (and thus risking his displeasure, given his great affection for Moschion); but Demeas' point (perhaps not made very clearly, but readily intelligible) is that the dialogue between the nurse and the young maid (255–61) showed that what the nurse had said was something that *was meant to have been* kept secret from Demeas. The repetition of λέγουσαν from 275 is yet another piece of linguistic carelessness; in between, too, we have had an echoing οὖσαν in the same metrical position as the first occurrence of λέγουσαν.

277 ἀποβλέψω: aorist subjunctive, like καταμάθω to which it is syntactically parallel.

278 τὴν ἀγαπῶσαν αὐτό: he means Chrysis, but these words would apply equally well to the old nurse; it is only the following phrase that disambiguates them. The baby is again referred to by a mere pronoun (265n.), though it has not been mentioned since 268.   **βεβιασμένην** 'who insisted', 'who strove mightily', cf. Lys. 9.16 βιαζόμενοι βλάπτειν ἐξ ἅπαντος λόγου 'striving to injure me at all costs'. As Lamagna notes, Demeas seems to have forgotten that it was Moschion who insisted that the baby (and Chrysis) should not be expelled: the prejudice that will lead to their actual expulsion is already apparent.

279 ἐξέστηχ' ὅλως 'I'm completely out of my mind': the dam of Demeas' self-control has finally burst – but he at once restrains himself again on seeing Parmenon and others approaching. Later (620) it will be Moschion who claims to have been driven out of his mind, using the same verb, by a much less powerful provocation – and his monologue, like Demeas' present one, ends with the arrival of Parmenon just when he is wanted (639–40).

280 Looking along Eisodos A, Demeas sees Parmenon approaching with at least two other persons, who will prove to be the Cook (283–390n.) and one or more assistants (the latter are never referred to separately, but their existence is proved by the plurals of 282 and 295). Probably the audience do not see them yet: the arrival of the cook, a character of predictable personality and the butt of predictable jokes (283–5n.), will have been a moment that comic audiences (especially perhaps the youngest of them?) looked forward to and wished to savour, and it would not be desirable to detract from its effect by having another character, as it were, speaking over it.   **ἀλλ'...γάρ** marking 'the appearance of a new character on the stage' (Denniston 1954: 103–4, citing many instances in tragedy and Aristophanes; in Menander cf. 639, *Dysk.* 607). The first particle indicates that the previous line of thought has been broken off, and the second that the speaker is explaining the reason for the break.   **εἰς καλόν** 'opportunely' (*Dysk.* 773, Soph. *OT* 78, Pl. *Men.* 89e). Parmenon's arrival is opportune because it will enable Demeas to question him immediately. **τουτονὶ προσιόνθ':** this, the reading of B, is supported by *Aspis* 247, *Dysk.* 47, 230, *Epitr.* 577, Anaxippus fr. 3.1–2, and is unlikely to have arisen by corruption.

281 ἰατέον: Demeas cannot question Parmenon about such delicate matters in the presence of the Cook, a complete stranger, so must wait to do so until the Cook and his assistant(s) have gone inside. Later, though, when his anger is at its height, Demeas will expel Chrysis from his house in front of the Cook (369–90), whom he treats merely as a nuisance and eventually threatens with violence (388–9).

282 παραγαγεῖν 'to show into the house'. Normally in Menander παράγω is intransitive ('go inside', as in 104), and Lloyd-Jones (*ap.* Austin) made it intransitive here by adding <θ'> after τούτους. But Demeas does not want Parmenon to go inside for any length of time – the intelligent young maid, or someone else, may warn him of what has happened and tell him to be on his guard if questioned – and in fact stops him just when he is about to do so (295). The verb is frequently transitive in fourth-century prose: cf. e.g. Dem. 18.170 τὸν ἥκοντα παρήγαγον 'they brought in<to the

ekklesia meeting> the man who had come <with news of Philip's seizure of Elatea>', [Dem.] 26.17 τίνα γὰρ παραγαγὼν εἰς τὸ δικαστήριον ... καὶ ᾔρηκεν;

282/3 Demeas withdraws to a spot where he is unlikely to be noticed; he is well away from his own door (304–5) and when he speaks at 295, Parmenon still has not seen him (296). This suggests that Demeas has placed himself well 'downstage'; and since his house is on the side nearer Eisodos A (see note on start of play), he has probably moved over to the other side.

Parmenon enters along Eisodos A, carrying his basket (190–1n., 297), now filled with his purchases, and accompanied by the Cook and his assistant(s) (280n.) Parmenon will be on the side of the Cook further from the *skene*, so that, looking towards the Cook with whom he is in lively conversation (61n.), his eye does not fall on Demeas. The Cook is easily identifiable as such by a distinctive mask (see next note) and also by carrying on him the tools of his trade, especially butcher's knives (284). Parmenon had also been instructed to buy an animal for sacrifice (190), and we can safely assume that he has done so. The animal is probably a sheep (cf. 399, *Dysk.* 393) and is probably being led along by (one of) the Cook's assistant(s); in contrast with the sheep bought by Nikeratos (399–404) it will be a good-quality beast with plenty of meat on it, and no attempt is made to draw the audience's attention to it.

283–390 Almost always in New Comedy, when a meat meal is to be prepared (which is to say, when an animal is to be sacrificed), a professional cook is hired; such cooks appear in *Aspis, Dyskolos* (Sikon), *Epitrepontes* (Karion), *Kolax* (F 1), *Misoumenos* (270–5 S = 671–6 A), and *Phasma* (73–74 as cited by Ath. 14.661e–f), as well as in seven plays of Plautus (but none of Terence). His social status is low (indeed he could sometimes be a slave, 194n.), and his occupation was considered disreputable (in Thphr. *Char.* 6.5 he is bracketed with brothel-keepers, tax-farmers and professional gamblers), but he is regularly represented as inordinately proud of his expertise and immensely loquacious, to the great annoyance of other characters whose complaints tend to include stereotyped puns on the verb κόπτειν (283–5, 292–3nn.). The figure of the comic cook was already well established in Middle Comedy (Nesselrath 1990: 297–309, Arnott 2010: 319–22); its development, typology and dramatic functions are discussed by Dohm 1964, Wilkins 2000: 369–414 and, for Menander, by Krieter-Spiro 1997: 26–31, 145–6, 162–6, 196–9. His appearance often, as here, heralds a kind of interlude that has no obvious bearing on the plot, while important issues are held in suspense (e.g. in *Aspis*, the question of who is to marry Kleostratos' sister); in *Samia* we know that Demeas is waiting to speak to Parmenon, undoubtedly to question him about the parentage of the baby. In this passage the Cook is not given much scope to display his stock characteristics, and when he exits at 295, having spoken only six or seven lines, we may not expect to see him again; but he will reappear (357) and make a surprise intervention in the action, attempting in vain to mollify Demeas (383–90) – whether out of sympathy for Chrysis and the baby, or out of apprehension that he may lose his job and fee for the day, we never discover – and drawing on himself the old man's anger at its peak.

In the Mytilene mosaic, the Cook is cross-eyed and has a dark face, with features that could well be intended as African, and with hair receding in front but falling to his shoulders in four long plaits on each side (they would now be called dreadlocks). Such a mask would correspond to Pollux's description of the 'slave Tettix' mask (Pollux 4.149–50) as 'bald, black, with two or three black locks on his head ... [and] cross-eyed'; 'slave' is probably an error here, since in the same passage Pollux speaks of the 'Maison' mask as that of a slave, and Maison was certainly a name associated with cooks (Athen. 659a – who also says that 'foreign' cooks were called Tettix), and undoubtedly Tettix ('Cicada', i.e. 'Chatterbox', cf. Alexis fr. 96) would be a good name for a comic cook. No mask similar to that in the mosaic has been identified in other surviving representations (Webster, Green and Seeberg 1995: 30–2), though there are a few portrayals of apparently comic characters with Negroid features from the fourth century onwards (Snowden 1970: 162–3). There is a character named Libys ('African'), who appears to be a cook, in com. adesp. 1093.188, 206, and there was another character of the same name in Menander's *Hydria* (fr. 359); in Roman comedy, we have the nurse Giddenis, *corpore aquilo*, in Plautus' *Poenulus* (1111–48), and an Ethiopian slave has a non-speaking role in Terence's *Eunuchus* (471). In real life there were certainly some black Africans to be found in the Greek world, even before Alexander's conquest of Egypt. Aristotle (*HA* 586a2–4, *GA* 722a9–11) reports what appear to be two variant versions of an account (set either in Elis or in Sicily) of a union between a Greek woman and an 'Ethiopian': their daughter was not of African appearance, but their grandson was. See further Snowden 1970: 101–9, 156–63, 184–5, Snowden 1983 (though he does not discuss our mosaic). We cannot, of course, know for sure what kind of mask/headpiece the Cook wore in the original production of *Samia*; but there is good evidence (see Introduction §11) that the Mytilene mosaics derive from a continuous iconographic tradition going back to Menander's own time or shortly afterwards, and it should be regarded as highly likely that Menander did represent the Cook in this play as a black African.

283–95 This short scene is not unimportant in the economy of the play: we are almost exactly half-way through the action, and this is the first time that two characters on stage have interacted in a hostile manner. Their hostility remains on a purely verbal level, and it would not have prevented subsequent cooperation between Parmenon and the Cook if Parmenon had not for quite other reasons fled from the scene at 324; but it foreshadows a long series of confrontations to come, starting with that between Parmenon and Demeas and then involving five of the six possible pairings among the four major characters (Demeas-Chrysis, Demeas-Moschion, Nikeratos-Moschion, Nikeratos-Chrysis, Nikeratos-Demeas), which will end only when first Demeas (527–31) and then Nikeratos (585–611) learn the truth about the baby. This and the short passage in which Nikeratos arrives with the other sheep (399–404) are the only purely comic episodes in Act III (cf. Arnott 1997: 76).

283–5 New Comedy's audiences seem never to have tired of jokes about cooks involving the verb (κατα)κόπτειν, literally 'chop up', idiomatically 'tire, bore, annoy' (Krieter-Spiro 1997: 136–7). They appear several times in the fragments of Menander's contemporaries and successors (Alexis fr. 177.12, Anaxippus fr. 1.23, Hegesippus fr. 1.3, Sosipater fr. 1.20). Menander himself seems to use them, in their simple form, only in his early plays (cf. 292–3, *Dysk.* 410); in *Dysk.* 398–9 he reverses the joke by having the cook himself, infuriated by an exceptionally uncooperative sheep, complain κατακέκομμ' ἐγὼ ὁ μάγειρος ὑπὸ τούτου, and in a cook-episode in *Aspis*, where the verb appears twice (228, 234), on neither occasion does it refer to anything said or done by or to the cook. Here there is a different kind of twist to the joke: in the punchline (285) κατακόψαι has to be understood simultaneously in its metaphorical sense (with λαλῶν) and in its literal sense (with πάντα πράγματ' 'everything', i.e. everything that a cook may need to cut up).

283 σύ: the subject of an indirect question may be placed, for emphasis, before the question-word (e.g. Pl. *Lach.* 190d ἐπιχειρήσωμεν ... εἰπεῖν ἀνδρεία τί ποτ' ἐστίν), but it is extremely abnormal for such a preposed subject – syntactically an integral part of the subordinate clause – to be separated from the question-word by verse-end. Contrast e.g. Soph. *Phil.* 572–3 τόνδε μοι πρῶτον φράσον | τίς ἐστίν where the subject of the indirect question has been 'raised' into the governing clause to serve as its object. Possibly the effect aimed at here, by thus isolating σύ, is to emphasize that the reference is to this man's individual characteristics, as if to say 'most cooks may need knives, but I don't see why *you* do!'

284 ἐφ' ὅ τι 'for what purpose'.

286 ἰδιῶτ' 'layman' (LSJ ἰδιώτης III), with the implication 'ignorant'. The term could be used in relation to any occupation or activity requiring special skill or training, from medicine (Thuc. 2.48.3) to cavalrymanship

(Xen. *Hipparch.* 8.1); but it doubtless seemed droll that a cook should use it to refer to non-cooks (cf. Poseidippus fr. 28.11) or to allegedly incompetent cooks (Poseidippus fr. 29.1), given the low repute in which their occupation was held (283–390n.).

287–92 Since a hired cook was normally going to have to slaughter an animal, and prepare a probably complicated meal, among strangers in a house he had never seen before, he might well have to ask many questions about the house and its facilities as well as about the catering requirements, and in comedy those of whom he asks the questions regularly find them irritating. Sometimes the questions are reasonably to the point, e.g. Diphilus fr. 17 (how many people have been invited, and are some of them foreigners – who, as the cook explains, tend to have different tastes in food?); sometimes they are fussy or worse, e.g. Alexis fr. 177.12–15 (is there a kitchen, and does it have a chimney?). In our passage the questions begin sensibly enough (the Cook obviously needs to know the size of the party and the time for the meal) but then progressively degenerate, and in any case they become irritating by their sheer number (seven).

287 εἰ πυνθάνομαι: he is interrupted before reaching the apodosis, but since the aim of the sentence is to explain why Parmenon can rightly be called an ἰδιώτης, the apodosis would have been something to the effect of 'I'm only asking the questions that any cook would ask, because I need to know the answers to them.' We are no doubt to understand that he had begun asking (some of) these questions before he and Parmenon came on stage, and that this had prompted Parmenon's annoyed reaction in 283–5.

287–8 πόσας τραπέζας μέλλετε | ποεῖν: the speaker in Men. fr. 409 complains that the cook has asked him this question three times, and retorts 'we're sacrificing *one* piglet, so what does it matter to you whether we have one table or two or eight?' Small portable tables were used, each serving for two or three persons, and brought into the dining-room with the food upon them: cf. Ar. *Wasps* 1216–21 (at least two tables for six diners), *Frogs* 518 (a single table for two diners).

288 πόσαι γυναῖκές εἰσι: normally men and (respectable) women did not dine together, but wedding feasts were an exception; the women, however, would have separate tables (cf. Euangelus fr. 1.1–2 where a cook is told to provide 'four tables for women and six for men') and also smaller portions of meat (cf. Xen. *Lac.* 1.3).

290 τραπεζοποιόν: a man hired by a cook (who would no doubt, if possible, recover the cost from his client) to prepare the tables and do other ancillary jobs (Antiphanes fr. 150 mentions washing up, preparing lamps and pouring libations); he would probably be needed only if the party was too large for the household servants, and the cook's regular assistant(s), to handle. A τραπεζοποιός is a minor character in *Aspis* (233–245).

290–1 εἰ κέραμός ἐστ' ἔνδοθεν | ὑμῖν ἱκανός: the question may at first sight seem rather insolent (and Parmenon may well think it so), but even a wealthy household might not have sufficient pots, pans or plates for a very large party, and there were stalls in the Agora at which cooks could hire crockery (Alexis fr. 259). Negligence in ascertaining, or estimating, what was required might result in the host or the cook having to borrow items from neighbours (*Dysk.* 456–521, esp. 490–2).

291 εἰ τοὐπτάνιον κατάστεγον: this, however, really is going too far: if it is absurd for a hired cook to ask whether his client's kitchen has a chimney (287–92n.), it is doubly so to ask whether it has a *roof!*

292–4 A second κόπτειν joke (283–5n.) following hard on the heels of the first, and once again moving back from the metaphorical to the literal sense of the verb, this time by the unexpected conclusion εἰς περικόμματα 'into mincemeat'.

292 γε introducing an interruption that completes the other speaker's sentence (Denniston 1954: 137), here supplying an apodosis to the Cook's protracted protasis; cf. Ar. *Peace* 444–6 (Ερ.) κεῖ τις ἐπιθυμῶν ταξιαρχεῖν σοι φθονεῖ εἰς φῶς ἀνελθεῖν... ἐν ταῖσιν μάχαις – (Τρ.) πάσχοι γε τοιαῦθ' οἷάπερ Κλεώνυμος, 450–2.

293 εἰ λανθάνει σε 'if you're not aware of it' (as evidently he is not).   **φίλτατ':** strongly sarcastic, as in Sosipater fr. 1.20 (likewise in a κόπτειν joke addressed to a cook); cf. also perhaps Araros fr. 16 οὐκ ἔσθ' ὅπως οὐκ εἶ παράσιτος, φίλτατε.   **εἰς περικόμματα:** cf. Ar. *Knights* 372 περικόμματ' ἔκ σου σκευάσω, 770 κατατμηθεὶς ἐψοίμην ἐν περικομματίοις (both spoken by the Sausage-Seller, respectively as a threat and an oath-curse).

294 οὐχ ὡς ἔτυχεν literally, 'not in a random manner' (cf. *Perik.* 338), i.e. 'with professional efficiency, thoroughly'. In this idiom the tense was originally variable (contrast Thuc. 5.20.2 ὅπως ἔτυχε with Eur. *Hipp.* 929 ὅπως ἐτύγχανεν), but by Menander's time it was invariably aorist.

294–5 τοῦτό γε | παντὸς ἕνεκ' 'that <I say> for every reason': γε signals that the speaker is 'reaffirming and supplementing his own preceding words' (Denniston 1954: 138). Parmenon can claim to have three reasons for disliking the Cook, who has irritated him by his endless questions, then insulted him (285–6), and now cursed him (294).

295 παράγετ' εἴσω: 104–5n.; here addressed to the Cook and his assistant(s). They now go into Demeas' house, taking the sacrificial animal with them; Parmenon is about to follow them when Demeas calls to him. For

COMMENTARY 296-7   193

such an aborted exit cf. *Epitr.* 857–8 (Pamphile about to go inside when Habrotonon calls to her) and see Frost 1988: 15.

296 ἐμέ τις κέκληκε; Parmenon turns round at the voice from behind him (282/3n.) and sees Demeas.   **ναιχί** in Menander (*Epitr.* 873; *Leukadia* 6 Arnott) appears to be a mere variant of ναί, conveying no attitudinal signals except through its intonation and context. It may be a colloquialism (see Dover 1987: 23), though it occurs once in tragedy (and in a lyric context at that) in Soph. *OT* 684: it never appears among the innumerable expressions for 'yes' in the genuine works of Plato (only in the spurious *Hipparchus*, 232a), and in Aristophanes it is found exclusively (six times) in the mouth of the Scythian archer in *Thesmophoriazusae* (1183–1218 – in the form ναικι, since the Scythian cannot cope with aspiration).

297 Demeas does not answer Parmenon's greeting (as he did Moschion's at 129, even though he was then in an angry mood) but merely gives him an order; similarly at 658 Moschion will brush aside Parmenon's χαῖρε σύ and send him inside to fetch a cloak and sword. Contrast *Georg.* 41 where Myrrhine reciprocates the greeting of Daos (her son's slave) with νὴ καὶ σύ γε.   **τὴν σφυρίδα καταθείς:** Parmenon takes this as an instruction to *go indoors*, put down the basket, and come back immediately. Blume 1974: 104 suggests that Demeas is to be understood as ordering Parmenon to put down the basket *at once*, outside the house, and that Parmenon deliberately misinterprets the order; but if Menander had meant his audience to understand the action thus, he would have helped them by making Demeas complain about Parmenon's behaviour, either during his absence or immediately after his return. Frost 1988: 107 points out that the basket has to be got rid of so that Parmenon can 'flee unencumbered' at 325.   **ἀγαθῆι τύχηι:** 116–17n. This is the only place in comedy where this phrase is used by one complying with an order, and it *may* be designed to indicate that Parmenon is here betraying apprehension that something may be wrong, warned by Demeas' peremptory order and tone of voice; but we cannot be sure of this, and Parmenon's attitude in 301–3 – giving an instruction in the imperative to Chrysis, a free person, and following this with a jaunty warning about the drinking habits of 'the old woman' – hardly suggests that he has a weight on his mind. *Epitr.* 223, often cited as a parallel, gives no support to the 'apprehension' hypothesis: Daos there is so sure of the justice of his case that he has accepted without hesitation Syriskos' proposal to go to arbitration, is completely indifferent as to who should be chosen as arbitrator (219–21), and now agrees for the dispute to be judged by a man of whom he knows nothing.
       Parmenon takes the basket into Demeas' house.

298–300 Menander takes advantage of Parmenon's brief absence by having Demeas explain why he wants to talk to him: if there has indeed been an affair between Moschion and Chrysis, Parmenon will certainly know of it.

298 γάρ is used because this sentence serves to explain what Demeas had said just before (his order to Parmenon to come back outside).

298–9 οὐδέν... | τοιοῦτον... πραττόμενον ἔργον is to be taken together as the subject of λανθάνοι... ἄν.

300 περίεργος 'nosy' (203–5n.).

300–1 τὴν θύραν | ... πέπληχε (367, 555, *Dysk.* 188, *Epitr.* 906) is used interchangeably with τὴν θύραν ψοφεῖ *vel sim.* (*Dysk.* 586, *Mis.* 206–7 S = 607–8 A, *Perik.* 316 etc.), ἐψόφηκε τὴν θύραν (669, *Epitr.* 875, Men. fr. 883), and ἡ θύρα ψοφεῖ (567), invariably when a character becomes aware that someone is about to come out of a house; similar expressions are already found in fifth-century comedy (Ar. *Knights* 1326, *Frogs* 603–4) and tragedy (Soph. *El.* 1322–3; Eur. *Ion* 515–16, *Hel.* 859–60). The absence of an expressed subject indicates that the speaker (thinks he) knows who is coming out (here Parmenon); see Melandri 2007: 6–11. The noise referred to was heard a little *before* the door actually opened; in Eur. *Hel.* loc. cit. no less than eight lines are spoken (857–64) between the time when Helen first hears the noise and the time when Theonoe comes out of the *skene* door. It probably represented the knocking away of the latch-pins (βάλανοι, cf. Ar. *Eccl.* 361 βεβαλάνωκε τὴν θύραν) which held in place the crossbar that kept the door shut (Furley 2009: 231–2, Neuburger 1919: 338–9). There is, of course, no need for any noise to have been audible in the theatre: the character's statement that (s)he has heard it will suffice.

301 Parmenon comes out of the house, talking back to those within (198n.), addressing the other slaves and even the free Chrysis in a confident, authoritative tone very different from the one he will adopt when he becomes aware that Demeas is angry with him (see Krieter-Spiro 1997: 187).   **δίδοτε, Χρυσί:** 252n.; Chrysis is specially addressed because she has, at least de facto, the power to organize and give orders to the slaves (cf. 730).

302 τὴν... γραῦν: the definite article would prima facie suggest that there was only one 'old woman' in the household, and if so, this would have to be Moschion's old nurse (232–61). However, the nurse had not been involved in the wedding preparations, since she had been upstairs (232) when they were in full swing. Moreover, when Demeas expels Chrysis from his house, he tells her 'You've got... the old woman' (372–3). Can this be the ex-nurse? Demeas had, to be sure, an absolute right to refuse any person (other than his wife, children or parents) lodging in his home, but he could not compel the ex-nurse, a free woman, to become Chrysis' attendant if she did not wish to (Krieter-Spiro 1997: 41 n. 5), and nothing elsewhere in the text indicates that she ever had had such a role. These considerations suggest that we are to understand there are *two* old women in the household. One, the ex-nurse, 'rushed off, I don't know where' at 261, and we do not hear of her again. The other is a slave, who has been working in the kitchen with her colleagues, and whom Demeas will later make over to Chrysis (cf. 381-2 προστίθημί σοι | ἐγὼ θεραπαίνας), perhaps seizing an opportunity to get rid of a slave who gives him much trouble and little work.

302-3 φυλάττετε | ἀπὸ τῶν κεραμίων: the stereotype of women as insatiable wine-drinkers goes back to Old Comedy (e.g. Ar. *Lys.* 193-239, *Thesm.* 347-8, 393, 628-32, 733-59, *Eccl.* 43-5, 132-57, 227); in Middle and New Comedy it is particularly associated with *old* women (*Perinthia* F 4, Men. fr. 412, Dionysius com. fr. 5, Alexis fr. 172, perhaps also Men. fr. 170 καὶ τὸ κεράμιον | ἀνέωιχας· ὄζεις, ἱερόσυλ', οἴνου πολύ – cf. *Epitr.* 1064, 1122 ἱερόσυλε γραῦ; Plaut. *Curc.* 96-138), see Arnott 1996b: 503-4. In the fifth century a wine-jar could be called a κεράμιον οἰνηρόν (Cratinus fr. 391; Hdt. 3.6.1; contrast κεράμιον ὀξηρόν Ar. fr. 743), but by Menander's time κεράμιον on its own could bear this meaning (Men. fr. 170, Alexis fr. 85).

303 τί δεῖ ποεῖν: Parmenon assumes that Demeas has some urgent orders for him.

304 τί δεῖ ποεῖν <σε>; It is common in comedy for a person who is asked a question to repeat the question before answering it. Sometimes, as here (and *Dysk.* 635), the repetition is in direct interrogative form, and sometimes, as in 481 (and *Dysk.* 363), an indirect interrogative is substituted; either way, as the second pattern shows, we are to understand that the echo-question means in effect 'Are you asking me ...?' (cf. 70-1n.). As transmitted, the line does not scan: one syllable (or two short syllables) must have dropped out after ποεῖν. Choice between the two proposed supplements (see apparatus) is difficult. Sudhaus thought he could detect in C traces of something that might be σε displaced to the end of the line, but this is very doubtful; however, σε is probably to be preferred on other grounds – it would have been slightly more at risk of accidental omission than ἴθι would, and an echo-question need not repeat the exact wording of the original question (cf. *Dysk.* 635 ποῦ γῆς ποτ' εἶ; – ποῦ γῆς ἐγώ;).

304-5 δεῦρ' ἀπὸ τῆς θύρας· | ἔτι μικρόν: Demeas wants to question Parmenon where there is no risk of their being overheard by those inside the house. Parmenon comes some way towards him, perhaps expecting that

Demeas will move to meet him; but Demeas stays where he is, and beckons Parmenon closer (ἔτι μικρόν). Cf. Plaut. *Men.* 158 *concede huc a foribus. –
fiat. – etiam concede huc. – licet.*

305 ἦν 'there you are', said by a person in the act of obeying an order or
request (687, *Epitr.* 391; Ar. *Peace* 327, *Frogs* 1390); contrast 313.   ἄκουέ
δή μου: cf. *Fab. Inc.* 27. The variant ἄκουε δή νυν (C) will be due to a scribe's
recollection of Euripides (*Hec.* 833, *Supp.* 857 and eleven other passages);
enclitic νυν is nowhere found in Menander.

306–7 is no doubt said in a tone which accurately conveys the message
that Parmenon *will* be flogged if he does not comply with Demeas' wishes.

306 μὰ τοὺς δώδεκα θεούς: the 'Twelve Gods' were the major Olympian
deities considered as a group; at Athens the group normally consisted
of Zeus, Hera, Poseidon, Demeter, Athena, Apollo, Artemis, Hermes,
Aphrodite, Ares, Hephaestus, and either Hestia (Pl. *Phdr.* 247a) or Dionysus (who takes her place on the Parthenon Frieze), and since 522/1 there
had been an altar dedicated to them near the northern end of the Agora
(Hdt. 6.108.4, Thuc. 6.54.6). See Guthrie 1950: 110–12. In surviving texts
before Menander's time the Twelve are only once invoked in an oath (Ar.
Knights 235; this is the first line spoken by Paphlagon, who represents
Cleon – was it a mannerism of the real Cleon's?); in New Comedy such
oaths appear at *Kolax* 127 S = E232 A and *com. adesp.* 1013.9.

308 συγκρύπτεις 'you are a party to concealing', 'you are helping to conceal' (Ant. 2.3.4, Andoc. 1.67, Isoc. 17.18).   πρός μ' 'from me': cf. Soph.
Phil. 587–8 λόγων κρύψαι πρὸς ἡμᾶς μηδὲν ὧν ἀκήκοας. It is possible that this
seemingly illogical use of πρός originated in negative contexts (note that
κρύψαι πρὸς ἡμᾶς μηδέν is equivalent to λέγειν πρὸς ἡμᾶς πάντα) and was then
generalized to non-negative ones. Riad 1973: 207 read C's damaged text as
πρᾱγμ', as in B; see however Sandbach 1980: 51. If it were indeed the only
transmitted reading πρᾶγμ' would be quite acceptable, but πρός μ' is better:
Parmenon's offence is not that he has participated in a deception, but that
he has participated in a deception *of his master.*   ἤι[σ]θημ' 'I am aware'
presupposes the factuality of the statement which is its object. Here and
throughout most of the interrogation (311, 316) Demeas pretends that he
knows that Parmenon is party to a cover-up and that Moschion is the baby's
father; then as now, a good way to secure a confession was to lead the suspect to believe that the interrogator was already in possession of other and
decisive evidence – and with Parmenon the ploy works beautifully (320).
And yet, at the same time as Demeas deceives Parmenon into overestimat-
ing his (Demeas') knowledge, he also deceives himself into overestimat-
ing his own knowledge: being certain that Chrysis is the baby's mother, he
cuts off Parmenon in mid-sentence (320–1) when, had he allowed him to

finish, Parmenon would probably have said something that revealed, or pointed the way to, the full truth (320n.).

309–10 Parmenon frenziedly – and quite falsely – swears his innocence in the name of four different gods. For other such serial oaths cf. *Dysk.* 666–7 (sheer excitement, at having been alone with Knemon's daughter for a few minutes); *com. adesp.* 1155.6–7 (likewise four gods – including two of the four invoked here – but this time, it would seem, in an affirmation of guilt by the accuser rather than of innocence by the accused: Handley 1996: 15–16); Eur. *Cycl.* 262–8 (an affirmation of innocence); and (with Plautine overkill) Pl. *Cist.* 512–16, *Bacch.* 892–5.

309 μά in an oath-formula can itself imply the denial of a statement, or a negative response to a question or command, even if there is no (other) negative word in the context, e.g. *Epitr.* 934–5 ἐπακροώμε[νος] ἕστηκας, ἱερόσυλέ, μου; – [μ]ὰ τοὺς θεούς, *Heros* 39 καταγελᾶις; – μὰ τὸν Ἀπόλλω, *Perik.* 309–310, *com. adesp.* 1084.1–2, Eur. *IA* 739 πιθοῦ. – μὰ τὴν ἄνασσαν Ἀργείαν θεάν.   **μὰ τὸν Ἀπόλλω τουτονί:** gesturing towards the pillar and altar of Apollo Agyieus which stood in front of the *skene* (444; Ar. *Wasps* 875ff; Pherecr. fr. 92; Aesch. *Ag.* 1081) as it stood in front of many real Athenian houses (see Parker 2005: 18); the same formula, or slight variants on it, appear in *Dysk.* 659, *Mis.* 314 S = 715 A, Men. fr. 884, *com. adesp.* 1155.7, and Ar. *Thesm.* 748.

310 **μὰ τὸν Δία τὸν σωτῆρα:** cf. *Epitr.* 359, *Perik.* 759, *com. adesp.* 1017.107, 1089.10, 1155.6. Zeus Soter had for centuries received the third libation after meals (Aesch. *Supp.* 26, *Ag.* 1386–7, *Cho.* 244–5, 1073, *Eum.* 759–60, fr. 55.4; Soph. fr. 425), but an actual cult of Zeus Soter and Athena Soteira appears to have been established, in the Peiraeus (Paus. 1.1.3), only in the late fifth century, perhaps during the period of the Peace of Nicias (421–413); Zeus Soter is never even mentioned in comedy before 411 (Ar. *Thesm.* 1009), and the seven oaths sworn by him in Aristophanes all date from 405 or later (*Frogs* 738, 1433; *Eccl.* 79, 761, 1045, 1103; *Wealth* 877). His priest is a character in Aristophanes' *Wealth* (1171–96), and by the 330s his festival, later called the Diisoteria, had become the biggest public sacrificial occasion in the Athenian year, to judge by the proceeds of the sale of victims' skins (*IG* II² 1496 A 88–9, 118–19). See Parker 1996: 238–41, 2005: 466–7.   **μὰ τὸν Ἀσκληπιόν:** the Athenian cult of Asclepius was established in 421/0 (*IG* II² 4960–1) and quickly became popular (see Sommerstein 2001: 8–13), but he is not found in comic oaths before the second half of the fourth century (Alexis fr. 168). For Menander μὰ τὸν Ἀσκληπιόν was a useful metrical resource – no other μά-oath could fill the slot between the hephthemimeral caesura and the end of an iambic trimeter – and it appears at *Dysk.* 160, 666, *Perik.* 336 (in the corresponding position of a trochaic tetrameter), Men. fr. 93, and also *com. adesp.* 1092.8.

311 παῦ: this shortened form of παῦε 'stop! stop it!', attested by Aelius Dionysius (π 28) and Photius (π 69), is not certainly found elsewhere in surviving texts, although it was conjectured by Bentley at Ar. *Knights* 821. The full form παῦε is frequent in Aristophanes (e.g. *Wasps* 37, *Peace* 648) but appears only once in later comedy, and then with a dependent participle (*Dysk.* 214 παῦε θρηνῶν).   **οὐ γὰρ εἰκάζων λέγω** 'I'm not speaking from guesswork', i.e. 'I'm speaking from certain knowledge' (308n.): εἰκάζειν and εἰδέναι are contrasted at *Mis.* 264–6 S = 665–7 A.

312 ἢ μήποτ' ἄρ': Parmenon reinforces his sworn denial (309–310n.) with what would have been, but for Demeas' interruption, an explicit curse that is to befall him if the denial is false. Menander will not have considered himself under any obligation to construct this interrupted sentence in such a way that it could be completed to make a valid iambic trimeter, but in fact Parmenon could have continued e.g. ἀγαθόν γέ μοι γένοιτό τι (cf. *Epitr.* 362). The surprising use of ἄρα (a regular variant of ἄρα throughout Attic poetry) in a wish-sentence probably originates with the idiom ἀπολοίμην ἄρα (vel sim.) for conditional self-curses 'in that case [viz. if I am not telling the truth] may I perish!' (Ar. *Lys.* 933, *Eccl.* 977, Eubulus fr. 115.7; possibly also *Dysk.* 94–5, see Handley 1965: 146–7). When the self-curse is introduced by ἤ (for which cf. Ar. *Knights* 409–10 οὗτοι μ' ὑπερβαλεῖσθ' ἀναιδείαι... ἢ μήποτ' ἀγοραίου Διὸς σπλάγχνοισι παραγενοίμην), the conjunction itself shows that the self-curse applies only if the assertion or promise made is false, and αρα is therefore redundant, but our passage shows that it was sometimes retained by analogy with self-curses of the other type.   **βλέπε δεῦρ':** Parmenon, by being unable to look Demeas in the face, has betrayed the fact that he is lying. Cf. Plaut. *Capt.* 570–1 *aspice agedum ad me... negas te Tyndarum esse?*; Ar. *Knights* 1239 (the Sausage-Seller describing the skills in which he was educated) κλέπτων ἐπιορκεῖν καὶ βλέπειν ἐναντίον; Soph. *Phil.* 110 (Neoptolemus shocked at the idea of lying his way to possession of Philoctetes' bow) πῶς οὖν βλέπων τις ταῦτα τολμήσει λακεῖν; Soph. *Trach.* 402 οὗτος, βλέφ' ὧδε is different, since the addressee, Lichas, had had no reason to look at the speaker, having been engaged in dialogue with a third party.   **ἰδού, βλέπω:** Parmenon does his best to meet Demeas' eye – but perhaps still fails. Cf. Eur. *Cycl.* 211–13 where the satyrs, ordered by the Cyclops to look ἄνω καὶ μὴ κάτω, 'obey' him by looking up at the sky!

313 ἤν 'help!' (spoken aside): Parmenon, tricked into believing that Demeas knows (308n.) he is lying about the baby, realizes that he now has little chance of avoiding painful consequences (except by flight). Photius (η 190) distinguishes between ἦν = ἰδού (305n.) and an aspirated ἦν which is used ἠθικῶς ('expressively'). The latter survives in Menander only here, but an extended form ἤην is used in precisely the same way in *Perinthia* 15 (again by a slave who is in peril because he has tried to deceive his master and been found out) and has been restored at *Dysk.* 465 (ην B, leaving the line a syllable short), where again the speaker is a slave. Here and in *Perinthia* the emotion expressed is mainly fear (cf. *Perinthia* 17–18: Daos has allegedly soiled himself from terror), and this may be the case in *Dyskolos* too (Getas is alarmed by the sudden sound of heavy, running footsteps as an infuriated Knemon rushes to the door: Knemon, until he falls into the well, terrifies everyone with whom he comes into contact). Luck 1965: 272–7 first drew attention to this Menandrian usage, but he was probably wrong to associate it with Terence's *hem* which is much more frequent, has a different pattern of use (it is not confined to slaves), and also differs semantically (it expresses 'surprise pleasant or unpleasant... or else...reflexion and hesitation', Shipp 1960: 129).

314 Χρυσίδος: Parmenon decides to stick to the agreed story; Demeas inevitably takes his answer as an evasion.

315 σόν, φ[ησίν]: by ascribing the assertion to Chrysis, Parmenon technically avoids telling a direct lie. The restoration φ[ησίν] is greatly superior to φ[ασίν]: having lived in the same house as Chrysis throughout the time when Demeas has been away, and being moreover notoriously περίεργος (298–300n.), it would be pointless for Parmenon to pretend that he did not know who Chrysis had said was the father of the baby, and proverbially it was the mother who best knew who the father was (*Odyssey* 1.214; Soph. *OT* 1171–2). **ἀπόλωλας** 'you're done for': the perfect is used proleptically, as ὄλωλα and its compounds often are (e.g. 324; *Epitr.* 906; Ar. *Clouds* 1077; Eur. *Andr.* 903), treating an event that has become inevitable as though it had already happened. **φενακίζεις:** φενακίζω 'cheat, con' is not otherwise found in comedy after the 380s (Ar. *Wealth* 271, 280; Theopompus com. fr. 9), though the verb was a favourite with Demosthenes who uses it (and its derivative φενακισμός) over fifty times (fourteen times in the one speech *Against Aristocrates*) and, more surprisingly, with Isocrates in his old age (8.36, 12.269 and five passages in the *Antidosis*).

316 εἰδότα γ': γε serves its common function of indicating that what is being said is the expansion of an (understood) affirmative answer to the question just asked: '<yes, you *are* cheating me>, because I know...' Demeas has no adequate warrant for saying he 'knows' that the three propositions affirmed in 317–18 are true (153–4, 308nn.); nevertheless they all *are* in fact true – though in two of the three cases (see below) he actually knows only part of the truth. Again at 466 and 477 he will assert knowledge which in fact he does not possess (Katsouris 1975b: 108).

317 Μοσχίωνός ἐστιν: by this, of course, he means that the baby is the son of Moschion *and Chrysis.* Parmenon, however, not knowing what Demeas has overheard in his absence, is almost bound to assume that Demeas has somehow discovered the full truth.

318 δι' ἐκεῖνον...τρέφει: Demeas means that Chrysis is rearing the baby (instead of exposing it, 132n.) out of affection for, and loyalty to, her supposed lover Moschion; Parmenon will again assume that he knows the full truth – that Chrysis is looking after (77–9n.) a baby not her own at Moschion's request. The words Demeas uses are fully compatible with both interpretations.

319 τίς φησι; – πάντες: Demeas continues to bluff. It is, in fact, reasonable for him to suppose that 'everyone' says that Moschion is the baby's father, since the soliloquy and conversation that he overheard pointed strongly to the inference that this was generally known by the household to be the case. He has not, however, heard anyone say that Parmenon was aware of it, or that Moschion was in any way responsible for the baby's being reared.

320 ταῦτ' ἐστίν; 'is that true?'; cf. Soph. *El.* 584 σκῆψιν οὐκ οὖσαν 'a false excuse'.   **ἔστι:** Parmenon is (truthfully) confirming the three propositions stated at 317–18. But he has not explicitly repudiated his earlier statement (314) that Chrysis was the baby's mother – he has not had the chance to do so, and in any case he is probably to be taken as believing that Demeas already knows the statement to be false (317n.); so Demeas will take this reply as further confirmation (if confirmation were needed) that Chrysis is indeed the mother.   **ἀλλὰ λανθάνειν – :** at this point it is highly likely that, had he not been interrupted, Parmenon would have said something that would, at the very least, have made Demeas aware that he was under a misapprehension. It is very much in Parmenon's interest to claim (though it is no more than a half-truth) that the objective of the scheme to which he was party was not so much to deceive Demeas, his master, as to deceive Nikeratos; and astute listeners will therefore have realized that he was about to mention Nikeratos (or 'the girl's father' or some equivalent expression) as the object of λανθάνειν. The complete sentence would have meant something like 'we wanted to keep Nikeratos in the dark until after the wedding' (cf. 529). Demeas would not have been able to make head or tail of what Parmenon was talking about, would have asked for an explanation, and the whole truth would have come out. But in fact, as soon as he hears the word λανθάνειν, Demeas takes it as an admission that Moschion, Chrysis and the slaves had plotted to keep *him* in the dark, and flies into a rage.

321 ἱμάντα: a leather strap, commonly used for the corporal chastisement of slaves (663, *Dysk.* 502, Antiphanes fr. 75.7–8; cf. also Ar. *Ach.* 723–4). **παίδων** 'of the boys', i.e. of the male slaves. The definite article can be omitted with terms denoting key persons and relationships within a household, e.g. κεκτημένη 'Mistress' (*Perik.* 262), παιδίον 'Baby' (*Epitr.* 403).   **τις δότω:** it was routine, both in drama (even tragedy, e.g. Aesch. *Cho.* 889) and in real life (Xen. *Cyr.* 5.3.49–50), for a master to call out to his slaves collectively an order for 'someone' (τις) to do so-and-so. Xenophon loc. cit. criticizes this practice on the ground that every slave would leave the order to be carried out by someone else, but if the practice were ineffective it would have disappeared, and it probably would have been effective if the slaves knew that if none of them obeyed, any of them at random might be punished. At any rate, in drama such orders are normally fulfilled (see Bain 1982); when in Aesch. loc. cit. Clytaemestra calls for an axe and does not get one, it is a sign that her authority is draining away. Hence we can reasonably assume that a slave does come out of Demeas' house (most likely between 322 and 323: Arnott 1998b: 14) with a strap which he gives to Demeas; the singular verb λάβ' (325) suggests that when Parmenon flees, this slave is sent off in (unavailing) pursuit. If so, Demeas will be left with the strap in his hand, and will retain it throughout his monologue (325–56), like the Sophoclean Ajax μαστιγοφόρος: he might even brandish it during his paratragic opening lines (325–6) and when he speaks brutally of expelling Chrysis (352–4). He can dispose of it when he goes inside at 360.

322 ἀσεβῆ is probably mere generalized abuse (like ἱερόσυλε, 678n., also addressed to Parmenon) and need not be taken as referring specifically to Parmenon's perjury at 309–12.   **μή, πρὸς θεῶν:** a plea to rescind the order just given (which therefore at this moment has not yet been fulfilled).

     A slave comes out of the house with a strap.

323 στίξω σε: probably 'I'll beat you black and blue', though its literal meaning is 'I'll tattoo you'. Slaves who ran away (and were recaptured), or committed other serious misdemeanours, might be tattooed on the forehead (Ar. *Birds* 760 δραπέτης ἐστιγμένος, Eupolis fr. 277, Herodas 5.65–79, Aeschines 2.79, perhaps Aesch. *Supp.* 839) as a mark of shame and to hamper repetition of the offence; hence the word στιγματίας (Ar. *Lys.* 331, Hermippus fr. 63.19, Eupolis frr. 159.14, 298.2; not found in Middle or New Comedy). Sometimes, however, στίζειν may be used of a severe beating which leaves the victim with so many bruises that he *looks as though* he had been tattooed (e.g. Ar. *Wasps* 1296). Parmenon later (654–7), attempting to justify his having taken to flight when (so he says) he had done nothing wrong, gives the impression that he took Demeas' threat literally, but it does not necessarily follow that the audience will. Tattooing requires the services of a specialist (cf. Herodas loc. cit.), so it could not have been done 'right away' (324); and Demeas can leave plenty of marks on Parmenon's body with his strap.   νὴ τὸν Ἥλιον: 'informal' oaths (Sommerstein 2007: 125) by the Sun are not found in comedy before Alexis (fr. 248), but they become very common in Menander, who has at least eleven instances (e.g. *Aspis* 399, 529; *Epitr.* 525, 631). Solemn oaths by the Sun are quite frequent in surviving treaty texts (e.g. *IG* II² 127, 281; Rhodes and Osborne 50) and are also found in tragedy (Soph. *OT* 660–2; Eur. *Med.* 746–53, *Supp.* 261, *HF* 858).

324 ἤδη γ' 'yes, right away!'   ἀπόλωλα: 315n. Parmenon now runs away down Eisodos B (see note at start of commentary).   μαστιγία: there may be a humorous point (on the dramatist's part) in making Demeas call Parmenon this when Parmenon has just *avoided* a flogging.

325–56 We expect Demeas, left alone, to be furiously angry against Moschion, and for a moment he is; but then he amazes us by declaring that Moschion 'has done [him] no wrong', that the supposed affair between Moschion and Chrysis is to be blamed entirely on the latter, and that *she* must be punished. He will expel her from his house, as he would have done earlier (133–6) but for Moschion's pleading; he will pretend that he is doing so for his original reason, Chrysis' disobedience in failing to expose the baby (354–5), and thus will avoid bringing on Moschion a dishonour which he believes Moschion does not deserve. As his soliloquy proceeds, however, it becomes evident that he is emotionally torn. Moschion is his only son and has given much evidence in the past of his good character (343–7); his ready acceptance of marriage to Plangon is now reinterpreted as showing that he was anxious to 'escape' from the clutches of Chrysis (333–7). But Demeas is also deeply in love with Chrysis – as she herself is well aware (81–2) – and has to lecture himself quite firmly on the need to face down and forget his passion (349–50, 356), so that we will be left wondering whether he will in the end have the mental strength to go through with his plan. Those spectators who have perceived a similarity between the situation in this play and in Euripides' *Hippolytus* plays will note that Demeas' attitude is the reverse of what Theseus' had been. Theseus, certain that his wife was a virtuous woman (and, at least in the surviving play, irritated by Hippolytus' tendency to make it obvious that he considered himself a morally superior being), implicitly believed her accusation of rape against Hippolytus; Demeas, certain that his adopted son is a virtuous young man (and irritated by Chrysis' apparent defiance of him in the matter of the baby), jumps to the conclusion that he must have been seduced by Chrysis rather than vice versa. This soliloquy is arguably the pivot of the play, triggering as it does the expulsion of Chrysis, the first overt act that seriously threatens to disrupt the wedding preparations.

The logic of the argument that establishes Moschion's innocence in Demeas' eyes leaves much to be desired. It is based essentially on two facts only: that Moschion has always shown himself to be a young man of good character (343–7) and that he readily, indeed eagerly (336 ἔσπευδεν), accepted Demeas' proposal that he marry Plangon. These facts are nowhere near sufficient to show that Moschion cannot have been at all to blame for the supposed affair between himself and Chrysis. Sexual temptation was notoriously a snare to young males, ὅταν ταράξηι Κύπρις ἡβῶσαν φρένα (Eur. *Hipp.* 969); and Moschion was in a situation of exceptional temptation, having been left at home with a very attractive ex-*hetaira*, quite possibly of about the same age as himself, as the only other free person in the house. We know, too, that he *did* in fact succumb to sexual temptation while Demeas was away, though not with Chrysis. Nor would an intentional seduction of Chrysis necessarily or even probably have caused Moschion to take a hostile attitude to Demeas when the latter returned (332–3), particularly if he had come, on reflection, to be ashamed of it as he is ashamed of his rape of Plangon (47, 67–8nn.). Moschion's willingness to marry Plangon does indeed show that he is not now in love with Chrysis; but Demeas has no grounds for rejecting (335–6) his own earlier belief that Moschion *is* in love with Plangon, except his determination to find reasons to maximize Chrysis' guilt and minimize or entirely eliminate that of Moschion. He has no actual evidence whatever that Chrysis forced, tricked, or intoxicated (339–42) Moschion into sleeping with her; his assertion that she is a χαμαιτύπη ... ὄλεθρος (348) is mere vituperation, based either on his assumptions about her way of life before he took her into his house, or on his certainty that she must have seduced Moschion. In short, the Demeas of this soliloquy is a man who will grasp at any straw if it enables him to exculpate his adopted only son; at one point he goes so far as to imply that Moschion ought not to be regarded as fully responsible for his actions even if it *was* he who took the initiative in the affair (330–1n.).

325 λάβ᾽ αὐτόν: if the slave who brought the strap at 322 is still on stage, this order will be addressed to him, and he will run off in (vain) pursuit of Parmenon (cf. *com. adesp.* 1032.10–11); but he may have already gone back into the house, in which case Demeas will be calling out 'to the world at large and no one in particular' (Gomme and Sandbach 1973) and there will be no response to his call (cf. Ar. *Thesm.* 1096).

325–6 "ὦ πόλισμα ... | ... ὦ –": a marginal note in B identifies this as a quotation (or adaptation) from Euripides' *Oedipus* (Eur. fr. 554b); it is not clear whether the note refers to the whole paratragic outburst or only to the first four words. In tragedy such apostrophes may express horror, as here, or may be appeals to man and/or nature to witness the speaker's suffering (e.g. [Aesch.] *Prom.* 88–92, 1090–3, Soph. *Ant.* 937–43); in either case one would expect any invocation of a πόλισ(μα) to name the city in which the speaker was currently located, and since all other indications are that Euripides' play was set at Thebes (note especially that Iocaste was a character, cf. frr. 545a, 551), it is likely that Euripides wrote Καδμείας χθονός (as e.g. *Phoen.* 1101) or Θηβαίας χθονός (as e.g. *Phoen.* 281, 776, 883) and that Menander has substituted an equally Euripidean phrase (cf. *Hipp.* 34, *Ion* 1571) appropriate for use in Athens. Demeas is so appalled by what Parmenon has revealed that he can find expression for his feelings only in the language of tragedy: every significant word he uses here is alien to the vocabulary of New Comedy and of ordinary speech. Any spectator who recognizes the source of the quotation may wonder whether Demeas' thoughts have flown to *Oedipus* because Oedipus usurped his father's bed as Demeas believes Moschion has done (cf. 496). We know his horror is due to a misapprehension; in a moment he himself will come to feel that it was excessive – but that change of feeling, too, will be based on entirely erroneous grounds.

326 ὦ ταναὸς αἰθήρ: αἰθήρ, the bright element that 'lies above and beyond the medium in which we live, between this medium and the sky' (Dover 1968: 135), featured prominently in the physics of Anaxagoras (frr. 2, 15, and test. 43, 70, 71, 73, 84, 89 D–K) and is much spoken of by Euripides, who uses the word and its derivatives over a hundred times, sometimes treating it as a virtual synonym of οὐρανός (e.g. *Hel.* 584, cf. 34), sometimes identifying it with Zeus (Eur. frr. 877, 941). He calls it ταναός (perhaps implying both 'widely outspread' and 'rarefied': Willink 1986: 139) at *Or.* 322, in a lyric passage; in iambics, however, he uses ταναός only in reference to long hair (*Bacch.* 455, 831), and this raises the suspicion that the phrase here may not be part of the *Oedipus* quotation but may have been created by Menander on the model of the *Orestes* passage, perhaps to suggest that Demeas is finding even normal tragic language inadequate to his needs and is straining for something still more high-flown.   **ταναός:** nominative for vocative, as in (and perhaps specifically imitated from) [Aesch.] *Prom.* 88 ὦ δῖος αἰθήρ.   **ὦ – :** Blume 1974: 120 attractively suggests that Demeas, trying to think of some yet more exalted expression to climax a threefold apostrophe, fails to find anything suitable, hesitates, and thus gives his rational self time to take control.   **τί, Δημέα, βοᾶις; :** with this self-admonition cf. *Dis Ex.* 23 ἐ[π]αν[αγε, Σ]ώστρατε and *Dysk.* 213–14 παῦε θρηνῶν, Σώστρατε. The speakers there are both young men; this passage and 349 are the only places in Menander where an old man apostrophizes himself (J. Blundell 1980: 65ff., Grant 1986: 180). Self-apostrophe is appropriate to a paratragic passage, being frequent in tragedy and especially in Euripides (Katsouris 1975b: 156–64).

327 τί βοᾷς, ἀνόητε; For the repetition cf. 465 (where again Demeas is trying to fight down his anger) Μοσχίων, ἔα μ᾽, ἔα με, Μοσχίων.   **κάτεχε σαυτόν, καρτέρει** has long been compared to Catullus 8.11 *sed obstinata mente perfer, obdura*, and Thomas 1984, noting some other parallels, argued that Catullus 8 was in fact based on this soliloquy (especially 349–56); it is at any rate likely enough that Catullus knew the passage and adapted some of its ideas and phrases to fit his own very different situation.

328 οὐδὲν γὰρ ἀδικεῖ Μοσχίων σε: well may Demeas call this statement παράβολος (see next note). How could Moschion have slept with Demeas' concubine and yet committed no offence against Demeas? Only if he somehow had no moral agency in the matter; and how does Demeas imagine that could have been so? We shall not be told until 339–41: Chrysis must have plied him with exceptionally strong drink (341 ἄκρατος) until he no longer knew what he was doing. The present sentence will be almost exactly repeated at 537, when Nikeratos' horrified report that he has seen Plangon breastfeeding the baby has confirmed Moschion's confession that she, not Chrysis, is its mother; the verb ἀδικεῖν is also used in connection with actual or imagined sexual transgressions in 68 (where see n.), 479 and 506.   **παράβολος** 'audacious, reckless, wild'; cf. fr. 784 on τοὺς παραβόλως πλέοντας who are likely to end up as 'either rich men or corpses', Ar. *Wasps* 192, Hdt. 9.45.3.

329 ἀληθινός: the statement is indeed true – almost the only true statement that Demeas will make in this soliloquy – but not for the reasons he gives!

330–1 might be paraphrased 'if Moschion in any way deserves to be blamed for what happened between him and Chrysis'. The manner in which Demeas enumerates the ways in which Moschion might have been blameworthy suggests that even on the worst assumption – that Moschion had taken the initiative in the supposed affair with Chrysis – Demeas is anxious to minimize his son's guilt, since he seems to distinguish between voluntary actions (βουλόμενος) and those performed under the influence of irrational feelings such as sexual desire (κεκνισμένος ἔρωτι) or hatred (μισῶν ἐμέ): Aristotle (*EN* 1111a22–b3), by contrast, insists that such acts (performed διὰ θυμὸν ἢ ἐπιθυμίαν) are voluntary.   **κεκνισμένος | ἔρωτι:** for κνίζω in an erotic context cf. Bacch. 17.8–10, Hdt. 6.62.1, Eur. *Med.* 568, Theocr. 4.59, Machon fr. 13.176–7 Gow.

331 μισῶν ἐμέ: truly a far-fetched idea, but apparently the only other explanation Demeas can think of, even hypothetically: that Moschion hates him like an enemy (presumably for some imagined wrong or slight) and has therefore set out to injure him by seducing his partner (as Aegisthus seduced Agamemnon's wife – and plotted to murder him – in revenge for what had been done to his father and brothers by Agamemnon's father Atreus).

332–3 Certainly one would expect Moschion – unless he was very crafty – to behave in an 'arrogant and hostile' manner towards Demeas, if he had seduced Chrysis out of hatred for his adoptive father. But on the far more likely supposition that he had acted out of (perhaps transient) erotic passion, he might have reacted in any number of different ways to Demeas' return; he might well, for example, have felt deeply ashamed (325–56n.).

332 ἦν ἄν 'he would now be'.   ἐπὶ τῆς αὐτῆς διανοίας 'in the same state of mind', cf. Dem. 21.213 τηρήσατε τὴν γνώμην ταύτην ἐφ' ἧς νῦν ἐστε, 8.14 μενεῖν ἐπὶ τῆς ἀνοίας τῆς αὐτῆς ὥσπερ νῦν.

333 ἐμοί … παρατεταγμένος: originally this participle meant 'drawn up in line of battle', and when it governed a dative it could refer, according to context, either to comrades fighting side by side (e.g. Pl. *Rep.* 556d ἀνὴρ πένης … παραταχθεὶς ἐν μάχηι πλουσίωι) or to hostile battle-lines facing one another (e.g. Xen. *Hell.* 4.3.5 ὡς … παρετάξαντο ἀλλήλοις). In this passage the original sense has been so far forgotten that the word denotes simply the hostile attitude of one *individual* towards another.   νυνὶ δέ 'but in point of fact'.   μοι: probably 'in my eyes', a dative of 'the person in whose opinion a statement holds good' (Smyth 1956: 344; often called the *dativus iudicantis*).

334 ἀπολελόγηται 'he has made out his defence', 'he has established his innocence'.   φανέντ' αὐτῶι 'that was revealed to him', implying that the idea of marriage to Plangon had not previously crossed Moschion's mind (whereas in fact, as we know, it had been *filling* his mind!) Gomme and Sandbach's 'sprung on him' catches the sense nicely.

335–7 We doubtless expected Demeas to say that Moschion's ready (indeed eager) acceptance of marriage to Plangon proved – as indeed it does – that he was neither in love with Chrysis (else he would not have given her up so easily) nor hostile to his father (whom he obeyed willingly and cheerfully). But he sees it, wrongly (325–56n.), as proving more than this – that Moschion was desperate to escape from Chrysis – and thereby as helping to establish that Chrysis was αἰτία τοῦ γεγονότος (338).

335–6 ὡς ἐγὼ | τότ' ὠιόμην: cf. 165–6.

337 Ἑλένην: undoubtedly the most notorious of the unfaithful wives of Greek myth – but also the woman of supreme beauty (e.g. *Iliad* 3.154–8;

Sappho fr. 16.6–7 Lobel-Page) whose husband could be imagined as stirred by her elopement not to anger but to desperate grief (Aesch. *Ag.* 408–28); see Offermann 1978: 152. It may well be felt (see e.g. S. R. West 1991: 17) that Phaedra would be a more appropriate *comparanda* (see Introduction §6): in at least one of the tragic treatments of her story (Sophocles' *Phaedra*), Hippolytus probably fled from her on discovering that she loved him (see Barrett 1964: 43, Talboy and Sommerstein 2006: 279–80, and cf. Seneca, *Phaedra* 728–9, [Apoll.] *Epit.* 1.18), whereas Paris of course fled *with* Helen. But here, as everywhere in the play, Menander carefully avoids explicit reference to the Phaedra-Hippolytus myth. This and αὕτη (338) are the only direct references to Chrysis in the first 23 lines of Demeas' speech (whereas the last nine lines will be centred entirely on her); they come exactly at the midpoint of his argument for Moschion's innocence (328–47). φυγεῖν βουλόμενος ἔνδοθεν implies that Moschion, on his marriage, would leave his father's house and set up a home of his own. This was by no means normal practice: the very strong Greek belief in the son's duty to maintain and care for his parents in old age would generally require at least one of a man's sons to continue living in the parental home after marriage (as did, for example, the adopted son and daughter-in-law of Menecles: Isaeus 2.18, 36). Demeas, however, might reasonably expect that Moschion would not wish to make his young wife live in the same house as an ex-*hetaira*, especially if the latter was also the mother of a child of his; he does not know that Plangon, her mother and Chrysis are already good friends (35–8). ποτε 'at last', cf. *Perik.* 162–7 'All this trouble was kindled...so that he [Polemon] might be roused to anger...and they [Glykera and Moschion] might at last discover their kin (τοὺς θ' αὑτῶν ποτε εὕροιεν).'

339 παρέλαβεν 'got hold of' with an implication of sinister intent; cf. *Perinthia* F 3 ὅστις παραλαβὼν δεσπότην ἀπράγμονα | καὶ κοῦφον ἐξαπατᾶι θεράπων; Eubulus fr. 48 παραλαβὼν ἀκράτωι κροῦε καὶ δίδου πυκνὰς [sc. κύλικας] | καὶ βότρυς τρώγειν ἀνάγκαζ' αὐτὸν ἐξ οἴνου ['soaked in wine'] συχνούς. **που...δηλαδή** 'evidently, I suppose'. This is the only passage in comedy where these two words are used together – not surprisingly, since one of them subverts the other: δηλαδή suggests that the statement is virtually certain to be true (González Merino 1983: 172), που reveals that it is guesswork.

340 ἐν ἑαυτοῦ 'in control of himself', cf. *Aspis* 307, Ar. *Wasps* 642, Pl. *Charm.* 155d. Underlying the expression (whose literal meaning is 'in his own home') is the idea that a person's mind is like a house in which he dwells or ought to dwell; cf. *Dysk.* 897 ἔξω...τῶν φρενῶν and Eur. fr. 144 = Ar. *Frogs* 105 μὴ τὸν ἐμὸν οἴκει νοῦν.

340–2 πολλὰ δ'...|...|... πλησίον 'neat wine and youth bring about many follies, when one [i.e. in this case Moschion] finds close at hand someone [i.e. in this case Chrysis] to conspire with them against him'. Chrysis, it is suggested, exploited and manipulated the risk factors to remove Moschion's normal inhibitions. For the textual problems see below on ἄν τις λάβηι and τὸν συνεπιβουλεύσοντα.

340 ἐξεργάζεται: it is not uncommon for a verb with two or more conjoined subjects to be singular (Smyth 1956: 265; Kühner and Gerth 1898–1904: I 79–80), either because the subject is viewed as a single complex entity or because one of the conjoined subjects is viewed as more important than the other(s). In this case Demeas may be thinking of ἄκρατος as the actual corrupting agent (it is always a bad thing to drink neat wine; it is not in itself a bad thing to be young). Cf., on the same topic, Ter. *Ad.* 470 *persuasit nox, amor, vinum, adulescentia* (i.e. the confluence of all these factors).

341 ἄκρατος: it had always been the custom to drink wine mixed with water (hence modern Greek κρασί 'wine'), but in the late fourth century a fashion seems to have developed (τοῦτο δὴ τὸ νῦν ἔθος, Men. fr. 401; cf. Alexis fr. 257) for drinking it neat, and Demeas predicts (392–7) that if Chrysis reverts to being a hired *hetaira* she will have to do so much more than is good for her health. It would be odd for Demeas to praise Moschion as κόσμιος καὶ σώφρων (344) immediately after speculating that he had drunk himself silly on neat wine, and we are probably therefore meant to understand that Demeas' assumption is that Chrysis plied Moschion with the strong drink without his being aware of it.　　　**ἄν τις λάβηι** (Luppe 1976) gives good sense, and accounts for the readings of the two papyri: τις fell out of the text, as short words often do, and the missing syllable was then 'restored' by extending ἄν to ὅταν (C) or ἐάν (B). If, with most editors, we accept one or other of the transmitted readings, we must either (a) *understand* τις as subject of λάβηι or (b) take the subject to be once again ἄκρατος καὶ νεότης; in case (b) τούτοις, which cannot refer to the subject of its own clause, would have to denote the πολλὰ ἀνόητα as the aim of the plot (Lamagna compares Lys. 28.8 τοιούτοις ἔργοις ἐπιβουλεύοντα 'plotting to do such deeds'), giving the sense 'when/if they find someone to conspire with them to that end'. Both (a) and (b) would be quite hard to understand in real time: Luppe's emendation economically obviates all difficulties.

342 τὸν συνεπιβουλεύσοντα 'someone to conspire with (συν-) them against (ἐπι-) him'; for this use of the future participle with article cf. Xen. *Anab.* 2.4.5 ὁ ἡγησόμενος οὐδεὶς ἔσται 'there will be no one to guide us', 2.4.22 τῶν ἐργασομένων ἐνόντων 'since there were men in the area to cultivate it' (Goodwin 1912: 330). There is no corresponding usage of the aorist participle: the transmitted reading τὸν συνεπιβουλεύσαντα would mean 'the person who has conspired', and Jacques' simple emendation (a one-letter substitution of a rarer inflection for a commoner one) is necessary. The participle is masculine because the statement is made in general terms, even though Demeas is primarily thinking of a particular case in which the 'co-conspirator' is a woman.

343–7 This argument – that Moschion's past character makes it incredible that he should have committed so grave a wrong against his adoptive father – is very reminiscent of two Euripidean passages, fr. 812 (from *Phoenix*) and fr. 1067 (most probably from *Hippolytos Kalyptomenos*): see Introduction §6. The Euripidean Phoenix and Hippolytus, accused of a crime similar to that of which Moschion is suspected, were both in fact innocent, but both their fathers were convinced of their guilt, at least until it was too late: Phoenix was blinded (cf. 498–500), Hippolytus was killed when Poseidon fulfilled Theseus' curse on him. Here, by contrast, the same argument for Moschion's innocence is brought up by the father himself.

343 πιθανόν 'credible', cf. 216.

344–5 εἰς... | τοὺς ἀλλοτρίους εἰς ἐμέ: if he behaves well towards all outsiders, a fortiori he can be expected to behave well towards his father, to whom his duty of respect is so much greater.

344 κόσμιον καὶ σώφρονα: cf. 18, 273.

346–7 These lines imply that it was widely believed that an adoptive son was more likely than a biological son to behave undutifully towards his father; similarly Lycurgus (*Leocr.* 48) treats it as a generally accepted proposition, on which an argument by analogy can be based, that 'not all [sons] show the same loyalty to adoptive fathers as they do to their natural begetters'. Demeas believes, as Moschion had professed to believe (140–3), that character matters more than birth: see Cusset and Lhostis 2011: 101–2.

346 οὐδ' εἰ δεκάκις and similar expressions are often used, especially by the orators, to assert emphatically that a statement is true no matter how often one may attempt to deny or disprove it, e.g. Isaeus 9.31 'Do you think that Astyphilus...would have adopted the son of an enemy, or left his property to him at the expense of his own kinsmen and benefactors? I certainly do not think he would have, εἰ καὶ δεκάκις ὁ Ἱεροκλῆς διαθήκας ψευδεῖς ἀποδεικνύει', Ar. *Lys.* 698 οὐ γὰρ ἔσται δύναμις, οὐδ' ἢν ἑπτάκις σὺ ψηφίσηι. The usage is then extended to contexts in which, as here, it cannot be understood literally, e.g. Polybius 12.6b.4 'From what has been said it is intelligible that those who emigrated from Locris and settled in Italy, εἰ καὶ δεκάκις ἦσαν οἰκέται, should have adopted the [Locrians'] friendship with Sparta as their own'; cf. already Eur. *Andr.* 634–6 'a boy who will bring grief to you and that daughter of yours... κεἰ τρὶς νόθος πέφυκε', and in English Shakespeare, *Hamlet* 3.2.324 (ed. Thompson and Taylor 2006) 'We shall obey, were she ten times our mother.'

348–56 Having established in his own mind that Moschion is innocent, Demeas turns his thoughts abruptly to Chrysis, to whom the remainder of his soliloquy is almost entirely devoted. The language used of her is in the starkest contrast to that in which Moschion has just been spoken of.

348 χαμαιτύπη 'a cheap whore', literally 'a ground-banger', i.e. a prostitute who does not even have a room to take her clients to and has to service them on patches of waste ground; cf. Aeschines 1.80–3, who claims that expressions like 'walls', 'tower', 'deserted place', 'building site' aroused ribald public laughter when used by or about Timarchus (allegedly a former male prostitute). The word is rare even in comedy (Men. fr. 472, Timocles fr. 24) but is used by the historian Theopompus (*FGrH* 115 F 225) in an extremely vituperative passage about the boon companions of Philip II. **ἄνθρωπος** (= ἡ ἄνθρωπος) is normally, like English 'the woman' or 'that woman', a disparaging expression. In the orators it almost invariably refers to a slave (e.g. Lys. 1.24, Isoc. 18.52–3, [Dem.] 47.4–17) or an actual or alleged prostitute (Isaeus 6.21–39, Alce; [Dem.] 25.57, Zobia; [Dem.] 59.46–72 *passim*, Neaera and Phano); the only exception, Dem. 19.197–8, relates to an Olynthian captive of good family (cf. Aeschines 2.154–5) who had allegedly been treated like a prostitute at a party attended by Aeschines. In comedy the usage is rare (*Mis.* 312 S = 713 A; Ar. *Lys.* 936) and in itself indicates nothing about the woman's status but only that the speaker is angry or impatient with her.   **ὄλεθρος** 'scum', literally 'destruction', i.e. one who deserves to be destroyed; cf. *Dysk.* 365–6 'he'll throw clods of earth at you and call you an idle ὄλεθρος', Men. frr. 164, 835.13, Ar. *Lys.* 325, *Thesm.* 860, *Eccl.* 934, Eup. fr. 406. Possibly χαμαιτύπη and ὄλεθρος should be taken closely together ('a damnable whore'); in Dem. 9.31 (ὀλέθρου Μακεδόνος) and 18.127 (ὄλεθρος γραμματεύς) there is an implication that to call someone a Macedonian ('from a place from which, in the old days, you couldn't even buy a decent slave'), or a pen-pusher, was *ipso facto* to call him worthless.   **ἀλλὰ τί;** 'but why <am I talking like this>?'; so again 450. As at the beginning of his soliloquy (326–7), Demeas checks himself from his angry outpourings.

349 οὐ... περιέσται 'she won't survive this', *sc.* as my partner – but the words may have grimmer overtones: a little later (390–7), speaking to Chrysis, Demeas will in effect predict that if she has to go back to her old life as an unattached *hetaira* she will have the choice between starvation and drinking herself to death. Catullus (327n.) may have understood the passage thus (Cat. 8.15 *scelesta, vae te, quae tibi manet vita?*). The verb περιεῖναι, not being used impersonally, requires a subject of some sort, and Chrysis is the only subject that the context allows us to supply; hence renderings like 'I'll gain nothing by it' (Capps, Jacques, Dedoussi) must be ruled out – if that was what Menander meant, he would have written οὐδὲν περιέσται.

349–50 νῦν ἄνδρα χρή | εἶναί σ': 64n. For a moment we may not understand why Demeas thinks he will need to show himself 'manly' in order to punish Chrysis; but the next five words reveal all.

350 ἐπιλαθοῦ τοῦ πόθου: to paraphrase other words of Catullus (85.1–2), Demeas *odit et amat…et excruciatur*. Will he, in the end, be able to conquer his passion?   **πέπαυσ'(ο):** the second-person perfect imperative 'is rare…[and] seems to be a little more emphatic than the present or aorist' (Goodwin 1912: 33–4). At 612 and Dem. 24.64 πέπαυσο is used by a speaker interrupting another; here too it may suggest that what is needed is an immediate and abrupt cut-off.

351–4 This sentence is important for the audience's understanding of the following scenes: neither Chrysis nor anyone else is to be told the real reason for her expulsion, since this would reflect badly on Moschion whom Demeas regards as innocent.

351 τἀτύχημα: applied to Moschion (contrast 218 where Demeas speaks of the same event as a μέγ' ἀτύχημα for *himself*) this is an extremely mild term to use (3n.), particularly on the lips of the man who has been wronged; it presents Moschion not as an offender but as a victim – which would be true enough if Demeas' reconstruction of events (338–42) were accurate. In Act IV he will have cause to think otherwise and will use ἀδικ-words (456, 506, 518; contrast 328) until Moschion confesses the truth.

351–2 κρύφθ' ὅσον | ἔνεστι: in fact he nearly fails to conceal it (371–2, 374–5), and at 447–9 he feels in need of divine support if he is to avoid revealing his distress; he nevertheless maintains his resolve even under what he sees as great provocation (460, 465–6, 470–1) until the apparent effrontery of Moschion's response to his accusation τὸ παιδίον σόν ἐστιν (477–9) causes him to burst out (481 βοᾶις) in the presence of Nikeratos. Even then he takes no steps actually to punish Moschion, as Nikeratos would have done (498–514); instead he begs Nikeratos to do him a favour by cooperating in the punishment *of Chrysis* (517–18).

352–4 Another 'ironical reversal of the conventional situation' (21ff n.): instead of a father putting pressure on his son to abandon a relationship with a *hetaira*, we find a father abandoning *his* relationship with an ex-*hetaira* to avoid embarrassing his son (so Lamagna).

353 ἐπὶ κεφαλήν 'head first, headlong' is governed by ὠθεῖν, as here, in Hdt. 7.136.1 and Pl. *Rep.* 553b. Not ἐπί τὴν κεφαλήν (C), which is not used in this sense.   **ἐς κόρακας:** 133n.   **καλήν:** before the discovery of B, C was thought to read κακην, but Austin and all subsequent editors have been satisfied that C actually has the same text as B. It is a far more powerful reading. Chrysis clearly *is* beautiful, and was courted by many men before Demeas took up with her (26); Demeas, it is equally clear, despite his anger, is still in love with her; but at the same time there is a bitter irony in the adjective – Chrysis' body may be beautiful, her soul is not. There may also be a suggestion that once she has been driven out ἐς κόρακας, she may not retain her beauty for long (349–50n., 390–6).

354 Σαμίαν: as at 337, the word that designates Chrysis stands alone, separated by a line-break from its article and adjective; and as there and at 265 (where see n.), Demeas does not refer to her by her name. Here the ethnic may not only highlight Chrysis' foreignness, but also evoke her past as a *hetaira* (21n.).

354–5 ἔχεις... | ἀνείλετ': 132n. To avoid revealing his actual reason for expelling Chrysis, Demeas will revive his complaint of the offence for which he had previously intended to do so, before Moschion dissuaded him. This risks arousing Chrysis' suspicions, and does indeed seem strange to her (413–16), since after discovering the baby Demeas had for some time behaved in a perfectly normal manner towards her (e.g. giving her instructions about the wedding preparations). But in itself it is evidently to be regarded as a valid reason for breaking off the relationship: Nikeratos too thinks Chrysis was foolish to keep the child (410–11).

355 ἀνείλετ' 'accepted', 'chose to rear' (instead of exposing). Normally, when used in connection with infants, ἀναιρεῖσθαι refers to the taking up and rearing of a child not one's own who had been exposed (*Epitr.* 250, *Perik.* 134, Ar. *Clouds* 531), but the extension is a natural one, appears to be found already in Menander's contemporary Epicurus (*ap.* Epict. 1.23.7), and becomes frequent in later Greek (e.g. Plut. *Mor.* 320e, 489f). Nevertheless, an irony is probably to be detected in Demeas' use of this word, since the truth of the matter is that Chrysis has indeed taken over a child not her own; this irony will be much stronger in 411 when the same verb is used by Nikeratos, whose daughter is the child's real mother. **ἐμφανίσῃς** 'explain, divulge'; this verb, very common in fourth-century prose, makes its first appearances in poetry here and at *Dysk.* 323 (Eur. fr. 797 is corrupt). The aorist subjunctive, regular in prohibitions, here precedes instead of following the negative μή.

356 δακών 'biting <your lip>': this ellipsis seems to occur only here, but δάκνειν is often used of a person forcibly restraining the open expression of pain or emotion, its object being sometimes χεῖλος or στόμα (e.g. Tyrt. fr. 11.22 West; Soph. *Trach.* 976–7; cf. *Od.* 1.381 ὀδὰξ ἐν χείλεσι φύντες), sometimes a noun referring to the feeling suppressed (e.g. Ar. *Clouds* 1369 τὸν θυμὸν δακών). It is left unclear whether the emotion to be suppressed here is anger or love – or a combination of both.   ἀνάσχου, καρτέρησον echoes 327 – though the imperatives here are aorist instead of present, perhaps suggesting that Demeas is trying to think only of steeling himself to the act of expelling Chrysis, blanking out the thought of his future life without her. As Thomas 1984: 311–12 notes, there is a similar piece of ring-composition in Catullus 8 (327n.), where line 11 (cited there) is picked up by the poem's last line (19) *at tu, Catulle, destinatus obdura*. It may well be no coincidence that Catullus in his penultimate line (18) refers to the biting of lips (*cui labella mordebis?*) – though the biter is not himself but Lesbia, and the lips are not her own but those of a hypothetical lover. Some in Menander's own audience, whose thoughts had been turned to Euripides' *Hippolytus* (325–56, 335–7nn.), may recall, in this final line of Demeas' soliloquy, the last words exchanged between Hippolytus and his father (*Hipp.* 1456–7): after the dying Hippolytus has released Theseus from the guilt and pollution of his death, Theseus begs him μή νυν προδῶις με, τέκνον, ἀλλὰ καρτέρει, but Hippolytus replies κεκαρτέρηται τἄμ’· ὄλωλα γάρ, πάτερ, asks Theseus to cover his face, and expires.   εὐγενῶς 'bravely' (Gomme and Sandbach 1973, Arnott), applied to the enduring of troubles in *Dysk.* 281 and Eur. *Tro.* 727.

357 The Cook comes out of Demeas' house, looking for Parmenon, whom he had expected to come in and assist him in his preparations; meanwhile Demeas, who had been well away from the house when talking with Parmenon (304–5) and had presumably remained in more or less the same place after his departure, moves back towards the house, meaning to carry out immediately his intention of expelling Chrysis. The Cook's appearance on stage at this point is necessary on technical grounds, to keep the action going when Demeas goes inside leaving the stage otherwise empty; but it also enables us to view Demeas' behaviour through the eyes of a more or less neutral third party, whom we expect to be a mere observer and commentator, but who in the end feels compelled by his sense of justice to attempt an intervention (383–90).   ἀλλ’...ἐνθάδ’: the absence of an expressed subject means that it will not be obvious that the Cook is looking for Parmenon until he calls out for him. It also implies that he had already been speaking about Parmenon before he came outside, either in soliloquy or to the other slaves or to Chrysis.   πρόσθε (B) or πρόσθεν (C)? The latter is the form normally found in contemporary inscriptions (Threatte

1980–96: II 402–4, Arnott 1998b: 15–16); but πρόσθε (an occasional variant in inscriptions from the mid fourth century onwards) is transmitted
in both papyri at 405 (in the same phrase) and at *Perik.* 299 (same phrase
again) and *Mis.* 68 S = 468 A, and πρόσθ' is guaranteed by metre at Alexis
fr. 103.15.

358 The Cook looks around, sees no sign of Parmenon, and calls out
loudly for him.   ἀποδέδρακέ με 'has run away from me'; the transitive
use of ἀποδιδράσκειν is fairly common (e.g. Ar. *Peace* 234, Soph. *Aj.* 167,
Thuc. 1.128.5). In fact Parmenon *has* run away, but not from the Cook
nor in order to evade work (Blume 1974: 130).

359 Blume 1974: 130 argues that realistically, in a household like
Demeas' with its many slaves, the Cook would be unlikely to find Parmenon's absence a cause of difficulty or complaint, particularly since he
also has at least one assistant of his own (280n.) and Parmenon had
instructed Chrysis and the others to give him everything he asked for
(301–2). We can suppose, if we like, that some question has arisen which
only Parmenon could answer, but the true explanation of this mild incongruity is simply that Menander needed an excuse to bring the Cook out
of the house.   ἀλλ' οὐδὲ μικρόν 'really not in the slightest' has become a
fixed phrase. Originally it formed part of a 'self-correction' trope in which
the speaker first said that something was 'of trifling value or importance'
(Denniston 1954: 24) and then interrupted himself with the correction
'no, not even trifling'; but by the fifth century the first part of the trope
was regularly omitted and only the 'correction' remained, complete with
the now logically redundant particle ἀλλ'. In a passage like the present,
even the basic notion of self-correction has been forgotten and ἀλλ' does
little more than add emphasis to the negative: cf. 655, Eubulus fr. 118.4,
Dem. 19.37, 21.114; also Ar. *Clouds* 1396 ἀλλ' οὐδ' ἐρεβίνθου 'not worth a
chickpea' and Diphilus fr. 61.8 τοῦτό μοι τὸ δεῖπνον ἀλλ' οὐδ' αἷμ' ἔχει where
'blood' will be taken as a self-correction of 'meat'.

359–60 Demeas rushes into his house, either barging the Cook out of his
way or forcing him to take rapid evasive action.   ἐκ τοῦ μέσου | ἄναγε
σεαυτόν 'get yourself out of the way!' For ἐκ τοῦ μέσου cf. *Dysk.* 81, *Sik.* 265;
for ἄναγε (σεαυτόν); Ar. *Birds* 1720, *Frogs* 853; Nicophon fr. 7.

360 Ἡράκλεις: 178n.   παῖ: most probably this is another attempt to call
Parmenon. It is true that παῖ in Menander (rather like '(oh) boy' in US
English) can be merely an interjection of surprise, and that it is usually
preceded or followed by τί τοῦτο; (691, 715, *Dysk.* 82, *Mis.* 216 S = 617
A, *Perik.* 316, fr. 110, *com. adesp.* 1096.21; *Sam.* 678 παῖ, τί ποιεῖς; can be
seen as a variant of this); but τί δέ μοι τοῦτο παῖ (362) can hardly be an
example of this idiom, and these two passages so close together cry out to

be treated as parallel. For Ἡράκλεις, τί τοῦτο; without παῖ cf. 405. Dedoussi takes both instances of παῖ, as interjections, with the sentences that *follow* (361 and 363 respectively); but elsewhere παῖ as an interjection invariably accompanies a question, not a statement.

361 μαινόμενος: this is also the impression that Demeas' behaviour makes on Chrysis (415) and, when he hears about it, Nikeratos (416–20); compare also Demeas' own words ἐξέστηχ᾽ ὅλως (279). Later it will be Nikeratos who rushes into and out of his house 'like a madman' after making a discovery connected with the baby (534, 563). **τις γέρων:** he is not yet aware that Demeas (who has been out of his house since before the Cook arrived) is the master of the house in which he, the Cook, is working.

362 ἢ τί τὸ κακόν ποτ᾽ ἐστί; 'or <if he's not mad> what on earth is the matter?' **τί δέ μοι τοῦτο;** The Cook reflects that the old man's seemingly crazy behaviour is no concern of his; soon he will be taking a different view, first in his professional capacity (364–6) and then on grounds of humanity (383–90). **παῖ:** the Cook dismisses the distraction caused by Demeas, and once again calls for Parmenon, in search of whom he had originally come outside.

363–8 The Cook is now imagined to hear Demeas 'shouting very loud indeed' (364) inside the house (though he cannot hear the actual words he is saying). Lamagna supposes that he is listening at the door (as Phaedra does in Eur. *Hipp.* 565–600); but the time-lag of more than a whole line between τὴν θύραν πέπληχεν (366–7) and μικρὸν ὑπαποστήσομαι (368) suggests that he is not so close to the door as to have to withdraw instantly when he perceives it is about to open. The same question arises when Demeas hears Nikeratos shouting indoors at 552–4, and the answer is probably the same there too, even though in that passage Demeas does hear some of Nikeratos' words. In neither passage is it necessary to suppose that the audience hear anything at all: compare Eur. *Hipp.* 575–90 where Phaedra, at the door, hears what Hippolytus is saying, the chorus hear the shouting but cannot make out the words (584–8), and the audience evidently hear nothing. From this point on, the Cook's thoughts are fixed on the words and actions of Demeas; Parmenon is mentioned only to be damned for having brought him to so disturbed a household (367–8).

363 μαίνεθ᾽ 'he *is* mad'.

364 κέκραγε . . . παμμέγεθες: i.e. more loudly than any sane man would, even if very angry. The adjective παμμεγέθης, fairly common in fourth-century prose, appears in comedy towards the end of the century (*Heros* 2, Timocles fr. 8.14, Sotades fr. 1.5); for its sense here cf. Aeschines 2.106 ἀναβοᾶι παμμέγεθες Δημοσθένης. **ἀστεῖον πάνυ** sc. ἂν εἴη, 'it would be really nice if…' (sarcastic); cf. *Dysk.* 568–9 ἔχει γὰρ ἀστείως *sc.* τὰ γύναια ταῦτα (who are not likely to let the speaker share their meal); Ar. *Clouds* 1064 ἀστεῖόν γε κέρδος ἔλαβεν ὁ κακοδαίμων (a knife, by being virtuous – in contrast with Hyperbolus who acquired great wealth by being a criminal).

365 τὰς λοπάδας… μου should be taken together; for an even more drastic hyperbaton with a genitive pronoun, cf. *Aspis* 420–1 ἀδελφός – ὦ Ζεῦ, πῶς φράσω; – σχεδόν τι σου | τέθνηκεν.   ἐν τῶι μέσωι: probably 'in his way', cf. 359.

366 ὄστρακα ποήσαι 'he were to smash up' (literally, turn into broken pieces of pottery). For the short form of the optative, 141n.   πάνθ' ὅμοια is best taken, with Gronewald 1995: 58–9, as a separate sentence, 'it's always the same!' (cf. Soph. *Aj.* 1366, Ter. *Phorm.* 264 *ecce autem similia omnia!*), i.e. whenever I get a job, something or other goes badly wrong (cf. *Aspis* 216–20). Previously these words had been taken as agreeing with ὄστρακα ('smash the dishes… into fragments – the whole lot alike', Sandbach), but then ὅμοια would be contributing little to the sense. B has ετοιμ[, which may well, as Jacques suggested, be due to a scribe's recollection of 223 (πάνθ' ἑτοίμως).

366–7 τὴν θύραν | πέπληχεν: 300–1n.

367–8 ἐξώλης ἀπόλοιο, Παρμένων, | κομίσας με δεῦρο: the Cook is afraid that the fracas may lead to damage to his property (364–6), the loss of his job and fee for the day, or both. Had Parmenon not hired him for this job, he might have got another, hopefully trouble-free one.

368 μικρὸν ὑπαποστήσομαι: expecting the old man to come out still in a rage, he moves away from the door to a spot where he can observe and listen unnoticed; he is still, however, close enough to intervene quickly when he decides to do so (383–4), and to go inside quickly when it becomes clear to him that he can make no impression on Demeas (389–90).

369–82 Demeas comes out of his house, driving Chrysis before him. She is carrying the baby, and has with her an old woman slave (373n.). This is the scene of the play that was chosen for representation in the Mytilene mosaic (see Introduction §11), where Demeas appears to be brandishing his walking-stick at Chrysis.

369 οὔκουν ἀκούεις; 62n. We are evidently to understand that this is said in reply to a question or protest by Chrysis; if the question she asked was the obvious one ('why?', cf. 372, 374), Demeas is refusing to answer it and merely insisting that she obey his order to go.   ποῖ γῆς: she has no kin in Attica and no other home to go to.   ὦ τάλαν: 252n.; here 'self-pity' is evidently uppermost.

370 ἐς κόρακας: 133n., 353; cf. Ar. *Birds* 990 οὐκ εἶ θύραζ' ἐς κόρακας;   **δύσ-μορος** *sc.* ἐγώ: similarly Ap.Rh. 3.783 (Medea).   **ναί, δύσμορος:** since δύσ-μορος in Menander is otherwise used only by women (69n.), Lamagna may well be right to suggest that Demeas here mockingly mimics Chrysis' tone of voice.

371 ἐλεεινὸν ἀμέλει τὸ δάκρυον 'tears stir pity, of course!' (223n.), ironically affecting to suppose that Chrysis' grief is mere play-acting. C has a *dicolon* after δάκρυον: since it can never have been imagined that there was a change of speaker here, the *dicolon* must be meant to mark change of addressee, i.e. that the present sentence is spoken 'aside' by Demeas to himself. If this is correct, the sentence might be taken (Barigazzi 1972: 203, followed by Lamagna) as indicating that Demeas is genuinely moved to pity, which he then suppresses; but if so, it would be the only sign of any such feeling in the entire scene. Barigazzi also saw here a reminiscence of *Odyssey* 8.531 and 16.219 ἐλεεινὸν ὑπ' ὀφρύσι δάκρυον εἶβεν/εἶβον.   **ἐλεεινόν** (BC) or ἐλεινόν (van Herwerden)? The shorter form is authentically Attic and regular in fifth-century drama, whose copyists are apt to replace it by the longer form (Soph. *OT* 672, Ar. *Ach.* 413; it has survived, however, at Ar. *Thesm.* 1063) even when it is guaranteed by metre (Soph. *Trach.* 528, *Phil.* 1130; Ar. *Frogs* 1063). The longer, however, is invariably found in Menandrian papyri (*Dysk.* 297, *Mis.* 387 S = 790 A) – always where it would be metrically admissible – and also in the MSS of Demosthenes (see MacDowell 1990: 400), and it became regular in the Koine, so the evidence tends to suggest that it became established in Attic speech during the fourth century.   **τὸ δάκρυον:** in a masked drama, tears must always be imagined, and it is therefore common for reference to them to be incorporated into the script. Cf. Ar. *Lys.* 127, 1034; Aesch. *Ag.* 270; Soph. *Ant.* 527; Eur. *Med.* 902–7.

372 ὡς οἴομαι – : Demeas hesitates, and this prompts Chrysis to ask what he was going to say, in the hope of learning what alleged offence she is being punished for. He had been about to say 'corrupting my son' or the like, but broke off on remembering that he must not mention anything that might be to Moschion's discredit (351–2, 355).   **οὐδέν** retrospectively cancels Demeas' interrupted sentence; so when Medea's nurse asks her children's tutor what he means by saying that Medea οὐδὲν οἶδε τῶν νεωτέρων κακῶν, he replies οὐδέν· μετέγνων καὶ τὰ πρόσθ' εἰρημένα (Eur. *Med.* 62–4). Of course this makes Chrysis aware that Demeas is trying to conceal something, but she has no idea what.

372–3 ἔχεις | τὸ παιδίον: the underlying thought may be 'you wanted to keep this baby, so keep it – only not in my house or at my expense!'

373 τὴν γραῦν: probably the slave mentioned at 302 (301–4n.). **ἀποφ-θείρου** 'go, blast you!'; cf. Ar. *Ach.* 460 φθείρου λαβὼν τόδ', *Knights* 892 and *Clouds* 789 οὐκ ἐς κόρακας ἀποφθερεῖ;, Eur. *Andr.* 708, 715. **ποτέ** indicates impatience; the logic of its use is clearer in the equivalent interrogatively-phrased expression οὐκ ἀποφθερεῖ ποτε; 'won't you ever go?' Cf. *Dysk.* 413 τὰς ὀφρῦς ἄνες ποτ', *Epitr.* 366 (after Daos has repeatedly failed to obey Smikrines' order to surrender to Syriskos the property in dispute between them) δός ποτ', ἐργαστήριον. C's ταχύ is either an intrusive gloss or a banalization.

374 ὅτι τοῦτ' ἀνειλόμην; This is the only offence that Chrysis knows herself to have committed against Demeas; she had expected it would anger him, at least temporarily (80–3), and it did (129–36), though we do not know what, if anything, he had said to her (indoors) at that time. On ἀνειλόμην, 354–5n.   **διὰ τοῦτο καὶ – :** again Demeas is about to blurt out the real cause of his anger; again he checks himself; again Chrysis asks what he was about to say; and again his answer is, in effect, 'nothing'.

375–90 On the Cook's asides in 375 and 383, and his subsequent intervention, see 357n.

375 τοιοῦτ' ἦν τι τὸ κακόν 'the trouble was something of that sort', i.e. something to do with a baby. For the imperfect referring to a fact which, though only now perceived by the speaker, has been true for some time past, see 70–1n. Both B and C are corrupt (and unmetrical) here, but fortunately they err at different points.

376 τρυφᾶν γὰρ οὐκ ἠπίστασ' 'you didn't know how to cope with luxury', i.e. I gave you a life of luxury (cf. 7) and it turned your head so that you fell into vicious ways. On the relationship between τρυφή and ὕβρις see Fisher 1992: 111–17.

377 τί δ' ἔσθ' ὃ λέγεις; Demeas' last accusation would be absurdly overblown if it referred only to Chrysis' not having exposed the baby, and so confirms her inference from his καί (374) that he has another serious complaint against her; but she still has no notion what it could possibly be.

377–9 Demeas reminds Chrysis how poor she was when he took her into his house, implying that she is basely ungrateful for all he has done for her.

378 σινδονίτηι: 'a linen χιτών' (Photius s.v. σινδονίτης χιτών): she did not have a ἱμάτιον to wear over it. Now, by contrast, she is richly attired: in the Mytilene mosaic she is wearing an inner and an outer garment, both of heavy material in bright and variegated colours.

379 λιτῶι 'cheap'. This adjective seems to have entered Attic not long before Menander's time (it is still not found in Plato or the orators). Cf. *Sik.* F 3 λιτόν ποτ᾽ εἶχες χλαμύδιον καὶ παῖδ᾽ ἕνα; Men. fr. 748 ἀπραξία γὰρ λιτὸν οὐ τρέφει βίον 'idleness won't keep a poor man alive'; Sotades fr. 1.8–9 λιτῶς ('sparingly') προσαγαγών | χλόην, κύμινον, ἅλας, ὕδωρ, ἐλάιδιον. In *IG* V (1) 1390.16–19 (Andania, early first century BC) free adult female candidates for initiation are to wear a χιτῶνα λίνεον under their εἱμάτιον, but young girls and slaves are to wear a καλάσηριν ἢ σινδονίταν.   **ἦν ἐγώ σοι πάνθ᾽:** cf. Aesch. fr. 132c.11 [εἰ]μ᾽ ἐγὼ τὰ πάντ᾽ Ἀχαιικῶι στρατῶι, Hdt. 3.157.4 πάντα δὴ ἦν ἐν τοῖσι Βαβυλωνίοισι Ζώπυρος, Thuc. 8.95.2, Dem. 18.43, Theocr. 14.47. The actor was probably instructed to emphasize ἐγώ in implicit contrast to Chrysis' alleged new lover; she is thus enabled to understand, for the first time, that she is being accused of infidelity.

380 νῦν δὲ τίς; Knowing herself innocent, Chrysis challenges Demeas to name the man he suspects.   **μή μοι λάλει:** these words may be almost screamed out. Demeas, desperate to protect Moschion's good name, cannot answer Chrysis' question; he can only silence her. And this he succeeds in doing: she will not speak again until she is left alone (398).

381–2 In between telling Chrysis to shut up and telling her to clear out, Demeas mockingly assures her that he is treating her correctly, indeed generously, so far as her property is concerned: not only is he allowing her to keep whatever belongs to her, he is even giving her maidservants and jewellery in addition. This apparent liberality, as Jacques saw (see also Thomas 1990), is almost pure rhetorical pretence: presently (390–7) Demeas will describe in detail, with some relish, the probable wretchedness of Chrysis' future life. When she came to him she possessed virtually nothing (377–9), and all the good things she has enjoyed since then were bought by Demeas and can be retained by him; τὰ σαυτῆς πάντα, therefore, refers primarily to the one possession of Chrysis that Demeas has no wish to keep – the baby, at which he doubtless points a finger. The jewellery is that which Chrysis is actually wearing (on the Mytilene mosaic she apparently has a tiara and a necklace): to insist that she give these up (let alone her expensive clothing) would cause delay and might require the use of physical force, and Demeas wants to get rid of Chrysis as quickly and quietly as possible. In view of 373 (τὴν γραῦν) it is unlikely that the plural θεραπαίνας is to be taken literally; to be sure, it is common in New Comedy for a *hetaira* to have two maidservants (e.g. Plaut. *Poen.* 222; Ter. *Eun.* 506, *Hec.* 793; cf. [Dem.] 59.35, 120; and see Fantham 1975: 65–6 n. 48), but these are prosperous or favoured *hetairai*. The expression θεράπαιναι καὶ χρυσία is almost formulaic in referring to a woman's personal possessions (see next note), and Demeas uses the formula to emphasize that he is 'giving' Chrysis everything that she would normally be entitled to take with her on separation.

382 θεραπαίνας, χρυσί': for this combination see *Mis.* A39–40 S = 39–40 A (a man's gifts to his slave partner) θεραπαίνας, χρυσία, | ἱμάτια δούς, Dem. 45.28 (bequest to wife in will) θεραπαίνας καὶ χρυσία, καὶ τἆλλα ὅσα ἐστὶν αὐτῆι ἔνδον ... Ἀρχίππηι δίδωμι, [Dem.] 59.35 (*hetaira* leaving her partner) συσκευασαμένη ... ὅσα ἦν αὐτῆι ... ἱμάτια καὶ χρυσία, καὶ θεραπαίνας δύο, 59.46. C's reading, without an apostrophe, is probably to be understood as the vocative Χρυσί. Hiatus after vocatives in -ι is admissible in comedy and related genres (cf. *Perik.* 983; Ar. *Ach.* 749; Herodas 1.84, 5.69; M. L. West 1982: 11), and Demeas addresses Chrysis by name three times in this scene (378, 385, 392) and three times more in the eighteen words he speaks to her in Acts IV and V (569, 575, 730); but the collocation of ΧΡΥΣΙ with θεραπαίνας can hardly be accidental, and if Chrysis is in fact wearing jewellery (see previous note) one would expect Demeas, in his present vein, to claim credit for allowing her to keep it (while implicitly reminding her – see previous note – that it was he who supplied her with it).

383 ἄπιθι: the brusque order of 369 is repeated. Evidently Chrysis has stood her ground thus far and is still close to the door, where she will remain during the altercation between Demeas and the Cook; Demeas' tongue-lashing of her continues at moments when he has browbeaten the Cook into temporary silence.   **τὸ πρᾶγμ' ὀργή τίς ἐστι:** i.e. Demeas is not insane, as the Cook had at first thought (361, 363), but merely angry, and so it may be possible to reason with him; see Groton 1987: 438 n. 4. **προσιτέον:** why does the Cook thus intervene in a quarrel that has nothing to do with him? Because (knowing now that Demeas is his employer) he fears losing his job and his fee (Stoessl 1969: 202 n. 33)? Because, like many comic cooks (cf. *Epitr.* F 2, *Dysk.* 409–19), he is unduly interested in other people's business (περίεργος, 298–300n.)? Or from indignation at Demeas' treatment of Chrysis and the baby? The audience cannot be sure.

384 βέλτισθ': 81–3n.; here evidently meant to be deferential; similarly in *Dysk.* 476 Getas addresses the angry Knemon as βέλτιστε in an attempt to pacify him.   **ὅρα** could stand by itself in the sense 'be careful' (cf. fr. 134 ὅρα τε καὶ φρόντιζε κἀπόστα βραχύ), but Demeas' anger will be brought out more strongly if he is made to interrupt the Cook (as at 388), who we may suppose was about to say something to the effect 'take care you don't regret this later' (cf. Hdt. 5.106.2 ὅρα μὴ ἐξ ὑστέρης σεωυτὸν ἐν αἰτίηι σχῆις).   **τί μοι διαλέγει;** said in an angry tone and probably with a threatening gesture, as the Cook's reply indicates.   **μὴ δάκηις:** so Getas at *Dysk.* 467, after Knemon, answering the door, has stormed at him for knocking.

385–6 We need not suppose that Demeas, who is still despite himself in love with Chrysis (350), actually envisages taking another mistress: he is speaking to reproach and wound her for (as he believes) showing such ingratitude to him after all he had done for her.

385 ἀγαπήσει 'will be content with', 'will appreciate'; for this meaning of ἀγαπάω cf. 617.

385-6 νή | καί 'yes, and', 'and what's more'; cf. *Epitr.* 1120-1. BC's νῦν is dull by comparison and contributes nothing to the sense.

386 τοῖς θεοῖς θύσει *sc.* in gratitude; cf. *Mis.* A88-9 S = 88-9 A ἀλλ' ἔγωγ' ἄν, φι[λοφρόνως] | κλη[θ]εὶς μόνον, θύσαιμι πᾶσι τοῖς θεοῖς. The corresponding English idiom is 'go down on her knees'.   **τί ἐστιν;** is rightly assigned by B to the Cook; for Chrysis to speak now would ruin the effect of her long silence after Demeas' μή μοι λάλει (380n.) terminated the long and fruitless series of questions she had put to him up to that point. The Cook, once 'bitten', is now making a tentative attempt to intervene again, which Demeas ignores; the Cook rather optimistically treats this as a good sign, since at least Demeas 'isn't biting yet' (387). Arnott takes his question here as an aside, but that makes οὔπω δάκνει unintelligible (Arnott's translation, 'Now he's not lashing out', would require the text to be οὐκέτι δάκνει). B has τίς ἐστιν; which has been adopted by several editors, but it gives no satisfactory sense. The Cook knows by now who Demeas is – the master of the house in which he is working; he has already met Chrysis indoors; and he can hardly be asking himself who is meant by ἑτέρα, since he has no reason to believe that Demeas has a particular person in mind at all. Sisti 2004: 156 adopts τίς ἐστιν; and gives it to Chrysis in the sense 'Who's this other woman?' (comparing her νῦν δὲ τίς; at 380); but even if it were otherwise acceptable for Chrysis to speak here (see above), it would not be desirable to have her voice a suspicion of which nothing is ever heard again.

386-7 ἀλλὰ σύ: contrasting Chrysis with the hypothetical ἑτέρα and implying (with sarcastic absurdity) that all she wanted out of her relationship with Demeas was a child (and that regardless of whether Demeas or Moschion was its father). Jacques and Lamagna, following O16, read ἀλλὰ τί; which Turner ([1967]: 189-90) had seen as a mannerism of Demeas, comparing 348 and 450; but in those passages the thought is quite different – each time Demeas, having given vent to his feelings, is reminding himself to focus on what he now needs to do. O16's τι probably originated from a correction of τίς (see previous note) written in the margin and wrongly thought to be a correction of σύ.

387 υἱὸν πεπόησαι 'you've had a son', cf. Pl. *Symp.* 203b ἡ οὖν Πενία ἐπιβουλεύουσα ... παιδίον ποιήσασθαι ἐκ τοῦ Πόρου: the active (πεπόηκας C) is not used in this sense before Roman times (Plut. *Mor.* 145d). The middle also means 'adopt' (cf. *Dysk.* 731 ποοῦμαί σ' υόν), so we are inevitably reminded of Demeas' relationship to Moschion and of the fact that he is unlikely ever to have a legitimate biological son – thoughts which may be in Demeas' mind too, and may give a particularly bitter tone to πάντ' ἔχεις. **πάντ' ἔχεις:** i.e. either 'you've got everything you wanted' (cf. Eur. *Med.* 569–70 'you women πάντ' ἔχειν νομίζετε if things are all right in bed') or 'you've got everything you need' (cf. Men. fr. 191.5 ὁ λογισμῶι διαφέρων πάντ' ἔχει). To have a son was indeed of enormous importance to a woman of citizen status: it gave her added respect in the eyes of her husband (cf. Lys. 1.6), and the son would have the duty of supporting her in her old age and of maintaining her tomb-cult after her death. It was quite otherwise for a *hetaira*, as Demeas must know perfectly well: she would be better off with a daughter, who could succeed her in her profession when she became too old to practise it remuneratively herself (cf. Plaut. *Cist.* 38–41, and see McClure 2003: 76–7). **οὔπω δάκνει** is followed in O16 by a *dicolon*, indicating that the Cook here changes from speaking 'aside' to addressing Demeas.

388 Emboldened by Demeas' failure to react to his tentative intervention at 386, the Cook tries to speak to him again, but this time he is cut off after only one word, Demeas brandishing his walking-stick (Blume 1974: 149) and threatening him with a beating. It is not clear what he is supposed to be trying to say. At the beginning of a speech in dialogue, ὅμως normally means 'despite what you have just said' (cf. *Aspis* 22, *Dysk.* 410, *Sik.* 147); Demeas' last words have indicated, no doubt by their tone as much as their content, that his anger is still strong, but the Cook may be hoping to persuade him to overcome it.   **κατάξω τὴν κεφαλὴν...σου:** Smikrines hurls the same threat at Sophrone in *Epitr.* 1062 (cf. 1068–9, 1072–5), but she is his slave and he has allowed her to utter (offstage) at least one complete sentence of criticism (which he quotes at 1064). The Cook here is a free man, and has now been silenced twice before he has had a chance to say anything meaningful.

389 νὴ δικαίως γ': ironic: the Cook is admitting that if he were to be beaten, he would deserve it – but he means that he would 'deserve' it, not for doing anything wrong, but for being imprudent; similarly Getas, when he offers assistance to Knemon in an emergency and is answered with a curse, comments καὶ μάλα δικαίως (*Dysk.* 602) – he 'deserved' the curse because, having already had experience of Knemon's character, he should have known better than to speak to him. Contrast *Epitr.* 249, where Syriskos' καὶ δικαίως (Smikrines having threatened him with a beating if he does not remain silent) is a recognition that he ought not to have interrupted Daos' speech. For the sequence νὴ...γε compare 129: C has καὶ δικαίως, a more common expression (cf. also Men. fr. 602.13) and therefore more likely to arise by corruption.

389–90 The Cook goes back into Demeas' house. His words ἀλλ' ἰδού, | εἰσέρχομ' ἤδη must be addressed to Demeas, apparently in order to assure him that he will make no further attempt to intervene between Demeas and Chrysis.

390–7 With the Cook out of the way, and Chrysis cowed into silence, Demeas can give free rein to his fury, and taunts Chrysis with the bleak future she faces as an ordinary *hetaira*, no longer maintained by a regular partner but dependent on casual hirings for parties, which she must accept or else starve. At these parties, in addition to hard drinking (394), she would also be expected to provide sexual services on demand; it is probably significant that Demeas does not mention this — his own passion for Chrysis is far from extinct. The juxtaposition between this speech and the abortive intervention of the Cook may prompt the reflection that, while cooks and *hetairai* both make a living by hiring themselves out for dinner parties, it will generally be the *hetaira* who finds it more difficult and disagreeable to satisfy her clients.

390 τὸ μέγα πρᾶγμ': sarcastic, 'the big shot!' 'the VIP!' That (Demeas alleges) is what Chrysis *imagines* herself to be, but she will soon discover the truth (390–1, 396–7). For the idiom cf. Dem. 35.15 (also sarcastic, referring to speaker's opponent) οὑτοσὶ... Λάκριτος Φασηλίτης, μέγα πρᾶγμα, Ἰσοκράτους μαθητής; Hdt. 3.132.2 ἦν δὲ μέγιστον πρῆγμα Δημοκήδης παρὰ βασιλέϊ. **ἐν τῆι πόλει:** implicitly contrasted with 'in my house' where she *had* been an important person.

391 ὄψει σεαυτὴν...ἥτις εἶ: the 'I know thee who thou art' construction (Mark 1.24 = Luke 4.34 οἶδά σε τίς εἶ: earlier e.g. *Odyssey* 4.832–4, Soph. *Phil.* 444, 573–4, Thuc. 1.72.1 τὴν σφετέραν πόλιν ἐβούλοντο σημῆναι ὅση εἴη δύναμιν; Kühner and Gerth 1898–1904: II 577–9), in origin perhaps a blend of the accusative + participle (or accusative + infinitive) and the indirect-question constructions. The verb is echoed by εἴσει (396) and γνώσει (397), to ironic effect: Demeas, who is so insistently reminding Chrysis that she will soon 'see' and 'know' her true worth and status, will himself soon learn that his present action was taken in almost complete ignorance of the facts of the situation.   **ἥτις εἶ:** viz. a common *hetaira*.

392 αἱ κατὰ σέ 'women of your sort', cf. *Heros* 18–19 παιδίσκην...κατ' ἐμαυτόν 'a girl of my own class', *Perik.* 710–11; Callim. *Epigr.* 1.12, 16 Pfeiffer (advice not to marry above one's station) τὴν κατὰ σαυτὸν ἔλα. B reads οὐ κατὰ σέ, which would have to mean 'not in accordance with your recent lifestyle', but this is hardly possible when Demeas has just used ἥτις εἶ to allude to a very different lifestyle.

392–3 πραττόμεναι δραχμὰς δέκα | μόνας: our best evidence for contemporary Athenian rates is *Kolax* 128–30 S = E233–5 A, where a πορνοβοσκός says that one of his girls makes three minae (300 drachmae) a day from a mercenary soldier, which is more than ten would earn ordinarily; i.e. a normal daily rate would be 25–30 drachmae. Demeas is thus classing Chrysis as cheap (as μόνας would in any case suggest). In *Epitr.* 136–41 Smikrines complains that his son-in-law Charisios is paying 12 dr. a day for the services of Habrotonon, but this does not prove that 12 dr. was an extravagant rate: Smikrines is a very stingy man, particularly when it is 'his' dowry money that is being spent, and his calculation (139–40) that 12 dr. could maintain a man for thirty-six days provokes another character to say, in a mocking aside, that this rate (two obols a day) 'was once [i.e. when prices were lower] enough to buy gruel for a starving man' (see Furley 2009: 131). These rates may still seem high, seeing that in 329/8 a skilled workman might make 2 to 2½ dr. a day (Loomis 1998: 111–13, citing *IG* II² 1672, 1673) and that a Menandrian cook is offered a fee of 3 dr. (*Aspis* 223); but a *hetaira* could not expect to be hired every day, and (as Lamagna notes) she would need to supply herself with clothing, perfumes and cosmetics. In the last years of the classical Athenian democracy, the daily rate for a female musician had been officially limited to 2 dr. ([Arist]. *Ath.Pol.* 50.2) and we hear of a prosecution for breach of this rule (Hyp. *Eux.* 3), but the system probably died with the democracy.

393 †ἑταῖραι†, which violates the metre, is here taken to have originated from a gloss on αἱ κατὰ σέ which displaced a word of the form ⏑ – (ἀεί Leo) or ⏑⏑ –. In B the word has been altered into ἕτεραι, which had indeed been proposed as an emendation long before B was discovered, and the corruption thus posited would be an easy one; but ἕτεραι, by sandwiching κατὰ σέ … μόνας between the article and the head word of the phrase, gives the inappropriate sense 'the others who, like you, charge only ten drachmae'. Chrysis is not yet at the stage of offering her services for ten drachmae: Demeas is *predicting* that she will discover (ὄψει 391) that that is the best price she will be able to command.   **τρέχουσιν ἐπὶ τὰ δεῖπνα:** for fear, presumably, that if they arrive late they may be forestalled by a competitor. Elsewhere the noun/adjective τρεχέδειπνος refers to parasites (Athen. 242c, possibly quoting Alexis, cf. Alexis fr. 173).

394 πίνουσ' ἄκρατον: 340–2n. These *hetairai* cannot afford to be choosy about which parties they attend or what they drink at them.   **ἄχρι ἄν,** not ἄχρις ἄν (BC): ἄχρι, and similarly μέχρι, are the only forms known in Attic inscriptions (Threatte 1980–96: II 669–71; cf. Phryn. *Ecl.* 6, Moeris

α 74), and they stand in hiatus before ἄν in a metrical inscription (*IG* II²
7873.8) and frequently in comedy (e.g. Men. fr. 748, Hegesippus fr. 1.26),
ἄχρι/μέχρι ἄν being perhaps treated as a single word on the model of ὅταν,
ἐπάν, ἐπειδάν.   **ἀποθάνωσιν:** probably the idea is that they drink themselves to death (395–6n.; cf. Hippocr. *Aph.* 5.5, *On Diseases* 3.8; Plut. *Alex.*
70.2; Dio Chrys. *Or.* 64.22); possibly it is merely that they will never get to
save enough money to be able to retire.

395 πεινῶσιν: there may well be a grimly sarcastic pun here on the roots
πιν- and πειν- (Blume 2001: 292): the *hetaira* has only the choice between
dying of drink or of starvation. At Ar. *Ach.* 751–2 Dicaeopolis mishears or
misunderstands the Megarian's διαπεινᾶμες 'we are constantly hungry' as
διαπίνομες 'we are constantly drinking'.

395–6 τοῦθ'... | ποῶσιν: i.e. τρέχωσιν ἐπὶ τὰ δεῖπνα καὶ πίνωσιν ἄκρατον.

396–7 Demeas repeats with emphasis his statement that Chrysis will learn
by bitter experience what she has lost by her folly. At the end of his tirade
she still has no idea what she has done to offend him, unless it was her
failure to expose the baby.   **οὐδενὸς... | ἧττον** 'no less than anyone',
i.e., by *litotes*, 'thoroughly well'. The phrase is not found in earlier poetry
(though cf. Ar. *Wasps* 1272–4 'he consorted with the *penestai* in Thessaly,
αὐτὸς πενέστης ὢν ἐλάττων οὐδενός) but is common in fifth- and fourth-
century prose (e.g. Thuc. 7.30.3, Pl. *Men.* 85c οἶσθ' ὅτι τελευτῶν οὐδενὸς
ἧττον ἀκριβῶς ἐπιστήσεται περὶ τούτων, Isoc. 12.83, Dem. 24.34).

397 τίς οὖσ' = ὅτι ἑταίρα οὖσα: cf. [Dem.] 59.115 ἐνθυμεῖσθε τοῦτο μόνον, εἰ
Νέαιρα οὖσα ταῦτα διαπέπρακται; Dickens 1837/1966: 103 (Bill Sikes to
Nancy) 'Do you know who you are, and what you are?' (viz. a prostitute, as
Dickens made explicit in a later preface, ibid. lxi).   **ἡμάρτανες:** after τίς
οὖσ', it will be fairly easy for Chrysis to (mis)understand this as referring
to her having behaved like a γαμετή (130) by not exposing 'her' baby; the
sentence expresses *less* well the meaning Demeas actually intends (referring to her supposed affair with Moschion), since sexual infidelity was at
least as heinous in a wife as in an unmarried live-in partner.

398 ἔσταθι (cf. Ar. *Birds* 206; *Odyssey* 22.489) 'stay where you are!', intransitive perfect imperative of ἵστημι: for the short form cf. ἑστάναι, ἑστώς, etc.
Demeas has turned to go back into his house, and Chrysis has evidently
made some move in the same direction (whether in the desperate hope of
being allowed back in, or with the intention of asking once again why she
has been expelled); he raises his hand (and probably his stick) to halt her.
He then goes inside, shutting the door firmly.   **τάλαιν' ἔγωγε τῆς ἐμῆς
τύχης** is, with minor variations, formulaic for Menandrian young women

in distress: cf. *Mis.* 247–8 S = 648–9 A, *Perik.* 810, and (with a more sub-stantial variation) *Epitr.* 855 τίς ἂν θεῶν τάλαιναν ἐλεήσειέ με; The trope (in which τύχης is causal genitive: Smyth 1956: 335) is of tragic origin; cf. Soph. *Aj.* 980 ὤμοι βαρείας ἄρα τῆς ἐμῆς τύχης, Eur. *Alc.* 393 ἰώ μοι τύχας, *Supp.* 1147 αἰαῖ τύχας, *El.* 1185.

398/9 Possibly Chrysis at this point approaches the door, tries to open it and finds it bolted against her (cf. 416 ἐκκέκλεικε); Sandbach (on 416) points out that this would provide extra time for the actor who played the Cook to change his costume and mask and make his way (with the sheep) from the *skene*, into which he exited at 390, to Eisodos A along which he will presently re-enter as Nikeratos.

399–420 Like 96–119a, this passage serves as a transition to the next Act. It also provides some further light relief in Nikeratos' grumbles about his scraggy sheep (399–404); and it then shows us Nikeratos at his best, tak-ing the distressed Chrysis into his house without question even though he thinks she made a bad mistake (411) in keeping the baby.

399–404 This passage combines two recurrent themes of comedy on the subject of animal sacrifice – complaints about the poor quality of prospec-tive victims, and reflection on the fact that the parts of the animal which are given to the gods are those which humans cannot eat or do not care to eat – which both also figure, but separately, in *Dyskolos* (393–9, 438–9; 447–53). For the first theme, cf. also *Birds* 890–902, Plaut. *Aul.* 561–8; for the second, Pherecrates fr. 28, Eubulus frr. 94, 127, *com. adesp.* 142. Here the old jokes are given a novel twist as Nikeratos complains that his sheep (evidently the least bad available at a price he could afford) contains *only* those parts reserved for the gods and no edible meat at all! But all the time the audience can also see Chrysis standing not far away, sobbing.

399 μέν is answered by δέ (403).

400 θυθέν: normal Attic would be τυθέν, with the aspirate dissimilated before another identical aspirate. In early Attic inscriptions aspirates tend, contrariwise, to *a*ssimilate nearby consonants to themselves (Threatte 1980–96: I 455–64), and forms like ἀνεθέθε̄ are occasionally found, but they become very rare after the fifth century and are virtually unknown in papyri and MSS of literary texts. However, in the aorist passive of θύω (and of τίθημι) such forms could have been created at any time by anal-ogy, and their very rarity makes it unlikely that they would arise by corrup-tion.   καὶ ταῖς θεαῖς is not formally necessary to the sense, since οἱ θεοί regularly refers to the whole of the pantheon regardless of gender, but, placed where it is as an addendum to the sentence, it emphasizes (like ἅπαντα) that the gods (unlike mortals) will be very well provided for by this sheep: it has enough blood, bones, etc., to satisfy not only all the male deities but all the female deities too! The joke is played the other way in Ar. *Birds* 898–902, where the chorus, after first declaring their intention to 'summon the Blest Ones' to share in a sacrifice, on second thoughts decide to summon 'just one of them' because the goat being offered is so skinny ('nothing but beard and horns') that there risks being nothing left for the worshippers.

401 αἷμα: the blood of a sacrificial victim was either allowed to flow on to the altar, or else was caught in a bowl (σφαγεῖον) and then poured over the altar: cf. Ar. *Thesm.* 695, 754–5, and see Burkert 1983: 5.　　**χολήν:** the gall-bladder was burnt on the altar, and omens could be drawn from the manner in which it burned: cf. *Dysk.* 452, *com. adesp.* 142.3, Soph. *Ant.* 1009–10.　　**ὀστᾶ:** the thigh-bones (cf. Ar. *Peace* 1021; Soph. *Ant.* 1008, 1011; *Iliad* 1.460–4) and the ὀσφύς or *os sacrum* with the tail (cf. *Dysk.* 451, Men. fr. 224.11–12, Ar. *Peace* 1053–5, Eubulus fr. 127, [Aesch.] *Prom.* 496–7) were wrapped in fat and burnt on the altar; Hes. *Thg.* 535–57 offers a mythical aetiology for the practice.

402 σπλῆνα μέγαν: the spleen is not elsewhere mentioned specifically as one of the gods' portions; it was probably included, with other internal organs, in the σπλάγχνα, which were shared between the god (cf. Ar. *Birds* 518–19, 1524, *Wealth* 1130; Athenion fr. 1.18) and the worshippers (cf. *Kolax* F 1.1; Ar. *Knights* 410, *Peace* 1102–16, *Birds* 654); see Gill 1974: 123–7. Enlargement of the spleen was recognized as a disease (σπληνιᾶν), cf. Ar. fr. 322.8, Arist. *PA* 670b9–10.

403 πέμψω ... τοῖς φίλοις: it was common practice to send round to friends portions of meat from sacrifices at weddings and other occasions; cf. Arist. *Ach.* 1049–50, Thphr. *Char.* 15.5, 17.2 (also 74–5n. on the distribution of portions of sesame-cake). Theophrastus' ἀνελεύθερος, by contrast, *sells* the meat from his daughter's wedding (*Char.* 22.4).

404 τὸ κώιδιον: a surprise: the sheep has no meat on it, or so little that none will be left over to send to friends.

　　Nikeratos now notices Chrysis, who has moved away from Demeas' door and is now close to his own (πρόσθε τῶν θυρῶν).

405 Ἡράκλεις: 178n.

405–6 πρόσθε ... | ... κλάουσ'; 'is this Chrysis, standing here sobbing in front of my door?' For this type of dialogue with oneself ('is this X? – yes, it is') cf. Plaut. *Poen.* 1299–1300 *estne illaec mea amica Anterastilis? et ea est certo,* Ter. *Eun.* 848 *sed estne haec Thai' quam video? ipsast.* In Greek, our passage (or a parallel one) is closely imitated by Lucian *Timon* 54 ἀλλὰ τί τοῦτο; οὐ Θρασυκλῆς ὁ φιλόσοφος οὗτός ἐστιν; οὐ μὲν οὖν ἄλλος, *Menipp.* 1; there is a very elaborate variant of the pattern in Soph. *OC* 310–21 where Antigone asks herself half a dozen questions about the woman she sees approaching on horseback (including ἆρ' ἔστιν; ἆρ' οὐκ ἔστιν; 316) before deciding that οὐκ ἔστιν ἄλλη (319) and then taking another two lines before naming her as Ismene.

406 Χρυσίς: Nikeratos, unlike Demeas (406), speaks of Chrysis not as ἡ Σαμία but by her name (so again 435).   **μὲν οὖν** emphasizing an affirmative response (Denniston 1954: 476–80).

407–8 'Why, that splendid friend of yours has thrown me out, of course!'

408 χρηστός: sarcastic, as in *Aspis* 75, *Epitr.* 1066, Ar. *Clouds* 8.   **τί γὰρ ἄλλ'(ο)**, appended to an answer, normally means 'what else could it be?', indicating that in the speaker's opinion the answer given is manifestly the only possible one; cf. Pl. *Tht.* 186d-e ('What name do you apply to seeing, hearing, smelling, feeling cold and feeling heat? – Αἰσθάνεσθαι ἔγωγε· τί γὰρ ἄλλο;'), *Meno* 77d; also Ar. *Clouds* 1087–8 ('What will you say if I refute you? – Σιγήσομαι· τί δ' ἄλλο;'). If that is the force of the expression here, Chrysis is maintaining her bitterly sarcastic tone, affecting to see Demeas' behaviour as perfectly natural and normal.

409 τίς; Δημέας; Obviously, if Chrysis has indeed been 'thrown out', it can only be Demeas who has expelled her; but Nikeratos' bewildered question makes it clear how hard he finds it to believe that the Demeas he knows could do such a thing.

410 τῶν γυναικῶν: i.e. from his wife and Plangon.

411 ἀνελομένη: 354–5n.   **ἐμβροντησία** '<that's> idiocy!' Properly ἐμβρόν -τητος means 'struck by lightning', whence it came to mean 'stupefied' and eventually 'stupid' (so already Ar. *Eccl.* 793; cf. *Dysk.* 441, *Perik.* 523; [Pl.] *Alc. II* 140c; Dem. 18.243 (to a doctor who reveals his recommended treatment only at the patient's funeral) ἐμβρόντητε, εἶτα νῦν λέγεις;). The reference is more likely to be to Chrysis' actions (which were the topic of the preceding sentence) than to those of Demeas (which, though seemingly irrational, could not exactly be called imprudent): it was indeed very hazardous for her, entirely dependent as she was on the goodwill of Demeas, to keep 'her' child when she knew he did not want her to. For the sentence consisting of a single nominative noun-phrase cf. *Dysk.* 481 ἀνδροφόνα θηρί' '<they're> man-eating beasts!'. Nikeratos expresses himself in characteristically blunt fashion, unmindful of the feelings of Chrysis and unaffected by the sight of the baby (whom, ironically, we know to be his grandson as well as Demeas') in her arms.

412 ἀλλ' ἔστ' ἐκεῖνος ἡδύς 'but he's a pleasant man' – and therefore, Nikeratos implies, even after Chrysis had disobeyed him in the matter of the baby, it would be out of character for him to expel her for that reason. For ἡδύς 'pleasant, agreeable' (of persons) cf. Alexis fr. 187, Diphilus fr. 86.2. The sense 'silly, gullible' (e.g. Pl. *Euthyd.* 300a, *Gorg.* 491e) is unlikely to be relevant; in Plato it typically appears in sneering remarks (ὡς ἡδὺς εἶ) by sophists and other negatively portrayed characters.

412–13 οὐκ ... | ...ἀρτίως are here continued to Nikeratos, and treated as interrogative, broadly in agreement with BC, which both indicate a change of speaker during 413 by placing a *paragraphos* under the line, though only C has a *dicolon* after ἀρτίως. Nikeratos is continuing his musings over Demeas' strange behaviour. Demeas must have discovered the baby as soon as he entered his house (at the end of Act I); yet when Nikeratos met him after that (169–87) he was not angry at all and was only thinking about making rapid arrangements for the wedding. Nikeratos infers that Demeas must have had an abrupt change of mind at some moment since then, and asks Chrysis if this is correct. Most editors before Jacques (and Arnott since) nevertheless gave these words, as statements rather than questions, to Chrysis, but there is no compelling reason to reject the evidence of the papyri, and the semi-tautologous (and quite unemotional) sequence οὐκ εὐθύς ... διαλιπών ... ἀρτίως is more suited to Nikeratos, trying to make sense of Demeas' seemingly senseless actions, than to the distressed and indignant Chrysis.

413 διαλιπών 'after an interval' (cf. *Dysk.* 783, *Epitr.* 890; Ar. *Clouds* 496). **ὃς καὶ φράσας** 'yes, after he'd actually told me ...': the sentence introduced by the 'connecting relative' (12n.) here serves to confirm and strengthen an assentient response, as in *Perik.* 471–2 ἧττον μεθύεις γάρ. – ἧττον; ὃς πέπωκ᾽ ἴσως κοτύλην [about 270 ml] and *Dysk.* 867–9.

414 εἰς τοὺς γάμους ... ποεῖν: cf. 221 τοῖς ἔνδον ἐκέλευσ᾽ εὐτρεπίζειν πάνθ᾽ ἃ δεῖ: Chrysis was regarded, and regarded herself, as being in charge of 'those inside' (301–4n.).

415 μεταξύ: i.e. while we were in the middle of making these preparations. **ὥσπερ ἐμμανής:** 361n.

416 ἐκκέκλεικε: 398–9n.   **χολᾶι:** one form of insanity was believed by fifth- and fourth-century medical theorists to be due to overheating of the body, and especially of the brain, caused by an overflow of bile into the blood (Hippocr. *On the Sacred Disease* 15, *On Diseases* 1.30); another form was attributed to a morbid darkening of the bile (Hippocr. *Airs* 10, *Epid.* 3.17.2). In popular parlance, both χολᾶν (*Epitr.* 393; Ar. *Clouds* 833; cf. Ar. *Peace* 66) and μελαγχολᾶν (563, *Aspis* 306–7, *Dysk.* 89; Ar. *Birds* 14, *Eccl.* 251, *Wealth* 12, 366, 903; Pl. *Phdr.* 268e; Dem. 48.56) had long been used indiscriminately to mean 'be insane'. See further Jacques 1998 and Ingrosso 2010: 308–10.

417 ὁ Πόντος οὐχ ὑγιεινόν ἐστι χωρίον: cf. 98n. and Hippocr. *Airs* 15 (Phasis), 19–22 (Scythia), though these passages do not refer specifically to *mental* diseases.

418 πρὸς τὴν γυναῖκα ... τὴν ἐμήν: it is not clear whether Nikeratos is assumed to know (as the audience do, 35–41) that his wife and Chrysis are on friendly terms; at any rate his wife is the obvious person to look after Chrysis, particularly since she has a baby and a female slave with her.

419 θάρρει: B has the non-Attic form θάρσει here, but the Attic form in 539 and (with C) in 677; θαρσ- is not otherwise found in any Menander papyrus. Apparently Chrysis is hesitating to accept Nikeratos' offer, doubtless because it will mean the end of the scheme, agreed before the two fathers returned, to keep Plangon's baby out of Nikeratos' house; Nikeratos perceives the hesitation, though he has no idea of its cause, and hastens to reassure her.   **τί βούλει;** follows θάρρει likewise at 677; as that passage shows, it means 'what <more> do you want?' and so here, in effect, 'you'll have everything you need' (viz. shelter, food and protection).

419–20 παύσεθ'... | ... λάβηι: it is possible that Nikeratos is still addressing Chrysis, supposing her to be afraid that he, poor as he is, will not be willing or able to maintain her indefinitely, and assuring her that the arrangement need only be temporary because Demeas is sure to relent soon; but he may be reverting to his own reflections (picking them up where he left off at 417).

419 παύσεθ': sc. χολῶν.   **ἀπομανείς** 'recovering from his madness'; cf. Aretaeus, *On the Causes and Signs of Chronic Diseases* 1.6.11 ἔνθεος ἥδε ἡ μανίη· κἢν ἀπομανῶσιν, εὔθυμοι, ἀκηδέες, ὡς τελεσθέντες τῶι θεῶι. The word cannot here be understood in its usual sense 'being/going completely mad' (e.g. Lucian, *Dial. Deorum* 20.1), since παύσεθ', which would then have to be taken as governing it, requires a present, not an aorist participle.

420 ὅταν λογισμὸν ... λάβηι 'when he thinks rationally about what he's now doing'. In fact, however, in this play, the effect of λογισμός tends to be the opposite of that here expected by Nikeratos. Demeas' present fury, indeed, is the result of two carefully articulated processes of reasoning, one (267–79) leading to the conclusion that Moschion must be the father of the baby (and to the cry ἐξέστηχ' ὅλως), the other (330–47) to the conclusion that sole responsibility for the supposed liaison rests with Chrysis (and to the decision to expel her ἐπὶ κεφαλὴν ἐς κόρακας, 352–4). Later, too, Moschion's reflections (λαμβάνω λογισμόν, 620) on the accusation mistakenly made against him will send him 'completely out of his mind' (ἐξέστηκα νῦν τελέως ἐμαυτοῦ, 620–1) in anger at his father's unjust suspicions. Nikeratos himself, ironically, as will be abundantly seen in the next Act, is not at all given to λογισμός, and can fly into literally murderous rages (cf. 560–1, 580–1) almost on the instant.

Nikeratos ushers Chrysis, the baby and the old woman into his house, and then follows them in, leading the sheep.

ACT IV

As appears to be common in Menander, Act IV brings the plot to a climactic point – and as in *Epitrepontes* and *Perikeiromene*, the climax crucially involves the discovery of the true parentage of a child, whether recently born (as here and in *Epitrepontes*) or already grown up (as in *Perikeiromene*). The act, 'by far the most complex and varied single act in surviving Menander' (Walton and Arnott 1996: 94), can be viewed as consisting of two halves. The first half (421–520) begins where Act III ended, with Chrysis and the baby safe in the house of Nikeratos. Moschion, returning from the city and learning from Nikeratos what has taken place in his absence, intercedes for Chrysis with his father, with disastrous results, as misunderstandings between them lead to Demeas becoming convinced that he was wrong to believe Moschion to be an innocent party in the supposed affair between him and Chrysis. Demeas does his best to keep this shameful information from Nikeratos (who has remained on stage), but eventually (480–1) he loses control of himself and begins shouting, and Nikeratos, listening to the quarrel and soon understanding what it is about, bursts out in even greater rage (492) against the libertine who had been minutes away from becoming his son-in-law. Demeas urges him to follow his own example and expel Chrysis from *his* home, and Nikeratos at once moves to do so, though Moschion makes an ineffective attempt to stop him (519–20). In sharp contrast with what will happen in the second half of the act, this is the first exit or entrance by any character since Demeas came on stage at 440. At this point everything seems in ruins, with the marriage cancelled, Moschion's shame revealed to a man who is all too likely to divulge it more widely (cf. 507–13), and Chrysis and the baby facing a very bleak future.

The second half begins with Moschion doing what he arguably should have done back in Act II – confessing to Demeas the truth about the baby: he is indeed its father, but its mother is Plangon. Now, however, it is necessary somehow to make this known to Nikeratos, and with Nikeratos in his present mood we expect this to be a very tricky business – not half as tricky as it becomes, though, when Nikeratos accidentally discovers the truth for himself (532–6). From this point on he is hardly sane; a terrified Moschion makes himself scarce almost at once, and Demeas is left to try and bring Nikeratos back to reason on his own. His attempts to do this fill the rest of

Act IV with a rich mixture of Feydeauesque farce (Arnott 1997: 74–5) and potential tragedy – for Nikeratos is now making credible threats of murder against the baby (553–5), Chrysis (560–1) and his own wife (580–1n.). Repeatedly he rushes in and out of his house: whereas there were no exits or entrances between 440 and 519, in the following sixty lines there are nine, six of which involve Nikeratos (whereas Demeas remains on stage throughout, conveniently reporting on what he can hear when Nikeratos is raging indoors). In the end it comes to violence (575–6) – the only physical confrontation between two old men in surviving Greek comedy, under cover of which Chrysis and the baby find refuge again in Demeas' house, back where they were to begin with and where they both belong.

Nikeratos' fury begins to abate when Demeas forcibly prevents him from rushing into his house for a fourth time (582–3) and Nikeratos accepts his offer to explain the situation (584–6). Demeas spins him a nonsensical yarn about Plangon possibly having been impregnated by a god; Nikeratos does not believe it (596, 598–9) and Demeas may not expect him to, but it does convey the message that Demeas thinks none the worse of him or Plangon on account of what has happened (it is surely, after all, a high honour to be like Acrisius (597) the grandfather of a god's son), as do Demeas' repeated assurances that Moschion still wishes to marry Plangon (586, 599, 610). Eventually (604–5, 611), as on previous occasions over the arrangement of the marriage and over its timing (168–88), Nikeratos yields, and once again (cf. 187) his surrender is accepted by Demeas with the assurance νοῦν ἔχεις (605, 611). The dangers threatening the marriage, which had been building up ever since Demeas overheard the unguarded words of the old nurse (245–61), have now vanished, and it can proceed as though nothing had happened – or so we think, until the arrival of a disgruntled Moschion at the start of Act V.

Thus the act is almost defined by the interaction between Demeas and Nikeratos. The first half begins with Nikeratos convinced that Demeas is mad (426–7, cf. 416–17) and hoping that Moschion can bring him to his senses; the second half begins with Demeas convinced (with better reason) that Nikeratos is mad, and soon finding himself deserted by Moschion; both halves end with Demeas successfully inducing Nikeratos to undertake two very different courses of action. All the male characters to some extent make fools of themselves. Demeas condemns Moschion unjustly (which in the circumstances is somewhat excusable), exposes him to the scarcely controllable fury of Nikeratos (which is not), and in the end is lucky not to find himself a helpless bystander at the murder of his partner and his grandson; his apology to Moschion (537–8) is humiliating for a father to have to make, and (as we shall see in the next act) it proves ineffective. Nikeratos behaves like one of the demented tragic heroes whose language he incongruously imitates (495–501, 516–17, 532–4), is narrowly prevented from killing three people including a baby whom he actually knows to be *his* grandson, and before the end is almost a child in the hands of Demeas, who soothes him with what can reasonably be called fairy-tales. And Moschion, though he tries to stand up for Chrysis (and therefore also for his own son) against an angry Demeas (452–80) and also briefly against an angry Nikeratos (519–20), comes clean with his father only when it is almost too late, and shortly afterwards flees in panic. In contrast, Chrysis (whom in this act we see only briefly) and Plangon and her mother (whom we do not see at all) form a united front (556–61) to defend the baby at the risk of their own lives, and they succeed.

The whole of Act IV is in trochaic tetrameters (as will be the last 68 lines of Act V). This metre can be used in any part of a Menandrian play: we find it in Act V of *Aspis* (521ff; the line-beginnings are lost, and the metre is inferred from the apparent length of the lines), in Act IV of *Dyskolos* (708–83), in Act III of *Sikyonioi* (110–49), in Act II of *Perikeiromene* (267–353), and apparently in Act I of *Phasma* (75–92 S, 75–98 A). It may be that the tetrameters were delivered in a fairly strict rhythm and to musical accompaniment, as were the trochaic *septenarii* of Roman comedy, but this is far from certain (Pickard-Cambridge 1968: 165): B inserts the stage-direction αὐλεῖ 'the piper plays' before the iambic tetrameters of *Dysk.* 880–958 but not before the trochaic tetrameters of *Dysk.* 708–83, let alone those in *Samia*. At any rate, trochaic tetrameters were clearly considered suitable both for farcical scenes (such as the latter part of the present act) and for passages of unusual solemnity (such as Demeas' speech in 694–712, or Knemon's in *Dysk.* 708–47). (Gomme and) Sandbach 1973: 36–7 may well have been right to generalize that 'passages in this metre are distinguished in tone from the adjacent iambics, but not always in the same way'. Here the effect may be to *signal in advance* an increase in dramatic tension which actually begins to occur only with the entry of an evidently agitated Demeas at 440. It has often been claimed that Menander's use of trochaic tetrameters decreased as his career advanced and that their extensive employment in *Samia* shows it to be an early play. *Samia* probably *is* in fact an early play (see Introduction §8), but the use of tetrameters is not strong evidence of this: *Halieus*, for example, from which there are three tetrameter citations (frr. 25–27), must have been produced after the death of Dionysius of Heraclea in 306/5 (Athen. 549a-d, citing fr. 25; D.S. 20.77.1).

421 Nikeratos comes out of his house, talking over his shoulder (198, 301nn.) to his wife, who has evidently been pestering him to protest to Demeas about his expulsion of Chrysis; she appears to be a person whose views and wishes it is difficult for her husband to disregard (see Introduction §4(d)).   παρατενεῖς 'you'll stretch me out, you'll prostrate me', not far short of (and sometimes glossed as) ἀπολεῖς 'you'll be the death of me'; cf. 544, Pl. *Symp.* 207a-b αἰσθάνηι...τὰ θηρία...τῶι λιμῶι παρατεινό-μενα ὥστε ἐκεῖνα ἐκτρέφειν 'you are aware that animals prostrate themselves with hunger so as to nourish [their young]'; Xen. *Mem.* 3.13.6 παρετάθη μακρὰν ὁδὸν πορευθείς 'he was exhausted after making a long journey [on foot]'.   βαδίζω νῦν 'I'm on my way now' suggests that Nikeratos' wife has been displaying impatience. We cannot tell whether he would in fact have gone to tackle Demeas immediately, since he is interrupted by the arrival of Moschion, who at his request makes the first move (451–2), both men supposing, wrongly but naturally, that he as Demeas' much-loved son is more likely to persuade him.   ἐκείνωι: Demeas.   προσβαλῶν: future participle of purpose, 'to confront' (cf. *Epitr.* 163).

422–3 οὐδ' ἂν ἐπὶ πολλῶι...|...ἐδεξάμην: lit. 'I wouldn't have accepted even at a high price', i.e. 'I'd never have wanted at any price' (Arnott). For this use of ἐπί (LSJ B.iii.4) cf. Ar. *Birds* 153–4 'I wouldn't become an Opuntius [i.e. a one-eyed man] ἐπὶ ταλάντωι χρυσίου'; for this use of δέχεσ-θαι cf. Aesch. *Eum.* 228 οὐδ' ἂν δεχοίμην ὥστ' ἔχειν τιμὰς σέθεν 'I wouldn't take your privileges as a gift' (Podlecki 1989); Andoc. 1.5 πάντα τὰ ἀγαθὰ ἔχειν στερόμενος τῆς πατρίδος οὐκ ἂν δεξαίμην.

422 μὰ τοὺς θεούς interrupts the noun-phrase τὸ γεγονός...πρᾶγμ(α): Sandbach's suggestion that this 'may be a sign of Nikeratos' agitation' finds some support in the two Menandrian passages that come closest to being parallels to this one, *Sam.* 565–6 (οὐδεπώποτ' εἰς τοιαύτην ἐμπεσών, μὰ τοὺς θεούς, | οἶδα ταραχήν) and *Dysk.* 151–2 (δέδοικα μέντοι, μὰ τὸν Ἀπόλλω καὶ θεούς, | αὐτόν), in both of which, as here (cf. 415, 419), the speaker is having to deal with a man who strikes him as being mad.

424 οἰωνός...ἄτοπος 'an untoward omen'; for this use of ἄτοπος as a euphemistic substitute for κακός, cf. *Dysk.* 288, *Epitr.* 704 Furley, 1099, fr. 602.6, and see Arnott 1964: 119–22. The evil omen consists not only in the weeping and distress of the women on what should be a day of rejoic-ing, but also in the event that has caused it: the expulsion from Demeas' house of a woman with a baby, on the day when Moschion is to take Plan-gon into that same house as his bride and the mother of his future chil-dren, might well be taken to bode very ill for the marriage. From this point of view the identity and status of the woman are of no consequence, and so Nikeratos refers to her merely as τις (425).

427 σκατοφαγεῖ 'is behaving like a lout (literally, shit-eater)'. A σκατοφά-γος was a person whose behaviour was as uncontrolled and indiscrimi-nate as allegedly were the dietary habits of the cattle in Boeotia (schol. Ar. *Wealth* 706) or Cyprus (*Kolax* F 8, Antiphanes fr. 124) who were sup-posed to eat each other's dung; at 550 Demeas will apply the term to

Nikeratos (also in his absence) when Nikeratos in his turn has lost control of himself through anger and indignation. In some other passages
(e.g. *Dysk.* 488, *Perik.* 394) the word comes to function merely as a generalized term of abuse.   οἰμώξεται 'he'll regret it', literally, 'he'll cry οἴμοι'.
In Old Comedy this future tense, either in the second or third person,
usually makes a strong prediction (often shading into a threat) of real
suffering or punishment for the person referred to (e.g. Ar. *Clouds* 217,
Birds 1207; *Thesm.* 248, *Frogs* 178, 707). In Menander the second person
of the verb (accompanied by μακρά) still functions thus (*Epitr.* 160, 1068 –
both spoken by Smikrines, each time addressing a female slave), and the
third person should probably be taken in the same way at *Aspis* 356 where
Chairestratos is horrified at the thought of his daughter being married to
his grasping, unfeeling brother Smikrines. Here it perhaps indicates that
Nikeratos' indignation is overblown: Demeas has not done him or his family any intentional harm, and Nikeratos will not be in a position to subject
him to anything worse than a verbal tirade.

428 σκαιός 'stupid, uncivilized', the opposite of δεξιός, found paired with
such adjectives as ἀγνώμων (*Epitr.* 918), ἀναίσθητος (Dem. 18.120), and
βάρβαρος ([Dem.] 26.17), and not a term that can often have been applied
to Demeas!   ὤν 'for being' (causal participle).

We expect Nikeratos now to go over and knock at Demeas' door, and
the resolute tone of his last sentence suggests that he is probably beginning to move in that direction, which is also the direction towards Eisodos
A (see note at start of commentary). But at this moment Moschion arrives
along Eisodos A from the city centre (432 ἐν ἀγορᾶι); he is conventionally
allowed a short entrance-monologue (119b-d n.) before he and Nikeratos
notice each other. He has been away since 162, at which time it had not
yet been agreed that the wedding would take place this day. We shall learn
presently (431–2) that he has now been given this news by Parmenon, having met him by chance in the Agora; but until we hear this, we may briefly
be mystified as to the reason for his impatience with the slow passage of
time – unless indeed the impatient bridegroom was already a comic cliché
(as may well have been the case, though no other example of it survives).

428 οὐ μὴ δύηι ποθ' ἥλιος; 'Is the sun *never* going to set?' Normally οὐ μή
+ subjunctive is used to make very strong negative statements, e.g. οὐ μὴ
βιῶ 'I'll die for certain' (*Aspis* 314); here, just as in 431 (νῦν ποοῦμεν τοὺς
γάμους;), the statement is converted into a question by means of an interrogative intonation. Compare Ar. *Clouds* 3, where a sleepless Strepsiades
asks οὐδέποθ' ἡμέρα γενήσεται; It was customary for a bridegroom to take
his bride home, by torchlight, 'when evening had sufficiently come on'
(ἑσπέρας ἱκανῆς, Photius ζ 28); cf. Ter. *Andr.* 581–2 *quor uxor non accersi-
tur? iam advesperascit.*   τί δεῖ λέγειν; 76–7n. What 'goes without saying'

here is the *reason* for Moschion's impatience (already evident at 158–9), of which he does not, and does not need to, speak directly.

429 ἐπιλέλησθ' (i.e. –σται) **ἡ νὺξ ἑαυτῆς:** Night, that is, has forgotten that it is her duty to darken the heavens at a certain time. In Lucian's *Dialogues of the Gods* (20.1 Macleod), contrariwise, Aphrodite complains to her son Eros about how he sometimes compels the Sun 'to dally with Clymene, forgetting his chariot-driving'; cf. also Men. fr. 222 (context unknown) ἐπελά-θεθ' αὐτὸν ὅστις εἴη. In Plautus' *Amphitruo* (271–8, 282–3), when the night is prolonged by Jupiter's command and the stars stand still, Sosias wonders if either Night or the Sun has got drunk and fallen asleep.   **ὦ μακρᾶς δείλης:** for this exclamatory genitive (Smyth 1956: 331) cf. 487; *Dysk.* 166, 498, 514; *Mis.* 258 S = 659 A; Ar. *Ach.* 64, *Clouds* 1476, *Birds* 1723–4; Eur. *Hipp.* 936, *Or.* 1666.   **δείλης:** δείλη 'afternoon', while common in the historians, occurs in comedy only here and at Philemon fr. 176. The term referred to the whole second half of the day, which could be subdivided into δείλη πρωΐα (Philemon loc. cit., Hdt. 8.6.1) and δείλη ὀψία (Thuc. 8.26.1, Dem. 57.9. Lyc. *Leocr.* 17).

429–30 τρίτον | λούσομ' ἐλθών: he has, then, bathed twice already. This does not refer to the ritual bathing of a bridegroom (124, 156–9nn.), since as late as 729 this has still not taken place. Rather, Moschion has been whiling away his time by visiting the public baths, and now decides to go back to the city centre (not into his house: he says ἐλθών, not εἰσελθών) and bathe yet again. He is on the point of leaving when Nikeratos hails him.

430–1 Μοσχίων, | χαῖρε πολλά: this is the first time Moschion and Nikeratos have met since the latter's return from abroad. It was a meeting that Moschion had earlier been anxious to avoid (161–2), and here it is Nikeratos who initiates contact, with notable cordiality (168–9n.); in a moment he will even be calling Moschion φίλτατε (436n.) – but before either of them has left the scene he will have called him a murderer (513–14), more wicked than the greatest criminals of myth and tragedy (495–7), and soon afterwards Moschion will again take to flight rather than face him (519).

431 νῦν ποοῦμεν τοὺς γάμους; Moschion does not return Nikeratos' greeting (contrast 128–9, *Georg.* 41, *com. adesp.* 1017.77–8) but turns immediately to the topic that fills his mind. We may well be surprised that he broaches the subject with such assurance, until we learn (in his next sentence) that he already knows that Nikeratos has agreed to the wedding being held today. The next time he and Nikeratos meet (713–16) their roles will be reversed, and it will be Nikeratos who is impatient for Moschion to come and take his bride.

431–2 ὁ Παρμένων | εἶπεν … ἄρτι μοι: we must be meant to suppose that this meeting took place while Parmenon was in the Agora shopping and engaging the Cook (between 200 and 283); when Parmenon fled from Demeas at 324, he did not go towards the Agora but in the opposite direction (see note at start of commentary). If Parmenon had met Moschion after fleeing from Demeas at 324, he would certainly have passed on the information that Demeas now knows Moschion to be the baby's father. It follows that ἄρτι should not be taken to imply that Moschion has come straight home after learning that the wedding was to be today; rather, a substantial interval has elapsed since he received the news – during which time, however, so far as he is aware, nothing of significance has happened. Cf. *Dysk.* 891, where Getas asks Sikon if he would like to take revenge on Knemon for 'what you suffered ἀρτίως', namely his ill-treatment by Knemon two acts earlier (499–514).

432–3 τί κωλύει | μετιέναι τὴν παῖδά μ' ἤδη; Encouraged, it would seem, by Nikeratos' friendly attitude, Moschion asks if he can take home his bride at once without waiting till sunset.

432 κωλύει: in tragic and comic iambics, the υ of κωλύω is short before a vowel if and only if the verb is not compounded (contrast *Dysk.* 421 μηδὲν ἐπικωλύετω) and is preceded (with or without intervening monosyllabic particles, articles or pronouns) by οὐδέν, μηδέν, τί or τίς, e.g. *Epitr.* 227 εἰ δή σε μηδὲν κωλύει, 238–9 τί γὰρ | τό με κωλύον; Before a consonant the υ is always long.

433 τὴν παῖδά: 'the girl' can be used to refer to any free, unmarried young woman, even if she is a mother (cf. 676) or is just about to become one (cf. *Georgos* 87).   **τἀνθάδ'** 'what has happened here' (sc. while you have been away).

434 ποῖ': 304n.   **ἀηδία τις … ἔκτοπος** 'an extraordinary and disagreeable event'.

435 Ἡράκλεις: 178n.   **τὴν Χρυσίδα:** 406n.

436 ἔνδοθεν 'from his house' (135n.).   **σου** is to be taken with ὁ πατήρ: the hyperbaton (365n.) is very moderate compared e.g. with Ar. *Peace* 1068–9 εἴθε σου εἶναι ὤφελεν, ὦ ἀλαζών, οὕτωσὶ θερμὸς ὁ πλεύμων.   **φίλταθ':** nowhere else in Menander is this highly affectionate form of address (Dickey 1996: 135–8) used by one man speaking to another (contrast 242, 630), except in 293 (where it is sarcastic, see ad loc.) and *Aspis* 289 (in an apostrophe to one absent and believed dead). The impression already created by the warmth of Nikeratos' greeting to Moschion (430–1n.) is strongly reinforced: he is treating his future son-in-law almost as if he were

the son he has never had, delighted at being able to marry his daughter
to such a rich and, he believes, virtuous young man.

437 οἷον εἴρηκας expresses the speaker's astonishment at what he has
heard; cf. *Dysk.* 75, *Perik.* 488 (both οἷον λέγεις) and the Homeric οἷον ἔειπες
(e.g. *Iliad* 7.455).   **τὸ γεγονός** sc. εἴρηκα, i.e. 'it's the truth'.   **διὰ τί; –
διὰ τὸ παιδίον** echoes 409. Moschion will (correctly) understand Nikeratos
to mean by this 'because she kept the child instead of exposing it'; he
thought he had persuaded Demeas not to expel Chrysis on this ground
(134ff), and will suppose that Demeas has for some reason changed his
mind.

438 εἶτα 'in that case', i.e. if it is as you have said; cf. *Aspis* 93, *Dis Ex.* 107,
Epitr. 468, *Perik.* 712, and (with ἔπειτα) 479, *Dysk.* 791, *Karch.* 37.   **ποῦ
'στι νῦν;** sc. ἡ Χρυσίς – though Moschion is also, indeed doubtless primarily,
concerned to know what has become of his own son.

438–9 ὢ δεινὸν λέγων | πρᾶγμα καὶ θαυμαστόν: literally, 'O you who say a
terrible and amazing thing!', i.e. 'What a terrible, amazing thing you're
saying!' This paratragic 'exclamatory participle' construction (e.g. Eur. *IT*
557 ὢ συνταραχθεὶς οἶκος, *Alc.* 407; Soph. *OC* 337–8) appears in Menander
only here and in 495–7 (see below), though *Mis.* 214 S = 615 A ὢ ποθού-
μενος φαν[είς,] | ὁρῶ σ' (at the moment when Krateia is reunited with her
father) is closely related; it indicates that Moschion's emotions are strongly
aroused. The pairing of δεινός with θαυμαστός (or its cognates) is also paratragic (Eur. *Hel.* 672; *Ba.* 667, 716; *IA* 942, 1538); cf. too Ar. *Birds* 1470–2.
There will be several echoes of this passage later in the scene. When Moschion intercedes with Demeas on behalf of Chrysis, Demeas repeatedly
says (aside) that this is δεινόν (454, 456, 462). Then, when Demeas tells
Moschion that he knows him to be the baby's father, Moschion, assuming
he also knows that Plangon is the mother, and unable to understand his
fury, argues that τὸ πρᾶγμα... | ἐστιν οὐ πάνδεινον (485–6), and Demeas
retorts that if he doesn't think it is δεινόν he will no doubt be willing to
tell Nikeratos all about it (489–90) – to which Moschion responds (aside)
that *that* will be particularly δεινόν (for a reason unknown to Demeas!).
Finally Nikeratos, realizing what Moschion has been accused of, and having heard him apparently admit it, exclaims ὢ πάνδεινον ἔργον and, in
an even more heavily paratragic reprise of the exclamatory-participle
construction, rails at Moschion as ὢ τὰ Τηρέως λέχη | Οἰδίπου τε καὶ
Θυέστου... | ...μικρὰ ποιήσας (495–7).

439 εἴ σοι δεινὸν εἶναι φαίνεται – : Nikeratos breaks off when Demeas comes
out. We are probably expected to guess that he was about to ask Moschion
to take the lead in trying to persuade Demeas to take Chrysis back (421n.;
cf. 451). The two men probably move further away from Demeas' side of

the stage; Demeas does not notice Moschion until the latter comes up and speaks to him (452), nor Nikeratos until he does likewise (463).

440-3 Demeas comes out of his house, still talking back angrily to the slaves within (198n.), who are distressed (some of them in tears, 440, 443) and probably protesting (see below on φλύαρος) at the expulsion of Chrysis. We may suspect that he is venting on them some of the anger that he will have to bottle up (447) when actually celebrating the wedding in the company of Moschion and Nikeratos. He has come outside to pray to Apollo Agyieus (444n.), and he may bring with him a small jar of incense to burn on the altar as an offering accompanying his prayer (cf. Ar. *Wasps* 860–2, *Frogs* 871–3; Soph. *OT* 912–13) – in which case he will probably also be wearing a myrtle garland (Ar. *Wasps* loc. cit., *Thesm.* 37), whose celebratory associations are distinctly incongruous with his mood and, increasingly as the scene goes on, with that of the others present also. We may be meant to be distantly reminded of Soph. *OT* 911–23 where Iocaste comes out, likewise complaining of unreasonable manifestations of distress within (by her husband Oedipus), to make a similar offering and prayer to Apollo. She immediately receives what seems to be very good news (Oedipus' supposed father, Polybus, has died peacefully at Corinth), only then to make a catastrophic discovery before the end of the scene (that Oedipus is in fact her own son). Demeas, contrariwise, will first 'discover' that things are even worse than he had supposed them to be, only then to learn, before the end of the scene, that neither Moschion nor Chrysis has done him any serious wrong at all.

440 ξύλον 'a cudgel' (cf. Ar. fr. 620, Hdt. 2.63.1); Plautus in comparably minatory contexts uses *fustis* (*Amph.* 358, *Aul.* 48). Demeas cannot mean an ordinary (walking-)stick, since he would have one ready to hand (as on the Mytilene mosaic) and ἂν λάβω would make no sense.

440-1 ποήσω τὰ δάκρυ' ὑμῶν... | ἐκκεκόφθαι 'I'll see those tears get knocked out of you!' It is unlikely to be coincidental that ἐκκόπτειν is regularly used to refer to injuries (however inflicted) that cause loss of the use of an *eye*; cf. Ar. *Ach.* 92–3, *Clouds* 24 (a thrown stone), *Birds* 342 (πῶς κλαύσει γάρ, ἢν ἅπαξ γε τὠφθαλμὼ 'κκοπῆις;); Dem. 18.67 (Philip II – an arrow wound, according to Theopompus *FGrH* 115 F 52). Euclio in Plautus' *Aulularia* twice (53, 189) threatens to *gouge* out the eyes of a female slave.

441 φλύαρος usually in Menander refers to nonsensical *speech* (so e.g. 586, 658 – but see 719n.); in *Perinthia* 15 Laches seems to be mockingly quoting Daos' own words back at him, cf. *Perinthia* F 3). We can thus infer that at least one of the slaves has spoken up in defence of Chrysis: Demeas at 456 will use the same words to Moschion after *he* has spoken up in her defence.

441–2 οὐ διακονήσετε | τῶι μαγείρωι; tells us that Demeas is still intending to go ahead with the wedding; otherwise the cook would have been sent away, as in *Aspis* 216–20.

442 πάνυ (no doubt said with a sarcastic intonation) marks the statement as ironic; cf. 364, *Perik.* 710–11, Ar. *Wealth* 565.   **γάρ** probably indicates that Demeas is answering his own question: 'Aren't you going to help the cook? <No,> because <you're lazy, and so> the loss of Chrysis is a great blow to you <because she treated your laziness with indulgence>.'

442–3 ἐστιν ἄξιον ... | ἐπιδακρῦσαι 'it [i.e. the expulsion of Chrysis] deserves to be cried over'.

443 ὑμῖν: she was a μέγα ἀγαθόν *for the slaves* – but not for Demeas.

444 αὐτὰ τἄργα δηλοῖ 'the facts speak for themselves' (Arnott): the slaves' neglect of their work (in failing to help the Cook) proves that the former mistress of the house had spoilt them. Cf. Ar. *Thesm.* 804 Ναυσιμάχης ... ἥττων ἐστὶν Χαρμῖνος· δῆλα δὲ τἄργα (viz. the fact that Charminus had recently lost a sea-battle, ναυμαχίαι ἡττήθη).   **Ἄπολλον:** addressing the pillar of Apollo Agyieus (309n.). Characters pray and make offerings to Apollo at this shrine in Ar. *Wasps* 860–90, Soph. *OT* 911–23, *El.* 634–59 – either for help in a difficult situation (as in Sophocles) or for blessing on an important venture (as in *Wasps*); Demeas desires both. **φίλτατε:** only here in Menander is this superlative (436n.) used by a man in addressing a god (Knemon's daughter uses it in *Dysk.* 197; in Men. fr. 247 the speaker is not praying to the goddess Ge but saying how great a blessing it is to own land). Demeas' anxiety for the success of the marriage, the well-being of Moschion, and the preservation of his good name, is evidently extreme, and only divine help, he feels, can secure these goals. It is striking that Demeas hardly ever uses the root φιλ- in reference to his relationships with other individual humans: only three times in all – twice when asking Nikeratos for a favour (184, 518), and once, almost at the end of the play (695), to express affection for Moschion.

445 ἐπ᾽ ἀγαθῆι τύχηι modifies the accusative-and-infinitive phrase τοὺς γάμους ... γενέσθαι. The expression is found (sometimes in the form ἐπ᾽ ἀγαθαῖς τύχαις) in comic prayers both to Apollo (Ar. *Wasps* 869, com. adesp. 1096.20–1) and to other or unspecified gods (Theopompus com. fr. 8, com. adesp. 1064.2), requesting that an enterprise about to be undertaken be blessed with good fortune. The similar-seeming phrase ἐπ᾽ ἀγαθαῖς συμφοραῖς (Ar. *Lys.* 1276, cf. *Knights* 655), on the other hand, though also found in ritual contexts, has the different function of noting that an act being or about to be performed (e.g. sacrifice, dance) is done in thanksgiving for a blessing already received. τε links the two imperatives χαῖρε and δός.

445–6 πᾶσι...|...ἡμῖν is meant to exclude Chrysis and the baby, whom Demeas no longer regards as part of 'us'. But in fact – as Apollo, being a god, knows, and so do the audience, but Demeas does not – Chrysis and the baby have been accepted into the household of which Moschion's bride is a member; and if we are meant to assume that the prayer is answered (and there are a surprising number of casual references to Apollo in the rest of this act to remind us of it: 455, 474, 567, 570, 596), then the god has benevolently interpreted it in accordance with the true state of affairs.

446 σύ is the last word of both the sentences in which Demeas petitions Apollo (cf. 449): is he, by the use of the emphatic pronoun, implying that it is vital that *Apollo* should ensure the wedding goes smoothly, since without divine assistance Demeas will find it very hard to carry through?

446–7 μέλλω...|...τὴν χολήν is not part of the prayer to Apollo, but an aside addressed to the audience (ἄνδρες, 5, 269nn.). We will already have inferred from the prayer itself (if not from 441–2) that the wedding is going ahead, but the aside serves to inform us that Demeas' mind is still in turmoil after the revelations in Act III and the expulsion of Chrysis, and that he is having difficulty in keeping control of himself. (The very fact that he interrupts himself in the middle of a prayer is probably designed to indicate the extent of his agitation: Blume 1974: 171.) As we shall soon see, it will take only a small push to send him over the brink.

447 καταπιών 'swallowing', i.e. suppressing. The phrase καταπίνειν τὴν χολήν appears to have been idiomatic; the Stoic philosophers Zeno and Chrysippus used it as evidence that the seat of the mind was in the breast and not in the head (Chrysippus *SVF* II 891). **χολήν** 'anger' (*Epitr.* 1126; Diphilus fr. 75; Ar. *Wasps* 403, *Thesm.* 468); literally 'bile' (cf. 416n.) **τήρ[ει δέ με]** 'and watch over me': the thought of the need for him to 'swallow' his anger leads Demeas to feel that he will need divine assistance to do so, and he accordingly turns back to Apollo to ask for this. The supplement proposed here is preferable to Austin's two suggestions (see apparatus) because τηρεῖν as an *intransitive* verb, at least in classical and early Hellenistic Greek, cannot govern a final clause with ἵνα + subjunctive (contrast Ar. *Wasps* 372, Isoc. 7.30, Arist. *Pol.* 1309b16–18, where it governs ὅπως + future indicative); for ἵνα + subjunctive after *transitive* τηρεῖν cf. [Dem.] 58.55 τηρητέον τοὺς ἐνθάδε παραβαίνοντας τοὺς νόμους...ἵνα μὴ δοκῆτε αὐτοὶ... συνειδέναι τι τούτοις ὧν πράττουσιν.

448 δέσποτ': cf. *Leukadia* 15 Arnott (Apollo of Leucas); Ar. *Wasps* 875 ὦ δέσποτ' ἄναξ γεῖτον Ἀγυιεῦ.

449 τὸν ὑμ[έν]αιον ᾄδειν: 125–6n. Demeas in his present mood will find it very hard to sing a song of rejoicing.   **εἰσανάγκασον:** a rare verb, probably attested otherwise only in Pl. *Tim.* 49a and Apollonius of Citium, *Comm. on Hippocr. On Joints* p. 72.2–3 Kollesch-Kudlien where it refers to forcing air into a bag through a tube. More frequent is ἐξαναγκάζειν (e.g. Ar. *Birds* 377; Soph. *El.* 620, *OC* 1179; Eur. *Or.* 1665).

450 [ἄ]ξ[ομ'] *sc.* τοὺς γάμους (681). Of alternative restorations, ᾄσομ' (Kamerbeek 1972: 386) would give excellent sense, but the traces of the second letter are consistent only with ξ or a mark of aspiration. Arnott 1998b: 16–17 proposed ἄρξομ', assuming that the ξ was at first omitted and then inserted above the line; if this is correct, the understood object will be τὸν ὑμέναιον.   <γάρ>, if correct, would come rather late in the sentence (fifth word); see 44n.   **ἀλλὰ τί;** 348n.

451 None of the proposed restorations at the start of this line is fully satisfactory. Jacques' supplement ('She won't come back') requires that Chrysis be understood as the subject of the sentence when she has not even been alluded to since 444; in any case, Demeas knows very well that Chrysis, whom he expelled by force, *would* come back if only he were willing to receive her. Sandbach's supplement ('Let anything happen now') would not be a true reflection of Demeas' feelings: he is very far from indifferent as to what is to happen now – he desperately desires that the marriage should go ahead and that Moschion's reputation should not be compromised. Dedoussi's [εἴθε μόνο]ν ἔλθοι 'I only wish he would come' has the drawback that Moschion has to be understood as the subject, and Demeas has made no mention of him; but Demeas' mind is focused on the wedding – Moschion's wedding – and the wedding cannot proceed without the bridegroom (Demeas is still unaware that Moschion has in fact returned and is only a few yards away from him). If a restoration on these lines is right, Demeas would probably look towards Eisodos A (with his back, therefore, to where Moschion and Nikeratos are standing) in the hope of seeing Moschion returning from the city centre.   **σὺ πρότερος... πρόσελθέ μου:** 421, 438–9nn. We need not suppose, with Sandbach, that Moschion and Nikeratos have been whispering to each other during Demeas' monologue. Nikeratos knows that Moschion too is appalled by Demeas' treatment of Chrysis, and can reasonably now, without preliminaries, ask him directly to approach his father. Both men will have wished to listen carefully to Demeas: his speech will have left them as mystified as ever about his motives, but they at least know (1) that he is still in a highly emotional state and (2) that he is determined to go ahead with the wedding.   **μου:** genitive of comparison, governed by πρότερος.

452–520 A connection has long been observed between this scene and the Theseus-Hippolytus scene in Euripides' *Hippolytus* (902–1101); see Introduction §6. Moschion the adopted son, like Hippolytus the bastard son, is condemned by his father for a sexual crime involving his stepmother (or equivalent) when there are facts that would exonerate him but about which he is unable to speak (in *Hippolytus* because he was deceived into taking an oath of secrecy, here because he dare not reveal the truth about Plangon and the baby); like Hippolytus too (see Katsouris 1975a: 132, Kovacs 1982: 46 n. 44, Sommerstein 1988: 34 n. 59), Moschion for a long time does not understand what he is being accused of (he is completely in the dark until Demeas tells him in 477 that he knows him to be the father of the baby, and it is only from Nikeratos' words in 507–17 that he will be able to infer that the mother is still assumed to be Chrysis, not Plangon) and as a result most of his attempts to clear himself only make things worse. This being a comedy, however, no irrevocable harm results, and although Demeas says at 521 that he will not listen to a word Moschion says, he violates this declaration immediately – and hears the truth.

452 [νὴ Δί']: Moschion must agree to Nikeratos' request; νὴ Δία is a regular formula for this purpose, and neatly fills the available space.
    Moschion now goes up to Demeas, who presumably turns round in surprise on hearing himself addressed as [ὦ π]άτερ: initially he will be pleased to see his son (and this will be made evident by the tone of his question ποῖα, Μοσχίων;), but his pleasure is of extremely short duration. **Μοσχίων:** Demeas addresses Moschion by name in this friendly question (cf. previous note) and at 459 and 465 when he is begging him to 'leave me alone'. Then, on the brink of losing control of himself, he says 'don't talk to me!' (466), and from that point on he never addresses his son by name again until he apologizes to him at 537.

453 διὰ τί Χρυσὶς οἴχετ' ἀπιοῦσ'; Moschion tactfully pretends to be unaware that Chrysis did not leave the house of her own volition, and makes no mention of the baby.

454–6 Demeas' first words (as far as δεινόν) are an 'aside' spoken to himself. Of the supplements proposed at the beginning of 454, δηλαδή 'evidently, apparently' is probably best; it is not usually placed first in its sentence, but cf. *Epitr.* 473, Eur. *Or.* 789. Austin's Ἡράκλεις (178n.) is also attractive, but may be just too long for the available space.

454 πρεσβεύεταί τις 'someone [i.e. Chrysis] is sending an emissary' (LSJ πρεσβεύω II 3); for the metaphorical use of this verb cf. *Perik.* 510, where

Polemon is begging Pataikos to intercede with Glykera on his behalf. Demeas still regards Chrysis as primarily responsible for the supposed intrigue, but now jumps to the conclusion that Moschion's intervention on her behalf shows him to be a willing accomplice of hers. He now not only avoids using Chrysis' name (265, 354nn.) but cannot bring himself to refer to her as ἡ Σαμία or even ἐκείνη (457), instead using an indefinite pronoun: before long (475) he will be referring to his son in the same way. πρός με: cf. 308, 719; πρὸς ἐμέ (B) would be inappropriate (contrast 479), since Demeas is not indignant because an emissary has been sent *to him*, but because he has been sent an emissary (he supposes) *by Chrysis*.

454-6 οὐχὶ σο[ν] | ... | ... [φλύ]αρος; : Demeas is now replying to Moschion's question of 453. In B these words are marked off by *dicola* at beginning and end, which here indicate change of addressee, not of speaker (see Introduction §13).

454-5 οὐχὶ σο[ν] ... | ... τοὔργον ἐστίν, ἀλλὰ παντελ[ῶς ἐμόν] 'that's no business of yours, it's entirely a matter for me'. Cf. *Aspis* 254 where Smikrines in similar language warns Chairestratos not to promise Kleostratos' sister in marriage to anyone (because she is an ἐπίκληρος and Smikrines has a legal right to marry her). In Soph. *El.* 1470, contrariwise, the disguised Orestes, ordered by Aegisthus to uncover the supposed corpse of Orestes, declines with the words οὐκ ἐμὸν τόδ᾽ ἀλλὰ σόν (Aegisthus being Orestes' kinsman).

456 [τίς ὁ φλύ]αρος; See 441n.: trying to conceal his terrible suspicions, Demeas affects to regard Moschion's concern for Chrysis as merely 'nonsensical' like that of the women slaves.   δεινὸν ἤδη: Demeas is now again speaking 'aside'. The addition of ἤδη indicates that he perceives the situation as having *now escalated* to a very serious level; cf. Ar. *Ach.* 315 (Dicaeopolis has not only made peace with the Spartans, but is even prepared to be an advocate for their cause!), *Wasps* 426 (the chorus are about to support Philocleon not merely with angry words, as hitherto, but with actual violence). It was bad enough when he had thought Moschion to be merely the victim of Chrysis' seductive wiles; now he is coming forward as her ally and agent!   συναδικεῖ: reversing his judgement of 328.   [τί φῄς;] The last thing preserved in this line in B (to be precise, in the Barcelona fragment) is a *dicolon* after ουτος, indicating that the lost final words of the line were spoken by Moschion; the restoration proposed by the first editors has been generally accepted. Moschion is of course assumed not to have heard Demeas' asides (cf. Bain 1977: 17); he is responding, uncomprehendingly, to the reply that Demeas had addressed to him (454-5) – and is entirely ignored by Demeas, who continues his train of thought (see next note) as though Moschion had not spoken.

457 [περιφα]νῶς goes very well with συναδικεῖ, being used frequently, especially in the orators, when a person is said to be manifestly guilty of some wrongdoing (e.g. Ar. *Wealth* 948, Andoc. 1.24, Lys. 16.8, [Dem.] 59.12); it is thus likely that Demeas is continuing his interrupted sentence, ignoring Moschion's question. For the continuation of a sentence over an interruption by another character cf. *Aspis* 355–6, *Dysk.* 751–2, Ar. *Frogs* 797–801. The alternative restoration [καταφα]νῶς (cf. καταφανῆ 500) is found, though less frequently, in similar contexts (e.g. Dem. 35.27, 42.30; Arist. *Probl.* 952b8); neither adverb appears elsewhere in Menander.

457–8 ἀσ[μένωι] | … γε[γονέναι] 'for he surely (δήπου) ought to have been pleased that this has happened': if, as Demeas had previously supposed, Moschion had been led astray by Chrysis and was an innocent party, he should have welcomed the expulsion of his corrupter from the house. With Sandbach's restoration this sentence follows on well from the preceding one (Moschion's action in approaching Demeas *on behalf* of Chrysis is the exact reverse of what one would have expected), and it also accounts for B's otherwise puzzling αυτῶ. For the construction ἀσμένωι (or ἀσμένηι) + dative (pro)noun + subject + verb cf. [Aesch.] *Prom.* 23–4 ἀσμένωι δέ σοι | ἡ ποικιλείμων νὺξ ἀποκρύψει φάος; Soph. *Trach.* 18–19; Eur. *Phoen.* 1043–6; Ar. *Peace* 582. Dedoussi's restoration, with ἀν[ακρινῶν] (punctuating at the end of 457, not after ἐκείνης) and γ' ε[ἰδέναι], gives good sense ('Why is he coming to inquire about her? He surely ought to know that [viz. the answer to his question]!'); but it requires the emendation of αυτῶ to αὐτόν, and αὐτόν is hardly likely to have been corrupted into a dative when on Dedoussi's view there was no other dative word in the sentence.

458 χρῆν, here a metrically necessary correction, occurs nowhere in the papyri of Menander, but is a likely emendation at *Aspis* 92 (χρη B). γε[γονέναι]: the gap in the papyrus is not long enough to accommodate this restoration, but Jacques plausibly supposed that the last three letters had been lost in B by haplography (from the middle Hellenistic period onwards νε and ναι were pronounced identically, as they are in modern Greek: Teodorsson 1977: 222–5, 253–5).

458–9 [τί τ]οὺς φίλους | προσδοκᾶις ἐρεῖν πυθομένους; 'What do you expect your friends will say when they find out?' This question implies that it was at least possible to argue that it was improper for a man to throw his partner into the street, even if she was an ex-*hetaira*, purely because she had disobeyed an instruction to expose their child, and that a man who acted thus might be embarrassed before public opinion. Demeas is indeed embarrassed by the question, but for a reason of which Moschion is unaware.

459–60 Of the restorations that have been proposed, those beginning with π[ροσδο]κῶ are much the best. Demeas begins to answer 'I expect my friends will…' and then realizes that he cannot complete his sentence without revealing what he 'knows' about Chrysis and Moschion, in the presence of Nikeratos (whom he will have seen as soon as he turned to face Moschion at 452); so he breaks off and tries to close down the discussion with ἔα με (see below). In the text as supplemented by Austin, μοι would be governed by the future infinitive (it might have been e.g. συμφήσειν) of which τοὺς φίλους would have been the subject if the sentence had not been aborted. In his subsequent responses to Moschion, Demeas several times again echoes his son's words (467, 468, 472, 481, 485). Alternative restorations mostly make Demeas say either 'Don't talk about my friends' (e.g. μ[ὴ λάλει] γ', ὦ Μοσχίων Jacques) or 'I don't care about my friends' (e.g. ο[ὐ προτι]μῶ, Μοσχίων Arnott): both, especially the latter, would bring Demeas dangerously close to asserting that he had no concern for his reputation – an attitude hardly consistent with his desperate anxiety to preserve the reputation of his son.

460 ἔα μ' 'let me be, leave me alone', desperately trying to induce Moschion to drop the subject of Chrysis for fear he will be forced to reveal what he is determined to keep secret; so again 465 *bis*, 470–1, and to the same effect 466 μή μοι διαλέγου.   **ἀγεννὲς ἂν ποι[οίη]ν ἐπιτρέπων** 'I'd be acting ignobly if I permitted it' (LSJ ἐπιτρέπω II 1). He cannot of course explain – certainly not in front of Nikeratos – *in what way* he would be acting ignobly (viz. betraying his own son, and Chrysis who had been the crucial figure in the plot to secure the child's future; cf. *Aspis* 304–5 προήσει τοὺς φίλους … οὕτως ἀγεννῶς;), and Demeas will understand him to be saying, monstrously, that he as Chrysis' lover has a moral duty to protect her from suffering the consequences of their affair. The adverb ἀγεννῶς will come to Moschion's lips again at 633, when he says – with very dubious justification – that he would be acting ignobly if he failed to punish Demeas for his unjust suspicions; this and the *Aspis* passage cited above are the only other places in Menander where ἀγεννής is used with reference to human behaviour (each time being applied not to an action but to a *failure* to act).

461–2 τοῦθ' | … | …δεινότερον: Demeas is yet further enraged at his son's audacity in presuming to lay down the law to him.

461 ὁρᾶ[θ';] With this restoration, Demeas will be addressing the audience, as at 447 (cf. also Ar. *Clouds* 1326, *Peace* 264, and see 488n.); with ὁρᾶ<ι>[ς], it has usually been supposed that he would be addressing himself (cf. Eur. *Med.* 404), though the singular form can in fact be used in addressing a group (Ar. *Thesm.* 496, 556; *Eccl.* 104). In either case one would normally expect Menander to insert a vocative (ἄνδρες, cf. 5n., or Δημέα, cf. 326, 349). If he is addressing the audience, however, he will be able to make it clear by gesture that he is doing so; and there is no instance of parenthetic ὁρᾶις in self-address in comedy.   [ὑ]περβολή 'the absolute extreme, the limit'; cf. Dem. 27.38 ταῦτ' οὐ μεγάλη καὶ περιφανὴς ἀναισχυντία; ταῦτ' οὐχ ὑπερβολὴ δεινῆς αἰσχροκερδείας;

462 τῶν δεινῶν... δεινό[τερο]ν: 438–9n. This is the last of Demeas' asides; henceforth, even when not actually addressing Moschion (473–5; note 476 τί δὲ λέγεις;), he makes no attempt to keep his thoughts private.

462–3 [ο]ὐ πάντα γὰρ | ἐπιτρέπειν ὀργῆι προσήκει: very true, and a cliché already in the time of Herodotus (3.36.1), but rather a presumptuous thing for a son to say to his father – and particularly galling to Demeas when he is in fact doing all he can to keep his anger under control.

463 ἐπιτρέπειν: here (cf. 460n.) 'yield to', 'give free rein to' (LSJ ἐπιτρέπω II 2; cf. Hdt. loc. cit., Pl. *Laws* 802b-c ταῖς... ἡδοναῖς καὶ ἐπιθυμίαις μὴ ἐπιτρέποντας ἀλλ' ἢ τισιν ὀλίγοις).   **Δημέα, καλῶς λέγει:** we probably already know enough about Nikeratos' character (29/30, 54nn.) to find humour in the fact that he chooses to second *this* particular statement by Moschion; from 492 (the very next time he speaks) until 584 he will be far outdoing Demeas in the unbridled displaying of anger.

464–6 Encouraged by Nikeratos' intervention, Moschion tells him to send Chrysis back home, not reflecting that he is thereby usurping from his father the role of master of the house (perhaps not the first time he has done so: 30–4n.). Demeas could well rejoin now, as he does a moment later (467–8), τῶν ἐμῶν οὐ κύριος ἔσομ' ἐγώ; Nikeratos does not fulfil Moschion's request; probably (so Dedoussi) he is moving towards his house to do so when Demeas' words πάντ' οἶδα (466) reveal to him that there is something relevant to the situation that *he* does not yet know, and he remains outside in the hope of discovering what this is.

464 ἀποτρέχειν 'come home', an idiomatic usage so long established that the verb's literal meaning had faded out completely; cf. *Aspis* 217, Ar. *Birds* 1162, 1549, Eubulus fr. 131, Alexis fr. 258.   **δεῦρ':** to be taken with ἀποτρέχειν, not with εἰσιών.   **εἰσιών** 'go in <to your house> and...'

465 Μοσχίων, ἔα μ', ἔα με, Μοσχίων: 459–460n. As in *Perik.* 506–7 (Γλυκέρα με καταλέλοιπε, καταλέλοιπέ με Γλυκέρα), the repetition (here with change of word order, at 470–1 without) indicates that the speaker is all but distraught; so again 535–6 ~ 540–1 where Nikeratos is made to repeat a ten-word sentence (with very complex changes to the word-order).

465–6 τρίτον λέγω | τουτογί: it is not clear whether this is to be taken as equivalent to a third ἔα με in quick succession, or whether it means in effect 'I have now said this three times' (viz. once in 460 and twice in 465). The former view is perhaps preferable, since 460 is now some distance back (there have been eight changes of speaker since then). For the emendation τουτογί cf. 172 [τ]αυτ[α]γί (if correctly restored).

466 πάντ' οἶδα 'I know all about it' (316n.). If what Demeas believed about Chrysis and Moschion were true, Moschion would certainly understand at once what he meant; as it is, he is completely baffled.   **ποῖα πάντα;** 'you know all about *what?*'   **μή μοι διαλέγου:** Demeas dare not answer the question, and in any case he still takes it for granted that Moschion knows the answer very well; so he again tries to break off the dialogue – though in comedy expressions of this type generally fail in that purpose (384, Ar. *Peace* 1061–2, *Frogs* 176).

467 ἀνάγκη: it is indeed an inescapable obligation for Moschion, because the future of his son is at stake. This time it is Demeas' turn to have no idea what Moschion means.   **ἀνάγκη;** 459–60n.

467–8 τῶν ἐμῶν οὐ κύριος | ἔσομ' ἐγώ; 464n. He may also be making an allusion (which he assumes Moschion will understand) to the 'fact' that Moschion, by consorting with Chrysis, has grossly infringed his rights as her κύριος. Cf. Eur. *Hel.* 1631–5 where Theoclymenus, about to put his sister Theonoe to death for 'giving my [intended] wife [Helen] to another' (1634), is obstructed by a courageous slave who says Theonoe gave Helen τοῖς ... κυριωτέροις, and rejoins κύριος δὲ τῶν ἐμῶν τίς; (1635), to which the slave replies 'The one to whom her father gave her.'

468 ταύτην ἐμοὶ δὸς τὴν χάριν: it is very bad tactics for Moschion to request the restoration of Chrysis as a favour *after* repeatedly speaking (458–9, 460, 462–3) in ways that amounted to accusing his father of doing her a wrong – though the request would have been futile in any case.   **ποίαν χάριν;** 'favour indeed!', 'a colloquial way of quoting the previous speaker's words with indignation or contempt' (Olson 2002 on Ar. *Ach.* 62–3), cf. 513, Ar. *Ach.* 109, *Knights* 162, *Lys.* 922.

469–70 'The way you expect *me* to quit my house and leave the two of you [Moschion and Chrysis] in possession!' This is not mere sarcasm: from Demeas' point of view Moschion's attitude only makes sense if he and Chrysis are in league, and later he will again speak of the pair in the second person plural (481) and describe them as conspirators (474–5). And Moschion has already once spoken (464) as if the house belonged to him. Moschion may possibly (so Lamagna) understand Demeas' words as meaning that since he cannot endure living in the same house as Chrysis, to demand Chrysis' return to the house is tantamount to demanding that Demeas leave it.

469 οἷον, as an adverb, may introduce any exclamatory sentence; cf. Ar. *Ach.* 321, *Knights* 367, 703, *Wasps* 901, 1328, *Thesm.* 704.

470–1 τοὺς γάμους … | … ἔα με ποιεῖν: 459–460, 465–6nn.

471 ἂν ἔχῃς νοῦν: 187n.

472 Moschion now retreats to the more modest request that Chrysis should be allowed to attend the wedding celebrations – though as 473 shows, he still hopes that this will merely be a stepping-stone to her permanent restoration.   <ἡμῖν>: metre shows that two syllables (– ×) have been lost, and B's χρυσιδ', with its elision, shows that the first of these syllables began with a vowel. Austin's supplement is supported by συμπαρεῖναι,

473 ἕνεκα σοῦ: Moschion knows how deeply Demeas had been in love with Chrysis (21–4, 81–2) and thinks that he may bitterly regret the breach with her when it becomes too late to heal it – and we already know what a blow the breach has been to him (349–56, 450). And, as ever, he is also thinking of the baby, who, after the wedding, will be not only his own legitimate son but also Demeas' legitimate grandson and ultimate heir. But by Demeas this assertion – made by the son whom he believes to have unurped his bed, on behalf of his supposed paramour – will be seen as a blatant falsehood and a crowning impudence.   γνώριμα: 267n.

474 μαρτύρομαί σε: usually in Old Comedy (e.g. Ar. *Wasps* 1436, *Peace* 1119), and at least once in Menander (576), μαρτύρομαι is a call to anyone present to bear witness (in a future trial) that the speaker has been wronged (typically by physical assault). When used to invoke *divine* witnesses, the word most often serves to confer on a statement the solemnity of an oath (Men. frr. 53, 884 – in the latter passage, as here, the god invoked is Apollo); here, however, the implicit request to Apollo seems to be that he punish those who are wronging Demeas, and the call would be tantamount to a curse on his son were it not that Apollo, being a god (and one who would not testify to a falsehood: Aesch. *Eum.* 615, Pl. *Apol.* 21b), presumably knows that Moschion and Chrysis are innocent. Λοξία: addressing the pillar of Apollo Agyieus (309, 444nn.). Λοξίας as a name for Apollo is very frequent in tragedy but rare in comedy (Ar. *Knights* 1047, 1072, *Wealth* 8, all referring to oracles; Mnesimachus fr. 1). In Men. fr. 893 (cf. also perhaps the corrupt fr. 44) this name is used, as here, in reference to Apollo Agyieus, and according to Photius (λ 395; *Bibl.* 535b33–8, citing Helladius of Antinoopolis) this was regular practice. Demeas in this act, in contrast with Nikeratos (495ff), does not dress up his indignation in paratragic language, and probably his use of the name here is merely an instance of the practice reported by Photius. The name Λοξίας has often been associated with λοξός 'oblique' and taken to refer to the indirectness and ambiguity of Apollo's oracles; such an allusion would be appropriately ironic in a scene in which almost every utterance has been misinterpreted by its addressee, but this etymology of Λοξίας was apparently unknown to Menander's younger contemporary Cleanthes the Stoic (*SVF* I 542) and the adjective λοξός is not applied to oracles or prophecies before Lycophron's *Alexandra* (14, 1467).

475 τοῖς ἐμοῖς ἐχθροῖς: i.e. Chrysis; on this 'generalizing' or 'allusive' plural see Katsouris 1977: 231–2, and cf. e.g. Soph. *El.* 652 φίλοισί τε ξυνοῦσαν οἷς ξύνειμι νῦν (i.e. with Aegisthus).   τις: 454n.; he cannot, in the presence of Nikeratos, identify Moschion as the guilty party.   καὶ διαρραγήσομαι 'I'm positively going to burst!' (for this use of καί see Denniston 1954: 320–1). In 519 Nikeratos, having been asked by Demeas to consider himself also a wronged party (συναδικοῦ, 518), will in his turn feel on the point of bursting with rage; cf. also Ar. *Knights* 340 where Paphlagon is infuriated because his opponent insists on being first to speak.

476 τί δὲ λέγεις; Moschion has heard what Demeas has just said (462n.) but cannot understand what he means (neither can the intently listening Nikeratos).   βούλει φράσω σοι; This colloquial construction (βούλει or βούλεσθε + first person subjunctive) occurs only here in Menander but is frequent in Old Comedy (e.g. Ar. *Knights* 36, *Birds* 813–14, *Lys.* 821; Cratinus fr. 270; Phrynichus com. fr. 9; Plato com. fr. 19).   δεῦρο δή: Demeas moves well away from Nikeratos, and beckons Moschion to follow him; Moschion has joined Demeas before he says λέγε. Nikeratos does not hear what Demeas and Moschion say to each other until Demeas' self-control finally snaps at 480–1.

477 ἀλλ' ἐγώ (sc. ἐρῶ) 'all right, I will' (cf. 733 – the only other surviving instance of this formula).   τὸ παιδίον σόν ἐστιν: having told Moschion this, Demeas assumes that Moschion now understands him to know the full 'truth', namely that he (Moschion) and Chrysis are the child's parents. And Moschion does indeed understand Demeas to know the full truth – this being, however, that he (Moschion) and *Plangon* are the child's parents. Hence the disastrous misunderstandings continue, only now they are a different set of misunderstandings (corresponding exactly to the mutual misunderstandings of Demeas and Parmenon in 316–21).

478 τοῦ συνειδότος τὰ κρυπτά, Παρμένοντος: in fact, Parmenon's admissions had only confirmed what Demeas had already learned with virtual certainty from other sources: his false statement that the baby's mother was Chrysis (314) passed unchallenged, since Demeas had no evidence that contradicted it and some evidence (265–6) that seemed to support it. Menander may here be planting a false scent in preparation for Act V.

Moschion now knows that Parmenon betrayed his secret, and many spectators may expect that he will later punish, or threaten to punish, Parmenon for this. Nothing of the kind happens. Moschion will in fact strike Parmenon (677–9), but for a completely different reason; and he will in fact attempt to get his own back for what he is now about to undergo – but from Demeas, not Parmenon (619–22, 633–8). **μηκέτι:** there is little to choose between this and ὥστε μή as corrections of B's unmetrical reading; but μηκέτι contributes more to the sense, by more clearly implying that up to now Moschion *has* been trying to fool Demeas.

479 πρὸς ἐμέ: 454n.; here, however, the emphatic pronoun has a point to it – Moschion has not merely been attempting a deception, he has been attempting a deception *of his father*.   **ἔπειτά σ' ἀδικεῖ Χρυσίς...;** This question, and Moschion's next, ought to have made Demeas aware that there was more to the situation than he yet knew. The mere fact that Moschion was the father of the child could not by itself absolve Chrysis from all guilt; that would require an additional fact, either (1) that Moschion had raped Chrysis (not seduced her, or been seduced by her), or (2) that nothing at all had happened between them and Chrysis was not the child's mother. Possibility (2) does not occur to Demeas, but as eventually becomes clear when he begs Nikeratos to expel Chrysis also (518), he does not believe (1) either. In other words, he is so certain that Moschion and Chrysis are both guilty that he fails to perceive that if they were, Moschion would have to be not merely wicked but insane to put his questions in the way he does.

480 ἀλλὰ τίς; σύ; 'Then who *is* the guilty party? You?' – i.e. 'Does that mean that you're taking the whole blame on yourself?' (cf. 482). Moschion, assuming that the reference is to his rape of Plangon, is of course perfectly ready to take the whole blame on himself, as he has done from the start (50–3).   **τί** 'in what respect?'   **γάρ** '<yes,> for' (Denniston 1954: 73–4).   **τί φῇς;** Demeas' anger at last defeats his determination to ensure that Nikeratos does not know what has happened, and he raises his voice to a shout (cf. 481 τί βοᾷς;). Moschion's insistence that Chrysis has done nothing wrong, and his casual acceptance of his own responsibility without an explicit word (leaving it to be implied by the assentient γάρ) or any apparent awareness that he is confessing to a very grave wrong against his father, have made it seem to Demeas that he is utterly shameless and have provoked him beyond endurance.

481 οὐδὲν ἐνθυμεῖσθε; 'Are you two [Moschion and Chrysis] completely without scruple?'. This use of ἐνθυμεῖσθαι (for which cf. Thuc. 5.32.1, 7.18.2) is to be connected with the noun ἐνθύμιον (e.g. Hdt. 8.54, Thuc. 5.16.1), which denotes 'the anxious anticipation of evil [particularly though not

exclusively] in consequence of evil deeds' (Parker 1983: 252–4). Once
again (cf. 470, 474–5) Demeas treats the supposedly guilty pair as a unit.
In B οὐδεν has been written twice, and there are *dicola* at the end of 480 and
after the first ουδεν: accordingly some early editors treated οὐδέν as Moschion's reply to τί φῄς; But Moschion would then be withdrawing his claim
that Chrysis was innocent, and 482 makes it clear that he has not done so.
Sandbach pointed out that the *dicolon* after ουδεν looks as though it had
been squeezed in after the letters had been written, and suggested that the
two *dicola* were inserted in an attempt to make an intelligible dialogue out
of the corrupt and unmetrical text with the duplicated οὐδέν.   ὅ τι βοῶ:
304n.   κάθαρμα σύ 'you piece of filth', literally, 'something removed by
cleansing'. The term occurs only here in Menander; cf. Ar. *Wealth* 454,
fr. 686; Eupolis fr. 384.8; *com. adesp.* 860; Dem. 18.128, 21.185; Aeschines
3.211. There may be a reminiscence (with comic lowering of register) of
Eur. *Hipp.* 959 (Theseus to Hippolytus) ὦ κάκιστε σύ (Katsouris 1975a:
134).

482 ἀναδέχει τὴν αἰτίαν: cf. Pl. *Hipp.Mi.* 365d ἀναδεχόμενος τὴν αἰτίαν; Dem.
19.36 ἀναδεχόμενος καὶ εἰς αὐτὸν ποιούμενος τὰ τούτων ἁμαρτήματα.

483 εἰπέ μοι: 170n. It is better to associate the phrase with the preceding sentence rather than with the following one, since it never begins any
but a very short sentence in Menander (Arnott 1998b: 17).   ἐμβλέπων
ἐμοί: it was a mark of shamelessness to (be able to) look someone in the
face while saying, or after having done, something disgraceful (312n., 519;
Men. fr. 821; *com. adesp.* 1017.41–3; Soph. *Phil.* 110, *OT* 1371–4).

484 This is the only trochaic tetrameter in Menander which does not
have a word-break (diaeresis) after its second *metron* (the point at which it
should have come falls in the middle of the word ἀπεγνω|κώς). Menander
has created this metrical abnormality 'to picture Demeas' seething mind'
(Sandbach *ap.* Austin 1969: 168).   ἀπεγνωκώς με τυγχάνεις; 'have you
really repudiated me?'; Moschion seems to be acting as though he no
longer recognized Demeas as his father. For ἀπεγνωκώς cf. Dem. 6.16 οὔτ'
ἂν εἰ νῦν ἀπεγίγνωσκε Θηβαίους: for this use of τυγχάνω cf. *Epitr.* 658–9 τοῦτο
μὲ[ν π]οήσω καὶ σχεδὸν | δεδογμένον μοι τυγχάνει 'That [taking my daughter
away from her husband] is what I'm going to do, and I've actually pretty
much made up my mind to do it.'   ἐγώ; Moschion becomes more and
more baffled.

485 διὰ τί; Understand τοῦτο λέγεις.   τὸ πρᾶγμα: Moschion means 'the
rape or seduction of an unmarried girl, provided it is followed by a confession and an offer of marriage'. See Introduction §5. But Demeas will take
him to mean 'the usurpation of one's father's bed'.

486 οὐ πάνδεινον: 438–9n.

486–7 μυρίοι... | τοῦτο πεποήκασιν: cf. Ter. *HT* 956–7 *quid ego tantum sceleris admisi miser? volgo faciunt; Ad.* 686–8 *virginem vitiasti... | iam id peccatum primum sane magnum, at humanum tamen: | fecere alii saepe item boni.* Moschion's statement is certainly true in the world of New Comedy plots; how true it was in real life we cannot tell, but there is reason to doubt whether it was very common for marriages to originate in this way. That speakers in the Athenian courts do not refer to such episodes in their own family histories is not surprising; but it may be significant that they do not refer to such episodes in their *opponents'* family histories, either. (A different view was taken in Sommerstein 1998: 112 n. 14; cf. also Brown 1993: 196–8.).

487 τοῦ θράσους: 429n.; cf. Ar. *Knights* 693 μορμώ, τοῦ θράσους. In 330–3 Demeas had reasoned that if Moschion had been a guilty party in the supposed affair with Chrysis, he would have continued to show himself θρασύς: now this judgement appears to be vindicated – Moschion has been proved (and confessed himself) guilty, and he is displaying extreme θράσος.

487–8 ἐναντίον | ... τῶν παρόντων: in effect 'before witnesses'. When something was done or said which might later be the subject of legal proceedings or have other grave consequences, it was common to call on anyone present (οἱ παρόντες) to be witnesses to the event; cf. Lys. 7.20, Isoc. 20.1, Isaeus 5.6, also *com. adesp.* 1032.24 (on which see Arnott 1996b: 836–7, 843–4), where a spokesman for a group (the chorus??) to whom such an appeal has been made (lines 17–20) speaks of the group as ἡμεῖς γ' οἱ παρόντες ἐνθάδε. In our passage the only person actually present is Nikeratos, but Demeas will doubtless have made an expansive gesture which would include anyone who might happen to be passing in the street – and would also include the theatre audience (446–7n.). By raising his voice at 480–1 he had *inadvertently* risked making the scandal public: he has now reached the stage at which he is prepared to do so *knowingly*.

488 δή: for the positioning of this particle at the start of a line of stichic verse, the only (near) parallel is Soph. *Aj.* 985–6 οὐχ ὅσον τάχος | δῆτ' αὐτὸν ἄξεις δεῦρο, an urgent order prompted by the information that the child Eurysaces has been left alone and in peril of being seized by his father's enemies. Here it presumably serves as a further marker of Demeas' agitation (446–7, 461–2, 465, 475, 480nn.), which is now so extreme as to make him entirely forget his earlier determination to keep Moschion's disgrace a secret (see previous note).

488–9 ἐκ τίνος τὸ παιδίον | ἐστί σοι; Demeas is of course asking this question not for information (he already knows the answer, or so he thinks) but to put Moschion to public shame, whether he answers or refuses to answer. He will quickly regret doing so (500).

489 Νικηράτωι τοῦτ' εἶπον: Demeas assumes, rightly (502–5), that if Nikeratos learns about Moschion's affair with Chrysis he will refuse to have him for a son-in-law, and assumes also that Moschion will think likewise. In fact, as we shall see in a moment (492ff), Nikeratos has come to an understanding of the situation (subject to the same misapprehension that Demeas himself is under) without needing to be told.   **εἶπον:** imperative of the weak aorist εἶπα: cf. *Dysk.* 410, Men. fr. 447, Pl. *Men.* 71d.

490 δεινόν: 438–9n.

490–1 Moschion is indeed terrified of the prospect of confessing to Nikeratos, but for an entirely different reason. This remark is an aside, not heard by either Nikeratos or Demeas.

490 νὴ Δί': despite the position of ἀλλά, this oath must be taken as emphasizing the sentence δεινὸν … λέγειν με ('indeed it *will* be terrible' tr. Arnott), since there is nothing in what Demeas has just said with which Moschion can at this point be expressing agreement; the comma printed after νὴ Δί' by most editors is thus potentially misleading, and has here been omitted. Cf. Ar. *Lys.* 927 (Κι.) ἀλλ' οὐδὲ δέομ' ἔγωγε. (Μυ.) νὴ Δί' ἀλλ' ἐγώ ('but *I do!*'). **οὕτω** should be taken with τοῦτο πρὸς τοῦτον λέγειν με in the sense 'just like that, without more ado' (Ar. *Wasps* 634, *Frogs* 625; Soph. *Ant.* 315, *Phil.* 1067; Eur. *Alc.* 680, *Heracl.* 374; Dem. 1.20). Moschion always knew that he would eventually have to confess the truth about the baby to Nikeratos; but to do so, at a moment's notice, *before* he is married to Plangon, is an appalling prospect.

491 χαλεπανεῖ: cf. 80. Moschion's apprehensions then, about Demeas' reaction to the proposed marriage, were mistaken; his apprehensions now about Nikeratos will be shared by Demeas (549) after he has learned who the baby's mother really is – and will prove to be mistaken also, but in the opposite direction, as Nikeratos' rage, far from being confined to angry words or even screaming (549 κεκράξεται), becomes a threat to several lives.

492 Nikeratos has now realized (no doubt from Demeas' question in 488–9) what Moschion is being accused of. He moves across to where father and son are arguing, confronts Moschion (to whom, or at whom, he is mostly speaking until 505), and bursts out with a ferocious denunciation, couched from the start in paratragic terms. Since we know that this diatribe is entirely based on a misapprehension, its extravagant tone adds a farcical element to the scene even while it increases yet further the pressure on Moschion; at the same time, primed by Moschion's fears just expressed, we wonder how Nikeratos will react when he discovers the actual truth. **ὦ κάκιστ' ἀνδρῶν:** cf. Eur. *Med.* 488, Soph. *Phil.* 974 (also Eur. fr. 472e.32 ὦ κάκιστ'(α) ἀνδρῶν φρονῶν); the phrase is not otherwise attested in comedy. In Euripides' *Hippolytus* Theseus, believing Phaedra's false allegation, twice calls Hippolytus κάκιστος (*Hipp.* 945, 959) and is afterwards himself called ὦ κάκιστε σύ by Artemis (1316). **ὑπονοεῖν ... ἄρχομαι:** if he is only 'just (μόλις 493) beginning to suspect/guess' what has happened, is he not exploding a little prematurely? Contrast Demeas' repeated assertions that he 'knows' the facts (466, 477).

493 τὴν τύχην καὶ τἀσέβημα 'the impious act', a poetic hendiadys of a kind alien to comedy. The use of τύχη in the sense 'action, event' is itself typically tragic (e.g. Eur. *Alc.* 137, *HF* 1116, *Or.* 1550); ἀσέβημα, on the other hand, while common in Attic prose from Antiphon (5.91, 93) onwards, occurs nowhere in archaic or classical poetry. **ποτέ** 'at length' (53, 335–7nn.).

494 Another aside, commenting on the implications of what Nikeratos has said. **τέλος ἔχω** 'I'm finished, I'm done for'; cf. 548 τέλος ἔχει 'it's all over'; probably derived from the fourth-century usage of τέλος ἔχειν = 'die' (Alexis fr. 145.16, Pl. *Laws* 772b–c). **τοίνυν** 'in that case', 'if that's so'. **νῦν αἰσθάνει ...;** When Nikeratos last spoke (463) it was to endorse Moschion's rebuke of Demeas for yielding too easily to anger; *now*, says Demeas, Nikeratos surely recognizes that his anger was justified. Demeas still seems content to let the scandal become public knowledge (488–9n.).

495–7 Continuing to speak in wild paratragic vein, Nikeratos absurdly claims that Moschion's supposed crime surpasses the worst sexual wickednesses of mythology. As elsewhere in the play (337n.), the highly relevant story of Hippolytus and Phaedra is conspicuous by its absence.

495 οὐ γάρ; '<Yes,> for <do I> not?' (480n.), i.e. 'I certainly do'; cf. Ar. *Birds* 610–1 (Ευ.) πολλῶι κρείττους οὗτοι τοῦ Διὸς ἡμῖν βασιλεύειν. (Πε.) οὐ γὰρ πολλῶι; **πάνδεινον:** 438–9n.

495–7 ὦ ... | ... | ... ποιήσας 'you who have made the debaucheries of Tereus and Oedipus and Thyestes and those of all the rest, all that we get to hear of as having happened, <seem> petty'. This elaborate participial vocative is extremely long even by tragic standards; the longest such expressions in Euripides, for example, run to about two iambic trimeters at the most (e.g. *Ion* 1512–14).

495 Τηρέως: Tereus, king of Thrace, married the Athenian princess Procne; later Procne asked him to fetch her sister Philomela from Athens to keep her company. On the journey, Tereus raped Philomela, and then cut out her tongue to prevent her revealing the crime; but Philomela managed to inform Procne by weaving the story into a garment (either in letters or in pictures), and the sisters took revenge on Tereus by killing Procne's son Itys and then tricking his father into eating his flesh. The story was dramatized in Sophocles' *Tereus* (see Fitzpatrick and Sommerstein 2006). λέχη: λέχος (literally, 'bed') is a purely poetic word which in tragedy can refer to any sexual relationship, including marriage.

496 Οἰδίπου: in Sophocles' *Oedipus Tyrannus*, Oedipus' incestuous marriage is repeatedly spoken of with more horror even than his parricide (*OT* 362–7, 457–60, 791–3, 1207–15, 1256–7, 1288–9, 1403–8). **Θυέστου:** Thyestes seduced Aërope, the wife of his brother Atreus; on discovering this, Atreus took revenge on Thyestes by treacherously inviting him to a feast at which he was served with the flesh of his two sons. Later, in exile, Thyestes (according to the most common account) raped his own daughter (having been told by an oracle that only thus could he beget a son who would avenge him), and she became the mother of Aegisthus, the future murderer of Atreus' son Agamemnon. Various parts of the story were dramatized in three plays of Sophocles and one of Euripides, and, like that of Oedipus, it became very popular in fourth-century tragedy (Arist. *Poet.* 1453a11; we know of at least six tragedies entitled *Thyestes* from that century). For the myth and its variants see Gantz 1993: 545–52.

496–7 ὅσα | γεγονόθ' ἡμῖν ἔστ' ἀκοῦσαι: literally, 'as many as it is possible for us to hear have occurred': ὅσα is the subject of an accusative + participle construction governed by ἀκοῦσαι. Athenians would 'hear' these stories told mainly in tragedy (cf. 589–90 οὐκ ἀκήκοας λεγόντων ... | τῶν τραγωιδῶν κτλ.; referring to the Danaë myth). The corruption γεγονασ' in B may be due to a misplaced supralinear variant (ἡμ)ᾶς for ἡμῖν in an earlier copy; Handley's emendation ὅσα γέγον', ὅσ' ἡμῖν ἔστ' ἀκοῦσαι is palaeographically neat, but Nikeratos is not trying to catalogue all the sexual crimes that had ever occurred (an impossible task) but those which myth had made memorable.

497 ἐγώ; This single weak word of protest is probably the only thing Moschion says out loud (his words at 494 and 515 are spoken aside) between the intervention of Nikeratos at 492 and his exit at 520.

498 τοῦτ' ἐτόλμησας σὺ πρᾶξαι: normal comic Greek, though elsewhere applied to words rather than actions (e.g. 483; Ar. *Ach.* 311, 558, 577). τοῦτ' [ἔ]τλης: *τλάω (ἔτλην, τέτληκα), on the other hand, while it was part of the language of Old Comedy (e.g. Ar. *Clouds* 119, 1387; *Thesm.* 544), is not otherwise found in Middle or New Comedy; in tragedy cf. e.g. Eur. *Med.* 796, 1328, 1339–40, *IT* 617, 862, 924.

Nikeratos now turns to Demeas; there is a *dicolon* in B, indicating change of addressee (not of speaker).

499–500 Ἀμύντορος | ... | ἐκτυφλῶσαι: alluding to the story of Amyntor and his son Phoenix, specifically the version found in Euripides' *Phoenix* (343–7n.), in which Phoenix was blinded by his father (Eur. fr. 816; cf. Ar. *Ach.* 421, [Apoll.] *Bibl.* 3.13.8) for having raped the latter's concubine; but Nikeratos forgets that in Euripides' play Phoenix was in fact innocent of this crime ([Apoll. loc. cit.; schol. A *Iliad* 9.453). Possibly he is confusing Euripides' version of the tale with Homer's (*Iliad* 9.447–80), in which Phoenix does sleep with his father's concubine (at his mother's urging); his father imprisons him (until he manages to escape) and curses him with childlessness, but he is certainly not blinded (cf. e.g. *Iliad* 16.196, 23.359–61), and indeed there is no evidence that blinding figured in any version of the story before Euripides. If Demosthenes (19.246) is to be believed, *Phoenix* was not a favourite play for revivals in the mid-fourth century.

500 διὰ σὲ τούτωι γέγονε πάν[τ]α καταφανῆ: Demeas makes no reply to Nikeratos, but instead rebukes Moschion for having made it possible for Nikeratos to learn about his supposed affair with Chrysis; cf. 706–8, where Demeas complains that Moschion is giving publicity to his father's 'error' of wrongly suspecting him. His present accusation seems somewhat unjust, since but for certain utterances of Demeas' own (480, 492nn.) Nikeratos would still have no idea what he and Moschion were quarrelling about, and he has recently himself been actively seeking to put Nikeratos in the picture (489, 494); he may now be beginning to realize that this was an error in view of Nikeratos' fiery personality, and be seeking to shift the blame to Moschion for having provoked him by acting as Chrysis' advocate.

501 Nikeratos turns back to Moschion.   **τίνος** might in principle be feminine ('from what woman?') or neuter ('from what crime?'). The former interpretation fits better with 502: if Moschion is so little in control of his sexual appetite that he will seduce or rape even his father's partner, there is a serious risk that in his pursuit of other women he will neglect his wife (cf. *Epitr.* 749–55, 793–6). For ἀπέχομαι in this connection cf. *Epitr.* 1060–1 τοιαυτησὶ γὰρ οὐκ ἀπέσχετ' ἄν | ἐκεῖνος ... ἐγὼ δ' ἀφέξομαι. **ποῖον** might possibly stand on its own, meaning 'what sort of thing?' (cf. Ar. *Wasps* 762), in which case Austin's [ἐργάσαι' ἔ]τι would be acceptable; but it would be more normal for it to have a noun to qualify, and Arnott's [αἰσχύνοις λ]έχ[ος] (cf. 507) is thus attractive. The surviving traces of the tops of one or two letters of the final word are extremely scanty.

502 εἶτ' 'in view of that'.

503 πρότερον 'sooner', i.e. 'rather'.   εἰς κόλπον δέ, φασί: sc. πτύω. With
these words Nikeratos spits into his bosom, an action well described by
Rusten 1993: 113 n. c as 'the ancient equivalent of knocking on [UK
'touching'] wood' which was done to avert superstitious dangers of various kinds (e.g. at the sight of a madman or epileptic, Thphr. *Char.* 16.14;
on speaking or thinking boastfully, Theocr. 6.34–40, with Gow 1950 ad
loc.; to drive away an unwanted suitor, Theocr. 20.11). Here the danger to
be avoided is that by mentioning the possibility of having Diomnestus for a
son-in-law, Nikeratos may cause that unwelcome prospect to become a real-
ity. For the ellipse of πτύω, typical of proverbial expressions, cf. e.g. *Mis.*
295 S = 696 A ὄνος λύρας (sc. ἤκουε).   φασί, like τὸ λεγόμενον (11n.), signals that the phrase is idiomatic or proverbial; cf. *Epitr.* 440 (ἀγνὴ γάμων),
Perik. 291 (ταῦτα…εὔχθω).   τὴν αδ[: Lloyd-Jones (*ap.* Austin) was probably right to restore here a reference to the goddess Adrasteia: to 'make
obeisance to Adrasteia' (τὴν Ἀδράστειαν προσκυνεῖν) was another means of
averting superstitious dangers, especially those arising from speech (*Perik.*
304; [Aesch.] *Prom.* 936; Pl. *Rep.* 451a; [Dem.] 25.37; cf. Men. fr. 226; [Eur.]
Rhes. 342, 468, Herodas 6.34–6). She is directly linked by Lucian (*Apol.* 6)
with apotropaic spitting: 'Adrasteia seemed to be standing over you…and
mocking you…because you were seeing fit to accuse [others] without first
spitting into your bosom.' In this role Adrasteia was sometimes replaced by,
or paired with, Nemesis (Men. fr. 226; Nicostratus com. fr. 35; Alciphron
Epist. 4.6.5).

504 ἐπί 'in the power of, dependent on': cf. Thuc. 6.22 μὴ ἐπὶ ἑτέροις γίγ-
νεσθαι, μάλιστα δὲ χρήματα αὐτόθεν…ἔχειν.   Διομνήστωι: this Diomnestus (*LGPN* 10) is otherwise unknown, but was evidently a contemporary,
since otherwise Nikeratos would not have thought it necessary to take
ritual precautions (503n.) against the risk of actually getting him as his
son-in-law. This rules out the suggestion (Dedoussi 1970: 167–8) that the
reference is to one Diomnestus of Eretria, supposed to have lived at the
time of the Persian wars (Heracleides Ponticus fr. 58 Wehrli). We cannot
tell what was objectionable about our Diomnestus, though the phrase ἐπὶ
Διομνήστωι γενοίμην (see previous note) suggests that he may have been
accused of practising blackmail or extortion on his father-in-law.   νυμφίωι: here 'son-in-law' as in *Dysk.* 795. If Austin's supplement [γὼ πενθερός]
(*vel sim.*) is correct, it will be another paratragic touch: πενθερός 'father-in-
law' was not a classical Attic word ([Dem.] 43.57 is cited from an archaic
law) but is found several times in tragedy (Soph. *OC* 1302, fr. 305; Eur. *El.*
1286, *HF* 14, 484).

505 ὁμολογουμένην ἀτυχίαν is a so-called 'accusative in apposition
to the sentence' (Smyth 1956: 268), more accurately an 'internal
acc[usative]…specifying that in which the action of a verb consists or

results' (Barrett 1964: 307): in this case the action of putting oneself in the power of Diomnestus as son-in-law will constitute, or result in, 'what all agree to be ill-fortune' (with this expression cf. Thuc. 6.89.6 (Alcibiades to the Spartans on democracy) ἀλλὰ περὶ ὁμολογουμένης ἀνοίας οὐδὲν ἂν καινὸν λέγοιτο).

505–6 ταῦ[τ   ] | ἠδικημένος κατεῖχον: is Demeas speaking to Moschion or to Nikeratos? Probably the latter, since Nikeratos in the second half of 506 seems to be replying to him and criticizing his attitude. In that case Demeas will most likely here be explaining to Nikeratos why he did not tell Chrysis the true reason for her expulsion, having realized that Nikeratos must have been misinformed about it by Chrysis and that otherwise he would never have joined Moschion in appealing for her to be taken back (463–4). Of the restorations proposed Arnott's is the best, since if Demeas were to admit to Nikeratos that he had suppressed the facts about Moschion's conduct in order to enable the marriage to go ahead, Nikeratos would be extremely (and justifiably) angry with him for his deception.

506 ἀνδράποδ[ον]: i.e. one 'who when wronged and treated like dirt is unable [or unwilling] to defend himself' (Callicles in Pl. *Gorg.* 483b, contrasting the behaviour of an ἀνδράποδον with that of an ἀνήρ (cf. 512)) – like a slave, who had no choice but to endure whatever treatment his master inflicted on him.

507–13 For Nikeratos this is an unusually elaborate sentence (Sandbach 1970: 121) – 'a measure of the strength of his indignation' (Ireland 1981: 187); but the mixture of paratragic and colloquial styles in it is thoroughly typical of him, as are the talk of selling a free woman (and perhaps also a male citizen) into slavery (509nn.), and the absurd description of Moschion's supposed crime as 'murder' (513n.).

507 ἐμὸν ἤισ[χυνε λέ]κτρον: cf. Eur. *Hipp.* 944 ἤισχυνε τἀμὰ λέκτρα. Both the word λέκτρον and the omission of the article are features of tragic language; λέκτρον occurs ninety-nine times in the thirty-two extant tragedies, in comedy only here.

507–8 οὐκ ἂν εἰς ἄλλον ποτὲ | ὕβρισ' (sc. Μοσχίων) is reminiscent of the words of Achilles in *Iliad* 1.232 (echoed by Thersites, 2.242) ἦ γὰρ ἄν, Ἀτρεΐδη, νῦν ὕστατα λωβήσαιο. Hippolytus' alleged rape of his stepmother Phaedra is spoken of as ὕβρις in Eur. *Hipp.* 1073 and probably in two fragments of the lost *Hippolytos Kalyptomenos* (Eur. frr. 437, 438).

508 οὐδ' ἡ συγ[κλ]ιθεῖσα 'nor would she who lay with him'. The verb συγκλίνομαι is rare even in tragedy (only Eur. *Alc.* 1090). **παλλακήν:** παλλακή was the regular term (Men. fr. 411; Ar. *Wasps* 1353; Cratinus fr. 279, of Aspasia; Strattis fr. 3; Lys. 1.31; Isaeus 3.39; [Dem.] 59.118, 122) for a woman (usually free, but cf. Ant. 1.14) who lived with a man in a more or less permanent relationship but was not married to him (usually because she was not a citizen); it was clearly differentiated from (γαμετὴ) γυνή (130n.) – though Demeas will call Chrysis his γυνή at 561 – and rather less clearly from ἑταίρα, since a παλλακή might often, like Chrysis, be a professional *hetaira* who had chosen to enter a long-term relationship (and might have to resume her old trade if the relationship foundered, 390–7). See McClure 2003: 18–21, Sommerstein forthcoming (*d*). The term is applied to Chrysis only here in the play. The omission of the definite article with παλλακήν and with υἱόν (510) may be a paratragic touch, stylistically incongruous in its context, since from this point on Nikeratos otherwise speaks almost entirely in the everyday language of comedy: παλλακή itself is not found in tragedy.

509 πρῶτος ἀνθρώπ[ω]ν ἐπώλουν: i.e. I would be the first to arrive at the slave market tomorrow morning, bringing her to be sold. In the surviving text we do not actually learn until 577 that Chrysis is a free woman, but we have heard that Nikeratos' wife and daughter have been socializing with her, apparently on more or less equal terms (35–8), and that Demeas' slaves regard her as the lady of the house (258n.), so Menander's audience will certainly have assumed that she is in fact free – in which case, selling her as a slave would constitute the capital crime of ἀνδραποδισμός (Isoc. 15.90, Xen. *Mem.* 1.2.62, [Arist.] *Ath.Pol.* 62.1). Nikeratos' readiness to take such drastic and illegal action is of a piece with his apparent suggestion that Moschion should be sold (see next note) or blinded (499–500), his equating Moschion's crime with murder (513), and his later threats to kill almost everyone within reach. Strictly speaking, to be sure, he is referring not to Chrysis but to a hypothetical παλλακή of his own, who theoretically might be a slave; but the whole point of this speech is that what Nikeratos would have done, Demeas should have done. **συναποκηρύττων:** probably 'auctioning together with her' (so Arnott). ἀποκηρύττω can mean either 'sell by auction' (Eupolis fr. 273, Pl. com. fr. 129, Lys. 17.7, Dem. 23.201) or 'formally disown' a son by public proclamation (Dem. 39.39, Pl. *Laws* 928e–929d), excluding him from the father's *oikos* and its cults and from any right of inheritance (D.H. *Ant. Rom.* 2.26.3). The latter procedure, according to Aristotle (*EN* 1163b22–3), would be used only in cases of exceptional depravity, but Moschion's supposed crime might well be thought to meet that standard, especially in Nikeratos' eyes. To sell into slavery one's son, an Athenian citizen, on the other hand, would be yet more monstrous than selling a free παλλακή, but even this is perhaps not too wild for Nikeratos in his present mood, and the prefix συν- tells in favour of this interpretation: Moschion would be taken down to the slave market *together* with Chrysis. On the other interpretation, the sale of

Chrysis and the disowning of Moschion would be two separate actions, and συν- would not be so appropriate.

510–11 μήτε... | μή (= μήτε... μήτε): a usage 'almost entirely confined to serious poetry' (Denniston 1954: 510; cf. Aesch. *Cho.* 291–2, Soph. *Ant.* 249–50, Eur. *Med.* 1348–9); another incongruous tragic touch, coming after μηθέν (a form of recent origin, unknown to the tragedians) and in a context of *stoai* and barbers' shops.

510 κουρεῖον: barbers' shops were favourite places for exchanging gossip; cf. Ar. *Birds* 1440–1, *Wealth* 337–9; Eupolis fr. 194; Lys. 23.3; Plut. *Nic.* 30.1–2; and see S. Lewis 1995.

511 στοάν: for στοαί (covered colonnades in public places, especially around the Agora) as places in which to loiter and chat cf. *Dysk.* 173, Thphr. *Char.* 2.2, 8.13. **κ[αθη]μένους:** cf. Ar. *Wealth* 338 ἐπὶ τοῖσι κουρείοισι τῶν καθημένων, Thphr. *Char.* 2.2 "ηὐδοκίμεις χθὲς ἐν τῆι στοᾶι"· πλειόνων γὰρ ἢ τριάκοντα ἀνθρώπων καθημένων.... **ἐξ ἑωθινοῦ:** cf. Ar. *Thesm.* 2, Alexis fr. 259.4, Xen. *Hell.* 1.1.5, Pl. *Phdr.* 227a.

512 λαλ[ε]ῖν: a decidedly colloquial verb, which in tragedy (and likewise in Plato and the orators) is rare and nearly always disparaging, whereas here it refers to deserved praise. **ἀνήρ:** 64, 506nn.

513 ἐπεξελθών: ἐπεξέρχομαι, in relation to crimes, normally means 'prosecute' by legal process, but for the sense 'punish, avenge' cf. Eur. *Bacch.* 1346. The construction with dative of the *crime* is found at Pl. *Laws* 866b; more usually this verb takes a dative of the *accused* (e.g. *Epitr.* 357, Ant. 1.1). **τῶι φόνωι:** an absurd exaggeration – nobody has been killed. If there *had* been a (wilful) murder, however, the penalty would be death – and before long Nikeratos will himself be turning executioner. **ποίωι φόνωι;** 'what do you mean, murder?' (468n.). Some editors have assigned this question to Moschion, but Moschion is too terrified (515) to put a question in this challenging tone – particularly when he must also be thinking out the implications of Nikeratos' words and coming to the realization that there has been a disastrous misunderstanding (515n.); it is better given to Demeas, whom Nikeratos has been addressing. B's speaker indications point the same way: it names Moschion as the speaker at 515, but not here.

514 'I judge it to be murder if someone rises in rebellion and does things like this.' **ὅστις** = εἴ τις (Smyth 1956: 565); cf. *Dysk.* 767–9; Eur. *IT* 605–7, *Hel.* 267–9, 271–2; Thuc. 2.44.1, 6.14. B's ὅσα τις, though it would give tolerable sense ('I judge things like this to be murder, anything that someone does when he rises in rebellion'), misses the point slightly: as Nikeratos has made quite clear, what has enraged him is not simply that

Moschion has rebelled against his father's authority, but that he has committed a heinous *sexual* wrong.   ἐπαναστάς: this verb 'often connotes
a desire to substitute one's own rule for that of the one to be deposed'
(Sandbach); cf. Andoc. 1.97 (citation of law) ἐάν τις τυραννεῖν ἐπαναστῆι,
Thuc. 1.115.5, 8.63.3, 8.73.2. Hippolytus was probably accused in Euripides' *Hippolytos Kalyptomenos* (and Sophocles' *Phaedra*) of aspiring to usurp
Theseus' throne (cf. Eur. fr. 434, Soph. fr. 683, and see Talboy and Sommerstein 2006: 259, 260–1, 282); in the surviving *Hippolytus* (1010–20)
he goes to some pains to rebut this charge even though it has not been
made. Demeas himself has spoken of Moschion as having repudiated his
authority (484).

515 Moschion is petrified with fear, not only at the intensity of Nikeratos'
anger and hatred, but also because he at last realizes what it is that he is suspected of. The implication (507) that Moschion has 'defiled [his father's]
bed', and the identification (508) of the παλλακή as 'she who lay with him',
make it evident that he is believed to be guilty of seducing Chrysis; and
he cannot possibly explain the truth of the matter in Nikeratos' presence
(cf. 490–1). Thus he seems completely trapped. Only Nikeratos' exit (520)
will give him a brief, but sufficient, opportunity.   αὖός εἰμι: with fear; cf.
Epitr. 901 αὖός εἰμι τῶι δέει, Theocr. 24.61 ξηρὸν ὑπαὶ δείους.   πέπηγα
'I'm frozen, I'm paralysed'; cf. Antiphanes fr. 166.7 πήγνυμαι σαφῶς (by
the high price of fish!).   τῶι κακῶι 'by this disaster'.

516 τοῖσιν: this long form of the 1st/2nd declension dative plural ending,
common in epic, tragedy and in Old Comedy, occurs only here in *Samia*
(though also found at *Perik.* 268 and *Theoph.* 25); cf. next three notes.
See Introduction §9.   τὴν τὰ δείν' εἰργασμένην: Chrysis; cf. Eur. *Or.* 396
σύνοιδα δείν' εἰργασμένος, *El.* 1204 δεινὰ δ' εἰργάσω. In Menander, except
here and at 642, the uncompounded verb ἐργάζομαι always means 'work'
(on the land, *Georg.* 47, *Dysk.* 163, 333; at another occupation, *Heros* 38,
Kolax 51) or 'achieve by labour' (*Koneiazomenai* 16); its use here as a synonym of ποιῶ, δρῶ or πράττω is thus paratragic.

517 εἰσεδεξάμην: cf. Eur. *Supp.* 876 οὐκ εἰσεδέξατ' οἶκον, *Phoen.* 261, 451,
Soph. *El.* 1128; the verb is not otherwise found in comedy (Ar. *Ach.* 392
is regarded by recent editors as corrupt).   μελάθροις τοῖς ἐμοῖς: μέλαθρον
(usually, as here, plural) appears in comedy only when tragedy is being
quoted, parodied or imitated (Ar. *Birds* 1247, *Thesm.* 41, 874). Here the
incongruity is heightened by its scansion, the cluster θρ being split between
two syllables so that the second syllable of the word is scanned long; such
a syllable split, in this and most other stop-liquid clusters, is normally alien
to comedy (cf. M. L. West 1982: 16–17). Even in tragedy this scansion
is not much favoured; in Euripides μελάθροισ(ιν) occurs twelve times in

lyrics or anapaests where the second syllable can be, and is, scanned short (e.g. *Alc.* 29, *Bacch.* 70), but only once in dialogue (fr. 362.12, where it is scanned long). It is particularly incongruous, too, that this lofty term, usually applied to the abodes of tragic kings, should be used in reference to Nikeratos' tumbledown house (cf. 593).

517–18 Demeas now asks Nikeratos to expel Chrysis from *his* house, presumably because her proximity will be hurtful to him and a temptation to Moschion. Nikeratos, we can already be sure, will need no urging.

518 συναδικοῦ 'feel yourself wronged together with me'. In 456 Demeas had used the active form of the same rare verb to say that Moschion and Chrysis were conspiring against him; here he uses the passive to invite Nikeratos to join him in the role of indignant victim. **γνησίως** 'nobly'; cf. Men. fr. 159 τά γ' ἀπὸ τῆς τύχης φέρειν δεῖ γνησίως τὸν εὐγενῆ, Pl. *Apol.* 31e, Dem. *Epist.* 3.32. **ὡς ἂν φίλος** 'like a friend', 'as a friend should' (not 'as if you were a friend'); cf. 702 ὡς ἂν ὑόν. It was the duty of a friend to help a friend in trouble (e.g. Eur. *Or.* 454–5, 665–6) – an idea comically stood on its head in Ar. *Birds* 128–34. On Demeas' use of the vocabulary of φιλία see 444n.

519 ὃς διαρραγήσομ' ἐπιδών: literally, 'I who will burst <with rage (475n.)> when I set eyes on her!', i.e. (approximately) 'Yes, absolutely – in fact I'll burst…'; as at 413, the connecting relative 'serves to confirm and strengthen an assentient response'. For ἐπιδών (ἰδὼν B, leaving the line a syllable short) cf. Men. fr. 1.3 ὅταν… τοὐμὸν ἐπίδω χωρίον (after a long absence); Eur. *Med.* 1413–14 οὓς μήποτ' ἐγὼ φύσας ὄφελον πρὸς σοῦ φθιμένους ἐπιδέσθαι (Jason on his dead children). Nikeratos will indeed be bursting with rage very shortly – but not because he has seen Chrysis!

Nikeratos now rushes towards his own house to carry out Demeas' request, but he finds that Moschion, in a desperate effort to save his child, has forestalled him and is blocking his way. **ἐμβλέπεις μοι:** 483n. **βάρβαρε:** the only surviving instance, at least before Roman times, of this vocative being used in addressing a Greek (though cf. Eur. *Tro.* 764 ὦ βάρβαρ' ἐξευρόντες Ἕλληνες κακά; in Athenion fr. 1.3 a cook is speaking to a slave). It implies that Moschion has ignored fundamental principles of behaviour that any Greek ought to observe. In *Epitr.* 898, 924 Charisios calls *himself* βάρβαρος for having walked out on his wife on learning that she had borne (as he thinks) another man's child, when he himself had sired a bastard not long before his marriage; in *Mis.* 311 S = 712 A Getas (a barbarian himself!) calls Krateia one for rejecting Polemon's offer of marriage (he is unaware that Krateia believes Polemon to have killed her brother).

520 Θρᾶιξ ἀληθῶς: not only a barbarian, but one of a particularly despised ethnicity: according to the speaker of *Aspis* 242–5 (a Thracian himself), the mills (to which slaves were sent as a punishment: *Heros* 1–3, *Perik.* 277–8, Eur. *Cycl.* 240, Lys. 1.18) were full of them, and Thucydides (7.29.4) says Thracians were 'among the most bloodthirsty of barbarians, when they think there's no danger'. In particular, Thracians had a reputation for extreme lustfulness: according to fr. 877 (again spoken by a Thracian), they were 'not very self-controlled' and had ten or twelve wives apiece. **οὐ παρήσεις;** (from παρίημι) 'let me pass, won't you?' The simple aorist imperative πάρες is used at *Dysk.* 81, *Sik.* 189 and *com. adesp.* 1032.7.

Nikeratos pushes Moschion out of the way and goes into his house. Moschion at once approaches his father.

520–32 Moschion now has no alternative but to confess the truth to his father and hope that Demeas will believe him, forgive him, and somehow persuade and mollify Nikeratos. Nikeratos' brief absence from the scene gives him just enough time to carry out his part of the task, and by 532 Demeas is on the way to being convinced that Moschion is now telling the truth – after which Nikeratos' reappearance, which might have been expected to disrupt Moschion's plan, instead provides the crucial evidence that removes any remaining doubts from Demeas' mind.

521 οὐκ ἀκούσομ' οὐθέν: we are doubtless meant to suppose that Demeas is expecting Moschion to offer further excuses (cf. 479–87) for behaviour which is beyond all excuse.

521–2 οὐδ' εἰ μηδὲν ... | γέγονεν 'not even if none of what you *think* has happened has *actually* happened?' It is necessary to emend this sentence (νηδι'οὐδεν, i.e. νὴ Δί' οὐδέν, B) into a conditional form because (1) only thus can Demeas' response πῶς μηδὲ ἕν; be accounted for, (2) νὴ Δία cannot accompany a negative statement (10–14n.). Possibly the sequence ΟΥΔΕΙΜΗΔΕΝ was telescoped into ΟΥΔΕΝ, and subsequently the missing letters were inserted above the line, brought back into the text in the wrong place, and finally 'corrected' into νὴ Δί'.

521 προσδοκᾶις: here 'believe'; cf. *Sik.* 151, 246, Eur. *Alc.* 1091.

522 ἄρτι γὰρ τὸ πρᾶγμα κατανοῶ echoes Nikeratos' words at 492–3, but this time – as the substitution of κατανοῶ for Nikeratos' ὑπονοεῖν indicates – the speaker really does understand the situation correctly.

523 This information, once he comes to believe it, changes the whole situation for Demeas, not only vis-à-vis Moschion but also vis-à-vis Chrysis: she has not wronged him after all, and he need no longer struggle to harden his heart against her. He never, on stage, admits to her, as he does to Moschion (537–8, 694–6, 702, 710), that he had suspected her unjustly; but it should be remembered that he is never henceforth alone on stage with her as he is with Moschion in the passages mentioned, and that from 615 to 690 they are together *off* stage.

524 τοῦθ' should probably be understood as internal object of χαρίζεται ('she's doing me this favour'), as in 525; the alternative would be to take it as subject of the indirect statement governed by ὁμολογοῦσ' ('professing that this <child is> her own'), but τοῦθ' would then not be really needed (τὸ παιδίον being easily understood from 523), and its position just before the diaeresis (484n.) encourages the hearer to link it grammatically with the preceding rather than with the following words.

525 τὰς ἀληθείας: this plural was idiomatic in the Attic of the middle and late fourth century (though avoided by Plato and Aristotle); cf. *Aspis* 372, *Epitr.* 579, *Theoph.* 25, Isoc. 2.20, 9.4, Dem. 42.8, 44.3, [Arist.] *Rhet. ad Alex.* 16.2. It probably developed on the analogy of expressions like ἀληθῆ λέγειν and ταῦτ' ἀληθῆ, which are far more frequent than the corresponding singular forms.

526–7 The answer to Demeas' question is actually 'because we didn't want Nikeratos to know the truth about the baby until after Plangon and I were safely married'; but this will only be intelligible once Demeas knows that Plangon is the baby's mother, and even now Moschion feels the need to prepare the ground a little before making this confession. In the end he never does explain to Demeas why he wanted the baby's parentage kept secret; the audience, who know the answer anyway, are unlikely to notice the omission amid the bustle and fury of the coming scene.

526 οὐχ ἑκὼν λέγω: Moschion still feels the inhibition of shame (47n.) at having to confess the rape, but (as he goes on to say) this is now the least bad option available (he would, of course, have had to do it sooner or later in any case). **μέν, ἀλλά:** for this sequence of particles cf. *Epitr.* 611–12, Ar. *Wasps* 482, *Birds* 1118–19, *Lys.* 1022–3; in three of these four passages, as here, the first limb of the antithesis contains a negative. **μεῖζον' αἰτίαν:** the charge of having usurped his father's bed.

527 λαμβάνω: here apparently 'I accept, I admit', though αἰτίαν λαμβάνειν usually means 'incur blame or criticism' (Eur. *Supp.* 606, Thuc. 2.18.3) or 'incur deserved blame, be guilty' (Thuc. 6.60.1, Lys. 12.57). By thus accepting his guilt, Moschion is opening the way for the moment when he will say λαμβάνω again (729) as part of the formula for accepting a bride (cf. *Perik.* 1014). **μικράν:** i.e. small by comparison with the other charge. It is not clear whether we are to understand Moschion as referring to the rape (palliated by his undertaking to marry the victim; see Introduction §5), or to his deception of his father and Nikeratos, or to both. **ἐὰν σὺ τὸ γεγονὸς πύθηι σαφῶς:** this clause in effect conditions μικράν: spelled out in full, Moschion is saying 'I am admitting a charge <which will be seen to be relatively> small if you learn accurately what happened.'

528 ἀποκτενεῖς 'you'll be the death of me', an exclamation of impatience (cf. Antiphanes fr. 55.5–6) equivalent to the ἀπολεῖς found at *Dysk.* 412 and frequent in Old Comedy (Ar. *Ach.* 470, *Wasps* 1449, *Thesm.* 1073, *Eccl.* 775, *Wealth* 390) and to Latin *enicas* (Plaut. *Merc.* 893, *Persa* 484; Ter. *Phorm.* 384). **ἔστι:** the subject (τὸ παιδίον) has not been mentioned since 523; Moschion is at last delivering the information that he omitted then.

529 λαθεῖν δὲ τοῦτ' ἐβουλόμην: cf. 320, where Parmenon was about to say something similar (presumably in the first person plural) but was not allowed to get beyond the first word (λανθάνειν). **ἐγώ:** Moschion's assumption of sole responsibility for the deception (which in fact involved the whole of Demeas' household, as well as Plangon and her mother) may be an attempt to shield Chrysis from any blame even for this lesser offence; we cannot infer from it that he was in fact responsible for the specific scheme of bringing the baby into his house and having Chrysis pretend to be its mother (on which see 57/8n.).

530 ὥσπερ πέπρακται: for a second time Moschion strongly affirms that he is telling the truth. **μή με βουκολεῖς ὅρα** 'mind you're not trying to hoodwink me' (596; *com. adesp.* 1007.35): βουκολεῖς is present indicative because Demeas fears that Moschion may be trying to deceive him *at this moment* (Goodwin 1912: 133), cf. Ar. *Clouds* 493, Soph. *Ant.* 1253–4, Pl. *Charm.* 163e.

531 Moschion points out that it would be pointless for him to lie, since the lie could be exposed easily (whether by questioning Plangon herself, or – more likely perhaps, since it would not require the cooperation of Nikeratos – by forcing the information out of one or more slaves). **οὗ** 'in circumstances in which'; for this use of οὗ (and ὅπου) cf. *Epitr.* 318, Antiphanes fr. 142.8–10 (praise of the parasite's life) οὗ γὰρ τὸ μέγιστον ἔργον ἐστὶ παιδιά... οὐχ ἡδύ; Soph. *Phil.* 1049–51. **ἔστι** 'it is possible' (= ἔξεστι). **τί κερδανῶ πλέον;** is a somewhat tautologous blend of the synonymous expressions τί κερδανῶ; (Ar. *Clouds* 259) and τί μοι πλέον; (Eur. *Ion* 1255; cf. Ar. *Eccl.* 1094, *Pl.* 531, Philemon fr. 77.7), both of which can be rendered 'what good will it do me?'

532 οὐθέν: with this one word Demeas has virtually accepted the truth of Moschion's confession – which is now about to be spectacularly confirmed. Here Demeas suddenly looks across towards Nikeratos' door. **ἀλλὰ τὴν**

θύραν τις – : he would have continued (unmetrically!) πέπληχεν (300–1n.), but is interrupted as a distraught Nikeratos bursts out of his house. Probably Nikeratos advances towards the audience and delivers his first two speeches (532–6) in their direction; he is not aware that Demeas and Moschion have heard him, as is shown by his near-repetition of 535–6 for Demeas' ears in 540–1. As τις shows, Demeas is not sure who is coming out; Lamagna notes that the audience would have been expecting to see Nikeratos driving out Chrysis (as Demeas had done in 369–98), and would have been surprised and mystified when he came out alone.   ὦ τάλας ἐγώ, τάλας: cf. Soph. *Aj.* 981, *OC* 847, also Ar. *Thesm.* 1038 in a parody of Euripides' *Andromeda*; Knemon expresses his grief (over the loss of a mattock!) in similar terms at *Dysk.* 596–7.

533–4 The paratragic tone of Nikeratos' exclamation is conveyed through the avoidance of all untragic vocabulary and metre; the use of one word (ἄχος) which is alien to comedy (except for tragic parody); the omission of the article before θυρῶν and καρδίαν; the hyperbaton ἀπροσδοκήτωι... ἄχει; and doubtless also through intonation and gesture. We are not yet told what has caused his distress, except that it is something he has seen (εἰσιδὼν θέαμα).

534 ἐμμανής: previously it was Demeas who had been driven out of his mind – in his own estimation as well as that of Nikeratos, Chrysis and the Cook (217, 279, 361–3, 415, 416, 419); now it will be Nikeratos' turn (cf. 563).

535–6 Nikeratos' second utterance is entirely in normal comic idiom, and includes two words (παιδίον and τιτθίον) never found in tragedy. We now learn what it is that he has seen, and it is indeed something shattering: he has discovered that his daughter is an unmarried mother. A coldly rational man would have linked this discovery with the fact, already known to him, that Moschion is the father of the baby, and realized that to solve the whole problem he need only go ahead and complete the couple's marriage; but Nikeratos is not the man to think things out rationally.

535 <ἄρτι>: Austin's supplement is inspired by 540–1, where Nikeratos repeats to Demeas what he has said here to the world in general, using almost exactly the same words differently ordered.

536 τιτθίον διδοῦσαν: just what Demeas had seen Chrysis doing in *his* house (265–6); but he (at first) controlled himself and came outside 'very quietly' (262–3n.).   τοῦτ' ἦν ἄρα 'so that *is* how it was!' Demeas realizes (70n.) that what Moschion has just told him conforms with this new evidence and is therefore certainly true. He is speaking to himself: for Moschion's next words (πάτερ, ἀκούεις;) show that he has not heard this remark. B has only a single (raised) point, not a *dicolon*, at the end of this line, and the earliest editors therefore gave τοῦτ᾿ ἦν ἄρα to Moschion; but B names Moschion as the speaker before πάτερ (not before τοῦτ᾿), and the omission of the second dot is therefore probably a mere slip of the pen.

537 πάτερ, ἀκούεις; An excited Moschion draws his father's attention (unnecessarily, as it happens) to the implications of what Nikeratos has said.   **οὐδὲν ἀδικεῖς, Μοσχίων, μ᾿:** 328n. Demeas formally reinstates his original judgement that Moschion is innocent (contrast 456, 506), but now this judgement is based on evidence instead of prejudice. Sandbach's insertion of μ᾿ (the single letter M could easily have dropped out after the preceding N) is supported by several arguments: (1) ἀδικῶ has to be understood with ἐγὼ δὲ σέ, and there it would be a transitive verb; (2) it is also transitive at 328, 456, 479 and 583; (3) while it is true that Moschion has not wronged Demeas, it is not true that he has done *no* wrong – he has wronged Plangon (67–8) and her father.   **ἐγὼ δὲ σέ:** a notable and somewhat humiliating admission for a father to make to his son – all the more so, given that Demeas' suspicions arose in the first place from a deception planned, as he has just been told (529), by Moschion himself. Even Theseus in Euripides' *Hippolytus*, though full of remorse for his fatal curse on Hippolytus, never admits to Hippolytus' face that he has wronged him. Hippolytus nevertheless fully forgives Theseus (Eur. *Hipp.* 1442–3, 1449–51): Moschion never explicitly forgives Demeas, and as late as 724–5 he is still criticizing him.

538 πρὸς σέ, Δημέα, πορεύομαι: Nikeratos now moves over towards Demeas and Moschion; Moschion is at once terror-stricken, though the fact that Nikeratos addresses himself initially to Demeas may indicate that he is not contemplating immediate violence against Moschion.

539 ἐκποδὼν ἄπειμι: Moschion moves towards Eisodos A (the exit furthest from Nikeratos' house: see note at start of commentary).   **θάρρει** 'don't worry', 'there's nothing to be afraid of': Demeas tries to dissuade Moschion from taking to flight. The tone of his reassurance may not be very confident or convincing: as Sandbach points out, he himself has no idea at this moment how to placate Nikeratos, since he thinks it will be too dangerous, at least at present, to come out with the truth (cf. 549). At first he merely stalls, making a futile attempt at persuading Nikeratos to disbelieve the clear evidence of his eyes (542–6); only at 566–7 does he decide that his one hope will be to tell the truth, and only at 584 can he begin to put this policy into action (but wrapping up the truth in a thick cloak of mythological nonsense).   **τέθνηχ᾿** sc. with fright; cf. 494, Dem. 4.45 τεθνᾶσι τῶι δέει, 19.81 τεθνάναι τῶι φόβωι. Moschion flees down Eisodos A;

this is the second time (cf. 161–2) that he has shown himself not to have the courage to come face to face with Nikeratos.

540–1 τί τὸ πάθος δ' ἐστίν; 'What's up with you?' (cf. 692). The particle δ' marks this as an answer to Nikeratos' words in 538, equivalent to 'you say you're coming to me, but why?' Demeas is pretending not to have heard what Nikeratos said in 532–6, so Nikeratos tells him what he has seen indoors, repeating 535–6 almost word for word, but with changes of word order whose effect is that out of the whole sentence only τῶι παιδίωι is in the same metrical position as before.

542 τυχὸν ἔπαιζεν 'perhaps she was just playing a game', i.e. *pretending* to be suckling a baby that was not actually hers.

543 κατέπεσεν 'she fainted' from shock and fear at being discovered. Other characters faint from shock at *Sik.* 363 and Ar. *Wasps* 995, from fear at Ar. *Birds* 61 (cf. 89). Plangon has recovered by the time Nikeratos next goes into his house at 547 (cf. 559).   **τυχὸν ἴσως:** this tautological idiom occurs six times more in Menander (e.g. *Aspis* 233, *Epitr.* 504) and in Timocles fr. 16.2 and *com. adesp.* 1000.9.   **ἔδοξε [:** the most likely restoration is ἔδοξέ [σοι] 'you imagined it', viz. that she was suckling the baby (desperate as Demeas is to persuade Nikeratos that he did not see what he plainly did see, he can hardly expect him to believe that he did not see Plangon faint). Cf. Aesch. *Cho.* 1051–3 τίνες σε δόξαι ... στροβοῦσιν; ... – οὐκ εἰσὶ δόξαι (i.e. they are not imaginary but real). Sandbach, proposing ἔδοξε [γάρ –], supposed that Demeas 'intended to advance a theory that [Plangon] imagined something, e.g. that the person entering was a stranger, but was interrupted before he could complete his sentence'; even if such a theory were true, however, it would not follow that Plangon was not actually suckling the baby, and Demeas' one aim throughout this short scene is to convince Nikeratos that she was not doing so.

544 παρατενεῖς: 421n.   **"τυχὸν" λέγων μοι πάντα:** lit. 'saying everything to me as τυχόν', i.e. qualifying everything you say with a 'perhaps'.

544–5 τούτων αἴτιός | εἰμ' ἐγώ: spoken aside, and not clearly heard by Nikeratos (hence his response τί φήις;). Once again (cf. 537) Demeas blames himself. This time it is possibly for having expelled Chrysis – but for that, the baby would not have been in Nikeratos' house and he would not have seen Plangon suckling it – but it is at least as likely (551n.) that he is still thinking of his unjust suspicions of Moschion, the discovery of which by Nikeratos was the cause of his going into his house at the moment when he did.

546 κορυζᾶις: κορυζᾶν means properly 'to have a runny nose', later 'to talk nonsense' (in Pl. *Rep.* 343a Thrasymachus plays on the word's two senses);

cf. Polyb. 38.12.5, Luc. *How to Write History* 31. The English verb 'drivel' has a similar semantic history (see *OED drivel* v.)   οὗτος οὐκ ἔστιν λόγος 'this is not mere words', 'this is not just something I'm saying', *sc.* but actual fact; for this sense of λόγος cf. Lyc. *Leocr.* 23 ἵνα … μὴ λόγον οἴησθε εἶναι ἀλλ' εἰδῆτε τὴν ἀλήθειαν, and the interjection *logi!* 'nonsense!' in Ter. *Phorm.* 493.

547 ἀλλὰ πάλιν ἐλθών – : no sooner are these words out of Nikeratos' mouth than he rushes back to his house without even finishing his sentence. We, and Demeas, are left to guess what his intentions are: to see whether his eyes had really deceived him, as Demeas has been insisting they must have done – or to take immediate drastic action?   τὸ δεῖνα 'the thing is –': a piece of verbal padding used when the speaker does not want to fall silent but is still thinking out what to say or how to say it. Cf. *Dysk.* 897, *Perik.* 335; Ar. *Wasps* 524, *Peace* 268, *Lys.* 921, 926, 1168. Here Demeas badly wants to keep Nikeratos outside but cannot think of anything to say that is likely to achieve this.   μικρόν: he would have added μεῖνον (cf. *Perik.* 336) had he not realized in mid-utterance that Nikeratos was gone and it was too late to say anything.   ὦ τᾶν (etymology obscure) is 'ostensibly a polite form of address … but very often with a note of condescension or impatience' (Stevens 1976: 42–3; see Dickey 1996: 158–60). Menander seems to use it for liveliness and urgency (*Dysk.* 247, Daos anxious to exculpate himself; *Dysk.* 359, Sostratos eager to learn whether he will see his beloved if he goes to work in the fields).

548 πάντα πράγματ' ἀνατέτραπται 'everything is ruined', cf. Dem. 18.143 τὸν … ἐν Ἀμφίσσηι πόλεμον … ὃς ἅπαντα ἀνέτρεψε τὰ τῶν Ἑλλήνων. Demeas assumes that when Nikeratos realizes what has happened he will call off the marriage, even though that will actually make things much worse for all concerned.   τέλος ἔχει 'it's all over' (494n.).

549 τὸ πρᾶγμ' ἀκούσας: Demeas probably means 'if I tell him the facts'. Sandbach thought he was anticipating that the women in Nikeratos' house would confess, but they are not otherwise mentioned in this speech. Once Demeas himself knew the true facts, the obvious next move, in normal circumstances, would be to explain them carefully to Nikeratos; but that is impossible with Nikeratos in his present mood.   χαλεπανεῖ: 491n.

550 σκατοφάγος: 427n.: Demeas unknowingly echoes the term which Nikeratos had earlier applied to him. But whereas Nikeratos had treated Demeas' strange behaviour as uncharacteristic and due to the effect of the Pontic climate (416–17), Demeas regards Nikeratos' behaviour as a product of his inherent character (τῶι τρόπωι, cf. 347). Presumably we are to suppose that Demeas had not previously seen Nikeratos when he was carried away by anger; otherwise he would hardly have chosen him as a father-in-law for his son.   αὐθέκαστος 'harsh' (cf. fr. 592), as sometimes in later writers (e.g. Plut. *Mor.* 11e, 529d, 823a; Luc. *Phal.* 1.2); this sense of the adjective developed (presumably via an intermediate stage 'blunt, tactless') from its literal meaning 'truthful' (i.e. αὐτὸ ἕκαστον λέγων 'calling each thing just what it is'), which is found in two contemporaries of Menander (Philemon fr. 93.6–7, Poseidippus com. fr. 41). Aristotle (*EN* 1127a20–6) used the word to denote a person who neither overstates nor understates his own good qualities.

551 'Ought I, villain that I am, to have suspected something like that – ought I?' Demeas now gives full vent to the self-denunciation which he was only able to make briefly and sotto voce while Nikeratos was present (544–5). The echo of 538 (ὑπονοῶν τοιαῦτα) suggests that he is thinking of his suspicions of Moschion rather than of Chrysis (544–5n.). Most editors before Lamagna punctuated the sentence as a statement; but it is implausible that Demeas should call himself a villain deserving death because he had *not* suspected (e.g.) that Nikeratos would be enraged (Austin 1967: 126) or that Chrysis was not really the baby's mother (Sandbach).   ἐμέ...ἐμέ: i.e. *myself* of all people (being Moschion's father). γάρ has been found puzzling, since the injustice of Demeas' suspicions is in no way an explanation of Nikeratos' character or of his likely reaction to being told the facts. Several solutions are possible. (1) The particle connects 551 not with the preceding *sentence* but with a preceding *gesture*, e.g. Demeas striking his head (Wilamowitz). (2) Demeas is resuming the train of thought he had begun in 544–5 (modifying a suggestion by Sandbach). (3) 'The connection of thought is ... lacking in logical precision' (Denniston 1954: 61) and may be articulated roughly as follows: 'a catastrophic situation has arisen (548–50) because <I proclaimed my suspicions, and> I ought never to have had those suspicions'.   τὸν μιαρόν: a very strong term of condemnation, found elsewhere in Menander only at *Aspis* 313–14 (of the avaricious Smikrines who is unconscionably insisting on his legal right to marry an heiress), *Georgos* 30 (of a rich young man who has raped a girl and is now about to marry someone else), and fr. 508.6 (an extreme misogynist denouncing all women).

552 νὴ τὸν Ἥφαιστον: this is the only affirmative oath by Hephaestus in surviving comic texts (the negative form μὰ τὸν Ἥφαιστον is found at *Dysk.* 718, *Sik.* 317; *com. adesp.* 1098.1; and Ameipsias fr. 18), significantly placed just before Demeas finds himself facing the prospect of his grandson being *burnt* to death.   δικαίως ἀποθάνοιμ' ἄν: so in Euripides' *Hippolytus* Theseus, having learned that he has caused the impending death of Hippolytus by believing Phaedra's false accusation, says to Artemis δέσποιν', ὀλοίμην (1325) and to Hippolytus himself εἰ γὰρ γενοίμην, τέκνον, ἀντὶ σοῦ νεκρός (1410). If this is how Demeas feels now, how much more strongly will he be condemning himself very shortly, when it seems that a false accusation made by *himself* is about to lead to the deaths of Chrysis and the baby?

552–3 Ἡράκλεις, | ἡλίκον κέκραγε: loud shouting is now heard from inside Nikeratos' house (cf. 364; for Ἡράκλεις, 178n., 360).

553 τοῦτ' ἦν: here (contrast 536n.) 'that's what I said' (cf. 549 κεκράξεται); Ar. *Ach.* 41 uses the fuller expression τοῦτ' ἐκεῖν' οὑγὼ λεγον.   **πῦρ βοᾶι** 'he's calling for fire'; cf. *Dysk.* 586–7 ταύτην [*sc.* τὴν δίκελλαν] πάλαι ζητεῖ βοᾶι τε, Eur. *Phoen.* 1154–5.

553–4 τὸ παιδίον | φησὶν ἐμπρήσειν: the destruction of infants born in dubious circumstances is frequently threatened in myth and tragedy (though they nearly always in fact survive), but here there is probably a specific allusion to Euripides' *Melanippe the Wise*, in which Melanippe, daughter of Aeolus, bore twins to Poseidon and hid them in her father's cowsheds, where his herdsmen found them being suckled by one of the cows and 'taking them for the monstrous offspring of the cow, brought them to the king [Aeolus] who, persuaded by the advice of his father Hellen, decided to burn the infants, and ordered his daughter Melanippe to dress them in grave-clothes' (*Melanippe the Wise* test. i Kannicht, cf. [D.H.] *Rhet.* 8.10, 9.11); Melanippe made a famous speech in their defence (from which come Eur. frr. 483–5), and the children were eventually saved (Melanippe's own fate in this play is uncertain). One of Menander's plays bore the title Ἐμπιμπραμένη and may have included an attempt to set a young woman on fire (as a punishment for alleged sexual misconduct, cf. *Perikeiromene*?).

554–5 υἱδοῦν ὀπτώμενον | ὄψομαι 'I'm going to see a grandson being roasted.' This short sentence contains two puns – υἱδοῦν ~ ὕδιον 'piglet' (cf. Xen. *Mem.* 1.2.31; see Keuls 1973: 14) and ὀπτώμενον ~ ὄψομαι – which help to remind us that this is a comedy and that nothing disastrous is actually going to happen. The word ὄψομαι is indeed only used for the sake of the pun, since Demeas has no reason to expect that the baby will be burnt in his presence.

555 πάλιν πέπληχε τὴν θύραν: another surprise; given Nikeratos' intentions as just reported, we would hardly have expected him to be coming outside at this moment.   **στρόβιλος** 'a whirlwind'.

556 σκηπτός: probably 'a tempest' (*Aspis* 402, Soph. *Ant.* 418 with scholia, Eur. *Andr.* 1046, Dem. 18.194) rather than 'a thunderbolt'. There may be a reminiscence of 206–9 where Demeas spoke of the 'sudden, unexpected storm' that had burst upon him.

Nikeratos again rushes out of his house.

556–7 echoes Demeas' words of 456 (δεινὸν ἤδη· συναδικεῖ μ' οὗτος) and 474–5 (συνόμνυται τοῖς ἐμοῖς ἐχθροῖς τις), which likewise referred to an alleged conspiracy involving Chrysis.

556 συνίσταται 'is in a conspiracy' (cf. Ar. *Knights* 863, *Lys.* 577).

558–60 With the life of the baby at stake, Chrysis, who once (84–5) declared herself ready to 'endure anything' to save it from coming to harm, has taken charge. She has seized the baby, refused to give it up, and told Plangon and her mother to admit nothing – which probably means refusing to answer questions like 'This baby is yours, isn't it?' and 'Who is its father?' They can no longer maintain the old fiction that the baby is Chrysis' child, which would be untenable now that Plangon has been seen feeding it. Most likely the audience will suppose that, in this dire emergency, Chrysis' plan is simply to ensure, if possible, that Nikeratos neither gets his hands on the baby, nor is given any information that may enrage him yet further, until he has had time to cool down.

560 οὐ προήσεσθαι 'that she won't let it go' (or perhaps 'betray it', cf. *Aspis* 304–5 προήσει τοὺς φίλους ... οὕτως ἀγεννῶς;).

560–3 Here we discover why Nikeratos has come outside: it is to give notice to Demeas (προειπεῖν 563) that he intends to murder Chrysis! He is not, of course, aware that Demeas now knows Chrysis to be innocent of the infidelity he had suspected, but even so this is not the conduct of a man in his senses, and it is entirely reasonable of Demeas to conclude that Nikeratos is mad (μελαγχολᾷ 563).

560 αὐτόχειρ, originally 'someone who acts with his own hands', had come to be used in discussions of homicide (e.g. Ant. 5.62) to distinguish one who personally committed a killing from one who procured, counselled, or shared in planning it, and by the mid-fourth century it could bear the meaning 'murderer' without any help from the context – indeed Demosthenes (21.106) can say that Meidias has been his αὐτόχειρ merely by inducing others to prosecute him with the object of destroying him politically and forcing him into exile.   **τῆς γυναικός** 'of my wife' (not 'of your wife': αὐτῆς can only refer to Chrysis, the subject of Nikeratos' previous sentence and in his mind the ringleader of the women's conspiracy). That Demeas can refer to Chrysis by this term is a powerful signal that his old affection for her is completely restored, perhaps even enhanced. He had once (130) spoken of her sarcastically as a γαμετὴν ἑταίραν because she had (as he supposed) kept their child instead of exposing it; now he applies to her a term that could be used to denote wedded wives in explicit contrast to παλλακαί like herself (cf. [Dem.] 59.122 ἔχομεν τὰς ... παλλακὰς τῆς καθ' ἡμέραν θεραπείας τοῦ σώματος [ἕνεκα], τὰς δὲ γυναῖκας τοῦ παιδοποιεῖσθαι γνησίως, ibid. 118 οὐ γυναῖκα εἶναι αὐτοῦ ἀλλὰ παλλακήν). So Achilles, when his captive Briseis was taken from him, called her his ἄλοχον θυμαρέα who was to him what Helen had been to Menelaus (*Iliad* 9.335–43; contrast 19.297–9, where Patroclus is reported as saying that he *would make* her Achilles' κουριδίην ἄλοχον by taking her to Phthia and holding a wedding feast there).

562 πάντα γὰρ σύνοιδεν αὕτη: Nikeratos has realized from Chrysis' actions that she is privy to the knowledge about the baby that is being withheld from him. Soon he will realize, from Demeas' defence of Chrysis, that Demeas is in possession of this knowledge too; he states this, in almost the same words, at 584.   **μηδαμῶς** 'don't do it!' (cf. 134).

563 προειπεῖν 'to give you notice'; cf. *Aspis* 158–9 τοὺς δὲ γινομένους γάμους | τούτους προειπεῖν βούλομ' αὐτοῖς μὴ ποεῖν. The same verb was used in reference to the public proclamation by the relatives of a murdered person, naming the alleged killer and warning him to stay away from certain public and sacred places (Dem. 43.57 [citation of law], [Dem.] 59.9): it is thus comically paradoxical that a killer should himself προειπεῖν his intentions to the κύριος of his prospective victim. Nikeratos bounds back into his house.   **μελαγχολᾶι:** 416n.

564 εἰσπεπήδηκεν 'he's rushed inside': cf. *Dysk.* 602, Philemon fr. 3.13, Ar. *Knights* 363, 545, and the antonym ἐκπηδᾶν (*Theoph.* 26, *Perik.* 527; Eriphus fr. 4).   **τί τούτοις τοῖς κακοῖς τις χρήσεται** 'what can one do with (literally, how will one use) this terrible situation?'

565–6 οὐδεπώποτ'...|...ταραχήν 'I'm not aware that I've ever run into trouble like this.'   **μέντοι:** 12n. Here too the particle is probably adversative ('however'); the situation is desperate, *but* Demeas can see one possible way out of it (539n.). He had previously thought that telling the truth was too dangerous (549); but nothing could be more dangerous than Nikeratos is at this moment.

567 Ἄπολλον: 100n.   **ἡ θύρα πάλιν ψοφεῖ:** this time Demeas is once again (532n.) unsure who is about to appear; in fact, for the first time in this act, it is Chrysis.

568–9 Chrysis rushes out of Nikeratos' house in terror, with the baby in her arms; Nikeratos follows in pursuit, brandishing his stick (577–9), at the end of 569. The stage-picture bears a considerable resemblance to that of 369–90; but this time the irate householder wants Chrysis to stay (and suffer violence) rather than to depart, and she will be defended not by the Cook (who can only intervene with words) but by Demeas, who is ready to use violence himself in her cause. At this moment, however, Chrysis still assumes that Demeas is an enemy, and sees no escape for herself.

568 ὦ τάλαιν᾽ ἐγώ: 245, 260, 398nn.   **τί δράσω;** The verb δρᾶν occurs
only here in Menander, and τί δράσω; comes very frequently to the lips
of tragic characters in grievous quandaries – twenty-two times in the surviving tragedies of Aeschylus, Sophocles and Euripides (e.g. Aesch. *Cho.*
899; Soph. *Aj.* 809, 920, 1024; Eur. *Alc.* 380, *Med.* 1042, 1271). δράσω,
like φύγω just afterwards, is aorist subjunctive (in a deliberative question),
not future indicative.   **ποῖ φύγω;** is also almost always tragic (Soph. *OC*
828, 1737; Eur. *IT* 291, *Ion* 1253); on its one other appearance in comedy
(Ar. *Birds* 354) it is accompanied by the high-poetic adjective δύστηνος. The
phrase is combined with τί δράσω; in Eur. *Med.* 1271, where the speaker
(offstage) is one of Medea's children about to be killed by their mother.

568–9 τὸ παιδίον | λήψεταί μου 'he's going to take my baby!' Once again
(cf. 558–60n.) it is probably instinct, not calculation, that is speaking here:
Chrysis, who has been caring for the baby almost since it was born, and
who loves it almost as if it were her own child, speaks of it, when its life is
in danger, *as* her own child. Very soon (579, 580) Demeas too will speak
of it as his, as Moschion, who really is its father, already has done (479):
everyone in both households is united in defending it, as part of their
families, against Nikeratos.

569 Χρυσί, δεῦρο: Demeas calls, and doubtless beckons, to Chrysis to take
refuge in his house.   **τίς καλεῖ μ᾽;** Chrysis is bewildered; so little does
she expect help to come from Demeas that she does not even recognize
his voice.   **εἴσω τρέχε:** Chrysis is still too baffled to obey, and hesitates;
thus when Nikeratos bursts out in pursuit, she has not reached the house
(574–5), but she has at least managed to get behind Demeas (or alternatively, Demeas has placed himself in front of her).

570 ποῖ σύ, ποῖ φεύγεις; is shouted at Chrysis. Demeas, now standing
between the two, faces up to Nikeratos.   **μονομαχήσω** 'I'm going to
be fighting a duel.' Most likely the allusion is to the armed single combats which had long been a feature of funeral games in Thrace (Hdt.
5.8), had been cultivated as an art in some Greek communities (Hermippus of Smyrna fr. 83 Wehrli: Mantinea, Cyrene; cf. already *Iliad*
23.798–825), attracted some interest at Athens in the late fifth or early
fourth century (Pl. *Lach.* 178a–184c, especially 182a ὅταν ... δέηι μόνον πρὸς
μόνον ... ἐπιθέσθαι), and were frequently sponsored by Macedonian rulers
in early Hellenistic times, as at the games given by Cassander at Aegae
in 316/15 (Diyllus *FGrH* 73 F 1; for the date, D.S. 19.52.5; for possible
implications for the date of *Samia* see Introduction §8). To Menander's
younger contemporary Poseidippus (fr. 23) these combats were so familiar that the life of οἱ μονομαχοῦντες had become a byword for wretchedness.
The contestants in such spectacles were of course young and vigorous men,

quite unlike Demeas or Nikeratos. Alternatively we may be meant to think of famous duels in myth such as those of Menelaus and Paris (*Iliad* 3), Hector and Ajax (*Iliad* 7), or Eteocles and Polyneices (e.g. in Euripides' *Phoenissae*); but the participants in these were men of heroic status and eternal fame, whereas Demeas, like the speaker in the Poseidippus fragment, clearly regards μονομαχεῖν as an unmitigated evil.

572-3 ἔα με ... | ... τῶν γυναικῶν: Nikeratos now intends, if he can get possession of the baby, to use it as a hostage to force Plangon, her mother and (if possible) Chrysis to tell him the truth about its parentage. We may be meant to think of Euripides' *Telephus*, in which Telephus seized the infant Orestes to force the Greek army to grant his request to be healed of his wound (Hyginus *Fab.* 101), an episode twice parodied by Aristophanes (*Ach.* 321–51, *Thesm.* 688–762).

573 μηθαμῶς: Demeas stands firm against Nikeratos, who will have been trying to get past him; he probably raises his stick in a threatening manner, though as yet there is no physical contact (otherwise Nikeratos would have said immediately what he says at 576: see Blume 1974: 231–2). Neither of the two transmitted readings (for μαινομαι as the reading of C, see Riad 1973: 207–9; it would have to be spoken by Nikeratos) is explicable as a corruption of the other: perhaps the greater part of the word was obliterated in an early copy, the text was supplemented by conjecture, and thereafter both the original and the conjectural reading survived in the tradition. Of the two readings, μηθαμῶς is preferable on two grounds. (1) If this were a conjectural supplement, it would probably have been spelt μηδαμῶς (see 140n. and cf. 562: μηθαμῶς indeed occurs nowhere else in *Samia*). (2) For Demeas to reply to Nikeratos' demand with a blunt 'Certainly not' is consistent with his attitude in the rest of the scene (especially in 579–82) and will help reassure the confused Chrysis that he is determined to protect her; it is, on the other hand, unlikely that Nikeratos would say 'I'm mad' at almost the only moment in this scene when he is *not* directly threatening murderous violence.

574-6 The assignment of lines to speakers hereabouts can be inferred from 573 (where Demeas makes evident his determination to defend Chrysis and the baby) and 576–7 (which show that it is Demeas, the speaker of 577, who was the first to use physical force). Nikeratos responds to Demeas' defiance of him by, in effect, warning him not to carry this to the point of violence. Demeas retorts that he does mean to use violence if necessary and, turning to Chrysis, urges her to get indoors at once. Chrysis still hesitates. Nikeratos advances another step or two towards Demeas, brandishing his stick again, and echoes Demeas' threat. Demeas shouts to Chrysis to run, and at last she does. Nikeratos tries desperately to get past

Demeas before Chrysis can disappear into the house, and Demeas either pushes him back or strikes him with his stick; either action would prima facie constitute the use of 'unjust violence' (χειρῶν ἀδίκων, see below), and Nikeratos calls on all and sundry to be witnesses to the assault. It seems as though Nikeratos, despite his threat, does not actually strike back; his demand at 578–9 that Demeas bring the baby out to him implies that by then, at least, he has given up the attempt to force his way through and seize the baby himself – presumably because he could not now do so except by entering Demeas' house without Demeas' consent (580n.) For what it is worth, the speaker-assignments adopted here are in conformity with the indications in B: the placement of *dicola* in C implies that, consistently with its reading μαίνομαι in 573, it assigns to Demeas all of 574–5 except for ἔγωγε.

574 θᾶττον is here an intensive ('really quick', 'quick and fast') rather than a literal comparative; this use of θᾶττον (cf. 658, 679, 720, *Perik.* 526 οὐκ εἰσφθερεῖσθε θᾶττον ὑμεῖς ἐκποδών; and Ar. *Clouds* 506, *Frogs* 94) is found also in high poetry (e.g. *Od.* 16.130, Soph. *Trach.* 1183). **εἰσφθάρηθι:** 373n.; this time, however, the use of –φθείρομαι does not connote detestation but merely impatience.

575 ἀλλὰ μήν 'all right then' (Denniston 1954: 342–3); cf. Aesch. *Ag.* 1652–3 εἶα δή, ξίφος πρόκωπον πᾶς τις εὐτρεπιζέτω. – ἀλλὰ κἀγὼ μὴν πρόκωπος. **κἀγώ σε** sc. τυπτήσω. We cannot tell whether Menander expected the actor to say κἀγώ σέ ('Then *I'll* hit *you*, too', Sandbach) or κἀγώ σε ('Then so will I'). **κρείττων ἐστί μου** is not necessarily to be taken as an accurate estimate of the two men's relative strength: Demeas is desperately anxious that Chrysis should go inside at once, and may be trying to scare her into doing so by warning her that he may not be able to resist Nikeratos if it comes to a fight. As there is probably no fight (see above), we will never discover whether he is indeed being over-pessimistic.

576 πρότερος ἅπτει μου: in a prosecution for assault (αἴκεια), the guilty party was the one who had 'been the first to use unjust violence' (ἦρχε χειρῶν ἀδίκων): cf. Lys. 4.11, Isoc. 20.1, Dem. 23.50, [Dem.] 47.40, 47. **ἅπτει** 'lay <violent> hands on'; cf. *Dysk.* 466 τί τῆς θύρας ἅπτει; (i.e. knock). **ταῦτ' ἐγὼ μαρτύρομαι:** 474n.

577–9 Demeas defends his use of force with the plea that he was protecting a 'free woman' whom Nikeratos was threatening to assault. We do not know whether the law contained a specific exemption covering such situations (e.g. for a person defending members of his household from imminent violence), but at the very least one might expect a jury to be sympathetic to the accused in such a case, in a society in which it was lawful to use *lethal* force against (among others) a thief, however petty, attempting to escape with his loot at night (Dem. 24.113). Demeas, of course, had probably himself – as the Mytilene mosaic suggests – raised his stick to Chrysis at some point(s) in the expulsion scene (369–98).

577 ἐλευθέραν γυναῖκα: 508n.

578 συκοφαντεῖς 'you're making a trumped-up accusation'. Elsewhere in Menander this verb always implies that the accusation is false (*Perik.* 378) and usually also that it was made for the sake of gain (*Georgos* F 1, *Epitr.* 218); it is therefore grotesque (but typical of him) that Nikeratos should speak thus of an accusation that is manifestly true.   **καὶ σὺ γάρ** (*sc.* ἐσυκοφάντεις) in a *tu quoque* or 'look who's talking' retort, implying that the addressee has no right to complain of what the speaker has done, since he has done the same thing himself to the speaker or others (cf. Ar. *Knights* 789, 1201). Demeas' accusation of συκοφαντία is as ill-founded as Nikeratos', since he certainly was the first to use physical force (otherwise he would have denied doing so, instead of attempting to excuse it): he too is getting carried away by anger, which he has now at different times displayed immoderately against every character in the play (Parmenon, 321–4; Chrysis, 369–98; the Cook, 388–9; Moschion, 481–9).

578–9 τὸ παιδίον | ἐξένεγκέ μοι: prevented by Demeas from seizing the baby in the street, Nikeratos is reduced to demanding that Demeas take it from Chrysis and bring it to him.   **τοὐμόν;** i.e. τοὐμὸν παιδίον ἐξενέγκω σοι; Demeas can hardly here be reverting to Chrysis' old fiction that he himself was the father of the baby; rather he is calling the baby his (as Chrysis in 568–9 called it hers) partly because it is a member of his *oikos* (and his eventual heir), partly because, in Moschion's absence, he (like Chrysis) has assumed the protective role of a parent, and partly because (also like Chrysis) he now cherishes it like a parent. Dedoussi's interrogative punctuation is essential; a statement ('it's mine!') would not be τοὐμόν but, as in 580, ἐμόν (*sc.* τὸ παιδίον).

580 ἰὼ 'νθρωποι: a call for help by a victim of crime (cf. D.L. 6.32). The act of uttering such a call was spoken of in Ptolemaic Egypt as βοᾶν ἀνθρώπους, a phrase found in several papyrus petitions (Bain 1981). The 'crime' of which he is complaining is the 'kidnapping' of his grandchild by Demeas; but he can more justly be regarded as himself the criminal, since he only wants to have the baby in order to extort information from its mother and grandmother by threatening its life.   **κέκραχθι** 'shout away', implying 'it'll do you no good', cf. Ar. *Ach.* 335, *Thesm.* 692 (both possibly deriving from Euripides' *Telephus*), also *Ach.* 186 οἱ δ'οὖν βοώντων.   **τὴν γυναῖκ'** 'my wife'. Having been forcibly prevented from doing what he wished to do (get possession of the baby), Nikeratos turns to what he sees as the only remaining alternative (τί γὰρ ποήσω;): he feels driven to vent his violent fury on *someone*, and with Chrysis, the ringleader of the alleged conspiracy against him (556–61), now inaccessible, his wife, who was also in the plot, can serve as a substitute. Arnott 1998b: 18–19 takes τὴν γυναῖκ᾿ to mean 'your partner', i.e. Chrysis, but this cannot be right. It was an extremely serious social offence to enter another person's house without the owner's consent or in his absence, except for a lawful purpose such as searching for stolen goods: it is striking that when Lysias' client Euphiletus had caught Eratosthenes in the act of adultery, knocked him down and tied him up, his first question was not 'Why have you seduced my wife?' but 'Why have you committed the *hybris* of entering my house?' (Lys. 1.25). If Nikeratos had announced his intention of doing this (let alone of killing Chrysis), Demeas' response τοῦτο μοχθηρὸν πάλιν· οὐκ ἐάσω would have seemed ludicrously feeble, when the threatened action was one that *no one* would tolerate: it applies much better to the unusual action of preventing a man from entering *his own* house for fear he may commit irreparable violence there.   ἀποκτενῶ: this is sometimes said hyperbolically by angry old men in Menander (*Dysk.* 931, *Epitr.* 1073; in both cases the prospective victim is an elderly female slave), and here it is certainly possible that Nikeratos 'only' intends to give his wife a beating, which in comedy is sometimes regarded as a husband's routine prerogative – cf. Ar. *Lys.* 160–2 (for refusing sex), 519–20 (for expressing an opinion on politics), Pl. com. fr. 105 (the only way to keep a wife well-behaved); but after his two previous murder threats (553–4, 560–1) it is quite understandable that Demeas fears Nikeratos may mean this one literally.

581 τί γὰρ ποήσω; 'What <else> am I to do?'

581–2 τοῦτο μοχθηρὸν πάλιν· | οὐκ ἐάσω: it is not clear whether this is spoken 'aside', or whether all or part of it is addressed to Nikeratos; in any case he takes no notice of it, and as Demeas is saying οὐκ ἐάσω Nikeratos begins to move towards his house, presumably to punish his wife (and, for all we or Demeas know, Plangon too). Demeas immediately runs after him.

582 ποῖ σύ; cf. 570; *com. adesp.* 1032.13.   μένε δή: either just before or just after saying this, Demeas grabs hold of Nikeratos' body or clothing, firmly enough to stop him completely.   μὴ πρόσαγε τὴν χεῖρά μοι: Nikeratos again complains of assault, but less strongly; from this point he begins to cool down. Demeas will retain his grip on him until satisfied that he is no longer dangerous – which may not take long: it is noteworthy that from 583 Nikeratos seems to forget about the women, against whom almost all his anger had been directed since he entered at 556, and complains only about Demeas (583–4, 596) and Moschion (585–6, 598–9, 612).

583 ἀδικεῖς... δῆλος εἶ = δῆλόν ἐστιν ὅτι ἀδικεῖς: cf. Ar. *Birds* 1407, *Lys.* 919, Pl. *Euthph.* 14b.

584 σύνοισθα: συν- implies that Demeas not only knows the full truth about the baby, but has been part of the conspiracy to conceal it from Nikeratos (Konstan 2011: 44).   **τοιγαροῦν ἐμοῦ πυθοῦ** 'that's why you should find out the facts from me'. The compound particle τοιγαροῦν (Denniston 1954: 566–8) is fairly frequent in Menander (e.g. *Dysk.* 347, 471, 761); Aristophanes by contrast uses it only once (*Wasps* 1098, in lyric).

585 τῆι γυναικί 'your wife' (580n.). In Menander ἐνοχλεῖν takes a dative of the person inconvenienced (713; *Dysk.* 232, 374, 458, 491, 693) except in *Mis.* 189 S = 589 A [τί] μ' ἐνοχλεῖς;

585–6 Throughout the previous fifty lines Nikeratos has made no mention, direct or indirect, of Moschion: 'when he saw that the child was Plangon's, the idea that Moschion was the father left his mind along with the idea that Chrysis was the mother' (Gomme and Sandbach 1973; cf. 535–6n.) Now he has calmed down sufficiently to remember that he had heard Moschion admit to being the father of the baby (479–87), and he at last puts two and two together.

586 ἐντεθρίωκεν 'has stuffed me like a fig-leaf'. A fig-leaf (θρῖον) stuffed with various savoury fillings was as popular a dish in Greece in antiquity as stuffed vine-leaves are today; cf. Ar. *Ach.* 1101–2, *Knights* 954, and see Dalby 1996: 79. Hesychius (ε 3328), evidently referring to this passage, glosses ἐντεθρίωκεν as ἐσκεύακεν (599), i.e. dealt with me as if I were a dish being prepared for the table. Demeas will pretend to take Nikeratos as meaning that Moschion intends to abandon Plangon; we are no doubt meant to understand that in fact Nikeratos is thinking of the violation itself, viewed as an offence against his honour.

586 φλυαρεῖς: here begins Demeas' attempt, which has succeeded by 613, to persuade Nikeratos that the circumstances of the baby's birth need bring no shame on him, and that the marriage of Moschion to Plangon can and should be allowed to go ahead. He does this by pretending to believe, and argue, that the baby's father may have been a god, as was so often the case in myth – and not only in myth: consider the case of Alexander the Great (see e.g. Plut. *Alex.* 27.8–10, Strabo 17.1.43, Hyp. *Dem.* 31–2). The mother of a god's son sometimes was, or became, the wife of a mortal (e.g. Alcmene of Amphitryon – or Olympias of Philip II), and this was seen (once the child's divine parentage was acknowledged) as an honour, not a disgrace, both to her husband and to her own family. Nikeratos does not actually believe Demeas' rigmarole (596, 598–9, 612); but 'the flattering comparison to a mythical king [Acrisius]... helps to defuse

Nikeratos' anger' (Gutzwiller 2000: 111), as does the humorous presentation of Chaerephon and Androcles as gods on earth, and the whole conversation gives him time to reflect and to realize that his best course of action is to carry on with the marriage.   λήψεται μὲν τὴν κόρην: so again 599 (in response to a similar outburst by Nikeratos), 610.

587 ἔστι δ' οὐ τοιοῦτον, placed where it is, can only be understood by Nikeratos as insinuating that Moschion is not really the father of the baby (it cannot mean that he will not betray Plangon, since that would not be in contrast with λήψεται... τὴν κόρην). Nikeratos will be mystified, as will the audience until they are reminded in 590–1 of the story of Danaë. περιπάτησον 'take a walk': by having himself and Nikeratos walk side by side, instead of standing face to face, Demeas hopes to reduce the tension between them.

588 περιπατήσω; Deliberative aorist subjunctive (569n.): 'you want me to take a walk?'   σεαυτὸν... ἀνάλαβε 'pull yourself together', cf. Isoc. 5.22.

589–90 οὐκ ἀκήκοας λεγόντων... | τῶν τραγωιδῶν: as in *Epitr.* 325–33, tragedy is appealed to as the prime source of mythological knowledge. Sophocles and Euripides both wrote plays entitled *Danaë* (Sophocles also an *Acrisius*, unless this was another name for the same play); Aeschylus' satyr-drama *The Net-Haulers (Diktyoulkoi)*, of which substantial papyrus fragments have survived, presented the arrival of Danaë and Perseus at Seriphos. The story was also the subject of comedies by Sannyrion, Apollophanes and Eubulus.

590 τῶν τραγωιδῶν: the performers of tragedy.

590–1 ὡς γενόμενος...|...ἐμοίχευσέν ποτε: Acrisius, having been told by the Delphic oracle that he would perish at the hand of a son of his daughter Danaë, shut her up in an underground chamber; but Zeus, being enamoured of her, impregnated her by pouring himself through the chamber roof in a stream of gold. When she was discovered to have given birth to a son (Perseus), her father set her and the child adrift at sea in a chest, which eventually came to land on the island of Seriphos. See Pherecydes fr. 10 Fowler; Aesch. *Pers.* 80; Soph. *Ant.* 944–50; Eur. fr. 228a.7–10; [Apoll.] *Bibl.* 2.4.1; Lucian, *Dial. Marini* 12. The story is assumed to be so familiar that Nikeratos (and the audience) will recognize it without any of the human characters needing to be named; in Menander's *Eunouchos* (cf. Ter. *Eun.* 583–91) a rapist may have compared his own actions to those of Zeus in this myth (see Garelli 2009).

591 ἐμοίχευσεν: cf. Ar. *Clouds* 1079–82, where Pheidippides is advised that if taken in adultery he should assert that he has done nothing wrong and that as a mere mortal he cannot be expected to be stronger than Zeus, who is always 'mastered by love and women'. This passage (cf. also 717) proves decisively (against Cohen 1991: 98–109) that the crime of μοιχεία included sexual violation not only of a man's wife but also of his unmarried daughter (and probably also of those other close female relatives whose seducer, under the law cited in Dem. 23.53, he was entitled to kill out of hand if caught in the act): Cohen does not mention the *Samia* passages, nor does Todd 2007: 46–9 in his survey of the issue.

592 ἴσως δεῖ πάντα προσδοκᾶν: i.e. perhaps one should regard nothing as impossible. Cf. Men. fr. 50 τὰ προσπεσόντα προσδοκᾶν ἅπαντα δεῖ ἄνθρωπον ὄντα, Alexis fr. 289, and the passage found at the end of several Euripidean plays (e.g. *Alc.* 1160–2) πολλὰ δ᾽ ἀέλπτως κραίνουσι θεοί· | καὶ τὰ δοκηθέντ᾽ οὐκ ἐτελέσθη, | τῶν δ᾽ ἀδοκήτων πόρον ηὗρε θεός.

593 ῥεῖ 'leaks': cf. Arist. fr. 558.1 [554 Rose] and 785 Gigon, Plut. *Mor.* 782e–f.

594 τοῦτο ... ἐκεῖν': τοῦτο = the state of Nikeratos' roof; ἐκεῖνο = the story of Danaë.   **χρυσίον** is here simply a less elevated synonym of χρυσός, as e.g. in Ar. *Wealth* 164, Pl. *Euthd.* 288e ὅπου τῆς γῆς χρυσίον πλεῖστον κατορώρυκται, Hdt. 3.97.3. Fourth-century comedians (589–90n.) may well have anticipated Horace's conversion of the stream of gold into a bribe to Danaë or to her guards (Hor. *Carm.* 3.16.8; cf. *AP* 5.31, 33, 34, Ovid *Am.* 3.8.29–34, all later than Horace); perhaps indeed in Euripides' *Danaë* Acrisius had suspected an intrigue of this kind (cf. Eur. fr. 324). Such an idea, however, would be irrelevant here, since bribery does not depend on a leaky roof.

595 ὕδωρ: rain comes from Zeus (e.g. *Mis.* A55–6 S = 55–6 A τοῦ Διὸς ὕοντος, Ar. *Clouds* 368–73, 1279–81), so it is no great stretch to conceive of Zeus as *turning himself into* rain-water.   **ὁρᾷς;** Cf. *Dysk.* 695; Ar. *Knights* 1164, *Clouds* 206, *Birds* 1616.

596 καὶ βουκολεῖς με; Cf. 530. καί introduces an indignant question (Denniston 1954: 311–12) as in *Phasma* 90 καὶ παρασκώπτεις μ'; and Ar. *Wasps* 1406 καὶ καταγελᾷς μου;

597 χείρων 'inferior to, less deserving than'. This is highly flattering to Nikeratos, since Acrisius was king of Argos ([Apoll.] *Bibl.* 2.2.1, Paus. 2.16.2, 2.25.7; cf. Bacch. 11.59–72).   **δήπουθεν** 'surely', 'presumably' (647, *Aspis* 397, Ar. *Wasps* 1296, *Peace* 1019); see Denniston 1954: 268–9. Demeas wishes to 'prove' that Zeus is the father of Plangon's child, and presents the following argument: Nikeratos is in no way the inferior of Acrisius; Zeus thought Acrisius' daughter worthy to be his mate (598n.); therefore Zeus might be expected to consider Nikeratos' daughter at least equally worthy. For δήπου(θεν) used in stating an argumentative premiss taken as self-evident cf. 456–8 (*Moschion ought to have been pleased at Chrysis' expulsion*; yet he is now pleading on her behalf; therefore he must be in league with her) and 485–7 (*many have done what I did*; therefore it cannot be such a very terrible thing).

598 ἐκείνην: Danaë (last mentioned, as καθειργμένην παῖδ', at 591). **ἠξίωσε** 'thought worthy of honour' (the honour of being the mother of a god's son, cf. [Aesch.] *Prom.* 648–9 γάμου τυχεῖν μεγίστου): for this sense of ἀξιόω cf. Soph. *Aj.* 1114, Eur. *Hec.* 319.   **τὴν γε σήν:** had Demeas not been interrupted, he might have continued εἰκός ἐστιν αὐτὸν ἀξιοῦν. **οἴμοι τάλας:** Nikeratos has at last understood what Demeas is saying – and has also realized that it is a smoke-screen covering Demeas' reluctance to admit openly that Moschion is the father of the baby.

599 ἐσκεύακεν evidently means much the same as ἐντεθρίωκεν (586) – on which, indeed, it is a gloss in Hesychius (586n.). A common meaning of σκευάζω is 'prepare (food) for serving', including cutting up, cooking, pouring on sauce etc., and one may compare English slang *carve up* 'cheat, swindle'.   **λήψεται μέν** *sc.* τὴν κόρην (cf. 586).

600 τοῦτο is probably to be taken as object of μὴ φοβοῦ, as the punctuation of C (adopted here) implies. Alternatively we might punctuate after 599, as B may have done (it has lost the end of the line), and take τοῦτο ... τὸ γεγενημένον together: the position of δέ is no objection to this (Dover 1985: 337–8).   **θεῖον ... τὸ γεγενημένον:** since θεῖος does not mean 'child of a god', τὸ γεγενημένον will mean 'the thing that has happened' (cf. Philemon fr. 109.3; Ar. *Peace* 704, *Eccl.* 457; Thuc. 2.5.4; Xen. *Hell.* 5.4.9; elsewhere τὸ γεγονός, 338, 351, 407, 422, 493, 527, 566) rather than 'the child that has been born' (cf. Arist. *HA* 584b13); cf. Hdt. 6.69.3 ὁ Ἀρίστων ἔμαθε ὡς θεῖον εἴη τὸ πρῆγμα (viz. that his wife had been visited by a phantom in his shape, later identified by seers as the hero Astrabacus).

601–2 Demeas undertakes to show that a divinely born child is nothing unusual: there are plenty of such individuals walking the streets of Athens! He argues, indeed, that Chaerephon and Androcles are *themselves* gods (604, 608), from which it follows automatically that they must have had at least one divine parent (like Dionysus – and Alexander, 586n.; most gods had two). His language (in particular μυρίους and δεινόν) echoes that of Moschion at 485–7, speaking about the same event; but Moschion's honest statement, being misunderstood, only made things worse for him, whereas Demeas' argument (and its insincerity) are perfectly well understood by Nikeratos and yet succeed in mollifying him.

601 εἰπεῖν ἔχω σοι 'I can mention to you.'   **ἐν μέσωι** 'in our midst',
'among the public'; cf. *Aspis* 345 'you'll be shut up in the house, σχῆμα
δ' ἐν μέσωι νεκροῦ | κεκαλυμμένον προκείσεταί σου'.

602 σύ δ' οἴει δεινὸν εἶναι τὸ γεγονός; I.e. seeing that such events are common, why should you be horrified when it happens to you? The passage
may be inspired by Eur. *Hipp.* 451–9 where Phaedra's nurse reminds her
that many gods and goddesses have had illicit love-affairs without loss of
reputation or self-respect and then asks σὺ δ' οὐκ ἀνέξηι; (cf. also Eur. *Phoen.*
543–7 'Sun and Night let themselves be governed by Equality without complaint, σὺ δ' οὐκ ἀνέξηι δωμάτων ἔχων ἴσον;' and *Supp.* 481–95 'To choose
war over peace is always stupid, wasteful and futile: σὺ δ' ἄνδρας ἐχθροὺς καὶ
θανόντας ὠφελεῖς, | θάπτων κομίζων θ' ὕβρις οὓς ἀπώλεσεν;').

603 Χαιρεφῶν (*LGPN* 3, *PAA* 975770) is frequently mentioned in late
fourth-century comedy (and related genres) as the typical parasite (Alexis
frr. 213, 259, Antiphanes fr. 197, Timocles fr. 9, Timotheus fr. 1; Machon
frr. 3, 4 Gow; Matron *SH* 534.9, 98; Lynceus of Samos *ap.* Athen. 584e); a
letter written by him, or in his name, to a fellow-parasite, describing a lavish
dinner, enjoyed sufficient circulation to be listed in Callimachus' great bibliography, the *Pinakes* (Callim. fr. 434 Pfeiffer). Of four other references to
him by Menander, all but fr. 215 are in plays otherwise known to be early
(fr. 304 from *Orge*, his first play; fr. 55 from *Androgynos*, produced not long
after the Lamian war (fr. 51); fr. 225 from *Methe*, produced before 318
(fr. 224.14, cf. Plut. *Phoc.* 35.5)). Two quotations by Athenaeus (243d-e)
in plays ascribed to Apollodorus of Carystus (frr. 29, 31), whose career may
not have begun till after Menander's death, are surprisingly late; but the
plays concerned may actually have been by Apollodorus of Gela, a close
contemporary of Menander (the first of them, *Hiereia*, is listed as his by
Suda α 3405). Thus all references to Chaerephon which are contemporary rather than retrospective probably come from the period 330–310.
In Nicostratus fr. 26, which is considerably earlier, there is no sign that the
Chaerephon who is addressed is a parasite. See Arnott 1996b: 610.   **ὃν
τρέφουσ' ἀσύμβολον** 'whom people feed without asking for a contribution'.
Dinner parties were often financed by contributions (συμβολαί) from all
those attending (cf. e.g. Ar. *Ach.* 1211, Eubulus fr. 72.3–5, Alexis fr. 15 with
Arnott 1996b: 86–98, Diphilus fr. 42.28–31); comedy constantly speaks
of parasites dining ἀσύμβολοι (e.g. Ephippus fr. 20, Alexis fr. 259 – of
Chaerephon – Timocles fr. 8.10, fr. 10, Diphilus fr. 74.8).

604 οὐ θεός σοι φαίνετ' εἶναι; because only gods could normally expect to
get their food (via sacrifices) without paying for it.   **τί γὰρ πάθω;** 'what
else can I do?', resigning himself to the inevitable; literally perhaps 'what
is <otherwise> to become of me?' (Dunbar 1995: 680). Cf. Ar. *Birds* 1432,

Lys. 884, *Eccl.* 860; Eur. *Hec.* 614, *Phoen.* 895; Pl. *Euthyd.* 302d. By accepting (or professing to accept) Demeas' nonsensical argument, Nikeratos shows that he accepts that Demeas is determined to make the marriage and that he has no real choice but to agree.

605 διὰ κενῆς 'to no purpose' (672, *Aspis* 373, 448, Ar. *Wasps* 929).   νοῦν ἔχεις: 187n.: this formula signals the re-establishment of Demeas' old ascendancy over Nikeratos.

606–11 are omitted by B, doubtless because a copyist's eye slipped from νοῦν ἔχεις (605) to the same phrase in 611. Blume 1998: 40 suggested that the lines were deleted by a producer at a time when the reference to a contemporary, Androcles, could no longer be understood; but only the first three of these six lines are about Androcles, and there would be no reason for a producer to cut the other three.

606 Ἀνδροκλῆς (*LGPN* 10) is not otherwise mentioned in comedy, unless he was the subject of Sophilus' play of that name – which was earlier than *Samia* (Sophilus is described by *Suda* σ 881 as a Middle Comedy poet). He was evidently an old man who looked and acted as though he were much younger. In view of πολὺ πράττεται (see below) it has long been found tempting to identify him, with Festugière 1970, as Androcles son of Xeinis of Sphettus (*LGPN* 55/57, *PAA* 128295), a rich man who made large maritime loans and other important financial transactions (cf. *IG* II² 1593.19–23), and the speaker of Demosthenes 35, delivered probably between 355 and 348 (MacDowell 2009: 262). The case for this identification has become much stronger since a rereading of *IG* II² 3073 revealed that this Androcles was director (*agonothetes*) of the City Dionysia (and set up an imposing monument to commemorate the fact) in 307/6, when he must have been in his seventies (Lambert 2003); his (younger?) brother Xenocles (*PAA* 732385), who had been a notable figure in Athenian public life since the mid 340s (*IG* II² 3019; see Lambert 2001: 52–9), was also prominent shortly after the fall of Demetrius of Phalerum, and was *persona grata* with the Macedonian Antigonids by whom Demetrius had been overthrown (*IG* II² 1492.100). This suggests that the family had been at odds with Demetrius' regime (cf. Bayliss 2011: 99, 102–3), so that between 317 and 307 Androcles would be a safe target for comic irreverence.

606–7 πολὺ | πράττεται 'he demands large payments' (cf. 392); we cannot tell what good or service he was supplying, but πράττεσθαι is often associated with interest on loans (Ar. *Thesm.* 843, Lys. 10.18, Lys. fr. 209 Carey, Thphr. *Char.* 6.9).

607 μέλας περιπατεῖ 'he goes around looking bronzed' (Ar. *Thesm.* 31; Dem. 21.71; Pl. *Rep.* 474e, 556d) from outdoor life and exercise (Bruzzone 2009); a dark complexion was associated with manliness and physical strength. Note that μέλας, like λευκός (e.g. Ar. *Thesm.* 191), when it qualifies a person, normally refers to the colour of his skin, not of his hair.

607–8 λευκὸς οὐκ ἂν ἀποθάνοι, | οὐδ' ἂν εἰ σφάττοι τις αὐτόν 'he wouldn't die pale, not even if you cut his throat' (Bruzzone 2009). This method of killing, as would be well known from its use in animal sacrifice, was the most efficient in draining the body of blood and making it resemble the pale wraiths in the underworld (cf. Ar. *Eccl.* 1071–3: a woman heavily made up with white lead is asked if she has 'risen up from among the majority', i.e. from the dead). Some men, such as Chaerephon the friend of Socrates, were so pale, even when healthy, that they were spoken of as living corpses (Ar. *Clouds* 103, 104, 503–4, *Wasps* 1413, *Birds* 1562–4; Eupolis fr. 253). But there was no way to make Androcles look like a corpse or a ghost: even if his throat were cut, his complexion would be as healthy as ever! And since, to that extent at least, death would not affect him, he must surely, by the logic Demeas is applying, be a god. Some editors have found it very tempting to improve that logic by punctuating after rather than before λευκός, to make Demeas say that Androcles 'would not die' even if his throat were cut, i.e. that he is immortal; but they have not offered any parallel to suggest that μέλας περιπατεῖ λευκός would be interpretable by an audience.

608 σφάττοι: Lambert 2003: 104 n. 18 suspects there may be a pun on Androcles' deme of Σφηττός (see above).   **οὗτός ἐστιν οὐ θεός;** For the unusual word order cf. Ar. *Peace* 672 κᾆσπευδεν εἶναι μὴ μάχας, *Frogs* 639 εἶναι τοῦτον ἡγοῦ μὴ θεόν. In those passages, however, the abnormality is due to the need to avoid the hiatus μὴ εἶναι: here, on the other hand, the normal order οὗτος οὐκ ἔστιν θεός; would present no metrical difficulty. And since C has placed words in the wrong order at 554 and 589 (and BC together at 590 and 653), Sandbach (*ap.* Austin 1967: 126) may well have been right to restore the normal order here.

609 ταῦτ' εὔχου γενέσθαι [σ]υμφέροντα: compare Dicaeopolis' prayer in Ar. *Ach.* 251–2 τὰς σπονδὰς δέ μοι | καλῶς ξυνενεγκεῖν τὰς τριακοντούτιδας. Such prayer or other ritual was particularly important if something had happened that was or might be ill-omened, such as the dream of Sostratos' mother in *Dyskolos* or of the Queen in Aeschylus' *Persians* (cf. *Dysk.* 417–18, Aesch. *Pers.* 216–223).

609–10 θυμία, | [σπένδε· τὴν] κόρην μέ[τε]ισ[ιν] echoes 158–9 σπείσας τε καὶ λιβανωτὸν ἐπιθεὶς [τὴν κόρην] μέτειμι: but this time it is Nikeratos who is envisaged as beginning the ritual preparations for the wedding feast. C appears to have read [την]τεκορην (Riad 1973: 211–12), but τε must be deleted: it gives dubious metre (resolution of the fourth syllable of a trochaic *metron* is very rare in Menander (Gomme and Sandbach 1973: 39)), and if any particle were needed δέ would be more appropriate here.

610 αὐτίκα: a somewhat overconfident statement, seeing that Demeas does not even know where Moschion is at this moment; over 100 lines later (714) Nikeratos will be wondering whether Moschion is ever going to appear.

611 πολλ[αχ]ῆι μὲν νοῦν ἔχει[ς] 'you show good sense in many ways' (cf. 605). The particle μέν shows that Demeas was going to say more but is interrupted; we cannot tell whether he would have said something like '…but particularly in this last decision' or something like '…but now let's get on with the preparations' (cf. 612–13).

612 εἰ δ' ἐλήφθη τότε – (*sc.* in the act of violating Plangon): there were various possible punishments, official and unofficial, that could be inflicted on a μοιχός (cf. 591; see MacDowell 1978: 124–5, Carey 1993), but one of them, if he was caught in the act, was summary killing (Dem. 23.53–5; Lysias 1), and the Nikeratos we have seen in this Act (553–5, 560–1, 580) is the sort of man who might do that – or at least the sort of man to *say* he would have done it. Demeas hastily interrupts him to forestall his saying anything so inauspicious. Later (717–18), Nikeratos will actually threaten (or pretend to threaten) to imprison Moschion as a μοιχὸς εἰλημμένος – though he could not have carried out the threat, since Moschion at that moment is armed and Nikeratos is not. The raising here of the counterfactual possibility of homicide may possibly recall Eur. *Hipp.* 1412–13 where Theseus wishes that he had never uttered the curse upon his son (in the false belief that Hippolytus had raped Phaedra) and the mortally injured Hippolytus replies 'Well, in that case you'd have killed me outright, you were so angry at that moment.' **πέπαυσο:** 350n.

612–13 πόει | τἄνδον εὐτρεπῆ: as Demeas had been doing (221) before he overheard the conversation that revealed to him that Moschion was the baby's father, leading to the almost catastrophic events that have filled Acts III and IV.

613 ποιήσω…πόει: Nikeratos has now completely subsided, and with these two one-word answers he agrees that the marriage shall go ahead as originally planned.

614 κομψὸς εἶ 'you're a smart fellow' (cf. *Perik.* 298), virtually synonymous with νοῦν ἔχεις (605, 611), though perhaps with a stronger (and flattering) suggestion that Nikeratos is not merely acting sensibly on this occasion but is sensible by nature. Nikeratos goes into his house – the fourth time he

has done so in this Act (not counting his abortive attempt at 580–1), but
the first time he has done so in a peaceable mood. Demeas' remaining
words are soliloquy; accordingly C has a *dicolon* after κομψὸς εἶ.

615 οὐθὲν…γεγονέναι: echoing the words of Moschion that began the
movement towards this dénouement, οὐδ᾽ εἰ μηδὲν ὧν σὺ προσδοκᾷς | γέγο-
νεν 521–2).

Demeas goes into his house to complete his side of the wedding preparations. All now seems settled, or so the two fathers think. The audience,
however, know that there is still a fifth Act to come in which some further
problem will arise (a common pattern in Menander – see next note), and
many will guess that this problem is likely to involve Moschion, who fled
from the scene at 539 and is unaware of what has happened since.

ACT V

If the fourth act of a Menandrian comedy generally brings the main issue
of the play to a climax and resolution (see opening note to Act IV), the
fifth act (Holzberg 1974: 121–6, 130–3, 177–8) may introduce a new
issue, or revive one from earlier in the play, which prevents the celebratory conclusion from being reached immediately. In *Dyskolos*, for example,
two such issues arise in succession – the reluctance of the newly-arrived
Kallippides to agree that *both* his children should marry into a relatively
poor family (784–96) and the refusal of Knemon to join the celebrations
(874–8) – one of which is resolved by persuasion, the other by coercion.
In *Epitrepontes* there are likewise two successive and separate movements
in the final act, and they involve two characters who return to the scene
unaware of crucial recent developments, Chairestratos (who is in love with
Habrotonon, but assumes he has lost her permanently to Charisios: Furley 2009: 241) and Smikrines (still trying to end the marriage between
Charisios and Pamphile). Here in *Samia* we also have two returning characters, Moschion and Parmenon, who are ignorant of the current situation; but although Parmenon is given a long and amusing monologue
(641–57), it leads to nothing, and there is only one new movement, initi-
ated by Moschion. As previously suggested (615n.), many spectators may
have anticipated as much, but they are unlikely to have guessed the nature
of the new development. They may well have expected Moschion to be
anxiously wondering whether the wedding has been called off; but in a
monologue of twenty-five lines he does not mention the wedding at all.
He has been brooding over recent events and become extremely indignant that his father should have suspected him of having had an affair
with Chrysis – indignation that is totally unjustified, given that half of what
Demeas believed was actually true (that Moschion was the baby's father),

that the other half (that Chrysis was the mother) was a lie in which Moschion himself had concurred, and that in any case Demeas had already (537–8) freely admitted to Moschion that he had done him wrong by suspecting him.

Sometimes in New Comedy a son at odds with his father will leave home to become a mercenary soldier, as in the back-story of Terence's (and presumably also Menander's) *H(e)auton Timorumenos* (93–118; Plaut. *Trin.* 597–9; similarly in Plaut. *Merc.* 660, 830–41 Charinus decides to go abroad, though not as a mercenary); see Zagagi 1988. Moschion has thought of doing this, but is too much in love with Plangon to be able to go through with it; so he has decided to *pretend* to be on the point of going abroad, to give his father a fright (it does not occur to him that he will be giving Plangon and her mother a fright as well, and probably further angering Nikeratos). This is the second deception in which Moschion has been involved, and it leads to nothing but humiliation for him, as he fails to foresee that others 'will either take his plan too seriously or not take it seriously at all' (Arnott 1997: 71). He first has to listen to a friendly yet severe lecture (694–712) by a Demeas who, unlike his son, is fully aware of his own errors, and then finds himself the target of well-deserved mockery (715–22) by a Nikeratos who is thus enabled to take some small revenge for Moschion's crime against his family – and who presently takes further revenge by announcing, in effect, that Moschion will receive no dowry (727–8). Thus scenes like the ragging of Knemon at the end of *Dyskolos* or of Smikrines at the end of *Epitrepontes* – or, further back, of a Lamachus or a Paphlagon in early plays of Aristophanes (Sommerstein 2000: 25–31) – find their counterpart in *Samia*, but, to the audience's probable surprise, it is the bridegroom, Moschion, who becomes the victim. Moschion himself seems to have learned nothing: his last word to his father is an ill-judged rebuke (724–5) before the play rapidly ends with a formal betrothal (726–9) and a joyful mass exit with the usual accompaniments of garlands and torches (731), an appeal for applause (733–5), and a prayer for victory in the festival competition (736–7).

Another feature apparently common in Menander's fifth acts is a prominent role for a slave character. In *Dyskolos*, Getas takes the lead in the merciless ragging of Knemon that fills the second half of Act V, and it is he who concludes the play; in *Epitrepontes* Onesimos seems to have been on stage throughout most of the act, and in its second half he toys with Smikrines at considerable length before eventually deigning to reveal to him that he has a legitimate grandson; and in the poorly preserved final act of *Misoumenos* Getas seems to have had an important role, perhaps with a major speech describing an alleged suicide attempt by his master Thrasonides (Kraus 1971: 26; Maehler 1992: 62; Arnott 1996a: 250–1, 339–41). In *Samia*, when Parmenon reappears, the audience may have been expecting something comparable; but after running away from the threat of a flogging by Demeas (321–5), he soon finds that he has returned only to suffer actual violence from Moschion (679), for no offence except having told him that all is ready for him to take his bride!

Up to 669 the dialogue is in iambic trimeters; but at 670 – when Parmenon comes out of Demeas' house bringing, not the requested sword and cloak, but the news that the wedding preparations are virtually complete – the metre changes to trochaic tetrameters (see opening note to Act IV), which continue to the end of the play.

Moschion returns along Eisodos A (539n.).

616 ἐγώ: an appropriate beginning for a monologue which reveals Moschion to be preoccupied with his own hurt feelings to the virtual exclusion of everything else: in twenty-five lines it contains ten first-person pronouns or possessives and eighteen verbs or participles of which Moschion is the subject. **ἧς εἶχον αἰτίας** = τῆς αἰτίας ἣν εἶχον 'of the accusation made against me' (50–1n.). **μάτην** 'falsely'. The adverb is found in this sense in tragedy (e.g. Soph. *El.* 63, 1298), but there is no other clear case in comedy, so this, like ἐλεύθερος (see next note), may be an early indication that Moschion is over-dramatizing his situation.

617 ἐλεύθερος in the sense 'cleared of an alleged wrongdoing' likewise occurs only here in comedy; in tragedy cf. Soph. *Ant.* 445, Eur. *Hipp.* 1450. **ἠγάπησα** 'I was content' (385n., *Dysk.* 745).

619–20 ἔννους γίνομαι | καὶ λαμβάνω λογισμόν: it is highly paradoxical that Moschion should become 'beside himself' *as a result of reasoned reflection*. It is true that this is more or less what happened to Demeas in Act III – though he did not actually use expressions like these – when the evidence of what he had heard and seen (267–79) forced him to conclude that Moschion must be the baby's father and to cry ἐξέστηχ' ὅλως: but Moschion in this speech produces no evidence or argument to show that his father's suspicions were not reasonable in the circumstances, and we may already suspect that what he speaks of as reasoned reflection was actually mere emotional brooding.

620–1 ἐξέστηκα νῦν | τελέως ἐμαυτοῦ: cf. 279; but the long, well-constructed, carefully contrasted pair of sentences that follows (623–32; see especially 623–5n.) suggests strongly that Moschion's statement here is a gross exaggeration.

621 παρώξυμμαι: contrast 612 μὴ παροξύνου – and Nikeratos, the addressee in 612, had far juster cause for indignation than Moschion has now.

622 μ' ὁ πατήρ (C) and ὁ πατήρ μ' (B) are both acceptable readings, but C's is to be preferred because it places the enclitic pronoun as early as possible in the sentence, in accordance with a very ancient tendency of the language (Wackernagel 1892 = 1955: 1–104), whereas B places it next to the verb that governs it; this is a case of the kind of corruption known as *simplex ordo* (Headlam 1902: 243–4).   **ἡμαρτηκέναι:** but, on his own showing (3), Moschion *had* committed a serious ἁμάρτημα, though not the one of which Demeas had supposed him guilty, and he had also committed the further ἁμάρτημα of attempting to deceive his father – an offence which he is now about to repeat. He never in this Act acknowledges any of these offences. Demeas himself, in contrast, even as he rebukes Moschion in 694–712, will refer three times to his own single and eminently forgivable error as a ἁμαρτία (703, 704, 707) and also as ἀδικία (696, 702), ἄνοια (708), and μανία (703).

623–5 This counterfactual conditional protasis is remarkably complex. It consists of two parallel clauses, the second of which has in apposition to its subject (τοσαῦτ') an asyndetic series of four nouns, three of which together (πόθος, χρόνος, συνήθεια) serve as the antecedent to a relative clause.

623 εἰ...καλῶς...εἶχε τὰ περὶ τὴν κόρην: from all we have heard in Acts I, II and IV about Moschion's feelings for Plangon, we would expect this to mean 'if I were sure that I would be allowed to marry her': after Nikeratos' frenzied denunciation of him (especially 502–5), followed by his discovery that Plangon is the baby's mother, he may well feel that his prospects are now poor. But as the sentence continues, we discover that εἰ καλῶς εἶχε actually means 'if I were not so much in love with her, and not bound by my sworn promise'. For the sake of punishing his father, in other words, he would cheerfully abandon Plangon and his infant son, were it not that *he* would then suffer the pangs of unfulfilled passion and run the risk of divine retribution for his breach of oath: so self-centred is his present attitude, and so much has his mind been warped by his ruminations on the 'wrong' done him by Demeas.

624–5 ὅρκος, πόθος, | χρόνος, συνήθει': this asyndetic series is an example of a common rhetorical trope for emphasizing the cumulative weight of several factors; cf. e.g. Dem. 18.124–5 οὗ μὲν ἦν παρ' ἐμοῦ δίκην... λαβεῖν...ἐξέλειπες, ἐν ταῖς εὐθύναις, ἐν ταῖς γραφαῖς, ἐν ταῖς ἄλλαις κρίσεσιν· οὗ δ' ἐγὼ μὲν ἀθῶιος ἅπασι, τοῖς νόμοις, τῶι χρόνωι, τῆι προθεσμίαι, τῶι μηδεπώποτε ἐξελεγχθῆναι...ἀδικῶν..., ἐνταῦθ' ἀπήντηκας; and Dem. 21.72 (cited for its vividness by Long. *Subl.* 20).

624 ὅρκος: see 52–3. **πόθος:** some spectators may remember the only other occurrence of πόθος in the play (350), when Demeas – whom Moschion now intends to punish for his unjust suspicions – urged himself to forget his πόθος for Chrysis, and expel her from his home, in order to spare the reputation of Moschion whom he believed, on no direct evidence, to be the innocent victim of her wiles.

625 χρόνος, συνήθει': a virtual hendiadys (so Sandbach), 'long familiarity': cf. *com. adesp.* 1017.28 ἡ μὲν συνήθει', ἡ φιλία, τὸ διὰ χρόνου, Dem. 18.125 (above) τοῖς νόμοις, τῶι χρόνωι, τῆι προθεσμίαι (= 'by the time-limitation which the law prescribes') and for the general sense Ter. *Hec.* 404 *amor me graviter consuetudoque eius tenet.* Moschion has been in regular (though, except on one occasion, not improper) contact with Plangon at least since the time their fathers went abroad (29/30, 30–4, 36–8, 57/8nn.). Long acquaintance was considered a desirable foundation for marriage: in *Aspis* (260–3) Smikrines, who is claiming the legal right to marry Kleostratos' sister (an ἐπίκληρος, after his supposed death), is urged to allow her to marry Chaireas instead because the young people had grown up together. **οἷς ἐδουλούμην ἐγώ** 'through which I gradually became enslaved', an early example of the theme, familiar from the Roman elegists, of love as enslavement (*servitium amoris*, on which see Copley 1947, Lyne 1979, Fitzgerald 2000: 72–7): cf. *Mis.* F 2 S = F 4 A, *Dis Ex.* 24–5, Men. fr. 791, Pl. *Symp.* 184b–c.

626–7 οὐκ ἄν... αὖθις ἠιτιάσατο | ... τοιοῦτ' οὐδέν: the aorist implies that Moschion *would already have taken action* (viz. leaving for abroad) which would have made it impossible for Demeas to do the same thing again: translate 'he wouldn't have had the chance to make another accusation like that'. **παρόντα... | αὐτόν** are to be taken together, 'when I was present in person', i.e. speaking in front of me and thus putting me maximally to shame.

626 αὖθις and αὖτις are both found elsewhere in Menander papyri, their distribution being apparently random, and it is impossible to tell with confidence which form the author used here.

627–8 ἀποφθαρεὶς | ἐκ τῆς πόλεως 'I'd have buggered off out of town ...': here (contrast 373n.) the use of (ἀπο)φθείρομαι does not imply a curse, only a rapid departure.

628–9 εἰς Βάκτρα ποι | ἢ Καρίαν ' ... to some place in Bactria or Caria'. Bactria (corresponding approximately to eastern Turkmenistan today) was one of the remotest parts of the new Macedonian world, and 'Moschion might take it for granted that soldiers would always be needed [there]' (Gomme and Sandbach 1973: 543). After he has thus emphasized his wish to be as far away from Athens and his father as possible, his mention of Caria, in south-western Asia Minor, comes as something of an anticlimax; but Caria (*Sik.* 6, 137; cf. Ter. *Eun.* 126, *HT* 608) and nearby Lycia (*Aspis* 23, 67, 225) seem to be particularly associated with mercenary service in the minds of Menander and his audiences, and there was a good deal of fighting in Caria between 315 and 313 (D.S. 19.62.5, 68.2–7, 75.1–5). On the possible bearing of these references on the date of the play, see Introduction §8.

629 διέτριβον αἰχμάζων ἐκεῖ 'I would be living the life of a spearman there'. αἰχμάζειν is an epic/tragic word (*Iliad* 4.324; Aesch. *Pers.* 756; Soph. *Trach.* 355, *Aj.* 97; [Eur.] *Rhes.* 444) found nowhere else in comedy.

630 νῦν δ' 'but as it is'.   **Πλαγγὼν φιλτάτη:** 436n.; other Menandrian lovers use φιλτάτη in *Mis.* 308 S = 709 A, *Perik.* 1020, fr. 96. For the apostrophe to a person not present cf. *Aspis* 2, 14, 284, *Dysk.* 220.

631 ἀνδρεῖον: 64n.; Moschion's grasp of the meaning of 'manliness' seems as uncertain as that of Demeas or Nikeratos. In this context, too, the word may make us wonder how well a young man who did not have the courage to tell the truth to his father until it was almost too late, and who then ran away from one unarmed old man, would be likely to fare as a soldier.   **οὐδ'** appears here to be equivalent to οὐ γάρ (Denniston 1954: 198 (cf. 169), on *Iliad* 9.372); Moschion's statement that to go abroad is 'impossible' badly needs an explanation, and none is offered except his love for Plangon.

632 This line is elevated in tone and (unlike the preceding four and following three lines) would be metrically acceptable in tragedy; cf. Eur. fr. 136 σὺ δ' ὦ θεῶν τύραννε κἀνθρώπων Ἔρως. Seneca (*Phaedra* 218) puts in Phaedra's mouth the line *Amoris in me maximum regnum puto*: is Menander here quoting or adapting a line from Euripides' *Hippolytos Kalyptomenos* (cf. Eur. frr. 428, 430)? Eros is spoken of as a personal god in *Heros* F 2 and Men. frr. 176, 339, 792.

633 μήν 'nevertheless' (Denniston 1954: 334–5). This is the only passage in comedy (unless Ussher's conjecture at Ar. *Eccl.* 756 is correct) where the particle μήν appears without the support of another particle (καί, ἤ, ἀλλά, οὐδέ or γε) preceding or following it; in tragedy cf. Eur. *Alc.* 1018, 1108, *IT* 889.   **ταπεινῶς οὐδ' ἀγεννῶς** 'cravenly or ignobly'. In fact it was not considered at all improper or unmanly to tolerate unjust treatment *by a parent*; Dover 1974: 273–4 gives ample evidence of the importance attached to filial obedience and submission. Aristotle (*EN* 1163b15–22, 1164b5) can equate the honour due to parents with that due to the gods, since to both alike one owes a debt which is beyond all repayment.

634 παριδεῖν 'overlook', cf. Dem. 21.123-4.   τοῦτ': Demeas' suspicion
and accusation.   τῶι λόγωι μόνον *sc.* τῶι δὲ ἔργωι οὔ.

635 εἰ μηθὲν ἄλλ' is to be taken closely with what follows: 'I want to *frighten*
him, if nothing else.' It should be remembered that, in general, to go
abroad as a mercenary soldier, especially if (like Moschion) one was an
only son, was to put one's life in the utmost jeopardy for purely personal
gain, and to leave one's parent(s) at risk of enduring a wretched old age
and leaving no son to tend their tomb. Kleostratos in *Aspis* is in a different
position: he had no parents living, and his objective in going on campaign
was to raise funds to provide a dowry for his sister (*Aspis* 8-10).

636 εἰς τὰ λοιπά is regular in Menander (*Dysk.* 320, 561) for earlier εἰς τὸ
λοιπόν (Ar. *Wasps* 748; Eur. *Andr.* 55, 1215).   γάρ: on the position of
this particle see 44n.

637 ἀγνωμονεῖν: the meaning of ἀγνώμων can range from 'without intelligence' (Aeschines 3.244, of inanimate objects) or 'foolish, stupid' (e.g.
Men. fr. 641, Apollodorus com. fr. 7.6) to 'heartless, unkind, cruel' (e.g.
Epitr. 918); this last sense is the most appropriate here, but the word is
anyway not one that a son should be using in reference to his father's
behaviour.

638 φέροντα μὴ παρέργως τοῦτ' 'not taking this casually', cf. Dein. 3.14
δεῖ μὴ παρέργως ἔχειν πρὸς τὰς ὑπὸ τῆς βουλῆς γεγενημένας ἀποφάσεις, ἀλλ'
ἀκολούθως ταῖς πρότερον κεκριμέναις 'the reports made by the Council [of
the Areopagus] should not be treated lightly, but in a manner consistent
with those on which judgement has already been given'.

639-40 Parmenon is now seen approaching along Eisodos B (see note at
start of commentary and 324n.). The fact that Moschion does not name
him suggests that by the time he speaks this line, Parmenon is already visi-
ble to the audience.   εἰς δέοντά μοι πάνυ | καιρὸν ... ὃν μάλιστ' ἐβουλόμην:
these expressions make it clear that Moschion intends to make use of Parmenon in some way to carry out his scheme of deception. The scheming
slave (Krieter-Spiro 1997: 96-102) was as familiar in Greek New Comedy
as in its Roman descendants – Daos in *Aspis* is an outstanding example –
and Menander may exploit the convention by creating the expectation
that a slave character will be of this type and then disappointing it: thus in
Dyskolos, when Sostratos is brutally rebuffed by Knemon, he feels sure that
his father's slave Getas will be able to help him (*Dysk.* 180-4), but Getas
in fact gives him no help at all, and he wins his beloved by an entirely different route. In this case it will prove that all Moschion wants Parmenon
to do is to bring him a cloak and sword (and then, perhaps, to make a

show of departing together with him towards the harbour). Because Moschion is looking to Parmenon to perform a role that is typical for slaves in comedy, it is unlikely to strike the audience as odd that he is putting his confidence in Parmenon when he knows (cf. 477–9) that Parmenon had betrayed his secret to Demeas (and does not know that this, for Demeas, was only confirmation of what he had already discovered).

641–57 While it is common in Greek drama (e.g. Eur. *Bacch.* 215–47, Ar. *Lys.* 387–97), and especially in Menander (J. Blundell 1980), for an entering character to deliver a monologue, addressed to no one in particular and sometimes ignoring the presence of other persons, there is no close parallel to this passage: Moschion has just told us that Parmenon is the very person he wanted to meet and has arrived at the right moment, yet he allows Parmenon to speak seventeen lines – which are of no particular interest to him, and to which he never subsequently refers – before accosting him. Presumably Menander calculated that this stretching of convention was an acceptable price to pay for the opportunity to create this monologue with its amusing combination of self-exculpation (in the matter of the baby, and the plot to conceal its true parentage), self-condemnation (for taking fright, and taking to flight, without good reason), and anticlimax (reminding himself, 654–7, that he *did* in fact, whether innocent or guilty, have good reason to flee). The monologue also has dramatic value in that it invites comparison with that of Moschion immediately before. Both Moschion and Parmenon were part of the conspiracy to deceive Demeas. Parmenon reviews the key events, and puts the entire responsibility on Moschion and Chrysis (the τις of 651). Moschion has condemned Demeas for his suspicions, as if the conspiracy had not been their main cause. Is it the free man or the slave who is more blatantly refusing to face up to the facts?

641 νὴ τὸν Δία τὸν μέγιστον: a weightier version of the usually casual oath νὴ (τὸν) Δία: it is frequent in New Comedy (e.g. *Dysk.* 835, *Sik.* 157, Men. fr. 397) but occurs only once in earlier texts (Dem. 48.2).

642 εὐκαταφρόνητον 'for which one might well be regarded with contempt': unconsciously ironic in the mouth of a slave, who could expect to be despised by his betters in any case.   ἔργον... εἰργασμένος: the *figura etymologica* ἔργον ἐργάζεσθαι is not infrequent in comedy (e.g. Men. fr. 296.2–3; Ar. *Ach.* 128, *Knights* 844), but with the perfect participle it tends to have an air of solemnity (*Epitr.* 895, Charisios rebuking himself; Ar. *Frogs* 1474, Euripides rebuking Dionysus; Ar. *Birds* 1175) and may be redolent of tragedy (cf. Aesch. *Pers.* 759, Soph. *Trach.* 706).

643 οὐθὲν ἀδικῶν: 328, 537nn.

644 τί δ' ἦν... πεποηκώς: when Parmenon asked Demeas the same question (307–8), Demeas replied συγκρύπτεις τι πρός μ', and Parmenon effectively admitted this when he spoke of λανθάνειν (320).

645 καθ' ἕν... οὑτωσί: perhaps Parmenon here lifts up a hand in front of him and in 646–652 counts off the events (there are four of them) on his fingers.

646 ὁ τρόφιμος 'my young master': properly the word denotes the son and heir of a slave's owner (e.g. *Dysk.* 413), but a slave would often continue to use the term after the old master's death (e.g. *Aspis* 2, *Epitr.* F 1). This sense of τρόφιμος, which is not found before Menander, will have developed from the word's earlier sense 'nursling' (Eur. *Ion* 684, Archippus fr. 25, Pl. *Polit.* 272b); the new sense may at first have been applied to the special relationship between a boy and his παιδαγωγός (or a girl and her nurse, cf. perhaps *Dysk.* 883).   **ἐξήμαρτεν:** 3n. In *Dysk.* 290–1, contrariwise, ἐξαμαρτεῖν is used of a woman yielding to the persuasion of a seducer.

646–7 ἐλευθέραν | κόρην: ἐλευθέρα κόρη (or παρθένος or παῖς) in Menander always denotes an unmarried girl *of citizen status*, eliding the many who were neither citizens nor slaves (*Georgos* F 4; *Dysk.* 50, 64, 290–1; *Epitr.* 495–6). In *Epitr.* 794 a contrast is drawn between an ἐλευθέρα γυνή and a πόρνη when, in the hypothetical situation envisaged, the latter (Habrotonon) would almost certainly have been given her freedom (cf. *Epitr.* 536–8 and probably 792 [γαμε]τῆς ἔχουσα σχῆμ').

647 ἀδικεῖ... οὐδὲν Παρμένων: this, and Parmenon's further third-person references to himself in 648 and 652, may well be imitations of Demosthenes' self-exculpation in his speech *On the Crown* (Dem. 18.303): 'if the power of some god, or of fortune, or the incompetence of military commanders, or the villainy of you people who were betraying the Greek states, or all these things together, assailed our whole position until it was wrecked, τί Δημοσθένης ἀδικεῖ;' This in turn may have been adapted from the language of court indictments (e.g. Xen. *Mem.* 1.1.1 ἀδικεῖ Σωκράτης... ἀδικεῖ δὲ καὶ...).   **δήπουθεν:** 597n.

650 ἤνεγκ' ἐκεῖνος: i.e. Moschion was *responsible* for its being brought (cf. 54 εἴληφ'); it would more likely have been Chrysis who actually carried the baby into Moschion's house.

651 τῶν ἔνδον... τις: Chrysis, like Plangon (646–7), is not named or precisely identified; Parmenon is presenting the sequence of events in entirely general terms, almost as if it were a draft plot for a drama (cf. Arist. *Poet.* 1455b16–23: τις = Odysseus, τινας = Telemachus, Eurycleia, Eumaeus and Philoetius). There is no need to suppose with Sandbach that he is trying to put Chrysis 'at a distance'.   **ὡμολόγησε** 'professed', cf. 524. C's ὡμολόγηκε will be due to anticipation of πεπόηκεν (652): throughout this passage the events that occurred are referred to in the aorist, and Parmenon asserts his innocence in non-past tenses (ἀδικεῖ... οὐδέν 647, οὐκ αἴτιος (sc. ἐστιν) 648, πεπόηκεν 652).   τοῦτο sc. τὸ παιδάριον.

652 Parmenon's rhetorical question cannot be taken as in itself proving that the plan for Chrysis to pose as the baby's mother was not his suggestion (57/8n.). Even if it was not, he was undoubtedly *party* to the deception. ἐνταῦθα 'in respect of that', cf. *Epitr.* 912, Soph. *OT* 582.

653 οὐθέν... ἔφυγες echoes 643–4 οὐθὲν ἀδικῶν... ἔφυγον.   οὕτως ἔφυγες: both papyri have these words in the reverse order, but that order is not metrically possible unless we read ἔφευγες (B), and the imperfect tense is not appropriate here – Parmenon is clearly thinking of his flight as a completed action (as it was – he did get clear away).

653–4 ἀβέλτερε | καὶ δειλότατε: both these epithets were earlier applied by Moschion to himself: he told Parmenon that he was feeling δειλός at the thought of approaching his father (65) and later said in soliloquy that he had been ἀβέλτερος to waste the opportunity of rehearsing what to say when he did approach him (126).

654 γελοῖον probably means 'that's an absurd question' (71, *Georgos* F 4) – because the answer (given directly afterwards) is obvious – rather than 'that (viz. running away) was an absurd thing to do'; if the latter were meant, Menander would probably have added δέ or ἀλλά to the next sentence, to make it clear that Parmenon was having second thoughts and arguing that his behaviour had *not* been absurd.

654–5 ἠπείλησέ με | στίξειν: 323n.   με: object of στίξειν: μοι (C), governed by ἠπείλησε, would be equally correct (cf. Lys. 3.28 ἠπείλουν αὐτῶι ἐγὼ ἀποκτείνειν), but the pronoun is more likely to have been linked in error with ἠπείλησε in the same line than with στίξειν in the next. Sandbach interpreted -σεμε as -σ' ἐμέ, implying that Parmenon is indignant that he alone should be singled out for punishment; but his reason for mentioning Demeas' threat is not that it was unjust (he will presently be saying that it makes no difference whether it was unjust or not) but that it explains and excuses his flight.

655 μεμάθηκας; 'You remember?' Cf. 378, and for the perfect tense *Dysk.* 419.   [ἀ]λλ' οὐδὲ γρῦ: for ἀλλ' οὐδέ see 359n.; for οὐδὲ (or μηδὲ) γρῦ cf. *Mis.* 291 S = 692 A, Men. frr. 265, 412, Antiphanes fr. 188.13, Ar. *Wealth* 17, Dem. 19.39. The literal meaning of γρῦ was disputed in antiquity, but it is likely to be connected with γρύζειν 'make a sound': οὐ(δὲ) γρύζειν (*Dysk.* 931; Ar. *Wasps* 741, *Lys.* 509, *Frogs* 913, *Wealth* 454) means the same as οὐδὲ γρῦ λέγειν.

657 ἀστεῖον 'nice, agreeable' (364n.)   οὗτος 'hey, you!', a brusque form of address (312, 675, 680), which in Menander is used only to or by slaves (and once in self-address, *Sik.* 401); see Dickey 1996: 154–8.

658 ἃ φλυαρεῖς ταῦτα 'this nonsense you're talking', referring to Parmenon's long speech, which on Parmenon's own showing (654–7) was based on an absurd premise (that he had had no good reason to run away from Demeas).   θᾶττον: 574n.   χλαμύδα καὶ σπάθην: the standard attributes of the stage soldier, cf. *Perik.* 354–5.   χλαμύδα: a type of cloak associated especially with soldiers (*Perik.* 354, *Sik.* F 3 S = F 6 A) and ephebes ([Arist.] *Ath.Pol.* 42.5, Philemon fr. 34, Antidotus fr. 2.2); see Stone 1981: 169, *BNP* s.v. chlamys.   σπάθην: σπάθη, originally meaning 'blade', became New Comedy's normal word for 'sword': ξίφος, once the standard term, is found only in *com. adesp.* 1085.9 and as a doubtful restoration in *Mis.* 109 S = 509 A. Likewise σπάθη is used at Thphr. *Char.* 25.4 (the only mention of a sword in the *Characters*). The word was later borrowed into Latin (as *spatha*) – though not attested before Tacitus (*Ann.* 12.35) – and eventually displaced *gladius*, becoming the ancestor of Italian *spada*, French *épée* etc.   τινά may not necessarily imply that Moschion 'is so little of a soldier that he has no sword of his own' (Sandbach), since he would probably have needed one while an ephebe (10n.), but together with Parmenon's question σπάθην ἐγώ σοι; it does suggest that he has rarely or never touched a sword since then.

660 καὶ ταχύ: 193n.

661–4 Parmenon's questions, and his slowness to obey Moschion's order, need not be entirely due to the strangeness of the order itself: he may also fear the possibility of encountering Demeas, whom he would presume to be still angry with him. He eventually complies with the order when faced with the near-certainty of physical punishment by Moschion if he dallies further.

661 σιωπῆι: i.e. without saying any more *to me*. Moschion does not mean that Parmenon is to be silent *while inside the house*, since (as 664–8 makes clear) he positively desires that his preparations for departure should be discovered by Demeas; but Parmenon apparently misunderstands him (688–9n.).

662–3 εἰ λήψομαι | ἱμάντα (cf. 321): he would have continued κλαύσει 'you'll be sorry for it' (cf. *Mis.* 220 S = 621 A), or the like, but Parmenon hastily interrupts him. The future indicative in a conditional protasis is often used to convey a threat, e.g. Aesch. *Eum.* 597, Soph. *Ant.* 324–6, Eur. *Med.* 351–4.

663 μηδαμῶς sc. λάβῃς ἱμάντα.   **βαδίζω:** he begins to move towards the door of Demeas' house, at first rather slowly.

664–8 Left alone, Moschion explains his plan. He expects that Demeas, discovering that his son is about to go abroad as a soldier, will beg him to stay; he will resist his father's pleas for a time, but eventually he will yield. His expectations – and the audience's – will repeatedly be cheated. At 670 and again at 686 it is not Demeas who appears but Parmenon, and then, when we had almost given up expectation of seeing Demeas (for Parmenon has said, 688–9, that nobody inside had seen him take the cloak and sword), Demeas comes out after all (690) – but not to beg or plead. See Katsouris 1976: 101–2.

664–5 δεήσεται | οὗτος καταμένειν δηλαδή 'no doubt (339) he'll beg <me> to stay'. The text has often been doubted, because (1) one would expect δεήσεται to be governing a genitive of the person appealed to (μου, added here unmetrically in C), as in 682–3, and (2) elsewhere in Menander δηλαδή invariably appears at the end of a line; but there is a parallel for (1) in *Dysk.* 676–7 ἐδεόμην γε μὴ ποεῖν τοῦθ' 'I begged <her> not to do that' (viz. cry, tear her hair etc.: 673–4) and for (2) in the possibly Menandrian *com. adesp.* 1093.119 (also Philemon fr. 73).

666 ἄλλως 'in vain', 'fruitlessly'.   **μέχρι τινός** 'up to a certain point' is a phrase not found before Aristotle but common in his writings (e.g. *EN* 1150a16–18 ἐπεὶ δ' ἔνιαι τῶν ἡδονῶν ἀναγκαῖαί εἰσιν, αἱ δ' οὔ, καὶ μέχρι τινός, αἱ δ' ὑπερβολαὶ οὔ...) and in those of Theophrastus (e.g. *HP* 2.6.10). It was restored by Lloyd-Jones 1966 in *com. adesp.* 1091.3 (μεχ[pap.)   **δεῖ γάρ:** sc. in order to give Demeas a real and prolonged fright (635).   **ὅταν δοκῆι** 'when I see fit'.

667–8 πιθανὸν εἶναι... | ...ποεῖν ἐγώ 'Only it's got to be credible <as a threat>, the thing [viz. going abroad] which, by Dionysus, I'm not capable of actually doing': cf. 630–1 οὐ ποήσω...οὐ γὰρ ἔξεστ'. This construal makes better sense than the alternative of taking ὅ to refer to τὸ πιθανὸν εἶναι: if Moschion thought that he could not make his pretence convincing even for a limited time, it would be pointless for him to make the attempt at all.

668 μὰ τὸν Διόνυσον: a particularly appropriate oath to be uttered by one who is about to act a part (see Blume 1974: 266). Compare, variously, *Aspis* 347 (Chaireas fails to understand the purpose of Daos' scheme for the family to 'perform a tragedy' (329) by faking Chairestratos' illness and death); Ar. *Clouds* 519, *Wasps* 1046 (the dramatist discussing his own career); and Ar. *Eccl.* 344, 357, 422 (all spoken by Blepyrus while dressed as a woman).

669 τοῦτ᾽ ἔστιν 'this is it!' Moschion has heard the sound of his door being opened (300–1n.), and assumes that Demeas is coming out to confront him.   ἐψόφηκε: here (contrast 567) ψοφεῖν is transitive as in *Dysk.* 586, 690, *Epitr.* 875 etc.; the subject is Demeas.

670 It is not, however, Demeas who comes out but Parmenon – and without the requested cloak and sword. On going inside he had found preparations for the wedding in full swing, and he cannot understand why Moschion should wish to go abroad when his dearest hopes are about to be fulfilled. (Moschion has not told Parmenon the reason for his request, but he can easily guess it, since only a soldier would need a sword.) The metre changes to trochaic tetrameters (see opening notes to Acts IV and V).   ὑστερίζειν: lit. 'to be behindhand compared with', i.e. 'not to be up to date with'.

671 τ᾽ (B), not δ᾽ (C): Parmenon is not making a fresh point, but restating and expanding on the point he has already made.   οὐδ᾽: here, however, C's reading is preferable: if we read οὔτ᾽ (B) the preceding τ᾽ would have to be taken as looking forward to it (cf. Eur. fr. 522, Pl. *Theaet.* 159e: Denniston 1954: 509) rather than as connecting this sentence with the previous one.

672 διὰ κενῆς: 605n.   ἀθυμίαν: knowing nothing of what has happened since his flight at 324, Parmenon can only assume that Moschion believes the projected marriage has fallen through and that he is taking up the life of a soldier out of despair.   τ᾽ could acceptably stand either before or after ἀθυμίαν, but both papyri write it in the latter place, and B's subsequent insertion of τ after εισ may well be a mere miscorrection of its original reading εισθαυμιαν, the corrector at first wrongly taking θ as an elided form of τε.

673 οὐ φέρεις; Moschion is only interested in his scheme to punish Demeas; as his next response to Parmenon will show, he is even giving it priority over his marriage.   κεράννυται: sc. ὁ οἶνος (a gloss οἶνος has actually found its way into the text of C). That the wine is now being poured into a κρατήρ and mixed with water shows that the drinking of it is expected to commence very soon; so in Ar. *Eccl.* 834–41 a herald, inviting the public to come immediately to a banquet, tells them that the tables are laden, the couches prepared, and κρατῆρας ἐγκιρνᾶσιν.

674 θυμιᾶτ᾽ 'incense is being burned' (158, 609–10nn.).   ἐνῆρκτ᾽ 'the sacrificial basket has been dedicated' (222n.). Note that this and the next verb are perfect, indicating that the stated parts of the sacrificial ritual have already been completed. ἀνῆρται (B after correction – though one suspects that its exemplar may have read ανηρκται) is a corruption due to the proximity of ἀνῆπτ(αι): Dedoussi, who prints it, offers no parallel for ἀνα(ε)ίρω with a dative in the sense 'lift up to/over'. **θύμαθ':** i.e. those parts of the sacrificial animal that were burnt on the altar (401n.); cf. Eur. fr. 781.261 θυμάτων πυρουμένων, Soph. *Ant.* 1006. The animal, then, has already been slaughtered, and the parts of it destined for the table are doubtless being cooked. B's σπλάγχνα θ' is unlikely to be right: the particle τε would destroy the balanced asyndetic series of four passive verbs (two present, two perfect), and the internal organs (σπλάγχνα) of a sacrificial animal were not burned but roasted, cut up and distributed to those present (cf. *Iliad* 2.426-7, Ar. *Peace* 1039-1126). That θῦμα is a word 'as much used in prose as in verse' (Sandbach) does not make it inappropriate company for Ἡφαίστου φλογί (see next note): θῦμα is about ten times as frequent in tragedy as in comedy, and its poetic air is enhanced by the fact that it is used in the plural (as in the two tragic passages cited above) and without a definite article. **Ἡφαίστου φλογί:** a highly poetic periphrasis (*Iliad* 9.468, 17.88; *Od.* 24.71; Ar. *Wealth* 661) which curiously does not appear in surviving tragedy ([Eur.] *IA* 1602 was written many centuries after Euripides' time). We cannot tell whether Ἡφαίστου is a possessive genitive (the flame belongs to Hephaestus as the god of fire) or a genitive of identity (the flame *is* Hephaestus, cf. *Iliad* 2.426, Soph. *Ant.* 1006-7 ἐκ δὲ θυμάτων (!) Ἥφαιστος οὐκ ἔλαμπε).

675 σε... <σέ> 'you – yes, *you*'. This is the likeliest restoration of the syllable which the metre shows to be missing: for the repetition cf. *Aspis* 455 σέ, σέ. **οὗτοι** is more likely to denote Demeas and Nikeratos (who arranged the marriage in the first place, and have now agreed once again to go ahead with it) than Demeas and his household; Parmenon will thus have made a large gesture towards both the two houses, rather than pointing specifically to Demeas' house. Both Demeas (690) and Nikeratos (714) will presently show themselves to be impatient with Moschion's apparent failure to return.

676 μετιέναι τὴν παῖδα: 158-9, 432-3nn. **μέλλεις;** Either 'are you going to...?' or 'will you waste more time before...?' Through the middle three Acts it had been Moschion himself who was eager to fetch his bride as soon as possible, and had complained about delays; now, as in Act I (67-75), though for an entirely different reason, it is Parmenon who is urging him not to delay further.

676-7 εὐτυχεῖς...|...τί βούλει; Four times Parmenon tries to reassure Moschion and induce him to go and take his bride; Moschion at first ignores him, then shows increasing signs of impatience and anger.

677-8 νουθετήσεις...|ἱερόσυλε; Typical for a master who is given good advice by his slave but has already made up his mind; cf. *Epitr.* 1063-4

(Smikrines to his daughter's old nurse Sophrone) νουθετήσεις καὶ σύ με; |
προπετῶς ἀπάγω τὴν θυγατέρ', ἱερόσυλε γραῦ;

677 ἱερόσυλε: literally, 'temple-robber', but in practice simply a term of
abuse; temple-robbers, together with traitors, were the only criminals who
were forbidden, after execution, to be buried in the soil of Attica (Xen.
Hell. 1.7.22). In Menander the term is normally (e.g. *Epitr.* 935, 952, 1064,
1100, 1122) but not invariably (*Dysk.* 640) used in addressing slaves; it is
not found as a form of address in earlier comedy. As he utters this word,
Moschion angrily strikes Parmenon in the face. Such onstage violence to a
slave is notably rare in comedy (Konstan 2011: 48): in *Epitr.* 1062–75 (cf.
previous note) Smikrines threatens to break Sophrone's head, to beat her,
and to drown her, 'if you say a word more' (1069) – but she remains silent
(being played by a non-speaking performer), and no violence occurs. Even
in Aristophanes there is only one instance of an actual blow being struck,
Peace 255–7 – and that may be an exception that proves the rule, since the
striker is War (Πόλεμος): the parallel passages cited by Olson 1998: 121–2
to show that 'Aristophanic masters routinely give their slaves spontaneous
blows' are all in fact instances of threats which are not carried out or are
evaded by flight.   **παῖ:** an exclamation of shocked surprise (see 360n.),
soon to be echoed by Demeas (691) and Nikeratos (715) also in reaction
to Moschion's behaviour.   **Μοσχίων:** 192–3n.; it is not uncommon for a
slave to address his τρόφιμος by name (*Dysk.* 95, 140; *Perik.* 272, 284, 335).

678–9 Moschion simply repeats his original order to Parmenon (and perhaps raises his fist again), thus implying that his answer to Parmenon's
question is 'I'm giving you what you deserve for not obeying me promptly.'
Parmenon still does not immediately comply, since he is feeling his face
for any injury.

678 διακέκομμαι τὸ στόμα 'I've split my lip'; cf. Ter. *Ad.* 558–9 *Ctesipho me
pugnis miserum . . . usque occidit . . . . em vide ut discidit labrum.* This is probably
spoken by Parmenon to himself, though Moschion hears it; it has to be
included in the script because only thus can the audience know of the
injury (the actor being masked).

680 ἔτι λαλεῖς: cf. *Dysk.* 504 καὶ λαλεῖς ἔτι;, *Epitr.* 1068–9 οἰμώξει μακρά | ἂν
ἔτι λαλῇς τι.   **βαδίζω:** 663n. Parmenon begins to move back towards the
door, but again slowly. After this word there is a *dicolon* in B, indicating that
Parmenon's next words are spoken to himself.

680–1 νὴ Δί' ἐξεύρηκά γε | τόδε κακόν 'this certainly *is* a spot of trouble that
I've got myself into!'; cf. Soph. *Trach.* 24–5 'I was terrified [when Heracles
and Achelous were fighting for my hand] μή μοι τὸ κάλλος ἄλγος ἐξεύροι
ποτέ'. Parmenon has returned home still apprehensive of what Demeas

might do to him (661–4n.), discovered unexpectedly that all is well, told Moschion the good news – and been hit in the face for it.

681 μέλλεις; 'Are you <still> dawdling?'   **ἄγουσι τοὺς γάμους ὄντως:** Parmenon still cannot understand why Moschion is so uninterested in taking his bride, and can only think that perhaps Moschion had not grasped, or had not believed, the news he gave him at 673–4; so he tells him again that the news really is true.   **πάλιν;** i.e. πάλιν τοῦτό μοι λέγεις; Cf. *Dysk.* 500 πάλιν αὖ σύ (sc. ἥκεις);

682 ἕτερον ἐξάγγελλέ μοί τι: these words may be spoken at Parmenon's departing back (cf. *Epitr.* 376; see Taplin 1977: 221–2, Frost 1988: 14) as he at last disappears into the house. Moschion merely means 'I don't want to hear any more about that from you', i.e. 'at this moment I'm only interested in getting the cloak and sword'. But taken literally, he is saying he would prefer that the wedding should *not* go ahead! This is also, of course, the message that his apparent intention to go abroad as a soldier is designed to convey to Demeas.   **νῦν πρόσεισιν** '*now* he [Demeas] will come to me'. Moschion, left alone, returns to his thoughts of 664–8.

682–4 ἂν δέ μου | ... | ... τί δεῖ ποεῖν; The possibility that Demeas might react by saying, in effect, 'all right, go and be damned to you' may seem a very remote one, particularly with the wedding preparations at such an advanced stage; but Moschion has had recent experience, from Demeas' behaviour both to Chrysis and to himself, of how his father can speak and act when his anger is aroused.

683 δέητ'... καταμένειν: the language is identical to that of 664–5. **ἄνδρες:** 5, 269nn.; here, as at 216–7, the speaker is ostensibly asking the audience to help him answer a difficult question he has put to himself. **ἀπογισθείς** 'in a burst of anger', cf. LXX *II Macc.* 5.17, the only other attestation of this verb. It could in principle mean 'recovering from his anger' (cf. 419n.), but the context precludes any potential ambiguity: Moschion has no reason to believe that Demeas is angry with him at this moment.

684 ἄρτι: i.e. in 664–8.   **τί δεῖ ποεῖν;** The question is unanswerable: Moschion would be forced to choose between a humiliating climb-down (686) and carrying out his threat – which is the last thing he wants to do (630–2, 668).

685 ἴσως is here nearer to 'probably' than to 'perhaps', as in *Dysk.* 730 οἴομαι [*sc.* ἀποθανεῖσθαι] ... καὶ κακῶς ἴσως ἔχω.   **ἐὰν δέ;** 'but if he does?' – the non-negative equivalent of the common ἐὰν (εἰ) δὲ μή.

685–6 πάντα ... | γίνεται 'anything can happen' (592n.).

686 γελοῖος ἔσομαι: which indeed happens, though not in the way Moschion or the audience expect (713–25n.).   **ἀνακάμπτων πάλιν** 'if I backtrack', 'if I make a U-turn'; cf. *Dysk.* 256.

687 Once again it is not Demeas but Parmenon who comes out, this time with the cloak and sword; the latter will be in a scabbard which in turn is attached to a belt. Moschion will put on the cloak as soon as it is handed to him (688), and will have buckled on the sword by the time Demeas appears (690), since at 693 Parmenon can say that his young master is completely ready for departure and indeed 'as you see, already...on his way'.

688–9 When Moschion asks whether anyone in the house had seen Parmenon taking the cloak and sword, he replies, twice, that no one did. He assumes that that was what Moschion wanted to hear; Moschion had failed to tell him that he *wanted* Demeas to discover that he was about to depart (664–8n.), and Parmenon had taken it for granted that his mission was supposed to be a secret one – particularly, no doubt, when he entered the house for a second time, knowing that Demeas was making all preparations for the wedding and would probably be angry to learn that Moschion was about to abscond. Parmenon thus expects Moschion to be pleased with his replies; Moschion is in fact furious, and curses him. This may well make Parmenon suspect that Moschion does not really intend to go abroad at all (690–4n.).

689 ἀλλά σ' ὁ Ζεὺς ἀπολέσαι (optative, 141n.): curses of this form, invoking either Zeus or '(all) the gods', are normally in Menander directed at slaves (*Dysk.* 139, 600–1, 927; *Epitr.* 424–5), except at *Dysk.* 221, where it is addressed to the absent Knemon for not properly protecting his daughter; cf. 677n.

690–4 Are we to understand that Parmenon really believes that Moschion is intending to go abroad as a soldier, or that he has perceived it is only a pretence? And if the latter, is he assisting in the deception, or trying to undermine it and embarrass his young master? The one word φλυαρεῖς (690) probably offers a key to understanding the passage. It can hardly be spoken by Moschion, since it would reveal to Parmenon (who might in turn reveal it to Demeas) that he was not in earnest about going away. It must therefore be *Parmenon* who is commenting on *Moschion's* words or behaviour, having perceived on his own that Moschion is play-acting. His suspicions having been aroused by Moschion's extreme annoyance on learning that Parmenon had not been seen while indoors (688–9n.), he tests them by urging Moschion to go at once (πρόαγ' ὅποι μέλλεις); Moschion does not move, and Parmenon is now certain that he is pretending (φλυαρεῖς). At this moment Demeas appears on the scene (see below). If

Parmenon now wanted to ruin Moschion's scheme, he would have said something which at least suggested to Demeas that Moschion was not really meaning to go away; instead he draws Demeas' attention to the 'fact' that Moschion has already taken his departure (693) and implies that he himself will be going with him (694). Parmenon is thus siding with Moschion against Demeas, as he did in the original deception scheme concerning the baby. Both father and son have abused him (Demeas with more justice than Moschion), but Parmenon apparently resents Moschion's cuff and curse less than he does Demeas' threat of a savage flogging (306–7, 321–4).

690 πρόαγ' ὅποι μέλλεις 'get a move on (cf. *Dysk.* 866, *Sik.* 146) to where you're meaning to go', i.e. (initially) to the harbour. Moschion remains motionless.

Demeas now comes out of his house, looking for Moschion. His surprise on seeing Moschion attired as a soldier (691) shows that Parmenon had been telling the truth about not having been seen taking the sword and cloak; he is seeking him simply because, with all now ready for the wedding, the bridegroom has apparently not yet arrived.   **εἶτα ποῦ 'στιν, εἰπέ μοι;** Demeas is speaking over his shoulder (198, 301, 421nn.) to someone (we may perhaps suppose it to be Chrysis) inside the house; (s)he may have just assured him that (e.g.) Moschion cannot have run away, and he irritably replies 'Well, in that case, tell me, where *is* he?' Cf. *Dis Ex.* 102–3 εἶτ' ἀκούσας ἐνθάδε | εἶναί με, ποῦ γῆς ἐστιν; 'well, if he's heard that I'm here, where on earth is he?'

691 παῖ: 360, 677nn.: Demeas is amazed to see Moschion wearing a military cloak and a sword. The parallels at 678 and 715 strongly suggest that παῖ is here the exclamation of surprise, not the vocative of παῖς (129, 148).   **πρόαγε θᾶττον:** if Parmenon is now assisting Moschion in his scheme (690–4n.), this will be said aside to Moschion, who needs to make a show of actually departing if he is to induce Demeas to eat humble pie as he desires. Moschion begins to move towards Eisodos A.   **ἡ στολὴ τί β[ούλετα]ι;** 'What's the meaning of this get-up?' (LSJ στολή II 1); cf. Ar. *Eccl.* 753 τί τὰ σκευάρια ταυτὶ βούλεται; Demeas is now addressing Moschion directly (otherwise this question would be mere repetition of his previous question τί τοῦτο;) Moschion ignores him, and in fact will not say anything to Demeas until 721.

692 τί τὸ πάθος; 540–1n. The end of this line cannot be restored with any confidence, and my suggestion [πρὸ τῶν γάμων] is meant merely to indicate one possibility.

693–4 With Moschion refusing to respond to his father's questions, Parmenon answers on his behalf, and elaborates the pretence by implying that he himself will be going away as Moschion's attendant (as Daos had accompanied Kleostratos on the expedition from which he returns without his master at the beginning of *Aspis*).

693 ἐν ὁδῶι: cf. Thuc. 2.12.2, Xen. *Cyr.* 5.3.54.   [νῦν δὲ δεῖ]: δεῖ is preferable to χρή, being ten times more frequent in Menander (Arnott 1998b: 19).

694 κἀμέ does not necessarily imply that Moschion has already bade farewell to the rest of the household (which Demeas would know to be false); Parmenon may be saying, in an elliptical but readily intelligible manner, 'I <will> also <be going with him, and therefore> must now take my leave of the people inside.'   προσειπεῖν 'bid farewell to', cf. *Dysk.* 884; at *Epitr.* 1113, on the other hand, it means 'greet'.   ἔρχο[μ' εἴσω] is probably preferable to the widely favoured alternative ἔρχο[μ' ἤδη]: a character making an exit into the *skene* normally says εἰσέρχομαι (390, *Mis.* 266 S = 667 A, *Perik.* 525) rather than simply ἔρχομαι. Parmenon now goes inside; the actor playing his part will shortly be needed in the role of Nikeratos (who enters at 713).

694-712 Demeas' speech is rather different from what Moschion had expected and hoped for. He neither pleads with Moschion not to go away (664-6) nor angrily tells him 'you can go for all I care' (683-4). In fact he never, throughout the speech, makes any explicit mention of Moschion's apparent intention to go abroad. Instead he focuses on its cause, Moschion's anger; this, he says, is quite understandable in the circumstances (695-6), and he had been very wrong to suspect Moschion as he did (696, 702-3, 710) – but he did his very best to keep his suspicions secret (705-6), whereas Moschion (if he leaves home) will be advertising the quarrel to the world (706-8); and besides, he is Moschion's father and greatest benefactor (698-700), and the 'one day in my life when I slipped up a bit' (709-10) is far outweighed by all the things he has done for Moschion in the past (698-700; we first heard of this beneficence from Moschion's own lips, 7-18). We could well understand it if Moschion was at a loss to answer this; there may be a noticeable silent interval before he is rescued from his embarrassment, for the moment, by the appearance of Nikeratos.

When Menander makes one of his characters give an ethical lecture to another, the seriousness of the argument is generally counterbalanced by some incongruity or inappropriateness in the relationship between speech and situation, as when the lecture is delivered by a son to his father (140ff, *Dysk.* 797-812), or by a slave to a free man (*Aspis* 189ff), or is based on a misapprehension (*Dysk.* 269-98), or has a concealed ulterior motive

(140ff again). Here none of these features is present. As Moschion's adoptive father, Demeas is the person who has the greatest right to rebuke his conduct; and while he has been himself partly to blame for the quarrel, he freely admits and even exaggerates his culpability. If there is a comic point in the passage, it must lie elsewhere, most likely in Moschion's reception of the speech. He shows no sign of appreciating Demeas' affection or contrition, nor any willingness to recognize that he himself bears any responsibility for the day's troubles. The only comment on the speech that we ever hear from Moschion comes at 724–5 when he says that if Demeas had asked Nikeratos sooner to bring out his bride to him, he 'wouldn't have been put to so much trouble moralizing (φιλοσοφῶν) just now' – entirely forgetting that he himself had previously rejected Parmenon's advice to go and fetch his bride at once (676). Perhaps during Demeas' speech Moschion shows obvious signs of boredom (e.g. by fidgeting or stretching his limbs; cf. Ar. *Ach.* 30, *Wasps* 642).

It appears from 707–8 that Demeas 'takes Moschion's apparent preparations for departure at face value' (Grant 1986: 173); his statement that Moschion is 'now' giving publicity to Demeas' mistaken actions can refer to nothing else. He understands correctly, however, without needing to be told, that Moschion is angry with him, and also the reason why: this is dramatically convenient (making it unnecessary for the audience to hear Moschion's explanation for a second time) and also highlights the 'profound emotional affinity between father and adopted son' (Zagagi 1994: 64).

694 [Μοσχίων]: it is all but essential, with Moschion seemingly determined to ignore Demeas' attempts to speak to him, that Demeas should now begin with a vocative in the hope of attracting his attention; he apparently succeeds.

695 ὅτι μὲν ὀργίζει, φιλῶ σε: this may seem a bold paradox, but it was considered proper, indeed manly, to feel angry when one was wronged or slighted, and one who did not could be thought 'foolish' or 'servile' (Arist. *EN* 1126a3–8; see Barigazzi 1970: 149); Demeas would not wish to feel he had a weakling for an adopted son.

696 ἀδίκως αἰτίαν. [: the last partly preserved letter is probably ε or σ, and is likely to be the remnant of some form of the verb ἔχειν: αἰτίαν ἔχειν (50–1n.) can mean either 'be accused' or 'bear responsibility, be to blame', and either sense is possible here, according to how we restore the end of the line. With a restoration like σ[χών, εὔλογον (Sandbach), ἀδίκως will modify αἰτίαν σχών and the line will mean 'If you feel hurt because you've been unjustly accused, that's entirely reasonable'; with a restoration like ἔ[γωγ' ἔχω] (Austin), ἀδίκως will modify λελύπησαι and the line will mean 'If you've been unjustly made to feel hurt, I'm the person who has caused it' (and we should then probably print a comma after ἀδίκως). Either alternative would fit the context well; Austin's is perhaps slightly preferable because it has Demeas make his disarming admission of blame at an early stage (otherwise he would not do so before 702).

697 θεώρει 'consider' (LSJ θεωρέω III 2), mainly a prose usage, but found at *com. adesp.* 1017.52.   **τίνι πικρο͞[**: the last partly preserved letter (necessarily a vowel) is either ο or ω. To Demeas' question the implicit answer must be 'your father' (cf. 698), though this need not have been spelled out in the text. With Dedoussi's restoration cf. Men. fr. 827 ὁ σκληρότατος πρὸς υἱὸν ἐν τῶι νουθετεῖν | τοῖς μὲν λόγοις πικρός ἐστι, τοῖς δ' ἔργοις πατήρ: with Kamerbeek's, Dem. 18.207 κελεύων ὑμᾶς ἐμοὶ πικρῶς ἔχειν, 21.215; with Lamagna's ('who do you think you're treating savagely?'), *Dis Ex.* 16 χρῆσαι πικρῶς. There is little to choose between them.

698 [ἀν]αλαβών 'adopting', cf. Arist. fr. 76.

699 εἴ σοι χ[ρόνος τι]ς γέγονεν ἡδύς: Demeas well knows – as does Moschion himself (7–18) – that almost the whole of Moschion's life hitherto has been pleasant; but such understatements are common in appeals to reciprocity whether addressed to humans or gods, e.g. Soph. *Aj.* 520–1 (Tecmessa to Ajax, whose faithful concubine she has been for several years) ἀνδρί τοι χρεών | μνήμην προσεῖναι, τερπνὸν εἴ τί που πάθοι, *Iliad* 1.40–1 (Chryses to Apollo, whose priest he has been for much of his long life) εἰ δή ποτέ τοι κατὰ πίονα μηρί' ἔκηα | ταύρων ἠδ' αἰγῶν.

700 δι' ὅν: the antecedent is τοῦτον (= τὸν χρόνον τὸν ἡδύν).   **ἀνασχέσθαι** 'endure, tolerate'.   **σε δεῖ** 'you ought to...' is preferable to σ'ἔδει 'you ought to have...', not only because B usually marks elisions and has not done so here, but also because Demeas is less concerned with recriminating about the past than with ensuring that Moschion does not *now* carry the quarrel to the point of a public breach; at 709–12 his words presuppose that Moschion's choice between defiance and obedience has not yet been irrevocably made.

701 τὰ λυπήσαντα 'things which have grieved you'.   **τι τῶν ἐμῶν:** more likely 'one of my actions' than 'one of my character traits', since Demeas is presenting his mistaken accusation as an untypical aberration; this is the first of several indefinite pronouns and adverbs (τι 702, 710; ποτε 705; cf. μίαν 710) which he uses to refer to it.

702 ὡς ἂν υόν 'as a son should' (518n.).

703 ἠγνόησ', ἥμαρτον, ἐμάνην: another asyndetic series (624–5n.) rising to a powerful climax.   **ἠγνόησ'** 'I was under a misapprehension'; the discussion of ἄγνοια in Arist. *EN* 1110b18–1111a21 puts the emphasis throughout on the agent's false belief (e.g. that his spear had its point capped, or that the drug he administered was medicinal when in fact it was poisonous). Similarly in *Perikeiromene*, when the goddess/personification Ἄγνοια, who speaks the (delayed) prologue, says that she provoked Polemon into anger (*Perik.* 162–5), she means that he became angry because he believed that Glykera had been seen kissing a lover when in fact she (though not the young man himself) knew he was her brother (*Perik.* 147–58). In the present case Demeas' misapprehension was that Chrysis was the mother of the baby; he chooses to disregard the fact, already admitted by Moschion (529), that Moschion himself had been party to the deception.   ἐμάνην: Demeas had said himself that the discovery that Moschion was the baby's father had driven him out of his mind (279), and his behaviour before and during the expulsion of Chrysis had seemed insane to the Cook, to Chrysis herself and to Nikeratos (361, 363–6, 415, 416, 419); he is thinking here, however, of his subsequent behaviour towards Moschion. He is again being extremely harsh with himself.   ἐκεῖνο[: the last partially preserved letter is most likely to be ι or ρ. Since ἡλίκη[ν] in the next line, if correctly read, comes too late in its clause to be taken as exclamatory, that clause (εἴς γε ... ἔσχον) must be taken as an indirect question (with the relative adjective taking the place of the indirect interrogative, as it often does: Smyth 1956: 601–2), and that points to something like Austin's ὀρ[θῶς σκόπει] 'consider properly' for the end of 703: ὀρθῶς σκοπεῖν governs an indirect question in Pl. *Laws* 801b (cf. *Charm.* 171b). The expression would echo ἀλλ' ἐκεῖν' ὅμως θεώρει (697), where likewise Demeas had just made a confession and was about to draw Moschion's attention to a countervailing consideration.

704 εἴς ... τοὺς ἄλλους ἁμαρτών: in his attempt to protect Moschion's reputation, Demeas acted wrongly towards at least five other people: to Chrysis and the baby, by expelling them from his house; and to Nikeratos, his wife and his daughter, by attempting to deceive them into finalizing the marriage of Plangon to Moschion in ignorance of important information, which Demeas firmly believed on reasonable grounds to be true, about Moschion's recent behaviour (note especially 470–1 τοὺς γάμους ἔα ποεῖν, τοὺς γάμους ἔα με ποιεῖν). See S. R. West 1991: 18.   τε is to be paired with τ' (705). The coordination is irregular, since its second limb (ἐν ἐμαυτῶι ... ἠγνόουν), unlike the first, is not expressed as an indirect question; but γε (Sandbach) does not remove the irregularity, and no other plausible emendation has been proposed. The anacoluthon does not impair intelligibility, and should be accepted; it might have been avoided, had metre allowed, by writing τηρῶν or θ' ὡς ἐτήρουν instead of τ' ἐτήρουν.

704–5 πρόνοιαν... | ἔσχον 'I showed concern'; cf. *Epitr.* 235, *com. adesp.* 1017.40, Eur. *Alc.* 1061.

705 ἐτήρουν 'I tried [conative imperfect: Goodwin 1912: 12] to keep secret'; cf. *Aspis* 382, Lys. 31.31. He did not succeed in keeping the information 'within himself' (cf. ἐν ἐμαυτῶι): it burst out when he raised his voice to Moschion (480–1) and then asked him 'in front of those present' who was the mother of his (Moschion's) child (488–9).   **τοῦθ' ὃ δή ποτ' ἠγνόουν** apparently means 'that misapprehension of mine, whatever it was', as if Demeas were eager to forget about it as far as possible: ὃ δή ποτε is equivalent to ὅ τι δή ποτε, cf. Dem. 44.65 καθ' ὃν δήποτε τρόπον ἐβούλοντο 'in whatever way they wished'.

706 οὐχὶ...ἐπιχαίρειν 'I didn't make it known to our enemies for them to rejoice over' (the infinitive is final-consecutive: Goodwin 1912: 306–7, 308–9). We have not previously heard of any (personal) enemies that Demeas has; it is simply taken for granted that *everyone* has enemies who wish him harm and will rejoice over any discomfiture he suffers (Dover 1974: 180–3). That Demeas' enemies did not learn of his son's supposed scandalous behaviour was, however, pure luck: Nikeratos knew of it, and he was not a man to guard his tongue (cf. 507–13).

707 ἐκφέρεις 'you are making public' (LSJ ἐκφέρω II 3), *sc.* by running away, which will make it evident that there has been a serious quarrel between him and his father.

707–8 μάρτυρας | ἐπ' ἐμὲ... λαμβάνεις: i.e. whether intentionally or not, you are making people aware of the family troubles and causing them to speak ill of me. The use of the forensic term μάρτυς implies that Moschion is acting as if he were Demeas' enemy (litigation opponent).

708 οὐκ ἀξιῶ 'I don't think I deserve <to be treated like that>' (LSJ ἀξιόω III 1), cf. Thuc. 4.86.2, Lys. 22.5; this leads up to Demeas' reiteration (709–10) of his earlier argument (698–702) that he is entitled to respect because of all he has done for Moschion hitherto.

709–10 μή negates the *whole* of the rest of the sentence: 'do not both remember *x* and forget *y*', 'don't remember *x* while forgetting *y*'. Usually in sentences of this semantic structure the first limb will contain the particle μέν (which Jacques suggested introducing here in place of μου), but in this case the absence of μέν will tend to suggest, correctly, that Demeas would prefer it if Moschion forgot today's blunder unconditionally.   **ἡμέραν... | μίαν:** the action of a Menandrian comedy, as of most tragedies in his time and earlier (Arist. *Poet.* 1449b12–13), is normally contained within a single day, and both in comedy and in tragedy characters sometimes reflect on how much has happened, or may happen, within that short time (e.g. *Dysk.*

187, 864; Carcinus fr. 5a = *Aspis* 417–18; Soph. *OT* 438, *El.* 919, 1363; Eur. *Med.* 373–5). Demeas' false suspicions of Moschion were actually of even briefer duration than that: they lasted only from 453 to 537.

710 διεσφάλην 'I slipped up', 'I failed', the earliest attestation of this verb in poetry; cf. [Arist.] *Ath.Pol.* 19.3 (on the attempts of the anti-Peisistratid exiles to regain a footing in Attica) ἔν τε ... τοῖς ἄλλοις οἷς ἔπραττον διεσφάλλοντο καὶ τειχίσαντες ... Λειψύδριον ... ἐξεπολιορκήθησαν.

711 πόλλ' ἔχων λέγειν ἐάσω, or its equivalent, is a forensic cliché near the end of a speech: cf. e.g. Dem. 57.66 πολλὰ δ' ἔχων καὶ ἄλλ' ἐπιδεῖξαι ... ἐάσω, 20.163, 45.86, 54.44.

711–12 καὶ γάρ ...| ... καλόν: the connection of thought is 'I could speak for longer, bring further arguments, and pressure you into reluctant compliance, but it will be better if I stop now and give you the chance to comply willingly.'

712 μόλις 'reluctantly', 'grudgingly'.   **πιθέσθ':** the strong aorist middle of πείθω is found in New Comedy only here and at Diphilus fr. 31.9, and is absent from the later orators (in Dem. 23.143 and Lyc. *Leocr.* 99 it is an unnecessary emendation); thus the present infinitive πείθεσθ' may well be right here.   **τὸ δ' ἑτοίμως** *sc.* τῶι πατρὶ πιθέσθαι.

713–25 Before Moschion can find anything to say in response to his father's homily, an impatient (and henpecked, 713n.) Nikeratos appears, and in a moment the mood is transformed from solemnity to farce. It is sometimes difficult to know to what extent the characters are in earnest, and to what extent they are merely trying to make game of each other. The interpretation adopted here, which in essentials follows Sandbach, is that Nikeratos genuinely believes that Moschion is trying to abscond, though (as in Act IV) his accusations and threats are sometimes hyperbolical; Moschion is attempting simultaneously to salvage some shreds of dignity from the situation and to ensure that his marriage does not fall through at the last minute; and Demeas is trying to ensure that things proceed smoothly and to prevent an explosion of rage from the volatile Nikeratos. The audience are unlikely to concern themselves much with reading the minds of the characters, content with enjoying the ludicrous situation – Moschion with a drawn sword (719n.) which he dare not use, Nikeratos threatening to imprison or otherwise maltreat the man who in a few moments will be his son-in-law, Demeas (with his grandson's fate still at stake) desperate to restore sanity but far from sure that it will be possible to do so.

713 μὴ 'νόχλει μοι: as at 421, Nikeratos comes out of his house talking back to his wife, who has again been pestering him. We are apparently to imagine that she has said something like 'What's happened to that boy?

If he doesn't come soon, there'll be no wedding' – to which Nikeratos replies (question-beggingly) 'We've had almost the whole of [*sc.* our part of] the wedding already – all that's needed is for him to come and take the bride away.'   πάντα γέγονε: i.e. all that part of the celebration that took place at the bride's home has been completed. (But, as Nikeratos well knows, it will all be meaningless if the bridegroom fails to appear.) λουτρά: i.e. the *bride's* ritual bath (124n.).   προτέλεια 'the pre-nuptial sacrifices' offered by or on behalf of the bride to Hera, Artemis, the Moirai, and probably the Semnai Theai (Pollux 3.38; Aesch. *Eum.* 834–6, Eur. *IA* 433–4, 718; Garland 1990: 219–20, Oakley and Sinos 1993: 11–12).   οἱ γάμοι: i.e. the wedding (or pre-wedding) feast in the bride's house, for which Nikeratos' scrawny sheep (399–404) will have supplied the main dish. This and the preceding rituals are imagined as having taken place partly in the interval between Acts III and IV (when Nikeratos' household was μεταξὺ τῶν γάμων ποουμένων, 423) and partly in the time since the end of Act IV (when Demeas had said to Nikeratos πόει τἄνδον εὐτρεπῆ, 612–13). Nikeratos' statement is nevertheless paradoxical, for while this (presumably not very lavish) feast may have been completed, the wedding as a whole (οἱ γάμοι in the more comprehensive sense) most certainly has not been.

714 ἂν ποτ' ἔλθηι: Demeas has repeatedly assured Nikeratos that Moschion will come back to take Plangon home (586, 599–600, 610), but much time has passed since then and he has still not come to Nikeratos' house.

715 παῖ, τί τοῦτ': 360, 677, 691nn. Nikeratos has just caught sight of Moschion in his military cloak. Apparently he does not at first see the sword, since at 716 he mentions only the cloak. This may indicate that from where he is positioned (presumably near his own door) he is looking at Moschion's left side (the sword, as always, being slung where he can draw it with his right hand). That, in turn, implies that Moschion, if facing the audience, will be further to their left (i.e. towards the east side of the stage) than Nikeratos is. Moschion and Demeas will be relatively close to their house, which is on the side nearer to Eisodos A (see note at start of commentary); Moschion, already 'on his way' towards the harbour (693), will if anything now be placed still further over towards Eisodos A (691n.). If these deductions are sound, therefore, Eisodos A (harbour and city) will in this play be the one on the east side (the spectators' left), Eisodos B (country) that to the west.   οὐκ οἶδ' ἔγωγε, μὰ Δία: true, strictly speaking, but misleading. Demeas does not know what Moschion's intentions are at this moment, but he certainly has more relevant information than Nikeratos does, as indeed his next brief remark will reveal. Possibly we are meant to understand that he is 'teasing Nikeratos by playing along with Moschion' (Arnott); more likely, however, he is simply being as non-committal as possible, to minimize the risk of angering Nikeratos. At any rate it is ironic that Demeas, who has spent so much of the play making mistaken claims of knowledge (153–4, 316nn.), should end it by making a deliberately misleading claim of ignorance (Katsouris 1975b: 108).

716 Nikeratos naturally assumes that Moschion is attempting to desert Plangon.   που 'apparently' (339n.).   φησὶ γοῦν: false, strictly speaking, but not misleading. Moschion has not spoken since Demeas came outside at 690, and it was Parmenon (693) who said that his young master was leaving home; but Moschion's accoutrements and actions had sent a clear message, and he has not yet given any indication of having changed his mind.

717 τίς δ᾽ ἐάσει sc. αὐτὸν ἀπαίρειν.   μοιχὸν ὄντ᾽ εἰλημμένον 'when he is a debaucher who has been apprehended'. Moschion is certainly a self-confessed μοιχός (591n.), and he has (now) been 'apprehended', but that does not make him a μοιχὸς εἰλημμένος since he has not been apprehended in the act of μοιχεία – an act which took place nearly a year ago. So far as we know, a μοιχός not taken in the act could not be imprisoned or physically maltreated but only prosecuted (Harrison 1968: 32–5).

718 ἤδη 'right away'.   δήσω: ever since Homeric times (*Odyssey* 8.295–359) a μοιχός taken in the act could be imprisoned until he, or someone on his behalf, paid (or gave security for) a ransom to have him released. The fifth-century Gortyn Law Code (*IC* IV 72.II.20–45) fixes the amount of ransom payable and requires it to be paid within five days, failing which 'the captors may deal with [their prisoner] as they please'. At Athens an alleged μοιχός who had secured his release could prosecute his captor for false imprisonment (ἀδίκως εἰρχθῆναι ὡς μοιχόν): if he won his case (by convincing the jury that he was not guilty of μοιχεία) he and any sureties were released from all liability (and probably – though no source explicitly says so – his captor was fined for unlawfully imprisoning an innocent free man), but if he lost he was to be handed over to his captor 'who may deal with him as he pleases, in the presence of the court, provided he does not use a knife' ([Dem.] 59.66). Nikeratos' threat here is one which he has no legal right to make, though it is less wildly exaggerated than his earlier description of Moschion as a murderer (513–14) and his various subsequent death threats; it expresses, though, his determination that Moschion shall not evade his duty of making an honest woman of his (Nikeratos') daughter and a legitimate child of his grandson. Cf. 612n. on what Nikeratos might have done if he *had* caught Moschion in the act (εἰ δ᾽ ἐλήφθη τότε).   οὐκ εἰς μακράν 'without delay' (lit. 'not at a long interval', cf. Ar. *Wasps* 454, Dem. 18.36).

719 δῆσον, ἱκετεύω: with these words Moschion draws his sword; but this clearly does not frighten Nikeratos in the least, and probably Moschion merely waves the weapon about in a manner which makes it plain that he has no idea how to use it effectively. Sandbach and Lamagna think that he is genuinely asking to be imprisoned, since this will enable him to avoid the embarrassment of admitting that his supposed departure for foreign parts was a mere pretence; but this interpretation will not account for the business with the sword. More likely, the brandishing of the sword and the tone of Moschion's voice will between them make it clear that he is being ironic ('I'd be delighted for you to try', as a modern equivalent might say) and reacting to the threat of imprisonment as any spirited young man might be expected to do. The incident may be modelled on Eur. *Hipp.*1084–9. There Theseus (who has sentenced Hippolytus to exile for life) orders his attendants to drag Hippolytus away; Hippolytus (drawing his sword?) retorts 'Any of them who touches me will regret it' and challenges Theseus to expel him with his own hands; but Theseus is adamant ('I'll do just that, if you don't obey me').   **φλυαρεῖς ... ἔχων** 'you keep acting nonsensically'; with this idiom cf. Pl. *Gorg.* 490e; Ar. *Frogs* 512 ληρεῖς ἔχων, 202, 524; *com. adesp.* 1018.25 σπαθᾷς ἔχων; Theocr. 14.8 παίσδεις ... ἔχων. Since ἔχων implies that the incident immediately complained of is part of a continuing history, and since Moschion has just spoken for the first time since Nikeratos appeared, it is likely that for once (cf. 441n.) φλυαρεῖν refers to behaviour generally, not just speech: Moschion was behaving absurdly towards Nikeratos (πρός μ') by attempting (as Nikeratos supposes) to evade marriage to Plangon, and he is now continuing on the same course by threatening violence.

720 Demeas, fearful that Nikeratos may be provoked to a fresh outburst of rage, intervenes to beg Moschion to calm down – thus fulfilling Moschion's original hopes (664–7, 682–6), though hardly in the way the young man had expected.   **πρὸς τῶν θεῶν** could in principle be taken either with κατάβαλε or with μὴ παροξύνηις: the former option, however, is supported by Ar. *Birds* 662–3 where the phrase is used, as here, by one speaker backing up a request by another (Πε. ... ἐκβίβασον ἐκ τοῦ βουτόμου τοὐρνίθιον. – Ευ. ἐκβίβασον αὐτὴν δῆτα πρὸς θεῶν.).

721 μὴ παροξύνηις: cf. 612 (to Nikeratos) μὴ παροξύνου.   **ἀφείσθω** (3rd sg. perfect imperative passive) 'away it goes!', literally, 'let it have been discarded', with an implication of finality (Goodwin 1912: 33). Moschion drops his sword.

721–2 καταλελιπαρήκατε | δεόμενοί μου 'you have begged and entreated me successfully'. Moschion had hoped that Demeas would beseech him (δεήσεται 664, 665, cf. 683); he now claims (somewhat unreasonably) that he has done better than that, since Nikeratos has beseeched him too! The sonorous octosyllable καταλελιπαρήκατε is the earliest surviving attestation of this verb by nearly half a millennium; it does not appear again before Lucian (*Kataplous* 4, 14; *Dialogues of the Gods* 24.2).

722 σοῦ δεόμενοι; δεῦρο δή: by his absurd claim to have made Nikeratos grovel, Moschion has managed to anger him after all; Nikeratos brandishes his stick at him and 'invites' him to come within range of it. **δήσεις μ' ἴσως;** 'I suppose you mean to tie me up?' – with a play on the two very similar verbs δέομαι 'beg' and δέω 'bind', and strong alliteration/assonance (five words in 722 begin with δ, followed each time by an *e*-vowel). This is probably to be understood as a taunt: Nikeratos' previous threat to confine Moschion had evaporated (or so Moschion professes to believe) when Moschion drew his sword, and Moschion, again speaking ironically, implies that he will not dare to try again (but prudently remains out of range). Seeing that there is considerable risk of another flare-up, Demeas hastily intervenes.

723 μηδαμῶς: i.e. 'don't get into a quarrel' (not 'don't tie him up'): Moschion's verbal aggression is as dangerous as Nikeratos' physical aggression, and Demeas needs to restrain both. Only after this does he address Nikeratos individually.   **δοκεῖ;** 'Is that agreed?' This question must be put to Moschion, not Demeas. Demeas has just asked for the bride to be brought out, which can only mean that he wants her to be handed over to Moschion immediately. Moschion himself, however, has not yet given any clear indication that he has abandoned his apparent intention to throw up the marriage and go abroad; and without his consent there can be no marriage. See also next note.

724 πάνυ μὲν οὖν: for the reason just stated, and despite B's explicit assignment of these words to Demeas, they must belong to Moschion. B's error will have resulted from mistakenly interpreting the *dicolon* after πάνυ μὲν οὖν as indicating change of speaker, when in fact it indicated change of addressee (Moschion speaking first to Nikeratos, then to Demeas).

As soon as Moschion has confirmed his willingness to proceed, Nikeratos goes back into his house to fetch the bride, and Moschion turns to Demeas.

724–5 εἰ τοῦτ' ἐποίεις...│...φιλοσοφῶν ἄρτι: we may well feel that this is an unreasonable complaint, particularly since Parmenon had already urged Moschion to go and bring his bride home (676–7) and he had refused; but it does serve to remind us, in these last moments of the play, that Moschion is genuinely and deeply in love with Plangon (see also 728–9n.) – on whom he is about to set eyes for the first time today, and who in a few minutes will be his wife. If Demeas, instead of delivering the lecture of 694–712, had simply knocked on Nikeratos' door and asked him to bring out Plangon forthwith, Moschion would have surrendered at once. All the same, Moschion forgets that Demeas could not have been expected to know this at the time.

725 φιλοσοφῶν 'moralizing'. φιλοσοφεῖν in late fourth- and third-century comedy means '"to theorise like a (professional) philosopher", usually with a pejorative implication that such activity is ill-judged, ill-timed, useless, irrelevant or bogus' (Arnott 1996b: 696); cf. *Aspis* 340 (a doctor spouting medical jargon), *Mis.* A17 S = 17 A; Anaxippus fr. 4.1; Theognetus fr. 1.9; *com. adesp.* 893. Here too Moschion is implying, indeed asserting, that Demeas' homily was 'ill-judged' and 'useless', since he could have achieved the same effect by an easier method.

Nikeratos comes out again, followed by Plangon, crowned and veiled as a bride (see Oakley and Sinos 1993: 16–18); she thus appears on stage for the only time in the play. A binding betrothal (ἐγγύη, 726–8n.) could be made without the bride being present (as in *Dysk.* 842–4 when Kallippides betroths his daughter to Gorgias), but here, where the ἐγγύη is combined with the actual transfer of the bride into her new husband's possession, her presence is obviously essential.

725 πρόαγε: either 'come forward' or 'come over here', depending on where Demeas and Moschion are standing.   **μοι** 'please', an ethic dative (128n.); cf. Pl. *Apol.* 27b μέμνησθέ μοι μὴ θορυβεῖν, Dem. 18.178 τούτωι πάνυ μοι προσέχετε τὸν νοῦν (see Smyth 1956: 342–3).

726–8 A contract of marriage was normally effected by the process termed ἐγγύη: the κύριος of the bride (her father if alive, otherwise another close relative or a guardian appointed by will) entrusted (ἐγγυᾶν or διδόναι) her to her husband-to-be (preferably before witnesses) and specified the amount of her dowry. The consent of the bride was not required, and a valid and binding ἐγγύη could be made without her presence (725n.) or even her knowledge (see Introduction, pp. 31–2). The ceremony is presented on stage in several plays of Menander, with slight variations in the formula (*Dysk.* 761–2, 842–4; *Mis.* 444–6 S = 974–6 A; *Perik.* 1013–15; Men. fr. 453; cf. *com. adesp.* 1010.10, 1045.8–9, 1098.4–6, also Hdt. 6.130.2). See Oakley and Sinos 1993: 9–10. The actual handover of the bride, and the accompanying wedding celebrations (γάμοι), could take place at any time after the ἐγγύη; here, exceptionally, owing to the haste with which the marriage has been arranged and the difficulties that threatened to wreck it, the ἐγγύη is performed when the γάμοι are already well under way.

726 μαρτύρων ἐναντίον occurs only here in a comic betrothal formula, though at *Dysk.* 761 Gorgias betroths his sister to Sostratos πάντων τῶν θεῶν ἐναντίον (probably because no potential witnesses are present); at *Aspis* 353–5 Daos predicts that Smikrines will betroth his niece to the first comer 'in the presence of three thousand witnesses' once he has the opportunity to claim the hand of another niece who is ἐπίκληρος of a bigger estate. Who are the witnesses here? Demeas will be one, but there are no other free adult males in either house (there has been no time to invite guests, 181), and women and slaves could not act as witnesses. Frost 1988: 117 must therefore be right to suppose that the additional 'witnesses' called in here are the theatre audience (cf. 487–8n.). δίδωμ' is the more common verb in this formula; the alternative ἐγγυῶ is used in *Dysk.* 842 and *com. adesp.* 1098.5, and Gorgias in *Dysk.* 762 uses both verbs in asyndeton. ἔχειν 'to have as his wife' (LSJ ἔχω I 4), a final-consecutive infinitive (706n.); not found elsewhere in comic betrothal formulae.

727 γνησίων παίδων ἐπ' ἀρότωι 'to raise a crop (literally, for the ploughing) of legitimate children'. This is the key phrase in the betrothal formula, because it specifies that the bride is being given as a lawful wife and not as a mere παλλακή (508n.); in surviving comic instances it is omitted only in *Dysk.* 761–2, which is irregular in other respects (there is no demonstrative or other expression, like τήνδ' here, to identify the bride, and nothing is said about the dowry). The order of words in the phrase may be varied for metrical reasons, and in Men. fr. 453, which as transmitted is corrupt, it is possible that a variant form παίδων γνησίων ἐπὶ σπορᾶι (conj. Mette) was used (cf. *Fab. Inc.* 29–30). The agricultural metaphor, common in tragedy (e.g. Soph. *Ant.* 569, Eur. *Med.* 1281), is at least as old as Hesiod (*Works* 812–13: the ninth of the month is ἐσθλὴ...φυτευέμεν ἠδὲ γενέσθαι ἀνέρι τ' ἠδὲ γυναικί). **προῖκα:** the specification of the dowry is normally joined by καί or τε to the making-over of the bride; here, apparently for metrical convenience, the two are coupled in asyndeton.

727–8 τἀμὰ πάνθ', ὅταν | ἀποθάνω γ' 'the whole of my property – when I die, that is'. In other words, Moschion will for the present receive no dowry at all, and even at Nikeratos' death his daughter will get only what she would have inherited in any case. It is not clear whether Nikeratos is being presented as too poor to afford a dowry (as perhaps Laches is in *com. adesp.* 1045), or whether he is withholding a dowry because Moschion as a self-confessed μοιχός (717–18) is in no position to insist on having one; he knows, at any rate, that Moschion is the heir to a substantial fortune and will be able to give his wife a high standard of living even without a dowry. In *Dyskolos* (844–7) the relatively poor Gorgias, having been given a dowry of three talents with Sostratos' sister, offers one talent to Sostratos as a dowry for his own sister, but Sostratos' rich father Kallippides tells Gorgias to 'keep it all yourself'; Sostratos himself had earlier (306–8) expressed

his willingness to marry Gorgias' sister without a dowry, 'since I have a sufficient livelihood'. Nikeratos, who has after all just returned from a long
and presumably successful business trip, would probably have been able to
get together (by borrowing, if necessary; see Millett 1992: 62–3) a dowry
of, say, twenty or thirty minae (a third to a half of a talent), which in real
life was a common figure (Schaps 1979: 99) – but dowries of that size do
not exist in comedy: every Menandrian bride who receives a dowry at all
receives at least two talents. It may be noted that no consideration seems
to be given to the possibility that the brotherless Plangon would become
an ἐπίκληρος at her father's death and be claimed in marriage by a kinsman; we know that it was sometimes possible in these circumstances for a
claimant to break up an existing marriage (Isaeus 3.64, 10.19), but *Samia*
gives support to the widely held view that this was not permitted if the
existing marriage had produced a son (see Schaps 1979: 28–9).

728 ὃ μὴ γένοιτ' 'which god forbid', a common formula for nullifying the
risk that the mention of some possible future evil might cause it to come
about; cf. *Mis.* 264 S = 665 A; Ar. *Lys.* 147; Aesch. *Seven* 5; D.L. 5.12
(Aristotle's will).   <εἰσ>αεί ζώιην may have been a set phrase typically
used in contexts like this (when a speaker had inadvertently or unavoid-
ably referred to his own death). This restoration of B's defective text is
somewhat dubious, since before the time of Augustus (e.g. D.H. *Ant.Rom.*
1.56.2) εἰσαεί is attested only in a few tragedies produced between *c.*450
and 425 BC ([Aesch.] *Prom.* 732; Soph. *Trach.* 1202, *Aj.* 342, 570, *OT* 275,
1013); but the only alternative that has been proposed, <εἴθ'> ἀεί, is even
less satisfactory, since the wishing particle εἴθε ought not to be attached to
the *second* of two connected wishes.

728–9 ἔχω, | λαμβάνω, στέργω 'I have her, I take her, I cherish her.' Mos-
chion doubtless suits action to word and takes Plangon by the hand or
perhaps (in a gesture seen in many vase-paintings symbolizing the possession of a woman; see Oakley and Sinos 1993: 32–3, 45) by the wrist (χεῖρ'
ἐπὶ καρπῶι). This is by far the fullest formal response to a betrothal declaration by a bridegroom in comedy: Polemon in *Perik.* 1014–15 merely says
λαμβάνω and thanks Pataikos for the generous dowry (καὶ καλῶ[ς ποεῖς]);
in *Dyskolos* neither Sostratos nor Gorgias says anything at all. Probably this
is because the formula found here (or a slightly different version of it –
logically λαμβάνω should precede ἔχω, but metre forbids this) was normally
used not at the ἐγγύη but at the actual transfer of the bride during the
γάμοι (indeed it would be inappropriate for the bridegroom to say ἔχω at
any earlier point), and it is only in exceptional circumstances such as those
of *Samia* that this transfer occurs during the action of a play. But in addition, as Moschion's last significant utterance in the play, the formula serves
to highlight once again (cf. 724n.) the deep devotion to Plangon which,

together with his equally strong commitment to the safety and welfare of their son (135–6, 453, 519nn.; see Introduction §4(a) and Sommerstein 2012), are the most appealing features of his character.

It is not clear whether Nikeratos now goes back into his house, or whether he remains on stage (in which case the audience would no doubt assume that Demeas had invited him to take part in the further celebrations). On the one hand, Plangon is now a member of Demeas' and Moschion's οἶκος, and Nikeratos has no further formal role to play. On the other hand, for Nikeratos to attend the feast given by his wealthy neighbour (whose οἶκος will one day merge with his, for Plangon's baby is the ultimate heir to both) would be in keeping with the spirit of solidarity across economic divisions which pervades this play (see Introduction §7) and would put the seal on his reconciliation with Moschion and Demeas, with both of whom he had quarrelled so fiercely in Act IV.

729 λουτρὰ μετιέναι 'to go for the bathing-water'. Since the bride has already been bathed (713), this will be taken to refer to the ritual bathing of the bridegroom (124, 157nn.). Normally this would have been done long since, but today this has not been possible; ever since it was agreed to hold the wedding this day (186–7), either Moschion has been absent or else (452–539) the wedding preparations have been at a standstill. Thus only now can the water for his bath be fetched from the Enneakrounos (124n.). Normally the procession to the Enneakrounos for this purpose would comprise only women (except for the piper, who might be a boy; see e.g. Oakley and Sinos 1993: pll. 14–19), but on this occasion Demeas, Moschion (with Plangon), and Nikeratos if he has remained on stage, will accompany them (731–2), and the procession, which will of course be returning to Demeas' house, will thus also perform the role of the wedding procession proper in which the bride was conducted to her new home. Thus Moschion, who came out of his house at the very beginning of the play, will end it without ever having re-entered that house.

730 Demeas goes to his door and calls into the house.   **Χρυσί:** this is the first mention of Chrysis in Act V, and confirms that she is fully restored to her position as the lady of the house and controller of its workforce (256, 258, 301nn.).   **πέμπε** 'arrange a procession of', cf. 124 and the phrase πομπὴν πέμπειν (Ar. *Ach.* 248–9, *Birds* 849, *Eccl.* 757). The expression neither entails nor excludes the personal participation of Chrysis in the procession, but as the woman of highest status in the household it would be surprising if she did not take part. (If she does appear, her mask will be worn by a mute performer.)   **λουτροφόρον:** a boy (Harpocr. λ 28 = Dinarchus fr. XIX 6 Conomis; cf. *POxy* 3966 (= Men. *Fab. Inc.* no. 9 Arnott) 7–16) or girl (Pollux 3.43, cf. 8.66) who carried the jar (also called a λουτροφόρος) in which the bathing-water was fetched. The λουτροφόρος (usually female) is often included in wedding scenes in vase-paintings (e.g. Oakley and Sinos 1993: pll. 14–19), and the jar was used in funerary sculpture on the tombstones of unmarried persons of either sex (cf. Dem. 44.18). Usually the bearer would be a relative of the bride or groom (Harpocr. loc. cit.), but in this case no such person is available and the role will be taken by a slave (cf. *POxy* 3966.16).   αὐλητρίδα: the procession to fetch the λουτρά was traditionally accompanied by a piper (*POxy* 3966.10; see Oakley and Sinos 1993: 15–16), as was the bridal procession itself (cf. Sappho fr. 44.24, Plaut. *Cas.* 798–9, Ter. *Ad.* 905–7; see Oakley and Sinos 1993: 33). Presumably this function too will be performed by one of Demeas' slaves – though in fact the mute performer taking this role will only need to mime, the actual playing being done by the regular piper who had played during the choral interludes and possibly accompanied the scenes in trochaic tetrameters (see note at start of Act IV).

731 δᾶιδα καὶ στεφάνους: a request for garlands and a torch (never provably more than one, though cf. Chrysippus com. fr. 1) is a standard feature at the end of a Menandrian play (*Dysk.* 964, *Mis.* 459–60 S = 989–90 A, *Sik.* 418–19; Men. frr. 908, 910.14; cf. Antiphanes frr. 197, 269, Poseidippus com. fr. 6.9); torches also appear at the end of Aristophanes' *Clouds* (1490–4), *Peace* (1317), probably *Birds* (a wedding procession with much talk of fire and light, especially 1709–17, 1747–50), *Frogs* (1524–5), *Ecclesiazusae* (1150), and *Wealth* (1194). To accommodate the semi-formulaic expression, a trochaic half-*metron* is exceptionally replaced by a dactyl (καὶ στεφά-); see Introduction §9.

732 συμπροπέμπωμεν 'we may join in escorting them'. A male slave (possibly recognizable from his mask as Parmenon, but in any case played by a mute extra) comes out of Demeas' house holding garlands (which he apparently gives to Demeas, who then puts one on himself and hands another to Moschion) in one hand and a lighted torch (which he will probably carry in the procession himself) in the other. By now, too, the λουτρά-procession will have come on stage, probably with Chrysis marshalling it and bringing up its rear (730n.).

732–3 πύκαζε σὺ | κρᾶτα (addressed to Moschion): tragic language (note the absence of the definite article), probably taken from the opening of Cassandra's speech celebrating her 'marriage' to Agamemnon in Euripides' *Trojan Women* (353; cf. also Eur. *Alc.* 831–2). The phrase appears elsewhere in comedy only amid the floral luxuriance of Cratinus fr. 105. The raising of the stylistic register prepares for the elevated language of the play's final lines.

733 καὶ κόσμει σεαυτόν: probably 'and <thereby> adorn yourself'. One might have expected Moschion to be supplied with a white γαμικὴ χλανίς (cf. Ar. *Birds* 1116, 1693) to wear instead of, or at least over, his χλαμύς; but no one has been ordered to bring him one, and he will therefore presumably be taking his bride home still dressed as if he were about to abandon her and go soldiering abroad.   ἀλλ᾽ ἐγώ *sc.* τοῦτο ποιῶ (477n.).

733–7 All Menandrian comedies whose conclusions we possess (*Dyskolos, Misoumenos, Sikyonioi*) end with an appeal to the audience (classified by age-groups) for applause followed by a prayer for victory in the dramatic competition. So did the plays whose endings are fragmentarily preserved as Men. frr. 908, 910, and the Ἀποκλειομένη of Poseidippus (fr. 6), a dramatist of the next generation; cf. also *com. adesp.* 925 (quoted by Augustus on his deathbed, Suetonius *Div. Aug.* 99.1). The speaker may be any male character (in *Dyskolos* it is a slave). Elsewhere in Menander the conclusion is regularly in iambic trimeters (in *Dyskolos*, after a long scene in iambic tetrameters, the metre actually reverts to trimeters for the last eleven lines), the appeal for applause normally ends with the imperative ἐπικροτήσατε, and the final prayer, except in fr. 910, follows a set formula (736–7n.). In *Samia* the metre remains unchanged (trochaic tetrameters), and the language is more distinctively poetic, especially in the last three lines.

733–4 παῖδες καλοί, | μειράκια, γέροντες, ἄνδρες: such comprehensive appeals to the various age-groups in the audience are found already in Aristophanes (*Peace* 50–1, *Eccl.* 1146; cf. Pl. com. fr. 222). Menander seems always to mention boys, youths and men; old men are mentioned as a separate category only here. In Old and New Comedy alike the listing is always exclusively of males, but this does not in itself prove that no women were present, and indeed there is positive evidence that some were (Ar. *Lys.* 1050–1; Pl. *Gorg.* 502b–d, *Rep.* 492b, *Laws* 658a–d, 817b–c); see Roselli 2011: 159–94, who refers to earlier literature (though not all the evidence he cites has much probative value).

733 παῖδες καλοί: forms of address such as ὦ καλὲ παῖ were originally erotic in tone (Thgn. 1280; Pl. *Phdr.* 243e, 252b; cf. the frequent use of ὁ παῖς καλός in vase inscriptions), but tended to become merely complimentary (Pl. *Euthyd.* 289b). By Menander's time the adjective in this phrase had become almost meaningless, and παῖδες καλοί could even be used in collectively addressing a group of slaves (*Dysk.* 462, 912). Young boys were always regarded as an important part of comedy's audience (cf. Ar. *Clouds* 539), and were thought to be particularly fond of the genre (Pl. *Laws* 658d).

734 εὐρώστως 'with healthy vigour': πάντες εὐρώστως ἅμα appears to have already been formulaic in this context (Antiphanes fr. 34); εὔρωστος and derivatives are not otherwise found in poetry before late antiquity.

735 εὐνοίας προφήτην 'as a harbinger of your goodwill', a high-poetic phrase (cf. Pind. *Nem.* 9.50 γλυκὺν κώμου προφάταν, of wine); elsewhere in comedy προφήτης is used in this sense only for parodic purposes (Antiphanes fr. 216.23, in a rhapsodic description of a banquet, calls hunger the προφήτης of dinner). **Βακχίωι φίλον** 'dear to the Bacchic god', patron of the current festival (whether it is the City Dionysia or the Lenaea). The name Βάκχιος for Dionysus, common in tragedy (it occurs thirteen times in Euripides' *Bacchae* alone), is found otherwise in comedy only in Ar. *Ach.* 263 (in a hymn to the phallus-god Phales, 'companion of Bacchius'), though it occurs as a poetic metonym for 'wine' in two somewhat dithyrambic passages, Ar. *Eccl.* 14 and Antiphanes fr. 234.

736–7 Appeals for victory in the dramatic competition are common already in Aristophanes (*Knights* 546–50, 581–94; *Clouds* 561–2, 1115–30; *Birds* 445–7, 1102–17; *Lys.* 1291–4*; *Thesm.* 971–2, 1229–31*; *Frogs* 389–93, *Eccl.* 1180–3*; the asterisked passages come at or very close to the end of a play). Three plays of Euripides, *IT, Phoenissae* and *Orestes*, end, as transmitted, with prayers to Nike to 'be in possession of my life, and never cease to crown it', which may have been inserted at the time of a revival in the fourth century (Barrett 1964: 417–18; Willink 1986: 360). In Menander the usual formula is ἡ δ᾽ εὐπάτειρα φιλόγελώς τε παρθένος | Νίκη μεθ᾽ ἡμῶν εὐμενὴς ἔποιτ᾽ ἀεί (words found in the *Samia* couplet are underlined). That formula can be understood as spoken in the name of all who had contributed to staging the performance, including the *choregos* (if any), the poet, and others as well as the actors, chorus and piper; the prayer we have here, like the one found in Euripidean texts, is spoken in the name of one person, presumably the poet (as often happens in the *parabasis* of Old Comedy, e.g. *Clouds* 518–62, and occasionally elsewhere).

736 καλλίστων ἀγώνων πάρεδρος 'who sits beside him [Dionysus] at this most splendid of contests' (not merely 'who attends the most splendid of contests': a πάρεδρος is always the assessor or associate *of* some central figure). Compare Ar. *Knights* 589, where Nike is χορικῶν ... ἑταίρα.   **θεά:** comedy normally uses θεός in both genders, but θεά appears in lyrics even in Menander (*Theoph.* (fr. dub.) 10 S = *Theoph.* 40 A) and can also be used in prayers (Men. frr. 163, 226; Ar. *Clouds* 265) or whenever it is desired to employ an elevated style (e.g. Ar. *Birds* 1718; Eubulus fr. 36).

737 Νίκη in this concluding formula was probably identified with Athena Nike as worshipped on the Acropolis; certainly εὐπάτειρα ... παρθένος in the standard version of the formula suggests Athena. Cf. Ar. *Lys.* 317–18, where the men besieging the Acropolis pray (unsuccessfully) to δέσποινα Νίκη (whose sanctuary would be visible from where they are supposed to be standing) to be their ally against the rebellious women.   χοροῖς: comedy still had a chorus (119a/b n.) – though it no longer took any part in the action – the dramatic competitions were still technically contests between choruses of 'comic singers' and of 'tragic singers' (κωμωιδοί, τραγωιδοί), and probably the herald still bade each contestant εἴσαγε τὸν χορόν as he had done in Aristophanes' time (*Ach.* 11); so it was still possible to use χορός as a synecdoche for 'dramatic composition' or 'dramatic performance'. A verse inscription by a victorious comic *choregos* from the deme of Anagyrus (*IG* II² 3101, mid fourth century) speaks of him as having won at the Dionysia ἡδυγέλωτι χορῶι.

The play ends with the departure of the λουτρά-procession, going to the Enneakrounos (124n.), probably along Eisodos A. The procession will be quite a fair-sized one, by the time it is complete: the torch-bearer (732n.); the λουτροφόρος; the girl piper; the women of Demeas' household, directed by Chrysis; Demeas, Moschion with Plangon, and Nikeratos if he has not exited previously. The chorus, if present, will have departed in the same direction, perhaps singing a hymeneal chant (cf. Ar. *Peace* 1329–end, *Birds* 1731–54, Plaut. *Cas.* 799–809, Ter. *Ad.* 905–7). We have no firm evidence as to whether Menander's choruses did in fact remain in the *orchestra* to the end of the play, rather than departing after their last entr'acte performance; but it might be argued that the presence of, and a song by, the chorus here would give added point to the final word of the play's script (see previous note).

F 1 This line is quoted from 'Menander in the *Samia*' by the grammarian Phrynichus in support of his (correct) view that the Attic word for frankincense is λιβανωτός, not λίβανος, in spite of Soph. fr. 595a. Someone (probably a woman, since she is attended by a female slave, Tryphe) asks to be given some incense, which she places on an altar and then tells Tryphe to kindle. It is just possible, as Gaiser 1976: 100–1 n.2 suggested, that the speaker is Chrysis, shortly after she has come on stage in the lacuna between 57 and 58, and that she is making an offering (to Apollo Agyieus? see 309, 444nn.) to accompany a prayer, perhaps for the safe return of Demeas; this would prove to be distinctly ironic, since for one thing, as is revealed shortly afterwards, Demeas' ship has in fact already arrived, and for another his return will lead to great tribulations for Chrysis. There is no sign of Tryphe after B's text resumes (58–85), but it is possible that she was sent indoors just before Moschion and Parmenon arrived; and if Chrysis is holding the baby (57/8n.), that might explain why she needs Tryphe to carry the incense (she herself merely needs to hold a pinch of it in her fingers for a second or two) and the flame. But it arouses suspicion that one of the only two other known mentions of λιβανωτός in Menander is also in *Samia* (158; the other is *Dysk.* 449). It may well be that Phrynichus' source cited *two* passages, *Sam.* 158 and another passage, and that Phrynichus has skipped over part of this material and given us the reference for one passage and the text of the other. The other passage may not even have been from Menander; a character Tryphe appears in a fragment of the Τοκιστής of Alexis (fr. 232), though it is not clear whether she is a slave or a *hetaira* (Arnott 1996b: 658).

Another papyrus fragment (*PBerol* 8450 = *com. adesp.* 1131) has also sometimes been attributed to *Samia* (e.g. by its first editors, Luppe and Müller 1983) because it contains mention of a woman named Chrysis (2) and expressions which might refer to the rape of a free young woman like Plangon (mention of a free person (6) and of someone tearing his/her hair (7, cf. *Epitr.* 488)). This evidence, however, is flimsy. The name Chrysis was not rare in New Comedy (Persius 5.165 with scholia, referring to Menander's Εὐνοῦχος; Plaut. *Pseud.* 659; Ter. *Andr.* 85), and the rape, if rape it was, is apparently said to have taken place 'the other day' (πρώ[η]ν), not, as in Plangon's case, nearly a year ago. Moreover, since Chrysis is referred to by name in the third person in line 2, she is unlikely to be speaking herself only three or four lines later, and yet no other character would be likely to know these particulars about Plangon's rape – except Moschion, who did not want to talk about them (47–50). Nor would we really expect to hear a detailed account of the rape when (in contrast with *Epitrepontes*) no question now arises of identifying the perpetrator, and when everyone, including Plangon herself, is in agreement that all difficulties will be at an end if she can be married to Moschion before their fathers know that the pair already have a child. The fragment should be regarded as coming from an unknown play – perhaps by Menander, perhaps not; its text has not been included in this edition.

WORKS CITED

Items marked with an asterisk may be referred to by the author's/editor's name alone.

Anderson, W. S. 1982. 'Euripides' *Auge* and Menander's *Epitrepontes*', *Greek, Roman and Byzantine Studies* 23: 165–77

Arnott, W. G. 1964. 'The confrontation of Sostratos and Gorgias', *Phoenix* 18: 110–23

1975. *Menander, Plautus, Terence*, Oxford

1979. *Menander I: Aspis to Epitrepontes*, Cambridge, MA

1993. 'Comic openings', in N. W. Slater and B. Zimmermann, eds. *Intertextualität in der griechisch-römischen Komödie* (Stuttgart) 14–32

1996a. *Menander: Volume II*, Cambridge, MA

1996b. *Alexis: the fragments – a commentary*, Cambridge

1997. 'Humour in Menander', in S. Jäkel et al., eds. *Laughter down the centuries: III* (Turku) 65–79

1998a. 'First notes on Menander's *Samia*', *Zeitschrift für Papyrologie und Epigraphik* 121: 35–44

1998b. 'Second notes on Menander's *Samia* (Acts II–V)', *Zeitschrift für Papyrologie und Epigraphik* 122: 7–20

1998c. 'Notes on Menander's *Phasma*', *Zeitschrift für Papyrologie und Epigraphik* 123: 35–48

1999. 'The length of Menander's *Samia*', *Zeitschrift für Papyrologie und Epigraphik* 128: 45–8

*2000. *Menander: Volume III*, Cambridge, MA

2001. 'Visible silence in Menander', in S. Jäkel and A. Timonen, eds. *The language of silence I* (Turku) 71–85

2004. 'Menander's *Epitrepontes* in the light of the new papyri', in D. L. Cairns and R. A. Knox, eds. *Law, rhetoric, and comedy in classical Athens: essays in honour of Douglas M. MacDowell* (Swansea) 269–92

2010. 'Middle Comedy', in G. W. Dobrov, ed. *Brill's companion to the study of Greek comedy* (Leiden) 279–331

Austin, C. F. L. 1967. Review of Dedoussi 1965, *Gnomon* 39: 122–7

*1969–70. *Menandri Aspis et Samia: I. Textus (cum apparatu critico) et indices* and *II: Subsidia interpretationis*, Berlin

1969. 'Notes on Menander's *Aspis* and *Samia*', *Zeitschrift für Papyrologie und Epigraphik* 4: 161–70

2010. 'Varia Menandrea', *Zeitschrift für Papyrologie und Epigraphik* 175: 9–14

Bain, D. M. 1977. *Actors and audience: a study of asides and related conventions in Greek drama*, Oxford

  1981. 'Menander, *Samia* 580 and "Not- und Hilferufe" in Ptolemaic Egypt', *Zeitschrift für Papyrologie und Epigraphik* 44: 169–71

  1982. *Masters, servants, and orders in Greek tragedy: a study of some aspects of dramatic technique and convention*, Manchester

  1984. 'Female speech in Menander', *Antichthon* 18: 24–42

Barigazzi, A. 1970. 'Sulla nuova e vecchia *Samia* di Menandro', *Rivista di Filologia e di Istruzione Classica* 98: 148–71, 257–73

  1972. 'La scena della cacciata di Criside nella *Samia* di Menandro', in *Studi classici in onore di Quintino Cataudella* (Catania) II 197–207

Barrett, W. S. 1964. *Euripides: Hippolytos*, Oxford

Bayliss, A. J. 2011. *After Demosthenes: the politics of early Hellenistic Athens*, London

Belardinelli, A. M. 1984. 'L'*Oreste* di Euripide e i *Sicioni* di Menandro', *Orpheus* 5: 396–402

Beroutsos, D. C. 2005. *A commentary on the 'Aspis' of Menander, part one: lines 1–298*, Göttingen

Blanchard, A. 1997. 'Destins de Ménandre', *Ktèma* 22: 213–25; revised version in Blanchard 2007: 9–27

  2007. *La comédie de Ménandre: politique, éthique, esthétique*, Paris

Blume, H. D. 1974. *Menanders Samia: Eine Interpretation*, Darmstadt

  1998. *Menander*, Darmstadt

  2001. Review of Lamagna 1998, *Gnomon* 73: 289–92

Blundell, J. 1980. *Menander and the monologue*, Göttingen

Blundell, M. W. 1989. *Helping friends and harming enemies: a study in Sophocles and Greek ethics*, Cambridge

Bond, G. W. 1963. *Euripides: Hypsipyle*, Oxford

Brown, P. G. McC. 1983. 'Menander's dramatic technique and the law of Athens', *Classical Quarterly* 33: 412–20

  1993. 'Love and marriage in Greek New Comedy', *Classical Quarterly* 43: 189–205

Bruzzone, R. 2009. 'Menander, *Samia* 606–8', *Classical Quarterly* 59: 640–2

Bugh, G. R. 1988. *The horsemen of Athens*, Princeton

Burkert, W. 1983. *Homo necans: the anthropology of ancient Greek sacrificial ritual and myth* (trans. P. Bing), Berkeley

  1985. *Greek religion, archaic and classical* (trans. J. Raffan), Oxford

Cahill, N. 2002. *Household and city organization at Olynthus*, New Haven

Canevaro, M. 2013. *The documents in the public speeches of Demosthenes*, Oxford

Cannatà Fera, M. 2003. 'Metateatro e intertestualità: lo *Scudo* di Menandro, *Elena* e *Ifigenia Taurica* di Euripide', in L. Belloni et al., eds. *L'officina ellenistica: poesia dotta e popolare in Grecia e a Roma* (Trento) 117–29

Carey, C. 1989. *Lysias: selected speeches*, Cambridge

1993. 'Return of the radish, or Just when you thought it was safe to go back into the kitchen', *Liverpool Classical Monthly* 18: 53–5

Cartlidge, B. forthcoming. *The language of Menander*, Oxford

Casanova, A. 2007a. 'I frammenti della "Fedra" di Sofocle', in R. Degl'Innocenti Pierini et al., eds. *Fedra: versioni e riscritture di un mito classico* (Florence) 5–22

2007b. 'Uso dell'aposiopesi nella *Samia* di Menandro', *Prometheus* 33: 1–16

2007c. 'Varianti equipollenti nei papiri della *Samia* di Menandro?', in J. Frösén et al., eds. *Proceedings of the 24th International Congress of Papyrology* (Helsinki) 153–66

Charitonides, S. et al. 1970. *Les mosaïques de la maison du Ménandre à Mytilène*, Bern

Christensen, K. A. 1984. 'The Theseion: a slave refuge at Athens', *American Journal of Ancient History* 9: 23–32

Cobet, C. G. 1876. 'Menandri fragmenta inedita', *Mnemosyne* n.s. 4: 285–93

Cohen, D. 1991. *Law, sexuality, and society: the enforcement of morals in classical Athens*, Cambridge

Collard, C. 1989. 'Menander, *Samia* 96–115 Sandbach', *Liverpool Classical Monthly* 14, 101–2

Collard, C. and Cropp, M. J. 2008. *Euripides, Fragments: Aegeus-Meleager*, Cambridge, MA

Copley, F. O. 1947. '*Servitium amoris* in the Roman elegists', *Transactions and Proceedings of the American Philological Association* 78, 285–300

1956. *Exclusus amator: a study in Latin love poetry*, Madison

Csapo, E. G. 1999. 'Performance and iconographic tradition in the illustrations of Menander', *Syllecta Classica* 10: 154–88

2010. *Actors and icons of the ancient theatre*, Chichester

Cusset, C. 2000. 'La fille d'à côté: symbolique de l'espace et sens du voisinage dans la "Samienne" de Ménandre', *Pallas* 54: 207–28

2003. *Ménandre ou la comédie tragique*, Paris

Cusset, C., and Lhostis, N. 2011. 'Les maxims dans trois comédies de Ménandre', in C. Mauduit and P. Paré-Rey, eds. *Les maxims théâtrales en Grèce et à Rome: transferts, réécritures, remplois* (Paris) 93–109

D'Aiuto, F. 2003. 'Graeca in codici orientali della Biblioteca Vaticana (con i resti di un manoscritto tardoantico delle commedie di Menandro)', in L. Perria, ed. *Tra Oriente e Occidente: scritture e libri greci fra le regioni orientali di Bisanzio e l'Italia* (Rome) 227–296

Dalby, A. 1996. *Siren feasts: a history of food and gastronomy in Greece*, London

Dale, A. M. 1964. Review of Bond 1963, *Journal of Hellenic Studies* 84: 166–7

Danoff, Ch. M. 1962. 'Pontos Euxeinos', *RE Suppl.* 9: 866–1175

Davidson, J. N. 1997. *Courtesans and fishcakes: the consuming passions of classical Athens*, London

2006. 'Revolutions in human time: age-class in Athens and the Greekness of Greek revolutions', in S. D. Goldhill and R. G. Osborne, eds. *Rethinking revolutions through ancient Greece* (Cambridge) 29–67

Dedoussi, Ch. V. 1965. *Μενάνδρου Σαμία: εισαγωγή, υπόμνημα, κείμενο*, Athens

1970. 'The *Samia*', in Turner 1970: 159–70 (discussion, 171–80)

1988. 'The future of Plangon's child in Menander's *Samia*', *Liverpool Classical Monthly* 13: 39–42

*2006. *Μενάνδρου Σαμία: εισαγωγή, κείμενο, μετάφραση, υπόμνημα*, Athens

Del Corno, D. 1975. Review of Jacques 1971, *Gnomon* 47: 753–7

Denniston, J. D. 1939. *Euripides: Electra*, Oxford

1954. *The Greek particles*, 2nd edn, Oxford

Detienne, M. 1972. *Les jardins d'Adonis: la mythologie des aromates en Grèce*, Paris

Dickens, C. J. H. 1837/1966. *Oliver Twist* (ed. K. Tillotson), Oxford

Dickey, E. 1996. *Greek forms of address from Herodotus to Lucian*, Oxford

Dillon, M. P. J. 2002. *Girls and women in classical Greek religion*, London

2003. '"Woe for Adonis" – but in spring, not summer', *Hermes* 131: 1–16

Dohm, H. 1964. *Mageiros: Die Rolle des Kochs in der griechisch-römischen Komödie*, Munich

Dover, K. J. 1968. *Aristophanes: Clouds*, Oxford

1974. *Greek popular morality in the time of Plato and Aristotle*, Oxford

1985. 'Some types of abnormal word-order in Attic comedy', *Classical Quarterly* 35: 324–43; reprinted in Dover 1987: 43–66

1987. *Greek and the Greeks. Collected papers, Volume I: language, poetry, drama*, Oxford

Dunbar, N. V. 1995. *Aristophanes: Birds*, Oxford

Dworacki, S. 1989. 'Die Interpretation ausgewählter Szenen aus der Samia von Menander', *Eos* 77: 199–209

Easterling, P. E. 1995. 'Menander: loss and survival', in A. H. Griffiths, ed. *Stage directions: essays in ancient drama in honour of E. W. Handley* (London) 153–60

Eyben, E. 1980/81. 'Family planning in Graeco-Roman antiquity', *Ancient Society* 11–12: 5–82

Fantham, E. 1975. 'Sex, status, and survival in Hellenistic Athens: a study of women in New Comedy', *Phoenix* 29: 44–74

Faraone, C. A. and McClure, L. K., eds. 2006. *Prostitutes and courtesans in the ancient world*, Madison

Feneron, J. S. 1974. 'Some elements of Menander's style', *Bulletin of the Institute of Classical Studies* 21: 81–95

Ferrari, F. 1998. 'Menandrea', *Zeitschrift für Papyrologie und Epigraphik* 121: 49–51

2004. 'Papiri e mosaici: tradizione testuale e iconografia in alcune scene di Menandro', in G. Bastianini and A. Casanova, eds. *Menandro: cent'anni di papiri* (Florence) 127–49

Festugière, A. J. 1970. 'Ménandre, *Samia*, 606 s.', *Revue de Philologie* 44: 93

Fisher, N. R. E. 1992. *Hybris: a study in the values of honour and shame in ancient Greece*, Warminster

2001. *Aeschines: Against Timarchos*, Oxford

Fitzgerald, W. 2000. *Slavery and the Roman literary imagination*, Cambridge

Fitzpatrick, D. G. and Sommerstein, A. H. 2006. '*Tereus*', in A. H. Sommerstein et al. *Sophocles: selected fragmentary plays I* (Oxford) 141–95

Foakes, R. A. 1996. *The revenger's tragedy (Thomas Middleton / Cyril Tourneur)*, Manchester

Fountoulakis, A. 2008. 'A note on Menander, "Samia" 98–101a', *Mnemosyne* 61: 467–76

2011. 'Playing with the dramatic conventions: Demeas' invocations in Menander, *Samia* 325–6', *Classica et Mediaevalia* 62: 81–98

Frost, K. B. 1988. *Exits and entrances in Menander*, Oxford

Furley, W. D. 2009. *Menander: Epitrepontes*, London

Gaiser, K. 1976. 'Die Akedeia Menanders'. *Grazer Beiträge* 5: 99–116

Gallo, I. 1983. 'Menand. *Sam.* 1 ss. S.', *Museum Criticum* 18: 199–201

Gantz, T. R. 1993. *Early Greek myth: a guide to literary and artistic sources*, Baltimore

Garelli, M.-H. 2009. 'Jupiter, l'eunuque et la pluie d'or (Térence, *Eunuque*, 550–614)', in J. P. Aygon et al., eds. *La mythologie de l'Antiquité à la Modernité: appropriation – adaptation – détournement* (Rennes) 73–83

Garland, R. 1990. *The Greek way of life: from conception to old age*, London

Gibert, J. C. 1997. 'Euripides' *Hippolytus* plays: which came first?', *Classical Quarterly* 47: 85–97

Gill, D. H. 1974. '*Trapezomata*: a neglected aspect of Greek sacrifice', *Harvard Theological Review* 67: 117–37

Goette, H. R. 1999. 'Die Basis des Astydamas im sogenannten lykurgischen Dionysos-Theater zu Athen', *Antike Kunst* 42: 21–5

Gogos, S. 2008. *Das Dionysostheater von Athen: Architektonische Gestalt und Funktion* (with appendices by G. Kampourakis) (trans. J. Rambach), Vienna

Goldberg, S. M. 1980. *The making of Menander's comedy*, London

Golden, M. 1995. 'Baby talk and child language in ancient Greece', in F. De Martino and A. H. Sommerstein, eds. *Lo spettacolo delle voci* (Bari) II 11–34

2005. Review of Lape 2004, *Classical Review* 55: 453–4

Gomme, A. W. and Sandbach, F. H. 1973. *Menander: a commentary*, Oxford

González Merino, J. I. 1983. 'Las partículas en Menandro', *Estudios Clásicos* 25: 163–84

Goodwin, W. W. 1912. *Syntax of the moods and tenses of the Greek verb, rewritten and enlarged*, London

Gow, A. S. F. 1950. *Theocritus*, 2 vols., Cambridge

Grant, J. N. 1986. 'The father-son relationship and the ending of Menander's *Samia*', *Phoenix* 40: 172–84

Green, J. R. 2010. 'The material evidence', in G. W. Dobrov, ed. *Brill's companion to the study of Greek comedy* (Leiden) 71–102

forthcoming. 'A scene from comedy', to appear in *Prometheus*

Gronewald, M. 1995. 'Bemerkungen zu Menander', *Zeitschrift für Papyrologie und Epigraphik* 107: 57–9

1997. 'Bemerkungen zu Menander', *Zeitschrift für Papyrologie und Epigraphik* 117: 19–20

Groton, A. H. 1987. 'Anger in Menander's Samia', *American Journal of Philology* 108: 437–43

Guthrie, W. K. C. 1950. *The Greeks and their gods*, London

Gutzwiller, K. J. 2000. 'The tragic mask of comedy: metatheatricality in Menander', *Classical Antiquity* 19: 102–37

Habicht, C. 1992. 'Der Kyniker Teles und die Reform der athenischen Ephebie', *Zeitschrift für Papyrologie und Epigraphik* 93: 47–9

1997. *Athens from Alexander to Antony* (trans. D. L. Schneider), Cambridge, MA

Hall, E. M. 1993. 'Drowning by nomes: the Greeks, swimming, and Timotheus' *Persians*', in H. A. Khan, ed. *The birth of the European identity: the Europe-Asia contrast in Greek thought 490–322 B.C.* (Nottingham) 44–80

Handley, E. W. 1965. *The Dyskolos of Menander*, London

1970. 'The conventions of the comic stage and their exploitation by Menander', in Turner 1970: 3–26 (discussion, 27–42)

1996. '4305. New Comedy: (?) Menander, *Synaristosai*', *The Oxyrhynchus Papyri* 62: 14–21

Harris, E. M. 2006. *Democracy and the rule of law in classical Athens: essays on law, society, and politics*, Cambridge

Harris, W. V. 1997. 'Lysias III and Athenian beliefs about revenge', *Classical Quarterly* 47: 363–6

Harrison, A. R. W. 1968. *The law of Athens: the family and property*, Oxford

Headlam, W. G. 1902. 'Transposition of words in MSS.', *Classical Review* 16: 243–56

Heap, A. M. 2003. 'The baby as hero? The role of the infant in Menander', *Bulletin of the Institute of Classical Studies* 46: 77–129

Holzberg, N. 1974. *Menander: Untersuchungen zur dramatischen Technik*, Nuremberg

Hunter, R. L. 1983. *Eubulus: the fragments*, Cambridge

Hurst, A. 1990. 'Ménandre et la tragédie', in E. W. Handley and A. Hurst, eds. *Relire Ménandre* (Geneva) 93–122

Hutchinson, G. O. 2004. 'Euripides' other *Hippolytus*', *Zeitschrift für Papyrologie und Epigraphik* 149: 15–28

Ingrosso, P. 2010. *Menandro: Lo scudo*, Lecce

Ireland, S. 1981. 'Prologues, structure and sentences in Menander', *Hermes* 109: 178–88

1983. 'Menander and the comedy of disappointment', *Liverpool Classical Monthly* 8: 45–7

Ireland, S. 2010. *Menander: The Shield (Aspis) and The Arbitration (Epitrepontes)*, Oxford

*Jacques, J.-M. 1971. *Ménandre, Tome I¹: La Samienne*, Paris

Jacques, J.-M. 1998. 'La bile noire dans l'antiquité grecque: médecine et littérature', *Revue des Études Anciennes* 100: 217–34

Jaekel, S. 1964. *Menandri sententiae; Comparatio Menandri et Philistionis*, Leipzig

1982. 'Euripideische Handlungsstrukturen in der Samia des Menander', *Arctos* 16: 19–31

Jernstedt, V. 1891. *Porfirievskie otryvki iz Atticheskoi komedii: paleografícheskie i filologicheskie etyudy* [*Archbishop Porfiry's Fragments of Attic Comedy: Palaeographical and Philological Studies*] = *Zapiski Istoriko-Filologicheskago Fakul'teta Imperatorskogo Sankt-Peterburgskago Universiteta* 26, St Petersburg

Jouan, F. and van Looy, H. 2002. *Euripide: Tragédies. Tome VIII, Fragments: 3ᵉ partie, Sthénébée-Chrysippos*, Paris

Kamerbeek, J. C. 1972. 'Problèmes de texte et d'interprétation dans la Samienne de Ménandre', *Mnemosyne* 45: 379–88

Karamanou, J. 2005. 'Euripides' *Alcmeon through Corinth* and Menander's *Periceiromene*: similarities in theme and structure', in J. F. González Castro et al., eds. *Actas del XI Congreso Español de Estudios Clasicos* II (Madrid) 337–44

Kassel, R. 1973. 'Neuer und alter Menander', *Zeitschrift für Papyrologie und Epigraphik* 12: 1–13

Kasser, R. and Austin, C. F. L. 1969. *Papyrus Bodmer XXV. Ménandre: La Samienne*, Cologny (Geneva)

Katsouris, A. G. 1975a. *Tragic patterns in Menander*, Athens

1975b. *Linguistic and stylistic characterization: tragedy and Menander*, Thessaloniki

1976. 'Menander misleading his audience', *Liverpool Classical Monthly* 1: 100–2

1977. 'Plural in place of singular', *Rheinisches Museum* 120: 228–40

Keuls, E. C. 1973. 'The *Samia* of Menander: an interpretation of its plot and theme', *Zeitschrift für Papyrologie und Epigraphik* 10: 1–20

Koenen, L., Riad, H. and Selim, A. el-K. 1978. *The Cairo codex of Menander (P. Cair. J. 43227): a photographic edition*, London

Konstan, D. 1995. *Greek comedy and ideology*, New York and Oxford

2011. 'Menander and cultural studies', in A. K. Petrides and S. Papaioannou, eds. *New perspectives on postclassical comedy* (Newcastle upon Tyne)
31–50

Konstantakos, J. M. 2008. '*Rara coronato plausere theatra Menandro?* Menander's success in his lifetime', *Quaderni Urbinati di Cultura Classica* 88:
79–106

Körte, A. 1910. *Menandrea ex papyris et membranis vetustissimis*, Leipzig
(rev. Thierfelder A.) 1957. *Menandri quae supersunt, Pars I: reliquiae in
papyris et membranis vetustissimis servatae (editio stereotypa correctior tertiae
editionis)*, Leipzig

Kovacs, P. D. 1982. 'Tyrants and demagogues in tragic interpolation',
Greek, Roman and Byzantine Studies 23: 23–50

Kraus, W. 1971. 'Zu Menanders Misumenos', *Rheinisches Museum* 114:
1–27, 285–6

Krieter-Spiro, M. 1997. *Sklaven, Köche und Hetären: Das Dienstpersonal bei
Menander*, Stuttgart

Kühner, R. (rev. Gerth, B.) 1898–1904. *Ausführliche Grammatik der griechi-
schen Sprache³. Zweiter Teil: Satzlehre*, Hannover

*Lamagna, M. 1998. *Menandro: La donna di Samo*, Naples

Lambert, S. D. 2001. 'Ten notes on Attic inscriptions', *Zeitschrift für Papyrologie und Epigraphik* 135: 51–62

2003. 'The first Athenian agonothetai', *Horos* 14–16: 99–105

Lape, S. 2004. *Reproducing Athens: Menander's comedy, democratic culture, and
the Hellenistic city*, Princeton

Lefebvre, G. 1907. *Fragments d'un manuscrit de Ménandre*, Cairo

Le Guen, B. 1995. 'Théâtre et cités à l'époque hellénistique: "mort de la
cité" – "mort du théâtre"?', *Revue des Études Grecques* 108: 59–90

Leurini, L. 1994. 'Echi euripidei in Menandro', *Lexis* 12: 87–95

Lewis, D. M. 1973. Review of Reinmuth 1971, *Classical Review* 23:
254–6

1997. *Selected papers in Greek and Near Eastern history* (ed. P. J. Rhodes),
Cambridge

Lewis, S. 1995. 'Barbers' shops and perfume shops: "symposia without
wine"', in C. A. Powell, ed., *The Greek world* (London) 432–41

2002. *The Athenian woman: an iconographic handbook*, London

Lloyd-Jones, H. 1966. 'POxy. 2329, 3–4', *Classical Review* 16: 275

1972. 'Menander's *Samia* in the light of the new evidence', *Yale Classical
Studies* 22: 119–44

Loomis, W. T. 1998. *Wages, welfare costs, and inflation in classical Athens*, Ann
Arbor

Lowe, J. C. B. 1962. 'The manuscript evidence for changes of speaker in
Aristophanes', *Bulletin of the Institute of Classical Studies* 9: 27–42

Luck, G. 1965. 'Elemente der Umgangssprache bei Menander und Terenz', *Rheinisches Museum* 108: 269–77

Luppe, W. 1972. 'Zum Prolog der Samia', *Zeitschrift für Papyrologie und Epigraphik* 9: 197–201

1976. 'Wein und Liebe mit einem Dritten im Bund: Nochmals zu Samia 340–2', *Zeitschrift für Papyrologie und Epigraphik* 21: 152

Luppe, W. and Müller, W. 1983. 'Zwei Berliner Papyri zu Komödien', *Archiv für Papyrusforschung* 29: 5–8

Lyne, R. O. A. M. 1979. '*Seruitium amoris*', *Classical Quarterly* 29: 117–130

McClure, L. K. 1995. 'Female speech and characterization in Euripides', in F. De Martino and A. H. Sommerstein, eds. *Lo spettacolo delle voci* (Bari) II 35–60

2003. *Courtesans at table: gender and Greek literary culture in Athenaeus*, London

MacDowell, D. M. 1978. *The law in classical Athens*, London

1990. *Demosthenes: Against Meidias*, Oxford

1994. 'The number of speaking actors in Old Comedy', *Classical Quarterly* 44: 325–35

2004. 'Epikerdes of Kyrene and the Athenian privilege of *ateleia*', *Zeitschrift für Papyrologie und Epigraphik* 150: 127–33

2009. *Demosthenes the orator*, Oxford

Macleod, M. D. 1970. 'A rare use of νή in Menander and Lucian', *Classical Review* 20: 289

Macua Martínez, E. 1997. 'La caracterización lingüístico-estilística en Menandro', *Veleia* 14: 145–61

Maehler, M. 1992. '3967. Menander, *Misoumenos* 381–403, 404*-418*', *The Oxyrhynchus Papyri* 59: 59–70

Major, W. E. 2004. Review of Lape 2004, *Bryn Mawr Classical Review* 2004.06.39

Melandri, E. 2007. 'Il "rumore" della porta all'uscita di un personaggio: sviluppo e valenza drammatica di un stereotipo menandreo', in R. Pretagostini and E. Dettori, eds. *La cultura letteraria ellenistica: persistenza, innovazione, trasmissione* (Rome) 3–24

Mette, H. J. 1969. 'Moschion, ὁ κόσμιος', *Hermes* 97: 432–9

Millett, P. C. 1992. *Lending and borrowing in ancient Athens*, Cambridge

Monk, J. H. 1813. Εὐριπίδου Ἱππόλυτος στεφανηφόρος / *Euripidis Hippolytus coronifer*, London

Moretti, J. C. 1997. 'Formes et destinations du proskènion dans les théâtres hellénistiques de Grèce', in B. Le Guen, ed. *De la scène aux gradins: théâtre et représentations dramatiques après Alexandre le Grand* = *Pallas* 47: 13–39

2001. *Théâtre et société dans la Grèce antique: une archéologie des pratiques théâtrales*, Paris

Nardelli, M. L. 1972. 'Morale e costume nel prologo della *Samia* di Menandro', *Atti dell'Accademia Pontaniana* 21: 459–64

Nervegna, S. 2013. *Menander in antiquity: the contexts of reception*, Cambridge

Nesselrath, H. G. 1990. *Die attische Mittlere Komödie: Ihre Stellung in der antiken Literaturkritik und Literaturgeschichte*, Berlin

Neuburger, A. 1919. *Die Technik des Altertums*, Leipzig

Nevett, L. C. 1999. *House and society in the ancient Greek world*, Cambridge

Nicole, J. 1898. *Le Laboureur de Ménandre: fragments inédits sur papyrus d'Égypte*, Basle/Geneva

Oakley, J. H. and Sinos, R. H. 1993. *The wedding in ancient Athens*, Madison

Offermann, H. 1978. 'Goldregen über Nikeratos' Haus (zu Menander Samia 589 ff.)', *Philologus* 122: 150–3

Ogden, D. 1996. *Greek bastardy in the classical and Hellenistic periods*, Oxford

Olson, S. D. 1998. *Aristophanes: Peace*, Oxford

2002. *Aristophanes: Acharnians*, Oxford

2007. *Broken laughter: select fragments of Greek comedy*, Oxford

Omitowoju, R. 2002. *Rape and the politics of consent in classical Athens*, Cambridge

2010. 'Performing traditions: relations and relationships in Menander and tragedy', in A. K. Petrides and S. Papaioannou, eds. *New perspectives on postclassical comedy* (Newcastle upon Tyne) 125–45

O'Sullivan, L. 2009. *The regime of Demetrius of Phalerum in Athens, 317–307 BC: a philosopher in politics*, Leiden

Papastamati-von Moock C. 2007. 'Menander und die Tragikergruppe: Neue Forschungen zu den Ehrenmonumenten im Dionysostheater von Athen', *Mitteilungen des Deutschen Archäologischen Instituts (Athenische Abteilung)* 122: 273–327

Parker, R. C. T. 1983. *Miasma: pollution and purification in early Greek religion*, Oxford

1996. *Athenian religion: a history*, Oxford

2005. *Polytheism and society at Athens*, Oxford

Patterson, C. B. 1985. '"Not worth the rearing": the causes of infant exposure in ancient Greece', *Transactions of the American Philological Association* 115: 103–23

Pernigotti, C. 2008. *Menandri sententiae*, Florence

Pfeiffer, R. H. 1949. *Callimachus I. Fragmenta*, Oxford

Pickard-Cambridge, A. W. 1968. *The dramatic festivals of Athens*, 2nd edn (rev. J. P. A. Gould and D. M. Lewis), Oxford

Pieters, J. T. M. F. 1971. Review of Austin 1969–70, *Mnemosyne* 24: 96–101

Podlecki, A. J. 1989. *Aeschylus: Eumenides*, Warminster

Poe, J. P. 1996. 'The supposed conventional meanings of dramatic masks: a re-examination of Pollux 4.133–54', *Philologus* 140: 306–28

Porter, J. R. 2000. 'Euripides and Menander: *Epitrepontes*, Act IV', *Illinois Classical Studies* 24–25: 157–73

Reinmuth, O. L. 1971. *The ephebic inscriptions of the fourth century B.C.*, Leiden

Riad, H. 1973. 'Das photographische Archiv griechischer Papyri: Mitteilungen über neue Lesungen an Kairener Papyri', *Zeitschrift für Papyrologie und Epigraphik* 11: 201–34

Roselli, D. K. 2011. *Theatre of the people: spectators and society in ancient Athens*, Austin

Rosivach, V. J. 1998. *When a young man falls in love: the sexual exploitation of women in New Comedy*, London

Rubinstein, L. 1993. *Adoption in IVth century Athens*, Copenhagen

Rusten, J. S. 1993. *Theophrastus: Characters*, in J. S. Rusten et al., eds. *Theophrastus: Characters; Herodas: Mimes; Cercidas and the choliambic poets*, Cambridge, MA, 1–195

Sandbach, F. H. 1970. 'Menander's manipulation of language for dramatic purposes', in Turner 1970: 113–36 (discussion, 137–43)

    1973. *See* Gomme and Sandbach 1973

    1980. 'Notes on the Cairo Codex of Menander (P. Cair. J. 43227)', *Zeitschrift für Papyrologie und Epigraphik* 40: 47–52

    1986. 'Two notes on Menander (*Epitrepontes* and *Samia*)', *Liverpool Classical Monthly* 11: 156–60

    1990. *Menandri reliquiae selectae²*, Oxford

Schaps, D. M. 1979. *Economic rights of women in ancient Greece*, Edinburgh

Schröder, S. F. 1996. 'Die Lebensdaten Menanders (mit einem Anhang über die Aufführungszeit seines Heauton Timoroumenos)', *Zeitschrift für Papyrologie und Epigraphik* 113: 35–48

Schwyzer, E. 1950. *Griechische Grammatik: Syntax und syntaktische Stilistik* (completed by W. Otto and A. Debrunner), Munich

Sehrt, Ae. 1912. *De Menandro Euripidis imitatore*, Giessen

Shipp, G. P. 1960. *Terence: Andria*, 2nd edn, Oxford

Sicking, C. M. J. and Stork, P. 1996. *Two studies in the semantics of the verb in classical Greek*, Leiden

Sisti, F. 2004. 'Varianti equipollenti e varianti di esecuzione nella tradizione papiracea di Menandro', in G. Bastianini and A. Casanova, eds. *Menandro: cent'anni di papiri* (Florence) 151–63

Smyth, H. W. 1956. *Greek grammar*, 2nd edn rev. by G. M. Messing, Cambridge, MA

Snowden, F. M. 1970. *Blacks in antiquity: Ethiopians in the Greco-Roman experience*, Cambridge, MA

1983. *Before color prejudice: the ancient view of blacks*, Cambridge, MA

Sommerstein, A. H. 1980. 'The naming of women in Greek and Roman comedy', *Quaderni di Storia* 11: 393–418; reprinted with updates in Sommerstein 2009: 43–69

 1988. 'Notes on Euripides' *Hippolytos*', *Bulletin of the Institute of Classical Studies* 35: 23–41

 1990. *The comedies of Aristophanes, Vol. 7: Lysistrata*, Warminster

 1995. 'The language of Athenian women', in F. De Martino and A. H. Sommerstein, eds. *Lo spettacolo delle voci* (Bari) II 61–85; reprinted with updates in Sommerstein 2009: 15–42

 1998. 'Rape and young manhood in Athenian comedy', in L. Foxhall and J. B. Salmon, eds. *Thinking men: masculinity and its self-representation in the classical tradition* (London) 100–14

 2000. 'Monsters, ogres and demons in Old Comedy', in C. Atherton, ed. *Monsters and monstrosity in Greek and Roman culture* (Bari) 19–40

 2001. *The comedies of Aristophanes, Vol. 11: Wealth*, Warminster

 2006. 'Rape and consent in Athenian tragedy', in D. L. Cairns and V. Liapis, eds. *Dionysalexandros: essays on Aeschylus and his fellow tragedians in honour of Alexander F. Garvie* (Swansea) 233–51

 2007. 'Cloudy swearing: when (if ever) is an oath not an oath?', in A. H. Sommerstein and J. Fletcher, eds. *Horkos: the oath in Greek society* (Exeter) 125–37

 2009. *Talking about laughter and other studies in Greek comedy*, Oxford

 2010. *The tangled ways of Zeus and other studies in and around Greek tragedy*, Oxford

 2012. 'The third father in Menander's *Samia*: Moschion and the baby', in G. Bastianini et al., eds. *Harmonia: scritti di filologia classica iin onore di Angelo Casanova* (Florence) 769–80

 forthcoming (*a*). 'The politics of Greek comedy', to appear in M. Revermann, ed. *The Cambridge companion to Greek comedy* (Cambridge)

 forthcoming (*b*). 'The authenticity of the Demophantus decree', to appear in *Classical Quarterly*

 forthcoming (*c*). 'Menander's *Samia* and the Phaedra theme', to appear in S. D. Olson, ed. *Ancient comedy and reception* (Berlin)

 forthcoming (*d*). 'Menander and the *pallake*', in A. H. Sommerstein, ed. *Menander in contexts* (London) chapter 2

Sommerstein, A. H. and Talboy, T. H. 2012. *Sophocles: selected fragmentary plays II*, Oxford

Spence, I. G. 1993. *The cavalry of classical Greece : a social and military history with particular reference to Athens*, Oxford

Stafford, E. M. 2000. *Worshipping virtues: personification and the divine in ancient Greece*, London

Stevens, P. T. 1976. *Colloquial expressions in Euripides*, Wiesbaden

Stoessl, F. 1969. 'Die neuen Menanderpublikationen der Bibliotheca Bodmeriana in Genf', *Rheinisches Museum* 112: 193–229

1973. 'Unkenntnis und Mißverstehen als Prinzip und Quelle der Komik in Menanders Samia', *Rheinisches Museum* 116: 21–45

Stone, L. M. 1981. *Costume in Aristophanic comedy*, New York

Storey, I. C. 2003. *Eupolis, poet of Old Comedy*, Oxford

Talboy, T. H. and Sommerstein, A. H. 2006. *Phaedra*, in A. H. Sommerstein et al. *Sophocles: selected fragmentary plays I* (Oxford) 248–317

Taplin, O. P. 1977. *The stagecraft of Aeschylus: the dramatic use of exits and entrances in Greek tragedy*, Oxford

Teodorsson, S. T. 1977. *The phonology of Ptolemaic Koine*, Göteborg

Thomas, R. F. 1984. 'Menander and Catullus 8', *Rheinisches Museum* 127: 308–16

1990. 'Menander, *Samia* 380–3', *Zeitschrift für Papyrologie und Epigraphik* 83: 215–18

Thompson, A. and Taylor, N. 2006. *The Arden Shakespeare: Hamlet*, London

Threatte, L. 1980–96. *The grammar of Attic inscriptions*, 2 vols, Berlin

Todd, S. C. 2007. *A commentary on Lysias, speeches 1–11*, Oxford

Traill, A. E. 2008. *Women and the comic plot in Menander*, Cambridge

Travlos, J. 1971. *Pictorial dictionary of ancient Athens*, London

Treu, M. 1969. 'Humane Handlungsmotive in der Samia Menanders', *Rheinisches Museum* 112: 230–54

Troupi, M. 2006. 'Menander, Euripides, Aristophanes: intertextual transformations of genre and gender', diss. Royal Holloway, London

Turner, E. G. [1967]. 'Menander, *Samia* 385–390 Austin (170–175 Koe.)', *Aegyptus* 47: 187–90 [actually published 1969]

1969. 'The *Phasma* of Menander', *Greek, Roman and Byzantine Studies* 10: 307–24

ed. 1970. *Ménandre: sept exposés suivis de discussions*, Geneva

1972. '2943. Menander, *Samia*', *The Oxyrhynchus Papyri* 41: 1–4

1979. 'Menander and the new society', *Chronique d'Égypte* 54: 106–26

Wackernagel, J. 1892. 'Über ein Gesetz der indogermanischen Wortstellung', *Indogermanische Forschungen* 1: 333–436

1955. *Kleine Schriften*, Göttingen

Walton, J. M. and Arnott, P. D. 1996. *Menander and the making of comedy*, Westport CT

Waterfield, R. 2011. *Dividing the spoils: the war for Alexander the Great's empire*, Oxford

Webster, T. B. L. 1995. *Monuments illustrating New Comedy*, 3rd edn rev. by J. R. Green and A. Seeberg, London

Weill, N. 1966. 'Adôniazousai ou les femmes sur le toit', *Bulletin de Correspondance Hellénique* 90: 664–98

1970. 'La fête d'Adonis dans la *Samienne* de Ménandre', *Bulletin de Correspondance Hellénique* 94: 591–3

West, M. L. 1982. *Greek metre*, Oxford

West, S. R. 1991. 'Notes on the *Samia*', *Zeitschrift für Papyrologie und Epigraphik* 88: 11–23

Whitehead, D. 1983. 'Competitive outlay and community profit: φιλοτιμία in democratic Athens', *Classica et Mediaevalia* 34: 55–74

Wilkins, J. 2000. *The boastful chef: the discourse of food in ancient Greek comedy*, Oxford

Willi, A. 2002. 'Languages on stage: Aristophanic language, cultural history, and Athenian identity', in A. Willi, ed. *The language of Greek comedy* (Oxford) 111–49

Willink, C. W. 1986. *Euripides: Orestes*, Oxford

Wilson, N. G. 1983. *Scholars of Byzantium*, London

Wilson, P. J. 2000. *The Athenian institution of the khoregia: the chorus, the city and the stage*, Cambridge

ed. 2007. *The Greek theatre and festivals: documentary studies*, Oxford

Wilson, P. J. and Csapo, E. G. 2012. 'From *chorêgia* to *agônothesia*: evidence for the administration and finance of the Athenian theatre in the late fourth century BC', in D. Rosenbloom and J. Davidson, eds. *Greek drama IV: texts, contexts, performance* (Oxford) 300–18

Winkler, J. J. 1990. *The constraints of desire: the anthropology of sex and gender in ancient Greece*, London

Zagagi, N. 1979. 'Sostratos as a comic, over-active and impatient lover', *Zeitschrift für Papyrologie und Epigraphik* 36: 39–49

1988. '*Exilium amoris* in New Comedy', *Hermes* 116: 193–209

1994. *The comedy of Menander: convention, variation and originality*, London

Zanker, P. 1995. *The mask of Socrates: the image of the intellectual in antiquity* (trans. H. A. Shapiro), Berkeley

Zwierlein, O. 2004. 'Senecas "Phaedra" und ihre Vorbilder nach dem Fund der neuen "Hippolytos"-Papyri', in O. Zwierlein, *Lucubrationes philologae* (Berlin) I 57–136

INDEXES

The abbreviation M stands for Menander. References to pages are in *italics*; all other references are to notes in the Commentary, except for the entry 'text (new proposals)' where the references are to the text and apparatus.

592: 148–9
Suppliants
839: 323
ALCAEUS (Lobel-Page)
  fr. 374: 73–4
ALCIPHRON
  4.6.5: 503
  4.18–19: *3*
ALEXIS
  fr. 15: 603
  fr. 85: 302–3
  fr. 96: 283–390
  fr. 103.15: 357
  fr. 145.16: 494
  fr. 168: 310
  fr. 172: 302–3
  fr. 173: 393
  fr. 177.12–15: 287–92
  fr. 187: 412
  fr. 211: *6 n. 33*
  fr. 213: 603
  fr. 232: F 1
  fr. 248: 323
  fr. 257: 341
  fr. 258: 464
  fr. 259: 290, 603
  fr. 263.9: 98
  fr. 269.6: 268–70
  fr. 289: 592
ANAXAGORAS
  fr. 2 D-K: 326
  fr. 15 D-K: 326
ANAXANDRIDES
  fr. 3: 209
ANAXIPPUS
  fr. 4.1: 725
ANDOCIDES
  1.5: 422–3
ANTHOLOGY
  Anthologia Palatina
  5.31: 594
  5.33: 594
  5.34: 594
  7.256.3–4: 102
ANTIPHANES
  fr. 34: 734
  fr. 55.5–6: 528
  fr. 124: 427
  fr. 142.8–10: 531
  fr. 150: 290
  fr. 166.5: 215
  fr. 166.7: 515
  fr. 191.1: 98
  fr. 192.15: 98

fr. 197: 603
fr. 216.23: 735
fr. 233.3: 98
fr. 234: 735
ANTIPHON
  1.1: 513
  1.14: 508
  5.62: 560
APOLLODORUS OF CARYSTUS
  fr. 29: 603
  fr. 31: 603
APOLLODORUS (OF CARYSTUS OR
  GELA?)
  fr. 7.6: 637
[APOLLODORUS] MYTHOGRAPHUS
  Bibliotheca
  3.13.8: 499–500
  Epitome
  1.18: 337
APOLLONIUS OF CITIUM
  Commentary on Hippocr. On Joints
  p.72.2–3 Kollesch-Kudlien: 449
APOLLONIUS RHODIUS
  3.783: 370
ARAROS
  fr. 16: 293
ARETAEUS
  Causes & Signs of Chronic Diseases
  1.6.11: 419
ARISTOPHANES
  Acharnians
  11: 737
  30: 694–712
  92–3: 440–1
  128: 642
  186: 580
  251–2: 609
  263: 735
  315: 456
  335: 580
  321–51: 572–3
  392: 517
  413: 371
  421: 499–500
  460: 373
  749: 382
  751–2: 395
  1049–50: 403
  1211: 603
  Birds
  61: 543
  128–34: 518
  153–4: 422–3
  342: 440–1

MENANDER (*cont.*)
Perikeiromene
121–80: 57/8
134: 355
147–58: 703
162–7: 337
162–5: 703
262: 321
267–353: *233*
268: 516
272: 677
284: 677
291: 503
298: 614
299: 357
304: 503
309–10: 309
335: 547, 677
354–5: 658
378: 578
471–2: 413
505: 91
506–7: 465
510: 454
532–6: 10–14
537–41: 94–5
550: 94–5
710–11: 392, 442
791: 53
805: 69
983: 382
1013–15: 726–8
1014–15: 728–9
1014: 527
1018: 100
Perinthia
15: 313, 441
F 3: 339
F 4: 302–3
Phasma
73–4: 283–390
75–92 S = 75–98 A: *233*
90: 596
95 S = 195 A: 46
Philadelphoi fr. 397: 641
Plokion fr. 296.2–3: 642
Pseudherakles
fr. 409: 287–8
fr. 411: 508
fr. 412: 85–6, 302–3
Sikyonioi
6: 628–9
110–49: *233*
135: 192–3

142: 192–3
146: 690
151: 521
157: 641
176–271: 9, 206–82
189: 265
246: 521
270–3: *49 n. 152*
363: 543
401: 657
F 3 S = F 6 A: 379, 658
Synaristosai fr. 339: 632
Thais fr. 163: 736
Theophoroumene
25: 516, 525
40 A = (fr. dub.) 10 S: 736
Thesauros fr. 176: 632
Thettale fr. 170: 302–3
Fabula Incerta (from the Cairo codex)
27: 305
29–30: 727
Fabulae Incertae (Arnott)
8: 140
9.7–16: 730
Unplaced fragments
fr. 447: 489
fr. 453: 726–8
fr. 472: 348
fr. 494: 272
fr. 508.6: 551
fr. 602.6: 424
fr. 641: 637
fr. 748: 379, 394
fr. 784: 328
fr. 790: 82–3
fr. 791: 625
fr. 792: 632
fr. 827: 697
fr. 835.9: 96
fr. 838: 163
fr. 877: 520
fr. 884: 474
fr. 893: 474
MNESIMACHUS
fr. 1: 474

NEW TESTAMENT
Mark
1.24: 391
Luke
4.34: 391
NICOPHON
fr. 7: 359–60

NICOSTRATUS
  fr. 26: 603
  fr. 29: 213
  fr. 35: 503

OVID
  Amores 3.8.29–34: 594
  Ex Ponto 3.8.15–16: 100
  Ibis 591: *4*

PAPYRI
  PAntinoop. inv. 4 (A2): *56*
  PBarcelona 45 (part of B): *54 n. 171*
  PBerol
  8450: *56, 324*
  21119: *49*
  PBingen 23 (A2): *56*
  PBodm 25 (B): *54–6*, 128, 140,
    168–9
  PCair J43227 (C): *55–6*, 140
  PKöln 203: 140
  PMich inv. 6222A: *38 n. 114*
  POxy
  1235.103–12: *3 n. 22*
  2831 (O16): *56*
  2943 (O17): *56*, 119b-d
  3966: 730
  4640: *38 n. 114*
  PSI 126: *54 n. 168*
  PVindob 29811: *49 n. 153*
PAUSANIAS
  1.1.3: 310
  1.2.2: *4*
  1.21.1: *4*
  1.29.16: *48 n. 148*
PERSIUS
  5.165: *324*
PHERECRATES
  fr. 28: 399–404
PHERECYDES OF ATHENS
  fr. 10 Fowler: 590–1
PHILEMON
  fr. 22: 138
  fr. 28: 206–8
  fr. 73: 664–5
  fr. 93.6–7: 550
  fr. 97.8: 148–9
  fr. 108.1: 128
  fr. 118: *36 n. 104*
  fr. 125: 55
  fr. 153: *36 n. 104*
  fr. 176: 429
PHILIPPIDES
  frr. 25–26: *5–6 n. 31*

PHILOSTRATUS
  Imagines 2.17: 209
  Life of Apollonius 1.21: 100
PHOTIUS
  Bibliotheca
  535b33–8: 474
  Lexicon
  ζ28: 428
  η190: 313
  λ395: 474
PHRYNICHUS COMICUS
  fr. 14: 126
PHRYNICHUS THE ATTICIST
  Eclogae
  137: *234*
PINDAR
  Nemeans
  9.50: 735
  Olympians
  12.2: 164
  Fragments (Snell-Maehler)
  fr. 139.6: 125–6
PLATO
  Apology
  27b: 725
  31e: 518
  Charmides 171b: 703
  Euthydemus
  289b: 733
  300a: 412
  Gorgias
  483b: 506
  491e: 412
  502b-d: 733–4
  Hipparchus 232a: 296
  Hippias Minor 365d: 482
  Laches 178a-184c: 570
  Laws
  658a-d: 733–4
  772b-c: 494
  801b: 703
  817b-c: 733–4
  866b: 513
  Meno
  71d: 489
  77d: 408
  85c: 396–7
  Phaedo
  61b8–d5: 198
  76c: 266
  Phaedrus
  243e: 733
  247a: 306
  252b: 733

PLATO (*cont.*)
276b: 38–50
Protagoras 314d: 256
Republic
338b: 242
343a: 85–6, 546
361b: 148–9
362a-b: 148–9
451a: 503
474e: 606
492b: 733–4
556d: 333, 607
Symposium
184b-c: 625
189c-193d: 69
203b: 387
207a-b: 421
Theaetetus
160e-161a: 132
186d-e: 408
Timaeus 49a: 449
PLATO COMICUS
fr. 105: 580
fr. 222: 733–4
PLAUTUS
Amphitruo
271–8: 429
282–3: 429
358: 440
Asinaria
746–809: 25
Aulularia
48: 440
53: 440–1
189: 440–1
561–8: 399–404
Bacchides
200: 21
574: 21
892–5: 309–10
Captivi
570–1: 312
Casina
798–9: 730
799–809: 737
Cistellaria
38–41: 387
59–95: 7 *n. 39, 31*
512–16: 309–10
Curculio
96–138: 302–3
Epidicus
165–73: 27
Menaechmi

158: 304–5
Mercator
660: *289*
830–41: *289*
893: 528
Persa
484: 528
Poenulus
222: 381–2
1111–48: 283–390
1299–1300: 405–6
Pseudolus
659: *324*
Trinummus
597–9: *289*
PLINY THE ELDER
Historia Naturalis
33.26: 189
PLUTARCH
Alcibiades
8.5: 38–50
Alexander
27.8–10: 586
70.2: 394
Moralia
11e: 550
145d: 387
320e: 355
489f: 355
529d: 550
712c: *30 n. 88*
753a: 73–4
782e-f: 593
823a: 550
Nicias
13.11: 38–50
Pericles
37.2–5: 135–6
Phocion
35.5: 603
POLLUX
3.43: 730
4.126–7: *96*
4.149–50: 283–390
8.66: 730
POLYBIUS
12.6b.4: 346
38.12.5: 546
POSEIDIPPUS
fr. 23: 570
fr. 25: 194
fr. 28.11: 286
fr. 29.1: 286
fr. 41: 550

3 GREEK WORDS

ἑορτή: 41
ἐπάγομαι: 218
ἐπαρκέω: 15–16
ἐπεξέρχομαι: 513
ἐπί + dat. (= 'in the power of'):
    504
ἐράω: 146
ἐργάζομαι: 516
εὔλογος: 5
εὐρώστως: 734
ἔχων 'persistently': 719

ἦ (interrogative): 286
ἡδύς: 412
ἤν (interjection): 305
ἤν (interjection): 313

θαρρέω/θαρσέω: 419
θεά: 400, 736
θεός: 163
θυθέν (aor. pass. part. of θύω):
    400

ἰδιώτης: 286
ἱερόσυλος: 677
ἱκετεύω: 203–5
ἱστεών: 234
ἰχθῦς (nom. pl.): 98

καθαρὰ ποῶ: 222
κάκιστος: 492
κακῶς of lovesickness: 81
καλός: 733
κατακόπτω: 283–5
καταλιπαρέω: 721–2
καταμανθάνω: 275
καταπίνω: 447
κεράμιον: 302–3
Κηδεία: 56–7
κόπτω: 283–5
κορυζάω: 546
κρᾶτα 'head': 732–3
κωλύω: 432

λάβρος: 207
λαλέω: 512
λαμβάνω: 28, 527
λέκτρον: 507
λέχος: 495
λιβανωτός: F 1
λιτός: 379
λογίζομαι: 4
λογισμός: 420
λόγον + adjective + λέγω: 136

λόγος 'mere words': 546
λοιπά, τά: 636

Λοξίας: 474

μά: 309
μαρτύρομαι: 474
μάτην: 616
μειράκιον: 272
μέλαθρον: 517
μέλας: 606–8
μέχρι(ς): 394
μήν: 633
μήτε...μή: 510–11
μιαρός: 551
μοιχός and derivatives: 591
μου avoided after –ου: 115
μῦς (nom. pl.): 98

ναιχί: 296
νοῦν ἔχειν: 187, 605

ξύλον 'cudgel': 440

ὅδε: 37
ὅστις (= εἴ τις): 514
οὐδέπω, elliptical use of: 196
οὐθείς: 140
οὐ μή + subjunctive in questions:
    428
οὗτος: 657

παῖ: 360
παῖς: 189, 433
πάλιν: 275
παλλακή: 508
παμμεγέθης: 364
παράβολος: 328
παράγω: 104–5, 282
παρατεταγμένος: 333
πάρεδρος: 736
παῦ: 311
παχύς: 13
πενθερός: 504
περί + acc.: 114
περίεργος: 203–5
πέφυκα: 12
πιθέσθαι: 712
ποιέομαι 'have (a child)': 387
πρᾶξις: 50
πράττω: 50
προάγω, προάγομαι: 214
προαιρέω: 230
πρός after verbs of hiding: 308